Capital cities of Australia and New Zealand
Capital cities of the states and territories
other cities
Outback
Indian Ocean
Pacific Ocean
Great Barrier Reef
Australia
Western Australia
Northern Territory
South Australia
Queensland
New South Wales
Victoria
Tasmania
Australian Capital Territory
Darwin
Uluru
Cairns
Brisbane
Perth
Albany
Adelaide
Sydney
Canberra
Melbourne
Hobart
Tasman Sea
New Zealand
North Island
South Island
Kerikeri
Auckland
Wellington
Christchurch
Queenstown
Milford Sound
0 250 500 750 1000 miles
0 500 1000 km

westermann

On Track

Englisch für Gymnasien
Ausgabe Bayern

5

von:
Friedrich Frenzel
Jon Hird
Claudia Maria Hugo
Heather Jones
Marc Proulx
Adrian Tennant
Agnes Tennant
Patricia Wedler
Story von Marcus Sedgwick mit Illustrationen von Pete Williamson
Graphic novel von Marcus Sedgwick mit Illustrationen von Steve Buccellato

herausgegeben von:
Helga Holtkamp

Begleitmaterialien zum Lehrwerk:

Workbook ISBN 978-3-14-040825-7
Medienpaket ISBN 978-3-14-062677-4
Ferienlektüre ISBN 978-3-14-040885-1
Schulaufgabentrainer ISBN 978-3-14-040895-0

BiBox – Digitale Unterrichtsmaterialien
Nähere Informationen unter www.bibox.schule

Vokabel-Apps sind online erhältlich.

westermann GRUPPE

Druck A[1] / Jahr 2021
Alle Drucke der Serie A sind inhaltlich unverändert.

Unter Mitarbeit von: Stacy Bentz, Udo Diekmann und Christine House

Beratung durch: Claudia Maria Hugo (Lindau), Günter Fischer (Mitwitz), Friedrich Frenzel (Bad Neustadt an der Saale), Dr. Mario Oesterreicher (Nürnberg), Christian Schulze (Lindau), Eva Maria Veitenhansl (München), Juliane Lobischer (Berlin), Margot Adami (Paderborn)

Redaktion: Dr. Martin Walter
Umschlaggestaltung: Detlef Möller, Paderborn
Coverfoto vorne: © Wim Wiskerke / Alamy Stock Photo. Sydney Opera House with Sydney Harbour Bridge
Coverfoto hinten: © Andrew Michael / Alamy Stock Photo. Surf school on Main Beach, Byron Bay, NSW, Australia
Druck und Bindung: Westermann Druck GmbH, Braunschweig

ISBN 978-3-14-**040805**-9

How to use this book Wie du dieses Buch benutzt

On Track 5 starts with a *Welcome* double-page spread. Then there are three regular workshops and one extra workshop. Every regular workshop has the same three parts. Parts one and two teach you new things, and part three helps you practise what you have learned. The activities and exercises have numbers and letters. Sometimes they have symbols, too.
On Track 5 beginnt mit einer *Welcome*-Doppelseite. Darauf folgen drei Hauptkapitel und ein Extrakapitel. Jeder reguläre Workshop besteht aus drei Teilen (*Parts*): In Teil 1 und 2 lernst du neue Dinge. In Teil 3 übst du, was du Neues gelernt hast. Die Aufgaben und Übungen haben Zahlen und Buchstaben. Einige haben auch Symbole.

Here is an explanation of the symbols: Hier findest du Erklärungen zu allen Symbolen:

audio	14	Listen to a dialogue, a text, song or story. Höre dir einen Dialog, Text, ein Lied oder eine Geschichte an.
video	2	Watch a film. Sieh dir einen Film an.
partner work		Work with a partner. Arbeite mit einem Partner / einer Partnerin.
group work		Work with two or more partners. Arbeite mit zwei oder mehreren Partnern / Partnerinnen.
mediation	M	Help an English person to understand German or a German person to understand English. Hilf einer englischsprachigen Person dabei, etwas auf Deutsch zu verstehen. Oder hilf einer deutschsprachigen Person dabei, etwas auf Englisch zu verstehen.
AE		American English (specific vocabulary or spelling) Amerikanisches Englisch (spezielle Wörter oder Schreibweisen)
revision	*	Grammar revision Grammatikwiederholung
step 1, 2, 3, …	S1	Activities with this symbol help you with a more complex task – step by step. Aufgaben mit diesem Symbol helfen dir Schritt für Schritt beim Bearbeiten einer komplexeren Lernaufgabe.
grammar	→ G14	There is more information about this grammar topic in the *Appendix*. Look up grammar rule 1 … 14. Zu diesem Grammatikthema findest du mehr Informationen im Anhang (*Appendix*). Schau die Grammatikregel Nummer 1 … 14 dort nach.
webcode	@ WES-40805-004	There is a webcode on the left-hand page of every workshop. This webcode helps you to find all the audio and video material. You also find transcripts of the audios and videos as well as solutions to the activities on the *Review* pages. In den Workshops steht jeweils auf der linken Seite ein Webcode, unter dem du alle Audio- und Videodateien findest. Hier stellen wir dir außerdem Transkripte der Audios und Videos sowie Lösungen zu den Aufgaben auf den *Review*-Seiten zur Verfügung.

How to use the webcodes Wie du die Webcodes benutzt

A webcode is like a small website. All the *On Track* audio and video material that you need for class or homework is here: www.westermann.de/webcodes. There is also extra material. You can listen and watch online or download everything. Type in the code for the workshop (**WES-40805-001**) without the @ and click "Aufrufen". There is your page for *Workshop 1*. There are webcodes in your workbook, too. Ein Webcode funktioniert wie eine kleine Webseite. Alle Audio- und Videodateien sowie Extramaterialien für die Arbeit in der Schule oder für Hausaufgaben sind hier www.westermann.de/webcodes. Du kannst online zuhören und schauen oder alles herunterladen. Gib den Code ohne @ ein (**WES-40805-001**) und schon bist du auf der Webseite von *Workshop 1*.

These are the webcodes in *On Track 5*: Dies sind die Webcodes in *On Track 5*:

Welcome: @ WES-40805-000
Workshop 1: @ WES-40805-001
Workshop 2: @ WES-40805-002
Workshop 3: @ WES-40805-003
Workshop 4: @ WES-40805-004

Contents

* grammar revision

* grammar revision

* grammar revision

English around the world

Look at the two flags. One flag is for Australia and the other for New Zealand. The Union Jack in the top left corner represents the historical link to the UK. Which one is the Australian flag?

Do the quiz and see how many questions you can get right. Compare your results in class.

Which answers surprised you the most? Which facts do you find most interesting? Explain why.

English language quiz

1. Approximately how many languages are there in the world?
   A 6,500
   B 380
   C 4,200

2. Which are the two most commonly spoken languages on earth?
   A English and French
   B Mandarin and Spanish
   C English and Spanish

3. Approximately how many English speakers were there in the world in Shakespeare's time?
   A 5–7 million
   B 15 million
   C 2–3 million

4. Approximately how many people speak English as a second language?
   A 51 million
   B 200 million
   C 510 million

5. What is the main reason why English spread and became a world language?
   A British colonialism
   B popular music
   C Shakespeare

6. You hear someone say 'No worries, mate.' Which country are they probably from?
   A Australia
   B South Africa
   C USA

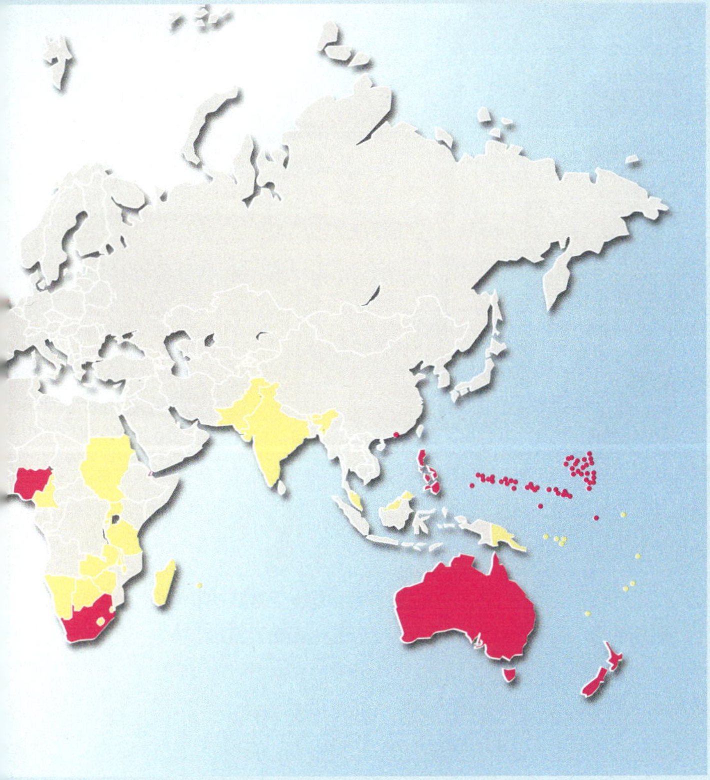

Watch the slideshow and take notes. Compare your answers.

1. Why do most Australians speak English as their mother tongue?
2. What is the Commonwealth?
3. List the factors that helped make English a global language.

Read and discuss what these teens say about different countries. Match them to these nations: *India, Australia, USA* and *South Africa.*

I said to a British friend, 'I like the color of your pants.' She looked horrified and replied 'Oh dear, are they showing?' That's when I realized we didn't speak the same language.

Brad

I told my friend we're having a braai just now and he said, 'Okay, let's go' and I said 'No, not now, just now.' He didn't seem to understand that 'just now' means 'later' where I come from!

Alain

When I first moved to this country, I often got confused by what people said. I remember standing at a bus stop one day and a boy saying 'How ya going?' When I answered, 'By bus,' they looked at me as if I were crazy.

Sanjay

'G'day! It's hot! Grab your togs and let's hit the beach.' If you need me to translate that … well, what do you wear at a beach? Yep, your swimwear.

Nicole

When I was visiting some relatives at my dad's birthplace, someone asked me, 'What's your good name, please?' I was really confused until I realized they just wanted to know my name. But when they asked if I had any doubts, I really hadn't got a clue.

Aesha

Aussies and Kiwis

Do this mini quiz to see how much you already know about Australia.

1. Who were the first Australians?
   A Maoris
   B Aboriginal people and Torres Strait Islanders
   C Indians

A

The State Barrier Fence (the rabbit proof fence), Western Australia

B

Aboriginal culture show at Tjapukai Cultural Centre, Queensland

2. Who gave Australia its name?
   A The Aboriginal people
   B The British
   C The Dutch

3. What is Australia's nickname? And do you know why it is called this?
   A Down Under
   B Down South
   C Deep Down

4. What is Australia?
   A A continent
   B A country
   C A continent, a country and an island

C

Kakadu National Park, Northern Territory

5. How big is Australia?
   A 12 times bigger than Germany
   B 16 times bigger than Germany
   C 22 times bigger than Germany

6. The population of Germany is about 80 million and of Australia ...
   A about 26 million
   B about 50 million
   C about 75 million

Aboriginal rock painting of the Rainbow Serpent, Kakadu National Park

7. What is the capital of Australia?
A Sydney
B Melbourne
C Canberra

Christmas on Bondi Beach, Sydney, New South Wales

8. There are more kangaroos than people in Australia.
A True
B False

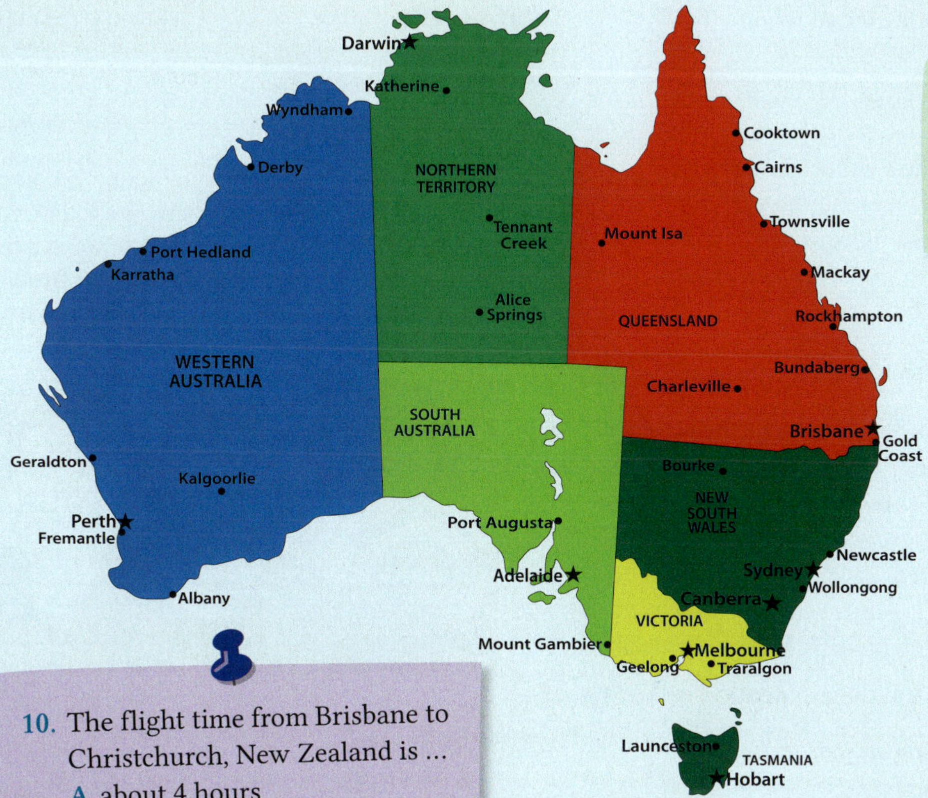

9. The interior of Australia is mainly desert and bush. What is its name?
A The Territory
B The Outback
C The Billabong

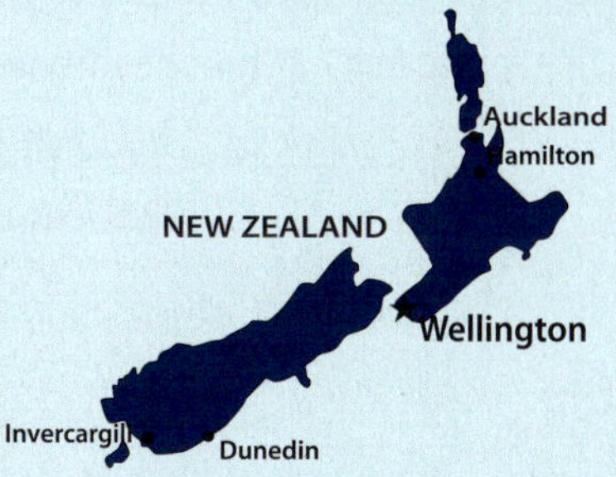

10. The flight time from Brisbane to Christchurch, New Zealand is ...
A about 4 hours
B about 6 hours
C about 10 hours

Auckland is New Zealand's biggest city.

2 Watch the video to check your answers. You will find out more facts about this amazing country, so watch the video again and then make three questions for another pair.

Jason's choice

1 The big news

a Jason Turner is a student at Bayview High School in Melbourne. He plays on the school rugby team together with his friend Ricky Bates. Read the story, then do the tasks.

1 Explain how the rugby team players feel and give reasons for your answers.
2 Describe the choice that Jason faces.

b Decide whether these statements are true or false. Correct the false ones.

1 Ricky and Jason are both excited when they hear the news.
2 At the end of rugby practice, the whole team feels the same.
3 Jason's dad wants to know who will pay for the trip.
4 Jason's mum understands Jason's dilemma.

1

The players were breathing hard and sweating as they gathered around Coach Hansen. 'Nice workout, guys,' he said. 'Now, I've got some big news.'
Jason and Ricky exchanged puzzled looks.
'Our partner school in Christchurch has invited us to play in their rugby tournament. It starts at the end of their school term,' he announced. 'Who wants to go to New Zealand?'
There was silence, then the whole team jumped and cheered. The noise echoed across the playing field and around the school campus.
'We're going to play against the Kiwis!' Jason said, giving Ricky a high five.
'Yeah, and we're going to *beat* them!' Ricky shouted.
When the coach announced the tournament dates, Jason's smile slowly disappeared. As they walked from the field, one thought kept going through his head: 'Nick and Eleni are celebrating their birthdays on 2 October'.

2 Sharing with a friend. Listen and do the tasks.

2

1 Describe what happens. Who is doing the sharing?
2 Compare how Jason and Ricky communicate with Eleni.
3 Choose one or more of these adjectives to describe Eleni's reaction: *happy, excited, shocked, supportive, uninterested, disappointed.*

3* Good friends

a Look at these sentences and the explanation in the box.

*You boyd **have been playing** so well.*
*We**'ve had** a good season so far.*

Explain why the progressive form is used in the first sentence and not in the second.

b Complete the text. Sometimes two forms are correct.

Jason [1] (*know*) Ricky since primary school. They [2] (*play*) rugby together since they were both ten. Jason and Nick Kourakis [3] (*be*) friends for a long time, too. He [4] (*work*) part-time at the Kourakis' Greek deli for the past year. Since then Jason and Eleni [5] (*spend*) more time together.

Remember

- We use the present perfect to express that an action is completed or to emphasize the result. *I**'ve texted** my mum ten times today, but she **hasn't answered**.*
- We use the present perfect progressive with action verbs like *go, talk, play* or *try* to emphasize the length of the action. *The coach **has been trying** to organize a trip like this for a while.*
- With state verbs like *have, know, want* or *understand* we use the present perfect, not the present perfect progressive. *He **has always wanted** to take the team to play in New Zealand.*

1

Words and phrases

g'day (AuE, NZeE) hello
mate (BrE, AuE) friend
puzzled not able to understand sth

→ Workbook, pages 8/9

2

At dinner Jason shared the news with his parents. 'That's brilliant, Jason!' his dad said. 'You boys have been playing so well, I'm not surprised.'
'Yeah, we've had a good season so far,' Jason said.
'Christchurch, New Zealand? That's quite a trip,' his mum said. 'Who's going to pay for it?'
'The school sports fund will pay for the plane tickets,' Jason said. 'And we'll be able to stay with the families of students from Papanui High School.'
'You don't look very enthusiastic. Is there a problem?'
Jason sighed. 'It's the same weekend when Nick's parents invited me to go to Sydney with them. It's Nick's and Eleni's sixteenth birthday.'
'Eleni?' his dad said.
'Nick's twin sister,' Jason's mum said.
'Ah, yes, the twins. Jason, I know Nick is your mate, but the team needs you,' his dad said.
'I think Jason needs to decide for himself what's more important,' his mum said. 'Eat up, Jason,' she added.
'Your film starts at 7.00, doesn't it?'
'It's OK,' said Jason. We're meeting at the cinema just before 7.00. Nick's going to book the tickets online.'

4* Planning to win

a Look at the sentences and read the explanation in the box. Why does Jason use the *going-to future* in the first and the *will future* in the second?

*We're **going to play** against the Kiwis.*
*The school **will pay** for the plane tickets.*

Remember
- We use *going to* to talk about plans or to say what we have already decided to do.
- We use *will* to offer or promise to do something or when we decide to do something while we are speaking.

We use both tenses to make predictions:
- *going to:* when we see what's going to happen
- *will:* when we think we know what will happen (but don't know for sure)

We can also use present tenses to express the future:
- We use the simple present to talk about timetables or programmes.
- We use the present progressive to talk about future arrangements.

b Jason is talking to his parents. Complete what he says with the correct future forms.

Mr T. Has your team started preparing yet?
Jason Yes, the coach gave us a new schedule. We [1] (*have*) extra training at weekends from next week.
Mrs T. What do you know about your opponent?
Jason Nothing yet, but we [2] (*meet*) them in a video call next week. I [3] (*try*) to find videos about the other school team on the internet. No matter what, we [4] (*ask*) the coach to work out the best strategy for our team.
Mrs T. I bet he [5] (*do*) that! I hope you [6] (*be able to*) go sightseeing in Christchurch as well. And how do you feel about the twins?
Jason I know I [7] (*not be able to*) go to Sydney, but I am sure Nick and Eleni [8] (*understand*). And they [9] (*have*) a barbie later in the year to celebrate their birthdays with everyone here.

5 So far and so close.

3 Jason gets a phone call that changes everything. Listen and do the tasks.

1 Describe what the rugby team has been getting ready for.
2 Explain why Ricky is so excited about the tournament.
3 Explain what Eleni's news means for Jason.

6 It's your turn: A sporting expert

a Which sport can you see in the picture? Look at this list (*Australian rules football, cricket, netball, rugby*), choose a sport and do some research. Then prepare a two-minute talk.

b Find a partner with another sport. Give your talks and ask each other questions. What didn't you know about your partner's sport before?

Grammar and structures

Tenses (revision) → G1
Eleni **hasn't known** about Aunt Koula's illness for very long.
The team **is going to practise** more, so I believe we**'ll be able to** win.

1 **a** Did you know that the word 'selfie' originates from Australia? Australians love to add 'ie' or 'y' to words to make them informal. Can you guess what the words in the box mean?

> Aussie ■ brekkie ■ footy ■ lappy ■ prezzie

3 **b** Now go to the webcode and watch the video. See if you can find another word like the ones in the box.

2 Australian English has many informal words and phrases. Read Jason and Eleni's conversation and match the numbered words and phrases with the standard English ones in the box. The context will help you. Compare your answers with a partner.

> afternoon ■ barbecue ■ Don't worry ■ food ■ great ■ Hello ■ How are you? ■ lots ■ Thanks ■ Well done

Eleni: **G'day** (1), Jason.
Jason: Hi, Eleni! **How ya going?** (2)
Eleni: Oh, I'm fine. It's so hot today, though. I hope it won't be like this all weekend.
Jason: Aw, **no worries** (3). They say it's going to get cooler.
Eleni: That's good. Hey, we're having a **barbie** (4) at our house this **arvo** (5). Would you like to join us?
Jason: That sounds **ace** (6). I'd love to come. Shall I bring some **tucker** (7) with me?
Eleni: Aw, no need – we've already done the shopping. We've got **heaps** (8) to eat.
Jason: **Good on ya.** (9) **Cheers!** (10) Then I'll see ya later.
Eleni: See you then!

3 Here are some more Australian words. Guess or find out what they mean. Use some of these words or those in **1** and **2** to write a short dialogue. Then share your dialogue in class. Can the others understand it?

> beauty ■ chockers ■ mozzie ■ nana ■ pom ■ roo ■ sickie ■ swimmers ■ ta

4 **a** Read part of an interview with Coach Hansen for the Bayview High School newspaper. Use the *present perfect* or the *present perfect progressive* to complete the sentences.

Q: Coach Hansen, you [1] (*coach*) the boys' rugby team for eight years. What do you like about the job and what [2] (*change*) since you started?
A: I [3] (*always, have*) the full support of the school principal and the teaching staff. The students and the parents [4] (*believe*) in me too. When we started, the inter-school competition in Melbourne wasn't well organized, but it [5] (*get*) better every year, so that [6] (*be*) a positive change.
Q: Why do you think the boys' team [7] (*be*) so successful this year?
A: We've got an amazing team with players like Ricky Bates and Jason Turner. These boys [8] (*play*) rugby for at least five years, so they understand how to be effective on the field. Also, we [9] (*try*) different game plans, and now I think we [10] (*find out*) what works.

b Read the next part of the interview. Use *will* or *going to* to complete the sentences.

Q: The team has been invited to Christchurch in New Zealand to play against their rugby team. Could you tell our readers how you are preparing for this trip?
A: There are a lot of things we [1] (*need*) to organize. First, we [2] (*have*) a meeting with the parents soon where we [3] (*try*) to answer all the questions. The school sports fund [4] (*pay*) for the plane tickets and once we are there the players [5] (*stay*) with host families. I am sure they [6] (*have*) a great time and [7] (*have*) the opportunity for sightseeing.
Q: Do you think you [8] (*win*) against the Kiwis?
A: I think we have a good chance. We [9] (*have*) extra practice at the weekends and [10] (*learn*) as much as we can about our opponents. It [11] (*be*) hard work but lots of fun at the same time. And I am sure the parents [12] (*support*) us.

@ WES-40805-001

→ Workbook, page 11

LISTENING AND VIEWING PRACTICE

1 Look at the pictures connected to Australia. With a partner speculate what they show. Make notes.

1

2

3

4

2 (4) Watch the slide show and check your ideas. What did you learn that you didn't know before?

3 **a** Put these events in the correct chronological order.

- Aborigines arrive in Australia.
- Captain Cook lands at Botany Bay.
- Gold is discovered.
- The Commonwealth of Australia is formed.
- The Dutch 'discover' Australia.
- The Eureka Rebellion takes place.
- The first settlement is established at Sydney Cove.

(4) **b** Watch the slide show again and check.

4 **a** Decide whether the underlined words and phrases are correct. Correct the wrong ones.

b Find eight factual mistakes in the text and correct them.

The first people to arrive in Australia were the Aborigines. They arrived between forty and sixty thousands[1] years ago. Then in 1506 a number of Dutch explorers 'discovered' Australia. They named this new land New Holland. In 1770 Captain James Cook landed[2] by[3] Sydney Cove. Sixteen years later the first colony has been[4] established at Sydney Cove with a lot of convicts sent from Britain. Between 1788 and 1868 around 64,000 convicts were transported by the ship[5] from Britain to Australia. In 1803 the Dutch explorer Mathew Flinders named it Terra Australis Incognita, which means 'unknown southern land'. In 1851, oil was discovered in New South Wales and thousands of free settlers arrived from around the world. In 1901 a competition is hold[6] to design a flag for the country. The Australian flag has four elements on a blue background. The first of these is the Union Jack in the top left corner showing that Australia was a British colony. Australia Day is celebrated on the first of January every year. This is the day that Australia became independently[7] of[8] Britain.

To move or not to move?

1 **Life in Australia.** Look at the picture. Speculate what is going on.

2 **Keira's email.** The Smiths are a family from the South of England. They have moved into the house next to the Turners. Keira, the daughter, is 15. She writes an email to her best friend back in the UK. Read the email, then do the tasks.

From: Keira Smith
To: Jasmine Roberts
Subject: Australia

Hiya,

So this arvo – that's Australian for afternoon – we are going to go for a barbie (you can guess what that means) with the Turners. They live next door to the place we're staying in and they've invited us round. I think Mrs Turner will ask us how we are settling in. And I bet Mr Turner will want to know if we are going to move to Melbourne for good. I wonder if they'll ask us what we kids think.
My dad says Fred and I have to like it here, too, and it is our decision as well. My mum has just told me not to worry, our opinion matters.
I'm not sure. I love it here. The weather is great, and the people are really friendly, but if I am asked, I will tell them that I don't want to leave my friends.

Jazz, what do you think I should say to my parents? I know they both love it here, but …
If we moved here, would you come over and visit?

Love K.
xxx

1 Explain why Keira is writing to Jasmine.
2 Speculate who Fred is.

Reported speech
We use reported speech to talk about what other people say.

- We start with reporting verbs, expressions such as: *He says / She asks / wants to know / wonders / has told (me), will ask*, etc.
- When the reporting verb is in the present, present perfect or future tense, we do not change the tense of what we report.
  We love the area.
  My dad ***says / has said / will say*** *(that) we* ***love*** *the area …*
- When we report questions we change them into a statement after the question word:
  So how are you settling in?
  She wants to know how we ***are settling*** *in.*
- To report *yes/no*-questions we use *if* or *whether* and invert the subject and the verb.
  Are *you* ***going to move*** *to Melbourne?*
  He wants to know ***whether we are going to move*** *to Melbourne.*
- For orders and requests we use the infinitive form of the main verb with *to*.
  Don't worry. → *My mum tells me* ***not to worry.***
- Be careful about the pronoun changes:
  So do ***you*** *think* ***you****'re going to move to Melbourne for good?*
  Mr Turner has just asked ***us*** *if* ***we*** *are going to move to Melbourne for good.*

Words and phrases

on your doorstep very close to where you live
to settle in to become familiar with a new way of life, place, job, etc.
to switch to change from one thing to another

→ Workbook, pages 12/13

3 A life-changing decision

5 **a** Listen to the conversation at the Turners' barbecue, then do the tasks.

1 Explain the big decision that the Smiths have to make. What do they have to think about?
2 Describe how Fred Smith feels and say why.

b Look at Jason's question and Fred's answer. Report what they both say.

Do you like sport, Freddie? Everyone's sport mad here.

Wow. That's great.

4 Decision time

a Back home after the barbecue Mrs Smith, Fred and Keira carry on talking about the move. Read the conversation and do the tasks below. (You will need the blue words and phrases for activity **b**.)

Fred — What's wrong with you, Keira?
Mrs S. — Please don't speak to your sister like that.
Fred — But mum! Why can't she decide?
Mrs S. — I know you want to move here …
Fred — Yes, I do. Just think of all the things I can do outdoors and I can join the rugby team and …
Mrs S. — Won't you miss your friends in England?
Fred — Sure, but I'll make new friends here.
Mrs S. — It's a big decision for everyone, Fred. Be patient with Keira!
Keira — It's not easy …
Mrs S. — No, it's not, Keira, but we don't have a lot of time. Can you think about it and make a decision by Wednesday?
Keira — Wednesday!? But that's only three days away.
Fred — I'll help you decide.

1 Explain why Fred is upset.
2 Analyse Keira's reaction to what Mrs Smith says.
3 Compare how Fred and Keira feel about the move.

b Keira is talking to her dad. Read the conversation again and complete what Keira tells him about it. The blue words in **a** can help you.

Mr S. — Are you OK?
Keira — Not really. Fred wants to know ___1___ and Mum has asked him ___2___.
Mr S. — So, you're not sure yet if you like it here?
Keira — No, but Fred is sure ___3___.
Mr S. — And what does your mother say?
Keira — Mum has told Fred ___4___. She wants me ___5___.
Mr S. — I'm sorry, I know it's hard for you. So, what are you going to do?
Keira — I'll talk to Fred. He has told me ___6___.

5 It's your turn: Going to Australia

a Think: Imagine you were going to spend a year abroad in Australia. How would you feel? What would you miss most? What would you be excited about? Makes notes.

b Pair: Tell a partner how you would feel if you were moving to Australia.

c Share: Report what your partner says to the rest of the class.

Grammar and structures

Reported speech in statements and questions in the present, present perfect and future → G2

My dad **says** we **love** the area …
Fred **has told** me he **will help** me decide.
Mrs Turner **will ask** us how we **are settling in**.

1 **a** The day after the barbecue you see Jason and Keira in the shopping mall. Listen to their conversation and do the tasks.

6

1 Say what Jason and Keira are talking about.
2 Explain why Keira thinks it is a great idea to be introduced to Jason's classmates.

b While you are listening to Jason and Keira's conversation, a friend rings you. Report what you hear.

Jason says ... *Keira admits that ...* *Jason wants to know ...*
Keira says that ... *Now Jason has offered to ...*
He thinks ... *He also says ...*
Keira looks happy! She tells Jason ...

2 At the barbecue, Mr Turner invited Bob Smith to visit him at his workplace. The following week, Bob went to see Adrian Turner. While he is there, Wendy phones him and asks him about the visit. Read the conversation and correct the underlined mistakes.

Wendy So, how is the visit with Adrian?
Bob It is interesting. You remember he mentioned working at a big factory that bottles fruit juice ...
Wendy Yes, I know from Judith he has an important job there.
Bob An important job! He owns the factory.
Wendy Wow! Have you ask[1] him about that?
Bob Yes, I have and he's[2] says he been[3] lucky as his dad started the company almost fifty years ago. He's just asked me what do I do[4] back in the UK and he seems to be happy that I am an electrician. He says that is great as he can always use electricians in the factory ...
Wendy What, you already have a job?
Bob No, of course not. But I think if we decided to move over here for good, there might be a job waiting for me.
Wendy That's wonderful news. What you[5] say to him if he asks?
Bob I'll say I think[6] about it ...
Wendy Bob!
Bob I'm joking, darling. I tell[7] him I'll be talk[8] to you and the kids more about moving to Melbourne ...

3 Jasmine discussed Keira's dilemma with her mum. Here are some of the things they said. Write an email from Jasmine to Keira in which you give her advice. Include some of the information and add your own ideas.

Has Keira been in Melbourne long enough to get to know the place?

Has she found anything she particularly likes?

I am sure she'll make friends there quickly.

You can use social media to keep in touch.

You will go and visit her as soon as you can.

What is the school system like there? – I think it's similar to ours.

Keira can join a school club. She'll meet lots of people.

Maybe she can start a blog about life in Australia.

→ Workbook, page 14

4 **a** Before they came to Australia Fred read this information leaflet. Read the leaflet and match the headings from the box to the paragraphs (A–F).

Deadly wildlife ■ It's absolutely massive ■ It's not just cities ■ Learn the slang ■ Sport mad ■ Sun and snow

Moving to the Land Down Under

Moving to a new country is always a big deal and it can take time to settle in. Here is some information you might want to know if you are considering moving to Australia.

A

Deciding where to live can be tricky. Australia is about the size of Europe and the distance between Perth in the west and Sydney in the south-east is 3,290 km. It takes more than four hours to fly from one city to the other!

B

Most people think of Australia as scorching. Sure, it can get hot, but not everywhere all year round. In fact, it's possible to go surfing and skiing on the same day. When it's summer in the south, it's usually the wet season in the north, while Melbourne is known for having 'four seasons in a day'.

C

Around 90 % of all Australians live in cities so there's a lot of empty space. There are more than five hundred National Parks, the world-famous Blue Mountains and vast areas of outback to explore.

D

It's true that Australia has more than its fair share of deadly animals, but it's often exaggerated. For example, there are only two species of deadly spiders in Australia and nobody has died from a bite since 1979! You're even quite safe in the sea. Stingrays have only ever killed two people, and on average there is only one shark attack per year.

E

Although English is the official language, it can often be difficult to understand an Aussie when they speak. It's not their accent that causes problems, but the amount of slang they use. Afternoon is *arvo*, when something is broken it's *cactus* and when you go for a *bogey*, it means you're going for a swim!

F

From Aussie rules to cricket and rugby, everyone is crazy about sport. But these are not the only sports. Melbourne hosts the Australian Open as well as one of the best known horse races in the world – the Melbourne Cup. Then, of course, there are all the beach sports from beach volleyball to surfing. Australia is a paradise for any sports lover.

b Find words or phrases in the text to match the definitions.

1 very hot
2 extremely big
3 to hold a special event
4 important or special
5 difficult, needing attention
6 informal language usually spoken by a particular group of people
7 making something bigger, more important, better or worse than it really is
8 thinking about doing something

c Read the leaflet again and do the tasks.

1 Explain why the leaflet says deciding where to live in Australia can be tricky.
2 Analyse what is meant by the phrase: Melbourne is known for having 'four seasons in a day'.
3 Outline why there is so much empty space in Australia.
4 Illustrate why the leaflet claims that it's an exaggeration that Australia is full of deadly animals.
5 Explain why Australia would be a 'paradise for any sports lover'.
6 Comment on why, even if you spoke good English, you might find it difficult to communicate in Australia.

1788

On January 26th, 1788 the First Fleet landed at Sydney Cove and established the first colony. The fleet consisted of 11 ships with 1480 people on board. Around half of these were convicts.

1851

In 1851 gold was discovered in Australia. A gold rush started with thousands of people arriving from different countries hoping to become rich. In just ten years, the population of Australia doubled!

1901

In 1901, the six territories joined together and formed the Commonwealth of Australia.
A new flag was designed for the new country.

1956

In 1956, sports mad Australia held the 13th modern Olympic Games in Melbourne. Australia won 35 medals, 13 gold. The star was 17-year-old Iain Murray Rose who won three swimming gold medals!

2008

In 2008, the Parliament of Australia made a formal apology to Indigenous Australians for the forced removal of their children by Australian government agencies. The apology was delivered by Prime Minister Kevin Rudd.

1 **a** Look at the infographic on the left. Then listen to Jason talking to Fred about Australian history and complete the tasks.

1. Name the two events in the infographic which Jason mentions.
2. Explain why Jason laughs at one point during the conversation.

b Later on Fred makes some notes about what Jason told him. Listen to the conversation again. Read the notes and correct the mistakes.

> Australia was once an American Colony.
>
> The first people from Europe arrived in 1856.
>
> The Olympic Games have been held twice in Melbourne.
>
> Australia won a lot of medals in wrestling.
>
> Australia was set up as a penal colony.

2 **a Think:** Choose one event from the infographic. Carry out some internet research and make notes. Use your notes to structure a short talk.

b Pair: Find a partner who has chosen the same event. Prepare your talk together.

c Share: Find two pairs with different events. Take turns and give your presentation. The others ask questions and give feedback. Then decide which event is the most interesting. Give reasons and present it to the class.

→ Workbook, page 15

3 Keira finds a book about the Aborigines that contains lots of information and also photos.
(8) Listen to her describing one of the photos to her mum. Which one is she talking about?

A

B

C

D

E

F

4 **a** Choose two different photos each and do some research. Make notes about each photo and any information you can find.

b Describe your photos to your partner and use your notes to explain what they show.

c Compare your photos. Discuss what they have in common. What do they tell you about Aboriginal culture?

d Have you learned anything new about Aboriginal culture through the photos? Discuss the importance of Aboriginal customs and traditions for the Australian society.

@ WES-40805-001
→ Workbook, page 16

Understanding new words and phrases

S1 Identifying main ideas. Before you start reading a text, first look at the title and any pictures to get an idea of what the text is about. Discuss your ideas for the text below.

S2 Working out the meaning of new words and phrases. Read the text carefully. First look at the **blue** words. Then read the tips and work out what they mean.

> **TIP**
>
> **How to work out the meaning of new words**
> First decide if you need to know the meaning of the new word to understand the text. If you do, then follow these tips.
> - Is the word similar to a German or an international word?
> - Can you guess the meaning from the words before / after it? Or does the text give an explanation (often inside commas)?
> - Do you already know part of the word or another form of the word?

Before and after

Australia's first peoples were hunter-gatherers who lived in small family groups and were **semi-nomadic**, systematically moving from place to place following the changes of the seasons. Each group lived in a defined **territory** with its own **distinct** history and culture. Although the hunter-gatherers didn't develop an **agrarian**, or farming, society, they managed the land and wild animals in various ways to make sure they had **predictable** supplies of food and water.

When the British arrived in 1788, about 770,000 Aboriginal people were living in Australia, with **approximately** 260 different language groups and 500 **dialects**. How did colonization **impact** these communities? The most immediate **consequence** was a wave of epidemic diseases such as smallpox, influenza and measles. These diseases killed many indigenous people because they had no **resistance** to them.

Many also died in **random** killings or organized **massacres**. Massacres often took the form of mass shootings or driving groups of people off **cliffs**. As a result, there was a drastic **decline** in the Aboriginal population. By 1900, it was estimated that only about 117,000 indigenous people were still living in Australia.

S3 Using dictionaries to find the meaning of new words and phrases

a Discuss these questions.

- How often do you use a dictionary? If not so often, why not?
- Do you use a printed dictionary or an online dictionary? Monolingual or bilingual? What are the benefits of each?
- What can you use a dictionary for? Make a list of your ideas and compare in class.

b Now look at the **red** words in the text in **2** and use a dictionary to find the right meaning in this context.

c You probably don't know the words *small pox*, *influenza* and *measles*. Why is it not necessary to check what they mean?

d What does *looking for trouble* mean? Explain the cartoon.

"He's been in here all day just looking for trouble."

@ WES-40805-001

→ Workbook, page 16

WORKSHOP TASK

Understanding texts on a new topic

S1 **Identify main ideas**

a Look at the title and the pictures. What do you think the text is about?

b Read and match the photos to the correct paragraphs.

Outback threatened by non-native species

Although much of Australia's interior is **arid** desert, it isn't empty of life. If you camp out in the outback, you'll hear the **howls** of dingoes, or wild dogs, **echoing** across the landscape. Dingoes were introduced into Australia around 4,000 years ago, and today they are both loved and **loathed**. They attack sheep and have caused the decline of many native species. In spite of this, it's exciting to see them **roam around** wild in Australia.

But they are not the only non-native species that have become serious **pests**, causing enormous ecological damage to Australia. You'll also **come across** the world's largest herd of **feral** camels. Introduced from Arabia and India for transport and work in the outback, they were **released** into the wild when they were no longer needed with the **advent** of powered engines. Other **invasive** species include foxes and rabbits, brought from Europe in the 19th century for sport hunting. They had few **predators**, so their populations **exploded**. Control **measures** have reduced their numbers, but they remain a big problem.

A

B

C

S2 **Work out the meaning of words and phrases.** Use the tips on page **24** to help you work out the meanings of the **blue** words. Then match the correct words to these definitions. What words in the text helped you guess?

1 allowed to go free
2 an action to achieve a particular aim
3 an insect or an animal that destroys plants, etc.
4 sounding again and again
5 the sound a wild dog makes
6 to get bigger very quickly

S3 **Use a dictionary to check the meaning of new words and phrases.** Now look at the words in **red**. Can you work out their meanings? Use a dictionary to check your guesses, or to find the correct meaning in the context. Compare your findings with a partner.

S4 **Use different kinds of dictionaries**

a In groups of three, read the last paragraph of the text. Note down any words or phrases you don't understand. Look at the tips on page 24 again and work out as many meanings as you can.

b Now each use a different method to check the rest of the list: (1) a monolingual dictionary, (2) a bilingual dictionary and (3) an online dictionary. When you have finished, compare your results.

Australia's prolonged drought is now driving large groups of camels out of the desert onto farms and into towns. In their desperate search for water, the camels demolish fences and foul critical watering holes, polluting the water and making it undrinkable. In an effort to defend farm properties, hundreds of camels are culled a day, leaving thousands of dead animals to rot. The culls are controversial. There is little agreement on a long-term solution.

Discovering Australia

1 Famous sites

a Look at the title, photos and the introduction and discuss what you think the texts will be about. Then one of you reads text A and the other one text B. Make notes under these headings:

- Location
- Importance to Aboriginal people
- Creation legend

b Outline what you have learned to each other. Then decide which place you would most like to visit and why.

Sacred sites of Australia

Aboriginal and Torres Strait Islander nations have their own Creation or Dreamtime legends which have been passed down by the Elders from generation to generation. The whole continent is covered with sacred sites that are extremely important in Aboriginal tradition and folklore. Find out about two of them.

A Uluru (was once called Ayers Rock)

Uluru is one of the most sacred sites in Aboriginal folklore. It's a large rock formation located close to the exact centre of Australia and has been designated a UNESCO World Heritage Site.
The rock resumed its original name in 1985 when the land was given back to the local people, the Anangu, by the Australian Government. They now own the Kata Tjuta National Park, which Uluru is part of. The Anangu had long wanted the title deeds to be returned. According to their leaders, 'this is how we can make sure the place is looked after properly for everyone'. Ancient Aboriginal paintings, which tell the story of the Dreaming, can be seen in caves in the rock.

Legend of Uluru according to the Anangu

Two tribes of ancient spirits were invited to a feast but didn't turn up. Their hosts were bitterly insulted. There was a great battle and many were killed. Uluru rose up to show that the land was deeply saddened by the bloodshed.

B Great Barrier Reef

The Great Barrier Reef is absolutely enormous. The size of about 70 million football fields, it's the only living thing on our planet that can be seen from space. It stretches 2,300 kilometres along the coast of Queensland and is home to a huge variety of marine creatures, including fish, seabirds, whales, dolphins and sharks. Fishing has been practised here for thousands of years by Aboriginal and Torres Strait Islanders, who are the traditional owners of the Great Barrier Reef region. Tourism is very important, but it's carefully controlled to limit damage to the reef.

Legend according to Yindingi clan

This story tells of two brothers who went out fishing and were ordered by Bhiral, the Creator, not to hunt one particular kind of fish. One of the brothers disobeyed and speared the fish. Bhiral was extremely angry, so he threw lava and hot rocks down from the sky. The lava made the sea rise and when the lava had cooled, it formed what is now the Great Barrier Reef. The story is very similar to what scientists believe really happened.

2 For and against

a Tourism can have advantages and disadvantages. Together brainstorm a list of arguments for and against it.

For	Against
brings money for the local community	???

b Share your ideas with the class. Discuss: Should tourism be banned completely in some places?

Useful expressions:
On the one hand, … on the other hand, … / For example, … / However, … / First of all, … / In my opinion, … / I'd like to point out that … / You have a point, but … / I'm not sure if … / The reason for this is that … / Finally, …

9 Words and phrases

to occupy a place to live or stay in a place **particular** one thing and not a different one **to stretch** to cover a large area of land

3* What's most important?

a Read the information in the box on the right. Find more examples of passive sentences in the texts about Uluru and the Great Barrier Reef. Then decide why the passive was used. Choose from this list.

1 The person or object doing the action is not known or not important.
2 To avoid using vague subjects like *Someone*, *People*, *They*.
3 The focus of the sentence is on the action, not the agent.

b Uluru is a very popular tourist destination. Use Fred's notes to write a paragraph about Uluru and tourism. Where possible, use passive forms as in the example.

- big tour companies bring busloads of tourists every day

Busloads of tourists are brought in every day by big tour companies.

- many visitors expect allow climb rock
- tourists ban climb sacred site since 2019
- reason: totally unacceptable to Aboriginal owners
- alternative activities develop for tourists since ban
- visitors offer walking tours around base Uluru by experienced guides
- Anangu not want tourism ban
- reason: one of main sources of income
- tourism industry should give Aborigine bigger share profits

Remember

- We form the passive with a form of *be* and a past participle.
  Each nation has its own Creation legends which ***have been passed down*** *by the Elders.*
- When a verb is followed by a preposition, it stays in the same position in the passive.
- When a verb has two objects, the passive sentence can begin with either the direct or indirect object. Verbs that take two objects include *give, offer, promise, show.*
  The land was given back to *the original owners.* OR
  The original owners were given back *the land.*
- We use the passive infinitive after modal verbs, and verbs like *expect, hope, like, need, want.*
  Ancient Aboriginal paintings ***can be seen*** *in caves in Uluru.*
  They had long wanted the title deeds ***to be returned****.*

4 A film trailer

a Your teacher is going to show you a trailer for the film *Walkabout*, which is set in the Australian outback. Look at the still from the film. What do you think the film will be about?

5 **b** Watch the trailer and write a short summary. You can use the ideas below.

The film tells the story of a sister and brother …
The two children have to …
They are saved by …
Suddenly a white man …
The siblings and the aboriginal boy …

5 **c** Watch again to check and add more details. What do you think happens at the end of the film? Present your ideas to the class.

Grammar and structures

Passive (revision) → G5

Passive with verb + preposition:	We can make sure the place **is looked after**.
Passive: verbs with two objects:	The land **was given back to** the local people.
Passive infinitive after *want*, *expect*, etc.:	The Anangu had long **wanted** the title deeds **to be returned**.
Passive infinitive after modal verbs:	Ancient Aboriginal paintings **can be seen** in caves in the rock.

→ Workbook, page 19

1 Look at the photos. What natural disasters do they show? Use a dictionary to find the English words you need. Then speculate how these disasters are connected to climate change and global warming.

A

B

C

2 **a** Read the article to find out how climate change is affecting Australia and complete the text with the appropriate passive forms.

b Outline the main effects of climate change in your own words. Show how the writer gives examples to illustrate them.

The climate reality

Australia is known for its stunning scenery, its fabulous beaches, and unique wildlife. Many animals such as koala bears, kangaroos, wombats **1** (*can, only, find*) in Australia. But scientists are warning that Australia is especially at risk from the climate crisis. This is the climate reality:

Heat and drought

Australia is already a very hot and dry country and it's expected to get a lot hotter and drier if no action **2** (*take*) on climate change. In January 2018, temperatures in Sydney soared to over 47 degrees. It was the hottest day that the city had experienced in 80 years. Climate change is making heatwaves much more common, more severe and longer-lasting than they have ever been. More heat means more droughts.

Bushfires / Wildfires

Drought creates the perfect conditions for bushfires. Plants dry up and die, providing the ideal fuel for fires. Bushfires are becoming much more frequent and more extreme, especially in the south and east. In the last few years, there were nearly 200 fires in Queensland. Conditions like these **3** (*never, see*) in its history.

Farming

As Australia's climate changes, every type of farmer **4** (*affect*). The climate crisis is making it more and more difficult for farmers to grow food and raise livestock. Queensland is one of Australia's most populated states, where much of the country's food **5** (*produce*). According to one farmer, 'Food security **6** (*endanger*) by climate change, there's no doubt about that.'

The ocean and the Great Barrier Reef

Our oceans are becoming warmer and more acidic. The Great Barrier Reef **7** (*hit*) incredibly hard by both factors. It **8** (*form*) over many millions of years by tiny animals called polyps. But these are dying due to the rise in sea temperature, and the future of the reef is in doubt.

Australia has a lot to lose. The causes of climate change need **9** (*tackle*) urgently.

WHO CAN CHANGE THIS? YOU!
JOIN THE CLIMATE FIGHT AND TAKE ACTION.

3 **a** Jason's schoolmate Ricky is very concerned about climate change, so he and his friends are taking part in a demonstration. A radio journalist interviews them. Read the questions.

1. Why are they at the demonstration?
2. What are the aims of the Seed Mob movement?
3. Why is the land important to Aboriginal people?
4. What are the main causes of climate change in Australia?
5. How does climate change affect Aboriginal people?
6. What do they want the Federal Government to do?

11 **b** Listen and make notes on the questions in **a**. Compare with a partner, then listen again to check and complete your notes.

c Compare the situation in Australia with Germany. Describe the similarities or differences of the problems. Outline how Germany is affected by climate change and how the people react to it. Write about 150 words.

10 **Words and phrases**

livestock	animals such as cows, sheep and pigs that are kept on a farm
stunning	very impressive or beautiful
to tackle sth	to try to solve a difficult problem
tipping point	the time when things start to happen in a situation, especially things that you can't change

→ Workbook, page 20

1 How often do you read blogs? Talk about these questions:

- Where and how often do blogs appear?
- What kind of topics can they cover?
- How are they structured?
- Who is the blogger's audience?
- What is a typical writing style for a blog (e.g. formal / informal, conversational, instructive, etc.)?

2 **a** Eleni is contributing to a website where teenagers post blogs about their home cities. Read her blog about Melbourne.

Melbourne is the place!

By Eleni Kourakis

Though I have lived in this magnificent city all my life, I can never get bored with it. If you asked me what I like about it most, I wouldn't know how to answer, there are so many attractions here. Let me take you on a virtual tour and show you the places I truly love. (If you ever come to visit, I am sure you'll love them, too.)

The narrow 'laneways' in the city centre are a good place to start. Do you like cool cafés, amazing street art and buskers playing great music? If so, then you'll enjoy Centre Place and Hosier Lane. What about colourful outdoor markets? I love Queen Victoria Market – it's an awesome place for shopping, yummy street food and just hanging out. Getting around in the city centre is really easy, too: you can ride the trams for free, or do what lots of people do – cycle! Cycling is my favourite way of exploring the city's back streets and hitting the beach at St Kilda. The list of cool and cheap things that you can do here goes on and on.

I've just mentioned St Kilda, so let me take you there. Do you want to soak up the sun on sandy beaches, cool down in the ocean or roller skate along the promenade? Have a picnic or relax in a café – whatever you want, it's there. Or just gaze at the Melbourne skyline? If you are lucky, you might see skydivers landing on the shore. It's an unforgettable experience and the best birthday treat I've ever had! And make sure you stay till sunset if you want to see the penguins. Just follow the crowd to the end of the pier where the sanctuary is.

Come check it out and this awesome city will win your heart, too.

b Say who the article is written for and explain what Eleni's aim is. Give examples of language she uses to achieve this. Include the line numbers.

c Look at the *TIP* box. Find examples in the article of the techniques that it lists. Compare and discuss with a partner.

d Write a blog entry (150 words or more) about your home town or city. Select features you like and use techniques to persuade the reader to visit these places / to make your reader interested in these places.

TIP

Here are some useful techniques when you are writing to persuade your readers:

- **Anecdotes** (short, personal stories) have an emotional effect.
- **Comparisons** show that you are balanced and honest.
- **Strongly positive or negative words** make the reader feel the same.
- **Personal pronouns** like 'I', 'you' or 'we' speak directly to the reader.
- **Direct questions** get the reader's interest and make him or her think.

12 **Words and phrases**

busker street musician

A New Zealand visit

A 

B 

C 

1 Away from home

14 **a** Paige Williams is in year nine at Papanui High School in Christchurch, New Zealand. She lives with her Aunt Christine and Uncle Tai. Look at the pictures and describe what they tell you. Listen, then describe the three scenes in more detail.

14 **b** Listen again and do these tasks.

1 List the topics Paige talks about in her video call.
- farm animals
- dad's health
- homesickness
- Paige's sister
- weather
- school
- Paige's aunt
- holidays

2 Explain why Paige lives with her aunt and uncle.

3 Name two things that their visitors find out during the conversation at dinner.

2 Life back home

a Paige says: 'I love baby goats.' Her teacher says: 'You can talk about your farm in Kerikeri.' Now look at these sentences and the rules in the box.

*She said that she **loved** the baby goats.*
*My teacher told me I **could** talk about our farm in Kerikeri.*

> **Reported speech**
> - In reported speech, when the reporting verb is in the past, the tense in the part of the sentence we are reporting moves one step back in time.
>   *It's pretty cool and wet here.* → *She said that it **was** pretty cool and wet there.*
> - In reported speech, you can leave out the word *that*.
>   *She told me **that** her subjects were tough.*
>   → *She told me her subjects were tough.*

b Later, Paige's dad told her more news from Kerikeri. Her aunt wants to know what he told her. Report what Mr Williams said. Remember: sometimes the pronouns change.

1 'Bella is doing a wonderful job with the vegetable garden.'
2 'Rachel texted me from Auckland yesterday. She texts at least every second day.'
3 'We've made the old shed into a guest house.'
4 'I can't come and visit because of the sheep.'
5 'We'll be able to come in the summer.'

> **CULTURE CORNER**
>
> **Aussies and Kiwis – a special relationship**
> Relations between Australia and New Zealand have often been compared to those of siblings or cousins.
> Even though the countries share common experiences like fighting side-by-side in two World Wars, they don't always get along. They have different personalities and sometimes serious political differences. They also have a huge sporting rivalry – mainly in cricket, rugby and netball, and they like joking about each other.
> However, when they are out in the big world, they often team together, and when they describe their relationship, they speak of the respect and trust they feel for each other.

13 Words and phrases

kinship	a feeling of being close or similar to another person
rivalry	a situation when people, countries, etc. compete for the same thing
sibling	a brother or sister
to tip over	(of a boat) to turn over in water
white water	river water that looks white because it is moving fast over rocks

→ Workbook, pages 21/22

3 South Island adventure

a Jason has been travel-blogging on social media. Look what he has posted. What do you find most interesting about each post? With a partner, compare and explain your thoughts.

b Think of a good heading for each post. Share your ideas.

jasonturner
4 October

Liked by **elenikourakis, nickkourakis, judithturner** and **7 others**

This is my NZ blog! Today after rugby practice a few of us went to Christchurch Adventure Park. You take a chairlift up to the top of the Port Hills. Amazing views of Christchurch, along the coast and all the way to the Southern Alps! Then we rode the zipline. It's the longest in NZ – over 1 km. It's fast and scary. My heart was racing! I asked one of the guys to take this photo of us.

jasonturner
5 October

Liked by **elenikourakis, judithturner** and **6 others**

Today we went to a place called Ko Tane. It's an interactive museum where Maori in costumes show how they lived before the Europeans came. We did the hongi greeting (nose to nose!), sang songs and watched this welcoming dance. Tai was such a great guide. We asked him what all the Maori words meant and he explained them. The best part was the hangi, a big meal cooked on hot rocks in the ground.

jasonturner
7 October

Liked by **elenikourakis, nickkourakis, judithturner** and **7 others**

The day after our game (they beat us by ONE point! 23 – 22 ☹), Coach Hansen organized a river rafting trip for us. The river was near some beautiful mountains where the Lord of the Rings trilogy was filmed! We practised paddling in the quiet part of the river, then we got to the white water. It was really moving fast! Our guide told us to paddle hard. We nearly tipped over once. At the end, we swam in the river in our wetsuits. Awesome!

4 An awesome trip

a Look at these examples from Jason's posts. What did Jason say directly to these people?

I asked one of the guys to take this photo of us.
We asked him what all the words meant.

Find one more example of indirect speech in Jason's posts and change it into direct speech.

Remember:

- To report *yes/no*-questions we use *if* or *whether* and invert subject and verb.
  ***Is Auckland** a big city?* →
  *I asked her **if Auckland was** a big city.*
- For questions with a *wh*-question word, the order is the same as in statements.
  ***What do** the Maori **words mean**?* →
  *He asked **what** the Maori **words meant**.*
- For orders and requests we use the infinitive form of the main verb with *to*.
  *Could you **repeat** the question?* →
  *She asked me **to repeat** the question.*

b Read these statements that other people made. What did Jason report to his parents?

Tai Show respect during the Maori rituals.
Guide Have you ever been rafting before?
Paige When are you going to visit us again?
Guide Keep your helmets on at all times.

5 It's your turn: A trip to Christchurch

a You and your partner are touring New Zealand and have two days in Christchurch. What will you do there? Form groups of four – **Pair A** and **Pair B**. Each pair should look at Jason's posts and do some more research about Christchurch. With your partner, discuss and agree on a plan.

b First **Pair A** presents their plan to **Pair B**. Then swap roles. Discuss the two plans and decide what you want to do in a group.

Grammar and structures

Reported speech in statements and questions in the past and in requests, offers, orders and advice → G3

Ricky **said** that he **wanted** to visit us again.
We **asked** Paige **to take** some photos.
They **asked** us **if** we **had enjoyed** the sightseeing.
Coach Hansen **told** us **not to be shy** on the river.
I **asked** them **where** the high school **was**.

Changes to adverbs of time and place in reported speech → G4

1 Do some research about five things or places that you find interesting, unusual or attractive about New Zealand. Get together in a group and discuss your choices. Rank them and present the top three to the class. Compare your results in class.

2 **a** Skim the text. Where would you find a text like this? Describe its function.

b Do these tasks.

1. Look at the map showing New Zealand on the front inside cover of the book. Find out which island the places are located on.
2. Outline what you learn about each place from the short programme description.

c **Think:** Collect ideas for a similar programme that looks at Germany. Include at least four places of interest and highlight one or two aspects of each place.

Pair: Compare your ideas and agree on a list of four places with highlighted aspects of each.

Share: Discuss and agree on a final list for your programme. Then, do a poster presentation of your places in class.

HOME | Programmes | Channels | Find a programme

Two Islands Make a Nation

Starting Wednesday, September 19 at 9 pm

Amanda Nguyen and Shane Alcott visit our neighbours across the Tasman Sea to find out what makes New Zealand's North Island and South Island distinctive, what challenges they face, and what they each contribute to this unique island nation. The six weekly segments are:

- Part 1 **Auckland and Wellington** – why these cities matter and what makes each special
- Part 2 **Queenstown** – why this little town has become a hot spot and how it began
- Part 3 **Rotorua** – the town's natural wonders and its cultural significance
- Part 4 **Christchurch** – the city's regional importance and the challenges it has faced
- Part 5 **Coromandel Peninsula** – what makes this area such a magnet for visitors
- Part 6 **Milford Sound** – a national treasure, its biological diversity and how it is being protected

3 **a** One day, Paige turns on the radio and listens to an interview by Kiri Snow. She is interviewing the filmmaker Shaun Reed. Listen and choose the statement that sums up best what the filmmaker says.

15

1. The film looks at how rugby is organized in New Zealand.
2. The film shows why the All Blacks are the best rugby team in the world.
3. The film describes how the game helped New Zealanders find their identity as a country.
4. The film shows how rugby has united the country's older and younger generations.

15 **b** Tai comes home from work and Paige tells him about the interview. Listen again, then look at the following sentences. How does Paige report them?

Why don't we see a lot of rugby action in this film.
Kiri asked why we didn't see a lot of rugby in this film.

1. It's about our relationship to the game and how it has shaped us as a country. *Shaun said ...*
2. Please explain what you mean by that.
3. The game was brought here in the late 19th century when our country was still very young.
4. Why did rugby become so important?
5. Our team showed the world that this small island nation could be the best at something.
6. Do the younger generations today still identify with the game?
7. It's still very big, with team and league competition on every level, both boys and girls.

c Now answer questions 4 and 6 from **b**.

→ Workbook, page 23

4 **a** Ricky has found a tourist website with information about Maori culture. Read the text and do the tasks.

1 Explain why Maori culture is protected by law.
2 Describe how to say 'hello' in the Maori language.
3 Explain what *whanau* means.
4 Outline what New Zealanders think is 'essential'.

b Find words or phrases that mean:

1 having always lived in a place
2 a group of people who officially control a country
3 get better
4 say hello to somebody
5 part of the customs or way of life of a group
6 how people live

Maori culture

To understand New Zealand and its people, it's important to understand the influence of Maori culture. As New Zealand's second-largest ethnic group, Maori make up 16.6 per cent of the country's population. But more than that, they are the indigenous people of New Zealand and their rights, culture and language have been protected by law since the country began in 1840. Although the government has not always respected those rights, relations between Maori and *Pakeha* (the Maori term for New Zealanders of European descent) have improved over time.

New Zealand Prime Minister Jacinda Ardern exchanging a *hongi* – the traditional Maori greeting.

Today the acceptance of Maori culture is felt everywhere in New Zealand. In everyday conversation, when someone says *kia ora*, he or she is greeting or thanking you; when people talk about *Aotearoa* ('Land of the Long White Cloud') they mean New Zealand; and when a Kiwi asks about your *whanau*, he or she wants to know how your family are doing. Official signs everywhere are in both Maori and English. The New Zealand national anthem is always sung first in the Maori language, *Te Reo Maori*, then in English. The national rugby team, the All Blacks, famously perform the *haka* before each game, and variations of this traditional Maori dance are performed by both men and women at official and unofficial events all over the country.

The All Blacks rugby team performing the *haka*.

Many believe that the Maori cultural influence is one reason for the success of New Zealand's multicultural society. A survey reported that New Zealanders of every ethnic group see Maori culture as an 'essential' part of the New Zealand way of life.

5 **a** Look at these two pictures of New Zealand. Take turns to talk about one or both of the pictures. Make notes about what your partner says.

b Work with a new partner. Report what your previous partner said about the pictures of New Zealand.

A

B

16

Words and phrases

anthem a song that has special importance for a country
influence the effect that sb or sth has on how people think and act
peninsula a large piece of land that sticks out into a lake or the sea

1 Read a newspaper article about climate change written by a teenager in New Zealand. Which paragraph does each picture on page **35** relate to? Give the line numbers.

What climate change means for New Zealand

A

As a Kiwi I'm really quite worried about climate change and what it will mean for me in the future. While New Zealand won't be as badly affected as other countries, particularly ones like the Pacific Islands, it will no doubt impact the way we live.

B

One reason for this is that two-thirds of people in New Zealand live within 5 km of the coast. As one consequence of climate change is increased sea levels, it's quite easy to understand that there will be an impact. We can already see results in some places like Moanataiari where the sea washed away parts of the road, and also in Kaiaua which experienced devastating floods. My aunt lives there and she told me it was the worst storm she had ever known, and she's lived there for over 40 years! One of the most surprising things was that they had no drinking water for ages. You'd think with so much water around it wouldn't be a problem, but apparently all the rain caused mudslides which contaminated the water in the reservoirs. Now, you might expect to have water shortages during a drought, and with climate change we are likely to experience more of those as well.

C

Hotter temperatures will lead to all sorts of problems. The elderly, the young and people with health issues are all likely to suffer as are people who have mental health issues. Why? Well, some people are already worried about climate change and, as the effects get worse, their anxiety levels will probably increase.

D

Higher temperatures have other consequences that people don't necessarily think about. For example, at the moment the climate in New Zealand is too cold for tropical diseases like malaria, but in the future that might not be the case. A warming climate also increases the frequency of extreme weather events such as storms, flooding, cyclones and forest fires. As many Kiwis love hiking in our beautiful nature, such events could really make a huge difference to the way we live and how we spend our leisure time.

E

However, it's not just the people who will bear the consequences of climate change. Many of our animals will also be at risk. I've already mentioned the threat of malaria from mosquitoes, but as temperatures rise the habitats where different animals live will also change. For example, at the moment it is too cold high up in the mountains for animals like rats, but as the snow melts then that might change. If it does, it will have a devastating impact on other animals that live there and don't have to worry about such predators yet.

F

Will everything connected to climate change be bad? Not necessarily. In the future, we may be able to grow crops that we can't at the moment. If you're like me and enjoy avocado on toast, then that might be good news! Recently, my best friend's uncle set up a touring company taking people out on boats in the new lake created by the melting of the Tasman Glacier on the West Coast. So, he's already making money from climate change. Sure, climate change will mean more challenges, but it could also mean some new opportunities.

→ Workbook, pages 24/25

2 Match the headings (1 – 6) to the paragraphs (A – F).

1 What about the people?
2 Not all bad
3 A Kiwi perspective
4 What about the animals?
5 Water – no water!
6 More extreme!

3 Find words or phrases in the text which have these meanings.

1 a powerful effect that something has on a situation or person
2 causing a lot of damage or destruction
3 to make something dirty or poisonous
4 a situation in which there is not enough of something
5 a feeling caused by worrying about something
6 to have to deal with something unpleasant
7 the natural environment in which an animal or plant usually lives
8 an animal that hunts, kills and eats other animals

4 Right, wrong or not in the text? Correct the false statements.

1 Other places will be worse hit by climate change than New Zealand.
2 Most people in New Zealand live in cities.
3 The writer's aunt lives in Kaiaua.
4 The elderly won't be affected by high temperatures.
5 New Zealand already has diseases like malaria.
6 The writer enjoys hiking in the mountains.
7 At the moment rats don't live high up in the mountains.
8 According to the writer, climate change could also have some positive effects.

5 Read the text again. Complete the tasks.

1 Explain why many people in New Zealand will be affected by rising sea levels.
2 Describe what happened to the writer's aunt.
3 Illustrate how people with health issues might be affected by climate change.
4 Describe what impact climate change might have on nature in New Zealand.
5 Comment on the last paragraph of the article. Do you agree with the writer? Say why or why not.

→ Workbook, page 26

Preparing to write an informative text

S1 Researching a topic and evaluating notes

a Your class has been asked to research and write an article about New Zealand for your international website. It should include information about New Zealand's history, geography, people and wildlife. Read the notes made by one student. Decide which information will be most useful and interesting for the readers.

- consists of two main islands – North Island and South Island
- 9th longest coastline in the world
- 600 smaller islands – largest = Rakiura island, also called Stewart Island
- first settled by the Maori people around 1300 – around 16% of population today
- first country to give women the vote in 1893
- unemployment 4%
- no snakes!

b Do some online research of your own and make more notes. You can also look back at the quiz questions on pages **12 – 13** for ideas about the kind of information to look for.

TIP

When doing research, use more than one source.
Write short notes in your own words: don't copy or cut and paste.
Bookmark your sources so can you find them again quickly.

S2 Making a plan

a Your text should have three main parts. Match the parts to their function and put them in the right order.

1 main body **2** introduction **3** conclusion

A summarizes key points or comments on the topic

B introduces the topic / purpose of the text

C provides the necessary information

b Organize the notes in **S1** into a logical sequence of paragraphs. The main body can be more than one paragraph.

S3 Using an appropriate style.

Look at the *TIP* box below. Then look at the two extracts from a student's text. Describe and evaluate the style of each paragraph.

TIP

When writing an informative text:
- choose the right style to suit your topic and audience, formal or informal, serious or chatty.
- use a variety of sentence lengths and types, simple and complex.
- include interesting facts to engage the reader.

What do you know about New Zealand? Can you find it on a map? Do you know which hemisphere it's in? Not sure? If you want to find out the coolest facts about this amazing country, read on!

As it is so remote, New Zealand has some very unusual wildlife that cannot be found anywhere else in the world. Nearly all the land animals are birds. Many of them lost the ability to fly as they had no predators.

Writing an informative text

S1 **Decide on a topic.** Look at the photos and tasks. Choose one of the topics to write about.

A

Write an informative article about High School exchange programmes for German students in Australia or New Zealand.

Divide your article into sections with headings to help the reader identify the key information. Headings could be typical questions which you give the answer to. Include this information:

- Reasons for going on a school exchange to Australia or New Zealand
- Organizations that arrange exchanges, what programmes they offer, their requirements (e. g. age, language level)
- What to expect at your High School – courses, after-school activities
- Benefits of staying with a host family
- Free time opportunities
- How to apply

B

Write an informative report about climate change in New Zealand. Choose a good title, e. g. *Climate change reality in NZ* or *No time to lose.*

Paragraph 1: Introduce the topic – concerns about climate change
Paragraph 2/3: Explain the main problems, causes and effects
Paragraph 3/4: Explain what is being done (by protesters / by the government)
Paragraph 4/5: Conclusion – say what is likely to happen in the future

TIP

- Use a chatty, personal style. Address your reader directly.
- Use adjectives like *great*, *exciting*, etc. to make your article more interesting and persuasive.

TIP

- Include key facts.
- Write in a neutral and factual style.
- Don't include your personal opinion.

S2 **Research your topic.** Look at the tips on page **36** and make notes. Then make a plan and order your notes.

S3 **Write and edit your text.** Use a dictionary to help you improve your text and check it for mistakes.

S4 **Evaluate your texts**

a Form groups of three or four. Take turns explaining which topic you chose, and how you researched your topic.

b Exchange your written products. Read them and give each other feedback. Have your classmates followed the guidelines in the *TIP* box?

What's in a dictionary?

- the right meaning of a word (monolingual and bilingual dictionaries often give more than one meaning, so choose the one that is right for the context)
- the correct spelling of a word
- grammatical information (e.g. part of speech, plural forms, verb patterns, which preposition to use, etc.)
- synonyms

1 Ricky gives a talk to his teammates before their rugby match against Papanui High School. Later one of his teammates phones his parents. Read what Ricky said and complete what the teammate said to his parents in your exercise book.

Hey guys! So, we are playing a match against Papanui High School. We know they are one of the best school teams in New Zealand, but we don't have anything to fear. Back home, we all practised really hard, and I am sure we can win. Remember, we've been playing together for over a year and we haven't lost any of our games. There is no reason this one will be any different. Do you agree?

Last night Ricky gave a short speech. He started by reminding us that we were playing a match against Papanui High School. He said …

2 **a** Read the story about the Rainbow Serpent and put the verbs into the appropriate tense.

The Rainbow Serpent

An Aboriginal tale from Australia

Australian aboriginal myths, also known as dreamtime stories, are traditionally told by the indigenous people of Australia. In one story, a group of Aboriginals 1 (*hunt*) in the outback. After they 2 (*hunt*) for many hours, they 3 (*decide*) to stop and rest. They 4 (*sit*) around, telling stories and warming their hands by the fire when one of them 5 (*look up*). There on the horizon was a beautiful multi-coloured rainbow. But the Aborigines 6 (*think*) that it was a serpent that 7 (*move*) from one waterhole to another, and they were frightened. They didn't want the huge serpent near their camp. They were grateful that he 8 (*not come*) too near their own waterhole.

One young man wanted to know more about the Rainbow Serpent so when he 9 (*return*) home, he asked the old men of his tribe why the hunters 10 (*be*) scared of the Rainbow Serpent when they were out hunting.

17 **b** Listen to what one old man told Ricky about the Rainbow Serpent. Then explain who the Serpent was, what he had done and what he might do again.

→ Workbook, pages 27-29 MORE PRACTICE

3 Complete the talk with the words from the box and the correct form of the verbs in brackets.

climate change ■ destruction ■ extinction ■ habitat ■ iconic ■ wildfires ■ to tackle

Today I'm going to talk about the [1] situation in Australia and the effect this [2] (*have*) on our unique wildlife.
In the last ten years, around 50 % of the animals [3] (*wipe out*). If we [4] (*carry on*) like this, animals that only live in Australia face [5]! Every year heatwaves, droughts and wildfires [6] (*report*) on the news, but what [7] (*cause*) this extreme weather?
One cause is deforestation. Trees are important for a number of reasons. One of these is that oxygen [8] (*release*) and CO_2 [9] (*capture*) by trees. Since the first European settlers arrived, more than half the trees [10] (*cut down*). Some of this [11] is also caused by [12]. Another consequence of this is the loss of [13]. A lot of experts say that around 45 million animals [14] (*kill*) each year because of tree cutting! The situation [15] (*can, not, ignore*) and action [16] (*must, take*) [17] it soon. If nothing [18] (*do*), not only will temperatures increase, but we will lose some of our most [19] animals such as koalas and even our kangaroos!

4 Use the notes to write a short article about Christchurch for your school magazine in your exercise book.

- largest city / South Island
- one of five 'gateway' cities / Antarctic exploration
- famous / street art
- tram or tourist bus / see the city
- street markets
- February 2011 earthquake / killed 185 / damaged or destroyed / buildings
- Hagley Park / third biggest / world
- slogan after earthquakes / 'Our city rocks!'
- southern Alps / 4-hour journey / film set 'Lord of the Rings'
- home / Canterbury Rugby Union team / most successful / New Zealand

5 Paige wrote a blog about the visit from the Australian school rugby team. She wrote too quickly and made some mistakes. Decide whether the underlined expressions are correct or wrong. Correct the wrong ones.

Last week a school rugby team from Australia came[1] to play against our school team. While they were hear[2], my Uncle Tai, took them out for a bit of an adventure and he asks[3] me to go with them. We visited most of the usual sides[4] – took the chairlift up the Port Hills, saw Ko Tane and did some withe[5] water rafting. One of the boys, Jason, told me he thinks[6] the hole[7] experience was awesome, so I told[8] him about my trip to Brighton last year. He asked me lot[9] of questions and seemed very interesting[10], but some of the questions were just silly. He asked me if I have meet[11] the Queen! I said him[12] I had[13] and he said[14] that he was jellous[15]. I don't know if he was joking or if he really tought[16] it was true! He asked me about the best part of the trip and I ansered[17] that apart from spending lots of time with Aimee, what I had enjoyed most was the visit to the *Mary Rose*.

M **Bernhard Holtermann**

a Anlässlich des australischen Nationalfeiertags im Januar möchte deine Schule eine Zeitung über Australien herausbringen. Die Schülerinnen und Schüler deiner Klasse schreiben dazu unter anderem Artikel über Deutsche, die nach Australien ausgewandert sind. Dir wurde Bernhard Holtermann zugeteilt. Benutze die abgedruckten Informationen, um über Holtermanns berufliche Tätigkeiten, seine Interessen und Anliegen und seinen Charakter zu schreiben (200 Wörter).

Bernhard Holtermann: Ein Leben mit vielen Kapiteln

Von André Leslie

[...] Christoph Heins neues Buch *Australien 1872: Wie ein Deutscher sein Glück fand und Fotogeschichte schrieb* erzählt die Geschichte von Bernhard Holtermanns Leben und zeigt bisher unveröffentlichte Fotos aus jener Zeit. Hein sprach mit André Leslie, dem Online-Editor des Goethe-Instituts Australien, über Holtermann und die Entstehung des Buchs.

Nachdem er mit Anfang 20 aus Hamburg nach Australien kam, scheint sich Bernhard Holtermann an zahlreichen Aspekten der australischen Gesellschaft aktiv beteiligt zu haben. Würden Sie ihn als Multitalent bezeichnen?

Ja, er war sehr vielschichtig. [...] Ich denke, Holtermann wusste immer, wie er sich mit dem, was er tat, einen Vorteil verschaffen konnte, aber das ist in Ordnung, denn er tat wirklich viel zum Wohl der Allgemeinheit. [...] Er wurde gewählter Politiker, setzte sich auf dieselbe Art, wie wir das heute tun könnten, für Einwanderung ein und hatte sehr fortschrittliche Ansichten. In den 1880er Jahren spendete er einen Teil seines Vermögens für den Bau einer Brücke, die später die Sydney Harbour Bridge wurde. Ja, er achtete auf seinen eigenen Vorteil, aber er hatte auch immer die Allgemeinheit im Sinn. Ich denke, das kann man heute mit Bestimmtheit sagen.

In Australien und insbesondere in Deutschland scheint es, als seien Holtermanns Leistungen etwas in Vergessenheit geraten. Würden Sie das auch so sehen?

Ich sehe das absolut so. In Australien haben wir die Leute im Holtermann Museum in Gulgong und die in der Provinzstadt Hill End in New South Wales, die noch in diesem Geist leben. Es gibt zudem ein paar neue, jüngere australische Künstler*innen, die mit den Fotos in der Holtermann Collection arbeiten. [...] In Deutschland ist Holtermann überhaupt nicht bekannt. So stieß ich beispielsweise in einem Hamburger Museum auf ein Fotoalbum mit Bildern, die wahrscheinlich Bayliss für Holtermann machte. Sie hatten das Album zwar, aber niemand wusste wirklich, was es war oder wie es dorthin gelangt war. [...]

Fotos scheinen für Holtermann sehr wichtig gewesen zu sein. Trotz der vielen verschiedenen Dinge, die er in seinem Leben machte, hat man den Eindruck, dass seine wahre Leidenschaft der Fotografie galt.

Ich denke, das ist richtig. Holtermann scheint sehr an neuer Technologie interessiert gewesen zu sein, er war Unternehmer. Er wollte die Nachricht davon, wie weit die Kolonie Australien damals entwickelt war, in die ganze Welt hinaustragen – und tat das auch buchstäblich. Australien war nicht mehr nur ein Ort für ehemalige Gefangene. Der beste Weg, das zu zeigen, war damals über Fotos. Fotografie war für ihn das richtige Instrument, um von Australien zu erzählen, und das tat er auch. Er gründete zudem ein Pharmaunternehmen und war im Import-Export der neuesten Maschinen tätig. Holtermann hatte immer einen guten Riecher für jede Chance, sich stärker zu profilieren. Er wurde berühmt, aber er wurde dadurch berühmt, dass er Australien dankte und der Welt zeigte, wie fortschrittlich das Land in den 1870er und 1880er Jahren war.
Er und der berühmte australische Fotograf Beaufoy Merlin, der ebenfalls stets auf der Suche nach den neuesten Trends war, hatten eine großartige Partnerschaft. Die beiden arbeiteten gut zusammen, sie waren Geistesverwandte. Holtermann freundete sich immer mit Leuten mit Fähigkeiten an, die er gerade brauchte. In dieser Hinsicht war er sehr clever.

→ Workbook, pages 30/31

Was, glauben Sie, können wir heute von Bernhard Holtermann lernen?

Niemand kann sich heutzutage sein ganzes Leben lang auf nur einen Beruf verlassen, es heißt, man müsse bereit sein, alle fünf Jahre etwas anderes zu machen. Holtermann wäre das perfekte Beispiel dafür. Er war alles Mögliche, und er war im wahrsten Sinne des Wortes ein Brückenbauer zwischen Europa und Australien. Er war ein Mann mit vielen Talenten und sehr mutig. Er wusste nie, ob er finanziellen Erfolg haben oder verarmt sterben würde. Er verließ Europa per Schiff, als er 20 Jahre alt war, ohne jede Ahnung, ob er es nach Australien schaffen würde, und er sprach damals kein Wort Englisch. Er stürzte sich da einfach hinein. Sein berühmter Goldfund ist ein gutes Beispiel. Sein Geschäftspartner Louis Beyers war nicht in Hill End, als das Gold ausgegraben wurde, und Holtermann schlief, als seine Leute es fanden. Aber es war immer als Holtermann Nugget bekannt. Das ist nicht ganz richtig. Sie hätten es zumindest Holtermann Beyers Nugget nennen sollen. [...]

Taken and adapted from: https://www.goethe.de/ins/au/de/kul/mag/21865525.html.

b Deine Mutter interessiert sich für den Artikel über Bernhard Holtermann und sagt, dass sie noch nie von dem Mann gehört hat. Als sie dich fragt, ob er in Australien heutzutage noch bekannt ist, berichtest du ihr vom Holtermann Museum in Gulgong. Du hast folgende Bewertungen im Internet gefunden. Deine Mutter möchte wissen, was die Besucher über dieses Museum denken. Beantworte die Frage deiner Mutter und gib die Gründe für die Bewertung der Museumsbesucher an.

Community museums rule! ★★★★★
This small museum is an inspiration. I was impressed by the community working together to save two heritage buildings in order to house the Holtermann Collection of photographs and showcase Gulgong during the 1870s Gold Rush. Really well displayed and engaging content and brilliant staff. Really important stop if you visit this heritage town.
July 2020

The Holterman Gulgong museum is first class. ★★★★★
This museum is well thought out with great touchscreens if you want to dive deeper into Gold Rush life.
The photographers hired by Holtermann, i. e. Merlin and Baylis, were masters of wet plate photography. The clarity of the enlarged photographs is superb, giving a great panorama of the gold fields. Well worth a visit.
June 2020

Excellent discovery! ★★★★☆
What history. It's all here and brilliantly presented. Almost too much to take in. Just immerse yourself in this snapshot of history in the goldfields, and then delve into photos of Sydney and Melbourne in the horse-drawn era.
June 2020

This UNESCO listed collection comes to life. Enter the door! ★★★★☆
What an amazing collection, and the presentation is stunning. Love that this significant historical collection is so accessible. And also so relevant – standing in Gulgong – it feels like you are back in history.
July 2020

Photography exhibition ★★★☆☆
An interesting photography museum primarily focused on the gold rush period. Rather small selection, but great photos. Our kids got bored anyway.
September 2020

Ready for Workshop 2?

1 **a** Look at these photos which are connected to the topics from this workshop. Say what you can remember about each of these topics.

A

Melbourne, Australia

B

Uluru

C

Australia / bushfire

D

Maori / Hongi

b Choose one of the topics from this workshop. Note down some information and use your notes to give a short (two-minute) talk to the rest of the class.

2 G1 G5 Complete the leaflet about the Great Barrier Reef with the correct form of the verbs from the box.

declare ■ hold ■ post ■ set up ■ not take ■ think ■ threaten ■ visit

The Great Barrier Reef is one of nature's wonders. It **1** that more than 1,500 species of fish live in the reef and it **2** a World Heritage site in 1981. Every year the Great Barrier Reef **3** by about two million people from around the world. Unfortunately, its very existence **4** by a number of issues connected to climate change.
If action **5** soon, it will be too late! A campaign **6** to help save the reef for future generations. A march **7** next Saturday. Information about the march **8** on different social media platforms, so come along and join us and help save the Great Barrier Reef.

→ Workbook, pages 32-34

3 Complete the conversation between Jack and Bruce with the correct form of the verbs in brackets.

G1 G5

Jack Hi, Bruce. What are you reading?
Bruce It's a book about Eddie Koiki Mabo.
Jack Who's he?
Bruce He [1] (*be*) a famous Aboriginal who [2] (*fight*) for the rights to land for his people.
Jack Sounds interesting. So what have you learned?
Bruce He was born in the Torres Islands off the North Coast of Australia, but in 1959 he [3] (*move*) to Queensland. He [4] (*live*) there for 13 years when he tried to return to Murray Island. He [5] (*hope*) to visit his father, but the government wouldn't let Eddie go because he [6] (*not, live*) there for so long that they said he was a non-Islander.
Jack Wow! That sounds terrible.
Bruce Yes, just six weeks later he [7] (*receive*) a message telling him his father [8] (*die*). After that he [9] (*spend*) the rest of his life trying to get equality for Aboriginal people in Australia.
Jack And what happened?
Bruce Well in 1993 the Native Title Act [10] (*pass*) by the Australian Parliament. The Act said the land did belong to the Aborigines.
Jack That was great. Eddie Mabo must have been happy.
Bruce Unfortunately, he [11] (*die*) the year before.
Jack That's just so unfair. Can I borrow the book after you [12] (*read*) it?
Bruce Sure.

4 Read this text a German student wrote for a school magazine. Are the underlined words correct or wrong? Correct the ones that are wrong.

G1

Earlier this year, I <u>have visited</u>[1] Auckland in New Zealand. We <u>had been</u>[2] on holiday in Australia for about a month when we decided to make the trip. <u>Interestingly</u>[3], Auckland is the largest city in New Zealand, but it isn't the capital. We stayed in a small hotel downtown, which was great for sightseeing. One day we <u>were going</u>[4] to Auckland Domain which is the <u>cities</u>[5] largest park and is on the side of <u>a extinct</u>[6] volcano. We also visited the iconic Sky Tower with <u>it's</u>[7] fantastic views of one of the two harbours. From <u>their</u>[8] we could see why Auckland <u>is known</u>[9] as 'the city of sails' because there are <u>thousands of yachts</u>[10] in the harbours. <u>I am</u>[11] a rugby fan since I first saw the All Blacks, New Zealand's national rugby team, <u>in TV</u>[12] a few years ago. So, for me the best part of the trip was when <u>we went</u>[13] to Eden Park, which is the largest sports stadium in New Zealand. It was so <u>good visiting</u>[14] Auckland, and <u>I hope</u>[15] that next year I can go back and also visit the South Island.

5 After the rugby game between Bayview High School and Papanui High School, Jason phoned his parents and told them a few of the things Coach Hansen said. What did Jason say to his parents?

G3 G4

You played really well.

What would you change for the next match?

You can't win every game.

I know you practised really hard yesterday.

1 The narrator of the song writes from the perspective of the First Nation people. Read the text and summarize what is being said about his / her people (4 – 5 sentences).

2 **a** The vocabulary below will help you understand and talk about the text. Look the words up in a dictionary and explain what they mean in the context of the song.

appropriation | Armageddon | to brainwash | compensation | demon days | exploitation | reconciliation | trauma | venom

b Find three more words you think are important to discuss the content of the song. Give reasons for your choice.

3 **a** Do some online research and find out how the natives in Australia were treated by the white settlers.

b Work on these tasks related to the song in groups of four.

1. Discuss how the actions of the white men may have been justified and how they were perceived by the natives.
2. Explain the idea of a 'nation within a nation'. What are they still waiting for?
3. Evaluate the four closing lines. Describe which view of the future the narrator has. Give reasons for your choice.

4

18 **a** Listen to the song. Comment on the music and how it supports the message.

b With a partner, talk about the emotions you felt while you were listening.

Midnight Oil, 'First Nation' (2020)

First nation, first nation
First to deserve an explanation
First nation, first nation
Last to receive an invitation

First nation, first nation
When we gonna start the conversation?
When we gonna start the celebration?
When we gonna end the exploitation?
When we gonna say the word invasion?

Out loud, we're waiting
Still waiting, nation within the nation
Still waiting, nation within a nation

Earth black the church lacked the first fact
80 thou turned demon days and a dirt nap[1]
Generate the trauma that made a kid rage[2]
Now the ment' capat[3] be filled with all that
Fall back
Why my cousin commit?
Why my uncle locked up?
Why my aunty forget, how to put a glass cup down?
Fighting the fit
We done been[4] brainwashed into fighting the temptay[5]
Fought Armageddon and I be out the next day
Of course I'm a get 'em[6] till the spirit run empty[7]
My corpse full of venom outcome of the invade
How dare you try to put me up in grave

Strong vision, tradition
No ticket, no admission
No government indecision
No token[8] recognition
First nation, so ancient

Let's sit down and talk about appropriation
Let's sit down and talk about compensation
Let's sit down and talk about reconciliation

Out loud, we're waiting
Still waiting, nation within a nation
Still waiting, nation within a nation

Nation, nation within a nation
Nation, nation within a nation
Nation, nation within a nation

When will the light switch?
24/7 in the crisis
White noise killed black thoughts I sense
There's a shift, it'll come by the night's end
When will the light switch?
24/7 in the crisis
White noise killed black thoughts I sense
There's a shift, see the ship sink like this

[1] **dirt nap** (*sl.*) death (literally 'sleeping in the dirt') – [2] **to rage** *toben, wüten* – [3] **ment' capat** = mental capability = head / mind – [4] **we done been** (*sl.*) we have been – [5] **temptay** = temptation – [6] **I'm a get 'em** (*sl.*) I'm going to get them – [7] **to run empty** = to run on empty, losing enthusiasm or motivation (like a vehicle with low fuel) – [8] **token** *Geste*

Aaradhna, 'Brown Girl' (2016)

I'm more than the colour of my skin
I'm a girl that likes to sing
All I know is what's within
Not just a brown girl in the ring[1]

Go to school and learn their ways
Told how to think and what to say
While my mother says to pray
I pray for better days

God, please help them see
They ain't no different from me
Not above, not beneath
Teach them equality

I'm not just a brown girl in the ring
I'm a girl that likes to sing
I'm not just a brown girl in the ring
I'm a girl that likes to sing

I'm more than what they think of me
More than the colour tones that they see
More than urban, R&B[2], more than a slang[3] that I speak
Close your eyes, don't say your word
Don't speak about what you seen or heard
Let's pretend that it's OK
Just the way the devil likes to play

Look in my eyes, look in my eyes
I can't lie, I can't lie
All these years of my life
I'm judged from the outside

I'm not just a brown girl in the ring
I'm a girl that likes to sing
I'm not just a brown girl in the ring
I'm a girl that likes to sing

And if you don't know by now
Time will show you what I'm talking 'bout
Said if you don't know by now
Time will show you what I'm talking 'bout
I'm talking 'bout

I'm not just a brown girl in the ring
I'm a girl that likes to sing
I'm not just a brown girl in the ring
I'm a girl that likes to sing

5 **a** Listen, then do the tasks.

19

1. For the singer it is important to be 'more than ...'. Find all the relevant lines and explain what they mean. Speculate which perspective for the future she develops.
2. In your own words, analyse her attitude towards education.

b Check the exact meaning of these words. Discuss to what extent they have a similar or a different meaning. Give reasons for your choices.

- prejudice
- stereotype
- discrimination
- bullying

c Find examples of the words in **b** from real life, either from your personal experience or from the news.

d Do some biographical research on the singer. Then prepare and give a two-minute talk.

6 Imagine you have just had a lesson on the German constitution. Your English teacher asks you to explain Article 3 to an exchange student from the USA:

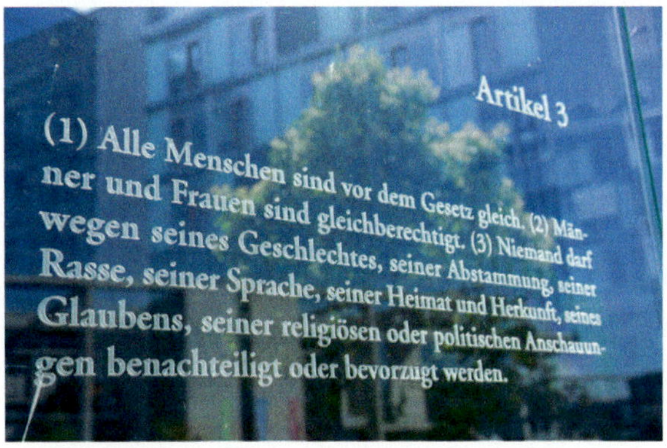

The law says ...
Relevant examples are ...
In my opinion, ...

---

[1] **in the ring** (*idiom.*) referring to ring games that children play, in which one child is singled out and 'in the ring', surrounded by the other children –
[2] **R&B** = Rhythm and Blues, a music genre typically including elements of blues and African American folk music and marked by a strong beat –
[3] **slang** = informal language register, can be used in a regional or social sense, showing your origin and belonging to a region or affiliation to a group

20 Marcus Sedgwick

Cudweed's Crush

ONE

I am a raven. I think I've told you *that* before? I like being a raven. If I haven't told you that before, then I apologize. I want to make this clear: I like being a raven. In fact, I love it! One of the main reasons that I love being a raven is that I do not have to get out of bed in the morning. I get up when I feel like it, and *not before*. On the other hand, you humans, you're always having to set an alarm clock, and rush off to school, or go to work, or something like that. I don't really understand why you do these things. Someone once told me that it's important to go to school to learn things, and that you have to go to work to earn money. But, from a raven's point of view, both of these things are overrated[1]. Ravens don't go to school, and we certainly don't go to work, and we get along just fine.

Now, why am I telling you all this? I'm telling you this because I do not like getting up in the morning, and as I said, I only get up when I feel like it. And if it happens that I feel like it at three o'clock in the afternoon, then that is when I get up. And finally, I am telling you this, because if I *do* get woken up early in the morning, and I haven't had enough sleep, then I become a Very Grumpy Raven. Indeed.

And that is just what happened last Tuesday morning.

I was sleeping the morning away, in one of my favourite places – the barrel[2] of an old cannon in a long corridor upstairs in the castle. I was having a really excellent dream about dead frogs. You know, when you see a frog on the road? A dead one? And it's totally flat, because it has been run over by a car? Well, ravens love a dead frog of this kind. They have a strange salty flavour[3], which is delicious, even if you do get a hint of[4] rubber along with it. In my dream there were hundreds of dead frogs on a nice empty road, and the sun was shining, which is wonderful because it warms up the frog nicely. And then, all of a sudden, Cudweed was standing on the road in my dream, shouting.

He was shouting, 'No, I won't! And you can't make me!'

I looked up from my tasty dead frog and I watched Cudweed shouting. He wasn't shouting at me, but as I looked at him, a strange thing happened: he slowly turned into a frog.

It was a bit weird. Then I realized that I was in a dream, and woke up. I could still hear shouting, and I was really, really grumpy.

The noise was coming from downstairs, and I could hear the shouting all the way upstairs.

Now, I admit, I was in a *very* bad mood, and I flopped out of the barrel of the cannon and decided to go and peck the head of the first person I met. And peck hard.

I flew along the corridor, turned the corner[5], headed for the stairs, and shot down them faster than an elephant on ice skates. I arrived in the dining room, the scene of all the noise, and who was the first person I saw? Cudweed!

So did I start pecking his head?

No, I did not.

Why?

Because the look on his face stopped me in my tracks. If I thought I was angry, it was nothing compared with the mood Cudweed was in.

---

[1] **overrated** überbewertet; überschätzt – [2] **barrel** Kanonenrohr – [3] **flavour** Geschmack; Aroma – [4] **a hint of** ein Hauch von – [5] **to turn a corner** um die Ecke biegen

His face was bright red, and there was steam coming out of his ears. (This last part is not actually true but it seemed to me that he was so angry that it was entirely possible his brain was boiling in his skull and was about to shoot out of his head.)

And he was shouting, 'No! I won't', over and over again.

There was one strange thing. One *other* strange thing, I mean. His trousers were slowly falling down. He was so angry, he hadn't noticed, but he made quite a sight as he kept shouting and we all got a good look at his underpants, which were, I was happy to see, the ones I chose for his last birthday, the ones with little ravens on them.

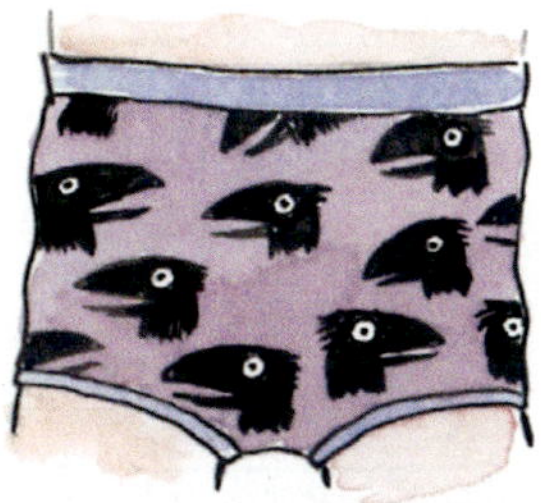

The rest of the family were staring at him, and the only one saying anything back was Minty.

'But you can't just stop like that,' she was saying. 'It's not right!'

I had no idea what was going on, so I landed on Solstice's shoulder to watch.

'Oh, good morning, Edgar,' she said. 'You're up early.'

'Grawk,' was all I had to say to that. And can you blame me? It was only ten o'clock! In the morning!

Solstice ignored my rude word and nodded at her little brother.

'He's a vegan,' she whispered.

I stared at Cudweed.

I stared at him hard. But he didn't *look* any different. But Solstice was telling me he was a vegan, so I looked again, harder, and this time, I realized something.

I didn't know what 'vegan' meant.

I pecked Solstice's ear and said, 'Arrk?'

And then she told me what 'vegan' means.

At first, I couldn't believe it. So I pecked her again and said, 'Kork?'

'Yes,' she said. 'He won't eat meat anymore. And not only meat, he won't eat anything that has come from an animal, and he won't eat anything that means an animal has been hurt making it, and he won't wear anything that's made from an animal either. Like his leather belt.'

So that explained the thing about his trousers, at least. His belt was lying on the floor and I assumed he had thrown it there, since then, his trousers had been going South[6].

'I refuse!' Cudweed cried, pointing one finger at the ceiling dramatically.

Minty was also not keeping calm.

'But I have just bought *four hundred* of your favourite hamburgers to put in the freezer! You can't just stop!'

'But I can!' shouted Cudweed. 'And I have! So there!'

'Well, couldn't you stop in a week or so?' asked Minty. 'Once you've eaten all the hamburgers?'

'No!'

'Well, what am I going to do with all these hamburgers!' screamed Minty, and I thought her head might fall off, she was so angry.

---

[6] **to go South** *here*: herunterrutschen

'I will bury[7] them in the back garden and we can all say sorry to the poor cows!'

With that, Cudweed tried to walk away, but the effect was ruined because he still did not know that his trousers were around his ankles. He fell flat on his face, said a rude word, got up, pulled his trousers up, and then stomped off[8] to his room.

'Well, well,' said Solstice.

'Ark,' I agreed. Because what else could you say?

I was so confused by the whole thing, that I couldn't get back to sleep. As the morning passed, I thought about being vegan... And I didn't like it. I didn't like it one little bit.

Now, as it happens, Solstice is already a vegetarian. She has been since she was a little girl. One day, when she was six, she told her parents she didn't want to eat animals anymore. She explained why. 'Edgar is a bird,' she said, 'and birds are animals. So that means Edgar is an animal. And if Edgar is an animal then I don't want to eat animals anymore. Because Edgar is my friend.'

It was very good logic, not bad at all for a six-year-old. I didn't like being called an animal, because you know, I'm a raven, and ravens are kind of special. And while I understood that it was very sweet of Solstice not to want to eat me, I didn't agree that that was the right way to behave. I mean, ravens *need* meat. We just do. I am in favour of people not eating *me*. And I am in favour of not eating *ravens in general*, but that's where I disagreed with Solstice. I think it's okay to eat *some* sorts of animals, and not others.

Anyway, from that day on Solstice was vegetarian. But now, here was Cudweed, a boy who has eaten more cows in a year than some small countries do, saying he was a vegan.

It was lunchtime.

Cudweed appeared. He was no longer angry, but he was still a little embarrassed by the thing with his trousers. He was the last to sit down at the dining table, and when he did, I saw that he had replaced his belt with a piece of string[9].

'What's for lunch?' he said, suspiciously.

Minty looked at him. She looked hopeful.

'Have you changed your mind yet, dear?' she asked.

'About what?'

'About being a vegan. I've made some nice meatballs and – '

'No!' he said. 'It's only been two hours. I have not changed my mind! I will eat salad!'

So he did, and this was very strange, too, because Cudweed is a boy who never eats salad unless his parents pay him to eat it. (They sometimes do, to make sure he is getting fresh vegetables.)

[7] **to bury sth.** etw. vergraben – [8] **to stomp** stapfen; stampfen – [9] **string** Schnur

So he ate a huge plateful of salad and as he did he simultaneously[10] stared at everyone and smiled at them, too. All while eating. It was a rather unpleasant sight, but when he was done, he got up from the table and made the following announcement.

'I shall be in my room. I shall be writing letters to various supermarkets and restaurants to inform them of their unethical behaviour towards animals. You will each be receiving a similar letter from me at dinner time. Until then, goodbye!'

And this time he stomped off with much more success than the first time, until the string in his belt broke, his trousers fell down and he fell flat on his face again.

It was later that afternoon that Solstice and I made our big discovery. Something was not right about this sudden change in Cudweed. If there is one thing you can be sure of about Cudweed, it is that he is *predictable*[11]. He likes the same things to happen on the same day at the same time. And one thing that he particularly likes is that his food is predictable, that it arrives when it's supposed to arrive. And that there are dead animals in it.

I agree with him about these last two points. Nothing is more stressful to me than a meal that arrives late, and then only contains *broccoli*. It's unbearable.

Strange. Cudweed's behaviour, I mean.

It seemed that Solstice was thinking the same thing, because just as I was trying (and failing) to fly at the height of Cudweed's keyhole, I heard her voice behind me.

'Edgar!' she said. 'Are you spying on Cudweed?'

'Urk,' I said, dropping to the floor.

'Good idea!' she said, and then she knelt and looked through Cudweed's keyhole, while I sat on her head and listened.

'I can't see anything,' she whispered, 'but I think he has someone in there with him. I think ... it's a girl!'

'A girl,' I thought, 'whatever next?!' But we had to be sure, so I flew out of the nearest window, circled around the castle walls, and came to rest outside Cudweed's window.

He didn't see me. As far as I could see he was alone in his room, but I saw that he was staring at his computer screen. He was talking to a girl. He was gazing[12] at her, his head was resting in his hands, and they were chatting away. I swear that a bomb could have gone off in his wastepaper basket, and he wouldn't have noticed.

There was only one explanation: Cudweed was in love!

[10] **simultaneously** gleichzeitig – [11] **predictable** vorhersehbar, durchschaubar – [12] **to gaze at sb.** jmd. anstarren

Youth matters

Young people around the world face lots of different challenges. Look at the pictures and discuss what issues each one shows.

21 Listen to six people talking about issues that affected them. Match each speaker to one of the pictures.

A

'If they don't like you for being yourself, be yourself even more.'
Taylor Swift, US singer-songwriter

'Blood makes you related; love makes you a family.'
unknown

B

In a government survey in 2019, over 90 per cent of Canadian citizens said that they would be comfortable if a neighbour were gay, lesbian or bisexual, and 87 per cent would be comfortable if that neighbour were trans.
from an LGBT+ news website

C

'To me, beauty is about being comfortable in your own skin. It's about knowing and accepting who you are.'
Ellen Degeneres, US TV host

'Every child is gifted. They just unwrap their packages at different times.'
Michael Carr, US author

'Hating our bodies is something that we learn, and it sure as hell is something that we can unlearn.'
Megan Jayne Crabbe, British blogger

'We are all different, which is great because we are all unique. Otherwise, life would be very boring.'
Catherine Pulsifer, US self-help author

'What I did in my youth is a hundred times easier today. Technology breeds crime.'
Frank Abagnale, US security consultant

21 Listen again and complete the sentences. Sometimes, you need more than one word.

The first speaker was thirteen when he first ___1___. The second speaker says his grandfather's views are rather ___2___. The third speaker is worried that her children might ___3___ when they are older. The fourth speaker's confidence is affected because she ___4___. The fifth speaker is surprised that ___5___ in the twenty-first century. The sixth speaker ___6___ to build his muscles faster.

Read the quotes. Discuss what makes people different.

We are family

1 Modern families

a Read the introduction to the article (lines 1 – 13). Summarize how family structures have changed.

b Read what Sadie and Mac say about their families and do the tasks.

1 Describe what kind of family Sadie and Mac each have.
2 Explain what difficulties each of them has experienced.
3 Outline what they feel is the best thing about their families.

Families have changed!

Families are becoming increasingly diverse in English-speaking countries as well as in other parts of the world. For a long time, a married couple and their children who live in the same household have been referred to as 'a nuclear family'. Today families can have many more different structures.
Up to half of marriages end in divorce, and many people get married again. This creates the blended family. In these cases, the children have to get used to living in a new unit.
Single-parent families, which may include a single mum or dad and their children, are increasingly common.
Same-sex marriage, which was legalized in Canada in 2005 and in 2015 in the USA, has led to even more family diversity. The 2020 US Census was the first that allowed respondents to indicate they are part of a same-sex couple, either married or unmarried.

We asked two teens, one from the US and one from Canada, about life in their new-style families.

I was twelve when my mom and dad divorced. My two older brothers, who I've always been very close to, went to live with my dad, and me and my sister Kristen lived with my mom.
I was upset about Mom and Dad splitting. But Dad made very clear that I'm still part of his family no matter what happens. Mom would always tell me the good parts of having two families so I didn't feel sad, like, 'You'll get two Christmas presents'. And I was just like, 'Oh yeah', and I was really happy.
On weekends I'd go to my dad's house. When my friends, who had known me before my parents divorced, came over, they'd ask, 'Why don't you live at this house?' and I'd just tell them about exactly what I just said and they'd be understanding, they'd just be like, 'Oh, okay'.
Sadie, 16 (US)

Some people, who were brought up in traditional families, would probably think my family is a bit irregular, because I have two moms. As in – gay moms. But to me, my family, which gives me safety, is just normal. We do things that every other family does. We are friends with people who think we are just average. It's a very easy-going family, not very uptight, but the best thing is that it's loving.
A harder thing about being part of my family is the fact that I experienced teasing and bullying at school in the past. No one wanted to play with me because they were afraid they'd be bullied like me. Kids who came over would ask sometimes, 'Where's your dad?', and I'd have to explain. But my family has taught me to be accepting of everyone, no matter what race, skin colour, gender or really anything.
Mac, 15 (Canada)

22 Words and phrases

respondent sb who fills in a questionnaire
to tease to make fun of sb or to laugh at sb in a playful, sometimes unkind way
uptight strict, not very relaxed

→ Workbook, pages 35/36

2 Giving information

a Look at the information in the box. Then find more examples in the text.

Relative clauses

- **Defining relative clauses** give important information about a person or thing. If we left out the relative clause, the sentence would be incomplete.
  *We do things **that** every other family does.*
  *We are friends with people **who** think we are just average.*
- **Non-defining relative clauses** add extra information. We use commas to separate extra information from the rest of the sentence. If we remove the clause, the sentence is still grammatically correct.
  *Single-parent families**, which may include a single mum or dad and their children,** are common.*
  *My two older brothers**, who I've always been very close to,** live with my dad.*

b Which relative pronouns in the grammar box examples can be left out?

3* Family matters

a Complete the sentences with relative pronouns. Add any missing commas.

1. My family really matters to me, so I feel sorry for kids ___ don't get on with theirs.
2. One issue ___ a blended family often has to cope with is different parenting styles.
3. Single parents ___ often have full-time jobs may have difficulties finding enough time to spend with their children.
4. Same-sex marriage in Canada ___ was legalized in 2005 is fairly common nowadays.
5. Children ___ come from same-sex marriages sometimes experience bullying at school.

b Read the two texts. Decide which relative clause needs a comma. Explain your decision.

A Extended family
The extended family consists of cousins, aunts or uncles and grandparents who live together and who help to raise the children and carry out household duties. Children who are brought up in such families often have a very close relationship to relatives other than their parents.

B Grandparent family
A growing number of children live with a grandparent or grandparents. Their parents cannot look after them for a variety of reasons. There are obvious difficulties with any arrangement that asks a lot from everyone. Grandparents might struggle to keep up with young kids whose needs can be tiring.

4 Family stories.

23

Valerie and Mike, two New Zealanders of immigrant descent, share their stories. Listen and do the tasks. Compare your answers with a partner.

1. Explain why Valerie's and Mike's relatives came to New Zealand.
2. Outline the difficulties Valerie's grandmother faced.
3. Illustrate how Valerie and Mike feel about their cultural heritage and identity.

5 It's your turn: Talking about my family.

Choose one of the topics. Make some notes.
Student A: Speak about your topic for a minute.
Student B: Use phrases from the *TIP* box to show you're listening to your partner.

- My grandparents / A grandparent
- Someone in my family who I am close to
- Family traditions
- What I like (best) about my family

TIP

Active listening can be used to encourage someone to speak, for example:
Go on. Tell me more. That's interesting. Really? Wow! I know what you mean.

Grammar and structures

Defining (revision) and non-defining relative clauses → G6
Mac and his family are friends with people **who think they are just average**.
Single-parent families**, which may include a single mum or dad and their children,** are increasingly common.

→ Workbook, page 37

1 **a Think:** Look at the cartoon. What gender expectations and roles are being challenged?

b Pair: Look at the list of typical household chores and activities. Draw a diagram like this and put them in the part of the diagram you think they belong.

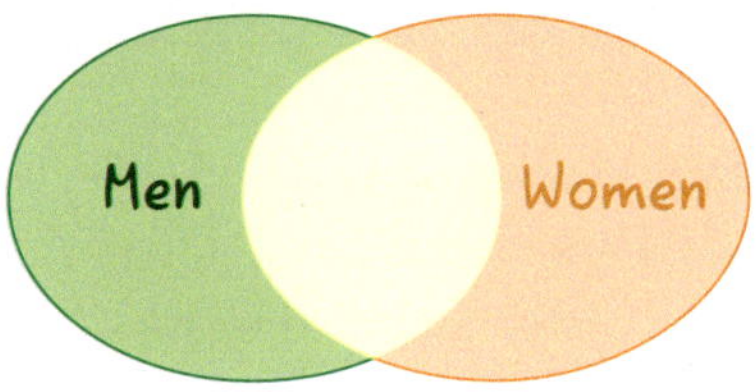

bake bread, cakes, etc. ■ do the dishes ■ do the grocery shopping ■ do the ironing ■ fix the computer ■ mow the lawn ■ prepare meals ■ raise the children ■ set up the internet ■ take the rubbish out ■ vacuum the house ■ wash clothes ■ wash the car

c Share: Compare your diagrams. Discuss the differences and similarities.

d Use your ideas after sharing and finish these sentences.

In the average family there are certain household chores and activities that are typically done by men and women.

- For example, men tend to …
- While women are often responsible for … , men …
- In some families, it is the men who … and the women who …

2 Read the extracts and identify

- typical gender stereotypes for boys and girls.
- how gender roles are learned and reinforced.
- how / why things are changing today.
- what parents do to raise gender-neutral kids.

Raising children gender-neutral

We used to raise girls and boys based on gender stereotypes. We believed that being a boy or a girl dictated who you were and what you could do. But ideas about gender identity have changed. More and more parents are raising their kids to be more gender-neutral. They are choosing clothes and toys that don't reinforce gender stereotypes. Some aren't even telling their children what gender they are. They want to give their children the freedom to choose their own gender identity when they are old enough.

Gender expectations

Research shows that children start to understand gender expectations as young as four. They develop these ideas by watching and copying how the people around them behave. So parents or carers who want to raise gender-neutral children should model what they want their kids to believe. For example, make sure household chores aren't gendered – i. e. mum cleans the house, dad mows the lawn; mum looks after the baby, dad goes out to work. This can help kids understand that gender doesn't determine what tasks they do.

Popularity of gender-neutral names

New US data shows a huge rise in gender-neutral names since 1985. In 2018, 'Harper' (traditionally a boy's name) pushed 'Abigail' out of the top 10 girls' names for the first time in 17 years. Parents who don't want their children to conform to stereotypical expectations – 'boys climb trees and girls play with dolls' – are giving their children a unisex or genderless name. This could be helpful later when applying for jobs, as gender bias still exists in the world of work.

24 **Words and phrases**

to reinforce	to give support to an idea and make it stronger
to conform to something	to behave in a traditional way

@ WES-40805-002

→ Workbook, page 38

LISTENING AND VIEWING PRACTICE

1 (6) You're going to watch a video about a 14-year-old teenager called Tayler. What do you think the title *My generation* refers to? Watch and find out about Tayler's journey.

2 Read what Tayler says and choose the correct meaning for the underlined parts.

1 I like … <u>mucking around</u> outside …
  - **a** spending time aimlessly, with silly things
  - **b** cleaning the dirt off the outside path
  - **c** playing in the mud

2 I never … <u>identified</u> with the girls.
  - **a** I never liked girls.
  - **b** I never knew who the girls were.
  - **c** I never felt I was a girl.

3 Everything … in my head … <u>clicked</u> …
  - **a** I had a strange noise in my head
  - **b** I understood everything clearly
  - **c** my head hurt

4 … felt like … <u>a huge weight</u> off [my] shoulders.
  - **a** I felt a lot better.
  - **b** I put down the weight I carried on my shoulders.
  - **c** My shoulders felt heavy.

5 It's … trying to <u>conceal</u> something.
  - **a** hide
  - **b** ignore
  - **c** deal with

CULTURE CORNER

LGBTQIA is an abbreviation used when referring to *lesbian*, *gay*, *bisexual*, *transgender*, *queer* (which is anyone who doesn't identify as heterosexual or 'straight'), *intersex* (that is people who have sex organs or hormones that don't match their gender) and *asexual* (a term for people who are not interested in sex). Together they are often seen as a group or community.

3 **a** Read the summary of Tayler's story, then complete it with the extra information below. Use relative clauses. Add commas when necessary.

Tayler is a 14-year-old trans boy from Wales. Tayler decided he wanted to make the transition to become a boy. He is currently on hormone-blocker medication.

He was helped by Stonewall. Fox Fisher from Stonewall came to Tayler's school to give a talk and tell the other kids about him. Tayler felt very relieved after Fox's visit.

His mum was surprised when Tayler first told her that he felt like a boy trapped in a girl's body. She remembered how she had tried to make Tayler wear dresses. Finally, she accepted him for who he is and now she feels very proud of him.

1 Tayler likes skateboarding, drawing and playing on his video console.

Tayler is a 14-year-old trans boy from Wales, who likes skateboarding, drawing and playing on his video console.

2 He realized that he wasn't supposed to be a girl when he was 10 or 11.
3 This prevents puberty from starting.
4 Stonewall is an organization that supports LGBTQ people.
5 Tayler had been worried about telling everyone himself.
6 His mum didn't think she had forced gender roles on him.
7 This had made him angry because he'd only wanted to wear trousers.

b Write a letter to a magazine about gender issues (250 words). Use vocabulary from this workshop.

(25) Words and phrases

tomboy a girl who takes part in activities and games that people think are more suitable for boys

Schools and diversity

1 A big decision

27 **a** Listen to the conversation between Deepak and his parents. Explain what they are discussing.

27 **b** Listen again and do the tasks.

1. Outline why the Ramesh family might be moving to the USA.
2. Explain why Deepak is worried.
3. Outline the solution they agree on.

2 Deepak's research

a Deepak found a short article comparing the education systems in the UK and USA. Read it and outline the differences between the two education systems.

b Match these definitions with words from the article.

1. directed towards something
2. a standard
3. studying a particular subject or skill more than any others
4. following a particular order / one after the other and not at the same time

One language, two systems

The UK system is very exam orientated with Key Stage exams at the ages of 7, 11 and 14. At the end of Year 11 (equivalent to Grade 10 in the USA) students sit their GCSEs (General Certificate of Secondary Education), where each subject has a separate exam. In the USA, students study for their high-school diploma, which they sit at the end of Grade 12. Different US states have their own systems, but often the criterion is to get enough credits from a range of subjects. In other words, in the UK the system is on specializing, while in the US it is geared towards generalization.

In the UK, there is a national curriculum, which all schools should follow. The exception is Scotland, where the schools operate with a framework that focuses on the natural relationship between subjects rather than prescribing exactly what is taught and when.

In the USA, schools can often set their own curricula, or at least one is set at state or district level. Another big difference is that in the US subjects such as math and science are taught sequentially. This means that in one grade students might study chemistry and in the following grade physics, but not both in the same grade.

At the end of high school, students can apply for college or university. Similarly to the UK, students pay tuition fees. The costs vary greatly in the US – while the average annual fee is comparable to that in the UK, famous universities such as Harvard or Yale are much more expensive. A big difference here is that in the US universities often offer scholarships to students who excel at a sport or music. This is very unusual in the UK, although there are some scholarships offered to students from disadvantaged families.

3* An email to Jeff.

Deepak is talking to Tariq about moving to the USA. Later, he emails Jeff about the possible move. Write the mail using the underlined information and non-defining relative clauses.

T. So explain it to me again.
D. <u>My father has been offered a job at Mass General. It's a hospital in Boston.</u>
T. But why would he want to leave the job he's got here in Durham?
D. <u>The job is connected to his research. It's a fantastic opportunity.</u>
T. Where would you go to school?
D. <u>Dad wants me to go to Boston Latin School. It's one of the best schools in Boston.</u>
T. And what do you think?
D. <u>I'm worried about my GCSEs at the end of this year. I want to pass them with good results.</u>
T. What does your mum think?
D. <u>Mum suggested we discuss the two school systems before we decide. She understands my concerns.</u>

26 Words and phrases

to excel (at sth)	to be superior or better than sb else
scholarship	support given to a student by a college (usually money)

→ Workbook, pages 39/40

4 A special place

28 **a** Listen to a presentation on a radio programme from the USA. Say what it is about and outline what the speaker says about these topics.

No Child Left Behind Act — Mainstream schools
Special training — Monroe High School

28 **b** Look at the explanation in the box. Then combine the information below to create commenting sentences. Listen again and check.

> **Sentence commenting relative clauses** tell us something about the situation described in the main clause.
> *The most important point came with the passing of the 'No Child Left Behind Act',* ***which was a real breakthrough.***

1 There are children from all sorts of ethnic backgrounds. I think that is really good.
2 I think all the children learn that they are all different and all special in their own way. It's a great lesson for life.

5 A special school.

Use the comments below to complete the extract from the Monroe High School website. Sometimes, more than one answer is possible.

> this creates an inspiring learning environment ■ this guarantees that no child at Monroe is left behind ■ this helps to make the world a better place ■ this means there is a place here for everyone ■ ~~this means we do not receive public funding from the state~~

Monroe High School in Lexington is a non-governmental school, *which means we do not receive public funding from the state*. Our students come from diverse backgrounds, **1**.
We provide the best education for all children whatever their background, ability or needs, **2**, including children with special educational needs (SEN). Integration is one of our key strengths, **3**. Our students learn the importance of respect and tolerance, **4**.

6 Special educational needs (SEN)

a In the programme, the woman spoke about different types of special educational needs. Read the explanations (1 – 4) and match them to the conditions (A – E). One condition isn't described.

A ADHD **B** autism **C** cerebral palsy
D dyslexia **E** dyscalculia

1 People with this often have problems with numbers. They can also have problems with concepts like bigger vs. smaller, estimating time, counting money or understanding that the number 5 and the word *five* are the same.

2 This is a range of conditions, so not everyone will be the same. However, generally people with this will have challenges with social interaction, both verbal and non-verbal communication, and will often have repetitive behaviours.

3 People with this often have problems with tasks like reading, writing and spelling. They also have problems matching letters to sounds. Often people with this condition will develop strategies to cope or to hide it.

4 When someone has this condition, it often impacts on the way they behave. They are often hyperactive, find it difficult to sit still for long periods or to concetrate. In the past, children with this were often labelled as 'naughty'.

b Do some research on the condition that was not described in **a**. Write a simple explanation.

7 It's your turn: Living with SEN.

Discuss what could be done to make life easier for students with SEN. Maybe you are one of these students or have a brother or sister or a friend who is. What do you think such students could benefit from? Come up with five suggestions.

Grammar and structures

Defining (revision) and non-defining relative clauses → G6
The language of instructions, **which is English,** is the same in the USA and UK.

Comment clauses → G7
There are children from all sorts of ethnic backgrounds**, which I think is really good**.

1 **a** Education is important, but what happens if you live hundreds of miles from the nearest school? Conny, who lives in a remote area of New South Wales, is talking about her school life. Look at the pictures and speculate about her life by finishing the sentences.

1 Conny doesn't go to a normal school because …
2 After breakfast Conny turns on the computer and waits for …
3 After her daily lesson, Conny …
4 Sometimes she gets help from …
5 All the learning materials are paid for by …
6 Twice a year Conny goes to a …

CULTURE CORNER

In some countries there are special SEN schools for students with learning difficulties. In New Zealand one such school for dyslexic students is the Summit Point School. In the UK there are several SEN schools offering specialized teaching.

29 **b** Listen and compare. Which parts of her school life were you right about?

2 30 **a** Listen to the conversation between Graham and Mike. Explain what they are talking about and what Steven Spielberg, the famous film director, and Graham's son Tim have in common.

G. Hi! We're your new neighbours. We've just moved in.
M. Hi! I'm Mike.
G. I'm Graham and that's my son Tim over there. We moved here because Tim has a new school.
M. A new school? Why's that?
G. Well, Tim has dyslexia.
M. Right, and what does that mean?
G. People with dyslexia have problems reading.
M. When did you find out he had dyslexia?
G. When he started school, he had a few problems. Then, one of the teachers realized. She also has a son with dyslexia.
M. Ah, that was lucky.
G. Yes, it was. Now he goes to a special school nearby. He gets really good support there.
M. What does he want to do when he finishes school?
G. He's planning on going to university to study drama.
M. Even though he's got dyslexia?
G. Yes, there are special programmes designed to help people with dyslexia when they are studying.
M. And after university?
G. He has several options, but he wants to become an actor.
M. And how do they manage reading long scripts?
G. Well, Tim's hero is the famous film director Steven Spielberg. He didn't find out he was dyslexic until he was 60!
M. Wow! Well good luck and I hope you like your new house and Tim likes his new school.

b Mike is writing to a friend about the conversation he had with Graham. He typed too quickly and made twelve mistakes. Find and correct them.

My new neighbour, who has just moved in, introduced me to his son, Tim who has dislexya. When Tim started school, they thaught he wasn't clever because he had problems reading. Lucky, one of Tim's teachers who's son also has the condition realized why Tim had problems. Apperently Graham and his family moved here so Tim could go to a new school. At his new school, which is nearbye, Tim get really good supports. After he finishes school, he plans to go to university. There he will be in a special programme, which is desined to help people with Tims' condition to study. Tim who wants to become an actor, is hoping to follow in the footsteps of his hero – Steven Spielberg.

→ Workbook, page 41

3 **a** Read the text about education in New Zealand and use the sentences in the box to complete it with relative clauses.

Maori accounted for just 8 % of the population in 1956 ■ It was originally based on the UK system ■ It's a shame ■ The Maori language is now taught in most state schools ■ They are called *köhaga reo* ■ It is a positive development

Education in New Zealand, 1, has undergone some radical changes in recent years. The biggest changes have been aimed at the indigenous Maori population. The number of Maori, 2, has grown and now makes up 16 % of the population of New Zealand. However, this increase is not the only reason for policy changes. While most Maori students are in mainstream education, there has been a shift in schools to focus on helping them reach their potential. Centres for early learning, 3, are now quite common. There has also been a revival of the Maori language, 4 and, as a consequence, the number of Maori medium schools has increased. Also, participation and attainment in schools among the Maoris has improved in recent years, 5. While these changes are welcome, the percentage of Maori going on to university is still extremely low, 6. It is hoped that the situation will improve and all students in New Zealand will have the same opportunities.

b Read the text again and do the tasks.

1 Name one reason why education in New Zealand has changed in recent years.
2 Describe how education has changed.
3 Assess the importance of the revival of the Maori language in terms of education.
4 Describe what further changes the writer would like to see in the future.

4 **a** Rachel has started training to be a teacher at a SEN school. She is reading about ways of helping children with SEN. Complete her notes with the words from the box.

aids ■ behaviour ■ breaks ■ copy ■ extra ■ instructions ■ places ■ points ■ real-life ■ schedule ■ steps ■ tasks

For students with autism
- Be consistent
- Stick to a 1
- Reward good 2
- Give them choices
- Find quiet 3

For students with dyscalculia
- Write out the problem
- Break tasks down into small 4
- Use 5 examples
- Review frequently
- Use visual 6 like graphs

For students with ADHD
- Seat them away from windows and doors
- Keep 7 short
- Try to do any difficult 8 first
- Use a variety of activities
- Have frequent 9

For students with dyslexia
- Provide 10 time to read or write
- Don't ask them to 11 from the board
- Use bullet 12

b Discuss with a partner which of the methods mentioned in **a** would help you be more efficient / happier / more relaxed in class.

CULTURE CORNER

In the USA, two different grading systems are used in schools. One is numerical and the other is with letters, A, B, C, D and F. These letters are usually connected to a percentage score with anything below C regarded as a fail.

5 Find out how much you can remember about the education systems in the UK and USA by doing this short quiz. Compare your answers.

1 What do the letters GCSE stand for?
2 Apart from at the end of Year 11, at what ages do children in the UK take exams?
3 When do students in the USA sit their high-school diploma?
4 What is one key difference in the approach to learning different subjects in the two systems?
5 What do all schools in the UK have to follow?
6 Who can get scholarships to go to college or university in the USA?
7 What do the letters SEN stand for?
8 What do people with dyscalculia have difficulties with?

PART 1
PART 2
PART 3

1 Describe what you can see in each picture. What's the connection between them?

A

B

C

D

2 **a** Marcus is an exchange student in the US. He's from Australia. Lindy, a reporter for her school's news website, interviewed him. Listen and put the photos in the order Marcus mentions them.

31

31

b Read Lindy's questions and listen again. How does Marcus answer them?

1 Can you please summarize the differences between the American and Australian school system?
2 How would you describe a normal school day?
3 Can you choose your own electives?
4 If you want to go to college or university, what do you do?
5 What do you like most about being here?
6 What are you looking forward to during the rest of your exchange year?

c Compare your answers with a partner. Then list similarities and differences between the Australian school system and the German system. What do you think are the advantages and disadvantages of each system? Give reasons for your answers.

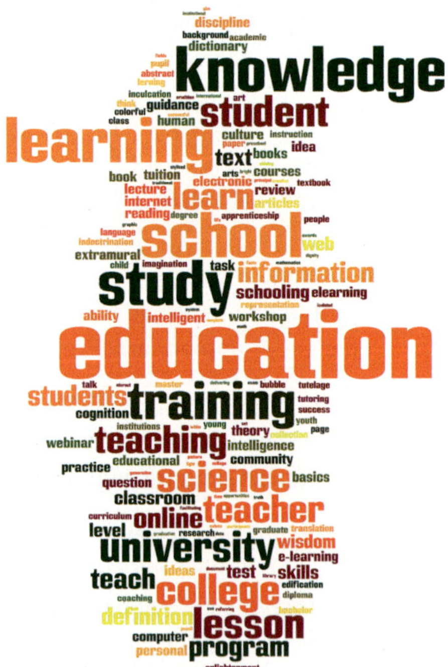

→ Workbook, page 42

3 **a** There are a lot of SEN schools in the UK. Here are three with some of the key features. Choose one of the schools and carry out some research to give a two-minute presentation about the school. Make notes to help with your presentation.

Name of school	**Abingdon House**	**Wilds Lodge**	**Gretton**
Location		Oakham, East Midlands	Cambridgeshire
SEN areas	Dyslexia, Dyspraxia and communication problems		Autism and Asperger's
Age range	5 – 17	5 – 19	
USP	Integrated therapy approach focusing on mental health and integration.	Has designated specialists for all needs. Includes an 'eco-school' focusing on the environment.	Focus on life and social skills. Has a 'forest' school where students explore the outdoors.

b Your teacher will put you in a group. Give your presentation in your group.

4 Look at these photos of special schools and read the text. Describe what each photo shows and discuss what you think is special about them.

Autism is a neurological disorder that affects the way a person's body and brain works. People suffering from autism are able to speak and learn, but they may have trouble with:

- **expressing feelings and understanding the feelings of others.** They might misunderstand other people's feelings or behaviour.
- **reading social cues.** They might not understand body language or facial expression.
- **handling sensory information.** Loud noises or crowds may bother them.
- **handling a new routine.** It might be hard for them to sit in a different seat or to react to people they don't know.

People with **Asperger's Syndrome** have difficulties relating to others socially. Generally, people with Asperger's Syndrome can speak with others and can perform fairly well in their school work, but their thinking patterns can be rigid and repetitive. Often, they develop specialized interests.

Cerebral palsy (CP) is a permanent moving disorder which includes difficulties in body movement and muscle coordination. For example, arms and legs can be stiff or forced into unusual positions. Many people with CP have difficulties with tasks such as tying shoes or grasping objects.

Down syndrome is a genetic disorder. People with Down syndrome have an extra copy of chromosome 21 and are often mentally impaired. However, many students with Down syndrome are educated in regular schools and some have a paid job in their later lives. Research has shown that children with this genetic disorder often learn better visually. For example, drawing may help with developing their reading or speaking skills.

A

B

C

D

Understanding diagrams (1)

S1 **Understanding the information.** Look at the line graph and the bar chart. How does each diagram present the information? Choose one diagram each and complete the description.

1 % children living with …

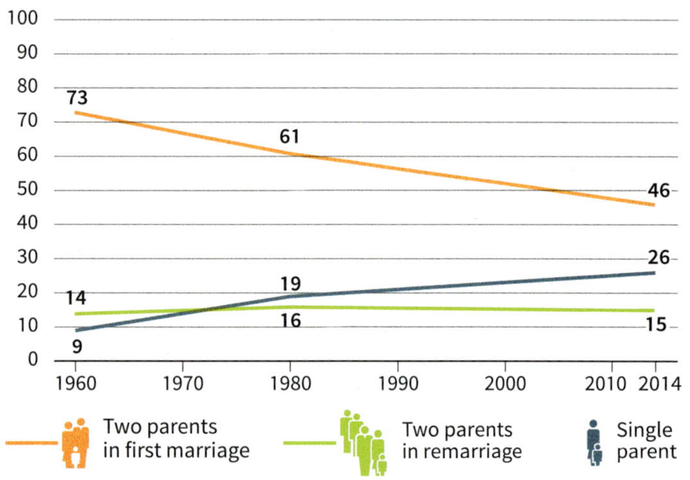

The graph gives information about changes in family life in the USA. In 1960, 73% of all children were living in a family with two parents in their first marriage. By [1], the number of children living in this type of family had declined to 61%. By 2014, the figure had fallen to less than [2] (46%). By contrast, there has been a dramatic rise in the percentage of children living with single parents. In 2014, [3] of children were living with one parent. The share of children living in a remarriage stood at [4], a small [5] from 14% in 1960.

2 % of people in 12 different countries who say over the past 20 years, equality between men and women in our country has …

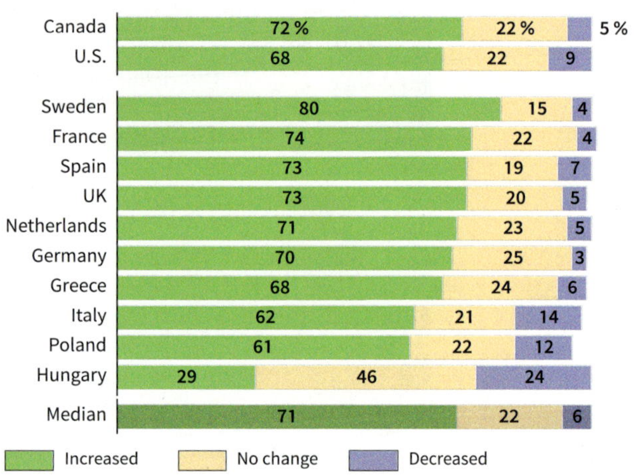

The chart compares the views of people in 12 countries on gender equality. It shows that a majority of people in all but [1] of the countries surveyed believe that gender equality has increased over the past few years. The countries with the [2] percentage holding this view are Sweden and France. In Sweden [3] of people say it has increased, compared with a tiny minority who say it has declined. In contrast, fewer than a [4] of Hungarians believe it has increased. [5] say it has not changed and [6] even says it has decreased.

Sources: (1) Pew Research Center, 2015; (2) Pew Research Center, 2020

S2 **Explaining the information.** Take turns to explain the information. Your partner should ask you to repeat and clarify if necessary.

TIP

Useful language for describing data

Describing the diagram:
The graph / bar chart is about … / shows … / gives information about … / figures for … / compares …

Describing / Explaining change:
By (date), the figure had fallen / declined / risen / increased to / levelled off / reached a peak.
There has been a (dramatic / rapid) rise / increase / fall / decline in (the number / percentage of) …

Comparing data:
The majority / A small / tiny minority of people think / believe that …
Less / More / Fewer than / Under (00) % / a half / a third think / believe that …
A smaller / larger / The highest percentage (of) … / 6 out of 10 / Smaller numbers of / Fewer (people) … compared with …
In contrast, …

Concluding:
Overall, … In conclusion, … In summary, …

Describing a diagram

S1 **Complete a description.** Skim the text in the yellow box. Explain what aspect of changing gender roles it talks about. Then complete the description of the line graph with words from the box in the correct form. You need some words more than once and others not all. Refer to the *TIP* on page **62** to help you.

decline ■ decrease ■ fall ■ fall below ■ fifth ■ higher ■ increase ■ less than ■ level off ■ lower ■ more than ■ reach ■ rise ■ stand at ■ third

S2 **Write a description.**

a Look at the description of the line graph. What words and phrases are used to link the different paragraphs? Make a list and add at least three useful words or linking phrases.

b Look at the bar chart. Describe the information. Refer to the TIP on page 62 to help you with language.

- Introduction: Say what information the chart gives and what the survey is based on.
- Paragraph 2: Describe the highest statistics.
- Paragraph 3: Describe the lower statistics and those that show no change.
- Conclusion / Summary: Say what can be seen from the survey.

S3 **Edit your description.** Exchange your text with a partner. Your partner reads and edits it. Rewrite your report if necessary.

1 % of mothers who are in the labor force with children …

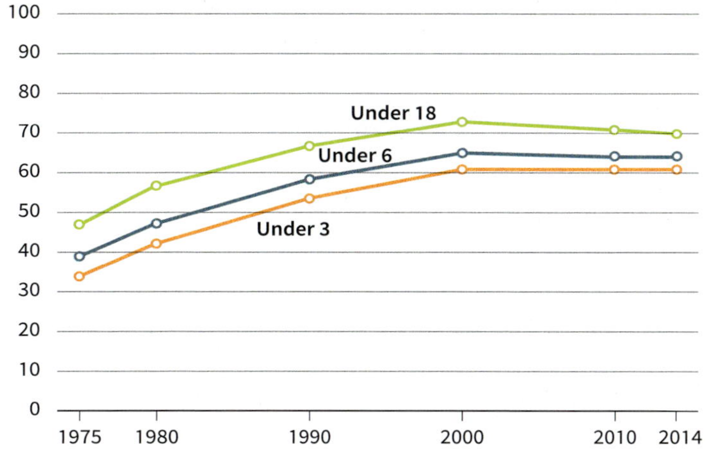

The graph shows the 1 in the number of mothers in the US labor force since 1975. It compares the percentage of working mothers with children under 3, 6 and 18.

As we can see, in 1975, 2 half of mothers with children younger than 18 were in employment. Only 40 % of those with children under 6 and about a 3 of those with children younger than 3 years old were working outside of the home.

However, those numbers 4 dramatically. By 2000, 73 % of all mothers were in the labor force. Since 2000, participation rates of mothers 5 and more or less 6 a peak. Labor force participation today 7 70 % among all mothers of children younger than 18, and 64 % of mothers with preschool-aged children.

In conclusion, we can see that the participation of mothers in the labor force has greatly increased since 1975. Although it 8 since 2000, it is far 9 it was four decades ago.

2 % who say over the past 20 years …

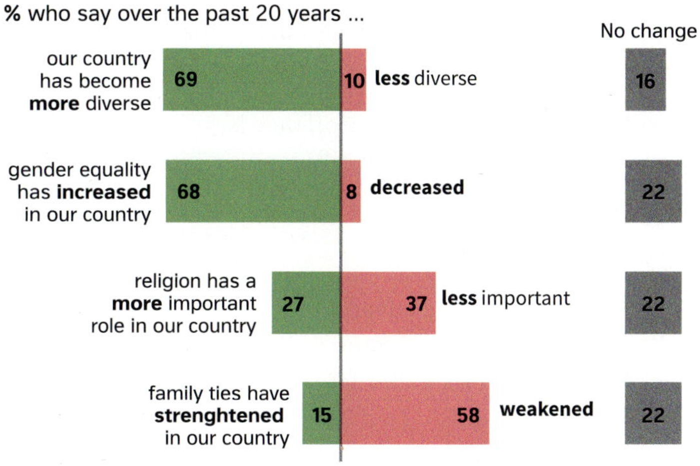

Sources: (1) California Cyrobank; (2) Office for National Statistics, UK 2020.

Teenage problems and the law

1 **Exploring the law.** Read the information about the Youth Justice System of England and Wales.

Legal rights for youth

The Youth Justice System guarantees the rights of young offenders aged 10 to 17. The main aims of the law are to:

- prevent future crimes by tackling the reasons for the offence
- help offenders become responsible members of their communities
- ensure offenders understand the effect of their actions and make amends
- keep the young person out of prison and only use custody for the most serious crimes
- intervene to deal with factors that put young people at risk of offending
- reinforce the responsibility of parents.

How can the law hold youth offenders accountable?
Before going to court:
For a first or non-serious offence, the police or Crown prosecutor may:

- give a warning – this is up to the police
- refer the young person to the Youth Offending Team (YOT) who will look at suitable community programmes or agencies for counselling
- require the young person to apologize to the victim/s, pay compensation or do community service to repair the harm done.

If arrested and found guilty in court:
Sentencing options apart from custody include: a fine, compensation to the victim/s, community service, probation or a combination of these. The judge must consider the circumstances of the case and decide on a fair sentence: seriousness of the offence, impact on the victim/s, if the offender has a criminal record and shows remorse.

1 Explain the main aims of the law.
2 Outline the measures that can be taken to achieve these aims.

2 **Jake's story.** Read about Jake, a teenager from the north of England. Think about what sentencing option/s you would choose if you were the judge. Look at these tasks before coming to a group decision.

1 Argue whether Jake's offence is serious enough to justify sending him to prison.
2 Outline the disadvantages of a prison sentence.
3 Summarize the advantages and disadvantages of community service.
4 Say what other alternatives could be considered.

Jake's Story

I'm 16 years old. I did something stupid and now I'm really in trouble. It all started out as fun. Some friends and I were hanging out and drinking beer one night. I don't have a driving licence, but somehow I got the idea of borrowing my sister's car and going for a joyride. I knew she often kept her car keys on the fridge. Deep down I also knew it was wrong to take them, but I did take them. Anyway, I got the keys and the car. Me and my mates were drinking and cruising along when it happened. I guess I'm not a great driver yet and the road was icy. I accidentally went up over a curb and drove into a group of people. Two of them had to be taken to hospital.The police and ambulance showed up and I was arrested. I had no excuse – I did drink and I did lose control of the car. I was charged with drunk driving and aggravated assault. What a mess. I do wish I could turn the clock back.

Words and phrases

compensation	money that is given to repay a victim
to hold accountable	to make sb feel responsible for their actions
to make amends	to do sth good to show you are sorry about sth you have done
probation	alternative to prison, offenders have to report to police

3 Strong words

a Look at these examples.

*I **did** drink and I **did** lose control of the car.*
*I **do** wish I could turn the clock back.*

How would you say these sentences in German? Discuss with your partner. Then complete the explanation in the grammar box.

> **Emphatic** *do / does, did*
> Adding the verb *do / does, did* to a positive statement emphasizes the ___. We do this when we want to contrast our statement with the one before, or when we want to add emotional emphasis.
> In spoken language *do / does, did* is always stressed.
> *I knew it was wrong to take them, but I **did** take them.*

b Read the statements by the people involved in the incident. Rewrite the sentences using *do / does, did* for emphasis. Say who said each sentence.

1. Believe me, I learned my lesson.
2. This lad behaved foolishly, but at least he admitted it when we arrested him.
3. While I understand why he took my car keys, he should have known better.
4. I know he regrets his action, he visited me in hospital.

4 What happened next?

33

a Jake went to the Youth Court. Listen to the recommendations of the prosecution lawyer and defence lawyer to the district judge. Do the tasks.

1. Summarize what new information you learn about the incident.
2. Describe how Jake shows he is sorry.
3. State what the prosecution lawyer recommends to the judge.
4. Outline what new information you learn about Jake from the defence lawyer.

b Explain whose recommendation you agree with. Give reasons for your answer. Has anything you heard changed your choice in **2**? Explain why / why not.

c Write down your views on both of the recommendations by the prosecution and the defence. Explain which one you agree with and give reasons for your answers.

CULTURE CORNER

The United Kingdom consists of England, Scotland, Wales and Northern Ireland. While England and Wales have the same Youth Justice System, Scotland has its own. The biggest difference between the two systems is that young offenders do not go to court in Scotland, but are dealt with by a special tribunal panel. The other key difference is that in Scotland a strong focus on early intervention is central to the system.

5 It's your turn: You be the judge

a Read the case on the right. Take the roles of the prosecution lawyer, defence lawyer and judge.

- Prosecution lawyer: Prepare your recommendations to the judge.
- Defence lawyer: Prepare your recommendations to the judge.
- Judge: List your options.

> Joe, 16, and his friend Hannah, 15, broke into a neighbour's house while the family were away on holiday. They waited until everyone in the neighbourhood was at work, then went to the backyard and threw a stone to break the glass window. They stole two laptops and some valuable watches. Joe had been on probation for theft before. This was Hannah's first offence.

b Role-play the court scene. The prosecution lawyer and defence lawyer present their recommendations. Use some of the phrases below as this is a formal speech. The judge then makes his / her decision.

> *… committed a serious offence / In view of the seriousness … /*
> *I recommend … / I would like to point out that … /*
> *… take these factors into account … / I have to consider …*

Grammar and structures

Emphatic *do / does, did* → G8
I **do** wish I could turn the clock back.

→ Workbook, page 46

1 Recently, Deepak has started worrying about his looks and what he eats. He does some research on the internet and finds some photos and interesting articles on body image. Look at the photos. Explain what issues they illustrate. Discuss how much looks or physical appearance matter in today's society.

A

B

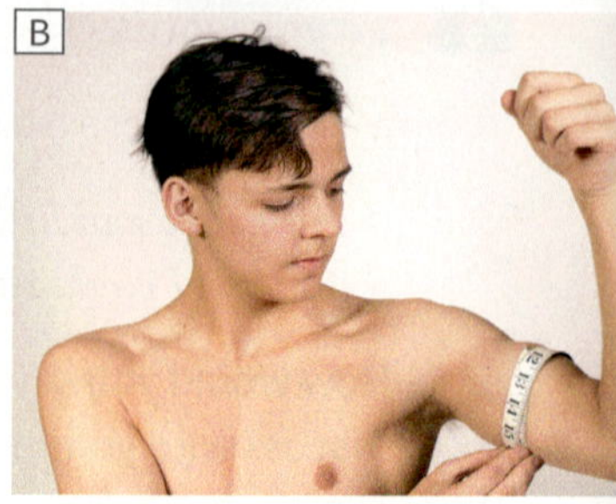

2 **a** Read the first paragraph (ll. 1 – 9) of the article from a website that offers advice to teens. Then skim the rest of the text. Summarize what it is about and explain the writer's intention.

Teen Healthline

Body image: Avoiding the dangers

Teens often have an ideal body image that isn't realistic. There's so much pressure to be perfect and conform to the standards we see in the media. Many teens go on crash diets or take diet pills to be super-thin like their celebrity idols. Boys are increasingly using supplements to help them bulk up and look like their superheroes. But extreme dieting and fitness supplements are bad for your health. Here are some tips on how to stay in shape AND healthy.

Dieting: Don't overdo it!

It's good to want to stay at a weight that's normal for your height – but it's dangerous to overdo it and go to drastic extremes trying to get super-model thin. The best way to achieve and maintain a healthy weight is to do regular exercise and follow a healthy eating plan. Experts recommend that teens do 60 minutes of physical activity every day, such as jogging, swimming or dancing. Your diet should include lean meats, fruit, vegetables, whole grains, and healthy fats. Avoid junk foods and fast food – they are full of bad fat and salt. Soda drinks contain large amounts of sugar and caffeine, so cut them out, too.

Body-building: It's not worth the risk!

It's good to do regular exercise, and strength training is an important part of physical fitness, but it can be dangerous if you don't practise it correctly or do too much. If you're under 16, your body is still developing. If you lift too much weight or lift weights incorrectly, you could injure yourself. Instead, build up your strength and fitness safely by following these simple tips. Check out your local gym and sign up for a strength training class to learn the correct techniques. Steer clear of common fitness supplements, including steroids. Using steroids can raise your risk of heart disease or liver damage. Eat a well-balanced diet. Don't try to count your calories, load up on protein, or cut out carbohydrates – this can slow down your growth and development.

b Read the article again carefully and make notes, using your own words.

1. Describe what the best ways are to achieve and maintain a healthy weight.
2. Explain the dangers of strength training for teenagers.
3. Outline how teenagers can develop their physical fitness safely.

c Find words in the text to match these definitions.

1. to do too much of something so it becomes dangerous
2. to increase something slowly
3. to stop eating something
4. to eat a lot of
5. to make something happen at a slower speed

3 Here are some comments readers left below the article. Add *do / does, did* to each sentence to make it more emphatic. You might need to change the verb form.

1. I knew I shouldn't take steroids, but I took them anyway.
2. I exercise regularly, but not as much as some of my friends.
3. I think that adverts that play on the idea of a perfect body image should be banned.
4. I worry about my weight, but there's nothing I can really do about it!
5. Most teenagers realize constantly dieting is not good for your health.

34 Words and phrases

lean (meat) meat with very little fat on it
to steer clear to avoid
steroids a drug that increases your muscles, often taken illegally in sports

→ Workbook, page 47

1 Look at the results of a survey about teens' attitudes concerning food in the US. Say what surprised you most.

Teen food attitudes survey

- Teens snack two to three times per day.
- Top 5 snack foods for teens:
  1 chips **2** fruit **3** pizza **4** frozen snacks **5** yoghurt
- The favorite meal among teens is dinner.
- The typical teen expresses dissatisfaction with a meal four times a month.
- More than 90 % of teens enjoy sitting down to a family meal.
- Parents are teens' number 1 source of food knowledge.
- 52 % of teens say meals served by their parents don't always suit their tastes or dietary lifestyle.
- 28 % of teens are interested in changing food preferences. Of those, most are interested in
  – low-carb 38 % – low-fat 35 % – vegetarian / vegan 32 %.
- Three times a week is the average number of times that teens help parents out in the kitchen.

2 **a** Read a letter written by a teenager to a news editor in reaction to the survey. Does she agree with the survey results? Give reasons for your answer.

b Complete the letter with the phrases from the box.

> but then I often skip breakfast ■ I stopped eating meat two years ago ■ I was surprised by some of the results ■ some of the results did ring true ■ some of your information doesn't match my habits at all ■ When I was young, I loved fast food

Dear Editor,

In a recent survey you published about teen food attitudes [1]. As a teenager, I really do not think the results reflect my own attitude, or that of my friends, towards food.

Of course, [2]. My favorite meal is dinner and I do enjoy sitting down with my family. It is sometimes the only time we get to spend together as both my parents work full-time. It's also true that what I like has changed as I've got older. [3], particularly pizza, but now I'm worried about my weight and want to have a healthy diet. [4], but love cheese too much to become vegan. However, [5]. For example, your survey results say that teens snack two or three times a day. I only snack once a day and that is a piece of fruit I have in the morning, [6]. In addition, every meal my parents cook is delicious. They've even changed what they eat because of me.

Georgina Harrison (15)

3 **a** Look at the survey again. Make a list of questions that were asked in the survey.

b In groups of five, choose one issue about teenage life (*family, gender, school, youth crime, body image*). What do you want to find out about it? Write a questionnaire.

c Find a group with another issue and interview them. Make notes about the answers. Then swap roles.

d Use your notes to write about the results from your group's survey. The phrases in the box can help you.

> **Useful phrases**
> *They all agreed that …*
> *They disagreed on …*
> *While some thought that …, some were of the opinion …*

35 **Words and phrases**

to ring true to sound correct or accurate

Advertising and Generation Z

1 Ads and us

a May likes to blog, particularly about technology. Read her blog post and do the tasks.

1 Describe the decision May made when she started blogging. Explain why she made it.
2 List the different kinds of advertising that May mentions.
3 Outline how May as a user reacts to these different kinds of advertising.
4 Explain why, in May's view, teens react differently to advertising by vloggers.

b Look at the mind map and copy it. Find more words in the blog and add them to your mind map.

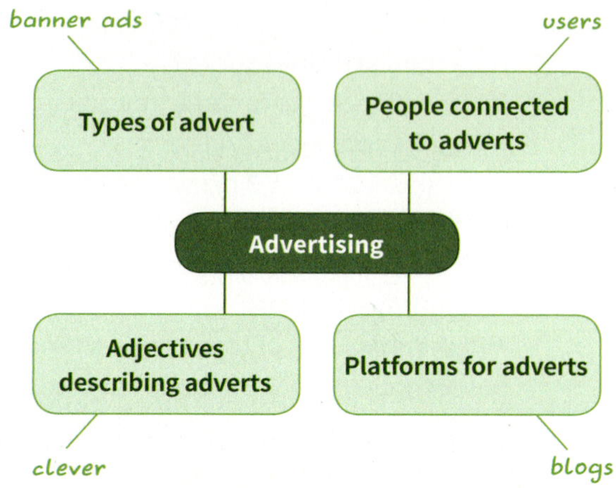

BLOG | ABOUT ME | GUEST BLOGGERS | COOL STUFF | ARCHIVE

Media Geek

Ads and us
by May

Maybe you've noticed there aren't any ads on my blog site. Cool, right? When I first started, I did think about advertising space, but I decided not to use it because I can earn money in other ways that don't take away from the user experience. It does annoy me when you see adverts everywhere.
Need some statistics? The average teenager sees 400–600 ads daily. In the UK, companies spend around £1 billion every year on marketing to teens. Businesses know that we, Generation Z, make up nearly a quarter of the population. So if they want to sell their products or services, they have to get our attention.
As 'digital natives' we socialize, shop and entertain ourselves online, and as users and consumers we're pretty savvy. We do know we're going to get blasted with ads for makeup, food, etc. every time we check our social media feeds. We see these banner ads and pop-up ads on webpages and blogs, too. Most of us scroll past them. Not once have I clicked or tapped on one of those ads.
Advertisers use lots of tricks, though, to get onto our screens and into our heads. Think about the paid content at the bottom of news sites, blogs and posts – they do look like serious articles with attention-grabbing headlines. The video ads that they slip in between the content we watch on video-sharing sites can be more interesting. I click past most of them, but if the music is cool or the ad speaks to me personally, I'll watch it and even share it with friends. This doesn't mean we go out and buy the product. What it means is that we enjoy clever content, even if it's advertising.
Some advertising is harder to separate from real content. When a film or TV show character is drinking a popular brand of cola or wearing stylish sneakers with a logo, they call this 'product placement'. Here's a tip: when you see or hear about a brand or product on social media or anywhere online, it's probably sponsored. The vloggers we know and love are often sponsored, too, but they're a special case. Sure, we know that brands pay them a ton of money to influence our buying choices, but we still watch and listen to them. Maybe because we feel close to them and trust that they wouldn't sell a product they didn't believe in. Also, most are open about it – they'll say, 'I'm getting paid to do this'. It's casual and personalized, and that makes it more authentic. The best vloggers don't really want to sell us anything. It's the advertisers who want our money.
Take my advertising mini-survey and leave a comment!

36 Words and phrases

banner ad an advert that is placed on a webpage and that links to a website
brand a type of product that is made by a particular company
to get blasted with to get hit with, bombarded with
pop-up ad an online advert that suddenly appears in a window on your screen
savvy (*infml.*) having practical knowledge or understanding about sth
sponsored paid by a company for advertising reasons

2 The thing about ads

a Explain what advertisers need to do to get teenagers' attention. Do you agree with May?

b Think of other ways that advertisers try to influence you online. Make a list. Compare and combine your lists in class to make a single list.

c Write a short comment (100 words) to post under May's blog.

3 Let me emphasize

a Look at these examples from May's blog and complete the explanations in the grammar box.

*I **did** think about advertising, but I decided …*
*This doesn't mean we go out and buy the product. **What** it means **is** that we enjoy clever content, even if it's advertising.*
*It's the advertisers **who** want our money.*

- We use a form of **1** when we want to emphasize a point we make.
- We can start a sentence with **2** or **3** to emphasize the subject or object.

b In a former draft of her blog post, May wanted to emphasize the underlined information. Rewrite the sentences using the word in brackets.

Those ads blocking the content are really annoying. (*What …*)
***What** is really annoying **are** those ads blocking the content.*

1 All the paid content I saw on other sites made me go ad-free. (*It …*)
2 The video ads get into your head. (*do*)
3 Advertisers should remember that teenagers like ads that feel authentic. (*What …*)
4 Influencers are good at introducing you to cool stuff. (*What …*)
5 It annoys me that usually the adverts load faster than the content. (*does*)

4 A mini-survey

a Answer the questionnaire that May included with her blog post. Write your answers in your exercise book.

Advertising and you

Hey! Let's find out how our experiences of online advertising compare. Just answer this questionnaire and I'll post the results in a few weeks. Thanks! May

1 Where do you notice advertising the most when you're online?
❏ social media feeds ❏ websites and blogs
❏ video sharing portals ❏ shows and films

2 Which of these ad types attract your attention the most? Rank them from 1 (= most) to 6 (= least).
❏ banners ❏ pop-ups ❏ paid content
❏ video ads ❏ product placement
❏ influencers

3 How often do you click on online ads?
❏ at least once a day ❏ 1 – 2 times a week
❏ once every two weeks ❏ seldom / never

4 How much influence do online ads have on what you buy?
❏ none at all ❏ not much ❏ some ❏ a lot

b Combine your group's results, then compare and discuss them.

5 It's your turn: Asking about ads

a Write four questions you would ask someone about the ads they know. Use the prompts to help, but you can also add your own ideas.

favourite | techniques / types | location | memorable | most popular | annoying

b Use your questions to interview a partner. Make notes about their answers.

c Get together in small groups. Compare your results and draw conclusions.

Grammar and structures

Emphatic structures → G9
What it means **is** that we enjoy clever content …
They **do** look like serious articles …
It's the advertisers **who** want our money.

1 Think about how you communicate in German when texting – the phrases, punctuation, symbols, etc. that you use. Compare this with the way you write, for example, for a school assignment. Talk about the differences.

2 **a** Skim the article and do the tasks below.

The way we write and how it's changing

by Katy McBride

English has always evolved. It's a living language. Now the internet has a big role in driving this evolution. It's where we talk most freely and naturally, and where we pay less attention to whether or not our grammar is 'correct'.

Should we be worried that English is being destroyed? Is it changing too quickly? Not really. Linguist David Crystal, author of *Internet Linguistics*, says: 'The vast majority of English is exactly the same today as it was 20 years ago.' Even e-communication isn't wildly different. 'Ninety per cent or so of the language you use in a text is standard English, or at least your local dialect,' Crystal says.

It's why we can still read and understand an 18th-century transcript of a speech George Washington gave to his troops, and why our grandparents don't need a translator when they send us an email.

However, the way we communicate – the punctuation, the sentence structure, the abbreviations we use or don't use – does depend on the context and the medium for communicating. There's a big difference between the casual way we talk in a text message or on social media and the way we put together sentences in an essay or an article. That's OK because they are very different text types. No one expects to see a casual comment in small letters and without punctuation in the *New York Times*.

On social media, emojis and creative texting make it possible to express ourselves in new and different ways. For example:

- new uses of punctuation such as full. stops. between. words. for. emphasis.
- abbreviated phrases like LOL and OMG
- words reduced to single letters, as in 'how r u?'
- or numbers that take the place of words, as in 'me 2' and '4 u'.

It's natural that language shifts and grows as a result of outside influences. The internet has only added a new dynamic to that process.

1 Outline where we communicate most freely and naturally.
2 Explain why we shouldn't be worried about changes in English.
3 Outline what the way we communicate depends on.
4 Name some examples of creative texting.

b Now read the complete article. Sum up the writer's main argument.

3 **a** Write the meaning of the texting abbreviations.

1 CUL **2** HBD **3** BTW **4** THX **5** ILY
6 NP **7** IMO **8** GR8 **9** BRB

b These letters sound like a word. Write the word for each in your exercise book.

Example: 2 = to / too

1 4 **2** B **3** C **4** I **5** O **6** R
7 U **8** Y

c Read this exchange between Deepak and Ranbir and discuss the meaning of the abbreviations. Rewrite the conversation in written English.

Hi! How RU? Want 2 C a film together? 2moro at my plc?

SRY, but 2moro I have lots 2 do. THX, anyway. BTW, RU free L8TR 2day? I have time 4 a kick around.

GR8! I'll wait 4 U at the usual plc at 3. Don't B l8.

NP. CU then.

37 Words and phrases

casual not formal
to evolve to develop gradually
a kick around passing the ball casually to each other by foot

→ Workbook, page 50

4 **a** May is drafting a blog post about the results of her mini-survey. Look at the extract. She has underlined sentences that she wants to rewrite to give them emphasis. Look at her notes in the margin and rewrite the sentences.

***What** really surprised me **is** the number of you who answered the questionnaire.*

b Complete these further sentences and parts from May's draft. Use emphatic structures. Sometimes there are several possibilities.

1. You notice advertising on social media feeds, but …
2. The most popular answer to question 4 was less of a shock: …
3. A yes / no question would also have been good.

The number of you who answered the questionnaire really surprised me. There were 8,681 respondents – that's awesome!	What …
Your answers sometimes surprised me, too.	did
Let's start with question 1: A lot of you say you notice advertising the most on social media feeds, but many more of you have a different experience: websites and blogs have the most advertising. Yeah. You hardly ever see a website that doesn't have advertising of some kind.	It's … that …
Your answers to question 2 were more unexpected. I thought most of you would say that influencers got your attention most,	did
but no: video ads really grab your attention. Interesting! For question 3, I asked how often you click or tap on online ads. I expected the largest number of you to choose 'seldom / never'. Surprise again!	It's … that …
Most of you say '1 – 2 times a week'. Hm, maybe those ads are more effective than I thought. The most popular answer to question 4 was no shock: online ads don't have much influence on what you buy.	What …
Of course! Our friends influence us most. I hope you had fun with this mini-survey – I sure did! One more question would have been good.	It's … that …
I should have asked 'Would you be happier without ads?' I think I already know your answer!	What …

5 Look at the picture about cyberbullying and do the tasks.

1. Look at the girl in her room. Describe the situation. What do her position and body language suggest to you?
2. Explain the purpose of the 'speech / thought bubbles'. What kind of messages do they convey?
3. Explain who you think the picture is aimed at. Give reasons for your answer.
4. Do you find the picture accurate / informative / shocking / thought-provoking / powerful, or doesn't it trigger any emotion?
5. Make notes and state the advice you would give to somebody who is experiencing digital extortion or cyberbullying.

6 Write a blog post (150 – 200 words) giving your views or experience of one of these: *online advertising*, *social media*, (the language of) *texting*, *cyberbullying*. Use emphatic structures if appropriate.

38 **Words and phrases**

extortion when you achieve sth by using force or threats

1 **a** Before you read the short interview with a teenage girl about mental health, write down six words you think will be in the text.

b Read the text and check your ideas.

Mental health is just as important as physical health. If you have good mental health, you can think, feel and react to different situations in life in a healthy, balanced way. Poor mental health can affect your body. For example, you cannot eat, cannot sleep, or your mood and behaviour can be erratic, and you can feel low, moody, etc.

A teen's perspective on mental health

Nura Mostaghimi, age 16, is a junior at Palo Alto High School in California. She spoke with *Stanford Children's Health* about mental health.

A

When I was in 8th grade, a friend of mine shared the news that another close friend was feeling really low. I knew what depression was at the time, but I wasn't familiar with how best to deal with the situation. There was a teacher at school who a few of us were close to, so we directed our friend to speak with that teacher and a school counselor. The experience of understanding my friend's thought process and going through that experience opened my eyes and made me consider questions like: 'What are the best approaches to having a conversation with the least amount of stigma possible? How can we make sure people are well educated and find a way to open a conversation about the subject?'

B

In my sophomore year, I learned about the Stanford Mental Health Innovation Challenge. Now my group are developing a video game designed for first to third graders to teach them about mental health. Later on, I took part in Stanford's second annual Adolescent Mental Wellness Conference.

C

I'm a bit biased, but I enjoyed the Youth Innovation panel that I was part of. The questions the audience asked were intriguing. There was one question from a lady who runs a youth mental health organization. She asked: 'Is there anything we can do to support you?'
The fact that mental health professionals in the community are ready to support us meant a lot. There's only so much we can do as students to help children learn about mental health.

D

Headspace, an online health company which focuses on mental wellness, has the capacity to make a powerful impact in the community. It will take cultural barriers into account. We want to make the centers easily accessible to the largest group of people, no matter what their background. As we work on mental health projects, it's important to think of the target audience. If changes need to be made so all cultural backgrounds have access to mental health support, then we should make these changes.

E

The best thing you can do is to get involved in something you're passionate about. Don't wait for someone to tell you. For me it is youth mental health, but it can be anything. When you have a desire to get involved, then pursue your passion right away.

→ Workbook, pages 51/52

2 The text is an interview. Each paragraph is the answer to a question. Match the questions (1 – 6) to the paragraphs (A – E). There is one question you don't need.

1 Why was the conference theme, 'Overcoming cultural barriers to access' important for the work you're doing on youth mental wellness?
2 Do you have any advice for young people who would like to help others?
3 Have you personally ever had any mental health issues?
4 How did you end up as an advocate for mental wellness?
5 What inspired your interest in youth mental health?
6 For you, which parts of the conference had the biggest impact?

3 **a** Choose the best synonyms for these expressions in this context.

1 approach (line 13)
a route **b** advance **c** gate
2 stigma (line 13)
a pity **b** shame **c** bad manners
3 to run something (line 22)
a to work for **b** be the head of **c** to escape from
4 to take into account (line 28)
a to consider **b** to count up to **c** to expect

b Find words in the text which have these meanings.

1 someone who is trained to listen to people and give them advice about their problems
2 preferring a particular person or thing and behaving unfairly as a result
3 very interesting because it is unusual
4 the ability to do a particular thing
5 able to be reached
6 to follow someone or something to try and catch or reach them

4 Read the text again and do the tasks.

1 Describe what happened to Nura to make her become passionate about mental health.
2 Outline the steps Nura took to try and help her friend.
3 Describe how Nura has become involved with helping people with mental health issues.
4 Explain why she was surprised by the question the lady asked on the panel.
5 Interpret the importance of taking into account cultural barriers when dealing with mental health.
6 Comment on Nura's advice in the last paragraph.

5 Look at these comments by different people. Which ones do you agree with? Give reasons for your answers.

A Physical exercise often helps reduce mental health issues.

B The use of social media by young people often causes mental health issues.

C Celebrities talking about their mental health really helps people realize that it's not something to hide and anyone can have a problem.

D In the past, there were far fewer people suffering from mental health issues.

E It's important to share and talk about your problems. Keeping things to yourself only makes things worse.

Patrick J. Kennedy, a nephew of J. F. Kennedy, is one of America's leading voices on mental health. He has suffered from bipolar disorder and alcohol addiction.

→ Workbook, page 53

Understanding diagrams (2)

S1 **Understand the information.** Choose one diagram each and use the notes to write a short description and analysis of the information shown.

1 The pie chart gives us information about [1] in the US. It is based on a sample of [2] in [3]. A tiny minority of teenagers [4]. Five times as many [5] as [6]. Just over a quarter [7]. The vast majority, almost [8], stated that [9].

2 The line graph compares [1] by [2] in England and Wales in a period between [3]. The number of young people who received sentences was [4] in each age group at the beginning of this period. In 2010, just over [5] 10 to 14-year-olds were sentenced. The figure for 15-year-olds (20,000) was about a [6] lower. The number in the other two age groups was between [7] and [8].
Overall, this 10-year period saw a steady [9] in the number of convicted young people for each age group. The largest drop was for the number of [10]-year-olds, from over 30,000 to 5,000.

3 The bar chart shows which factors motivate teenagers to [1].
While film stars are the [2] for both genders, they are more important for boys [3].
The next most important factor for both boys and girls is [4], but they [5] girls more than boys. Both genders agree, however, that print ads are the [6] motivating. This is followed by [7] and [8] for boys.
In conclusion, there is not a [9] difference in what motivates boys and girls to do physical exercise. However, almost [10] girls as boys list reading as an important factor.

Sources: (1) Cyberbullying Research Center, US 2016; (2) Ministry of Justice, UK 2020; (3) Journal of Clinical Nutrition and Dietetics, India 2018.

[1] Bullied others in school and online (US, 12–17-year-olds, 2016)

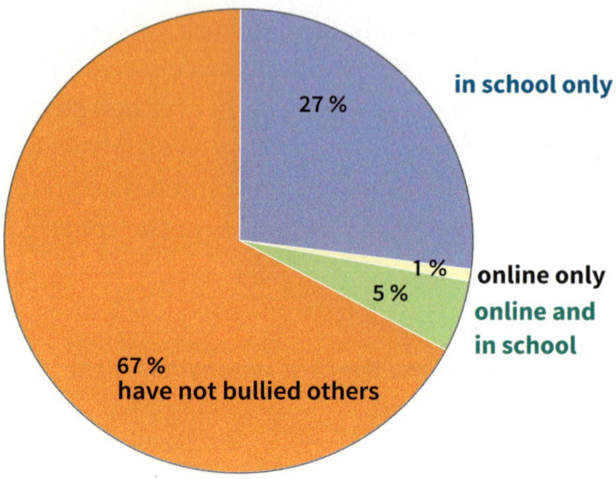

[2] Number of children receiving a sentence by age (England and Wales)

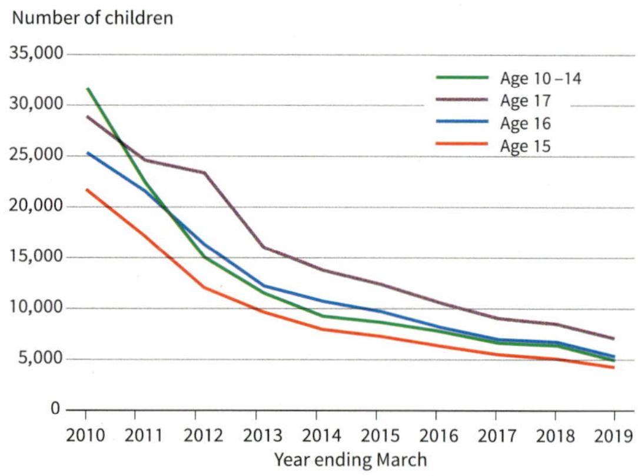

[3] Factors motivating teens to do physical exercise

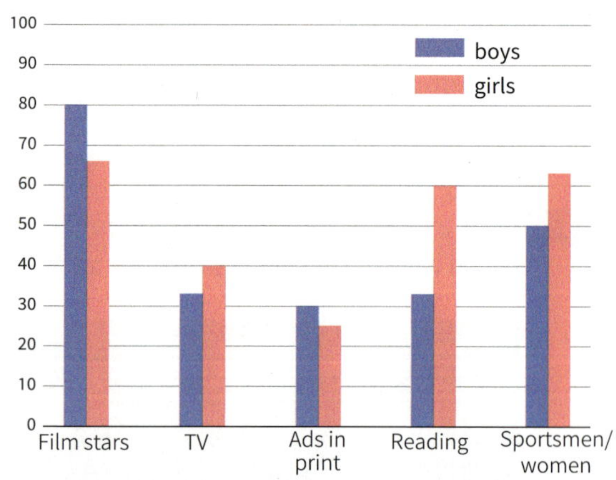

S2 **Discuss the data.** Think about the reasons behind the trends. Discuss and compare what you know about the same topics in Germany.

→ Workbook, page 53 **WORKSHOP TASK**

Presenting information from a diagram

S1 **Choose a diagram.** With a partner, discuss the two diagrams below and choose one to describe. Refer to the *TIP* on page **62** for useful language and look at the descriptions on page **74**.

S2 **Write a description.** Organize your description into the following parts:

- Introduction: say what the diagram shows / is about
- Main body: explain and describe the key information
- Conclusion: summarize the main point(s) expressed in the diagram

1

Who influences children to decide which products to buy? (UK/US, 2019)
Based on a survey of more than 4,000 children aged 6–16, 50% in the UK, 50% in the US

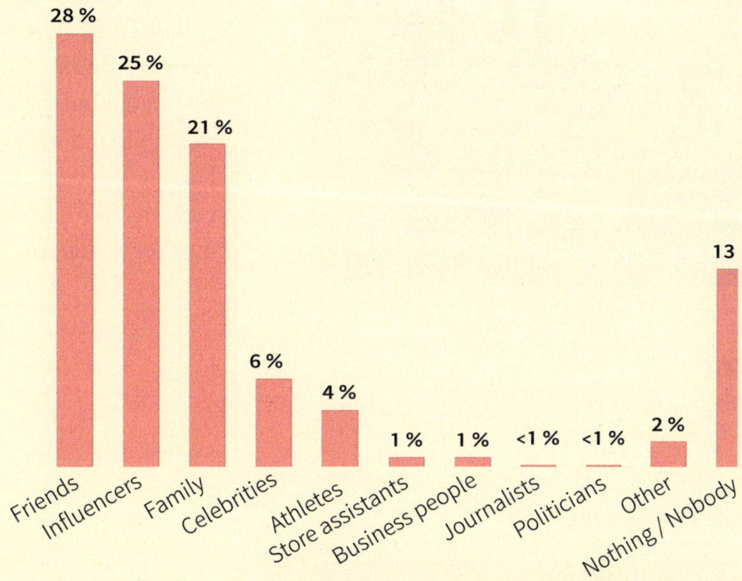

2

Cyberbullying statistics (England/Wales, 2020)
Frequency of online bullying experienced by children aged 10–15 in the previous 12 months (by type of behaviour).

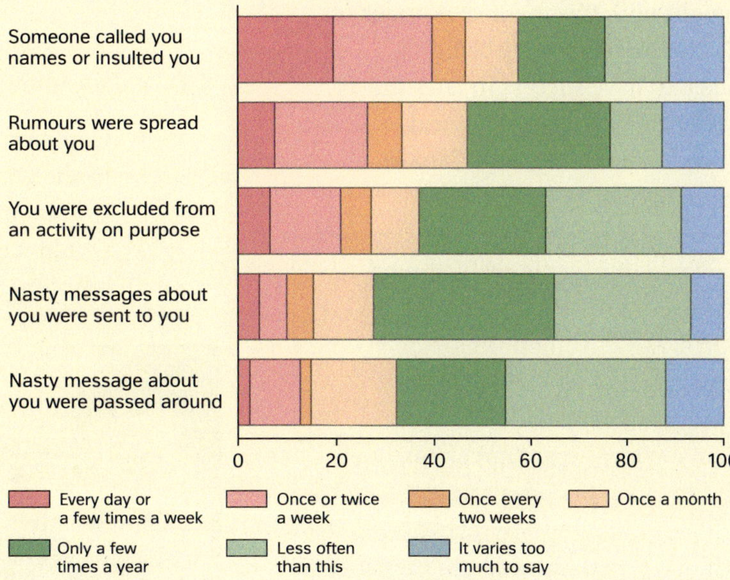

Sources: (1) Wunderman Thompson Commerce; (2) Office for National Statistics, 2020

S3 **Edit another description.** Swap texts with a pair who looked at the other diagram. Give each other feedback, then correct and improve your original text. Use your description to explain the data to the class. Prepare to comment on the data and start a discussion on the topic.

S4 **Give a presentation.** Use your description to explain the data to the class. Prepare to comment on the data and start a discussion on the topic.

1 **a** Make a mind map about families and complete it with words connected to family. Look back at the workshop to help you.

b Complete the text about Sandie's family life with words connected to families. Use your mind map to help you.

After my parents got [1], we were a [2] family for a while. Then my mum met her new partner. Her name is Cathy and she has a son, a year younger than me. We moved in with them, and now I am part of a [3] family with two mums. At first I was worried that I'd get bullied, but all my friends accepted it. In fact, my best friend told me that his favourite uncle is in a [4] relationship with a guy called Tony, who I know from my community centre. Meanwhile my dad found a new wife, too. They have just had a baby so I guess, for now, they are a typical example of a [5] family.
For me the best time is when, on special occasions, I see my [6] family, the Chinese relatives on my mother's side and also my dad's family.

---

2 **a** Do you remember the Moving EDGEucation programme from last year? It is a different approach to learning. Complete the text with the phrases from the box.

are taught with this method ■ focus on the students' well-being ■ is a key to have success in later life ■ is tiring and feels unnatural ■ originated in Toronto, Canada

How would you like to walk around the classroom while you learn maths or skip along reciting poems? This special method, which [1], would allow you to do just that. Students who [2] are not obliged to sit still for long periods of time, which [3]. Moving EDGEucation uses movement and social-emotional learning techniques that [4]. This innovative approach can be used for all subjects and in all schools. It helps to develop creativity, confidence, and allows every student to perform to their best ability, which [5].

b Find the opposites of these words. They are all in the text.

failure ■ inability ■ insecurity ■ old-fashioned

c Read the text again and do the tasks.

1. Compare the Moving EDGEucation approach to the way you learn at school.
2. Comment on whether you think this approach would work for you. Give reasons for your opinion.

→ Workbook, pages 54-56 MORE PRACTICE

3 Tina, who was accused of shoplifting, is in court. Her defence lawyer makes a short closing speech to the court. Decide whether the underlined phrases are grammatically correct or wrong. Correct the wrong ones.

> My client does accepting responsibility[1] for her actions. On the day when she was committed[2] shoplifting and an assault on the security guard, she was very keen impressing[3] her friends. She understands now that people, who encourage[4] criminal activity are not real friends. Also, she knows she behaved[5] foolishly. In her defence, I like to point out[6] that when the police arrested her she didn't resist[7] or blame anybody else. Also, she has never in trouble before[8], which should be considered in the sentencing. She does regret[9] her actions and will like to make[10] amends. Her family are disappointed but fully supporting[11] her. She also has the support by[12] her school and the wider community.

4 39 **a** Listen to a radio programme about body image. What do the following words and expressions from the radio programme mean? Use a dictionary if necessary.

1 to skip meals | 2 to have something substantial | 3 to snack | 4 a high-energy breakfast | 5 overrated | 6 a quick fix | 7 peer pressure

39 **b** Listen again and do the tasks.

1 Explain what Amanda means when she says breakfast 'sets you up for the day'.
2 Describe how eating breakfast can help you with your weight.
3 Assess why eating breakfast is important for Stacey.
4 Explain why David takes food supplements.
5 Evaluate the advice the two experts give David.

5 **a** May posted this blog on her website. Complete it with the phrases from the box and emphatic *do* and *did*.

are relatively new ■ I listed in my last blog ■ you all praised me for ■ you recognize

b Now rewrite the underlined sentences with *It's …* or *What …* for emphasis.

> Hi everyone!
>
> I wanted to catch up with you after you completed my survey. I must say the number of you who responded (1) surprise me. Let me summarize the main findings for you, which (2).
> You all acknowledge that the advertisers who (3) (4) all look for an opportunity for free advertising. You also point out that some adverts are so unusual that they (5) get into our heads. However, we can all agree that we want to focus on the content, not the adverts. You also share my feelings that personalized ads, which (6), (7) annoy us a lot. But we do not mind product placements in films.
> Finally, I am proud that there are no ads on my blog site, which (8).

1 Nachhaltigkeit in der Textilindustrie

M

a Zusammen mit eurer englischen Partnerschule hat deine Klasse ein Projekt zum Thema Nachhaltigkeit ins Leben gerufen. Deine Gruppe ist für das Thema „Nachhaltigkeit in der Textilindustrie" zuständig. Du hast einen interessanten Blogeintrag gefunden, den du für deine Gruppe auf Englisch zusammenfasst – konzentriere dich dabei besonders auf die Probleme, die durch *fast fashion* entstehen. Schreibe etwa 180 Wörter.

b Mache deiner Gruppe einen Vorschlag für eine Definition des Begriffs *fast fashion*.

Fast Fashion

[...]

Entstehungsgeschichte und Ursachen für Fast Fashion

Ihren Ursprung hat die schnelle, verschwenderische Mode in den 1980er Jahren. Damals entstand in vielen Branchen [...] die sogenannte Quick Response Strategie. Durch den beschleunigten Austausch von Information und Ware wurde die Reaktionszeit auf Veränderungen [...] am Markt stark reduziert. Designer konnte[n] rasch auf Trends reagieren und die Nachfrage nach bestimmten Stilrichtungen, Farben, Mustern [...] im Rekordtempo erfüllen. Rund um den Jahrtausendwechsel war das höchstmögliche Tempo erreicht. [...] Zwölf Kollektionen pro Jahr war[en] plötzlich keine Seltenheit mehr. [...]

Fast Fashion in Daten und Zahlen

[Eine] Unternehmensberatungsfirma [...] hat im Jahr 2016 das Kaufverhalten von Kunden in westlichen Länder[n] untersucht. Zwischen 2000 und 2014 [...] ist die Anzahl der gekauften Kleidungsstücke pro Jahr um 60 % gestiegen. Gleichzeitig werden die einzelnen Stücke nur mehr halb so lang getragen wie noch vor 15 Jahren. Die gleiche Studie fand heraus, dass [eine der bekanntesten Mode-Ketten] mittlerweile 24 Kollektionen pro Jahr auf den Markt bringt. [...] Das Aufkommen der Fast Fashion Konzerne hat dazu geführt, dass die durchschnittliche Anzahl an Kollektionen pro Jahr in Europa von nur zwei im Jahr 2000 auf fünf im Jahr 2011 angestiegen ist. [...]

Die Folgen

[...] Fast Fashion wirkt sich negativ auf soziale, ökologische und ökonomische Faktoren aus.

Der Einsturz einer Modefabrik in der Stadt Dhaka in Bangladesch am 24. April 2013 hat auf tragische Weise die Aufmerksamkeit der Welt auf die Arbeitsbedingungen der Modeindustrie geworfen. Bei dem Vorfall kamen 1135 Menschen ums Leben, mehr als 2000 weitere Personen wurden verletzt. [...] Hergestellt wurde in der Fabrik vor allem Kleidung für den westlichen Markt. Die Behörden schlossen nach den Ereignissen 18 weitere Textilfabriken, die sich in ähnlich desaströsen Zuständen befanden. Die Nachfrage nach immer mehr, immer günstigerer Kleidung führt zur Ausbeutung von Textilarbeitern und Textilarbeiterinnen in Entwicklungsländern. [...] In diesem Zusammenhang sei allerdings kurz erwähnt, dass auch viele

→ Workbook, pages 57/58

höherpreisige Unternehmen, die nicht unter den Begriff Fast Fashion fallen, ihre Kleidung in derartigen Fabriken herstellen lassen. [...]

Für die Umwelt hat das Geschäft mit der schnellen Mode ebenfalls schwere Auswirkungen, die weit über den reinen Transport der Ware [...] hinausgeht. Jährlich verursacht die gesamte Modeindustrie über eine Milliarde Tonnen CO^2, weit mehr als der gesamte Flugverkehr. Billige Kleidung aus Kunstfasern belastet die Umwelt durch mikroskopisch kleine Elemente (Mikroplastik), die bei jedem Waschgang abfallen und so in den Wasserkreislauf gelangen. Kleidung für Sport und Outdoor [...] werden wiederum oft mit giftigen Chemikalien hergestellt [...]. Selbst das T-Shirt aus 100 % Baumwolle verursacht in der Herstellung einen enormen Wasserverbrauch von 15.000 Liter[n] pro Kilo. [...]

Lösungsansätze für mehr Nachhaltigkeit in der Mode

[...] Unter dem Begriff Slow Fashion haben eine Reihe an Herstellern den Gegenentwurf zu Fast Fashion entwickelt. Diese Art der Mode konzentriert sich auf lediglich zwei Saisons pro Jahr, nutzt möglichst schonend hergestellte und recycelbare Materialien und achtet darauf, dass die jeweiligen Kleidungsstücke länger haltbar sind. Auch die Arbeits- und Menschenrechte in den Herstellungsländern haben Priorität. [...] Für diese Kleidungsstücke müsst Ihr ein wenig tiefer in die Tasche greifen. Die lange Lebensdauer gleicht diesen Umstand aber wieder aus. [...]
Nachhaltige Mode lässt sich aber auch ohne großes Budget verwirklichen. Second Hand Shops sind eine tolle Möglichkeit, den aussortierten Kleidungstücken von anderen ein zweite[s Leben] zu geben. Ist das neue, gebrauchte Outfit bei Euch zu Hause, verlängert Ihr mit richtigem Waschen die Zeit, bis sich Löcher [und] Co im Stoff zeigen. [...]
Viele moderne Kleidungsstücke lassen sich nur schwer recyceln. Als Alternative wurde das sogenannte Upcyling entwickelt. Dabei werden Kleider in ihre Einzelteile zerlegt und zu neuen Designs zusammengesetzt. Ebenso innovativ sind mittlerweile die Möglichkeiten, Kleidung für kurze Zeit [– zum Beispiel für besondere Anlässe –] zu leihen. [...]

Quelle: https://peppermynta.de/fair-fashion/fair-fashion-greenpeace-modekonsum-fast-fashion/

2 Fast Fashion und die Umwelt.

M Bei einem Projekttag eurer Schule soll deine Klasse das Thema „Nachhaltigkeit in der Mode" präsentieren. In einem englischen Blog hast du bei deinen Recherchen die folgenden Information zum Thema *Fast Fashion* gefunden. Mache dir Notizen und bereite auf Deutsch eine Kurzpräsentation vor.

Fast Fashion: Environmental impact

Did you know...?

- 1.5 trillion liters of water are used by the fashion industry each year.
- 200 tons of fresh water are needed to dye one ton of fabric.
- 750 million people in the world do not have access to drinking water.
- 15% of our clothing are recycled or donated.
- 5,2% of the waste in our landfills are textiles.
- 3 years is the average lifetime of a piece of clothing today.
- 23 kg of greenhouse gases are generated for each kilo of fabric produced.
- 70 million oil barrels are used each year to produce polyester.
- 400% more carbon emissions are produced if we wear a piece of clothing five times instead of 50 times.

Quelle: Mathilde Charpail, "Fashion's Environmental Impact", paragraphs on "Fashion and Water Consumption", "Fashion and Waste Accumulation", "Fashion and Greenhouse Gas Emissions", 2017, https://www.sustainyourstyle.org/old-environmental-impacts

Ready for Workshop 3?

1 G 6 Use the clauses from the box to complete Sam's blog entry about his family. You will need to add the correct relative pronouns.

are typical in many parts of the world ■ changed our lives completely ■ is famous for its diversity ■ is far from being traditional ■ makes him indigenous ■ makes the place really vibrant ■ shows how unconventional my new family is ■ was the only home I'd known

My name is Sam and I live in a city [1]. We have people from all over the world, [2]. It also means that people are a lot more tolerant here. Diversity does not only mean lots of different nationalities, it is also reflected in the family structures. Traditional families, [3], are almost rare here. My family, [4], is a good example to illustrate what I mean. My mother is a second-generation Chinese and my father is from a first nation tribe, [5]. However, this is not all. Two years ago my parents made a decision [6]. They got divorced. We had to move out of the big house [7]. And that's not all. I am going to tell you a story [8].

2 G 6 G 7 Read the mail from Deepak to a local newspaper. Rewrite it with the information in the sentences below. Use relative clauses.

- The article was written by one of your journalists.
- I felt the general statements about teenagers were unfair.
- The journalist seems to think all teenagers do is sit around playing computer games.
- The public service adverts should focus on issues that concern my generation.
- Blaming teenagers is what the journalist seemed to do.

Dear Editor,

I'm writing in response to a recent article in your newspaper. In the article, there were lots of sweeping statements about teenagers. The journalist suggested that in the future there would be a public health crisis because of lifestyle choices. However, she failed to realize that many of these choices are made because of the constant advertising targeted at teenagers. If there were more public service adverts, I think we would all be better informed and would be able to make better choices. Rather than blaming teenagers for everything, it would be better to look at the real causes of the problems.

Deepak Ramesh
Durham

3 **a** Deepak is organizing his notes about the UK and US educational systems. Copy the table and complete it with his notes. Then fill in the last column for Germany.

	UK	US	Germany
Curriculum	???	???	???
Exams	???	???	???
Science	???	???	???
Certificates	???	???	???
Scholarship	???	???	???

- Set nationally
- Common
- Excel in sports, music
- Separate for each subject
- At the end of Year 11
- High school diploma
- Credits
- Taught sequentially
- GCSE
- Set by state or district
- At the end of Grade 12
- Disadvantaged students
- Unusual

b Argue why it would be easy or difficult for Deepak to continue his studies in the US. Give reasons for your answer.

c Compare the German school system to that of the UK and US. Outline which of the two is closer to the German one. Give reasons for your answers.

→ Workbook, pages 59-61

4 G 8 Tina is in a youth court accused of shoplifting and punching a security guard who tried to stop her. Here is a newspaper report about what happened in court. Rewrite the report without the emphatic *do / does* or *did*.

As our readers will know, we do pride ourselves at the Echo for reporting on local news stories. This one is about Tina, a local teenager accused of shoplifting and punching a security guard. In court she admitted she had behaved badly. She said at the time she didn't think she was wrong but that she does see it now. She said she had gone to the shopping centre with two friends and that when they said nobody would get hurt, she did believe them. However, everything went terribly wrong, and now she does need to take responsibility for her actions. Tina admitted that she did punch the security guard in the face and said she would like to apologize to him. Finally, she did promise that it would never happen again and that she wouldn't give in to peer pressure in the future.

5 G 1 G 6 Read the two online texts asking for advice. Decide whether the underlined words and phrases are correct or wrong. Correct the wrong ones.

I'm a 15-year old girl from Tulsa, in the USA. I need some advices[1] about bullying. There are some girls at my school which tease me[2] about the clothes I wear. I come from a single-parent family, because my parents got divorced[3] when I was young. My mom does her best, but money is always a problem. She has two jobs and usually gets home lately[4]. The priorities are food and pay the bills[5]. So, most of my clothes are second-hand. What should I do[6]?
Kathryn

My name's Tom and I'm sixteen. I spent[7] a lot of time to play[8] games on my computer and surfing the web. However, recently I was experiencing[9] online bullying. I've been to a website about cyberbullying and tried to follow[10] the advice, but it hasn't had much effect. Of course, one suggestion was not to go online, but I don't want giving up[11] my hobby. Do you have any advice[12] for me?
Tom

6 Read these comments by teenagers. What are they talking about? Choose one comment you all agree on – or come up with your own. Present your comment to the class. Support your choice with reasons, examples, etc.

A *I don't even notice them anymore.*

B *I do hate the fact that social media sites are full of the stuff.*

C *What's annoying is that you can't avoid them.*

D *It's worrying just how much they influence what you do or buy.*

Karen McManus, *One of us is lying* (2019), Chapter Twenty

One of us is lying. Who? Only one? To whom? Why? Four teenagers at Bay View High are confronted with these questions as they try to find out how their schoolmate Simon could be murdered while they were all together in detention. Now prime suspects, the secrets each of them has been hiding are slowly revealed and values such as true friendship are put to the test. One of the four is Cooper, who is aspiring to become a professional baseball player. As events unfold, he has to face the consequences of deceiving others as well as himself. He is sitting at dinner with his dad.

Tuesday, October 16, 5:45 p.m.

'Pass the milk, would you, Cooperstown[1]?' Pop[1] jerks his chin at me during dinner, his eyes drifting toward the muted television in our living room, where college football scores scroll along the bottom of the screen. 'So what'd you do with your night off?' He thinks it's hilarious that Luis posed as me after the gym yesterday. I hand over the carton and picture myself answering his question honestly. Hung out with Kris, the guy I'm in love with. Yeah, Pop, I said guy. No, Pop, I'm not kidding. He's a premed freshman at UCSD[2] who does modeling on the side. Total catch[3]. You'd like him. And then Pop's head explodes. That's how it always ends in my imagination. 'Just drove around for a while,' I say instead. I'm not ashamed of Kris. I'm not. But it's complicated. Thing is, I didn't realize I could feel that way about a guy till I met him. I mean, yeah, I suspected. Since I was eleven or so. But I buried those thoughts as far down as I could because I'm a Southern jock[4] shooting for an MLB[5] career and that's not how we're supposed to be wired. I really did believe that for most of my life.

I've always had a girlfriend. But it was never hard to hold off[6] till marriage like I was raised. I only recently understood that was more of an excuse than a deeply held moral belief. I've been lying to Keely for months, but I did tell her the truth about Kris. I met him through baseball, although he doesn't play. He's friends with another guy I made the exhibition rounds with, who invited us both to his birthday party. And he is German. I just left out the part about being in love with him. I can't admit that to anybody yet. That it's not a phase, or experimentation, or distraction from pressure. Nonny[7] was right. My stomach does flips when Kris calls or texts me. Every single time. And when I'm with him I feel like a real person, not the robot Keely called me: programmed to perform as expected. But Cooper-and-Kris only exists in the bubble of his apartment. Moving it anyplace else scares the hell out of me. For one thing, it's hard enough making it in baseball when you're a regular guy. The number of openly gay players who are part of a major league team stands at exactly one. And he's still in the minors. For another thing: Pop. My whole brain seizes[8] when I imagine his reaction. He's the kind of good old boy who calls gay people 'fags[9]' and thinks we spend all our time hitting on straight[10] guys. The one time we saw a news story about the gay baseball player, he snorted in disgust and said, 'Normal guys shouldn't have to deal with that crap in the locker room.'

If I tell him about Kris and me, seventeen years of being the perfect son would be gone in an instant. He'd never look at me the same. The way he's looking at me now, even though I'm a murder suspect who's been accused of using steroids[11]. That he can handle. 'Testing tomorrow,' he reminds me. I have to get tested for steroids every damn week now. In the meantime I keep pitching[12], and no, my fastball hasn't gotten any slower. Because I haven't been lying. I didn't cheat. I strategically improved. It was Pop's idea. He wanted me to hold back a little in junior year, not give my all, so there'd be more excitement around me during showcase season[13]. And there was. People like Josh Langley noticed me. But now, of course, it looks suspicious. Thanks, Pop. At least he feels guilty about it. I was sure, when the police got ready to show me the unpublished *About That* posts[14] last month, that I was going to read something about Kris and me. I'd barely known Simon, only talked with him one-on-one a few times. But anytime I got near him, I'd worry about him learning my secret.

Last spring at junior prom he'd been drunk off his ass, and when I ran into him in the bathroom he flung an arm around me and pulled me so close I practically had a panic attack. I was sure that Simon – who'd never had a girlfriend as far as I knew – realized I was gay and was putting the moves on me[15]. I freaked out so bad, I had Vanessa disinvite him to her after-prom party. And Vanessa, who never passes up a chance to exclude somebody, was happy to do it. I let it stand even after I saw Simon hitting on Keely later with the kind of intensity you can't fake. I hadn't let myself think about that since Simon died; how the last time I'd talked to him, I acted like a jerk because I couldn't deal with who I was. And the worst part is, even after all this – I still can't.

1 **a** Summarize the conversation at dinner time in three to five sentences.

b Describe the atmosphere. Speculate about Cooper's and his father's feelings.

c Examine the constellation of characters (family, friends, classmates) you read about in the excerpt. Make a mind map with Cooper in the centre and arrange the characters according to their closeness to the protagonist. Differentiate between emotional and physical distance.

d Collect the information you get from the text about Cooper's character and write a short characterization about him. Quote from the text in order to justify your statements. Make sure that you include descriptive adjectives.

e Analyse the relationship between father and son and evaluate it by comparing it to your understanding of a healthy parent-child relationship.

Literary terms

- **Narrator:** the person who tells the story in a book or play (NOT the author!)
- **Plot:** the sequence of events that forms and unifies the main story of a novel, play or film
- **Point of view:** the perspective from which a story is told. The point of view of a first-person narrator like Cooper in this excerpt allows the reader to see through the narrator's eyes, to hear and listen through his ears, to read the thoughts in his mind …
- **Protagonist:** the main or most important character in a story of a book, play or film
- **Setting:** the time when and place where the events in a book or film happen

2 **a** With a partner, discuss the problems of coming out in today's society.

b Comment on one of the following statements:

The truth may hurt for a little while, but a lie hurts forever.

Better to be slapped with the truth than kissed with a lie.

Three things cannot be long hidden: the Sun, the Moon, and the Truth.

3 Cooper's thoughts are written in the form of an interior monologue. He verbalizes all of his jumbled thoughts. Imagine yourself at a decisive point in your life. It might be happy or sad, something difficult you are afraid of or something you are looking forward to. Look at the text again and write down an interior monologue of your own in a similar style. Write between 150 – 200 words.

- **Step 1:** Collect adjectives that express your feelings.
- **Step 2:** Think of verbs that express what you might / could do or don't dare to do.
- **Step 3:** Then, think of three people that could get involved in your life at this point and describe their potential reactions to your situation.
- **Step 4:** Write the monologue.

Interior monologue is the technical literary term for a character's train of thought and is usually found in a novel. For the reader it is like looking into a character's mind, gaining insights into the ideas and feelings in real time. The character's inner voice is speaking (self-talk) and often internal secrets are revealed.

---

[1] **Cooperstown / Pop** nicknames for Cooper and Cooper's father (from 'poppa' = dad) – [2] **premed freshman at USCD** Kris is a first-year-student at the University of California, San Diego. – [3] **catch** (*infml.*) a desirable person to start a relationship with ('a good catch') – [4] **jock** (AE, *infml.*) a student who practises a lot of sport but is less interested in or talented for an academic career – [5] **MLB** Major League Baseball, the American baseball league – [6] **to hold off** to delay sth, *here*: not to have sex before marriage – [7] **Nonny** = Grandma – [8] **my brain seizes** my brain stops working – [9] **fag** (AE, *slang*) taboo word for a homosexual man – [10] **straight** heterosexual – [11] **steroids** substances that should make your muscles grow and get stronger – [12] **to pitch** to throw the ball (in baseball) – [13] **showcase season** talent scouting: young players are keen to present their talents in order to be recruited for a well-reputed professional league club – [14] ***About That* posts** *About That* is a gossip app that Simon, one of the students at school, has been running, feeding it with ugly news and revealing secrets about his classmates until his death – [15] **to put the moves on someone** to try and develop a (sexual) relationship with someone you have a crush on

TWO

It was dinnertime.

'Ask Cudweed why he's become a vegan, mother,' said Solstice to Minty.

It was the first thing anyone had said in twenty minutes. Solstice was eating a toasted peanut butter and jelly sandwich. The twins were eating spaghetti with a cheese sauce. I say 'eating,' but most of it was in their hair or on the floor, and very little of it in their stomachs. Valevine and Minty were eating steaks, with bacon on the side. Valevine was making a lot of fuss about how delicious the meat was, that it was juicy and so on. He kept offering more slices of bacon to Minty, and at first she said yes, but then she started to actually look like she might be sick, and concentrated on a piece of lettuce that was on her plate instead. So Valevine helped himself to the rest of the bacon and then grabbed the rest of the twins' cheese sauce and poured that all over his steak and bacon. He kept looking at Cudweed, and I finally realized that he was trying to get him to give up the idea of being a vegan, and eat something that came from an animal.

But Cudweed took no notice. He kept chewing away on a bowl of salad that seemed to stay the same size, no matter how much he ate. (That's one of the things I have noticed about salad; no one ever finishes it.) He didn't look once at his father, or his mother, and he especially didn't look at their plates of food, not even when Valevine picked his plate up and began licking it clean. This was very strange indeed, because he has a set of rules about how to behave at the dinner table. He's always talking to the children about their behaviour. If *they* had licked their plates, they would have been in big trouble.

Now, if Valevine's food wasn't having any effect on Cudweed, it certainly was having a big effect on *me*. Another of Valevine's rules at the dinner table is one I really don't like: No Ravens Allowed. I don't like this rule at all, or understand it. As a result, I usually stay away while the others are eating, but the smell of all this lovely bacon was too much, and I had flown into the dining room, secretly.

I was sitting on a chandelier high above the dining table, watching what was going on, and waiting for a chance to grab a piece of bacon or a forkful[1] of steak. Now Valevine had finished eating approximately half a cow, and I was disappointed. But I was still hopeful about Minty's plate, because it looked like she was about to give up. I just had to wait for my chance.

And then Solstice said, 'So, Mother, why don't you ask Cudweed *why* he's suddenly become a vegan?'

Minty stared at her daughter for a moment, then realized that this was actually a very good idea.

'Well, Cudweed?' asked Minty. 'What do you have to say for yourself?'

Cudweed was chewing away at his salad, then he shrugged, swallowed[2], and said very calmly, 'Eating meat is unethical.'

'What's that?' cried Valevine, 'Unethical? You don't even know what that means!'

Cudweed put down his fork.

'Unethical: not morally[3] correct,' he said, sounding like a talking dictionary, 'lacking moral principles, in this case inflicting[4] unnecessary cruelty and death upon sentient[5] creatures.'

---

[1] **a forkful** eine Gabel voll – [2] **to swallow** hinunterschlucken – [3] **morally** moralisch – [4] **to inflict** zufügen – [5] **sentient** empfindsam

Valevine's mouth fell open.
Solstice's did, too.
'But I told you that it was *unethical* to eat animals years ago!' she yelled. 'And all you said was "but I really like bacon"! So what's changed?'
'Yes, dear,' said Minty, trying to be understanding, 'what's changed?'
Cudweed opened his mouth to speak, but his sister was too quick!
'I'll tell you what's changed,' she said. She was getting a little bit upset now, and she pointed a finger straight at her brother. 'He's in LOVE!'
She said it like it was a really bad thing. And she wasn't finished.
'He's in love with a GIRL!'
Cudweed glared[6] at his sister and I moved to a different chandelier, one that was directly above Minty's plate. I had a feeling that my chance was coming.
'So what?' cried Cudweed.
'In love?' cried Minty. 'Is this true? You didn't tell us!'
'Why should I?' Cudweed asked, looking mad. 'Do I have to tell you everything?'
'Yes!' cried Minty. 'Well, no, but ... this girl, she's made you become a vegan, has she?'
'She hasn't *made* me do anything!' Cudweed shouted, and stood up. He was on the verge[7] of storming out of the room again and I only hoped for his sake that he had fixed the problem of a belt by now. I took a good look, and as far as I could see, he had wound some Sellotape[8] across the top of his trousers. Clever, I thought. Not bad at all.
'Well,' asked Solstice, 'is *she* a vegan?'
Cudweed glared at his sister.
'Yes,' he said, eventually, 'but all she did was tell me about certain things. Things about how we treat animals so badly, in farms and so on. And now I know it is only right to be a vegan.'
'But I told you all that! And you just kept moaning about sausages!'
'I do not moan,' said Cudweed, moaning. 'Now, if you'll excuse me, I have to go and call Joanna.'
'Oooh, "Joanna", is it?' said Solstice, and I was surprised, because she suddenly started acting very childishly. Even for a child. 'Oooh, Cudweed loves Joanna, Cudweed loves Joanna.'
And I love bacon, I thought, and if I am not mistaken[9], I am about to get some. Hee hee.
I hopped to the back of Minty's chair, and with everything that was going on, no one paid me any attention at all.
'Now see here, young man,' said Valevine, doing his best impression of being an angry parent. 'You will leave the table when I say so! And not before!'
'Really?' said Cudweed.
'You've already spent all day talking to her,' said Solstice. 'Why do you need to talk to her again?'
'Because I want to,' said Cudweed.
That started Solstice again.
'Cudweed loves Joanna,' she sang, 'Cudweed loves Joanna.'
'So what?' asked Cudweed. 'Just because you don't have a boyfriend!'
Uh-oh. That did it.
I should explain that Solstice had just broken up with her boyfriend Douglas, about three weeks before this. She was still feeling sensitive about it, poor thing. And she burst into tears.
Then Valevine started shouting at Cudweed; Cudweed turned and ran out of the room, the Sellotape snapped and his trousers fell down; Minty ran over to put her arms around Solstice; and I jumped onto Minty's plate and stole three enormous slices of bacon.

'That bird is so irritating!' shouted Valevine, but I was gone. Like a jet plane, out of the dining room, and upstairs, and into the cannon where no one would be able to stop me eating the bacon, not even with a very long pole.

[6] **to glare at sb.** jmd. zornig anstarren – [7] **to be on the verge of** kurz vor etw. sein – [8] **Sellotape** Klebestreifen – [9] **to be mistaken** sich irren

It was quiet after dinner time. I snoozed in my cannon for a while, fat and happy after my success with the bacon. But it does make you thirsty, and I decided to pay a visit to the kitchen to see if I could find some water to drink. There is usually a pile of pots and pans in the kitchen sink with some washing-up water left in, and I was in luck! There was a huge soup pan, left soaking in the sink, half full of water.

I was standing on the edge and taking a sip of water flavoured with pea soup, when I heard someone come in behind me.

It was Valevine. He was in his pyjamas and dressing gown, so I guessed it was late. He was not angry at me for drinking from the sink, which he usually would have been.

He was holding two huge white pills in one hand, and an empty glass in the other.

'Ah, hello, bird,' he said. 'I'm sorry for shouting at you earlier.'

'Awwk,' I said. I wasn't angry with him; I knew that everyone had been upset at dinner time.

'Funny thing about that son of mine,' he said. And he shook his head.

'Kark,' I agreed.

'Love!' he shouted, suddenly.

'The boy is in love. And when we are in love, well ...'

I knew what he meant.

Maybe drinking cold pea flavoured water from the sink had done something to my brain, but I suddenly felt a little romantic myself. You know, I was in love once. Well, maybe more than once, but the most important time I fell in love was when I met Mrs Edgar. I mean, that wasn't her name when I met her. Her real name was Eulalia Lillibella, but that was hard for everyone to remember, and even harder to say, and when we got married, everyone just called her Mrs Edgar instead. It sounds sexist[10] now, but times were different then. Anyway, I loved Mrs Edgar from the day I met her to the day she fell out of a tree and the dogs ate her. Sigh.

Poor Mrs Edgar, I thought, poor, poor Eulalia, and a single fat tear rolled down my beak, and fell into the soup pan, with a loud plop!

That woke us both up, Lord Valevine and me, I mean, and he turned on the tap[11] and filled his glass of water. He showed me the large white pills in his hand.

'I have terrible stomach ache,' he said, 'I can't think why.'

But I knew why. Stupid human. He had eaten too much meat, and, I had to admit, that Cudweed and his girlfriend had a point – eating too much meat isn't good for you.

I went to sleep. It was very late by now, and maybe because I had already had a little nap after dinner, or maybe because I had eaten too much bacon before bedtime, I had trouble falling asleep.

[10] **sexist** sexistisch – [11] **tap** Wasserhahn

When I finally did, I had terrible dreams. In my dreams, I was being chased all around the countryside by a giant sheep that had Cudweed's face. The sheep-that-was-Cudweed was crying out, 'I'm going to eat you! All of you! Even your beak!' and as hard as I tried, I couldn't get away from him. Then he turned into a giant cheese, a Swiss one, I think, because he was full of holes. He started breaking large lumps[12] off himself and eating them. As he was doing that, it began raining broccoli from the sky, and then in the next moment, the whole family was there, and everyone was sitting around a dining table on the hillside. They were all holding knives and forks and had serviettes tucked under their chins. I was sitting in the middle of the table, and they were staring at me, grinning. Then I saw that I was sitting on a serving plate, and then I woke up squawking like a parrot with a problem.

If that nightmare wasn't bad enough, things got worse on Wednesday morning. I woke up very late, and I flew around trying to find someone to annoy. Finally, I found Solstice. She was in her room, and because I felt stupid for not looking there first, I decided to peck her ears.

'Don't Edgar,' she said, but she wasn't mad. In fact, she seemed sad, really sad.

'Kork?' I asked.

'I don't understand,' she said. 'I told Cudweed all about how bad it is to eat animals, and he took no notice[13]. And now this stupid girl tells him and suddenly ... bam! He's a vegan!'

'Rurk,' I pointed out.

'I know!' she said. 'But I thought he loved me, too! I'm his big sister!'

'Ork,' I added.

'Well, anyway,' said Solstice. 'We're going to find out what she's like. She's coming here. Cudweed has invited her to come and meet everyone. Tomorrow.'

'Arrrk?' I said.

'Yes, Edgar, "arrk".'

We stared out of her window for a while, and I suppose we were both thinking about Cudweed. It seemed that young Cudweed was growing up.

'Hey Edgar,' said Solstice suddenly. 'Do you want to hear a joke? It's very, very funny.'

'Rork,' I said, though I didn't much feel like a joke.

'How do you know if someone is vegan?' she asked.

'Ark,' I said, because I had no idea.

'They tell you!' she said. Then she started laughing and didn't stop.

[12] **lump** Brocken; Klumpen – [13] **to take notice** etw. wahrnehmen

@ WES-40805-003

Workshop 3

Routes to your future

Have you thought about what you want to do when you leave school? Look at the stickers on the board and check the words you don't know in a dictionary. Is there anything you would write on the empty stickers? Explain your choice.

Attending a careers fair is a good way to find out what career options are available to you and help you identify different routes into employment.

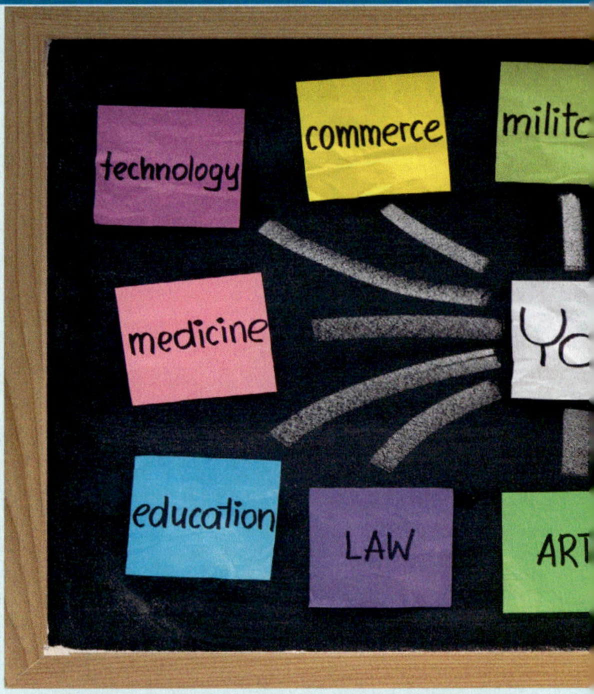

Describe what you can see on the signpost. What routes does it show and what do you know about them?

41 Emily, Sammy and Lucas are at the Skills London Careers Fair. Read their career goals. Then look at the infographic and listen to the advice they get at the fair on how they can achieve their goals.

My goal is to work with animals. I want to find out what my options are after I've taken my GCSEs.

Emily, 15

Sammy, 17

I'm studying languages and I'd like a career where I can use them.

I'm interested in a career in engineering. I want to get some advice about what to do after A-levels.

Lucas, 18

Take turns to explain each students' option. Use the infographic and the phrases below.

Career options

- to take GCSE / A-Level exams
- to get good grades / exam results
- to apply for / to do an apprenticeship / an internship / a degree course
- to study for vocational qualifications
- to learn practical skills
- to get academic qualifications / a degree in (engineering / ...)
- to spend a year abroad
- to graduate from (university)

Think about and discuss the advantages and disadvantages of each route, e. g.:

You can earn money while you study for vocational qualifications.
You may have to move away from home.

New directions

1 What's next?

a *New Directions*, a career website for students and school leavers, has asked students to share their hopes and plans after they finish secondary school. Look at the options. Which seem most interesting or attractive to you? Rank them in order from 1 to 8 and explain the reasons for your ranking.

internship | gap year | work experience | international volunteer work | university | apprenticeship | business school | start-up

b Read what five students have said. Match the options in **a** with the students – Amir, Daniela, Lauren, Ben and Sisi.

Home | Further education | Undergraduate | Alternatives | Careers

NEW DIRECTIONS ▸ **Planning the next step**

Amir, 16, from London, England

I want to go to university. In the student activist group that I'm in, we focus on looking at social issues like discrimination. I like reading about current issues and discussing them in our group. I can see how lawyers can make a difference. My Uncle Nasir is a lawyer. He's suggested doing work experience in a lawyer's office. I need to find out if I like the job. I haven't decided yet. I'm going to think about it.

Daniela, 18, from Munich, Germany

Next spring I'll finish my Abitur – that's like A-levels. After that I want to study medicine. But first my best friend and I are going to go to Australia for the summer. We hope to have a great adventure before I start my studies. Medical students usually do an internship in a hospital. I'd like to do mine in the UK or Ireland.

Lauren, 17, from Dublin, Ireland

Next year most of my friends will be doing a university course or an apprenticeship. I'm not ready for that yet. I'd like to take a gap year to work and get some ideas about what to do next. I've been reading about au pair work. Hopefully a year from now I'll be working as an au pair somewhere in the US or Canada.

Ben, 18, from Cardiff, Wales

I'm determined to find a computing job. My parents advised me to go to university first, but you don't really need a degree to start in computing. I'd much prefer to learn the skills on the job. I've managed to get an interview at a tech start-up. I think I have a good chance of getting the job. As soon as I've finished doing my A-level exams, I will be ready to start the apprenticeship.

Sisi, 17, from Manchester, England

A friend and I have a business idea. We are both passionate about buying vintage clothes, making changes to them and then selling them at markets. We hope to turn this into an online fashion business. It sounds crazy, I know. We're going to apply to a start-up incubator for training and help with our idea. They also offer money. It's a three-month programme. We will be taught how to build our website and also how to get started. If it doesn't work out, I'll probably go to business school.

c Complete the sentences in your own words.

1 Amir is interested in ...
2 The first thing that Daniela wants to do is ...
3 Lauren doesn't want to ... yet.
4 Ben disagrees with his parents about ... because ...
5 Sisi and her friend are going to need ...

42 Words and phrases

degree	the qualification that you get when you finish college or university
gap year	a one-year break between secondary school and university
to learn sth on the job	to learn skills in a practical way
long-term	taking or lasting a long time
start-up incubator	a programme that helps people develop their business ideas

→ Workbook, pages 62/63

2 Choices, choices

a Choose the option that you identify with most – university, apprenticeship, gap year or own business. Explain your choice to a partner.

b Write a short text (150 – 200 words) about your choice to send to an advisor who works for *New Directions*. Include any questions you may have.

3* A bright future.

Sisi is telling her class why she's applying to the local start-up incubator for training. Read what she says and complete the sentences with the correct form of the verbs. You can check with the remember box.

How did I become interested in 1 (*create*) something new and fashionable from vintage clothes? I was about 10 years old when I learned 2 (*do*) basic sewing from my grandmother. I remember 3 (*change*) the buttons on my dresses and 4 (*decorate*) my jeans with patches. Then I discovered a stall at the local flea market that sold vintage clothes. I got a beautiful dress from there and started 5 (*experiment*) with it. I enjoyed 6 (*work*) on it so much that I wanted 7 (*get*) more – and I did. Now I've decided 8 (*turn*) my hobby into serious business. That's why I am looking forward to 9 (*learn*) all the skills I'll need to make a living out of my hobby.

Remember:
Some verbs are always followed by a gerund (*having*) and others by a *to*-infinitive (*to have*). Some verbs can be followed by either a gerund or an infinitive. In these cases the meaning sometimes changes.
- verb + gerund: *finish, imagine, practise*
- verb + preposition + gerund: *carry on, look forward to, be interested in, believe in*
- verb + infinitive: *agree, decide, learn, plan*
- verb + gerund or infinitive with no change in meaning: *continue, hate, like, prefer*
- verb + gerund or infinitive with a change in meaning: *forget, remember, stop, try*

4 Work. Explore. Grow.

43 **a** Listen to the *New Directions* podcast. Why do many school leavers choose to take a gap year? List at least three reasons. Compare your answers.

43 **b** Listen again. Are the statements true or false? Correct the false statements.

1 Lucy is planning to go to university in September.
2 She will need to save money for university.
3 In March Lucy plans to travel to the US.
4 Simon has already done work experience at a publishing company.
5 He preferred working at the publishing company to being a volunteer.
6 He hopes to get a place on a degree apprenticeship programme.

c Compare Lucy's and Simon's motivations for taking a gap year. Describe the similarities and differences.

5 It's your turn: The next step

a Interview a partner about his / her hopes and plans after finishing school. Make notes.

What ...? Where ...? How long ...?
How are you going to pay for it?
What will you do if ...?
What are you afraid of most?

b After two minutes, change partners and tell your new partner what your first partner said.

Grammar and structures

Different use of gerund and *to*-infinitive (revision) → G10
I think I have a good **chance of getting** the job.
That's why I am **looking forward to learning** all the skills I'll need ...
I **learned to do** basic sewing from my grandmother.
I want to get some ideas about **what to do** next.
I **remember changing** the buttons on my dresses.

→ Workbook, page 64

1 Discuss with a partner. If you could do work experience in any job or organization, what would it be and why would you choose it?

2 **a** Look at this job advert from a UK employment website. Do the tasks.

1. Describe the opportunity that is offered.
2. Outline the advantages described.
3. Explain how to apply for the work placement and how much you can earn.

b Decide which of the students from page **90** could be interested in the advert. Explain why.

> **Work experience placement**
>
> Putney Legal Advice Centre, London
>
> Putney Legal Advice Centre is pleased to offer an unpaid work experience placement to a candidate between 15 and 19 years old who shows an interest in one of the careers we offer.
>
> This is a great opportunity to learn about the work of a legal professional and about how a legal advice centre protects the rights of people who cannot afford a lawyer. We can also help you explore career options in the legal profession.
>
> Apply in writing to Amanda.Cowley@putneylegal.co.uk.

3 **a** Amir has seen the advert and written an email about it to his Uncle Nasir. Complete his email with the correct form of the verb from the box.

do ■ follow ■ get ■ look ■ search ■ show ■ talk

> Hi Nasir,
>
> I enjoyed __1__ on the phone last week. Thanks for all your advice! You suggested __2__ work experience to find out if I like legal work. I've decided __3__ your advice. I've started __4__ at job ads. I want __5__ you this advert I saw online. Have you heard of the Putney Legal Advice Centre? Do you think I should apply? Mum says I should, but I'd prefer __6__ your opinion first. For now I'll keep __7__ the job ads!
>
> Best, Amir

b Read Nasir's reply to his nephew. Look at the underlined phrases and decide whether they are correct or wrong. Correct the wrong ones.

> Hi Amir,
>
> Thank you for your email. I've looked at the job advert and I definitely think you should apply. I've heard a lot of good things about this legal centre and I even remember to meet[1] lawyers who work there at a conference. They tried to persuade[2] me to go and work for them but, as you know, I am happy at my company. I can tell you they believe in helping[3] the community. The work they do is very varied, so if you'd like having[4] experience in different areas of the law then it's the right place for you.
>
> If you do decide to apply[5], then remember including[6] all the articles you've read about social issues. I am sure they'll be impressed.
>
> When you write the cover letter, don't forget mentioning[7] what you are doing in the student activist group. I hope your application will be successful. But if I were you, I would try looking for[8] other opportunities as well. Have a look at this link: Londonlawfirms.com. You might find other similarly suitable positions. Good luck!
>
> Nasir

4 Role-play a student and careers expert at a fair. Follow these steps:

1. Decide together who is the expert for traineeships and who is the expert for self-employment. Then read your text.
2. Close your books and do the role-play. One of you (A) is the expert, the other person (B) is the student. B asks specific questions about the topic, which the expert tries to answer. You can start like this:
   A: *Hello. How can I help you?*
   B: *Hello, I'm interested in finding out about …*
   A: *Yes. What would you like to know?*
3. Swap roles and do the role-play again.

Traineeships	Self-employment
Traineeships are short, flexible education programmes for 16–23-year-olds who don't have the skills and experience to get a job or an apprenticeship.	Being self-employed means you run your own business. You are both the boss and the employee.

44

Words and phrases

to boost to increase or make better

failure when sth doesn't succeed

@ WES-40805-002

→ Workbook, page 65

LISTENING AND VIEWING PRACTICE

1 Look at these pictures and describe the people in them. Pay attention to the body language. Speculate what the situation is in each picture. How do you know?

2 **a** Estella, Lucas and Hailey are talking to their school counsellor about their part-time jobs. In groups of three, each of you should focus on one student. Copy the table, then watch the video and complete it.

7 8 9

	Estella	Lucas	Hailey
How is the job?	???	???	???
How is school?	???	???	???
How is the work-school-life balance?	???	???	???

b Compare notes in your group.

1 Summarize what the three students have in common.

2 Explain in what ways they are different.

c Find a partner from another group who also focused on your student. Compare your notes and your profiles. Then read the *TIP* box before you watch the video again. This time pay attention to non-verbal communication.

1 Are your answers similar or different? Talk about the differences.

2 How did your student's non-verbal communication help you reach your conclusions?

TIP

Identifying attitudes through non-verbal communication
What a person communicates non-verbally is just as important as what he or she actually says. So what should we listen and watch for to learn about how somebody feels about something?

- **Tone of voice:** Does the person speak loudly or softly? Fast or slowly? Does the intonation go up and down or is it flat and monotone?
- **Eye contact:** Does the person look straight at you when speaking or being spoken to? Are his or her eyes fixed, or do they move around a lot?
- **Facial expression:** Is the person's face relaxed or tense? Do his or her eyes, mouth or eyebrows move a lot or not? Are his or her facial expressions positive (e.g. smiling) or negative?
- **Body language:** Are the person's shoulders relaxed or tense? Does he or she sit up with a straight back or slump in the chair? With crossed arms or legs? Does the person use hand gestures? If so, what kind of gestures?

45

Words and phrases

monotone ≠ lively **to slump** ≠ to sit straight **tense** ≠ relaxed

Applying for a job

1 Doing it right

a Amir is looking at the *New Directions* website for information about job applications. Read the website and complete it with the phrases from the box.

> Conclude with a call to action ■ Highlight your qualities and explain why you're the right person ■ Include the essentials ■ Know your options ■ Show who you are ■ Talk about relevant skills

Home | Further education | Undergraduate | Alternatives | Careers

NEW DIRECTIONS ▸ **The application process – Tips for teenagers**

The written application

For students or school leavers with little experience, applying for work is always a challenge. Whether it is work experience, a training programme or an actual job, you will have to apply in writing. This means an up-to-date Curriculum Vitae (CV) and a cover letter. Briefly, let us look at how you can get the most from your CV and cover letter.

A winning CV

Be clear and brief. Your CV should have a clear format and structure. It should also be detailed but not too long. Normally, for teens with little or no work experience, one page is enough.

____1____. In some countries, you don't have to give personal details in your CV that could be used to discriminate against you because of your race, nationality, gender or a disability. In the UK, you are not obliged to include a headshot photo. Similarly, your date of birth is also optional. However, in some European countries you're supposed to include this information. If an employer wants to see a headshot, you'll be forced to add one. Check what is expected in the country where you are applying.

____2____. Employers are interested in your education, work experience and skills. These details must be in your CV. No hiring manager will be willing to consider your application without them.

____3____. You can show more of your personality by listing hobbies and interests. If you have skills, awards or other achievements, you ought to highlight them here. You can also add a short statement near the top of your CV. For example:
I have strong communication and interpersonal skills and work well as part of a team. My interests include climbing and skiing – in both, my drive and competitive nature are clear to see. I am looking for a position where I can learn new skills and develop.

An effective cover letter

A cover letter can help you sell the skills and knowledge that you have. To make your cover letter effective:
Introduce yourself clearly. Explain who you are, the position you are applying for, and how you found out about the opportunity.

____4____. Don't just say that you think you're right for the job. Give a real-life example that shows *why*.

____5____. Identify the skills you've gained in part-time jobs, school activities and sports. Explain how you'll be able to use those skills. Remember: soft skills (e. g. listening and communicating well) are not to be confused with hard skills (e. g. doing maths and using computer programs).

____6____. You need to leave a strong final impression, so invite the employer to contact you. For example:
As you can see from my cover letter, I am very interested in the position so hope to hear from you soon.

b Find out more. Read the text again and complete the tasks.

1. Explain why a job applicant's CV doesn't always have to include a photo.
2. Outline why it is an advantage to list your hobbies in your CV.
3. Describe why a cover letter is useful.
4. Explain how you should end a cover letter.

c Which information in the article do you find especially useful? Explain why.

d Agree on the top three tips in the article. Make notes, then share your ideas in class.

46 Words and phrases

achievement sth very good and difficult that you manage to do
to be willing to to be ready or happy to (do sth)
drive desire and energy to do sth
essentials things which are absolutely necessary in a situation or an activity

→ Workbook, pages 66/67

2* Planning the application

a Look at the grammar box and say which of these functions the modals have: *advice, certainty, lack of obligation, obligation, prediction.*

Remember:
- *Amir **can** speak Bengali.* = ability.
- *You **can** sit over there.* = permission.
- *... you **don't have to** give your personal details in your CV ...* = 1
- *No hiring manager **will** be willing to consider your application ...* = 2
- *Explain how you'll **be able to** use those skills.* = 3
- *If you have skills, awards or achievements, you **ought to** highlight them here.* = 4
- *These details **must** be on your CV.* = 5

b Amir is planning his first written application. Complete his thoughts with modals. Remember that modals can change their forms in different tenses.

1. My cousin Salma said she ___ (*must*) include a headshot with her last application.
2. After I get my A-level results, I ___ (*can*) add them to my CV.
3. When I spoke to Uncle Nasir, I ___ (*should*) asked him which skills are important.
4. Maybe I ___ (*should*) ring him after dinner and get more information.
5. I hope that some day employers ___ (*not, can*) discriminate so easily.

3 In other words.

There are other ways of expressing the German verbs *sollen* and *müssen* in English. Look at these examples from the text. Find the German equivalents for the phrases in **bold**.

1. In the UK, **you are not obliged to** include a headshot photo.
2. In some countries, however, **you're supposed to** include this information.
3. If you have skills, **you ought to** highlight them here.
4. **You need to** leave a strong final impression.

4 The job interview: Dos and don'ts

47 **a** In this *New Directions* podcast, a hiring manager gives advice about interviewing for a job. Listen to part 1 and do the tasks.

1. Explain why Rose focuses on the most basic do's and don'ts.
2. Outline how you should 'do your homework'.
3. Describe what you ought to do if you're not sure how to dress.
4. Explain why Rose says 'Don't feel obliged to act overly cheerful'.

48 **b** Now listen to part 2 and sum up the five pieces of advice Rose gives the listeners.

c Discuss which advice is helpful.

TIP

The word *advice* is uncountable, so we say:
He gave me some advice / a piece of advice.
How much advice were you given?

5 It's your turn: Good advice.

Practise giving each other advice. First, think of a difficult situation or decision you have to make. You can use the ideas in the box or your own. Then take turns to describe your challenge and ask for advice. Remember to use the expressions for giving advice from **4**.

You're late for a job interview because the bus hasn't come. ■ You've lost your mobile. ■ You forgot to do an important piece of homework. ■ You forgot a good friend's birthday. ■ A good friend has asked you to join him / her at a summer camp.

Grammar and structures

Modal verbs, modal substitutes (revision) → G11

You **can't** always choose which details to include in your CV.
Your information **must** be correct and up to date.
Applicants **should** plan their cover letter carefully.

Ways of expressing the German verbs *sollen* and *müssen* → G12

Sollen: should, ought to, be to, be supposed to
Müssen: must, have to, need to, be forced to, be obliged to

@ WES-40805-003

1 Amir is applying for the work experience placement advertised on page **92**. Look at his CV and complete it.

address ■ date of birth ■ education ■ mother tongue(s) ■ other skills and interests ■ work experience

TIP

Writing a great CV
- Check that all information is correct and up to date.
- Include exam grades if a placement or job requires them.
- Give details about your work experience.

CURRICULUM VITAE

Personal information	Amir Shah
[1]	11a Grantley St, London E1 4BN United Kingdom
Mobile:	+44 7146549876
Email	a.shah@mail.co.uk
[2]	5 April 20..
Job applied for	Work experience placement
[3] and training	
Sep. 20.. – present	Langdon Park Sixth Form, London E14 ORZ
20.. – 20..	Swanlea School, London E1 5DJ Completed GCSEs including English (7), Maths (6+)
[4]	
Jan. – June 20..	Part-time typist and transcriber, Fuse Universal, Tower Hamlets, London *Helped transcribe listening materials for learning software.*
August 20..	Volunteer, RSPCA (animal rescue shelter), East London *Looked after rescued dogs and cats.*
Oct. 20.. – June 20..	Writer, school newspaper club, Swanlea School *Wrote about social, political and sport topics.*
Personal skills	
[5]	English, Bengali
Other language(s)	French B1
Computer skills	Competent in most office programs
[6]	Active in school clubs (student newspaper, community activism). Interested in local politics and culture. Member of the school football team.

2 **a** Write your own CV for the job advertised on page **92** or this one.

Part-time waiter (m/f/d) wanted

Homely café is looking for a part-time waiter (m/f/d) to work two evenings a week and Saturdays. No experience necessary.

This is a great opportunity to earn a little extra money and to learn about working in the hospitality sector. All employers look to see if you have any work experience. Candidates must be at least 15 years old.

b Swap CVs and give feedback. How complete is the information? Is it up to date? Are there gaps in the dates?

3 Writing a CV is about presenting yourself in the most positive way possible. What strengths, interests and skills do you have that employers might be interested in? Name two and explain how they might be useful in a job.

4 Amir's uncle is giving him advice about becoming a legal aid lawyer. Complete his email. Sometimes more than one answer is possible. Don't forget to use the right verb form.

be able to ■ be obliged to ■ be supposed to ■ have to ■ need to ■ ought to ■ should

You'll [1] work hard as a legal aid lawyer, but it's a very rewarding job. The government [2] provide legal aid to people who can't afford it. However, the government has cut this support in recent years. As a result, some law centres closed and there are fewer jobs for legal aid lawyers. But there are still opportunities. To become a legal aid lawyer, you [3] follow the standard career route, which includes a university degree, a one-year Legal Practice Course and training in a law office. If your degree is not a law degree, then you will also [4] to complete a Post-Graduate Diploma in Law. I think you [5] also get some real-world work experience. I [6] do this when I was a law student. Volunteer for a non-profit organization – then you'll [7] learn about giving advice and solving problems.

49 **Words and phrases**

rewarding making you happy because you're doing sth useful or important

→ Workbook, page 68

5 **a** Amir has written a cover letter to send with his CV. How are the activities and skills he mentions useful for the placement he is applying for?

b Look again at the tips for writing a cover letter in the article on page **94** (lines 39 – 57). Look at Amir's letter and describe what he has done differently.

11a Grantley St
London E1 4BN

Hiring Manager
Putney Legal Advice Centre
129 Putney High St
London SW 15

20th November 20..

<u>Application for work placement</u>

Dear Ms Cowley

I am 16 years old and a student at Langdon Park Sixth Form in London. I am applying for the work placement which you advertised on the website *youngjobs.co.uk* on 19th November.

I think I am the right person for this placement because I feel strongly about standing up for people's rights. I am doing active student work in this area and would like to do similar work as a career. I am interested in learning about the work that your lawyers do at Putney Legal Advice Centre.

At school, I am in a student activist group that deals with social issues like discrimination. Basically, we gather information, help inform students and others in the community and support people who are affected by these issues. Additionally, I am active as a writer for the school newspaper. I think that these activities, together with my computer skills, make me a good candidate for this work placement.

Thank you for considering my application. I look forward to hearing from you soon and hopefully being asked to come in for an interview.

Yours sincerely
Amir Shah

6 **a** Find the sentence adverbs in Amir's cover letter in **5a**. The article on page **94** also contains sentence adverbs. Find them and add them to your list.

Sentence adverbs (for example *thankfully*, *ideally*) express how someone feels about the content of a sentence; or they put the sentence in a certain context (*technically*, *politically*). They usually come at the beginning of a sentence.
Surprisingly, *the hiring manager called me the next day.*
Theoretically, *I could begin next week.*

b Choose the best sentence adverb to complete each sentence. One of the adverbs doesn't fit.

Basically ■ Fortunately ■ Ideally ■ Naturally ■ Normally

1. I have a lot of camping experience. ____, I am an enthusiastic rock climber.
2. ____, I have visited Glasgow several times, so I know the city well.
3. ____, I don't include a video CV with my job applications, but this is a special case.
4. ____, I would like to begin in July, but of course I could start sooner if necessary.

7 **a** Write a cover letter for the CV that you wrote for **2**.

b Swap your cover letter with a partner. Think about the content, language and structure of a formal letter as well as the tips from the article on page **94**. Give your partner feedback on the letter. For tips on how to give feedback, look at pages **144 / 145**.

TIP

Writing a formal letter

- Use a formal opening and closing.
  Dear Ms Smith
  Yours sincerely
- Use polite forms.
  I would like …
  Please send me …
  Could you please …?
- Avoid short forms.
  I am (~~I'm~~); advertisement (~~ad~~)
- Write complete sentences.

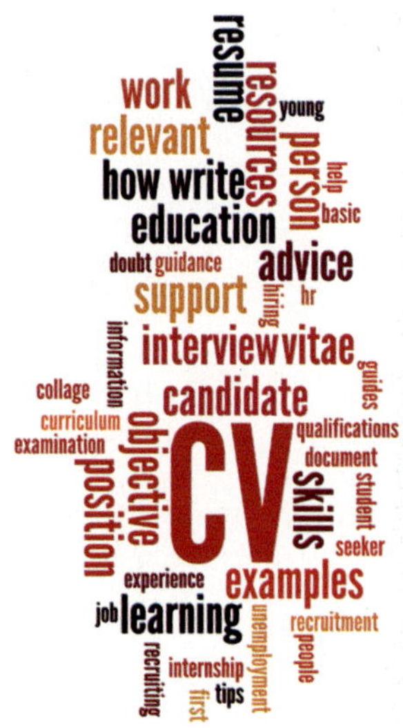

1 **a** You are going to read an article about work. Write down three things you think you will read about and compare your ideas with a partner.

b Skim the article and choose the best heading.

c Read the article in detail. Are all your ideas included? What does the article not mention? What had you not thought of?

1 The future of work | 2 The changing nature of work | 3 A job for life | 4 Women in the workplace

In the 1980s, when my parents were young, getting a job wasn't too difficult. Once you had a job, that was often where you stayed for the rest of your working life, at least with the same organization or field of work. The same cannot be said of the situation today. A recent survey revealed that it is taking young people two years longer to get their first job than it did twenty years ago. On top of that, they are likely to change jobs far more often than in previous generations. In a recent poll, 21% of millennials said they had changed jobs in the last year, while on average people will have had five different jobs by the age of 35! So, what does this all mean for young people today?

Firstly, it means they are often in an insecure position, at least in terms of finances. It is a lot harder to put money aside for those big-ticket items like a car, an apartment or a house. The lack of financial security also has an impact on starting a family, which may explain why many people are waiting until much later than in the past. Secondly, living from pay-check to pay-check can have an impact on your mental health. For many youngsters it is incredibly stressful not knowing if you'll have enough money to pay the bills next month.

One consequence of this situation is that young people feel less loyalty towards their employers. Why should you give your all if you aren't sure you'll have a job in the future? Another consequence is the idea of trying things out until you find something you like. For many, this isn't seen as a negative consequence, but actually something that is a positive.

I can remember a close friend of mine saying, 'My dad lived to work and he never really enjoyed his job. Whereas I work to live – if I don't like my job – I quit and look for another one.'

So, one question might be: How important is it that it's harder for young people to find work and to stay in the same job for long? It could be argued that young people today have far more freedom as there isn't the expectation to leave school, then get a job and settle down straight away. On the other hand, the uncertainty means that there is often little incentive to think of a long-term career. A result of this might be that youngsters don't see the point in investing in a degree that has a narrow specific focus, but will choose something that has transferable skills, leaving them with more options later on.

Finally, while there are both obvious advantages and disadvantages to the situation most youngsters find themselves in today when it comes to work, one thing can be said with certainty: the world of work and our attitude towards it have changed and continues to change.

2 **a** Read the text again and find words and phrases that match the definitions.

1 an area of activity or interest
2 a study in which people are asked their opinions about a subject / person
3 born in the 1980s, 1990s or early 2000s
4 not having confidence, not fixed or safe
5 things that are expensive to buy
6 to stop doing something or leave a job or a place
7 what you believe or hope will happen (in the future)
8 that can be used in a different situation or for a different purpose

b Write down all the words whose meaning you are not sure of. Compare your list with a partner. Are there any words you are both not sure of? Work out their meaning together. Check the tips on page **24**.

→ Workbook, pages 69/70

3 Read the article again and do the tasks.

1 Name two of the changes outlined in the article between the 1980s and nowadays.
2 Explain why young people are more likely to change jobs than previous generations.
3 Describe some of the consequences of not having a steady job.
4 Read lines 43–49 again. Comment on what the author writes. Do you agree with the statements made here? Say why or why not.

4 **a** Read the quotes connected to work below. Choose one quote and spend two minutes preparing to explain it.

b Explain the quote you chose to the rest of your group. Then discuss which one you can most identify with and why.

Your talent determines what you can do. Your motivation determines how much you're willing to do. Your attitude determines how well you do it.

Lou Holtz (*1937), former American Football player, coach and analyst

Someday is not a day of the week.

Janet Dailey (1944 – 2013), American novelist

I haven't failed. I've just found 10,000 ways that won't work.

Thomas Edison (1837 – 1931), American inventor

The only way to do great work is to love what you do. If you haven't found it yet, keep looking. Don't settle.

Steve Jobs (1955 – 2011), co-founder of Apple Inc

If you don't design your own life plan, chances are you'll fall into someone else's plan and guess what they've planned for you? Not much!

Jim Rohn (1930 – 2009), American entrepreneur, author and motivational speaker

5 **a** Look at these factors. Rank them from 1 – 8 in terms of which are the most important (1) to the least important (8) when considering a job.

- the pay
- adds value to the world we live in
- your colleagues
- you feel valued and appreciated
- it's something you love doing
- it's challenging
- there is a good work-life balance
- flexible hours

b Compare your rankings in your group and try to agree on the top three.

c Share your top three. Give reasons for your choices and then vote as a class.

→ Workbook, page 71

Identifying communication strategies

S1 **Optimize communication.** You are going to listen to extracts from two job interviews. The job candidates Ron and Sunita are both interviewing for the same apprenticeship. First look at the *TIP* box. Copy the table in your notebook, then listen. Identify the strategies the speakers use (✓). Compare your table with a partner.

50

	Strategy 1	Strategy 2	Strategy 3	Strategy 4
Interviewer	???	???	???	???
Sunita	???	???	???	???
Ron	???	???	???	???

TIP

How to communicate effectively in conversation

Here are some common strategies:

- Speak clearly and use plain language.
- If you didn't hear what was said, ask the speaker politely to repeat it.
- Ask for clarification, if necessary.
- Rephrase a statement in your own words to confirm understanding.

S2 **Avoid misunderstanding.** Listen to Ron and Sunita again and complete the phrases in your exercise book.

50

- **Asking for repetition**
  Could you 1 *that, please?*
  Sorry, I didn't 2 *that.*
- **Asking for clarification**
  What do you 3 *by …?*
  I'm not 4 *what you mean (when you say …).*
- **Rephrasing**
  Sorry, let me 5.
  In other 6, …
- **Confirming understanding**
  I 7.
  I understand.
  Right.
- **Making time to think**
  Well, …
  So, …
  …, you 8, …
  Let me 9 */think …*

S3 **Role-play: Make yourself understood**

a Choose your roles from the cards on the right. Use at least two communication strategies from **S2**. Then start your role-play. You can start like this:

A *Hi (B's name), I'm (name).*
B *Hi.*
A *Thanks for coming. So, you'd like to be our DJ?*
B *…*

b Find a new partner and swap roles.

A
You are in a student group that is organizing a school dance. Your group is looking for a DJ and you've heard that Student B works as a part-time DJ. You've asked him / her to come for an interview.

You want to find out:
- if he / she has experience
- the kind of music he / she plays
- equipment
- his / her favourite music
- his / her fees
- …
- …

B
You have turned your music hobby into a part-time job as a DJ. A student group in your school is organizing a dance and they have heard about you. Student A has asked you to come for an interview.

Your partner wants to know:
- How long you've done the job
- The music you play
- Your equipment
- Your favourite music
- Your fees
- …

→ Workbook, page 71

Communicating effectively in an interview

S1 **Prepare to evaluate an interview.** Copy this interview evaluation sheet in your exercise book. Discuss at least two further evaluation points based on the strategies on page **100** and the *TIP* box on the right. Add them to your evaluation sheet.

	very good	OK	needs work
1 The person speaks clearly.	???	???	???
2 He looks confident and calm.	???	???	???
3 He asks for repetition when he hasn't heard what was said.	???	???	???

TIP

Non-verbal strategies in an interview – dos and don'ts

- Look confident and calm.
- Don't slump in your chair.
- Don't cross your arms over your chest.
- Make eye contact.
- Don't forget to smile occasionally.

S2 **Evaluate Amir's interviews**

a You are going to watch two interviews with Amir. The first interview is a practice one with his uncle. The second interview is for a work experience placement. Watch the first interview and make notes on your evaluation sheet.

b Watch the second interview and do the same.

c Compare the two interviews using the observations on your evaluation sheet.

S3 **Role-play: Do your own interview**

a In groups of three, take turns as a candidate interviewing for a job, an interviewer and an observer. First look at the instructions. Decide on the roles and take a few minutes to prepare. Then begin the interviews. If possible, make a video of each interview.

Theme Park Work Experience Programme

Awesome Adventure Parks
You will experience every aspect of our theme park operation. One day you will take bookings for holidays or sell theme park tickets, and the next day help to operate a ride and serve guests their lunch.
Our work experience placement is a fantastic way to learn what it is like to work in our different departments. You will get practical training to expand your skills and a certificate at the end of your placement.
Are you interested in a career in the leisure industry? Then apply now.

The candidate: Look at the job advert. You have applied for this placement and will be interviewed. Think about how to answer these questions:

- Why do you want this work experience placement?
- What skills would you like to learn?
- Why do you think you're a perfect candidate?
- What questions do you have?

The interviewer: Your interview should look like this.

1 Greet the candidate.
2 Ask questions including follow-up questions like *Can you give me an example?* or *What do you mean?*
3 Conclude the interview.

The observer: Use the evaluation sheet from **S1** to make notes about how effectively the candidate is able to communicate.

b Use your observer's notes to give each other feedback. Watch the video of each interview if you recorded them. In your group, discuss who communicated most effectively in the interview and why.

The changing world of work

A

B

C

D

1 New ways of working.
'Generation Z' – those born between 1997 and 2012 – face a world of work that is very different from that of their parents or grandparents. Describe and compare the photos. Explain what they show about changes in working life.

2 A job for life?

a Read the text from an online forum and summarize the main points in five to six sentences. Include information about

- how the world of work has changed,
- what the 'gig economy' is,
- what opportunities the gig economy offers.

b Discuss and make notes on the possible disadvantages of the gig economy.

c Compare your notes with the class.

security | social interaction stress | holiday pay | workers' rights | working conditions

Wendy Jones
10 September

How has the world of work changed?

Right up until the 1980s, most workers used to expect to stay with the same company for life. But that's not the norm today. 'Job hopping' – changing jobs frequently – is much more common than it used to be, especially among young people. Also, many companies now prefer to hire independent contractors for short-term work instead of taking on permanent employees. So people are only paid for the 'gigs' they do. Gig work can range from well-paid consultants to on-demand drivers or food delivery couriers. These days many office workers have meals delivered to the office, but that didn't use to be the case.
For young people, the gig economy has advantages, especially flexible work schedules and independence. You can take on a full-time job and just do a few part-time gigs on the side to top up your income. Apps that hire independent workers provide ways of working only when you want to. Or you can work on your own projects in your free time – running your own business as a sideline is increasingly common. Or, finally, you can go freelance full-time. Freelancer platforms allow you to set up a personal profile and bid for jobs that match your skills.

Used to, didn't use to, would

- We can say *used to* + infinitive when we talk about actions that happened regularly in the past, but don't happen now.
  Workers ***used to*** *expect to stay with the same company …*
- We can use *would* + infinitive instead of *used to* + infinitive for repeated actions in the past, but not for states.
  People ***would*** *commute to the office every day.*
- We can say *didn't use to* + infinitive when we talk about states or situations that weren't true in the past but are true now.
  These days many office workers have meals delivered to the office, but that ***didn't use to*** *be the case.*

51 **Words and phrases**

to bid for work	to offer to do work for a specific price
independent	not permanently employed by a company
menial	work that needs no skill, is not important and is boring
peer	sb who is the same age or has the same job as you
a sideline	an activity that you do as well as your main job, to earn more money

→ Workbook, pages 72/73

3 **In the past.** Complete the sentences with *used to, didn't use to* or *would and* compare with today.

1 When they had to get in touch, people ___ type or handwrite letters. Today …
2 Women ___ wear trousers or jeans to work. They ___ wear dresses or skirts and tops.
Today …
3 People ___ be allowed to smoke in the office. The rubbish bins ___ catch fire regularly. Today …
4 There ___ be so many self-employed workers. Today …
5 In the past, my dad ___ stay late at work and he ___ get paid overtime. Today …
6 Women ___ do menial tasks like making coffee for the boss. Today …
7 People ___ get food delivered to their desks. They ___ go to the company canteen for lunch. Today …
8 When my dad started working in an office, he ___ spend an hour a day commuting to work. Today …

4 **The way it was**

52

a For a school project, Ben from Cardiff asked his grandmother about working life in the past. Listen. In what order does she talk about these topics?

main industries | technology in the office | gender pay gap | new ways of working | length of the working day

52

b Choose a topic from **a**. Listen again and make notes. Tell a partner what you've learned about your topic.

5 **Not just work.** Ben asks his grandmother what her personal life was like when she was young. Complete her answer with *used to, didn't use to* or *would*.

We were five children and we [1] share two rooms. My dad, your great-grandfather, was a coal miner. He [2] work down the pit. He [3] leave the house at five thirty and walk or cycle to work. In later years, he [4] go down the pit, he [5] work as a driver. Then, after he had retired, he [6] look after his pigeons. Did you know that pigeon racing was a Welsh tradition? My mum [7] go out to work, she was a housewife. She [8] do all the chores around the house: cooking, cleaning, washing the clothes … she [9] do that once a week because it was a big task. All of us [10] help her.

6 **It's your turn: Things I used to do**

a Write a paragraph of about 120 words comparing how you were as a child with how you are now. Include one fact that isn't true.

When I was a kid, I used to eat meat but now I'm a vegetarian. I used to have long hair, but now I have short, spiky hair. I used to stay at my grandparents' every weekend, but now I don't visit them that much.

b Read out your paragraphs. The other members of the group guess which fact isn't true.

Grammar and structures

***Used to, didn't use to, would* to describe past habits and states** → G13

Most workers **used to** expect to stay with the same company for life.
People **would** commute to the office every day.
Many office workers have meals delivered to the office, but that **didn't use to** be the case.

→ Workbook, page 74

A

B

C

1 Match the headlines to the photos and describe what you see. Explain what social issues they illustrate and what the connection might be.

3 Food poverty now a public health emergency

1 Gap between rich and poor grows while UK's total wealth is on the rise

2 Stabbing fears stop children going out

2 Read the report about the growing gap between rich and poor in the UK. Are the underlined phrases correct or wrong? Correct the wrong ones.

While it's true that there <u>would be</u>[1] a gap in the past between the richest and poorest, it is now wider than ever before. Bosses <u>use to get</u>[2] paid more than their employees, but the difference <u>didn't used to be</u>[3] as big as today. Two other areas connected to rich and poor are house prices and food security. Today it is much harder to get on the housing ladder than it <u>used to be</u>[4] for previous generations. In the 1960s, people <u>would buy</u>[5] their first home when they were in their 20s, today the average age of a first-time buyer is 33. The other shocking statistic of recent years is the rise in the use of food banks. Originally only the homeless or the unemployed <u>would to use</u>[6] food banks. However, in the last few years, the kind of people who <u>didn't use to visit</u>[7] such places, such as low-paid working people, has changed.

3 **a** How does Gen Z feel about giving money to charity? A not-for-profit organization did some research. Before you listen, look at the words. Which ones do you know? Explain their meaning.

disadvantaged ■ to donate ■ financial means ■ to get caught up in something ■ a loan ■ stability ■ to survive ■ tuition fees ■ violence

53 **b** Listen to the interview and watch out for the words you didn't know. Try to work out their meaning from the context.

53 **c** Listen again and describe at least two different ways the students are supporting charities. The words in the box can help you.

campaigning to raise awareness ■ collect bags ■ offering support ■ volunteering time

4 **a** Your class wants to set up a class charity group. Discuss the issues below and come up with a plan and a name for a charity. Outline its purpose and what you want to do. Make notes.

1. Discuss the social problems in your area. Which issue are you *all* interested in?
2. Argue what you can do to help. How will you make it happen? Plan your campaign.
3. How will you get the word out there? For example: you could make posters to stick up on walls, write a blog on social media, etc.

b You are going to decide what your class charity should be. Each group presents their ideas in a two-minute talk. Comment on the presentations and choose the best three. Then take a vote.

→ Workbook, page 75

1 Nikki has written a report about her 6th form College Charity Group for the local charity newsletter. Speculate what information she will include. Discuss your ideas with a partner.

2 Read the report and check your ideas. Did she include anything you didn't mention?

The College Charity Group was founded a year ago. The aim of the group is to campaign to raise awareness about a range of different social issues. This month our campaign has focused on collecting re-useable carrier bags for a local food bank. The food bank found itself in a position where it did not have enough bags to distribute food to the people who needed it.

We started the campaign by thinking how we could reach the largest number of students. We designed posters, which were placed on noticeboards, and we also recorded a short message that could be played on the radio. We are fortunate to have a radio station at our 6th form college, which is run by student volunteers. Initially the response was disappointingly slow, however, by the middle of week three we had collected more than 5,000 carrier bags, far surpassing our original target of 2,000.

Despite the success of the campaign, many of us in the group feel there is far more we could do to help alleviate food poverty. The result of this is that next month we are going to run a new campaign targeting food donations. The hope is that every student who can will donate at least one packet or tin of food each week to the food bank. These items can then be distributed using the carrier bags we have collected during the current campaign.

3 Read the report again and do the tasks.

1 Describe the purpose of each paragraph and how they are connected.
2 Does Nikki use formal or informal language? Give examples to support your answer.
3 Explain the link between the photograph and the report.
4 Explain the meaning of the following words from the report: *distribute*, *surpassing* and *alleviate*.

4 **a** Sam (A) and Harper (B) both volunteer at a charity. Look at their notes and decide which charity you would like to support. Then write a report for a school newsletter about the charity. Describe why you think the charity should be supported and what you think can be done by the school (150 words).

A

YoungMinds – founded 1993
Leading charity: children's mental health and well-being
Issues: bullying, eating disorders, body image, exam stress, etc.
Resources: booklets, leaflets, toolkits, statistics, etc.
How you can help: donations, volunteering, raising awareness

B

Rock Benefit – founded 2020 as a result of Corona pandemic to help young bands and singers
Activities: gives loans to young musicians, organizes studio sessions for recordings, supplies a platform for virtual concerts
regularly features new talent
How you can help: subscribe to platform, support on social media, join virtual concerts

b Exchange your report with a partner and give each other feedback. Is it well written? Are there any mistakes? Can the writer convince the reader about the importance of the charity?

An internship abroad

1 **Daniela in Ireland.** Daniela did a summer internship in Ireland, arranged by a local organization in Dublin. Skim her blog. Then briefly summarize the benefits of doing the intern programme in Ireland, and explain why she recommends it.

Remember:
- Present participle: the *-ing* form of the verb (*staying, buying, ...*)
- Past participle: the 3rd form of the verb (*stayed, bought, ...*)

Medical internship in Dublin, Ireland with InternIreland

Daniela
Age 19, Germany

Preparation

I came across a fantastic organization while researching internships abroad. This organization, run by an Irish government agency, helps young people find their ideal placement and provides support before, during and after their stay. Wanting a hands-on experience before making the final decision about my university course, I contacted them. They set up an eight-week medical internship for me during the summer and I'm really grateful for everything they did. You don't need any experience to apply for the internship programme, but you have to be over 18. First, I filled in an online application and sent my CV and letters of reference. After completing that part, I had a video interview with them. I felt really nervous about it, but they were so positive that I was able to relax.

The experience

Before arriving, I received lots of information and answers to any questions I had. When I got there, I stayed in a beautiful house with other student interns. The team were always available if anyone had a problem. However, they didn't try to act like your parents, and I lived and worked completely independently. Having managed to work out where all the facilities I needed were, I felt quite proud of myself!

Wanting to get hospital experience, I shadowed a doctor at one of Dublin's top hospitals. She was really great at explaining things to me and letting me watch her both in clinic and in surgery. I also met students at the hospital already studying medicine. They were happy to answer all my questions about their course.

My internship helped me to gain practical work experience while also allowing me to experience life in Dublin and Ireland. Never having been to Ireland before, I was determined to do and see as much as I could. From Dublin, I could take a bus or train to wherever I wanted to go in the country. The Irish countryside is really beautiful, with some breathtaking scenery. If asked about it, I'd say it was the prettiest place I've ever visited.

Summary

After I have spent eight wonderful weeks there, I can thoroughly recommend doing an internship in Ireland. True, as you are not getting paid while you are working as an intern means you have to cover the cost yourself and it's expensive to live abroad, but in my opinion, it's worth it. When I look back on it, I can genuinely say I had a fantastic experience. I came home with more confidence in my career choice and my abilities. I met some great people and still keep in touch with some of them. If I was given the opportunity, I would do it again.

54 Words and phrases

to come across	to find sth by chance
confidence (*n.*) / **confident** (*adj.*)	being certain that you can do sth
to shadow	to follow sb closely at work to see what they are doing

→ Workbook, pages 76/77

2 Daniela's review

a Look at the first box below and read the first part of Daniela's review (ll. 1 – 8). Find the examples from the box in the text.

1

Participle constructions help us to give information using fewer words. They are typically found in written English.
We use present participle constructions
- for simultaneous actions, carried out by the same person. (*while researching …*)
- for adverbial clauses of time. (beginning with *before*, *after*, *while*, *since*) (*after completing …*)
- for adverbial clauses that give reason for an action. (*wanting a hands-on experience …*)

We use past participle constructions for reduced relative clauses when we shorten a non-defining relative clause. (*…, run by an Irish government agency*)

b Look at the second grammar box. Then read the second part of Daniela's review (ll. 9 – 24) and find more examples of participle constructions.

2

- We also use present participle constructions to shorten a defining relative clause. (*already studying medicine*)
- We use perfect participle constructions for actions that finished before the action in the main clause. (*having managed …*)
- We use past participle constructions to shorten *if* clauses, mainly when the verb is in passive. (*if asked about it …*)

c Read the last part of Daniela's review (ll. 25 – 30). Rewrite the underlined parts using participle constructions. Check your solution with a partner.

3 Travelling the world

12

a Before you watch Sarah and Jermaine talking about their internships, look at the questions. While you watch, listen for the answers.

1. Why did they decide to do an internship?
2. Where did they choose to do it and why?
3. What interesting and exciting things did they do and see?
4. Did they face any challenges?
5. How do they rate their experience?

12

b Watch again and note down the key information. Then take turns to ask each other the questions in **a** about Sarah and Jermaine. Help each other to correct or add information. Say which destination you think sounds most interesting. Explain your reasons.

4 It's your turn: Where will you go?

a You have decided you would like to do an internship. Think about all the countries / cities you have learned about. Decide where you would like to do it and why. You can use the questions below.

- Why do I want to do an internship abroad?
- Why do I want to intern in (name of place)?
- What am I interested in doing and seeing?
- What do I hope to gain from this experience?

b Share the results with your group.

Grammar and structures

Participle constructions instead of adverbial clauses (present, past and perfect) → G14

Before arriving, I received lots of information.
You aren't paid **while working** as an intern.
If asked about it, I would say …
Wanting to get hospital experience, I shadowed a doctor.
Having spent eight wonderful weeks there, I can thoroughly recommend …

1 **a** Look at these three photos and describe the situations. What do the pictures have in common?

A

B

C

b Read the article and find out what the young people are applying for.

c Read the article again and do the tasks.

1 Describe what many internships have in common.
2 Explain why young people are often willing to do an internship even if they aren't paid.
3 Justify the popularity of the internship programme.
4 Summarize the purpose of the article.
5 Comment on the idea that unpaid internships discriminate against some people.

There are many reasons why young people might do an internship and there are lots of different types. However, one very common feature is that they are almost always unpaid. Even in countries with fairly strict labour laws, many companies have managed to keep unpaid internships going by claiming that they are providing training and therefore they can't be regarded as work.
This raises a number of issues as it can often cost the intern a lot of money to take up this programme. Often they will need to pay for their accommodation, travel and food during the stay. This has led to some people claiming that unpaid internships discriminate against young people from poorer backgrounds.
Despite this the popularity of internships has never been higher. In the USA, the number of university and college students doing an internship was a record 62% in 2017. This was up from 50% ten years before and 45% higher than in 1992!
Of course, some are paid, but it certainly is not the norm. Whether or not they are paid, internships are here to stay. According to one recent survey, people who have done one are 14% more likely to get an interview for a job than those who have not.

2 Read the extract from a report written by Daniela's supervisor at the hospital. Make the supervisor's sentences shorter and more formal by using participle constructions to replace the underlined clauses.

End of internship report

Background
Before Daniela chose this programme, she knew that she wanted to live abroad. She's always wanted to visit Ireland, so she felt this was the perfect opportunity for her.

Initial concerns
Her main concerns were that she was going to a new place and she didn't know anyone. But after she moved in, she realized that wouldn't be a problem. She made a lot of friends while she was living here.

Evaluation
After Daniela had overcome her initial reservations, she was able to get the most out of the programme. If we were given the opportunity, we would love to employ Daniela in the future.

55

Words and phrases

to discourage sb (from doing sth)	to try to stop sb from doing sth
to drop out	to leave college before your course has finished
outstanding	excellent, extremely good
to tend to	to be more likely to do something

→ Workbook, page 78

3 Internships are just one route into a career. Complete this text with the words from the box. There are three you do not need.

apprenticeship ■ business ■ colleagues ■ employment ■ entrepreneurs ■ gap year ■ interview ■ start-up ■ training ■ university ■ volunteer ■ work experience

After finishing school, I decided to take a [1] before going to university. A lot of my friends were going travelling, but I opted for getting some [2], so I took part in an international [3] programme.

Knowing what I wanted to do, the biggest obstacle was getting enough money to begin my own business. I applied for a [4] fund for young [5] and luckily was given a grant of £5,000 towards my [6] idea.

Not being very academic, I decided not to apply for [7]. Instead, I found an [8] with a local company. It's great – I get [9] and paid at the same time!

4 **a** Read about the IBYE competition, then read the information about three past finalists. Edit the texts to make them shorter and more formal so they are suitable for IBYE's website. Use participle constructions.

b Imagine you are a private investor and you are looking for a promising start-up to put money into. Choose one of the three finalists and explain why you think they have the best idea. Discuss your ideas as a group and choose one to invest in.

c Many students around the world start their own businesses while they are studying. Research one of them and write a short description explaining why people should invest in the business.

Ireland's Best Young Entrepreneurs Competition

Are you a young entrepreneur with an outstanding and innovative business? Then the IBYE Competition is for you. There's a €2 million Investment Fund and personal business support to help you develop your business idea. Send in your application with a short description of your business idea or start-up enterprise.

Orla Stafford – IZMOO

Orla trained in gelato-making during her transition year at school and went on to study E-Commerce in Retail. She came up with the idea for Izmoo after she visited many gelaterias around the world, and set up her first store in Drogheda. She grew up in the food business, so she was able to bring a lot of knowledge and experience to this new venture.

Wendy Oke – TEACHKLOUD

Wendy gained a first-class degree and PhD in Early Childhood learning and wanted to put her knowledge into practice. She is passionate about child development and she wants every child to receive a high-quality education in order to reach their full potential. Based on this, she created TeachKloud. This cloud-based platform allows teachers to work smart and spend less time on paperwork and at the same time improve the quality of teaching.

Darragh Lucey – YOONI

Every year millions of students go to college, but up to 60 % of them drop out because they have chosen the wrong course. Darragh saw the drop-out problem first hand while he was taking his Electrical & Electronical Engineering degree at university, and he wanted to help. Since they graduated, Darragh and his friend Nathan have developed the Yooni platform, which uses AI (Artificial Intelligence) algorithms to empower school-leavers to make the right choice of course.

PART 1
PART 2
PART 3

1 Look at the illustration. Briefly describe it, then analyse and comment on its message.

2 **a Think:** Look at the infographic. Describe and analyse what it shows. Why do you think there is such a big difference in the statistics?

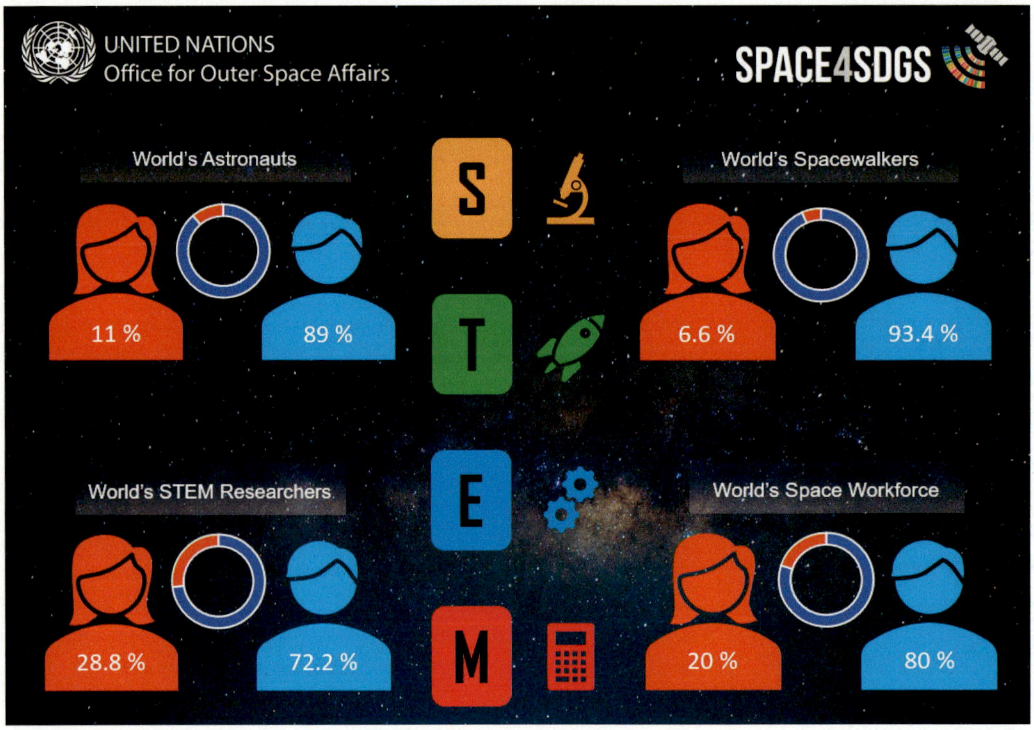

b Pair: Discuss your ideas about the infographic and try to agree on what it shows and why.

c Share: Share your ideas as a class. Did you come to the same conclusions?

3 **a** Listen to what three teenagers say about gender and work, then do the tasks.

56

1. List the issues each teenager speaks about.
2. Explain what Lauren means by 'It's about time people were judged on merit, … .'
3. Analyse the reasons Mike gives for the gender pay gap.
4. In your own words, explain what is meant by the term 'glass ceiling'.
5. Explain what Dana means by '… they are the exception, not the rule'.

b Discuss which of the issues you feel is the most important. Give reasons for your answer.

→ Workbook, page 79

4 **a** Look at the photos and describe the jobs they show. Is there anything you find unusual?

A

B

C

D

E

F

b Look at these facts and figures about women in the workplace. Which ones surprise you the most? Discuss with a partner. Did you have the same ideas?

- Of the top 100 companies in the UK, only 6 had a female CEO in 2020.
- 30% of CEOs in Thailand are female.
- In 2020, 33% of the workforce were female, but only 26% of the senior executive positions were held by women.
- In 2019, just 15% of nursery and primary school teachers were male in the UK.
- In the US, only 26% of jobs in computing or maths-related jobs are occupied by women.
- Israel is one of the few countries around the world where women also have to do military service.
- The first female leader of a country was elected in 1960. Since then, there have been 90 around the world and in 2020 21 countries were led by a woman.
- In 2019, only 5% of airline pilots were female, but in India women made up 13% of commercial pilots.
- In 2021, for the first time in 40 years, women in Russia were allowed to work as train operators again.

c Choose one area mentioned and carry out some research about the situation in Germany. Make notes.

d Work in groups. Present your research.

→ Workbook, page 80

Practising workplace communication

S1 **Paraphrasing.** Paraphrasing is a useful communication strategy in the workplace, where you can be faced with new or uncommon words and concepts. When we don't know the word for something, we can use other words to describe it. Match the quotes from an interview with the words they describe.

1 He just copied her words and called them his own!
2 I think the job is a good, erm, chance to do something.
3 It's cold in here. Where's the switch to make it warmer?
4 What do you use to check that something is horizontal?
5 I think collecting money for the project is our best option.

a thermostat
b spirit level
c plagiarized
d fundraising
e opportunity

A forklift? What's that?

You know, that small electric vehicle that can lift heavy boxes and things.

What's it called when a new employee is shown around the workplace on the first day?

That's an induction.

TIP

Ways to talk about something you don't know the word for

- Use vocabulary that you already know. *It's a device you use to put two holes in a piece of paper.* (hole punch)
- Describe the concept. Explain who uses it, why it's used, or where. *What's that machine where employees can get a drink of water?* (water dispenser)
- Use a synonym. *Let's meet at the reception. – Sorry, what's that? – That's the front desk.*
- Use a more general category word (fruit, clothing, etc.) *Is there one of those vehicles that sells lunch food near here?* (food truck)

S2 **Follow Amir on his first day at work**

57 **a** It's the first day of Amir's work experience at the legal advice centre. The office is new to him, so he's getting an induction. Listen to the dialogue. Put the items A–G in the order in which they are shown to Amir.

A kitchen
B Amir's desk
C shopping rota
D open-plan areas
E supply room
F conference room
G breakout areas

57 **b** Listen again and complete these sentences. Compare your answers.

1 ... everybody sits together in one big office.
2 ... that we can use the room when it is empty?
3 ... that look like giant TVs?
4 ... that some things in the fridge are shared and some things aren't?
5 ... a sharing system.
6 ... everyone takes turns shopping for tea, coffee and milk.

@ WES-40805-003

→ Workbook, page 80

Role-playing an induction

S1 **Identify verbal strategies**

58 **a** Listen to the second part of Amir's introdcution at his workplace. Which of the items in the list does Amir learn about and in which order?

- fire escapes
- toilets
- legal pad
- cleaning supplies
- fire extinguisher
- car park
- printer
- first-aid kit

58 **b** Listen again. What strategies is Amir using when he is not quite sure what Jackie is talking about? Make notes and compare your answers.

S2 **Practise paraphrasing.** In small groups of three, look at the worksheet that your teacher will give you. Check that you know the words for all of the objects and activities. Take turns describing them. The other group members guess which picture is being described.

S3 **Expand your communication strategies.** Communication strategies can also be non-verbal. Look at these objects and concepts. Discuss how you could describe them also using the non-verbal strategies shown in the *TIP*.

TIP

Verbal communication strategies

- **Paraphrasing using statements and questions**
  It's a thing for …-ing. / It's a thing that you use to … / It's sort / kind of like a …
  What do you call the thing that you use to …? / What's it called when you …?
- **Asking for repetition**
  Sorry, what was that? / I'm sorry, what did you say?
- **Asking for clarification**
  Does that mean that …? / Have I got it right that …?
- **Rephrasing**
  What I mean is … / To put it another way, … / What you're saying is …

Non-verbal strategies: showing and demonstrating

Showing or demonstrating something is sometimes more effective than trying to describe it with words. You can do this by …

1 pointing or using a gesture
2 demonstrating an action or a sound
3 using paper to draw a simple picture.

1 e-scooter
2 rucksack
3 research
4 frisbee
5 sightseeing
6 yoga
7 painting
8 emoji

S4 **Role-play: School induction**

a A British exchange student is being shown around your school. Choose your roles, then begin your tour of the school. Add as many different rooms, places and objects as you like.

Student A

You want to show **Student B**, an English exchange student, some of the rooms, places and objects listed below. He or she doesn't speak German yet, and you don't know the English names of these things in your school (even if in reality you do). Choose five items from the list and add two of your own to show **Student B**:

- Sekretariat
- Serverraum
- Hausmeisterraum
- Kollegstufenraum
- Mensa, Cafeteria
- Soziale Arbeit
- Aufenthaltsraum für Schüler/innen
- Raum der Schulleitung
- Fachraum Chemie
- großer Mehrzweckraum

Student B

You are trying to learn German, so you want to find out the names of different places and things in your school – more than just the ones **Student A** explained to you. You can show to **Student A** or you can paraphrase with questions like:

- *What do you call the place where you / the students …?*
- *What's the thing that you use to …?*

b **Student A**, find somebody from another pair who was **Student B**. Swap roles and do the role-play again.

1 After the careers fair, Leslie, a new adviser at the fair, writes a report for her manager. Replace the underlined parts with participle constructions to make it shorter and more formal.

As I had never advised at the careers fair before, I was amazed at just how many young people who visit the fair have no idea about their future plans. While I was preparing for the fair, I read the reports which had been written by my colleagues in previous years. The fair, which is attended by boys and girls from local schools, has clearly been growing in importance in recent years. This event, which was extended by one extra day this year, plays a crucial role in guiding students who are searching for the right career path.
Before I actually spoke to anyone, I had the feeling from previous reports that the wish to study is increasing. If you consider the high tuition fees, this is rather surprising. My initial impression, which was confirmed during my discussions, highlighted the need to encourage young people to really ask themselves what they wish to do with their degree. If they are shown other options and if they are asked the right questions, some of them either start to reconsider their wish to go to university or think about choosing a path which will enable them to gain more practical experience. In addition, if they are given the chance to earn some money while they are studying, some of them rethink their original choices.

2 Emily found an advert on the website youngjobs.co.uk. She decided to apply for the apprenticeship. Read the advert and write her cover letter. Use some of the words and expressions from the box.

additionally ■ applying for ■ basically ■ considering ■ have been ■ hearing ■ ideally ■ naturally ■ passionately ■ which you advertised ■ Yours sincerely

Apprentice wanted! 22 November

Are you passionate about horses? Do you want to earn while you learn?

We are a well-established, family-run riding school, catering for all age groups.
We are currently looking for an enthusiastic, dedicated apprentice to join our friendly, hard-working team.
The successful candidate will be assisting with the day-to-day running of the yard, riding lessons and the daily care of the horses.
What we offer is a real job, with hands-on experience and a chance to train while you work.
Interested? Send your CV and cover letter to
Penelope.Croxley@croxleystables.co.uk

The Grange
Horsham RH12 1AE
Surrey

Croxley Stables
Horsham RH12 4PX
Surrey

25 November 20

Application for apprenticeship

Dear Ms Croxley

I am 16 years old and a student at Thorton Lane Sixth Form College in Surrey. …

Emily Sullivan

→ Workbook, pages 81–83 MORE PRACTICE

3 Choose two of the pictures and prompts to write short statements about how work has changed using *used to*, *didn't use to* and *would*. Write between 60 and 80 words for each.

A

office desk / typewriter / dial phone

B

laptop / mobile phone

C

meetings / meeting room / face-to-face

D

online – virtual

E

male boss / gender roles

F

female boss / mixed team

4 Complete the conversation about social issues with the words and phrases from the two boxes. There are more phrases than you need, but you may have to use some twice.

1
hunger ■ hungry ■ poor ■ poverty ■ stereotypes ■ the elderly ■ the homeless ■ the unemployed ■ the young

2
another idea is to ■ as a result of ■ due to ■ lead ■ means ■ on top of that ■ one idea is to ■ one reason for ■ so ■ that's why

Liam Did you see that programme on TV about social issues today?
Aimee Yes, it was shocking. Which issues do you think are the worst?
Liam It's got to be [1] and [2]. The two are clearly linked.
Aimee Oh, I'm not so sure. Farmers in lots of countries are [3], but they aren't [4].
Liam Yes, but I thought about people with nowhere to sleep like [5] and [6] who don't work.
Aimee Well, there are also many single-parent families who go to food banks. [7] this is the jobs they have are really badly paid [8] they can't afford to buy food. It showed that certain groups of people like [9] and women were more likely to use food banks than other people.
Liam Why is that?
Aimee The cost of university has increased so much, and many leave university very [10]. In the case of women it's often because they are in the lowest paid jobs. Although [11] are changing it's still unusual to find a man working in a nursery with young children or in a care home with [12]. That means these jobs are done by women and they get paid less.
Liam What's the solution?
Aimee [13] pay people in these jobs more. [14] encourage more women to study STEM subjects like maths and science. That [15] to more opportunities.

5 Write an email to a friend about your class charity group. Include answers to these questions:

- What social problem does your charity focus on?
- Why is this an important issue for you?
- What reasons are there for the issue?
- What do you hope your charity will be able to do?

1 M **The Bavarian school system.** Eure englische Partnerschule macht im Moment ein Projekt zum Bundesland Bayern. Ihr gestaltet eine Wandzeitung mit Besonderheiten, die Bayern auszeichnen. Diese Wandzeitung möchtet ihr eurer Partnerschule schicken, damit diese sie in der Aula aufhängen kann. Deine Aufgabe ist es, das bayerische Schulsystem zu beschreiben. Benutze die Grafik unten und schreibe einen Text über das bayerische Schulsystem (200 Wörter). Du hast bereits folgende Vokabeln im Wörterbuch nachgeschaut:

Übertritt an weiterführende Schulen	*entrance to secondary schools*
Mittlerer Schulabschluss	*intermediate school-leaving certificate*
Ausbildungsberuf	*occupation requiring vocational training*
höherer Berufsabschluss	*higher vocational qualification*

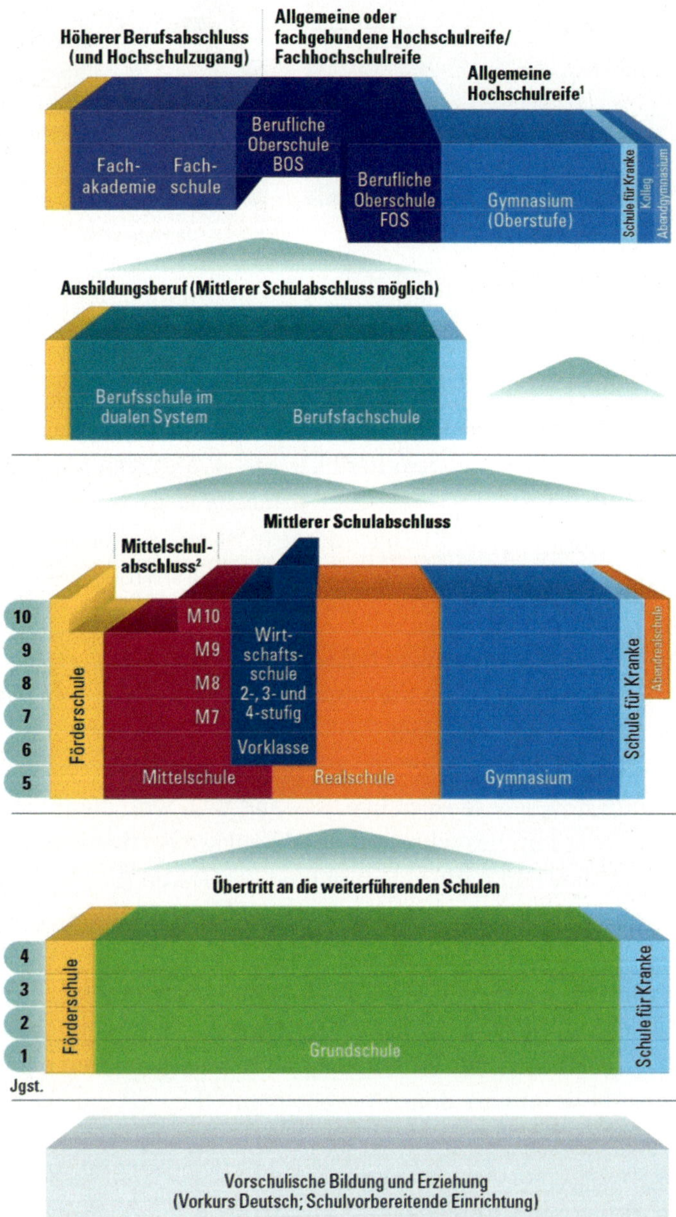

Diese Schularten ermöglichen einen Hochschulzugang.

Diese Schularten ermöglichen einen mittleren Schulabschluss.

Die Grundschule ist die erste und gemeinsame Schule.

Die vorschulische Bildung bereitet auf den Übergang in die Grundschule vor.

[1] Die Umstellung auf das neue neunjährige Gymnasium erfolgte zum Schuljahr 2018/19 mit den Jgst. 5 und 6. Der erste Jahrgang des neunjährigen Gymnasiums legt im Schuljahr 2025/26 das Abitur in Jgst. 13 ab. Die Möglichkeit, die Lernzeit individuell auf acht Jahre zu verkürzen, wird eröffnet.

[2] Erfolgreicher oder qualifizierender Abschluss der Mittelschule

Quelle: Bayerisches Staatsministerium für Unterricht und Kultus, https://www.km.bayern.de/schularten

→ Workbook, pages 84/85

2 M **Summer jobs.** Dein amerikanischer Austauschpartner Elijah wird dich in den Sommerferien besuchen. Ihr wollt zusammen Geld für einen gemeinsamen Urlaub verdienen. Deshalb schaust du dich nach Stellenangeboten für Jugendliche in deiner Gegend um. Auf der Internetseite eurer Lokalzeitung hast du mehrere interessante Inserate gefunden. Elijah ist 15 Jahre alt und spricht wenig Deutsch. Schreibe ihm eine E-Mail (120 Wörter), in der du ihm die Ferienjobs vorstellst. Begründe, für welches dieser Jobangebote du dich entscheiden würdest.

Die Stadt Amberg vermittelt folgende Ferienjobs für Schülerinnen und Schüler und Studierende. Interessenten melden sich bitte telefonisch bei Frau Gebhardt im Rathaus. Frau Gebhardt kann Ihnen weitere Fragen, u.a. zur Bezahlung, beantworten.

Zeitungszusteller/in (m/w/d, Teilzeit, bis 20 h / Woche)

Für die Zeit vom 30. Juli bis 15. September sucht das Amberger Stadtpanorama Aushilfen für die Zustellung der täglichen Zeitungen an Privathaushalte. Die Zeitungen müssen am Zeitungsladen in der Hauptstraße abgeholt und verteilt werden. Dafür werden mehrere Leute eingesetzt, denen jeweils ein Stadtbezirk zugewiesen wird. Handwagen werden gestellt. Die Zustellung erfolgt in den Morgenstunden bis 7 Uhr.

Helfer/in im landwirtschaftlichen Bereich (m/w/d)

Der Landwirtschaftsbetrieb Sievers in Raigering sucht für die Zeit der Sommerferien nach Schülerinnen und Schülern, die ihren Hof unterstützen möchten. Die Aufgaben reichen von einfachen Erntetätigkeiten (Obst, Gemüse), Unterstützung bei der Weiterverarbeitung der Produkte bis zur Mithilfe im Hofladen sowie Stallarbeiten. Vorerfahrung ist von Vorteil, aber keine Voraussetzung. AG zahlt den gesetzlichen Mindestlohn.

Pizzaboten (m/w/d, 16 h / Woche)

Die Pizzeria Pinocchio am Marktplatz ist auf der Suche nach Pizzaboten, die telefonisch bestellte Speisen mit dem Fahrrad oder dem Roller ausliefern können. Wichtig sind ein sicherer Fahrstil sowie Zuverlässigkeit und schnelles Arbeiten. Die Arbeitszeit verteilt sich unter der Woche auf die Abendstunden sowie am Wochenende sowohl mittags als auch abends. Mitarbeiter/innen dürfen kostenlos in der Pizzeria essen.

Umfragen durchführen (je nach Bedarf)

Das Referat Jugend, Senioren und Soziales sucht nach jungen Leuten zur Durchführung einer innerstädtischen Umfrage von Jugendlichen unserer Stadt. Umfragebögen werden gestellt. Wer mithelfen möchte, wird in der Fußgängerzone Personen zwischen 8 und 18 Jahren ansprechen und ihnen Fragen zum Angebot unserer Stadt stellen. Ziel der Befragung ist es, herauszufinden, ob es ein ausreichendes Freizeitangebot für Jugendliche bietet, wie das bestehende Angebot genutzt wird und welche weiteren Angebote sich junge Menschen wünschen.

Mitarbeit in Claudias Boutique (m/w/d, 10 h / Woche)

Claudia Menges ist auf der Suche nach zwei Personen, die sie in den Sommerferien in ihrer Boutique unterstützen können. Die Boutique hat sich auf klassische Mode und ausgefallene Schuhe und Accessoires spezialisiert. Frau Menges braucht Hilfe beim Auspacken und Einräumen der Waren und der Dekoration ihres Ladens.

Ready for the next level?

1 G 10 Read what five young people said about their plans for the future. Complete the sentences with a verb in the correct form (gerund or *to*-infinitive).

The careers advisor suggested **1** *a gap year while I decide what to do.* — Lee

I start a course at a Further Education College next year. I'm really looking forward to **2** *lots of new people and* **3** *new skills.* — Marcie

When I finish university, I'm planning **4** *to the USA and take an MBA.* — Rick

School isn't for me. I hate **5**. *It's so boring. All my friends are going to start sixth form, but I hope* **6** *a job and start earning.* — Emma

I remember **7** *to my father about what I should do after finishing school. He said, 'Remember* **8** *something you like because you don't want to have a job that doesn't interest you.'* — James

2 Getting to know you. Find a partner you don't normally work with. Ask him or her questions. Record the interview, then swap roles.

1. Can you describe something you recently finished?
2. What are you are interested in?
3. What is a decision you recently made?
4. Is there anything you do now that you plan to continue in the future?
5. What is something you often forget?

3 Read Ben's cover letter. Rewrite it so the language is more appropriate.

33 Parkway Avenue
Cardiff
CF10 1DE

Human Resource Manager
TRT Computing
Cardiff
CF10 1AT

Your job ad

Hi Mr Jones

I'm 17 years old and a student at City Sixth Form College in Cardiff. I am applying for the work placement in your ad on the website *youngjobs.co.uk*.

I think I am the right person for this work placement because I will become an engineer. This has been my dream for many years. I am studying engineering at college and I have always been interested in mechanical things. I believe that this work placement would give me the opportunity to learn more. Tell me more about the job.

Thank you for liking my application. I look forward to you offering me the job soon.

All the best
Ben Evans

→ Workbook, pages 86-88

4 G 13 Eileen Jameson is a journalist from Portmarnock near Dublin. Read her blog and complete it with *used to*, *didn't use to* and *would*. When you can, use *would*.

My name's Eileen Jameson. I'm from Portmanock and I have a younger sister, Lauren, who I share a small house with. I work as a freelance journalist. I started working in the gig economy just over five years ago. Before that, I **1** work for a local Dublin newspaper. I **2** get up at around six in the morning and I **3** commute to work on a very crowded train from Portmanock to Dublin. I **4** sit in a big office full of people. Now I work from a small room in my house. I guess the one advantage of the job at the newspaper was that I **5** work at the weekend. However, there were lots of disadvantages. First of all, I **6** usually be told what stories to cover. I **7** often work through my lunch break, so I **8** have food delivered to my desk. It was very stressful, but at least I **9** worry about money, as I **10** always be paid at the end of the month. Anyway, there's no going back now. Small newspapers like the one I **11** work for are finding it hard nowadays. Freelance journalism is definitely the future.

5 *New Directions* is planning an advice column about internships. Use the notes to write a short and interesting text that can be published on the website. Think of ways to structure your text.

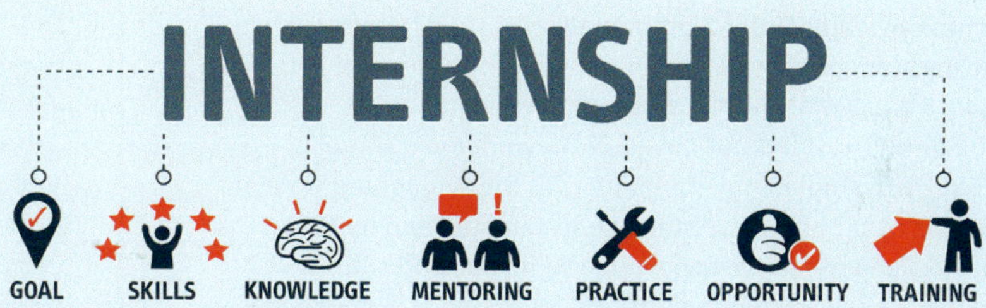

Are you interested in applying for an internship? If so, then read our advice before starting your application.

- no work experience not a problem / transferable skills
- future career plans / influence the programme
- list of clubs and societies / stand out at interview
- join forum / post questions
- wait / contact person / in touch
- waiting / consider other options

6 You've been asked to write a short article (200 words) for your school magazine about gender issues in the workplace. Use the infographic to help you.

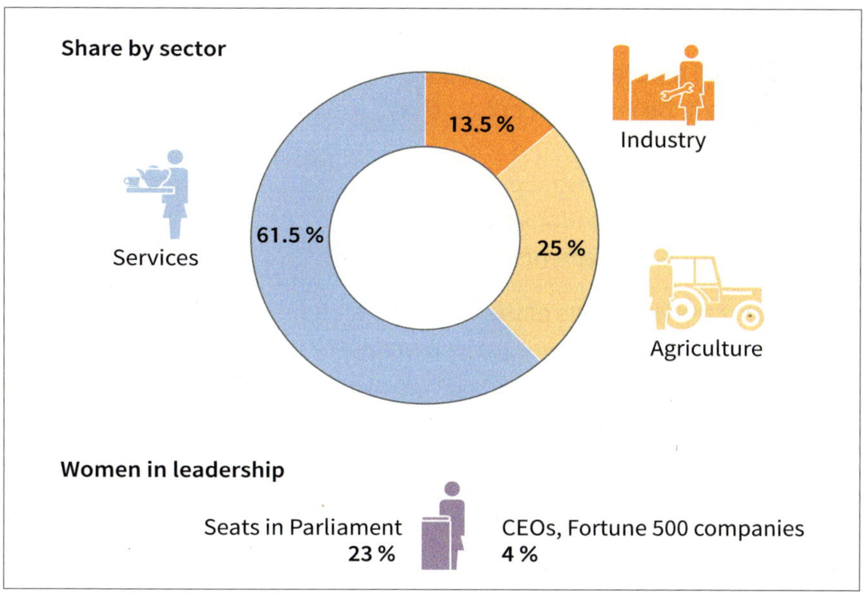

Margaret Atwood, 'There Was Once' (1992)

Margaret Atwood (*1939) is a Canadian novelist who also writes short stories, poems and essays. After studying English language and literature at the University of Toronto and then later at Harvard, she started a career as a university lecturer but soon began to publish her own works. She is well known on the international literary scene and has been awarded numerous prizes and honours. These include: The Man Booker Prize in 2019, which she won for a second time (the first time was in 2000); the Peace Prize of the German Booktrade; the famous Commonwealth Order 'Companions of Honour', awarded for having made a long-lasting, major contribution to the arts, as well as several lifetime achievement awards. One of her most famous novels is *The Handmaid's Tale* (1985), a dystopian novel dealing with the subjugated[1] role of women in a totalitarian[2] state. Multi-talented and multi-faceted, she has published a huge variety of works, from graphic novels to children's books, television scripts or even non-fiction publications. She is also actively engaged in a lot of other issues, like the environment and animal rights.

'There was once a poor girl, as beautiful as she was good, who lived with her wicked stepmother in a house in the forest.'

'Forest? Forest is passé, I mean, I've had it with all this wilderness stuff. It's not a right image of our society, today. Let's have some urban for a change.'

'There was once a poor girl, as beautiful as she was good, who lived with her wicked stepmother in a house in the suburbs.'

'That's better. But I have to seriously query this word poor.'

'But she was poor!'

'Poor is relative. She lived in a house, didn't she?'

'Yes.'

'Then socio-economically speaking, she was not poor.'

'But none of the money was *hers*! The whole point of the story is that the wicked stepmother makes her wear old clothes and sleep in the fireplace –'

'Aha! They had a *fireplace*! With poor, let me tell you, there's no fireplace. Come down to the park, come to the subway stations after dark, come down to where they sleep in cardboard boxes, and I'll show you *poor*!'

'There was once a middle-class girl, as beautiful as she was good –'

'Stop right there. I think we can cut the beautiful, don't you? Women these days have to deal with too many intimidating[3] physical role models as it is, what with those bimbos[4] in the ads. Can't you make her, well, more average?'

'There was once a girl who was a little overweight and whose front teeth stuck out, who –'

'I don't think it's nice to make fun of people's appearances. Plus, you're encouraging anorexia.'

'I wasn't making fun! I was just describing –'

'Skip the description. Description oppresses. But you can say what colour she was.'

'What colour?'

'You know. Black, white, red, brown, yellow. Those are the choices. And I'm telling you right now, I've had enough of white. Dominant culture this, dominant culture that –'

1 **a** Before you read the story, look at the first sentence. Say what it reminds you of and speculate what might happen in the story. You can discuss it with a partner, draw a picture, or make notes.

There was once a poor girl, as beautiful as she was good, who lived with her wicked stepmother in a house in the forest.

b Now read the story and talk about your first reaction to it. Do you like it or not? Use at least five adjectives to justify your reaction. Ask three of your classmates to what extent the story has matched their expectations from **1**, then summarize their statements and add your own.

c Outline the key points of the story. Think about the following aspects:

- Who are the people involved (characters)?
- Where and when does the story take place (setting)?
- What are they talking about (summary of the content)?

[1]**subjugated** being under sb's control – [2]**totalitarian** a political system in which the state, usually a dictator, attempts to assert total control over the lives of its citizens – [3]**intimidating** making you feel frightened – [4]**bimbo** a young woman considered to be attractive but not intelligent

'I don't know what colour.'

'Well, it would probably be *your* colour, wouldn't it?'

'But this isn't about me! It's about this girl –'

'Everything is about you.'

'Sounds to me like you don't want to hear this story at all.'

'Oh well, go on. You could make her ethnic[5]. That might help.'

'There was once a girl of indeterminate[6] descent[7], as average-looking as she was good, who lived with her wicked –'

'Another thing. Good and *wicked*. Don't you think you should transcend[8] those puritanical[9] judgmental[10] moralistic epithets[11]? I mean, so much of that is conditioning[12], isn't it?'

'There was once a girl, as average-looking as she was well-adjusted, who lived with her stepmother, who was not a very open and loving person because she herself had been abused in childhood.'

'Better. But I am so *tired* of negative female images! And stepmothers – they always get it in the neck! Change it to step*father*, why don't you? That would make more sense anyway, considering the bad behaviour you're about to describe. And throw in some whips and chains. We all know what those twisted, repressed, middle-aged men are like –'

'Hey, just a minute! I'm a middle-aged –'

'Stuff it, Mister Nosy Parker. Nobody asked you to stick in your oar[13], or whatever you want to call that thing. This is between the two of us. Go on.'

'There was once a girl –'

'How old was she?'

'I don't know. She was young.'

'This ends with a marriage, right?'

'Well, not to blow the plot, but – yes.'

'Then you can scratch the condescending[14] paternalistic[15] terminology. It's woman, pal. Woman.'

'There was once –'

'What's this was, once? Enough of the dead past. Tell me about now.'

'There –'

'So?'

'So, what?'

'So, why not here?'

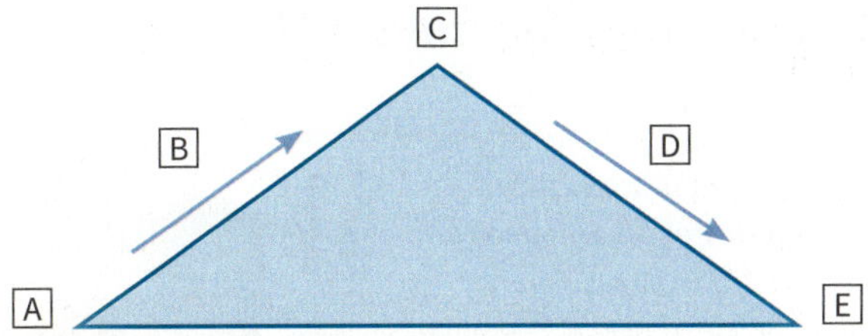

TIP

Every story has a 'story arc', that means the path the story follows. Usually, it provides a beginning, a middle and end of the story. It is typically shaped like a hill.

- **Exposition** (A). This is the reader's introduction to the story. The exposition offers background information about the main character(s), the setting, and time period.
- **Rising action** (B). This is when conflict begins to develop. It is usually a series of events that put the main events of the story in motion.
- **Climax** (C). This is the highest point of tension and usually the point with the greatest intensity in a story.
- **Falling action** (D). The falling action is the opposite of rising action, i.e. all the events that happen after the climax and lead the readers to the solution.
- **Resolution** (E). This is the end or conclusion of the story. Depending on the genre, it can be happy or tragic.

2 **a** Read the *TIP* box, then examine the plot of the story. With a partner, discuss if the story follows the traditional story or narrative arc.

b Analyse the conflict and how it enforces the development of the theme. Look at the objections and corrections the listener makes.

c Why do you think the two characters remain anonymous? What is their function?

d Comment on the target audience. Who might the story be intended for?

3 **a** Discuss the message you think the author wants to convey. In your group, write down what you can agree on.

b Do some research and give a definition of the two popular literary devices, irony and satire. Analyse how Atwood uses them to convey her message.

c Discuss whether fairy tales are old-fashioned and outdated. Give reasons for your opinion.

---

[5] **ethnic** relating to a particular race or nation and their culture, customs and traditions – [6] **indeterminate** vague, imprecise – [7] **descent** sb's family origin and nationality – [8] **to transend** to go beyond; rise above – [9] **puritanical** relating to the Puritans – [10] **judgmental** being overly critical towards others – [11] **epithet** ['epɪθet] label, description – [12] **conditioning** the act of training sb / sth to behave in a particular way or for a particular purpose – [13] **to stick your oar in** to get involved, often giving an opinion without being asked – [14] **condescending** thinking that you are better, more intelligent, etc. than other people and looking down on them because of it – [15] **paternalistic** a rather controlling manner of leadership where you restrict the ability of other people to make their own decisions and live as they choose

@ WES-40805-003

Ben Ockrent, *Hacktivists* (2015)

Ben Ockrent and his wife, the British actress Jemima Rooper

Ben Ockrent is an award-winning writer and director for theatre, film, television and radio. Some of the UK's leading actors have worked with him and he has had his work produced and broadcast all over the world.

In a recent interview he spoke about his motivation:

Finally, what is your main motivation when writing a play? Is it simply to entertain the audience, or do you also want to encourage them to think?

It depends on the project, but ultimately both. Though there's an arrogance in assuming that you have any new insights that will challenge the audience to question what they really think. Entertainment is what it is. It's not a lecture. I want people to have a good time and to leave thinking … I don't know what else we should aspire more to in life than just enjoying an experience with other people. To be able to live in a culture where we can access that and to do a job where I can at least aspire to be a part of that experience for other people, that's the inspiration or the dream.

1 **a** Describe the illustration and say what effect it has on you. Include at least five adjectives modified by an adverb, e.g. 'fairly frightening'.

b Now analyse the text in the illustration. Who is talking and what is the message? Do you agree? Consider the stylistic device of personification in this context.

Scene Two

Music cuts and throwies[1] are extinguished simultaneously[2] to lights up on Archie and Beth facing each other adversarially[3]. Eloise enters, followed by Mark, Steve and Cath. The atmosphere is tense …

BETH (*Understatement*). Well, that was embarrassing.

ARCHIE. It's his house. He was free to decide who he lets in.

BETH. But not to humiliate[4] me.

ARCHIE. He didn't humiliate you.

ELOISE. He made you get down on your knees in front of the entire party and beg you to let us in.

ARCHIE. He was just having a laugh. So what? That's fine.

ELOISE. And did you find it funny?

ARCHIE. Yeah, maybe I did, actually.

ELOISE. You're lying.

ARCHIE. Alright then, no, I didn't find it 'funny', exactly –

CATH. Then why did you do it?

Hugs enters, followed by Jenny, Tania, Nisha, Seb, Pez and Drew.

HUGS. It's all over YouTube.

STEVE. What is?

NISHA. Archie on his knees in front of everyone at the party. Someone filmed it from a window.

MARK. We should make it stop now before it's trending[5].

ARCHIE. Take it down and we make it look like Daniel Cooper's got to us[6]. Don't give him the satisfaction. (*To Hugs and Beth*) You were right. We weren't invited. I accept that. But you know what? I don't care. We're better than him. We're better than all of them.

BETH. Then maybe it's about time they found out.

HUGS. How?

BETH. By teaching this Daniel Cooper a lesson.

ARCHIE. Now, hang on a minute –

BETH. We agreed. If he didn't let us in, we'd start putting this place – all of your talents – to real use. You can't go back on that.

[1] **throwie** a form of LED light art used for creating non-destructive graffiti and light displays – [2] **simultaneous** at the same time – [3] **adversarially** facing each other like enemies – [4] **to humiliate** to show no respect and embarrass sb, especially in the presence of other people – [5] **to trend** to go viral on the internet – [6] **to get to sb** (*coll.*) to make so. feel upset and angry

HUGS (*To Archie*). Mate, a deal's a deal.

ARCHIE. We said we'd turn this into a real hackerspace. We never said anything about teaching anyone a lesson.

BETH. I'm sorry, but can anyone remind me why the Headmaster let you have this place?

PEZ. Because she wants us to become the next tech giants?

BETH. Sorry, tech what?

ELOISE. Giants.

BETH. Oh, giants! Because that's what geeks[7] can be these days. (*To Mark*) Can't they, Mogul?

MARK. Potentially.

BETH. So long as what?

MARK. They know what they're doing.

BETH. Pez, you said you could take down that video.

TANIA. They've made it into a song. Used a re-mix of that Madcon[8] song 'Beggin'.

DREW. Quite catchy, actually.

NISHA. (*Glancing at her phone*) Uh-oh.

MARK. What?

NISHA. Someone's posted it on Twitter.

PEZ. What's the hashtag?

NISHA. (*Reading her phone*) HashtagMassive BellEnd.

HUGS. Amazing.

ARCHIE. But I can't have been down on my knees for more than ten seconds!

JENNY. They're fairly liberal with the slow-mo.

CATH. And the rewinds[9].

TANIA. And the freeze-frames[10].

ARCHIE. But why would they do that?

HUGS. Coz it's funny?

NISHA. It's not funny, Hugs. It's mean.

PEZ. I could probably hack into the YouTube account and take down the video if you want?

STEVE. Do it.

ARCHIE. No. Leave it up. I don't care.

STEVE. Mate, it's probably not even been seen by that many people yet.

DREW. (*Reading his phone*) Twenty-three thousand, four hundred and nineteen ... twenty ... twenty-one ...

c Read the quotation below. Discuss Hug's and Beth's attitude towards the issue of hacking, e.g. Is it positive or negative, moderate or extreme …?

ARCHIE. Alright, then what is the point?

HUGS. Freedom.

BETH. ... That's what hacking is. It's breaking down barriers. Overcoming limitations.

2 **a** Plays are intended to be performed on stage. Get together in a group and imagine you're on a stage. Do a role-play and read the text aloud.

b Sum up the scene in three to five sentences and outline the overall topic of the conversation.

3 Now read the excerpt again and do the tasks.

1. Examine the various attitudes towards what has happened to Archie.
2. Describe the atmosphere and tone of their meeting.
3. Characterize Beth and Archie and define their role in the play.
4. Cyberbullying has become quite common these days. Examine the way it is practised here, the reasons for it and its effects.

4 The setting in the *Hacktivists* is described as a 'hackerspace' in a Portacabin on the school grounds where the students of the computer club meet at lunchtime. Use your imagination and design the interior. You can either draw a picture or describe it.

TIP

Setting and stage directions
Instructions for the setting and stage directions give information about how the actors have to move, behave or what tone their voices should have, etc. They are special to the genre of drama and are usually given by the author.

---

[7] **geek** (*coll.*) a computer nerd who is an expert on the one hand but doesn't know how to behave socially on the other hand – [8] **Madcon** a Norwegian musical duo, playing hip hop, dance pop and rap; one of their songs is called "Beggin'" with the line "I'm beggin' on my knees" in it – [9] **rewind** backward movement – [10] **freeze-frame** picture in a standstill

59

THREE

Joanna came to lunch on Thursday. Looking back, I think it might have been better if she had not been invited to a meal, not at first. Things were difficult right from the start.

In order to make his girlfriend happy, Cudweed had demanded that the lunch was 100% vegan. He had spent the whole morning in the kitchen, looking at the lists of ingredients in sauces and salad dressings and anything else that had a label on it. At one point, I even saw him holding up a cabbage and staring at it hard. He was still staring at it when Solstice walked by.

'Why are you staring at that cabbage?' she asked.

Cudweed looked worried.

'Cabbages are vegan, right?' he asked.

'Of course cabbages are vegan!' she replied.

'Well, you never know,' said Cudweed.

'Yes, you do. Cabbages are vegan, it's very simple.'

Cudweed sighed.

'I thought it was simple, but it isn't,' he said. 'I thought honey would be okay, but Joanna says it isn't. People seem to argue about all sorts of details.'

Solstice ignored him.

'I see you've solved the problem of your trousers,' she said, looking at his belt. Cudweed had replaced the Sellotape with a cord[1] from one of Minty's dressing gowns. It was a rather nice red colour, and I thought it looked quite stylish, but then Solstice said, 'You know that's made of silk[2], don't you?'

Cudweed looked even more worried.

'It is …?' he said, 'And silk …?'

'Isn't vegan!' said Solstice. 'It's made by little worms. Silkworms! If you are going to be an ethical vegan, you can't wear silk!'

'A what?' asked Cudweed.

'A dietary[3] vegan only avoids animal foods, an *ethical* vegan avoids *all* animal products. I thought you would know that.'

'I told you it wasn't simple!' cried Cudweed and ran off to find something to replace the silk with.

At lunch time, Joanna arrived. I was fascinated to see what she looked like, and so I snuck up[4] onto the chandelier in the dining room again.

She didn't *look* vegan. I mean, you couldn't have guessed just by looking at her. She didn't have horns[5], or stripes[6], or anything. In fact, she was quite pretty, and I could see why young Cudweed had fallen in love. I started to wonder if I was wrong about vegans. Maybe they're not so different from anyone else. They just don't eat animals.

No one was speaking very much. Valevine was in a terrible mood, from being forced to eat nothing but tomatoes and avocados. Solstice was sulking. Cudweed was very nervous. But Minty tried to make conversation.

'So, Joanna,' she said, 'how did you two meet?'

'On the internet, Mrs Otherhand,' she said.

'Internet,' Cudweed added.

And that was the end of that conversation.

'So, er …' Minty tried again. 'Have you been vegan a long time?'

'All my life,' she said. 'My parents raised me as a vegan. I have never eaten an animal.'

'She's never eaten an animal,' added Cudweed.

'Never!' said Valevine, exploding. 'That's not possible!'

'I assure you it is possible, Mr Otherhand,' Joanna said.

'It is possible,' added Cudweed.

[1] **cord** Band – [2] **silk** Seide – [3] **dietary** Ernährungs-; diätisch – [4] **to sneak up (snuck, snuck)** heranschleichen – [5] **horn** Horn – [6] **stripe** Streifen

'But, but ...' said Minty. 'It's not healthy, is it? I mean, it's one thing for adults to stop eating meat, but children need certain things.'

'Certain things?' asked Joanna.

'Certain things?' added Cudweed.

'Yes,' said Minty. 'Certain things ... to grow up ... right.'

Joanna put down her fork.

'All the vital[7] components necessary for the healthy development of a child can be obtained[8] from a vegan diet, given the addition of certain vitamins and proteins through dietary supplements[9].'

'... the addition of certain vitamins and proteins through dietary supplements,' added Cudweed.

I wasn't the only one who had noticed he was repeating everything Joanna said, and I wasn't the only one who was finding it annoying. Solstice was glaring at her little brother.

'Oh,' said Minty, 'I see. Well. That's nice. Chocolate cake anyone?'

'*Vegan* chocolate cake,' added Cudweed, seeing the look on Joanna's face. 'I made it myself. It's totally vegan. It has no eggs, or milk in it. Or flour, it's gluten free, too.'

'What does it have in it?' asked Valevine suspiciously. 'Chocolate, I suppose?'

He started to laugh at his joke until Cudweed said, 'No. Actually it doesn't have any chocolate in it. It has vegan chocolate instead.'

Valevine looked like he might faint, but Minty got the chocolate cake, and everyone had a slice. The room was filled with silence as everyone chewed the cake.

'Very ... very nice dear,' said Minty to Cudweed, looking like she might be sick. Solstice pushed her plate away, the cake half-finished. Valevine took one look at his and that was that. Only Joanna ate all of her slice of cake.

'Excellent,' she said. 'And doesn't it taste so *much nicer* knowing that no animals were harmed to make it?'

'No animals were harmed to make it,' added Cudweed. 'So much nicer, isn't it?'

'No,' said Valevine, 'it isn't.'

It looked as if Joanna might start arguing with Valevine. Cudweed saw it coming, and tried to do something.

'Why don't we go to my room, Joanna,' he said, 'and design some posters for veganism? Or something?'

Joanna was about to reply, when something bad happened.

It's a little embarrassing for me to tell you what happened next. I am really very ashamed. It was a total accident, I swear, but well ... It's like this. I had eaten those three large slices of bacon. Then, the following day, I found that someone had left the fridge door open and there was a huge bowl of cheese sauce in there. Not all ravens like cheese sauce, but I do ... And then, when Cudweed was making his chocolate cake, he found out that he couldn't put normal chocolate in it, and he left the bars[10] of chocolate out of the cupboard. Three of them, and I ... Well, you can imagine.

So now, after three days of food like that, things were 'not right' in my poor old raven's stomach. In fact, as I sat on the chandelier, I suddenly felt something moving in my insides.

Ark! I thought. I need to excuse myself! I need to leave the room! I need to ...

But it was too late, and I released a small amount of raven poo. All over Joanna's head.

She screamed and looked up to see me, and then she screamed again.

'What is that?' she yelled. 'And what is this?' She added, wiping at her hair with her napkin.

'Edgar!' cried Minty, 'What are you doing in here?'

'That thing has a name?' cried Joanna.

Thing? I thought. Who is she calling a *thing*?

'That's Edgar,' said Solstice, angrily, 'And he is our raven.'

'You have a pet?' said Joanna.

No, I thought, I am not a pet, but I could see no one was interested in my opinion.

'You are keeping a living animal as a slave in your house? A prisoner? Unable to be free, as it would be in nature?'

---

[7] **vital** lebensnotwendig – [8] **to obtain** erhalten – [9] **supplement** Ergänzung – [10] **bar** Riegel

'... would be in nature?' added Cudweed, and I suddenly wanted to leave something on his head, too.

'Edgar is not our pet,' said Solstice. 'He lives here. With us. It's his choice.'

'Oh, really?' said Joanna. 'And he told you that, did he?'

'Did he?' asked Cudweed. Then he added, 'Actually, did he tell us that?'

'Not exactly,' said Solstice, 'but this is his home. He doesn't want to go anywhere else!'

Well, I do like a nice holiday every once in a while, I thought, and I told them so.

'Korrrrk!' I said, and Joanna stared at me.

'It's very ugly, isn't it?'

Well, that was that.

Solstice stood up and started shouting at Joanna, Valevine started shouting at Solstice not to shout, Minty put her head in her hands, and Cudweed stood up, grabbed Joanna's hand and pulled her away from the table.

He was flustered[11].

'I'll take you to my room and you can wash my hair,' he said.

Everyone stared at him.

'I mean, we can wash your hair,' he said to Joanna, correcting himself.

They started to walk off and then I saw that Cudweed's trousers were held up by an extremely long elastic band[12]. But not long enough. As he reached the stairs, the rubber band snapped, and down came his trousers again. I saw that he was still wearing the raven underpants, which was very sweet, but I made a note to tell him that if he was going to have a girlfriend, he might need to learn to change his underwear from time to time.

There was silence in the house for some time. Everyone had disappeared. Cudweed and Joanna had gone to his room and hadn't been seen since. I flapped around the castle, very bored, but also very angry at being called ugly. I was also still very embarrassed by what had happened at the dinner table. What I had done, I mean.

I decided to go for a long fly over the lake and back. It does me good to get out into nature when I am in a bad mood. I do it whenever I am feeling grumpy, or depressed, or worrying. I spend a lot of time in nature. Anyway, when I got back, I was feeling a little better, and as I flew along into the Small Hall, I saw Solstice sitting in an armchair reading a book.

'Oh, hello, Edgar,' she said, and I went to see what she was reading.

It was a book called 'A Young Person's Guide to Philosophy.'

'Kark?' I said.

'I'm trying to be a better person,' she said. 'I am reading about morals. And ethics; about how we know what the right thing to do is. Stuff like that.'

'Kark,' I said, because Solstice is the best person I know, and I didn't think she needed a book to help her be any better.

Then Cudweed appeared, and he wandered[13] over. He looked extremely miserable.

'Cudweed?' asked Solstice. 'Is everything okay?'

'Yes,' he said. Then, 'No. It isn't okay. It's very difficult. I totally love Joanna, but we have been arguing. I understand why it's a good idea. For example, did you know that the world would have enough food for everyone if everyone was even just a vegetarian? That there would be less global warming?'

Solstice rolled her eyes.

'Yes, I told you that about a million times!'

Cudweed wasn't listening.

'But it's so hard to be a vegan,' he said, 'Joanna says I can't even eat chocolate on my birthday, not the kind with milk in, which is my favourite. And right now, she's going through all my books, and I'm going to have to throw half of them away because the glue in the older ones is made from dead horses.'

'Ewww,' said Solstice, 'horse glue. Ugh.'

I thought that sounded rather tasty, but I decided it wasn't the right moment to say so.

'Cudweed,' said Solstice. 'Just because she's your girlfriend, it doesn't mean you have to do *everything* she says.'

Cudweed looked at his sister.

'But I'm afraid that if I don't, she won't go out with me anymore.'

'Well, you are going to have to make a decision,' said Solstice. 'Milk chocolate, or Joanna. She might even respect you more for standing up for yourself.'

And just then, Joanna appeared.

'Oh, there you are, Cudweed,' she said.

'Joanna, I have something to say –' began Cudweed, but Joanna interrupted him.

'Wait! I have something to tell you,' she said. 'Cudweed, I don't think we can go out anymore.'

'What??' cried Cudweed. 'Why not?'

---

[11] **flustered** durcheinander – [12] **elastic band** Gummiband – [13] **to wander** umherziehen; wandern

'Because we are not right for each other. And you are keeping an animal prisoner in your house.'

'Kork!' I said, and looked for somewhere I could sit right above her head.

'I ... oh,' said Cudweed. 'Oh.'

'Now, what was it you wanted to tell me?' asked Joanna.

'Oh,' said Cudweed. 'I was going to say I don't think I can be a vegan anymore. It's too hard for me.'

Joanna shrugged.

'It is difficult for some people. But if you believe in something, it's really quite easy. Anyway, you must do what you think is right.'

Cudweed looked very sad. Joanna said she was sorry and that she had enjoyed the cake, and then she left. And that was that.

Solstice and I spent the rest of the day trying to cheer Cudweed up.

'Chocolate?' suggested Solstice, and he smiled. 'Milk chocolate?'

'Okay,' he said, and we all went to the kitchen to see what we could find.

As he was eating the chocolate, Solstice chatted away.

'You know, I think it was very sweet of you to try to be a vegan for your girlfriend,' she said, 'but you don't have to change yourself to be liked, you know.'

'No?'

'No,' said Solstice. 'One day, you'll meet someone who likes you for who you are.'

'I will?'

'You will. And I will, too.'

She smiled at the idea.

'Now,' she said, 'how about we ask for sausages for you, for dinner?'

'Erm, actually,' said Cudweed, 'No.'

'No?' said Solstice.

'Krark?' I said.

'No,' said Cudweed. 'I have decided not to be a vegan, but I am going to be a vegetarian from now on.'

'You are?'

'I am,' said Cudweed.

'But why?'

Cudweed shrugged.

'Because I think it's the right thing to do. Veganism is a great idea, but even being vegetarian helps the planet a lot. It's healthier. But most of all I don't want to eat animals anymore.' And he tickled the feathers under my chin.

So that was that, how Cudweed became a vegetarian. And it's only been a week, but I think it suits him already. He's already lost a little weight, but he's using a belt again, so at least his trousers have stopped falling down.

THE END

@ WES-40805-004

A Glimpse of the Death Saint (Before and while reading)

1 Famous graphic novels

a Read these descriptions of four famous graphic novels. Find the covers on the internet. Tell your group which one you would like to read and why. Did you make similar choices?

***Watchmen* by Alan Moore**
This award-winning graphic novel has an exciting murder mystery plot and an amazing art style. The story features a cast of six superheroes who carry out brave deeds while struggling with personal problems and a lack of confidence.

***The City of Ember* by Jeanne DuPrau**
Originally a dystopian novel that was later turned into a graphic novel, this is the story of two children who grow up in darkness in an underworld city. By following clues left by the builders of the city, they manage to escape.

***Persepolis* by Marjane Satrapi**
This is the memoir of a young girl coming of age in Iran in a time of conflict, oppression and war. The simple black and white pictures tell a powerful and unforgettable story about home and public life. At times funny, it is also heart-breaking.

***I am Alfonso Jones* by Tony Medina**
Young African American Alfonso Jones is shot and killed by police, but his spirit lives on in the afterlife, along with other victims of police shootings. Meanwhile Alfonso's family and friends fight for justice for him.

b What types of story are the graphic novels in **a**? What other types do you associate with graphic novels?

mystery, …

c Are you a fan of graphic novels? Why? / Why not?

2 The Death Saint

a Look at the title of the graphic novel. Explain what you think it means.

A 'glimpse' means …
I think people get a glimpse of the Death Saint when …

b Look at the picture of the Death Saint. Describe and analyse what further information you get from the picture. For example, is the Death Saint male or female? Good or evil? Explain the reasons for your ideas.

The picture shows …
I think the figure looks …
The figure is holding its hands like that because …
In my opinion, the Death Saint …
I would say people fear / respect / love / …

c Share your ideas from **a** and **b** with the class.

3 The characters, setting and plot

a Look at the illustrations on pages **130 / 131** of the graphic novel and make notes.
- **Student A:** Who are the characters on these pages?
- **Student B:** Where does the story take place (the setting) and what is happening (the plot).

b Share your ideas from **a** with another pair. Discuss how you think the story continues. Together, write three questions you have about the story.

4 Attitudes and feelings

a Now read the first two pages of the graphic novel and check your ideas from **3**. Add more information to your notes.

b Describe the attitudes of the man from the water company, the reporter and the camera guys towards the group of people. Use adjectives from the cloud and your own ideas. Explain why you get this impression.

c Explain why the girl doesn't want to give her name. Describe how you think she is feeling now.

5 Were you right?

Were you right? Read the rest of the story and check your ideas from **3b.** Were your three questions answered in the story?

6 The girl's story.

The girl's story. In your exercise book, write notes under each heading.

- Where the girl was born
- Living / Economic situation of her family
- What happened to her father and brother
- What happened to her mother and why
- Her journey to the border of 'El Norte' (the USA)
- Her life at the border
- How she crossed the border

7 After the interview.

After the interview. What happened when the girl was talking to the reporter after the interview? Decide if these sentences are true or false, and correct the false sentences.

1 Immigration officials suddenly appeared.
2 They had weapons.
3 The immigrants were all adults.
4 The coyote disappeared.
5 Everyone crossed the border.
6 The girl crossed the border with another immigrant.

CULTURE CORNER

ICE is the USA's **I**mmigration and **C**ustoms **E**nforcement. Its function is to prevent illegal immigration and border crime such as drug smuggling.

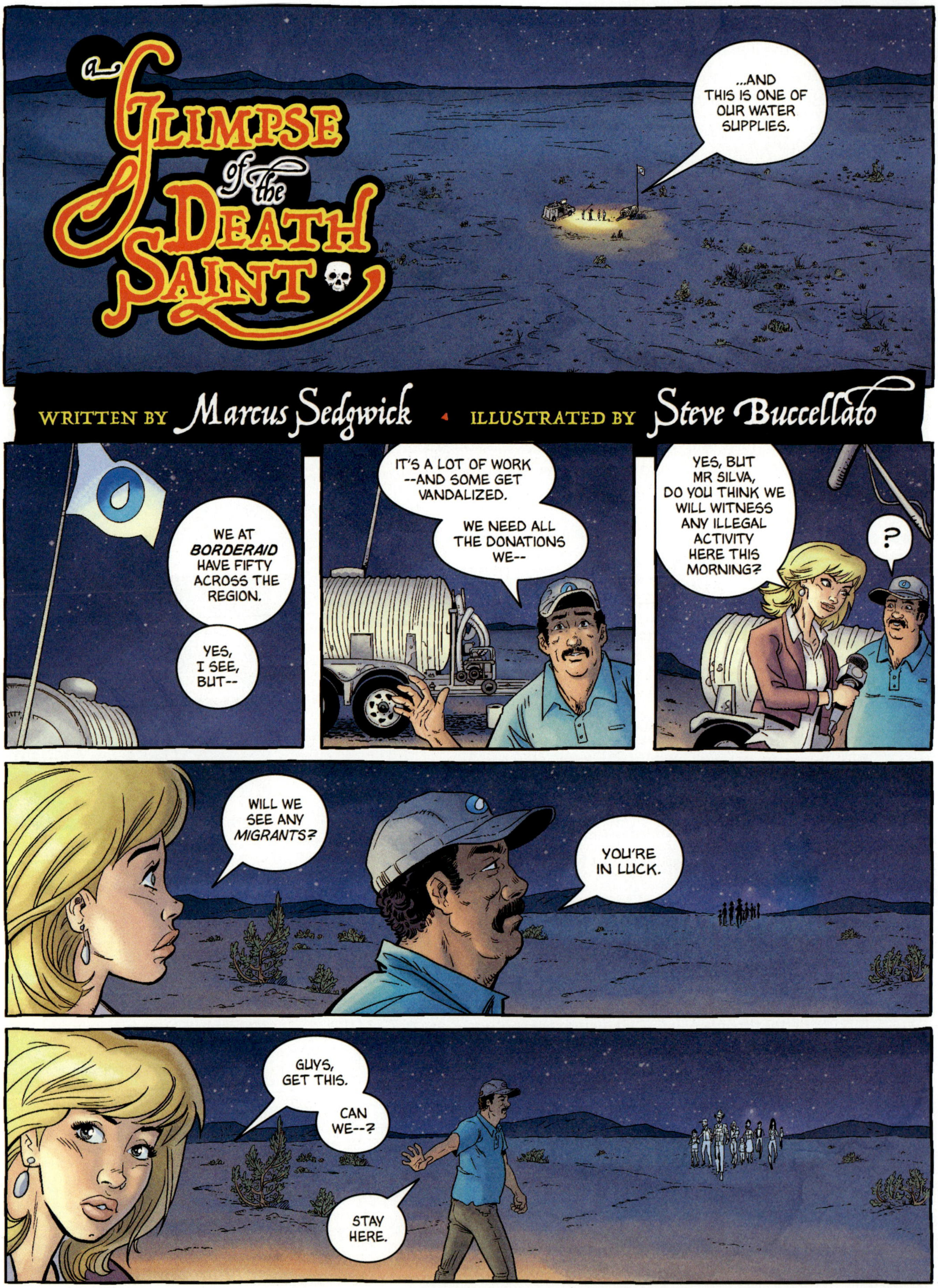
a Glimpse of the Death Saint
...AND THIS IS ONE OF OUR WATER SUPPLIES.
WRITTEN BY Marcus Sedgwick
ILLUSTRATED BY Steve Buccellato
WE AT BORDERAID HAVE FIFTY ACROSS THE REGION.
YES, I SEE, BUT--
IT'S A LOT OF WORK --AND SOME GET VANDALIZED.
WE NEED ALL THE DONATIONS WE--
YES, BUT MR SILVA, DO YOU THINK WE WILL WITNESS ANY ILLEGAL ACTIVITY HERE THIS MORNING?
?
WILL WE SEE ANY MIGRANTS?
YOU'RE IN LUCK.
GUYS, GET THIS.
CAN WE--?
STAY HERE.

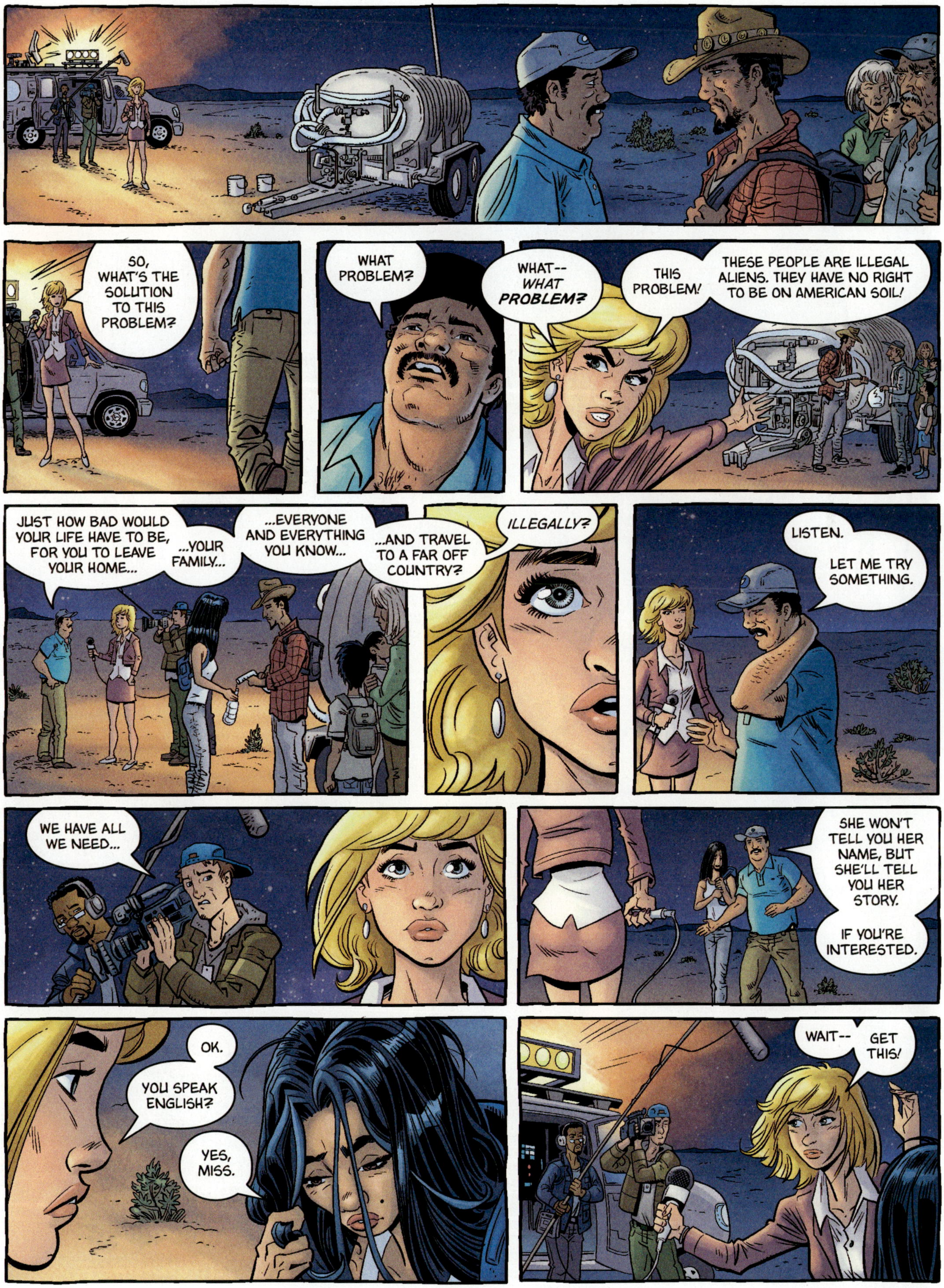
SO, WHAT'S THE SOLUTION TO THIS PROBLEM?
WHAT PROBLEM?
WHAT-- WHAT PROBLEM?
THIS PROBLEM!
THESE PEOPLE ARE ILLEGAL ALIENS. THEY HAVE NO RIGHT TO BE ON AMERICAN SOIL!
JUST HOW BAD WOULD YOUR LIFE HAVE TO BE, FOR YOU TO LEAVE YOUR HOME...
...YOUR FAMILY...
...EVERYONE AND EVERYTHING YOU KNOW...
...AND TRAVEL TO A FAR OFF COUNTRY?
ILLEGALLY?
LISTEN.
LET ME TRY SOMETHING.
WE HAVE ALL WE NEED...
SHE WON'T TELL YOU HER NAME, BUT SHE'LL TELL YOU HER STORY.
IF YOU'RE INTERESTED.
OK.
YOU SPEAK ENGLISH?
YES, MISS.
WAIT--
GET THIS!

I WAS BORN IN GUATEMALA AND GREW UP IN THE SLUM OF LA LIMONADA.
I never knew my father. My mother did what she could to make money, like making clothes.
CHOSA POP
She couldn't get any other work. No one would give her a job, once they knew we lived in La Limonada.
My brother scavenged in the tips for things to sell.
But it was never enough.

There's only two ways you make money in La Limonada...
If you're a man, you join a gang.
And then, sooner or later, you get killed.
That's what happened to my father...
...And then it happened to my brother, too.
If you're a woman, or just a girl, it's worse.
After my brother was killed, my mother went crazy.
She went and picked a fight with the boss of the gang.
I never saw her again...

That's when three of us decided to find a better life.
In El Norte.
And someone had told us about how to get there. Someone had told us about La Bestia.
The Beast!
But The Beast is dangerous, too...
...bad things happened.

It's thousands of miles to El Norte, and the roads are dangerous.
So lots of people ride The Beast instead.
THUNK
I saw more than one man die that way.

But sometimes we were helped by kind people.
¡BUENA SUERTE!
On the train we met this guy. His name was Bastian. He seemed different from everyone else. Confident...
He said he had a contact who could get us work when we got to the US. He told us to stick with him and he'd look after us.
He said we should follow the drugs north, to America.
WHERE THE DRUGS GO, THAT'S WHERE THE MONEY IS!
Bastian said he worshipped the lady of death, *Santa Muerte.*
He said we should, too, that she protects poor people like us, runaways...
But as we got close to the border, our luck ran out.

There was a police raid.
A fight...
They kept rocks on the roof of the train ready for this...
It was hell.
As the police moved in, we ran!
But I lost my friends.

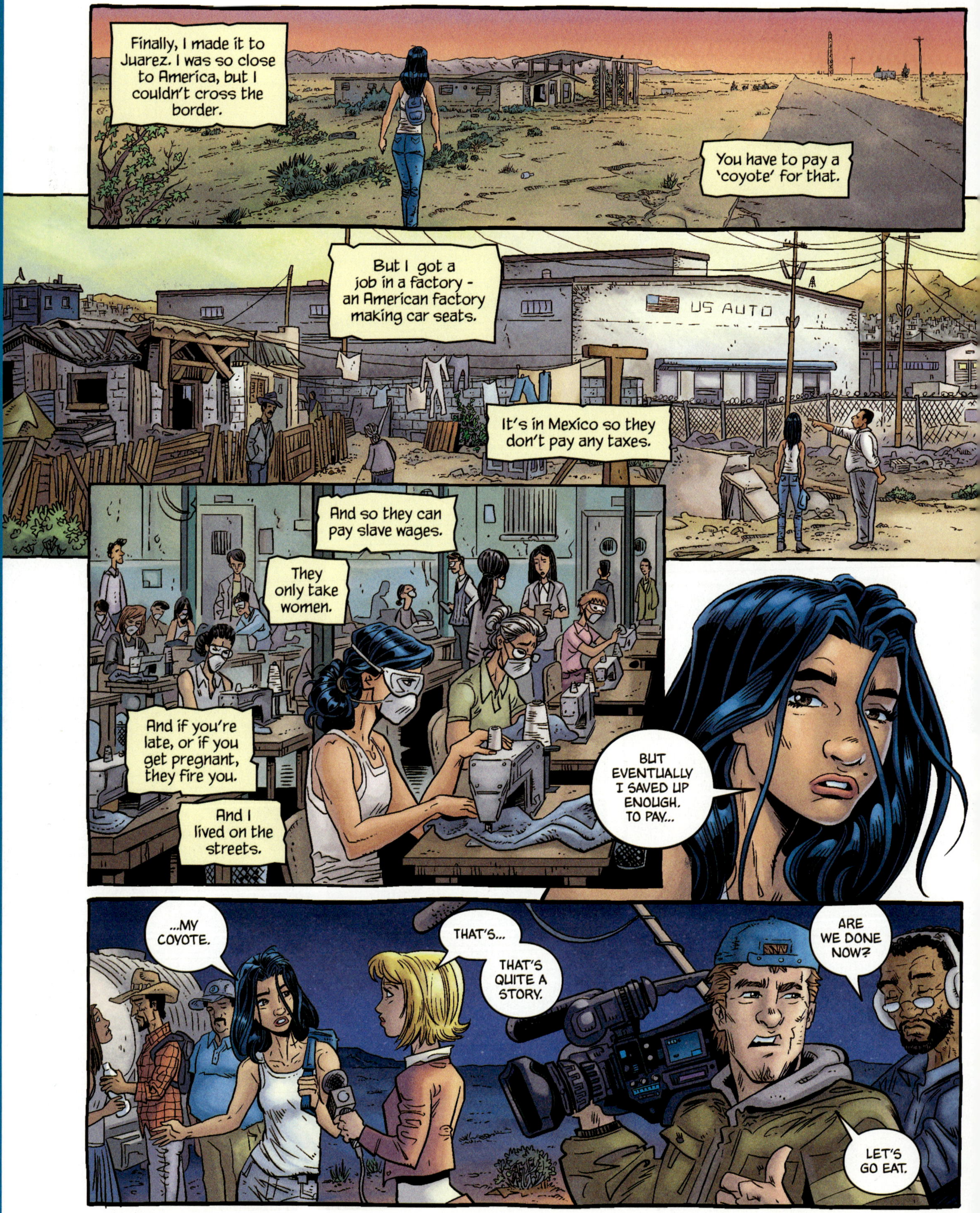
Finally, I made it to Juarez. I was so close to America, but I couldn't cross the border.
You have to pay a 'coyote' for that.
But I got a job in a factory - an American factory making car seats.
US AUTO
It's in Mexico so they don't pay any taxes.
And so they can pay slave wages.
They only take women.
And if you're late, or if you get pregnant, they fire you.
And I lived on the streets.
BUT EVENTUALLY I SAVED UP ENOUGH. TO PAY...
...MY COYOTE.
THAT'S...
THAT'S QUITE A STORY.
ARE WE DONE NOW?
LET'S GO EAT.

NO, GUYS, WAIT, THIS IS...
... BUT WHERE ARE YOU GOING? WHAT ARE YOU GOING TO DO?
I DON'T KNOW. I WILL FIND SOME-THING.
BUT YOU CAN'T JUST-
WAIT!
RUN!
EVERYONE, RUN!
GOOD LUCK.
WHOEVER YOU WERE.
the end

@ WES-40805-004

A Glimpse of the Death Saint (After reading)

1 Your reaction and opinion

a Tell a partner how you felt while reading the story and why. Give specific examples from the story which made you feel like that.

When I read ..., I felt ...
The part about ... made me feel ...
I really identified with / sympathized with ... when ...
To give another example, ...

b The girl crossed the border into the USA illegally, which is a crime. Analyse how the graphic novel makes us sympathize with the girl's story.

c What do you think about the issue of illegal immigration from Mexico into the USA? Discuss your opinion.

In my view, ...
On the one hand, ... on the other hand, ...
Although ...

2 Attitudes.

Attitudes. Look back at **4b** on page **129** and the last two pages of the story. Explain how the attitude of the reporter and the attitude of the cameramen changed or didn't change after hearing the girl's story.

The reporter / cameraman asks / looks / says / wishes ...

3 What does it mean?

a Write a definition for the following names in the story. Explain why you think the thing or person has this name.

1 The Beast (pages 134 / 135)
2 a coyote (pages 138 / 139)

b Match these words with the correct explanations. There are two definitions you don't need.

1 to scavenge (page 132)
2 to stick with (page 136)
3 to worship (page 136)
4 raid (page 137)
5 slave wages (page 138)
6 to fire (page 138)

a to stay close to somebody
b a very low amount of money for work
c extremely violent behaviour
d to beg for something
e a surprise attack
f to take away somebody's job
g to offer prayers to
h to look for something among rubbish

4 **An American factory in Mexico**

a Read the description of the girl's work on page **138** again. Describe the working conditions there and why they can't be improved.

b When you buy a product such as jeans, trainers or electronic equipment, how can you be sure that it was made under conditions that did not harm the workers and the environment? Think about where it was made, specific brands, certified labels and logos, etc.

5 **The reporter's article.** Write the reporter's article for an online website. Use your notes in **7** on page **129** to tell the girl's story. Make sure to include details about the girl's living conditions and working conditions at the border. Start like this:

It's shocking but it's true. Every day, immigrants from Central America risk their lives to cross the border into the USA. I spoke to one girl, let's call her …, who told me her thought-provoking story.

6 **La Limonada**

a La Limonada in Guatemala is the largest city slum in Central America. Do some research online and make notes about the following questions.

- How many people live there?
- When and why did people move there?
- What is it like to live there?

b Exchange information with the class.

7 **It's your turn: What happened to the girl?**

Choose one of these tasks below. Then present your pages or your story to your partner.

A Continue the graphic novel. Make a page or two pages where you show what happened to the girl after the interview. Draw pictures and write speech bubbles. You can use a similar style or your own style.

B You are the girl many years later. You tell your children the story of how you crossed the border, why you did it and what you did afterwards. Think about your story and make notes.

8 **Graphic novels as a genre**

a **Think:** What are the characteristics of graphic novels and how are they different from text-based stories? Think about *A Glimpse of the Death Saint* and other graphic novels that you know. Use the notes in the box to help you.

character development ■ expression of feelings and attitudes ■ illustrations ■ text style ■ use of frames ■ who tells the story

b **Pair:** Exchange your ideas with a partner, giving examples from *A Glimpse of the Death Saint*.

c **Share:** Discuss ideas with the class. Agree on a definition of a graphic novel together.

9 **A presentation of a graphic novel.** Present a graphic novel you have read to your group. Talk about the characters and the story as well as the style of the illustrations and their effect.

@ WES-40805-004

More about Australia

1 **The Great Barrier Reef.** Read the text about the Great Barrier Reef. What else would you like to know about it? Do some research and create a fact file about Australia's great natural wonder.

Damage to the Great Barrier Reef has reached a 'critical' level due to climate change

The conservation status for Australia's Great Barrier Reef has declined from 'significant concern' to 'critical' due to increasing impacts associated with climate change, a new report has found. The damage to the reef is a result of ocean warming, acidification[1] and extreme weather, which has resulted in coral bleaching[2], according to the International Union for Conservation of Nature's (IUCN) 2020 World Heritage Outlook report [...]. The process of coral bleaching occurs when water is too warm and the algae[3] the corals expel[4] [...] cause them to turn completely white.

The decline of the coral has also resulted in decreasing populations of certain marine species [...]. The reef is the most extensive in the world with more than 1,500 species of fish.

A third of the natural World Heritage sites are currently being threatened by climate change, the IUCN reported. [...] After climate change, the next two significant threats to these natural sites are invasive[5] alien species and tourism impacts. [...] .

'Natural World Heritage sites are amongst the world's most precious places, and we owe it to future generations to protect them,' Bruno Oberle, the IUCN director general, said in a statement. 'The IUCN World Heritage Outlook 3 reveals the damage climate change is [doing to] natural World Heritage, from shrinking glaciers to coral bleaching to increasingly frequent and severe fires and droughts. As the international community defines new objectives to conserve biodiversity, this report signals the urgency with which we must tackle environmental challenges together [on such a large] scale.'

Source: abc NEWS, Julia Jacobo, "Great Barrier Reef has deteriorated to 'critica' level due to climate change", 6 December 2020, https://abcnews.go.com/International/great-barrier-reef-deteriorated-critical-level-due-climate/story?id=74569794 [31.08.2021]

2 **Steve Irwin – The Crocodile Hunter.** Read about a famous Australian and sum up his life in about 120 words.

In 1969, at the age of just six, Steve Irwin caught a brown poisonous snake. While most people would try to avoid such an encounter, for the young Irwin this moment was the start of a lifelong interest that tragically ended when he was just 44. It was probably natural that Irwin should show a fascination with such creatures as his parents had run what was later called the Australian Zoo since 1970. This love of animals and his ability to skilfully handle them led to a career, first managing the park from 1991 and then making TV documentaries. Irwin became famous worldwide when the TV documentary series *The Crocodile Hunter* became a global hit.

In 2006, Irwin went to film another documentary in Queensland's Batt Reef. Little did he know that this would be his last adventure and that it would be an ocean creature considered to be fairly harmless that would ultimately kill him. During a delay in filming , Irwin and cameraman Justin Lyons decided to go off and do some filming of their own. While they were filming, they noticed an eight-foot wide stingray[6]. 'Stingrays are normally very calm. If they don't want you around them, they'll swim away ,' Lyons explained. Everything seemed to be fine, so the two friends thought they'd do one more shot. With the stingray between Irwin and Justin, Irwin would swim toward the camera and Justin would film as the ray swam away. Unfortunately, things didn't go as planned. 'All of a sudden, it started stabbing[7] wildly with its tail, hundreds of strikes in a few seconds,' Lyons remembers. Irwin was killed by a stab through the heart.

After the tragedy, many people said that Irwin must have been behaving irresponsibly for such an accident to happen. But Justin had a different opinion, 'It probably thought Steve's shadow was a tiger shark, who [eat] them pretty regularly, so it started to attack him.'

When news of his death spread around the world, many were surprised that it was a stingray and not something more dangerous like a crocodile or shark which ultimately led to Irwin's death. If there is one consoling fact, it's that he died doing something he loved and not in a more mundane[8] way.

With information from: Biography.com, Rachel Chang, "Steve Irwin: The Devastating Death of 'The Crocodile Hunter'", 25 August 2020, https://www.biography.com/news/steve-irwin-crocodile-hunter-death [31.08.2021]

[1] **acidification** Übersäuerung – [2] **coral bleaching** Korallenbleiche – [3] **algae** Algen – [4] **expel** ausstoßen – [5] **invasive** invasiv; *hier*: gebietsfremd und gefährlich für dort beheimatete Arten – [6] **stingray** Stachelrochen – [7] **to stab** stechen – [8] **mundane** alltäglich; banal

3 **The Australian system of government.** Read the text and match the following terms and definitions.

1 representative | 2 constitution | 3 currency | 4 legislative

a money that is in use in a certain country or region

b the basic principles and laws of a state that define the powers and duties of the government and guarantee certain rights to the people

c a politician that has the voters' authority to act and speak for them

d the part of government that has the power to make laws

Australia has three levels of government that work together to provide [...] the services [needed]. The three levels are:

- Federal Parliament – makes laws for the whole of Australia
- six state and two mainland territory parliaments – make laws for their state or territory
- over 500 local councils – make local laws (by-laws) for their region or district.

Each of the three levels of government has its own executive that puts laws into action. How the federal and state parliaments work together is sometimes referred to as the division of powers. Each level of government has its own responsibilities, although in some cases these responsibilities are shared.

Australians aged 18 years and over vote to elect representatives to federal, state and territory parliaments, and local councils to make decisions on their behalf. This means Australians have someone to represent them at each level of government.

Federal Parliament

The Constitution established an Australian – federal – Parliament. The 227 members of the Australian Parliament – 76 in the Senate and 151 in the House of Representatives – are responsible for making federal laws. [These laws relate to issues such as for example trade and commerce, foreign policy, weights and measures, currency, copyright, marriage, and immigration.] [...]

Parliament House in Canberra, the seat of the legislative branch of the Australian Government

State and territory parliaments

Australia has six state parliaments. It also has two territory parliaments known as legislative assemblies. These parliaments are located in Australia's eight capital cities. [...]

State and territory parliaments make laws that are enforced within their state or territory. [...] State laws relate to matters that are primarily of state interest such as [for example schools, roads and railways, public transport, electricity, agriculture, community services, police and prisons.] [...]

Councils

There are over 500 local government bodies across Australia. They are often called councils, municipalities or shires. Local governments consist of two groups who serve the needs of local communities:

- elected members, who normally have four-year terms
- staff who work for the council.

On average each council has nine elected members who are usually called councillors or aldermen, while the chair or head of the council is usually called the mayor or president. These smaller legislative bodies make by-laws about local matters and provide services. For example, councils are responsible for: [rubbish collection and recycling, parks, sport fields and swimming pools, childcare and aged care, libraries, art galleries and museums, town planning and land and coast care programmes.] [...]

Source: Parliamentary Education Office, "Three levels of government: governing Australia", Based on: https://peo.gov.au/understand-our-parliament/how-parliament-works/three-levels-of-government/three-levels-of-government-governing-australia/ [15.09.2021]

More about the Commonwealth

1 **The Commonwealth of Nations.** Take a look at the photograph. What do you think? Where, when and why was it taken?

CULTURE CORNER

The Commonwealth of Nations, or Commonwealth, is a political association of 54 states. Most of these were once part of the British Empire. The countries share certain basic values, English as their common language and are historically connected.

2 **From Empire to Commonwealth**

13 **a** Watch this video and answer the following questions.

1 What country in the Commonwealth is the biggest as far as population is concerned?
2 What two things do all Commonwealth countries share?
3 What is the function of the Commonwealth Charter?
4 Why is the discussion about climate change especially important for the Commonwealth?

b The video was made in 2015. Find out which country or countries joined the Commonwealth after that date.

3 **The history of the Commonwealth Games.** Did you know that there are many international games like the Olympic and the Paralympic Games? Think of the Pan American or the Asian Games. The Commonwealth Games are a big event with more than 70 teams competing.
Read the text and find out about the history.

The concept

The concept of a united Commonwealth sporting event had been talked about amongst Commonwealth nations since the rebirth of the Olympic Games [held in Athens in 1896]. [...]

[The 'Festival of Empire']

In 1911, the 'Festival of Empire' was held in London to celebrate the coronation of King George V. As part of the festival, an Inter-Empire Championships was held in which teams from Australia, Canada, South Africa and the United Kingdom competed in events such as boxing, wrestling, swimming and athletics. A trophy in the form of a silver cup, 2ft 6in high and weighing 340oz, the gift of Lord Lonsdale, was presented to the winning country, which was Canada.

The first Games

[...] The first Commonwealth Games, known as the British Empire Games at the time, were held in Canada in 1930 in Hamilton, Ontario. [...] The events at this meeting included track and field athletics, swimming, rowing, boxing and wrestling, and lawn bowls. While no points were [awarded], [athletes from Great Britain won the most events].

Ongoing Games

[...] From 1930 to 1950 the Games were known as the British Empire Games, then the name was changed to the British Empire and Commonwealth Games until 1962. From 1966 to 1974 they had the title of British Commonwealth Games and from 1978 onwards they have been known as simply the Commonwealth Games.

The Friendly Games

While other Games around the globe have been founded on geographic or climatic factors such as the Asian, Pan Am, African Games and Winter Olympics, the Commonwealth Games [have] been founded on history. A unique characteristic of the Commonwealth Games is being the only Games which share a common language. All athletes and officials can converse with each other in English, creating an atmosphere that has led to the Commonwealth Games being long known as the 'Friendly Games'.

Olympics vs Commonwealth Games

While both events take place every four years there are some major differences. The most obvious of these is who competes. The Olympics is open to competitors from all countries around the world. However, to compete in the Commonwealth Games competitors need to come from one of the 54 Commonwealth countries. Another difference is which sports are included. The Commonwealth Games include sports traditionally played in Commonwealth countries such as netball, squash and lawn bowling – events you won't find at the Olympics.

Moments to remember

The Commonwealth Games have often had really special moments that live long in people's memories. Here are a few:

In 1954 in Vancouver, England's Roger Bannister beat Australia's John Landy in a race known as 'The Miracle Mile'. Earlier in the year Bannister had been the first man to run a mile in under four minutes. A few weeks later Landy also ran under four minutes and set a new world record. The race in Vancouver was the first time two men ran under four minutes in the same race.

In the 1988 Commonwealth Games held in Kuala Lumpur, Australian swimmer Ian Thorpe won four gold medals. One thing that makes this really remarkable is that he was only 15 at the time.

At just 16 Cathy Freeman became the first Aboriginal athlete to win a gold medal at the 1990 Games in Auckland, New Zealand. Four years later, she won individual gold medals in both the 200 and 400 metre events. After both races, she displayed both the Australian and Aboriginal flags.

Sources: paragraphs 1-5: Robert Wood, "History of the Commonwealth Games", Topend Sports Website, 2010, https://www.topendsports.com/events/commonwealth-games/history.htm [15.09.2021]; paragraphs 6-7 with information from differencebetween.info, "Difference between Commonwealth Games and Olympic Games", http://www.differencebetween.info/difference-between-commonwealth-games-and-olympic-games [15.09.2021]; commonwealth sport, "Top 10 Commonwealth Sport Moments", https://thecgf.com/stories/top-10-commonwealth-sport-moments [15.09.2021]

@ WES-40805-004

More about New Zealand

1 **Jacinda Ardern.** Read the text about the first female New Zealand prime minister. Then do some online research to find out whether her call to introduce compulsory instruction in the Māori language in schools has been successful.

[Jacinda Ardern was born in Hamilton, New Zealand on July 26, 1980. In October 2017, at age 37, she became the country's youngest prime minister in more than 150 years.]

Even before [finishing university], Ardern began her association with the Labour Party. In 1999, at age 17, she joined the party and […] became involved in the re-election campaign of Harry Duynhoven […]. [Then,] following graduation, Ardern became a researcher for another Labour MP, Phil Goff. That experience would lead to a position on the staff of Prime Minister Helen Clark, the second woman to hold New Zealand's highest office and Ardern's political hero and mentor.

In 2005 Ardern embarked on an 'overseas experience,' an extended – usually working – trip to Britain, which is a traditional rite of passage[1] for the children of New Zealand's middle and upper class. Instead of working in a London pub or warehouse and then touring the Continent, […] Ardern worked for two and a half years in the cabinet office of British Prime Minister Tony Blair […].

[On returning to New Zealand in 2008,] Arden was chosen as Labour's candidate for MP of the Waikato district, a seat[2] that historically had been beyond the party's reach[3] and that Ardern lost by some 13,000 votes. Nevertheless, she entered parliament as a list candidate. New Zealand's mixed member proportional (MMP) election system allows candidates who run for a district seat also to be on a party's list of candidates, from which 49 MPs are chosen in proportion to the number of votes received by their parties. At age 28, Ardern entered the House of Representatives as its youngest member. In her [first] speech she called for the introduction of compulsory instruction in the Māori language in New Zealand schools and she [criticized] the New Zealand government for what she characterized as its 'shameful' response to climate change. […]

[…] [As] the general parliamentary election scheduled for September 2017 approached, Labour's showing in preference polling was [terrible]. […] With fewer than two months left before the election, [the Labour party leader] Little stepped down as leader but not before [getting Ardern to agree] to stand as his replacement (reportedly, she refused seven times before agreeing). [Ardern was the only candidate and] was elected leader on August 1.

[…] As 'Jacindamania' swept the country, pundits[4] began characterizing Ardern as a 'rock star' politician in the mode of Canadian Prime Minister Justin Trudeau and former U.S. president Barack Obama. […]

[In the election, no party gained a majority so a coalition government was formed.] Ardern found out at the same time as the rest of the country that she was about to become its 40th prime minister, and she was sworn in on October 26.

In June 2018, Ardern gave birth to her first child, a girl. She thus became the first leader of a country, [since Benazir Bhutto in Pakistan nearly 30 years before], to give birth while in office. […]

[In September 2020 during the height of the coronavirus[5] pandemic, voters rewarded Ardern for her 'go hard, go early' approach] by handing her a landslide victory. Having captured some 49 per cent of the vote, Labour […] [became] the first party since the introduction of proportional representation in 1993 to be able to form a majority government without a coalition partner. […]

In her victory speech, Ardern reached out to all New Zealanders:

We are living in an increasingly polarized world. A place where, more and more, people have lost the ability to see one another's point of view. I hope that this election, New Zealand has shown that this is not who we are. That, as a nation, we can listen and we can debate. After all, we are too small to lose sight of other people's perspective.

Source: Encyclopedia Britannica, Jeff Wallenfeldt, "Jacinda Ardern", 11 August 2021, https://www.britannica.com/biography/Jacinda-Ardern [15.09.2021]

---

[1] **rite of passage** Übergangsritus – [2] **seat** regionale Verwaltungseinheit – [3] **reach** Reichweite – [4] **pundit** Experte/Expertin – [5] **coronavirus** *hier*: das SARS-CoV-2 Virus, das die potentiell tödliche Atemwegserkrankung COVID-19 auslösen kann und im Jahr 2019 eine weltweite Pandemie auslöste

2 Some signs in Māori. Look at these Maori words and research their meaning.

A

B

C
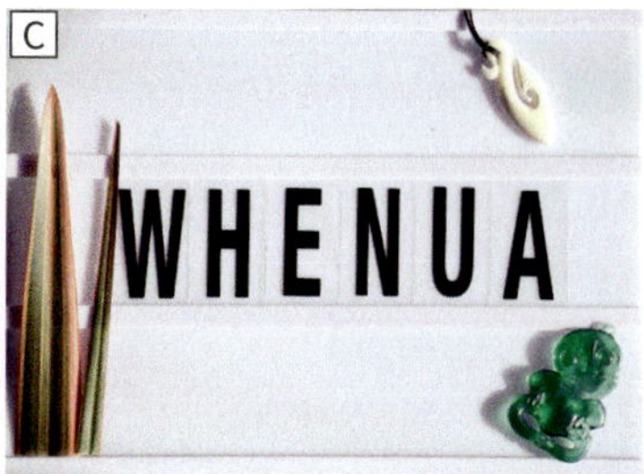

3 **A Maori filmmaker.** Read the text about Taika Waititi. After reading, summarize why Taika Waititi felt it was so important to include indigenous people in the making of his film.

All The Ways That Taika Waititi Pushed for Indigenous Representation On The *Thor: Ragnarok* Set

[The film *Thor: Ragnarok* is a movie based on the Marvel Comic character of Thor. It was directed by the Maori director Taika Waititi, but was filmed in Australia.] [As the director] Taika Waititi not only made a career leap[6] for himself, but a huge leap for indigenous representation behind the camera. With a budget of approximately $180 million, *Ragnarok* is the sort of opportunity that big studios almost never hand to an indigenous director – and so Waititi used his position to include others. From Easter eggs[7] to shadowing[8] opportunities for indigenous filmmakers, from an opening Karakia ceremony to avoiding appropriation[9], Waititi worked to bring better representation and inclusion to the *Ragnarok* set.

Waititi is Māori […] from New Zealand, and so he had some understanding of what it meant for *Thor: Ragnarok* to film on land that traditionally belongs to indigenous Australians. 'You wouldn't really start a movie in New Zealand without asking the local tribe to come in and bless you and send you to work with some good mojo[10],' Waititi told *Screen Australia*, 'Especially if you're on their land, you're in their backyard.'

So on the first day of production – July 4, 2016 – he invited members of the Yugambeh mob to perform [the opening ceremony]. […]

In addition, Waititi wanted to include indigenous people behind-the-scenes, such as hiring an Aboriginal company to supply[11] water for the cast and crew. […]

Waititi also insisted on providing creative opportunities for indigenous aspiring[12] filmmakers. 'I just said to Brad [Winderbaum], whenever I do my films I make sure we try to get any locals who might be interested in the film industry to come in and get some work experience, or just to sit around on set and see how it's done,' […]. As a result, eight indigenous interns […] were brought on board to shadow Waititi and experts in other departments, including stunt work and set design. […]

Indigenous Australian and Māori actors were also hired for the cast, including Rachel House as Topaz, Shari Sebbens as an Asgardian mother, and Stephen Oliver as cousin Carlo.

Designers for *Ragnarok* were also inspired by the native art of Australia and New Zealand, but Waititi was careful to warn them against crossing the line into appropriation. 'I was very careful in these design meetings,' he said, 'You need to follow-up by saying "don't copy that, but use it as inspiration", because the next thing you know you have 50 people who have appropriated[13] all these like beautiful ancient designs without asking what they mean, or who owns them, or for any permission.'

Lastly, Waititi also included little Easter eggs to amuse himself and other indigenous viewers. […] 'I wanted to fill it with a few in-jokes and things for Kiwis and Australians […] so while I'm making this giant Marvel movie I could look around and go, "That spaceship – that's painted with the Aboriginal flag colors. No one else knows that but us."'

Source: The Mary Sue, Marykate Jasper, "All The Ways That Taika Waititi Pushed for Indigenous Representation On The *Thor: Ragnarok* Set", 22 October 2017, https://www.themarysue.com/taika-waititi-indigenous-representation-thor-ragnarok/ [15.09.2021]

---

[6] **leap** Sprung – [7] **Easter egg** versteckte Anspielung oder Witz in einem Film oder ein Zusatzkapitel/-level in einem Computerspiel – [8] **to shadow** auf Schritt und Tritt begleiten – [9] **appropriation** kulturelle Aneignung – [10] **mojo** Glücksbringer; *hier im Sinne von* Karma – [11] **to supply** mit etw. versorgen – [12] **aspiring** aufstrebend – [13] **to appropriate** sich etw. bemächtigen; sich etw. zu eigen machen

Feedback and peer editing

1 Look at the illustration below. Make a list of the different forms of feedback that exist.

Giving feedback: Dos and don'ts

Giving and accepting peer feedback can help you write good texts or give interesting presentations. Use the feedback you receive to reflect on your work and revise it. When you give feedback, pay attention to these rules:

- **Be polite:** Before you start it is important to recall the 'Code of Conduct', i.e. don't be rude! Show respect and consideration for the writer's feelings. Only appropriate, clear and constructive comments are helpful.
- **Be balanced:** Point out the strengths as well as the weaknesses of the document / presentation / speech, etc. It is a good idea to follow a three-step approach:
  1. Complimenting (start with something positive that develops trust and encouragement)
  2. Suggesting (make a suggestion for something that could be improved)
  3. Correcting (tell the writer where he / she should correct aspects that are wrong)
- **Be constructive:** You can offer a solution or raise questions, but remember that your own opinion or point of view is not relevant. Of course, personal criticism should be avoided, i.e. your comments should not be biased.
- **Be precise:** Vague feedback like 'This should be more interesting' is not helpful at all. Instead, you should always be as clear and detailed as possible, for example: 'A description of the protagonist's outer appearance / character / behaviour could help the reader to imagine him / her better.'

2 Peer editing is a particular useful form of feedback. It is often used with writing tasks. Students exchange drafts of material they have written and provide each other with suggestions for improvement. Peer editing can be used at any point in the writing process, at the concept or draft stage or for the almost finished product. Choose a text you have produced lately and give it to your partner, then discuss possible improvements.

Feedback is a message that you send to somebody. It is always interactive and there are numerous ways of conveying the message. When giving feedback, non-verbal communication, e.g. body language or facial expression, is as important as explicitly verbal communication, like opinions, criticism or suggestions. Remember that criticism has to go beyond just giving a 'thumbs up or down' or using emoticons – it has to be constructive and clearly voiced. The phrases below may be helpful for giving feedback on a presentation or a written text.

Phrases for giving feedback

Starting and summing up

- *What I really like(d) about your talk / presentation / essay / piece of writing is (was) that …*
- *Generally I like(d) the way you… but in particular the way you …*
- *What I like(d) most about … is (was) …*
- *My favourite part is (was) …, because …*

Expressing an opinion / Asking for an opinion

- *From my point of view …*
- *For me … came across as …*
- *I'm worried because this may lead to / might result in …*
- *… is interesting / relevant / only partly true.*
- *Have you considered …?*
- *I had not seen … from that angle before but what do you think about …?*

Suggesting and asking for ideas

- *I think your pronunciation / intonation / body language / vocabulary / grammar … needs some improvement.*
- *Why don't you (use) …?*
- *I suggest that you add / leave out …*
- *It could make a big difference if you …*
- *It might be helpful if you always check … first / at the end.*
- *Have you got any ideas how I could this differently in the future?*
- *How do you suggest improving on this next time?*
- *What could I do to …?*
- *How else could I …?*
- *Can you think of any alternatives …?*

Talking about positive and negative points

- *I thought … was very effective.*
- *… surprised me positively / fascinated me because …*
- *I was impressed by the fact that you …*
- *The logical structure of … is not evident …*
- *At several points I recognized …*
- *Of course … it is important that …, but …*
- *When you presented …, I noticed that …*
- *… annoyed me / made me angry because …*

Asking for clarification

- *When I listened to your talk / presentation, I didn't quite understand …*
- *When I read your essay / text, I could not place … in a meaningful context.*

Linking arguments

- *First of all / Second / Third …*
- *There are various reasons for …*
- *Moreover, … / Furthermore, … / In addition, …*
- *Although it is true that …, it would be wrong …*
- *Another point to mention / clarify / explain more clearly is …*

Giving an example

- *Let me give you an example of what I mean by …*
- *A good example is …*
- *Let me explain … with the help of an example.*
- *An example I can offer to illustrate …*
- *Take …, for instance, …*

Mediation

1 **What is the difference between mediation and translation?** Mediation is transferring important information from one language to another. This information may be in English or German, in a spoken or a written text, for example an interview, an informative text, an infographic or a leaflet.

You don't have to mediate everything, only the facts the other person (the addressee) needs to do a certain task. This will be explained in the instructions. They will also tell you how you should mediate, for example in an email or an article. Look at the mediation on page **40** and answer these questions. Then make notes and do the task.

- Do you have to mediate in English or in German?
- How is the information presented?
- Who is the addressee?
- Which information is important for the task?
- How should you present the facts you mediate?

2 **How do you deal with culture-specific words in a mediation?** A culture-specific word is one which you only find in one language or culture – often there is no direct translation, so you have to explain the word. Such a word may not even be important, for example if *Currywurst* occurs as an example of one of the many sausages Germans like in an article about German eating habits. If your mediation task is to explain the kind of food Germans eat, then you don't need to specifically mention *Currywurst*. But it is important if you are at an *Imbissbude* with a friend who doesn't speak German and *Currywurst* is on the menu. Look at this menu and decide which items you can translate and which you need to explain.

- Currywurst od. Schaschlik mit Pommes rot-weiß
- Schweinebraten mit Knödeln und Rotkohl
- Fischfrikadellen mit Kartoffelsalat
- Kartoffelpuffer mit Apfelmus

- Apfelsaft – Wasser – Bier – Schorle

3 **How formal or informal should your mediation be?**

a The kind of English, or register, you use depends on the situation and on the addressee. Is it a friend, your parents, a teacher, a future employer? What kind of English should you use? Match the expressions (1 – 3) with the situations (a – c).

1 informal chatty English (*Hi, gonna, wanna, gotta, ain't, cool, …*)
2 neutral, factual English (*Hello, going to, want to, have got to, isn't, interesting, …*)
3 formal English (*Dear Mr/Ms, going to, would like to, have to, is not, intriguing, …*)

a in written communication with somebody you don't know, e. g. a new employer or an official
b with a friend in spoken communication
c in spoken and written texts for almost any situation

b Look at the German article about fast fashion on page **78**. Decide who will write a more formal and who a more informal text, then each write about 120 words. Compare your texts and give each other feedback about register and style.

TIP

Make sure you understand the difference between a mediation and a text production task.

Text production
Be creative and express your own ideas or arguments.

Mediation
Listen or read carefully and transfer the important and relevant ideas from the original text(s).
- Don't add arguments or facts that are not in the text(s).
- Don't make comments.
- Don't give your opinion.

Speaking

1 **Identify situations in which you need to speak English.** Sometimes you have time to prepare before you speak English and sometimes you don't. Look at the situations below and decide if they are spontaneous or not. Can you add more examples?

- **Monologue:** giving directions, giving a presentation, …
- **Dialogue:** asking for and giving information, talking on the phone to one speaker, …
- **Multilogue:** participating in a group discussion or an online meeting, …

2 **Speak confidently in a presentation**

a When you give a presentation, there are some dos and don'ts. With a partner, make a list.

b It's not easy to speak freely for more than one or two minutes. Prompt cards help you remember the main points. Look at this prompt card about toads. What is your first impression? Discuss how you could improve the card.

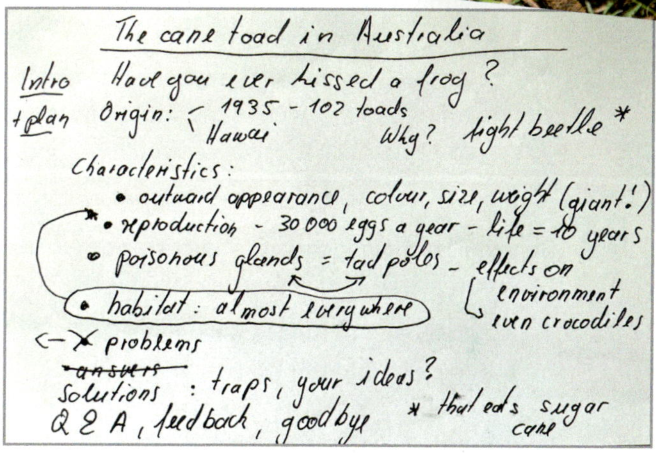

c A good presentation needs a clear structure with signposting language to guide the audience. Discuss what makes a good structure and come up with some useful phrases for each part.

d It is also important to engage your audience. How can you do this? Put the strategies in the box next to the examples.

> Ask rhetorical questions ■ Encourage your listeners to ask questions ■ Explain special terms ■ Repeat important information or messages ■ Use emphasis ■ Use question tags

1 This isn't a frog, is it?
2 What is unbelievable is the fact that …
3 Is it important to distinguish between frogs and toads? Yes, it is because …
4 Today there are 200 million toads in Australia. Yes, 200 million.
5 I'll be very happy to take questions at the end of my talk.
6 The cane toad has poisonous glands. These are small organs …

3 **Useful expressions for a dialogue or discussion.** When you speak to other people, it is not always possible to prepare beforehand. If you use some of these expressions, your English will sound more authentic. Can you add more?

- If you need to collect your thoughts before you speak: *Well, … / Let me think … / …*
- Sometimes you want other people to say something, too: *What about you? / And what is your opinion on …? / …*
- Or you would like to say something yourself: *Can I say something? / May I interrupt you for a second? / …*

4 **Improve your speaking skills.** Look at the ideas below. Which strategies do you already use? Which ones could be useful in the future? Use the language from **3** to discuss your opinions.

- Communicate with native speakers.
- Read English books, listen to English songs, or watch English films.
- Learn new words and phrases in their context: learn collocations, e.g. *give a presentation, hold a speech* or, if a word is followed by a preposition, learn it that way, e.g. *spend time on sth., be used to doing sth.*
- Work with the audios. Listen, stop and guess the next word, then listen and compare.

Language awareness

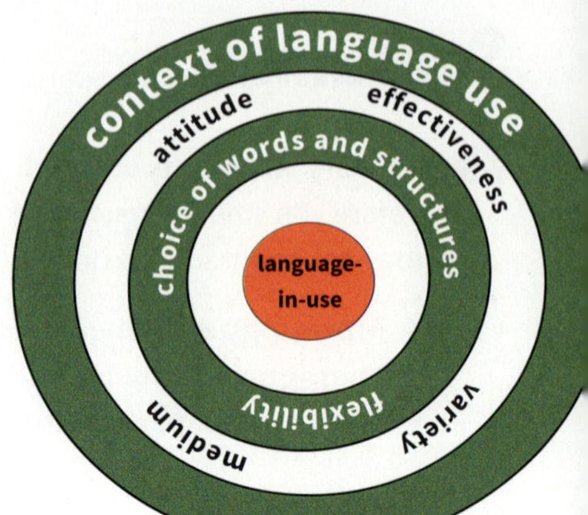

1 What is language awareness?

a Language awareness is a complex subject, but a basic understanding of it can help you to improve your English and make your learning more efficient. Look at these simplified definitions and decide which one(s) best describe(s) language awareness.

A understanding grammar rules and using them correctly
B deciding which new words and phrases you need to learn
C knowing when it is appropriate to use certain words and phrases

b Create your own language awareness target. Copy this illustration and complete it for yourself, based on your learning goals as well as the situations and contexts in which you need English. Here are some ideas, but yo can add your own, too: *correct structures, intonation, dialect, context, register, intercultural competence*.

2 Be aware of how incorrect structures or words can create misunderstandings.

Look at these pairs of sentences. What is the difference in meaning?

1 **a** Ben moved to the US for two years.
b Ben moved to the US two years ago.

2 **a** I'm in Paris for five days.
b I've been in Paris for five days.

3 **a** I'm looking for the kids in the park.
b I'm looking after the kids in the park.

4 **a** Emily stopped taking photos.
b Emily stopped to take some photos.

A

B
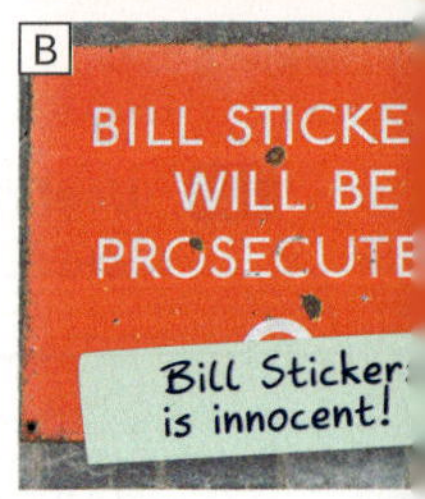

3 Be aware of which words and phrases you need to understand and learn

a In *On Track 5*, you have covered various topics. Each one has its own specialist vocabulary. Choose a topic which particularly interests you and note down words and phrases linked to that topic which you feel are important. You will need them in **4c**.

b If you chose the topic 'law' in **a**, you will probably understand the verb *prosecute* in **sign A**. If your 'knowledge of the world' is not enough to help you with the word *trespasser*, a dictionary will give you the meaning. Which words would you put in your vocabulary book to actively learn?

c To understand **sign B** and the 'joke', you first need to check the various meanings of 'bill' in a dictionary as the first meaning 'Rechnung' clearly doesn't fit here. But you need to know more than the dictionary can tell you, for example that 'Bill' can also be a name or that *-er* added to a verb often denotes a person (e.g. *teach* > *teacher*). Can you explain the handwritten message?

4 Be aware of the appropriate register

a Certain words are inappropriate in some situations. Who do you think is talking in this dialogue?

A Hi Tim! Got your sports stuff?
B F***, no! I dumped it all on my bed, then this morning was like, you know. My mum was like nagging me cos I was late and I just like forgot.
A I have an extra shirt. Wanna borrow it?
B Cool! Cheers mate.

b If Tim was talking to a teacher, how would the dialogue differ? Rewrite it in the correct register.

c Tim uses the word *like* three times in **a**. Why? Many young people overuse this word and aren't aware that they do so. Take turns to talk about the topic you chose in **3a**. Your partner should check if you use *like* and, if so, how often. Together, improve your talk if necessary.

Literary analysis

When analysing a literary text, you do not only pay attention to its form (a poem, a novel, a play, etc.) but also to stylistic devices. They are used to achieve a certain effect:
- to emphasize a certain aspect and make the text lively,
- to grab the reader's interest and make them think, to surprise them or to provoke a particular response,
- to criticize a situation, a person, an idea or event.

Here are ten common devices often found in literary texts:

Literary devices: Definitions

- **alliteration:** repetition of a sound at the beginning of neighbouring words
- **climax:** highest point of tension in a storyline
- **irony:** saying the opposite of what you really mean
- **metaphor:** a figure of speech that directly compares one thing to another for rhetorical effect
- **parallelism:** deliberately using similar or identical words, phrases or structures in neighbouring lines, sentences or paragraphs (= repetition)
- **personification:** presenting ideas, objects or animals as human beings
- **register:** a particular type of language used in a specific situation or for a specific purpose
- **rhetorical question:** question to which no answer is expected because it is obvious
- **rhyme vs. free verse:** using words that repeat syllable sounds vs. poetry without a regular metre or rhyme
- **symbol:** an idea or image that stands for something abstract

The analysis of dramatic texts differs from that of novels or poems. Remember that a dramatic text is not just written to be read but is meant to be performed on a stage or in a theatre. It often contains a conflict between characters and encourages the audience to identify with them, so that they can participate in their experiences. There are two main types or genres of drama: tragedy (= which usually has a sad ending, often leading to the death of one or more protagonists) and comedy (which usually has a happy ending). Usually, a play is made up of five acts and, like short stories, each one is centred around one important event. Below you will find some important keywords for analysing dramatic texts:

Dramatic texts: Keywords

- **act and scenes:** the formal structure of a play; each act usually consists of one or more scenes
- **dialogue:** a conversation between characters
- **monologue (= soliloquy):** a character revealing his / her thoughts and emotions, ideas, sorrows, fears to the audience
- **playwright:** the author of a play
- **properties ('props'):** items used by actors on stage
- **stage directions:** what the author wants the actors to do on stage, e.g. dance, a description of their outward appearance e.g. costumes, their voice, intonation, facial expression. They can also describe the scenery and the effects.
- **flat and round characters:** the characters act in a predictable way and do not develop in the course of actions (flat) or have a complex personality and undergo transformation (round)
- **inner and outer system of communication:** communication among the characters (inner) and communication between the playwright and the audience (outer)
- **dramatic irony:** a situation in which the audience knows something that the characters don't, for example, the words or actions of a character may have a special meaning for the audience that the characters are unaware of
- **reported action:** relevant background information about the characters, the setting or the plot that is provided by the actors for the audience
- **comic relief:** a means of including humurous elements in the plot, often to relieve tension. It can be an amusing scene or character, a comic remark or incident. They are often found in Shakespeare's tragedies.

@ WES-40805-004

Poetry

When talking about the particular way in which a poem can be understood, analysed and explained (= interpretation) you can approach it in different ways. Although there is no fixed approach and you should and will develop your own, the following procedure might be helpful for a successful and satisfying leap into the world of poetry.
And, of course, you can read the lyrics of a song like a poem. However, the music can add further meaning to the text and have an effect on the audience. Remember: poetry is always meant to be read or recited aloud so that the power of its words can be properly experienced and understood. So, start by reading out the poem and listening to how it sounds.

A 10-step poetry analysis

First steps

1. Try to express the impression that reading the poem has made on you and write down some key words or phrases for the main idea you associate with the text.
2. Note words and phrases you remember word for word.
3. Is there a personal message for you in the text? Does it appeal to your senses? What can you hear, see, taste and feel?

Analysis

4. Check unknown words in order to understand their literal meaning as a basis for interpretation. It is important to be aware that words in poetry often convey images or metaphors, so sometimes the literal meaning is not what the writer intended to express.
5. Point out formal aspects, e. g. structure (stanza), rhyme scheme, …
6. Define stylistic devices, explain their function in the text and the effect on the reader (see page **146**)
7. Analyse figurative language and motifs.
8. Research the poet's personal background (biography) and find out any facts that might have influenced his or her way of seeing and writing about the world.

Summary

9. Sum up your results to write a critical evaluation of the poem in about 120 words.
10. Say the lines again aloud and try to memorize the first stanza and the last (or an adequate number of lines if there is no division into stanzas). If you want to, you can learn the complete poem by heart.

Information (1975)

By David Ignatow (American poet, 1914 – 1997)

This tree has two million and seventy-five thousand leaves. Perhaps I missed a leaf or two but I do feel triumphant at having persisted in counting by hand branch by branch and marked down on paper with pencil each total. Adding them up was a pleasure I could understand; I did something on my own that was not dependent on others, and to count leaves is not less meaningful than to count the stars, as astronomers are always doing. They want the facts to be sure they have them all. It would help them to know whether the world is finite. I discovered one tree that is finite. I must try counting the hairs on my head, and you too. We could swap information.

I, Too (1925)

By Langston Hughes
(American poet and activist, 1902 – 1967)

I, too, sing America.
I am the darker brother.
They send me to eat in the kitchen
When company comes,
But I laugh,
And eat well,
And grow strong.

Tomorrow,
I'll be at the table
When company comes.
Nobody'll dare
Say to me,
'Eat in the kitchen,'
Then.

Besides,
They'll see how beautiful I am
And be ashamed

I, too, am America.

Trees (2005)

By Mark Haddon (British novelist and poet, *1962)

They stand in parks and graveyards and gardens.
Some of them are taller than department stores,
yet they do not draw attention to themselves.

You will be fitting a heated towel rail one day
and see, through the louvre window,
a shoal of olive-green fish changing direction
in the air that swims above the little gardens.

Or you will wake at your aunt's cottage,
your sleep broken by a coal train on the empty hill
as the oaks roar in the wind off the channel.

Your kindness to animals, your skill at the clarinet,
these are accidental things.
We lost this game a long way back.
Look at you. You're reading poetry.
Outside the spring air is thick
with the seeds of their children.

The Journey (1986)

By Mary Oliver
(American poet, 1935 – 2019)

One day you finally knew
what you had to do, and began,
though the voices around you
kept shouting
their bad advice
though the whole house
began to tremble
and you felt the old tug
at your ankles.
'Mend my life!'
each voice cried.

But you didn't stop.

You knew what you had to do,
though the wind pried
with its stiff fingers
at the very foundations,
though their melancholy
was terrible.

It was already late
enough, and a wild night,
and the road full of fallen
branches and stones.

But little by little,
as you left their voices behind,
the stars began to burn
through the sheets of clouds,
and there was a new voice
which you slowly
recognized as your own,
that kept you company
as you strode deeper and deeper
into the world,
determined to do
the only thing you could do
determined to save
the only life you could save.

Appendix

Grammatical terms

Here are some of the most important **grammatical terms** in English:

active	aktiv
adjective	Adjektiv
adverb **adverb of frequency** **adverb of manner** **adverb of place** **adverb of time**	Adverb Adverb der Häufigkeit Adverb der Art und Weise Adverb des Ortes Adverb der Zeit
article **definite article** **indefinite article**	Artikel bestimmter Artikel unbestimmter Artikel
aspect	Aspekt
auxiliary	Hilfsverb
clause **adverbial clause** **comment clause** **contact clause** ***if*-clause** **main clause** **relative clause** **defining relative clause** **non-defining relative clause** **subordinate clause (of time)**	Teilsatz Adverbialsatz nicht notwendiger Relativsatz, der sich auf den gesamten Satz bezieht notwendiger Relativsatz ohne Relativpronomen Bedingungssatz; Konditionalis Hauptsatz Relativsatz notwendiger Relativsatz nicht notwendiger Relativsatz Temporalsatz
comparative	Komparativ; Vergleichsform
conditional **conditional type I, II, III, mixed**	Konditionalis; Konditionalsatz
demonstrative determiner	Demonstrativbegleiter
future **future perfect** **future progressive** **future with *going to*** **future with *will*** **present progressive with future meaning** **simple present with future meaning**	Futur; Zukunft Futur II Verlaufsform des Futur Futur mit *going to* Futur mit *will* Verlaufsform des Präsens mit Zukunftsbezug einfache Form des Präsens mit Zukunftsbezug
gerund	Gerundium
imperative	Imperativ; Befehlsform
infinitive ***to*–infinitive**	Infinitiv; Grundform *to*-Infinitiv
modal **modal substitute**	Modalverb Ersatzform eines Modalverbs
negative	negativ; verneinend
noun **countable noun** **uncountable noun**	Substantiv; Nomen zählbares Substantiv nicht zählbares Substantiv

object **direct object** **indirect object**	Objekt direktes Objekt indirektes Objekt
participle **participle construction** **past participle** **perfect participle** **present participle**	Partizip Partizipialkonstruktion Partizip Perfekt *having* + Partizip Perfekt Partizip Präsens
passive ***by*-agent**	Passiv Handelnde(r) im Passivsatz
past **simple past** **past progressive**	Präteritum; Vergangenheit einfache Form der Vergangenheit Verlaufsform der Vergangenheit
past perfect **past perfect (simple)** **past perfect progressive**	Plusquamperfekt einfache Form des Plusquamperfekts Verlaufsform des Plusquamperfekts
plural	Plural; Mehrzahl
positive	positiv; bejaht
possessive *'s*	*s*-Genitiv
possessive determiner	Possessivbegleiter
preposition **preposition of place** **preposition of time**	Präposition Präposition des Ortes Präposition der Zeit
present **simple present** **present progressive**	Präsens; Gegenwart einfache Form des Präsens Verlaufsform des Präsens
present perfect **present perfect (simple)** **present perfect progressive**	Perfekt einfache Form des Perfekt Verlaufsform des Perfekt
pronoun **indefinite pronoun** **interrogative pronoun** **object pronoun** **personal pronouns** **possessive pronoun** **reciprocal pronoun** **reflexive pronoun** **relative pronoun** **subject pronoun**	Pronomen Indefinitpronomen; unbestimmtes Pronomen Interrogativpronomen; Fragepronomen Objektpronomen Personalpronomen Possessivpronomen; besitzanzeigendes Pronomen Reziprokpronomen Reflexivpronomen Relativpronomen Subjektpronomen
prop word *one/ones*	Stützwort *one/ones*
quantifier	Numeral; Zahlwort
question **question tag**	Frage Frageanhängsel; Bestätigungsfrage
reported speech **backshift**	indirekte Rede Rücksetzung der Zeitform um eine Stufe
singular	Singular; Einzahl
statement	Aussagesatz
subject	Subjekt
superlative	Superlativ
tense	Zeitform
verb **irregular verb** **regular verb**	Verb; Tätigkeitswort unregelmäßiges Verb regelmäßiges Verb
word order	Wortstellung

Grammar

Do you have a question about grammar?
The **grammar appendix** explains all the grammar that you learn in this book.

G 1 Tenses (revision)

Workshop 1, pages 14 – 15

Present tenses

Simple present

- We use the simple present to talk about something that happens all the time or that is always true.
  My mum ***works*** *as a nurse.*
  I ***love*** *my dog.*
  We normally ***watch*** *the football on Saturday afternoon.*

- We make negatives and questions with a form of *do*.
  They ***don't go*** *to the cinema very often.*
  He ***doesn't live*** *here anymore.*
  Who ***does*** *this dog* ***belong*** *to?*
  Don't *you* ***like*** *this movie?*

Present progressive

- We use the present progressive to talk about what is happening now when we are speaking.
  *They****'re playing*** *tennis now.*
  We ***aren't eating*** *lunch at the moment.*
  Are *you* ***reading*** *the newspaper or can I have it?*

- Some verbs do not have a progressive form, for example *know*, *like*, *want* or *understand*.

Past tenses

Simple past

- We use the simple past to talk about things that happened at a time in the past. We often use expressions of time like *yesterday, last Thursday, two months ago,* etc. With regular verbs, we add *-ed* to the infinitive of the verb to make the simple past. We form the negative with *didn't* and questions with *did*.
  We ***stayed*** *in Australia for two months last summer.*
  The British ***arrived*** *in Australia in 1788.*
  They ***didn't treat*** *the Aboriginals respectfully.*
  When ***did*** *they* ***close*** *Uluru for tourists?*

- Some verbs don't add *-ed* in the simple past. They are irregular (see the list on pages 177/178).
  We ***went*** *to the beach yesterday.* NOT ~~*We goed to the beach*~~.
  He ***sent*** *me an email an hour ago.* NOT ~~*He sended me an email*~~.

Past progressive

- We form the past progressive with *was / were* + *-ing*. We form the negative with *wasn't / weren't* + *-ing*. For questions, we put the subject between *was / were* and the *-ing* form.
  My parents met when they ***were living*** *in Spain.*
  Sorry, I ***wasn't listening****. What did you say?*
  Were *the others* ***waiting*** *when you arrived?*

- We often use the past progressive together with the simple past to give background information.
  It ***was raining*** *when I got up.*
  While we ***were cycling*** *home from training last week, I had an accident and fell off my bike.*
  Jack went home from school early yesterday because he ***wasn't feeling*** *well.*
  What ***were*** *you* ***doing*** *when I saw you in town last Saturday?*

+ see next page!

Present perfect

- We form the present perfect with *has / have* and the past participle. We form the negative with *hasn't / haven't* and the past participle. For questions, we put the subject between *has / have* and past participle.
  *She **has called** several times.*
  *I **haven't seen** Morgan in school today.*
  *How long **have** you **lived** here?*

- We use the present perfect in two main ways.
  - To talk about something in the past which is connected with or has consequences in the present. We often use the present perfect in this way with *yet* and *already*.
    ***I've** already **booked** the tickets.*
    *I **haven't seen** the exhibition yet.*
    ***Has** she **given** her presentation yet?*
  - To talk about something that started in the past and continues now. We often use the present perfect in this way with *for* and *since*.
    *He**'s lived** in this house for ten years.*
    *We**'ve been** friends since we were seven.*

Present perfect progressive

- We form the present perfect progressive with *has/have + been + -ing*. We form the negative with *hasn't/haven't + been + -ing*. For questions, we put the subject between *has/have* and *been*.
  ***I've been playing** the guitar for three years/since I was 11.*
  *We **haven't been playing** very well since our trainer left.*
  *How long **have** you **been learning** English?*

- We often use the present perfect progressive to talk about an action or a situation which started in the past and continues to the present. We use it with *for*, *since* and *all* as well as in questions with *How long*.
  ***I've been living** here for years/since 20.. .*
  *The kids **have been playing** in the garden all afternoon.*
  *Sorry, I'm late. – Don't worry. We **haven't been waiting** long.*
  *How long **have** you **been working** here?*

Past perfect

- We form the past perfect with *had* and the past participle. We form the negative with *hadn't* and the past participle. For questions, we put the subject between *had* and the past participle.
  *I was late and the exam **had** already **started**.*
  *He **hadn't told** me he was Meg's friend.*
  ***Had** you **seen** the film before?*

- We use the past perfect to show that one event happened before another one in the past. We use the past perfect for the event that happened first and the simple past for the more recent event. We often use sequence adverbs such as *when*, *before*, *after* and *until* to link the two events.
  *A few hours after we **had started** along the trail, my father **fell** ill.*
  *We **had hoped** to reach this place sooner, but the bad weather **slowed** us down.*
  *The boy **had** just **had** his 8th birthday when he **fell** and **died**.*

- We also use the past perfect to show that something happened before a time in the past.
  *We**'d travelled** over 200 miles by 12 o'clock.*
  *I **hadn't met** him before the concert last June.*

Past perfect progressive

- We form the past perfect progressive with *had* + *been* + *-ing*. We form the negative with *hadn't* + *been* + *-ing*. For questions, we put the subject between *had* and *been*.
  *We'**d been playing** for 20 minutes when it started to rain.*
  *I **hadn't been waiting** long when the bus came.*
  ***Had** you **been looking for** an internship for long before you got one?*
- We use the past perfect progressive to focus on the length of the earlier action and to show that it was in progress before the second action started.
  *I'**d been playing** rugby for three years when I became captain.*
  *We **hadn't been driving** for long when dad realized that he didn't have his phone.*
  *How long **had** the others **been waiting** when you finally arrived?*

Future tenses

Will future

- We use *will* to offer or promise to do something for somebody. The verb form always stays the same. For negatives we use *won't*.
  *I'**ll help** you with your homework this evening.*
  *There isn't any milk in the fridge. – Don't worry. I **won't forget** to buy some this afternoon.*
- We use *will* when we decide to do something while we are speaking.
  *You look hungry. We'**ll buy** a sandwich.*
  *I'm so tired, I **won't stay up** much long.*
- We use *will* for predictions that are based on personal feeling or opinion.
  *You'**ll love** it in Canada!*
  *It **won't take** long.*
  *It'**ll take** you longer than you think.*

Going to future

- We use *be going to* for decisions and future plans that were made before the time of speaking.
  *I'**m going to join** the school drama club next term.*
  *Have you packed? – No, I **am going to pack** after dinner.*
  *We'**re going to book** our train tickets at the weekend.*
- We use *be going to* for predictions that are based on present evidence. In other words, there is something in the present that indicates something in the future.
  *Look at the traffic. We'**re going to be** late.*
  *It looks like it'**s going to be** a lovely day.*

The simple present

- We use the simple present to talk about future events when the statements are based on present facts, and when these facts are something fixed like a timetable, schedule or calendar.
  *The bus **leaves** at 6.30, please hurry up.*
  *The soccer match **starts** at three o'clock on Sunday.*

Present progressive

- We use the present progressive with a future time to talk about future arrangements.
  *Next week, I'**m seeing** my cousin to discuss my internship.*
  *We'**re meeting** at the pizzeria this evening.*
  *When **are** Chris and Jo **going** to the USA?*

+ see next page!

Future perfect

- We use the future perfect (*will have* + past participle) to talk about something already completed by a point in the future. We often use the future perfect with *by*.
  *The apprenticeship starts in September. I'**ll have finished** my A-levels by then.*
  *I'm sure we'**ll have arrived** by midnight.*
  ***Will** you **have had** dinner by 8.30?*
- We can use the future perfect to talk about something not completed by a point in the future.
  *I'm afraid I **won't have finished** my report by Friday.*
  *I **won't have had** time to do much research before the interview.*

Future progressive

- We use the future progressive (*will be* + *-ing*) for an action in progress at a specific time in the future.
  *Next year most of my friends **will be doing** a university course or an apprenticeship.*
  *Hopefully by September I'**ll be working** somewhere in the US or Canada.*
  *This time tomorrow, I'**ll be having** my interview.*
  *At 3 o'clock, we'**ll be driving** to the airport.*

The passive (all tenses)

- We use the passive in different tenses when we focus on the action and not on who does the action. We use *be* in the appropriate tense + past participle.

Simple present (*am* / *is* / *are* + past participle)
*The internet **is used** by billions of people every day.*
*Today, most goods **are paid for** electronically.*

Simple past (*was* / *were* + past participle)
*It's hard to imagine life before electricity **was invented**.*
*The first emails **were sent** in the 1970s.*

Present perfect (*has been* / *have been* + past participle)
*The way we communicate **has been revolutionized**.*
*Today, many cashiers **have been replaced** by self-service check-outs.*

***Will* (*will be* + past participle)**
*Autonomous drones **will be used** to deliver parcels to our doors.*
*Many jobs **will be lost**.*

Modal verbs (*can be* / *might be* / *had to be* + past participle)
*Our homes will be full of smart appliances that **can be controlled** remotely.*
*The new website **might be launched** soon.*
*Until the early 20th century, all household chores **had to be done** by hand.*

G 2 Reported speech in statements and questions in the present, present perfect and future

Workshop 1, pages 18 – 19

We sometimes report a person's exact words or the general idea.

Statements:

- We can use *say* and *tell* to report what someone says.
  *He **says** that he loves the area.*
  *Thomas **tells** me that you're going back to the UK.*
- We can use *that* after *say* and *tell*. There is no rule about *that* and it is usually personal choice.
  *She **says** she's not hungry.* OR *She **says that** she's not hungry.*
- We use an indirect object (e. g. *me, us*) after *tell*.
  *He tells **me** they are hoping to set off at about 6.30.*
- As well as *say* and *tell*, we can use the present tense of verbs such as *admit, agree, assure, claim, deny, inform, suggest, think*, etc.
  *He **admits** he's wrong.*
  *She **agrees** it's a good idea.*
- When we use the present, the present perfect or the future with reporting verbs, we generally keep the information we are reporting in the same tense as the original comment. This is usually to show that something is still true, relevant or important.
  *I**'ll be** home in ten minutes.* → *She says she**'ll be** home in ten minutes.*
  *It**'s** Jenna's birthday today.* → *Alice tells me it**'s** your birthday today.*
  *I think Sam **left** about an hour ago.* → *He thinks that Sam **left** about an hour ago.*
  *We**'re going** to the beach.* → *Luke says they**'re going** to the beach.*
- We sometimes need to change pronouns *(we → they)* and other words such as *here → there*, etc.
  ***I**'ve lived **here** since **I** was 13.* → ***He** says **he**'s lived **there** since **he** was 13.*

Questions:

- We can report a question with verbs such as *ask, want to know* and *wonder*.
  Fred: Is everything OK? → *Fred **wants to know** if everything is OK.*
  David: When are we leaving? → *David**'s asking** when we're leaving.*
  Jessica: Where are we going next? → *She**'s wondering** where we are going next.*
- For a *yes/no*-question (without a question word) we use *if* or *whether*.
  *He **is asking** me **if** I know his brother.*
  *Olga **has asked** me **whether** I can give her a surfing lesson.*
- The word order is different from direct questions but the same as in statements.
  *Where **does he live**?* → *She wants to know where **he lives**.*
  *When **are we leaving**?* → *He keeps asking when **we're leaving**.*
  NOT ~~*She's wants to know where does he live.*~~ • ~~*He keeps asking when are we leaving.*~~

Examples

*Oliver **wants to know** if you can give him a lift to the airport.*
*The receptionist **is saying that** he's not expecting us until tomorrow.*
*Magdalena **tells me** you're applying for Australian citizenship.*

G 3 Reported speech in statements and questions in the past and in requests, offers, orders and advice

Workshop 1, pages 30 – 31

Statements and questions

When reporting speech, we often use the past tense forms *said, told, asked, wanted to know, was wondering, assured, admitted, denied, suggested, promised,* etc. We usually 'backshift' the tense (move the tense one step back in time) in the statement, comment or question we are reporting.

- present tense → past tense
  *I **work** in Adelaide.* — *She told me she **worked** in Adelaide.*
  What's wrong with you? — *Keira asked Fred what **was** wrong with him.*
  *OK, I admit I**'m** wrong.* — *He admitted he **was** wrong.*
- past tense / present perfect → past perfect
  *I **didn't want** to go.* — *She told us she **hadn't wanted** to go.*
  *We**'ve** just **arrived**.* — *He said they**'d** just **arrived**.*
- *will* — *would*
  *I**'ll call** you later.* — *She said she**'d call** me later.*
- *can* — *could*
  *I **can't find** it.* — *He told me he **couldn't find** it.*
- *must* — *had to*
  *We **must leave** now.* — *She said they **had to leave**.*

We sometimes use the past tense forms *said*, *told*, *asked*, *wanted to know*, *was wondering*, etc and we do not change the tense. This is usually to show that something is still true, relevant or important.

*Sam **left** about a hour ago.* → *He said that Sam **left** about an hour ago.*
*I**'ll** be home in ten minutes.* → *She said she**'ll** be home in ten minutes.*
*Where's Jamie **going**?* → *She was wondering where Jamie's **going**.*

Requests, offers, orders and advice

- We can report a request with verbs such as *asked* and *want* + indirect object + *to*-infinitive.
  Can you wait here? → *She asked **us to wait** here.*
  Could you repeat the question? → *She wanted **me to repeat** the question.*
- We can report an offer with *offer* + *to*-infinitive.
  I can give you a lift if you like. → *Maria offered **to give** us a lift.*
  I'll help you if you like. → *He offered **to help** us.*
- We can report an order or advice with *told* + indirect object + (*not*) + *to*-infinitive.
  You should apologize to them. → *She told me **to apologize** to them.*
  Don't be late again. → *He told me **not to be** late again.*

We can also use the present tense of the reporting verbs:
*Gareth **wants** me **to help** him.*
*She's **asking** us **to wait** here.*
*Petra's **offering to give** us a lift.*
*The life guard **is telling** us **not to swim** here.*

Examples *He said he **was** from Wellington.* • *She said they **were going to have** a barbecue.* • *He asked me if I **was** OK.* • *Olga asked me if I **could give** her a surfing lesson.* • *He wanted to know where I **worked**.* • *Oliver wants me **to phone** him.* • *The receptionist asked us **to wait** a few minutes.* • *I offered **to help** them with the tidying up.* • *The teacher told the children **not to run** in the corridors.*

G 4 Changes to adverbs of time and place in reported speech

Workshop 1, pages 30 – 31

When we are reporting, we sometimes need to change adverbs of time and place.
I saw Anders ***yesterday****. → She mentioned she'd seen Anders* ***the day before****.*
I'll call you ***next week****. → She said she'd call me* ***the following week****.*
This is the first time I've been ***here****. → He said it was the first time he'd been* ***there****.*

Common changes include:
yesterday → the day before
tomorrow → the next day / the day after
last weekend / week / month / year → the weekend / week / month / year before
next weekend / week / month / year → the following weekend / week / month / year
here → there

G 5 Passive (revision)

Workshop 1, pages 26 – 27

Use

- We often use the passive when we do not mention who does an action, as we are more interested in what happens than who does the action. This is usually because who does the action is obvious, unknown or not important. The passive also means we can avoid using vague subjects like *someone, people* and *they*.
  Canberra ***was chosen*** *as the capital of Australia in 1908.*
  The Rugby World Cup ***is held*** *every four years. It* ***was*** *first* ***held*** *in 1987.*
- However, we can use the passive with *by* to say who does the action. This is often when we are giving new information about an existing topic. The passive enables us to put the existing information first and the new information second.
  Each nation has its own Creation legends which have been passed down ***by the Elders****.*
  New Zealand was first settled ***by the Maori people*** *as early as 1300 AD.*

Form

- We form the passive with the appropriate form of *be* + past participle.
  Rugby Union ***is played*** *by two teams of 15 players.*
  Relations between Australia and New Zealand ***have*** *often* ***been compared*** *to those of siblings.*
  The Olympics ***were held*** *in Australia in 1956 and 2000.*
  The museum ***will be opened*** *by the Prime Minister.*
- We use *be* + past participle after modal verbs.
  Ancient Aboriginal paintings ***can be seen*** *in caves in Uluru.*
  You ***won't be contacted*** *unless you give us permission.*
- We use the passive infinitive *to be* + past participle after verbs that are normally followed by *to*-infinitive (e. g. *allow, ask, expect, hope, like, need, want*).
  The Anangu had long wanted the title deeds ***to be returned****.*
  I hope ***to be invited*** *to the opening ceremony.*
- We form a question by putting the subject after the auxiliary verb *be* or between the auxiliaries if there are two of them.
  When ***was*** *Parliament House* ***built****?*
  Has *the World Cup ever* ***been held*** *in Australia?*
  What time ***will*** *we* ***be collected*** *from the hotel?*

+ see next page!

- When a verb is followed by a preposition, the preposition stays in the same position in the passive.
  We can make sure the place ***is looked after****.*
  At the hotel, all diets ***are catered for****.*

- When we use the passive in a relative clause, we can sometimes omit the relative pronoun and *be*.
  There are some amazing carvings (which are) made from wood, ivory and sandstone.
  I took part in a sponsored run for a charity (which is) called ResCom.

- When a verb has two objects, the passive sentence can begin with either the direct or the indirect object. The direct object is usually a thing and the indirect object is usually a person. When we begin with the direct object, we use the preposition *to* or *for* before the indirect object.
  The land *was given back* ***to the original owners****.* OR ***The original owners*** *were given back* ***the land****.*
  Four seats *were saved* ***for us****.* OR ***We*** *were saved* ***four seats****.*

- Verbs that take two objects include:
  buy • find • get • give • offer • make • promise • send • show • teach

Australia ***was*** *first* ***named*** *Terra Australis, which was later abbreviated to the current form.*
Tasmania ***can be reached*** *by boat in about ten hours from Melbourne.*
They've arranged for us ***to be met*** *at the airport.*

G 6 Defining relative clauses (revision) and non-defining relative clauses

Workshop 2, pages 52 – 53

Defining relative clauses

- A defining relative clause defines, identifies or gives necessary information about a person or thing. A defining relative clause comes immediately after this person or thing and begins with a relative pronoun. We use *who* for people and *which* for things. We can use *that* for both people and things. We use *whose* to show possession.
  Kids ***who came over*** *would ask sometimes, 'Where's your dad?'*
  Is this the book ***which your parents gave you as a birthday present****?*
  Mac and his family do things ***that every other family does****.*
  This is my friend ***whose paintings I showed you****.*

- A relative pronoun can be the subject or the object of a relative clause.

	relative pronoun / subject	verb	object	
There's the man	***who***	*helped*	*us*	*yesterday.*

	relative pronoun / object	subject	verb	
There's the man	***who***	*we*	*helped*	*yesterday.*

- We can omit *who, which* or *that* when it is the object of the relative clause.
  There's the man (who) we helped yesterday. NOT ~~*There's the man helped us yesterday.*~~
  Is this the picture (which) your parents gave you as a birthday present?
  Mac and his family do things (that) every other family does.
  Is this the café (that) Luke mentioned the other day?

Non-defining relative clauses

- A non-defining relative clause gives extra non-essential information about a person or thing. The non-defining relative clause comes immediately after this person or thing and begins with a relative pronoun. We don't use *that* in a non-defining relative clause. We always separate a non-defining relative clause from the main clause with commas.
  My two older brothers, ***who I've always been very close to,*** *went to live with my dad.*
  Single-parent families, ***which may include a single mum or dad and their children,*** *are increasingly common.*
  My best friend, ***whose parents divorced when she was a baby,*** *was brought up by her mum.*
  He was born in Avalon, ***which is a small town near Los Angeles.***

Non-defining relative clauses are more common in writing and in more formal spoken contexts.

Where and *when*

We can use the relative adverbs *where* and *when* in relative clauses. We use *where* to identify a place and *when* to identify a time.
The hotel ***where we stayed*** *is in the city centre.*
Thanksgiving is a day ***when families and friends get together.***
Carmel, ***where we went the other week,*** *is one of my favourite places.*

The girl ***who is on the right*** *is my little sister.*
The couple ***that live in the flat above us*** *are very noisy.*
What's that game ***we were playing*** *last night?*
Mr Jones, ***who also actually taught my mum,*** *is my maths teacher.*
Christmas is usually a time ***when families come together.***

G 7 Comment clauses

Workshop 2, pages 56 – 57

- We can use a non-defining relative clause beginning with *which* to comment on the whole of the previous clause. The comment clause is similar to a non-defining relative clause and is separated from the preceding clause by a comma.
  There are children from all sorts of ethnic backgrounds, ***which I think is really good.***
  I was at a school reunion last weekend, ***which was great fun.***
  The school became co-ed in the 1980s, ***which was a major step forwards.***
  I missed the bus, ***which was really annoying.***
- Whereas non-defining relative clauses are more common in writing and in more formal spoken contexts, comment clauses are quite common in spoken and more informal English.

Examples

Maria offered to help, ***which was very kind of her.***
I found my phone, ***which was a huge relief.***
The meal was €10, ***which was quite cheap to be honest.***

G 8 Emphatic *do / does, did*

Workshop 2, pages 64 – 65

We can use a form of the auxiliary verb *do* (*do, does, did*) to give emphasis to a statement. In speaking, we stress *do, does, did*. We use *do* in this way for two reasons:

- to emphasize our feelings or emotions
  *I **do** wish I could turn the clock back.*
  *I **do** like Mexican food.*
  *Anna **does** have some great ideas.*
  *I **did** enjoy that film.*
- to emphasize a contrast
  *I don't do any sport, but I **do** like watching it on TV.*
  *He doesn't drive, but he **does** have a motorbike licence.*
  *I knew it was wrong to take them, but I **did** take them.*

With tenses and forms that already have an auxiliary verb, we stress the auxiliary verb to express emphasis in a similar way.
*I **am** looking forward to seeing them.*
*We really **have** had a great time, thank you.*

Examples
*I **do** agree with you. Please believe me!*
*I **did** enjoy that meal. Did you?*
*It's not easy, but I **am** trying!*

G 9 Emphatic structures

Workshop 2, pages 68 – 69

We can use sentences beginning with *It ...* or *What ...* to give emphasis to what we are saying. This helps to focus attention on or 'spotlights' the important information.

Neutral sentence	→	Sentence with emphasis
I didn't delete the files.		***It wasn't** me **who** deleted the files.*
All the advertising annoys me.		***What** annoys me **is** all the advertising.*

The main forms are:

- ***It is / was ... that / who / which ...***
  ***It's** all the advertising **which** annoys me.*
  ***It's** the advertisers **who** want our money.*
  ***It's** the video ads **that** really catch your attention.*
  ***It was** Jenny **who** phoned, not Maria.*
- ***What ... is / are / was / were ...***
  ***What** it means **is** that we enjoy clever content, even if it's advertising.*
  ***What** is really annoying **are** those ads blocking the content.*
  ***What** we needed **was** a better internet connection.*
  ***What** we needed **were** more options to choose from.*

Examples
***It was** clicking on the ad **that** caused the virus.*
***It wasn't** Masha **who** phoned, it was Olga.*
***Was it** Professor Jones **who** retired last month?*
***What I** don't understand **is** why no one said anything to her.*
***What** annoys me **is** his lazy attitude.*

G 10 Different use of gerund and *to*–infinitive (revision)

Workshop 3, pages 90 – 91

A gerund is the -ing form of a verb. A gerund followed by an object or an adverbial is called a gerund clause.

- We can use a gerund or a gerund clause as the subject of a verb. This is when the subject is an activity or action. We often use the gerund as a subject in signs and notices. To form the negative, we put *not* before the gerund.
  ***Spending** a year abroad is very popular among young people.*
  ***Not knowing** what to study is a fairly common problem among teenagers.*
  ***Parking** here is forbidden.*
- We can use a gerund or a gerund clause as the object of certain verbs. This is when the object is an activity or action.
  *I don't mind **waiting** for you.*
  *I like **seeing** how people live here.*
  *I regret **not going** to the school prom.*

Sometimes we use two verbs together. The second verb adds information to what is expressed by the first verb. When one verb follows another verb, the second verb is usually the gerund (-ing) or the to-infinitive.

- We use the gerund (*-ing*) after certain verbs. These include:
  admit • avoid • consider • deny • don't mind • enjoy • fancy • feel like • finish • imagine • involve • keep (on) • mention • miss • practise • recommend • risk • spend time • suggest
  *Did you **enjoy reading** the book?*
  *I **miss seeing** my old friends.*
- We use the *to*-infinitive after certain verbs. These include:
  agree • aim • appear • arrange • can('t) afford • choose • claim • decide • demand • (be) determined • expect • help • hope • intend • learn • manage • need • offer • plan • pretend • promise • refuse • seem • tend • threaten • want • would like / prefer

  *He **hopes to get** a place on a degree apprenticeship programme.*
  *I've **decided to look for** a new job.*
  *Did you **manage to finish** your assignment on time?*
  *Lucy is **planning to go** to university in September.*
- Some verbs can usually be followed by the gerund or the *to*-infinitive with little or no difference in meaning. These include:
  begin • continue • hate • like • love • prefer • start

  *I **hate getting up** early.* OR *I **hate to get up** early.*
  *I **prefer studying** alone.* OR *I **prefer to study** alone.*
  *I **like reading** about current issues.* OR *I **like to read** about current issues.*

  However, we can sometimes use *like* + *to*-infinitive to say that something is a good or sensible idea.
  *I **like to get** my assignments finished before the deadline.*
  *I **like to eat** plenty of fresh fruit and vegetables.*

+ see next page!

- Some verbs can be followed by a gerund or the *to*-infinitive but there is a difference in meaning. These verbs include:

  <u>*Try*</u>
  We use *try* + gerund when we do something to see what the results will be.
  If you're unhappy at work, you should ***try talking*** *to your boss.*
  I ***tried turning*** *the computer on and off, but the program still didn't work.*

  We use *try* + *to*-infinitive when we make an effort to achieve something.
  They ***tried to persuade*** *me to work for them, but I am happy at my company.*
  I'm ***trying to learn*** *the drums, so that I can join a band.*

  <u>*Remember* and *forget*</u>
  We use *remember / forget* + gerund to talk about memories.
  I ***remember changing*** *my password.*
  Do you ***remember going*** *to school for the first time?*
  I'll never ***forget visiting*** *London. It was a wonderful trip.*

  We use *remember / forget* + *to*-infinitive to say we do or don't do something.
  If you decide to apply, then ***remember to include*** *all the articles you've written about social issues.*
  Oh no! I ***forgot to mention*** *my hobbies in my CV.*

  <u>*Stop*</u>
  We use *stop* + gerund to talk about something ending or stopping.
  I ***stopped eating*** *meat ten years ago.*
  I hope it ***stops raining*** *soon.*

  We use *stop* + *to*-infinitive to express the reason or purpose.
  Sorry I'm late. I ***stopped to get*** *some petrol on the way here.*
  I was working, but I ***stopped to watch*** *TV for a while.*

  <u>*Go on*</u>
  We use *go on* + gerund to say we continue to do something.
  Jack ***went on studying*** *even though he wasn't really enjoying the course.*

  We use *go on* + *to*-infinitive to say we do something new.
  When she didn't get a place to study medicine, Jen ***went on to train*** *as a physiotherapist.*

- Some verbs are followed by an object + *to*-infinitive. These include:
  advise • allow • ask • choose • encourage • expect • help • invite • need • order • persuade • tell • want • would like

  My boss ***wants me to apply*** *for the new position.*
  Do you ***need someone to help*** *you?*

  Note that we can use some verbs (e. g. *ask, choose, expect, help, need, want*) without or with an object.
  We ***expect to arrive*** *on Friday. We* ***expect them to accompany*** *us on Friday.*

  Note that when these verbs are in the passive, they are followed directly by the *to*-infinitive.
  As a child, I ***was*** *always* ***encouraged to work*** *hard.*

- Prepositions are always followed by a gerund, not a *to*-infinitive. These include:
  after • against • before • by • without
  Did you do these tasks ***without using*** *a smartphone?*

- Some combinations of adjectives, nouns and verbs with prepositions are also followed by a gerund. These include:
  to believe in • capable of • to carry on • to focus on • good at • importance of • interested in • look forward to • reason for
  *Some young people don't understand the **importance of voting**.*

- A lot of nouns can be followed by a *to*-infinitive. These include:
  chance • idea • opportunity • plan • time
  *It was **time to start**.* • *It's a good **idea to check** the information.*

- We can use some verbs + question word + *to*-infinitive. These include:
  ask • decide • discover • discuss • explain • find out • forget • know • learn • remember • talk about • understand • wonder
  *Let's **talk about where to stay**.*
  *I can't **decide who to invite** to the party.*

- We can also use certain phrases + question word + *to*-infinitive.
  *I'm not sure **where to go**.*
  *I have no idea **how to install** the software.*
  *Let me know **what to buy**.*
  *Do you know **how to get to** the station?*

- We can also use a *to*-infinitive after *whether*.
  *We need to decide **whether to go** by train or by bus.*
  *I'm not sure **whether to stay** here or **go with** them.*

- We use the infinitive to explain why we do something – in German 'um … zu'.
  *I went to the careers fair **to get** some advice.*
  *Paula looked at her phone **to check** the time of her interview.*

Examples

*I don't **feel like studying** today.*
*We **hope to arrive** around 6.30.*
*I **hate being** late for anything.*
*I **tried to order** online, but the website was down.*
*Did they **ask** Jack **to go** with them?*

G 11 Modal verbs, modal substitutes (revision)

Workshop 3, pages 94 – 95

The modal verbs are *can, could, may, might, must, shall, should, will* and *would*. We also use the modal substitutes *be able to, have to, need to* and *ought to*.

- A modal verb always has the same form. The ending never changes.
  She can speak English. NOT ~~*She cans speak English.*~~

- We use an infinitive without *to* after a modal verb.
  I will help you. NOT ~~*I will to help you.*~~

- To form a question, we put the modal verb before the subject.
  Can you help me? NOT ~~*Do you can help me?*~~

- To form a negative, we put *not* or *n't* after the modal verb.
  You mustn't do that. NOT ~~*You don't must do that.*~~

+ see next page!

affirmative	*She can speak German.*	*It might rain.*	*They should go.*
negative	*She can't speak German.*	*It might not rain.*	*They shouldn't go.*
question	*Can she speak German?*	*Might it rain?*	*Should they go?*

Can, could and *be able to*

We use *can, could* and *be able to* in a number of ways.

- We use *can* and *be able to* to talk about ability. We use them:
  - to talk about general abilities and skills.
    *Amir **can** play the guitar.*
    *I **can** speak French and Spanish. But I **can't** speak Italian.*
    *Some people **are able to** speak several languages.*
  - to talk about ability at a particular time.
    *I **can't** read this. The writing is too small.*
    ***I'm not able to** fix the problem, I'm afraid.*

  The past tense of *can* is *could* and the past tense of *be able to* is *was/were able to*.
  *I **could** speak some English when I was four years old.*
  *Unfortunately, I **wasn't able to** find his office.*

  We use *be able to* (not *can*) with *will* and the present perfect.
  *I'm sure you **will be able to** find a great job.*
  ***I've been able to** speak English since I was four.*

- We use *can* to talk about permission.
  - to talk about rules and laws.
    *You **can't** park here. But you **can** park over there.*
    *You **can** leave school when you are 16.*
  - to talk about permission given by an individual.
    *You **can** leave when you have finished the report.*
    ***Can** I use the printer?*

  The past tense of *can* is *could*.
  *Sorry I'm late. I **couldn't** leave work any earlier.*
  *We **could** wear jeans at work in my last job.*

  We sometimes use *be allowed to* as an alternative to *can* to talk about permission.
  ***Are** you **allowed to** wear jeans at work?*
  *I **was** never **allowed to** stay up late on a school night.*

- We use *can* to talk about possibility.
  *We **can** have the meeting on Thursday or Friday.*
  *You **can** show more of your personality by listing hobbies and interests.*
  *A cover letter **can** help you sell the skills and knowledge that you have.*
  ***Can** we book tickets in advance?*

May and *might*

We use *may* and *might* to say that something is possible or likely. *Might* is more common in informal contexts, such as conversation. The negative is *may not* and *might not*. We use them:

- to say what is possible or likely in the future.
  *It **might** rain later.*
  *I **might not** go to the meeting.*
  *There **may** be a slight delay with your order.*

- to say what we think is possible or likely in the present.
  *This **might** be Nina's office. But I'm not sure.*
  *She didn't answer the phone. She **might not** be at home.*

Must, have to and *need to*

- We use *must, have to* and *need to* to talk about what is necessary or what is required. When they are used in this way, there is usually little difference in meaning, e. g. *I **have to** prepare for my interview / I **need to** prepare for my interview. / I **must** prepare for my interview.* We use *must not* (or *mustn't*) to express a negative idea.
  *Education and work experience details **must** be included in your CV.*
  *Your information **must** be correct and up to date.*
  *You **need to** show some ID to get in the building.*
  *Does your dad **have to** wear a tie for work?*
  *You **mustn't** be late! You **need to** leave by 5.30 at the latest.*

- In more informal contexts, such as conversation, we can use *have got to*.
  *I**'ve got to** prepare for my interview.*
  *What time **have** we **got to** leave?*

- The past tenses are *needed to* and *had to*. We use *had to* as the past tense of *must*.
  *Sorry I'm late. I **needed to** stop at the shops on the way here.*
  *I **had to** stay at work later than usual today.*

- We use *don't have to* and *don't need to* to say that something isn't necessary.
  *We **don't need to** leave until midday.* NOT ~~*We mustn't leave until midday.*~~
  *In some countries, you **don't have to** give personal details in your CV.*
  *I **didn't need to** go to work today.*

Should and *ought to*

- We use *should* to give advice and to say what we think is the best or correct thing to do. The negative form is *shouldn't*.
  *Your CV **should** have a clear format and structure.*
  *You **should** try to exercise at least once a week.*
  *What **should** I do?*

- We can sometimes use *ought to* as an alternative to *should*.
  *You **ought to** exercise at least once a week.*
  *I think we **ought to** leave now.*

Will and *shall*

We use *will* in a number of ways. Note that *will* is often contracted to *'ll*. The main uses of *will* are:

- to express spontaneous choices and decisions.
  *I**'ll** help you if you want me to.*
  *I think I**'ll** take a short break.*

- to express predictions or assumptions about the future, present or past.
  *I'm hoping I**'ll** finish the report by Friday.*
  *Hurry up! The taxi **will** be waiting.*
  *I think the meeting **will** have finished by now.*

- to talk about things we see as inevitable or certain.
  *I**'ll** be at work all day tomorrow.*
  *She**'ll** be 21 in January.*
  *No hiring manager **will** be willing to consider your application without a CV.*

- We mainly use *shall* in the form of a question to make offers and suggestions. We use it in this way with ***I*** and *we*.
  ***Shall** I help you?*
  *What time **shall** we meet?*

See also Ways of expressing the German verbs *sollen* and *müssen* → G12

G 12 Ways of expressing the German verbs *sollen* and *müssen*

Workshop 3, pages 94 – 95

The German verbs *sollen* and *müssen* are commonly expressed as *should* and *must* in English. However, there are other words and phrases we can use to express the same ideas.

Sollen: *should, ought to, be to, be supposed to*
*What time **should** we be there?*
*We**'re supposed to** arrive by 8.30.*
*Soft skills **are not to** be confused with hard skills.*

Müssen: *must, have to, need to, be forced to, be obliged to*
*You **must** be honest on your CV. You **mustn't** invent or exaggerate anything.*
*You **are obliged to** attend all weekly meetings.*
*The company insists that no employees will **be forced to** resign.*

Note that *be to, be obliged to* and *be forced to* are generally used in more formal contexts, such as professional, business, current affairs and legal communication.

Examples
*Who **are** we **supposed to** contact when we get to the university?*
*You **are obliged to** pay 50% of your fees before enrolling on your course.*
*At school, we **were forced to** go outside at break times even if it was raining.*

See also Modal verbs, modal substitutes (revision) → G11

G 13 *Used to, didn't use to, would* to describe past habits and states

Workshop 3, pages 102 – 103

Used to
We use *used to*–infinitive to talk about past actions or situations that no longer exist. These could be:

- past actions, habits and routines
  *My dad **used to spend** an hour a day commuting to work.*
  *I **used to drive** to work, but these days I usually cycle.*
  *Do you work in advertising? – No, but I **used to**.*
- past states
  *'Job hopping' is much more common than it **used to be**.*
  *There **used to be** a cinema here.*
  *I **didn't use to go** to the gym.*

Note that there is no final *'d'* in negatives and questions.
*I **didn't use to like** football.*
*What **did** people **use to do** before mobile phones?*
***Didn't** Jamie **use to work** in marketing?*

Would
We use *would* + infinitive to talk about past actions, habits and routines. *Would* is usually contracted to *'d* after pronouns.
*People **would commute** to the office every day.*
*In my old job, we**'d have** a meeting almost every day.*

We do not, however, use *would* to talk about past states.
NOT ~~*'Job hopping' is much more common than it would be.*~~

<u>Frequency adverbs</u>
Note that we can use frequency adverbs such as *never, always, usually, often, sometimes,* etc. with *would* and *used to*.
*I **never used to play** computer games.*
*I **sometimes used to wear** a tie in my old job.*
*He**'d often arrive** late for work.*

Examples *My dad **used to have** a beard.*
***Didn't** there **use to be** a café here?*
*As a child, I**'d spend** hours climbing trees.*
*We**'d often stay up** all night when we were students.*

G 14 Participle constructions instead of adverbial clauses (present, past and perfect)

Workshop 3, pages 106 – 107

There are two main types of participle:
- the present participle (the *-ing* form of the verb)
  *Before **arriving**, I received lots of information.*
  ***Wanting** to become a teacher, he volunteered in his local school.*
- the past participle (the regular *-ed* form or an irregular form)
  *I came across a fantastic workshop, **organized** by an Irish government agency.*
  ***Given** the opportunity, I would do it again.*

Other participle forms are:
- the perfect participle (e. g. *having done*)
  ***Having spent** eight wonderful weeks there, I can thoroughly recommend it.*
- the perfect passive participle (e. g. *having been done*)
  ***Having been postponed** twice, the conference finally took place in December.*

To form the negative, we put *not* or *never* before the participle.
***Not wanting** to be late, they set off in plenty of time.*
***Never having been** to Ireland before, I was determined to do and see as much as I could.*

We can use present participle constructions:
- when two events happen at the same time or when one is immediately followed by another.
  *I fell asleep **watching** TV last night.*
  *Luke's in the library **researching** his assignment.*
- in clauses beginning with *before, after, while, since, when,* etc.:
  *Make sure you turn the computer off **before leaving**.*
  *She's worked here **since finishing** university.*
  *I came across a fantastic organization **while researching** internships abroad.*
- when we express the reason for or the result of an action:
  ***Wanting** some hands-on experience before university, I contacted them.*
  ***Not earning** much at the factory, he took a second job working in a café.*
  *She did well in the exam, **passing** with grade A.*

Note that in the above present participle constructions, the events in both clauses are carried out or experienced by the same person.

+ see next page!

- in reduced relative clauses when we shorten a defining relative clause. This can be:
  - in progressive tenses when we remove the relative pronoun and *be*.
    I also met students at the hospital ***already studying medicine****. (= I also met students at the hospital who were already studying medicine.)*
    Who are the people ***talking to Harry****?*
  - in place of a relative pronoun + simple tense that express a fact, state or permanent situation.
    I work in an office ***overlooking the river****. (= I work in an office that overlooks the river.)*
    The students ***living next door*** *are very friendly.*

We can use past participle constructions

- in reduced defining or non-defining relative clauses. We remove the relative pronoun and the verb *be* in passive structure.
  It's a local business, ***run*** *by the same family for over 200 years. (= It's a local business which has been run by the same family for over 200 years.)*
  Have they found money ***stolen*** *from the office?*
  Cars ***parked*** *here will be removed.*
- in shortened *if* clauses to give passive meaning, usually without *if*.
  If ***asked*** *about it, I'd say it was the prettiest place I've visited so far. (= If I was asked about it, …)*
  Given *the chance to take the exam again, I'd do it without hesitation. (= If I was given the chance to take the exam again, …)*

We can use perfect participle constructions when one event happens before another event. We use the perfect participle to emphasize that the first event is completed before the second or that there is a time interval between the two events.
Having finally finished *their exams, they organized a big party.*
Having met *the staff, he was even more keen to get the job.*
Having overslept*, she was late for work.*
Having managed *to work out where all the facilities were, I felt quite proud of myself.*

Note that beginning a sentence with a participle clause is more common in more formal writing and literary contexts.

Examples

Louise is in the kitchen ***making*** *a coffee, I think.*
After ***leaving*** *university, he got a job in a bank.*
Living alone*, Fred always looked forward to the few visitors he had.*
Having *suddenly* ***quit*** *his job, he now needed to look for something else.*
Bags ***left*** *unattended will be destroyed.*
Given *the chance, I'd love to live abroad for a year or two.*

Irregular verbs

infinitive	simple past	past participle	German
to **be**	**was / were**	**been**	sein
to **beat**	**beat**	**beaten**	schlagen
to **become**	**became**	**become**	werden
to **begin**	**began**	**begun**	beginnen, anfangen
to **bet**	**bet**	**bet**	wetten
to **bite**	**bit**	**bitten**	beißen
to **blow**	**blew**	**blown**	blasen
to **break**	**broke**	**broken**	brechen
to **bring**	**brought**	**brought**	bringen
to **build**	**built**	**built**	bauen
to **burn**	**burnt / burned**	**burnt / burned**	(ver)brennen
to **buy**	**bought**	**bought**	kaufen
to **catch**	**caught**	**caught**	fangen
to **choose** [uː]	**chose** [əʊ]	**chosen** [əʊ]	auswählen
to **come**	**came**	**come**	kommen
to **cost**	**cost**	**cost**	kosten
to **cut**	**cut**	**cut**	schneiden
to **deal**	**dealt**	**dealt**	handeln
to **dig**	**dug**	**dug**	graben
to **do**	**did**	**done**	machen, tun
to **draw**	**drew**	**drawn**	zeichnen
to **dream**	**dreamt / dreamed**	**dreamt / dreamed**	träumen
to **drink**	**drank**	**drunk**	trinken
to **drive** [aɪ]	**drove** [əʊ]	**driven** [ɪ]	fahren
to **eat**	**ate** [et], [eɪt]	**eaten**	essen
to **fall**	**fell**	**fallen**	fallen, stürzen
to **feed**	**fed**	**fed**	füttern

infinitive	simple past	past participle	German
to **feel**	**felt**	**felt**	(sich) fühlen, spüren
to **fight**	**fought**	**fought**	kämpfen
to **find**	**found**	**found**	finden
to **fly**	**flew**	**flown**	fliegen
to **forget**	**forgot**	**forgotten**	vergessen
to **forgive**	**forgave**	**forgiven**	vergeben
to **freeze**	**froze**	**frozen**	frieren
to **get**	**got**	**got / gotten (AE)**	bekommen, holen
to **give**	**gave**	**given**	geben, schenken
to **go**	**went**	**gone**	gehen, fahren
to **grow** [əʊ]	**grew** [uː]	**grown** [əʊ]	wachsen, anbauen
to **hang**	**hung**	**hung**	hängen
to **have (got)**	**had**	**had**	haben
to **hear** [ɪə]	**heard** [ɜː]	**heard** [ɜː]	hören
to **hide** [haɪd]	**hid** [hɪd]	**hidden** [hɪdn]	(sich) verstecken
to **hit**	**hit**	**hit**	schlagen
to **hold**	**held**	**held**	halten
to **hurt**	**hurt**	**hurt**	wehtun
to **keep**	**kept**	**kept**	(be)halten
to **kneel** [niːl]	**knelt** [nelt]	**knelt** [nelt]	knien
to **know** [nəʊ]	**knew** [njuː]	**known** [nəʊn]	wissen, kennen
to **lead** [liːd]	**led** [led]	**led** [led]	führen
to **learn**	**learnt / learned**	**learnt / learned**	lernen
to **leave**	**left**	**left**	verlassen
to **lend**	**lent**	**lent**	leihen

infinitive	simple past	past participle	German
to **let**	**let**	**let**	lassen
to **lie**	**lay**	**lain**	liegen
to **light**	**lit / lighted**	**lit / lighted**	anzünden, anmachen
to **lose** [uː]	**lost** [ɒ]	**lost** [ɒ]	verlieren
to **make**	**made**	**made**	machen, herstellen
to **mean** [iː]	**meant** [e]	**meant** [e]	bedeuten
to **meet**	**met**	**met**	(sich) treffen, kennen-lernen
to **mow**	**mowed**	**mown / mowed**	mähen
to **pay**	**paid**	**paid**	bezahlen
to **put**	**put**	**put**	stellen
to **quit**	**quit**	**quit**	aufhören
to **read** [iː]	**read** [e]	**read** [e]	lesen
to **rebuild**	**rebuilt**	**rebuilt**	wieder aufbauen
to **rewrite**	**rewrote**	**rewritten**	umschreiben
to **ride**	**rode**	**ridden**	fahren, reiten
to **ring**	**rang**	**rung**	klingeln, anrufen
to **rise**	**rose**	**risen**	ansteigen, (sich) erheben
to **run**	**ran**	**run**	laufen, rennen, leiten
to **say** [eɪ]	**said** [e]	**said** [e]	sagen
to **see**	**saw**	**seen**	sehen
to **sell**	**sold**	**sold**	verkaufen
to **send**	**sent**	**sent**	schicken
to **set**	**set**	**set**	setzen, stellen, legen
to **shake**	**shook**	**shaken**	schütteln
to **shine**	**shone** [ɒ]	**shone** [ɒ]	scheinen

infinitive	simple past	past participle	German
to **shoot**	**shot**	**shot**	schießen
to **show**	**showed**	**shown / showed**	zeigen
to **sing**	**sang**	**sung**	singen
to **sink**	**sank**	**sunk**	sinken
to **sit**	**sat**	**sat**	sitzen
to **sleep**	**slept**	**slept**	schlafen
to **smell**	**smelt / smelled**	**smelt / smelled**	riechen
to **speak** [iː]	**spoke** [əʊ]	**spoken** [əʊ]	sprechen
to **spend**	**spent**	**spent**	verbringen, ausgeben
to **split**	**split**	**split**	sich trennen
to **spoil**	**spoilt**	**spoilt**	verderben
to **spread**	**spread**	**spread**	sich ausbreiten, etw. verteilen
to **stand**	**stood**	**stood**	stehen
to **steal**	**stole**	**stolen**	stehlen
to **stick**	**stuck**	**stuck**	kleben
to **sting**	**stung**	**stung**	stechen
to **swim**	**swam**	**swum**	schwimmen
to **take**	**took**	**taken**	nehmen, dauern
to **teach** [iː]	**taught** [ɔː]	**taught** [ɔː]	unterrichten
to **tell**	**told**	**told**	sagen, erzählen
to **think**	**thought**	**thought**	denken, glauben
to **throw**	**threw**	**thrown**	werfen
to **understand**	**understood**	**understood**	verstehen
to **wake up**	**woke up**	**woken up**	aufwachen
to **wear** [eə]	**wore** [ɔː]	**worn** [ɔː]	tragen
to **win**	**won** [ʌ]	**won**	gewinnen
to **write**	**wrote**	**written**	schreiben

Vocabulary

Here are all the words from the workshops. They are in the same order as in the workshop.

There is the page number and the activity.

A ▢ at the side is for words from the listening text. A ▢ is for words from videos.

Words in **grey** are important for one text or they are culture-specific. You don't have to be able to use them actively and you can always find them in the dictionary list at the end of the book

The phonetic transcription [ ] tells you how you say a word.

The example sentence shows you how we use a word.

= shows words with the same meaning

≠ shows words with the opposite meaning

! shows words with the same meaning in French, Latin or Spanish or it gives other interesting information about the word.

When you work with the *Vocabulary*, cover the German, look at the English word and the example and say the German word. You can also cover the German and the example sentences to practise the English.

page	exercise	Welcome Workshop		
10		**flag** [flæg]	*The flag on top is the national flag.*	Fahne
		de facto [ˌdeɪ ˈfæktəʊ]	*There are many countries where English is an official or de facto official or national language.*	de facto
		approximately [əˈprɒksɪmətli]	*Approximately how many languages are there in the world?*	ungefähr; etwa
		commonly [ˈkɒmənli]	*Which are the two most commonly spoken languages on earth?*	gewöhnlich; häufig
		colonialism [kəˈləʊniəlɪzəm]	*British colonialism helped to spread English around the world.*	Kolonialismus
		worry [ˈwʌri]	*If the problem isn't big, your friends will say 'no worries'.*	Sorge
11		**slideshow** [ˈslaɪdʃəʊ]	*Watch the slideshow and take notes about the topic.*	Diaschau
		to list [lɪst]	*List the factors that helped make English a global language.*	auflisten; listen
		apart [əˈpɑːt]	*The USA and Australia are far apart.*	auseinander
		to decline [dɪˈklaɪn]	*When native cultures declined, many languages disappeared.* **!** *Fr. 'decliner'*	verfallen
		tie [taɪ]	*Many countries have ties to Great Britain.*	Verbindung
		human right [ˌhjuːmən ˈraɪt]	*Bruce is a famous Aboriginal who fights for human rights.*	Menschenrecht
		influence [ˈɪnfluəns]	*Britain's influence around the world was very big.* **!** *Lat. 'influere (influo, influxi, influxum)' = to flow into*	Einfluss
		trade [treɪd]	*Global trade is mostly done in English.*	Handel

page	exercise	Welcome Workshop		
		to come to know [kʌm tə nəʊ], **came, came** [keɪm, keɪm]	*After the two world wars, the world came to know more American products.*	erfahren; kennenlernen
		mass [mæs]	*English became the language of entertainment for the masses.*	Masse
		status ['steɪtəs]	*Its role in popular culture gave English a special status.*	Status
		like [laɪk]	*We went to the movies and, like, we got home really late.*	halt
		matter: no matter [nəʊ 'mætər]	*We wanted to win the game no matter what.*	was auch immer; egal wie
		to come from [kʌm frəm], **came, came** [keɪm, keɪm]	*The internet and most developments in computer technology came from the United States.*	kommen aus
		computer [kəm'pju:tər]	*I turn on the computer and go online.*	Computer
		lexicon ['leksɪkən]	*The lexicon of the digital world is in English.*	Wortschatz
		pants [pænts]	*I like to wear pants with crazy colors.* ! *BE = trousers*	Hose
		horrified ['hɒrɪfaɪd]	*She looked horrified and replied, 'Oh dear, am I late?'*	entsetzt
		swimwear ['swɪmweər]	*You see all sorts of swimwear at the beach.*	Badebekleidung
		doubt [daʊt]	*I have no doubts that he's a nice guy.*	Zweifel

page	exercise	Workshop 1		
12		**mini** ['mɪni]	*Do this mini quiz to see how much you already know about Australia.*	klein; winzig
		proof [pru:f]	*There is a rabbit-proof fence in western Australia.*	...sicher; undurchdringlich
		continent ['kɒntɪnənt]	*Australia is the only country in the world that covers an entire continent.*	Kontinent
		times [taɪmz]	*How many times bigger is Australia than Germany?*	mal
13		**rainbow** ['reɪnbəʊ]	*When the sun shines while it's raining you can see a rainbow.*	Regenbogen
		serpent ['sɜ:pənt]	*= snake*	Schlange
		interior [ɪn'tɪəriər]	*The interior of Australia is huge and very dry.* ! *Lat. 'interior, - oris'*	Binnenland; das Innere
		bush [bʊʃ]	*A large part of Australia is desert or bush.*	Busch; Gebüsch; Buschland
		outback ['aʊtbæk]	*You have to be careful when travelling in the vast and dry Australian Outback.*	Busch; Hinterland
		therefore ['ðeəfɔ:r]	*The training was voluntary and therefore not considered as work.*	daher; deshalb; darum

page	exercise	Workshop 1		
		underneath [ˌʌndəˈniːθ]	*The ancient Greeks believed the world was round, so there must be land underneath in the south to balance the known world.* *≠ above*	unterhalb; darunter
		equator [ɪˈkweɪtər]	*Germany is north of the equator.*	Äquator
		hemisphere [ˈhemɪsfɪər]	*There is a group of five stars that can only be seen in the southern hemisphere.*	Hemisphäre
		globe [gləʊb]	*The globe is an object shaped like a ball with the map of the world on it.* **!** *Fr. 'globe' (m.)* *Sp. 'globo' (m.)*	Globus; Erdkugel
		to balance [ˈbæləns]	*We added more weight in front to balance the load.*	ausgleichen
		platypus [ˈplætɪpəs]	*If you want to see a platypus in the wild, you have to go to Australia.*	Schnabeltier
		koala [kəʊˈɑːlə]	*Many animals such as koala bears, kangaroos and wombats can only be found in Australia.*	Koala
		kookaburra [ˈkʊkəbʌrə]	*The call of the kookaburra, an indigenous bird in Australia, sounds like laughter.*	Kookaburra; Lachender Hans
		creepy [ˈkriːpi]	*And now for a really creepy fact: Australia is home to some of the deadliest animals on the planet.*	gruselig
		deadly [ˈdedli]	*There are deadly snakes in Australia.*	tödlich
		to unite [juˈnaɪt]	*Australia's colonies united to create one nation.*	sich vereinigen
		downhill [ˌdaʊnˈhɪl]	*Skiing downhill can be dangerous when there are too many people.*	bergab
		cross-country skiing [ˌkrɒs ˌkʌntri ˈskiːɪŋ]	*Aussies love winter sports especially downhill skiing, cross-country skiing and snowboarding.*	Langlaufen; Skilanglauf
14	1a	**to exchange** [ɪksˈtʃeɪndʒ]	*We can exchange our email addresses.*	austauschen; wechseln
		puzzled [ˈpʌzld]	*Jason and Ricky exchanged puzzled looks.*	verblüfft; verwirrt
		silence [ˈsaɪləns]	*There was silence, then the whole team jumped and cheered.* **!** *Lat. 'silentium, -i' (n.)*	Schweigen; Ruhe
		to echo [ˈekəʊ]	*The noise echoed across the playing field and around the school campus.*	nachhallen; nachklingen
	1b	**dilemma** [dɪˈlemə]	*Jason's mum understands his dilemma and wants to find a solution.*	Dilemma
	2	**nut** [nʌt]	*There is a lot of protein in nuts.*	Nuss; *hier*: Verrückte(r)
		alright [ɔːlˈraɪt]	*Is everything alright at home?*	in Ordnung

page	exercise	Workshop 1		
		supportive [səˈpɔːtɪv]	*My mother has always been supportive and helped me.*	unterstützend
		uninterested [ʌnˈɪntrəstɪd]	*He was uninterested in books and never read.*	desinteressiert
	3	**part-time** [ˌpɑːt ˈtaɪm]	*Women with children are more likely than men to work part-time.*	nebenberuflich; teilzeitlich
		to emphasize [ˈemfəsaɪz]	*Emphasize the results of the survey when you write about it.*	betonen
15	1a	**to sigh** [saɪ]	*Jason sighed, then took out the garbage as his mother had asked.*	seufzen
	3b	**deli** [ˈdeli]	*You can buy sandwiches and ready-made foods at a deli.*	Feinkostladen
	4b	**introductory** [ˌɪntrəˈdʌktəri]	*We will have an introductory video call with the other team next week.*	Anfangs...; Einführungs...
		strategy [ˈstrætədʒi]	*My company's strategy includes a lot of advertising.* ! *Fr. 'stratégie' (f.)*	Strategie
	5	**godmother** [ˈgɒdmʌðər]	*My mother's best friend is my godmother.*	Patentante
		fanatic [fəˈnætɪk]	*I like the game, but I'm not a fanatic.* ! *Lat. 'fanaticus, -a, -um'*	Fanatiker(in), fanatisch
	6	**sporting** [ˈspɔːtɪŋ]	*They have sporting events at my school every season.*	sportlich; Sport...
		netball [ˈnetbɔːl]	*Two of the biggest sports in Australia are netball and cricket.*	Netzball
16	1a	**informal** [ɪnˈfɔːml]	*Australian English has many informal words and phrases.*	informell
	1b	**to slip on** [slɪp ˈɒn]	*When you sit in the sun at the beach, slip on a shirt to protect your skin from the sun.*	rasch anziehen
		to slop on [slɒp ˈɒn]	*Slop on some sunscreen or you'll get a sunburn.*	schwappen
		to slap on [slæp ˈɒn]	*When you go to the beach, be sure to slap on a hat.*	draufklatschen
		to seek [siːk]	*If the heat becomes too much for you, seek shade immediately.*	suchen
		to slide on [slaɪd ˈɒn]	*Slide on some sunnies to protect your eyes from the sun.*	aufschieben
		shade [ʃeɪd]	*In the afternoons we sit in the shade of the tree in the garden.*	Schatten
	2	**standard** [ˈstændəd]	*She speaks standard English, not a dialect.*	standardmäßig; normal
		heap [hiːp]	*We've got heaps to eat.*	Haufen
17		**to establish** [ɪˈstæblɪʃ]	*They named the new land New Holland, but they didn't establish a settlement.*	gründen

page	exercise	Workshop 1		
		convict ['kənvɪkt]	*Convicts and their families were brought from britain to settle Australia.*	Verurteilte(r)
		uncommon [ʌn'kɒmən]	*Fighting between the indigenous Aborigines and the settlers wasn't uncommon.*	ungewöhnlich; selten
		smallpox ['smɔːlpɒks]	*The biggest threat to the Aborigine were diseases like smallpox, which killed tens of thousands.*	Pocken
		gold rush ['gəʊld rʌʃ]	*A gold rush started with thousands of people arriving from different countries hoping to become rich.*	Goldrausch
		to double ['dʌbl]	*In just ten years the population of Australia doubled.* ❗ *Fr. 'doubler'*	sich verdoppeln
19				

Aussie slang

ace [eɪs]	klasse	**nana** ['nænə]	Banane
arvo ['ɑːvəʊ]	Nachmittag	**pom** [pɒm]	Brite / Britin
bogey ['bəʊgi]	Schwimmen	**prezzie** ['prezi]	Geschenk
brekkie ['breki]	Frühstück	**roo** [ruː]	Känguru
chockers ['tʃɒkərz]	voll	**sunnies** ['sʌniz]	Sonnenbrille
footy ['fʊti]	Fußball	**sickie** ['sɪki]	Krankheitstag
g'day [gə'deɪ]	guten Tag	**tog** [tɒg]	Sachen; Zeug
lappy ['læpi]	Laptop	**tucker** ['tʌkə]	Essen
mozzie ['mɒzi]	Mücke		

page	exercise	word	example	translation
	3a	**vibrant** ['vaɪbrənt]	*It's a really vibrant city where lots of young people live.*	dynamisch; lebhaft
		switch [swɪtʃ]	*It won't be easy to make the switch from UK to Australia.*	Umstellung; Umstieg
		drive [draɪv]	*It's an hour's drive from the city to the beach.*	Fahrt
		doorstep ['dɔːstep]	*If something is on your doorstep, it's very near.*	Türschwelle
		undecided [ˌʌndɪ'saɪdɪd]	*I'm pretty much undecided about whether I want to move or not.*	unentschieden; unentschlossen
20	1a	**sleep** [sliːp]	*I'm tired, as I didn't have much sleep.*	Schlaf
		to admit [əd'mɪt]	*Keira admitted that she had forgotten my birthday.* ❗ *Fr. 'admettre'* *Sp. 'admitir'*	zugeben
	2	**workplace** ['wɜːkpleɪs]	*At the barbecue, Mr Turner invited Mr Smith to visit him at his workplace.*	Arbeitsplatz
		electrician [ɪˌlek'trɪʃn]	*I am an electrician and work in a factory.*	Elektriker(in)
21	4a	**deal** [diːl]	*Moving to a new country is a big deal.*	Geschäft; *hier*: Angelegenheit
		to settle in ['setl ɪn]	*They moved to a new city but settled in really quickly.*	sich eingewöhnen

page	exercise	Workshop 1		
		scorching ['skɔ:tʃɪŋ]	*Most people think of Australia as scorching hot.*	glühend
		exaggerated [ɪg'zædʒəreɪtɪd]	*The number of deadly animals in Australia is often exaggerated.*	übertrieben
		species ['spi:ʃi:z]	*There are only two species of deadly spiders in Australia and nobody has died from a bite since 1979.* **!** *Lat. 'species, -ei' = view, look*	Spezies; Art
		stingray ['stɪŋreɪ]	*Stingrays are often seen in the Great Barrier Reef.*	Stachelrochen
		on average [ɒn 'ævərɪdʒ]	*Stingrays have only ever killed two people and on average there is only one shark attack per year.*	im Durchschnitt
		cup [kʌp]	*Melbourne hosts the Australian tennis open as well as one of the best known horse races in the world – the Melbourne Cup.*	Meisterschaft
		volleyball ['vɒlibɔ:l]	*There are a lot of beach sports, from beach volleyball to surfing.*	Volleyball
		paradise ['pærədaɪs]	*Australia is paradise for any sports lover.* **!** *Fr. 'paradis' (m.)* *Sp. 'paraíso' (m.)*	Paradies
22	1a	**penal** ['pi:nl]	*Australia was set up as a penal colony.*	strafrechtlich
23	3a	**didgeridoo** [ˌdɪdʒəri'du:]	*A didgeridoo is a large bamboo or wooden trumpet of the Australian aborigines.*	Didgeridoo
24	S2	**hunter-gatherer** [ˌhʌntə 'gæðərər]	*Australia's first peoples were hunter-gatherers who moved from place to place following the seasons.*	Jäger und Sammler
		semi... ['semi]	*When you put 'semi' before a word it means a part of something.*	Teil...
		systematically [ˌsɪstə'mætɪkli]	*Semi-nomadic people systematically move from place to place following the seasons.*	systematisch
		distinct [dɪ'stɪŋkt]	*Each native group has its own distinct history and culture.* **!** *Lat. 'distinctus, -a, -um'*	eindeutig; eigenständig
		agrarian [ə'greəriən]	*The hunter-gatherers didn't develop an agrarian, or farming, society.*	landwirtschaftlich
		predictable [prɪ'dɪktəbl]	*The future is not predictable.*	vorhersehbar
		colonization [ˌkɒlənaɪ'zeɪʃn]	*How did colonization impact these communities?*	Kolonialisierung
		immediate [ɪ'mi:diət]	*The most immediate problem was providing housing and fresh water.*	unmittelbar; umgehend
		epidemic [ˌepɪ'demɪk]	*An epidemic is a disease that spreads quickly and affects many individuals at the same time.*	epidemisch

page	exercise	Workshop 1		
		influenza [ˌɪnflu'enzə]	*There was an influenza epidemic in 1918.*	Grippe; Influenza
		measles ['mi:zlz]	*Measles infections have been increasing in the world.*	Masern
		resistance [rɪ'zɪstəns]	*These diseases killed many indigenous people because they had no resistance to them.* ❗ *Fr. 'résistance' (f.)*	Widerstand; *hier*: Resistenz
		random ['rændəm]	*They died in random killings that were motivated by racism.*	zufällig; willkürlich
		massacre ['mæsəkər]	*Many Aborigine died in random killings or organized massacres.*	Massaker
		to drive [draɪv], **drove, driven** [drəʊv, drivn]	*They drove people off the land.*	treiben
		cliff [klɪf]	*Cliffs are high areas of rock with a steep side.*	Klippe; Felsen
		drastic ['dræstɪk]	*Air traffic caused a drastic rise in pollution.*	drastisch; extrem
		decline [dɪ'klaɪn]	*Pollution can cause a decline in the insect population.*	Rückgang
	S3a	**printed** [prɪnt]	*Do you use a printed dictionary or an online dictionary?*	gedruckt
		monolingual [ˌmɒnə'lɪŋgwəl]	*A monolingual dictionary gives definitions but no translations.*	einsprachig
25	S1	**arid** ['ærɪd]	*Although much of Australia's interior is arid desert, it isn't empty of life.*	dürr; trocken
		to camp out [kæmp aʊt]	*If you camp out in the Outback, you'll hear the howls of dingoes, or wild dogs.*	zelten
		howl [haʊl]	*The howls of wild dogs can be heard in the Outback.*	Geheul
		dingo ['dɪŋgəʊ]	*The dingo is a kind of wild dog mainly living in Australia.*	Dingo
		to loath [ləʊð]	*= hate* *≠ love*	hassen; verabscheuen
		in spite of [ɪn spaɪt əv]	*We had a nice hike in spite of the rain!*	trotz
		to roam [rəʊm]	*You can see dingoes roam around wild in Australia.*	herumschweifen; durchschweifen
		pest [pest]	*Animals that are not indigenous can become a pest when they have no enemies.*	Plage; Schädling
		ecological [ˌi:kə'lɒdʒɪkl]	*Non-native species are causing ecological damage to Australia.* ❗ *Lat. 'oecologicus, -a, -um'* *Fr. 'écologique'*	ökologisch
		herd [hɜ:d]	*The land is protected and a herd of wild horses live there.*	Herde
		feral ['ferəl]	*You'll come across the world's largest herd of feral camels.*	wild

page	exercise	Workshop 1		
		camel ['kæml]	*In desert counties camels are used to ride on.* **!** *Lat. 'camelus, -i' (m./f.)*	Kamel
		advent ['ædvent]	*With the advent of engines, animals were no longer needed to do work.*	Beginn; Einführung
		invasive [ɪn'veɪsɪv]	*Other invasive species include foxes and rabbits, brought from Europe in the 19th century for sport hunting.*	invasiv
		predator ['predətər]	*When there aren't any predators, a species can grow uncontrollably.*	Raubtier; Räuber
		to explode [ɪk'spləʊd]	*They had few predators, so their populations exploded.* **!** *Fr. 'exploser'*	explodieren
		measure ['meʒə]	*We have to take measures to save the environment.*	Maßnahme
	S2	**aim** [eɪm]	*Our aim is to raise awareness about social issues.*	Ziel; Absicht
	S4	**prolonged** [prə'lɒŋd]	*A prolonged drought is creating multiple ecological problems.*	anhaltend; verlängert
		drought [draʊt]	*When it doesn't rain for a long time there is a danger of draught.*	Dürre
		to demolish [dɪ'mɒlɪʃ]	*Before building the highway they had to demolish several houses.*	abreißen
		to foul [faʊl]	*The camels foul water holes and make the water undrinkable.*	verschmutzen; verseuchen
		watering hole ['wɔ:tərɪŋ həʊl]	*Watering holes are important to the people who live in the Outback.*	Wasserstelle
		to pollute [pə'lu:t]	*Industry is polluting water all around the world.*	verschmutzen; verseuchen
		undrinkable [ʌn'drɪŋkəbl]	*The water from the river is dirty and undrinkable.*	untrinkbar
		to defend [dɪ'fend]	*Be ready to defend yourself walking home alone at night.* **!** *Lat. 'defendere (defendo, defendi, defensum)'*	verteidigen
		to cull [kʌl]	*When there is a disease, animals are often culled to stop the spreading.*	keulen; selektiv schlachten
		to rot ['rəʊtə]	*After they are culled, thousands of dead animals are left to rot.*	verfaulen
		cull [kʌl]	*The culls of animals are controversial.*	Schlachten; Keulen
26	1a	**creation** [kri'eɪʃn]	*Do you know the Aboriginal people creation legend?*	Schöpfung
		dreamtime ['dri:mtaɪm]	*Aboriginal myths, known as dreamtime stories, are told by the indigenous people of Australia.*	Traumzeit
		folklore ['fəʊklɔ:r]	*The sacred sites are extremely important in Aboriginal tradition and folklore.*	Folklore

page	exercise	Workshop 1		
		formation [fɔ:'meɪʃn]	*Uluru is a large rock formation located close to the exact centre of Australia.*	Formation
		to resume [rɪ'zju:m]	*The sacred rock resumed its original name in 1985 when the land was given back to the local people.*	übernehmen; wieder annehmen
		deed [di:d]	*A title deed proves that you are the owner of a property.*	Urkunde
		bitterly ['bɪtəli]	*She cried bitterly when she hurt herself.*	bitterlich
		to insult ['ɪnsʌlt]	*It is easy to be insulted by things people write online.*	beleidigen; verletzen
		saddened ['sædnd]	*I was deeply saddened when I heard he was dead.*	betrübt
		bloodshed ['blʌdʃed]	*When a lot of people are killed, we call it bloodshed.*	Blutvergießen
		reef [ri:f]	*The reef is home to many species of fish and a tourist attraction.*	Riff
		marine [mə'ri:n]	*The Great Barrier Reef is home to a huge variety of marine species.*	marin; Meeres...
		creature ['kri:tʃər]	*Divers can see marine creatures, including dolphins and sharks.* ! *Lat. 'creare (creo, creavi, creatum)' = create*	Geschöpf; Lebewesen
		seabird ['si:bɜ:d]	*Many seabirds live near the reef.*	Seevogel
		clan [klæn]	*Their clan has many legends about their people.*	Stamm
		creator [kri'eɪtər]	*In many religions God is the creator of the world.*	Schöpfer(in); Erschaffer(in)
		to spear [spɪər]	*The brave boy speared the lion and saved his sister.*	aufspießen
		lava ['lɑ:və]	*The Great Barrier Reef was formed from cooled lava.*	Lava
		to cool [ku:l]	*When the hot lava cooled, it formed the Great Barrier Reef.*	abkühlen
27	3a	**vague** [veɪg]	*Avoid using vague subjects like 'someone', 'people' and 'they' in your description.*	unbestimmt; vage
		agent ['eɪdʒənt]	*The focus of the sentence is on the action, not the agent.*	Mittel
	3b	**busload** ['bʌsləʊd]	*Big tour companies bring busloads of tourists every day.*	Busladung
		ban [bæn]	*There is a ban on rock climbing at the sacred site.*	Verbot; Sperre
		unacceptable [ˌʌnək'septəbl]	*It was totally unacceptable to allow tourists to climb in the sacred site.*	inakzeptabel
		alternative [ɔ:l'tɜ:nətɪv]	*They have developed alternative activities for tourists since the ban on climbing the mountain.*	alternativ

page	exercise	Workshop 1		
		base [beɪs]	*We will meet at the base of the mountain after the hike.* ❗ *Fr. 'base'* *Sp. 'base'*	Fuß; Basis
		income ['ɪnkʌm]	*Tourism is an important source of income for many countries.*	Einkommen
	4a	**trailer** ['treɪlər]	*I saw a trailer advertising a new film that is set in the Australian outback.*	Trailer
	4b	**sibling** ['sɪblɪŋ]	*The film tells the story of two siblings, a sister and brother.*	Geschwister(kind); Bruder; Schwester
		civilized ['sɪvəlaɪz]	*We live in a civilized society.* ❗ *Lat. 'civis, -is' (m./f.) = citizen*	zivilisiert; kultiviert
28	2a	**reality** [ri'æləti]	*The reality of climate change can really be felt in Australia.*	Realität
		stunning ['stʌnɪŋ]	*The views from the top of the mountain are stunning and the air is fresh.*	toll; atemberaubend
		wombat ['wɒmbæt]	*A wombat looks like a little bear.*	Wombat
		degree [dɪ'gri:]	*In January 2018, temperatures in Sydney soared to over 47 degrees.*	Grad
		heatwave ['hi:tweɪv]	*Climate change is causing more and longer heatwaves.*	Hitzewelle
		bushfire ['bʊʃfaɪər]	*Drought creates the perfect conditions for bushfire.*	Buschfeuer
		frequent ['fri:kwənt]	*It's good for children to take frequent breaks during the school day.*	häufig
		livestock ['laɪvstɒk]	*The climate crisis is making it more and more difficult for farmers to grow food and raise livestock.*	Vieh; Viehbestand
		populated ['pɒpjuleɪtɪd]	*Queensland is one of Australia's most populated states.*	bevölkert; besiedelt
		security [sɪ'kjʊərəti]	*Climate change is going to make food security a major issue in the future.* ❗ *Fr. 'securité' (f.)*	Sicherheit
		to endanger [ɪn'deɪndʒər]	*Climate change endangers many species.*	gefährden
		acidic [ə'sɪdɪk]	*Our oceans are becoming warmer and more acidic.*	sauer
		polyp ['pɒlɪp]	*Polyps are tiny animals.*	Polyp
		due to [dju: tə]	*Coral are dying due to the rise in sea temperature.*	wegen
	3a	**demonstration** [ˌdemən'streɪʃn]	*They are very concerned about climate change, so they're taking part in a demonstration.*	Demonstration
		mob [mɒb]	*We call ourselves a mob movement because we organize lots of activities together to raise awareness.*	Meute
	3b	**faraway** ['fa:rəweɪ]	*This isn't a faraway problem.*	fern

page	exercise	Workshop 1		
		exporter [ek'spɔ:tər]	*Australia is the world's biggest exporter of coal and gas.*	Exporteur(in)
		to dig [dɪɡ]**, dug, dug** [dʌɡ, dʌɡ]	*Companies want to dig more massive coal mines in Queensland.*	graben
		to frack [fræk]	*When you frack, you open cracks in the ground to get out oil or gas.*	fracken
		homeland ['həʊmlænd]	*Aboriginal people are being moved off their homelands.*	Heimat
		wheat [wi:t]	*Wheat is a plant we use for making flour for bread.*	Weizen
		bushland ['bʊʃlænd]	*People need to stop destroying forest and bushland.*	Buschland
		tipping point ['tɪpɪŋ pɔɪnt]	*We've only got a few years before we reach the final tipping point in climate change.*	Kipppunkt; Trendwende
29	1	**to structure** ['strʌktʃə]	*How buildings are structured determines whether they can survive an earthquake.*	strukturieren; aufbauen
		conversational [ˌkɒnvə'seɪʃənl]	*I think about conversational topics before going on job interviews.*	Gesprächs...
		instructive [ɪn'strʌktɪv]	*The style of the video is instructive.*	instruktiv; lehrreich
	2a	**to contribute (to)** [kən'trɪbju:t]	*Eleni is contributing to a website where teenagers post blogs about their home cities.*	mitarbeiten (an); beitragen (zu)
		magnificent [mæɡ'nɪfɪsnt]	*I live in a magnificent city, but I can get bored of it.* **!** *Lat. 'magnificus, -a, -um'* *Fr. 'magnifique'*	großartig; herrlich
		virtual ['vɜ:tʃuəl]	*Let me take you on a virtual tour and show you the places I truly love.*	virtuell
		laneway [leɪnweɪ]	*There are many small 'laneways' in the city centre.*	Sträßchen
		busker ['bʌskər]	*Do you like cool cafés, amazing street art and buskers playing great music?*	Straßenmusiker(in)
		yummy ['jʌmi]	*This is where you can get the most yummy street food in the city.*	lecker
		to ride [raɪd]**, rode, ridden** [rəʊd, 'rɪdn]	*Getting around is really easy, too; you can ride the trams for free.*	fahren
		to soak up [səʊk ʌp]	*On my days off, I go to the beach to soak up the sun and read.*	aufnehmen; hier: (Sonne) tanken
		sandy ['sændi]	*I don't like lying around on a sandy beach in the sun.*	sandig
		roller skate ['rəʊlə skeɪt]	*When I was a kid, there were rinks where you could go roller skating.*	Rollschuh
		promenade [ˌprɒmə'nɑ:d]	*There are beautiful houses on the promenade close to the sea.* **!** *Fr. 'promenade' (f.)*	Promenade
		to gaze [ɡeɪz]	*You can relax on the beach and gaze at the city skyline.*	blicken

page	exercise	Workshop 1		
		skydiver ['skaɪdaɪvər]	*If you are lucky, you might see skydivers landing on the shore.*	Fallschirmspringer(in)
		unforgettable [ˌʌnfə'getəbl]	*I still remember the unforgettable story she told me.*	unvergesslich
		treat [tri:t]	*It's an unforgettable experience and a wonderful birthday treat.*	Genuss; Vergnügen
		pier [pɪər]	*To find the sanctuary, just follow the crowd to the end of the pier.*	Kai
		sanctuary ['sæŋktʃuəri]	*The bird sanctuary is home to thousands of migrating birds.*	Schutzgebiet
	TIP	**comparison** [kəm'pærɪsn]	*Comparisons show that children have better grades when they are happy.*	Vergleich
30	1a	**sweetheart** ['swi:thɑ:t]	*My sweetheart sent me flowers!*	Liebste(r); Liebes
		challenge ['tʃælɪndʒ]	*Applying for work is a challenge if you never finished school*	Herausforderung
		guy [gaɪ]	*He's a good guy.*	Kerl; Typ
		weed [wi:d]	*I'm taking out all these weeds around the tomatoes.*	Unkraut
		veggie ['vedʒi]	*You can show how much you know about animals and organic veggies.*	Gemüse
		drop kick ['drɒp kɪk]	*We worked on our drop kicks at rugby practice.*	Dropkick
	1b	**homesickness** ['həʊmsɪknəs]	*I have homesickness whenever I'm away from home too long.*	Heimweh
	CC	**relation** [rɪ'leɪʃn]	*Talk about the impact that rugby has had on race relations.*	Beziehung; Verhältnis
		rivalry ['raɪvlri]	*They also have a huge sporting rivalry – mainly in cricket, rugby and netball.*	Konkurrenz
		respect [rɪ'spekt]	*Respect and trust are important for every relationship.* **!** *Lat. 'respectare (respecto, respectavi, respectatum)' = to look back, to turn around*	Respekt
31	1a	**chairlift** ['tʃeəlɪft]	*You can take a chairlift up to the top of the mountain.*	Sessellift
		to race [reɪs]	*The movie was so exciting, my heart was racing.*	rasen
		dance [dɑ:ns]	*A student group in your school is organizing a dance.*	Tanz
		trilogy ['trɪlədʒi]	*A trilogy consists of three parts.*	Trilogie
		to film [fɪlm]	*The 'Lord of the Rings' trilogy was filmed here.*	drehen; filmen
		to tip over [tɪp 'əʊvə]	*We nearly tipped over in the canoe and lost the camera in the water.*	umkippen
	4a	**to invert** [ɪn'vɜ:t]	*Sometimes you can invert the subject and verb in a sentence to form a question.*	umkehren; umstellen

page	exercise	Workshop 1		
	5	**to tour** [tʊə]	*We were in New Zealand for four weeks and toured most of the country.*	besuchen; besichtigen
		individually [ˌɪndɪˈvɪdʒuəli]	*Solve the problem individually.* *= on your own* *≠ in groups*	einzeln
32	1	**attractive** [əˈtræktɪv]	*Which places in New Zealand are most interesting or attractive to you?* **!** *Fr. 'attractif'*	reizvoll
	2a	**to skim** [skɪm]	*Skim the article and answer the questions below.*	überfliegen
		distinctive [dɪˈstɪŋktɪv]	*What makes New Zealand's North Island and South Island distinctive?*	unverwechselbar; ausgeprägt
		segment [ˈsegmənt]	*The six weekly segments each focus on a different game.*	Segment; Abschnitt
		significance [sɪɡˈnɪfɪkəns]	*The town's natural wonders are of great significance.* **!** *Lat. 'significare (significo, significavi, significatus)'*	Bedeutung; Wichtigkeit
		regional [ˈriːdʒənl]	*The article highlights the city's regional importance and the challenges it has faced.*	regional
		peninsula [pəˈnɪnsjələ]	*Many rare and endangered water birds live on the peninsula.*	Halbinsel
		biological [ˌbaɪəˈlɒdʒɪkl]	*The biological diversity of Australia is a national treasure.*	biologisch
	2c	**to collect** [kəˈlekt]	*We collect and recycle old plastic bags.*	sammeln; einsammeln
		to highlight [ˈhaɪlaɪt]	*Include at least four places of interest and highlight one or two aspects of each place.*	betonen
	3a	**studio** [ˈstjuːdiəʊ]	*Documentary filmmaker Shaun Reed is here in the studio to talk about his new film.*	Studio
		phenomenon [fəˈnɒmɪnən]	*The new documentary film 'Beyond the Black,' looks at the rugby phenomenon in our country.*	Phänomen
		intense [ɪnˈtens]	*The film shows the intense rivalry between two schools.*	stark; ernsthaft
		college [ˈkɒlɪdʒ]	*My mom left New Zealand as soon as she finished college and spent a lot of time travelling before coming back.*	Universität; Hochschule
		talented [ˈtæləntɪd]	*There are so many strong and talented players.*	begabt; talentiert
		to adopt [əˈdɒpt]	*The team adopted the Maori war dance as a ritual before games.*	annehmen
		pride [praɪd]	*The All Blacks are a source of pride for the whole nation – for Maori and non-Maori.*	Stolz

page	exercise	Workshop 1		
33	4a	**ethnic** ['eθnɪk]	*The Maori are New Zealands' second-largest ethnic group.* ! *Fr. 'ethnique'*	ethnisch
		descent [dɪ'sent]	*Two third-generation children of immigrant descent will share their stories.*	Abstammung
		acceptance [ək'septəns]	*Today the acceptance of Maori culture is felt everywhere in New Zealand.*	Akzeptanz
		anthem ['ænθəm]	*The New Zealand national anthem is always sung first in the Maori language.*	Nationalhymne; Hymne
		variation [ˌveəri'eɪʃn]	*There are different variations of this traditional dance.*	Variante; Variation
		unofficial [ˌʌnə'fɪʃl]	*It's an unofficial event, you don't have to dress up.* ≠ *official*	inoffiziell
	5b	**previous** ['pri:viəs]	*Why are young people more likely to change jobs than previous generations?* ≠ *following*	früher
34	1	**to relate to** [rɪ'leɪt tə]	*Which paragraph does each picture on page 35 relate to?*	mit etw. in Zusammenhang stehen; sich auf etw. beziehen
		increased [ɪn'kri:st]	*Increased sea levels means that islands will disappear.* ≠ *decreased*	erhöht
		devastating ['devəsteɪtɪŋ]	*This area has experienced devastating floods.* = *enormous*	verheerend
		mudslide ['mʌdslaɪd]	*The mountain sides were wet and the rain caused mudslides.*	Schlammlawine
		to contaminate [kən'tæmɪneɪt]	*The rain caused mudslides and they contaminated the water.* ! *Lat. 'contaminare (contamino, contaminavi, contaminatus)' Fr. 'contaminer'*	verunreinigen; kontaminieren
		reservoir ['rezəvwɑ:r]	*The water reservoirs keep our drinking water.*	Reservoir; Behälter
		shortage ['ʃɔ:tɪdʒ]	*You can expect to have water shortages during a drought.*	Mangel
		anxiety [æŋ'zaɪəti]	*Anxiety about climate change is growing in many countries.*	Sorge; Ängstlichkeit
		malaria [mə'leəriə]	*Malaria is an illness caused by mosquito bites.*	Malaria
		to increase [ɪn'kri:s]	*Climate change increases extreme weather conditions.*	erhöhen
		flooding ['flʌdɪŋ]	*Global warming is causing flooding in some areas of the world.*	Fluten; Flut

page	exercise	Workshop 1		
		cyclone ['saɪkləʊn]	*A cyclone is a very bad tropical storm.*	Zyklon
		to bear [beər]	*People and animals will bear the consequences of climate change.*	ertragen
		habitat ['hæbɪtæt]	*The habitats of wild animals are in danger.*	Habitat
		avocado [ˌævə'kɑ:dəʊ]	*If you're like me, you enjoy avocado on toast.*	Avocado
35	2	**perspective** [pə'spektɪv]	*You can look at these issues from different perspectives.* ! *Lat. 'spectare (specto, spectavi, spectatus)' = to see*	Sichtweise; Perspektive
	3	**poisonous** ['pɔɪzənəs]	*Wearing boots provides protection against bites from poisonous snakes.*	giftig
		unpleasant [ʌn'pleznt]	*Getting stung by the spider was a really unpleasant experience.*	unangenehm
36	S1	**coastline** ['kəʊstlaɪn]	*We walked for hours along the coastline and watched sea birds.*	Küstenlinie; Küste
		vote [vəʊt]	*New Zealand was the first country to give women the vote in 1893.*	Wahlstimme; Stimme; Wahlrecht
	S2a	**purpose** ['pɜ:pəs]	*What is the purpose of the underlined clauses in these sentences?*	Zweck
	S2b	**logical** ['lɒdʒɪkl]	*Organize the notes into a logical sequence of paragraphs.*	logisch; folgerichtig
	TIP	**to suit** [su:t]	*Choose the right writing style to suit your topic and audience.*	passen; sich eignen (für)
		chatty ['tʃæti]	*When I talk to customers I use a chatty personal style of speaking.*	gesprächig
		to engage [ɪn'geɪdʒ]	*Include interesting facts in your writing to engage the reader.*	fesseln; engagieren
37	S1	**requirement** [rɪ'kwaɪəmənt]	*Think about the requirements of the school exchange programme.*	Voraussetzung
	TIP	**to address** [ə'dres]	*Address your reader directly.*	ansprechen
		persuasive [pə'sweɪsɪv]	*Provide details to make your article more interesting and persuasive.*	überzeugend
38	1	**to fear** [fɪər]	*We know they are good but we don't fear hem.*	befürchten
	2a	**horizon** [hə'raɪzn]	*There on the horizon is a beautiful multi-coloured rainbow.* ! *Fr. 'horizon' (m.)*	Horizont
		waterhole ['wɔ:təhəʊl]	*Lakes are big waterholes.*	Wasserloch
	2b	**to crawl** [krɔ:l]	*= to move slowly* *≠ to race*	krabbeln; kriechen
		rainstorm ['reɪnstɔ:m]	*There was a rainstorm when we walked home and we got really wet.*	Regenschauer; Gewitter
39	3	**to wipe out** ['waɪp aʊt]	*In the last ten years around 50% of the animals have been wiped out.*	vernichten
		deforestation [ˌdi:ˌfɒrɪ'steɪʃn]	*Deforestation is leading to climate change.*	Abholzung

page	exercise	Workshop 1		
		oxygen ['ɒksɪdʒən]	*Trees capture carbon dioxide and release oxygen.* *! Fr. 'oxygène' (m.) Sp. 'oxígeno' (m.)*	Sauerstoff
	4	**gateway** ['geɪtweɪ]	*Where is the gateway for the Great barrier Reef?* *= entrance*	Zugang; Gateway
		exploration [ˌeksplə'reɪʃn]	*The Antarctic exploration starts from the island.*	Exploration; Erforschung
42	2	**march** [mɑːtʃ]	*Information about the march is posted on different social media platforms.*	Marsch
43	3	**equality** [i'kwɒləti]	*He spent the rest of his life trying to get equality for Aboriginal people in Australia.*	Gleichberechtigung
		act [ækt]	*The Act said the land belonged to the Aborigine.*	Gesetz; Verordnung
	4	**sail** [seɪl]	*Auckland is known as 'the city of sails' because there are so many yachts in the harbour.*	Segel
		yacht [jɒt]	*The harbour is full of luxurious yachts.*	Jacht; Yacht

page	exercise	Workshop 2		
50		**shoplifting** ['ʃɒplɪftɪŋ]	*Shoplifting is a crime.*	Ladendiebstahl
		to progress ['prəʊgres]	*It started with shoplifting, but then progressed to more serious crimes.*	fortschreiten
		to fall in love [fɔːl ɪn lʌv], **fell, fell** [fel, fel]	*You can't choose who to fall in love with.*	sich verlieben
		confidence ['kɒnfɪdəns]	*People can lose confidence when they are bullied.*	Selbstvertrauen
		self-belief [ˌselfbɪ'liːf]	*Self-belief is as important as confidence.*	Selbstwertgefühl; Selbstbewusstsein
		anxious ['æŋkʃəs]	*I'm anxious all the time and I know that isn't healthy for me.*	besorgt; ängstlich
		gay [geɪ]	*Being gay and black means I face a lot of problems.*	schwul; früher: fröhlich
		tolerance ['tɒlərəns]	*Society shows more tolerance to people who are different.*	Toleranz
		obsession [əb'seʃn]	*It started off just as a way of getting fit, but then it became an obsession.*	Obsession; Besessenheit
		steroid ['sterɔɪd]	*Steer clear of common fitness supplements, including steroids.*	Steroid
		songwriter ['sɒŋraɪtər]	*Taylor Swift is a US singer-songwriter.*	Texter(in); Liederkomponist(in)
51		**lesbian** ['lezbiən]	*Lesbians continue to fight for basic rights, including the right to marry.*	Lesbe

page	exercise	Workshop 2		
		bisexual [ˌbaɪ'sekʃuəl]	*Most Canadian citizens said that they would be comfortable if a neighbour were gay, lesbian or bisexual.*	bisexuell
		trans [trænz]		trans...
		LGBT (lesbian, gay, bisexual, transgender)	*LGBT is an abbreviation used when referring to lesbian, gay, bisexual and transgender people.*	LGBT
		gifted ['gɪftɪd]	*Every child is gifted in his or her way.*	begabt
		to **unwrap** [ʌn'ræp]	*They just unwrap their packages all at once.*	auspacken
		to **breed** [bri:d] [bred, bred]	*Some say new types of technology breeds new kinds of crime.*	brüten; züchten
		consultant [kən'sʌltənt]	*Frank is a technology security consultant.*	Berater(in)
52	1a	**increasingly** [ɪn'kri:sɪŋli]	*Families are becoming increasingly diverse.* *= more and more* *≠ less*	zunehmend
		blended ['blendɪd]	*There are five kids and three parents in my blended family.*	gemischt
		sex [seks]	*Same-sex marriage has led to even more family diversity.*	Geschlecht; Sex
		to **legalize** ['li:gəlaɪz]	*Same-sex marriage was legalized in Canada in 2005.*	legalisieren
		respondent [rɪ'spɒndənt]	*How many respondents were there in the census?*	Befragte(r)
		unmarried [ˌʌn'mærid]	*Many unmarried couples live together and have children.*	unverheiratet
		uptight [ˌʌp'taɪt]	*You should relax and not be so uptight.* *≠ easy-going*	verklemmt
53	2a	**incomplete** [ˌɪnkəm'pli:t]	*Without the subject the sentence would be incomplete.*	unvollständig
	3a	**full-time** [ˌfʊl 'taɪm]	*My mother has a full-time job, but she works from home.*	ganztags
		to **experience** [ɪk'spɪəriəns]	*Talk to your parents if you experience cyberbullying.*	erfahren; erleben
	3b	**extended** [ɪk'stendɪd]	*There are cousins, aunts and uncles in the extended family.*	erweitert
		arrangement [ə'reɪndʒmənt]	*When you have made an arrangement, you should stick to it.*	Vereinbarung
		cooperation [kəʊˌɒpə'reɪʃn]	*Cooperation is important to solving big problems.*	Zusammenarbeit
		to **struggle** ['strʌgl]	*Grandparents might struggle to keep up with new technologies.*	sich anstrengen; sich bemühen
	4	to **descend (from)** [dɪ'send]	*His family are directly descended from African slaves.*	abstammen (von)

page	exercise	Workshop 2		
		to immigrate ['ɪmɪgreɪt]	*Her parents wanted to give their daughter a better life than they had, so they immigrated to New Zealand.*	einwandern
		to step up [step ʌp]	*After my father died, my grandma stepped up to take his place.*	vortreten
		to envy ['envi]	*When I was younger, I used to envy my friends' families a lot.*	beneiden
54	1b	**to mow** [məʊ], **mowed, mowed / mown** [məʊd], [məʊn]	*On Saturdays I mow my grandma's lawn.*	mähen
		lawn [lɔ:n]	*We don't like to mow the lawn too often.*	Rasen
		to vacuum ['vækju:m]	*I have to vacuum the house and do the dishes before I can hang out with my friends.*	staubsaugen
		ironing ['aɪənɪŋ]	*My weeks are so busy, I have to do the ironing on the weekend.*	Bügeln
	1d	**to tend to** [tend tə]	*In the past, men tended to work outside the home while women were responsible for managing the house.*	zu etw. neigen
	2	**stereotype** ['steriətaɪp]	*Read the extracts and identify typical gender stereotypes for boys and girls.*	Stereotype; Klischee
		to reinforce [ˌri:ɪn'fɔ:s]	*Describe how gender roles are learned and reinforced.*	verstärken; bekräftigen
		to dictate [dɪk'teɪt]	*Being a man or a woman long dictated what you could be in life.* ! *Lat. 'dictare (dicto, dictavi, dictatum)'* *Fr. 'dicter'*	bestimmen
		carer ['keərər]	*Children who don't have parents are raised by carers.*	Betreuer(in)
		gender-neutral [ˌdʒendə 'nju:trəl]	*Gender-neutral means suitable for all sexes.*	geschlechtsneutral
		gendered ['dʒendəd]	*Household chores aren't gendered.*	geschlechtsspezifisch
		data ['deɪtə]	*Data from a survey shows new developments.*	Daten
		to conform (to) [kən'fɔ:m]	*There's so much pressure to be perfect and conform to the standards we see in the media.*	(sich) anpassen an; übereinstimmen (mit)
		stereotypical [ˌsteriə'tɪpɪkl]	*I do not want to conform to stereotypical expectations.*	stereotypisch
		unisex ['ju:nɪseks]	*It makes a lot of sense to have unisex bathrooms that everyone can use.*	Unisex...; nicht geschlechtsspezifisch
		genderless ['dʒendələs]	*Some people want to give their children a unisex, or genderless, name.*	geschlechtslos
		bias ['baɪəs]	*Gender bias still exists in the world of work.*	Voreingenommenheit
55	1	**BMXing** [ˌbi: em 'eksɪŋ]	*BMXing is a popular sport.*	BMX-Rad fahren

page	exercise	Workshop 2		
		to muck around [mʌk əˈraʊnd]	*I like skateboarding and mucking around outside with my friends.*	Spaß haben; vertrödeln
		armed [ɑːmd]	*My brother is in the armed forces.* ! *Sp. 'armado'*	bewaffnet
		transition [trænˈzɪʃn]		Wechsel; Übergang
		hormone [ˈhɔːməʊn]	*He is currently on hormone treatments to stop the sex hormones that don't match his gender.*	Hormon
		blocker [blɒkər]	*I started on the treatment of hormone blockers which stop my male hormones.*	Blocker
		to conceal [kənˈsiːl]	*I no longer try to conceal my true gender.*	verbergen
		to trap [træp]	*Some people feel trapped in their bodies.*	fangen
		tomboy [ˈtɒmbɔɪ]	*They thought she was a tomboy because she was interested in things that boys generally like.*	burschikoses Mädchen; Wildfang
		to force [fɔːs]	*You shouldn't force people to do things.*	zwingen
		dress [dres]	*I don't like wearing dresses, I prefer trousers.*	Kleid
		disgusted [dɪsˈgʌstɪd]	*The boy was disgusted when his mother fed him vegetables.*	empört; angewidert
	CC	**transgender** [trænzˈdʒendər]	*My uncle is transgender, so it's never felt unusual to me that people might not feel comfortable with their sex.*	transsexuell
		queer [kwɪər]	*Someone who is 'queer' doesn't identify as heterosexual or 'straight'.*	schwul; queer
		heterosexual [ˌhetərəˈsekʃuəl]		heterosexuell
		straight [streɪt]	*People who identify as heterosexual are often called 'straight'.*	heterosexuell
		intersex [ˈɪntəseks]	*Intersex people have sex organs or hormones that don't match their gender.*	Intersex
		organ [ˈɔːgən]	*The skin is the human body's largest organ.* ! *Fr. 'organe' (m.)* *Sp. 'órgano' (m.)*	Organ
		asexual [ˌeɪˈsekʃuəl]	*Asexual is a term for people who are not interested in sex.*	asexuell
	3a	**medicine** [ˈmedsn]	*My grandma takes a lot of medicine.*	Medizin
		puberty [ˈpjuːbəti]	*Puberty is the transition from being a child to becoming an adult.* ! *Fr. 'puberté' (f.)*	Pubertät
56	1a	**compatible** [kəmˈpætəbl]	*I have an old computer and hope that it's compatible with the software.*	kompatibel
	2a	**orientated** [ˈɔːrɪənteɪt]	*The UK system is very exam orientated.*	orientiert

page exercise

Workshop 2

equivalent (to) [ɪ'kwɪvələnt]	*Year 11 is equivalent to grade 10 in the USA.*	entsprechend
criterion [kraɪ'tɪəriən], **criteria**	*There are a lot of criteria for getting into this university.*	Kriterium
credit ['kredɪt]	*You have to get credits to be able to take the exam.*	Credit; Notenpunkt
geared: to **be geared towards** [bi gɪərd tə'wɔ:dz]	*The UK system focuses on specializing, while in the US the system is geared towards generalization.*	auf etw. ausgerichtet sein
generalization [ˌdʒenrəlaɪ'zeɪʃn]	*The US educational system focuses on generalization.*	Generalisierung
exception [ɪk'sepʃn]	*Powerful women in the world, such as Hillary Clinton are the exception, not the rule.*	Ausnahme
to **focus on** ['fəʊkəs ɒn]	*The schools focus on the natural relationship between subjects rather than dictating what is taught.*	sich konzentrieren
to **prescribe** [prɪ'skraɪb]	*The educational system here prescribes exactly what is taught.* ❗ *Lat. 'praescribere (praescripto, praescripsi, praescriptus)'*	vorschreiben; festsetzen
district ['dɪstrɪkt]	*Every state is divided into districts.*	Bezirk
chemistry ['kemɪstri]	*Chemistry is part of natural science.*	Chemie
physics ['fɪzɪks]	*I'm interested in a career in engineering and am expecting to get good grades in maths and physics.*	Physik
tuition [tju'ɪʃn]	*University tuition is very high in the USA.* ❗ *used in the singular*	Studiengebühr(en)
to **vary** ['veəri]	*The costs of an education vary greatly in different parts of the world.* *≠ to stay the same*	variieren
annual ['ænjuəl]	*This year the annual conference is in September.* ❗ *Lat. 'annuns, -a, -um'* *Fr. 'annuel'*	jährlich
comparable to ['kɒmpərəbl tə]	*The average annual fees for university in the USA is comparable to the fees in the UK.*	vergleichbar mit
scholarship ['skɒləʃɪp]	*Who can get scholarships to go to college or university in the USA?*	Stipendium
disadvantaged [ˌdɪsəd'vɑ:ntɪdʒd]	*There are some scholarships offered to students from disadvantaged families.*	benachteiligt

page	exercise	
57		

Workshop 2

Special educational needs (SEN)

attention deficit hyperactivity disorder (ADHD) [əˌtenʃn ˈdefɪsɪt haɪpəræk'tɪvəti dɪsɔ:də]
Aufmerksamkeitsdefizit-Hyperaktivitätsstörung

autism ['ɔ:tɪzəm]	Autismus
cerebral palsy [sə'ri:brəl 'pɔ:lzi]	zerebrale Kinderlähmung
disorder [dɪs'ɔ:də]	Störung
Down syndrome ['daʊn sɪndrəʊm]	Downsyndrom
dyscalculia [ˌdɪskæl'kju:liə]	Dyskalkulie
dyslexia [dɪs'leksiə]	Legasthenie
dyslexic [dɪs'leksɪk]	legasthenisch
dyspraxia [dɪs'præksiə]	Dyspraxie
genetic [dʒə'netɪk]	genetisch
hyperactive [ˌhaɪpər'æktɪv]	hyperaktiv
impaired [ɪm'peəd]	beeinträchtigt
neurological [ˌnjʊərə'lɒdʒɪkl]	neurologisch

exercise			
4a	**integration** [ˌɪntɪ'greɪʃn]	*Integration in schools helps children to learn that everyone has strengths and weaknesses.*	Integration
	mainstream school ['meɪnstri:m'sku:l]	*Parents of a child with special educational needs can send their child to a mainstream school.*	Regelschule
	provision [prə'vɪʒn]	*An expert is talking about the special educational needs provision in schools in the USA.*	Maßnahme
	policy ['pɒləsi]	*What are the key policies in the act?*	Politik; politische Linie
	assistance [ə'sɪstəns]	*The school provides assistance for special needs children.*	Unterstützung
	additional [ə'dɪʃənl]	*Often children are given additional support if they have dyslexia.*	zusätzlich; ergänzend
	dyslexia [dɪs'leksiə]	*Dyslexia makes learning to read difficult.* ! *Fr. 'dyslexie' (f.)*	Legasthenie
	dyscalculia [ˌdɪskæl'kju:liə]	*Children are given additional support in school if they have dyscalculia.*	Dyskalkulie
	attention deficit hyperactivity disorder (ADHD) [əˌtenʃn 'defɪsɪt haɪpəræk'tɪvəti dɪsɔ:də]	*Try to seat students with attention deficit hyperactivity disorder away from windows and doors.*	Aufmerksamkeitsdefizit-Hyperaktivitätsstörung
	autism ['ɔ:tɪzəm]	*When working with students with autism, be consistent.*	Autismus
	to pride oneself [praɪd wʌn'self]	*It's a fantastic school that prides itself in being at the heart of the community.*	Stolz auf etwas sein
	cerebral palsy [sə'ri:brəl 'pɔ:lzi]	*There is a girl with cerebral palsy in my class, who sometimes uses a wheelchair.*	zerebrale Kinderlähmung
6a	**verbal** ['vɜ:bl]	*Verbal and non-verbal communication are both important.*	verbal; mündlich

page	exercise	Workshop 2		
		repetitive [rɪˈpetətɪv]	*People with Asperger's Syndrome can perform fairly well in their school work but their thinking patterns can be rigid and repetitive.*	repetitiv; sich wiederholend
		to cope [kəʊp]	*Often people with this condition will develop strategies to cope or to hide it.*	zurechtkommen
		hyperactive [ˌhaɪpərˈæktɪv]	*They are often hyperactive and find it difficult to sit still for long periods or to focus their attention.*	hyperaktiv
58	CC	**dyslexic** [dɪsˈleksɪk]	*With help dyslexic children can be great students.*	legasthenisch
	1b	**streaming** [ˈstriːmɪŋ]	*We've got live video streaming to help with long-distance learning.*	Streaming
		headset [ˈhedset]	*I've got a headset with a microphone so that I can actively take part.*	Headset; Kopfhörer
		microphone [ˈmaɪkrəfəʊn]	*Be careful not to put your lips to close to the microphone when you speak.*	Mikrofon
		to demonstrate [ˈdemənstreɪt]	*Our teacher demonstrated some problems on the whiteboard.* ! *Lat. 'demonstrare (demonstro, demonstravi, demonstratum)'*	zeigen; vorführen
	2a	**to account for** [əˈkaʊnt fər]	*In 1956 Maori accounted for just 8 % of the population.*	ausmachen
		shame [ʃeɪm]	*Shame is a painful feeling about oneself.*	Schamgefühl
		to undergo [ˌʌndəˈgəʊ], **underwent, undergone** [ˌʌndəˈwent, ˌʌndəˈgɒn]	*We have undergone some radical changes in recent years.*	durchmachen
		shift [ʃɪft]	*There has been a shift in schools to focus individual learning.*	Veränderung
		revival [rɪˈvaɪvl]	*The revival of the Maori language in schools is important for New Zealand culture.*	Wiederbelebung
		participation [pɑːˌtɪsɪˈpeɪʃn]	*The participation of mothers in the labor force is increasing.*	Beteiligung
		attainment [əˈteɪnmənt]	*Attainment refers to the highest level of education a student gets.*	Leistungen
59	3b	**to type** [taɪp]	*He typed too quickly and made twelve mistakes.*	tippen
		footstep [ˈfʊtstep]	*There are footsteps in the snow.*	Fußstapfen
	4a	**aid** [eɪd]	*Use visual aids to help people understand your ideas.* ! *Fr. 'l'aide' (f.)*	Hilfe; Unterstützung
		consistent [kənˈsɪstənt]	*My teacher is consistent about classroom rules.*	konsequent

page	exercise	Workshop 2		
		to stick to [stɪk tə], **stuck, stuck** [stʌk, stʌk]	*Young children do better if you stick to a schedule.*	dabei bleiben
		to reward [rɪ'wɔːd]	*It is more important to reward good behaviour than to punish bad behaviour.*	belohnen
		to break down [breɪk daʊn], **broke, broken** [brəʊk, 'brəʊkən]	*It helps if you break down big projects into steps.*	in Schritte unterteilen; aufschlüsseln
		graph [grɑːf]	*Use visuals like graphs to help listeners understand information.*	Diagramm
		to seat [siːt]	*Seat the audience twenty minutes before the concert begins.*	setzen
	4b	**efficient** [ɪ'fɪʃnt]	*Which method of learning is most efficient for you?* **!** *Fr. 'efficace'*	effizient; wirksam
	5	**approach** [ə'prəʊtʃ]	*What is the best approach to make sure people are well educated?*	Vorgehen; Ansatz
	CC	**grading** ['greɪdɪŋ]	*In the USA, two different grading systems are used in schools.*	Noten...
		numerical [njuː'merɪkl]	*One is numerical and the other is marked with letters, A – D.* **!** *Lat. 'numerus, -i' (m.) = number*	numerisch
		score [skɔːr]	*What was your score in the test?*	Note
60	2a	**polo shirt** ['pəʊləʊ ʃɜːt]	*In most high schools you wear a white polo shirt.*	Polohemd
		blazer ['bleɪzər]	*Our uniform consists of trousers, a polo shirt and a blazer.*	Blazer; leichte Sportjacke
		badge [bædʒ]	*We wear a blazer with the school badge on the top pocket.*	Abzeichen; Plakette
		tuck shop [tʌk ʃɒp]	*A tuck shop is a shop on the grounds of a school.*	Laden; Kiosk
		production [prə'dʌkʃn]	*I'm taking a course in theatre production – it's my favourite.*	Produktion; Inszenierung
		emphasis (on) ['emfəsɪs]	*There's a lot more emphasis in Australia on study-life balance.*	Betonung (auf)
		homecoming ['həʊmkʌmɪŋ]	*Homecoming is a special week at school and includes a student dance.*	traditionelles Event in Highschools
61	3a	**dyspraxia** [dɪs'præksiə]	*Dyspraxia can make writing difficult.*	Dyspraxie
		therapy ['θerəpi]	*I have therapy twice a week now that my leg has healed.*	Therapie
		specialist ['speʃəlɪst]	*There is a specialist for this problem at the hospital.*	Spezialist(in); Experte/Expertin
	4	**neurological** [ˌnjʊərə'lɒdʒɪkl]	*= having to do with nerves*	neurologisch
		disorder [dɪs'ɔːdə]	*Autism is a neurological disorder that affects the way a person's body and brain works.*	Störung

page	exercise	Workshop 2		
		to misunderstand [ˌmɪsʌndəˈstænd], **misunderstood, misunderstood** [ˌmɪsʌndəˈstʊd, ˌmɪsʌndəˈstʊd]	*They might misunderstand other people's feelings or behaviour.*	missverstehen
		cue [kjuː]	*It's important to learn to read social cues.*	Hinweis; Stichwort
		sensory [ˈsensəri]	*Some people have a more difficult time dealing with sensory information than others.* = *relating to the five senses*	sensorisch
		routine [ruːˈtiːn]	*I am pretty good at handling new routines.*	Routine
		rigid [ˈrɪdʒɪd]	*Their thinking patterns can be rigid and unflexible.*	starr; rigide
		stiff [stɪf]	*Her legs were stiff and she couldn't move.*	steif; starr
		to tie [taɪ]	*He stopped walking and tied his shoes.*	binden; zubinden
		to grasp [grɑːsp]	*I grasped the cup when it fell.*	greifen; festhalten
		Down syndrome [ˈdaʊn sɪndrəʊm]	*Children with Down syndrome often go to a mainstream school.*	Downsyndrom
		genetic [dʒəˈnetɪk]		genetisch
		chromosome [ˈkrəʊməsəʊm]	*Humans have 23 chromosomes.*	Chromosom
		impaired [ɪmˈpeəd]	*When you are visually impaired, you can't see well.*	beeinträchtigt
62	S1b	**to decrease** [dɪˈkriːs]	*The number of two-parent households decreased in the past ten years.*	fallen; zurückgehen
		median [ˈmiːdiən]	*The graph shows the individual countries and the median.* = *average*	Median; Durchschnitt
		remarriage [ˌriːˈmærɪdʒ]	*Remarriage is common and results in blended families.*	Wiederverheiratung
		to survey [ˈsɜːveɪ]	*The groups surveyed believed that gender was formed by social cues.*	befragen
	TIP	**to level off** [ˈlevl ɒf]	*The data on the graph levels off this year.*	sich ebnen; abflachen
		overall [ˌəʊvərˈɔːl]	*Overall, we can see that bullying is a problem among teenagers.*	allgemein
63	S1	**labour** [ˈleɪbər]	*The graph shows the number of mothers in the US labor force.* ! *AE = labor*	Arbeits...
		preschool [ˈpriːskuːl]	*It's difficult for mothers with preschool-aged children to work fulltime.*	vorschulisch

page	exercise	Workshop 2		
64				

The law

to accuse [ə'kju:z]	beschuldigen; anklagen
aggravated assault [ˌægrəveɪtɪd ə'sɔ:lt]	schwere Körperverletzung
amends [ə'mendz]	Wiedergutmachung; Schadensersatz
assault [ə'sɔ:lt]	Angriff; Überfall
caution ['kɔ:ʃn]	Verwarnung; Warnung
to charge (with) [tʃɑ:dʒ]	anklagen (wegen)
client ['klaɪənt]	Mandant(in); Kunde/Kundin
compensation [ˌkɒmpen'seɪʃn]	Entschädigung
to convict [kən'vɪkt]	verurteilen
conviction [kən'vɪkʃn]	Verurteilung
counselling ['kaʊnsəlɪŋ]	Beratung
criminal record [ˌkrɪmɪnəl 'rekɔ:d]	Vorstrafregister
custodial sentence [kʌ'stəʊdiəl 'sentəns]	Freiheitsstrafe
custody ['kʌstədi]	Verwahrung; Schutz; Sorgerecht
defence [dɪ'fens]	Verteidigung
guard [gɑ:d]	Sicherheitsbeamter(in); Wächter(in)
to hold accountable [həʊld ə'kaʊntəbl], **held, held** [held, held]	zur Rechenschaft ziehen
joyride ['dʒɔɪraɪd]	Spritztour (mit einem gestohlenen Auto)
justice ['dʒʌstɪs]	Justiz
to legalize ['li:gəlaɪz]	legalisieren
offender [ə'fendə]	Täter(in)
offence [ə'fens]	Straftat
to plead guilty [pli:d 'gɪlti]	sich schuldig bekennen
probation [prə'beɪʃn]	Bewährung
prosecution [ˌprɒsɪ'kju:ʃn]	Staatsanwaltschaft
prosecutor ['prɒsɪkju:tə]	Staatsanwalt / -anwältin
remorse [rɪ'mɔ:s]	Reue
to sentence ['sentəns]	verurteilen
sentence ['sentəns]	Verurteilung; Strafe
supervision [ˌsu:pə'vɪʒn]	Überwachung; Aufsicht
shoplifting ['ʃɒplɪftɪŋ]	Ladendiebstahl
theft [θeft]	Diebstahl
tribunal [traɪ'bju:nl]	Tribunal; Gericht
victim ['vɪktɪm]	Opfer

exercise	word	example	German
1	**justice** ['dʒʌstɪs]	*Read the information about the Youth Justice System of England and Wales.* ❗ *Lat. 'ius, iuris' (n.) Sp. 'justicia (f.)*	Justiz
	offender [ə'fendə]	*The Youth Justice System guarantees the rights of young offenders aged 10 to 17.*	Täter(in)
	offence [ə'fens]	*The main aims of the law are to prevent future criminal offences.*	Straftat
	amends [ə'mendz]	*Offenders must understand the effect of their actions and make amends.*	Wiedergutmachung; Schadenersatz
	custody ['kʌstədi]	*With young people custody should only be considered for the most serious crimes.*	Verwahrung; Schutz; Sorgerecht

page	exercise	Workshop 2		
		to intervene [ˌɪntəˈviːn]	*It's important to intervene to prevent young people from committing crimes.*	eingreifen
		to hold accountable [həʊld əˈkaʊntəbl] [held, held]	*How can the law hold youth offenders accountable?*	zur Rechenschaft ziehen
		prosecutor [ˈprɒsɪkjuːtə]	*The police or Crown prosecutor may only give a warning for a first or non-serious offence.*	Staatsanwalt/-anwältin
		counselling [ˈkaʊnsəlɪŋ]	*For a first or non-serious offence, the police refer youth to an agency for counselling.*	Beratung
		victim [ˈvɪktɪm]	*They require the young person to apologize to the victim.* ! *Lat. 'victima' (f.) Fr. 'victime' (f.)*	Opfer
		compensation [ˌkɒmpenˈseɪʃn]	*Sentencing options apart from custody include: a fine, compensation to the victim, community service or probation.*	Entschädigung
		to repair [rɪˈpeər]	*So now Jake, I have to consider what sentence will best help you to repair the harm you have done.*	beheben; reparieren
		to sentence [ˈsentəns]	*He was sentenced to do community work.*	verurteilen
		probation [prəˈbeɪʃn]	*Joe had been on probation for theft before.*	Bewährung
		circumstance [ˈsɜːkəmstəns]	*What were the circumstances of the crime?* ! *Lat. 'circumstare (circumsto, circumsteti)'*	Umstand; Lage
		seriousness [ˈsɪəriəsnəs]	*The seriousness of the offence influences the sentencing.*	Ernsthaftigkeit
		sentence [ˈsentəns]	*She got a lesser sentence than expected.*	Verurteilung; Strafe
		criminal record [ˌkrɪmɪnl ˈrekɔːd]	*Because he has been sentenced, he now has a criminal record.*	Vorstrafregister
		remorse [rɪˈmɔːs]	*Does the offender understand the seriousness of the crime and show remorse?*	Reue
	2	**joyride** [ˈdʒɔɪraɪd]	*I took my sister's car keys and went for a joyride.*	Spritztour (mit einem gestohlenen Auto)
		icy [ˈaɪsi]	*I guess I'm not a great driver yet and the road was icy.*	eisig
		curb [kɜːb]	*You can't park your car on the curb.*	Bordstein
		excuse [ɪkˈskjuːs]	*I had no excuse – I did drink and I did lose control of the car.*	Entschuldigung
		to charge (with) [tʃɑːdʒ]	*He was charged for murder.*	anklagen (wegen)
		aggravated assault [ˌægrəveɪtɪd əˈsɔːlt]	*I was charged with drunk driving and aggravated assault.*	schwere Körperverletzung

page	exercise	Workshop 2		
		assault [ə'sɔ:lt]	*There was an armed assault on the shop.*	Angriff; Überfall
65	3b	**incident** ['ɪnsɪdənt]	*A few people were involved in the incident.*	Vorfall; Ereignis
		lad [læd]	*He was a young lad, maybe 16 or 17.* = *guy*	Bursche; Kerl
		foolishly ['fu:lɪʃli]	*He behaved foolishly, but at least he admitted what he had done.*	unvernünftig
	4a	**prosecution** [ˌprɒsɪ'kju:ʃn]	*What sentence did the prosecution lawyer recommend to the judge?*	Staatsanwaltschaft
		defence [dɪ'fens]	*The defence lawyer spoke after the prosecution.*	Verteidigung
		to **plead guilty** [pli:d 'gɪlti]	*Jake, you have pleaded guilty to drunk driving and aggravated assault.*	sich schuldig bekennen
		dumb [dʌm]	*I was young and a bit dumb.* = *stupid*	blöd; dumm
		harmful ['hɑ:mfl]	*The effect on his victims has been very harmful.*	schädlich
		custodial sentence [kʌ'stəʊdiəl 'sentəns]	*It is a serious offence and I recommend a short custodial sentence.* ! *Lat. 'custos, -odis' (m./f.)* = *prison guard*	Freiheitsstrafe
		supervision [ˌsu:pə'vɪʒn]	*As he was a first-time offender, the judge ordered probation and supervision.*	Überwachung; Aufsicht
	CC	**tribunal** [traɪ'bju:nl]	*Tribunals are minor courts that deal only with specific cases.*	Tribunal; Gericht
		intervention [ˌɪntə'venʃn]	*Early intervention is central to the Scottish system.*	Eingriff; Eingreifen
	5a	**backyard** [ˌbæk'jɑ:d]	*In the summer we eat dinner in the backyard.*	Garten hinter dem Haus; Hinterhof
		theft [θeft]	*Theft is a crime and can get you in serious trouble.*	Diebstahl
66	2a	**intention** [ɪn'tenʃn]	*Summarize what the text is about and explain the writer's intention.*	Absicht
		standard ['stændəd]	*There's so much pressure to conform to the standards we see in the media.*	Standard
		crash diet ['kræʃ 'daɪət]	*Crash diets aren't effective and very unhealty.*	Crash-Diät
		pill [pɪl]	*Taking diet pills can be bad for your health.*	Tablette
		super ['su:pər]	*I used to starve myself trying to be super-thin.*	super; besonders
		celebrity [sə'lebrəti]	*Many teens want to look like the celebrities in the media.* ! *Lat. 'celebrare (celebro, celebravi, celebratum)' = to celebrate*	Prominente(r)

page	exercise	Workshop 2		
		idol ['aɪdl]	*My idols have always been rock stars.*	Idol
		food supplement ['fu:d ˌsʌplɪmənt]	*There are lots of different kinds of food supplements, but many of them are not good for you.*	Nahrungsergänzungsmittel
		to **bulk up** [bʌlk ʌp]	*Boys are increasingly using supplements to help them bulk up and look like their superheroes.*	Masse zusetzen; hier: Muskeln aufbauen
		superhero ['su:pəhɪərəʊ], **superheroes**	*The comics are about six superheroes.* ❗ *Lat. 'heros, -ois' (m.)*	Superheld
		dieting ['daɪətɪŋ]	*Extreme dieting and fitness supplements are bad for your health.*	Schlankheitskuren; Diäten
		fitness ['fɪtnəs]	*Build up your strength and fitness safely by following these simple tips.*	Fitness
		to **overdo** [ˌəʊvə'du:], **overdid, overdone** [ˌəʊvə'dɪd, ˌəʊvə'dʌn]	*It's good to stay at a weight that's normal for your height – but it's dangerous to overdo dieting.*	übertreiben
		lean [li:n]	*Your diet should include lean meats, fruit, vegetables, whole grains and healthy fats.*	mager
		grain [greɪn]	*Your diet should include lean meats, fruit, vegetables, whole grains and healthy fats.*	Getreide
		junk food [dʒʌŋk]	*Avoid junk foods and fast food – they are full of bad fat and salt.*	Junk Food
		soda ['səʊdə]	*Soda drinks contain large amounts of sugar and caffeine, so cut them out too.*	Limo; Sprudel
		caffeine ['kæfi:n]	*Tea and coffee contain caffeine.* ❗ *Fr. 'caféine (f.)*	Koffein
		incorrectly [ˌɪnkə'rektli]	*If you operate the machine incorrectly, you could damage it.*	falsch; fehlerhaft
		liver ['lɪvər]	*Using steroids can raise your risk of heart disease or liver damage.*	Leber
		calorie ['kæləri]	*You are active, so a high-energy breakfast with a lot of calories will give you energy.*	Kalorie
		protein ['prəʊti:n]	*Foods such as eggs, fish, and meats are rich in protein.*	Protein
		carbohydrate [ˌkɑ:bəʊ'haɪdreɪt]	*If you want to loose weight, cut out carbohydrates.*	Kohlenhydrat
		growth [grəʊθ]	*Counting calories all the time can slow down your growth and development.*	Wachstum
	3	**emphatic** [ɪm'fætɪk]	*Add 'do' or 'did' to each sentence to make it more emphatic.*	emphatisch
		dissatisfaction [ˌdɪsˌsætɪs'fækʃn]	*The typical teen expresses dissatisfaction with family meals.*	Unzufriedenheit

page	exercise	Workshop 2		
		taste [teɪst]	*My tastes are really specific, I don't like green vegetables.*	Geschmack
		dietary ['daɪətəri]	*Many teens say meals served by their parents don't always suit their tastes or dietary lifestyle.*	diätetisch
68		**archive** ['ɑ:kaɪv]	*Articles written last year are still available in the archive.*	Archiv
		geek [gi:k]	*My best friend is a geek and helps me with my homework.*	Geek; Spezialist(in)
		to annoy [ə'nɔɪ]	*It does annoy me when you see adverts everywhere.*	ärgern; aufregen
		marketing ['mɑ:kɪtɪŋ]	*In the UK, companies spend around £1 billion every year on marketing to teens.*	Marketing
		consumer [kən'sju:mər]	*Companies address consumers through adverts.* ! *Lat. 'consumere (consumo, consumpsi, consumptum)'* *= to consume*	Verbraucher(in)
		savvy ['sævi]	*= clever* *≠ stupid*	klug; schlau
		to blast [blɑ:st]	*My friends and I get blasted with ads for makeup.*	bombadieren
		makeup ['meɪk ʌp]	*My mother says I can start wearing makeup when I'm 14.*	Schminke
		to tap [tæp]	*Not once have I clicked or tapped on one of those ads.*	tippen
		trick [trɪk]	*Advertisers use lots of tricks to get onto our screens and into our heads.*	Trick
		brand [brænd]	*When you see a brand social media, it's probably sponsored.*	Marke
		sneaker ['sni:kə]	*Many people buy sneakers because of the logo.* ! *BE = trainer*	Turnschuh
		placement ['pleɪsmənt]	*Product placement is when a popular brand appears in a movie or TV show.*	Platzierung
		casual ['kæʒuəl]	*A text message is more casual than an article.*	locker; lässig
		to personalize ['pɜ:sənəlaɪz]	*If ads are personalized it makes them more authentic.*	personalisieren
69	3b	**former** ['fɔ:mə]	*In a former draft of her blog post, Mary emphazided different information.* *= earlier* *≠ later*	frühere(r)
		to block [blɒk]	*Those ads blocking the content are really annoying.*	blockieren
		influencer ['ɪnfluənsə]	*Video influencers make money off of product placement.*	Influencer(in)

page	exercise	Workshop 2		
	4a	**portal** ['pɔ:tl]	*You can post your film on the video sharing portal.* ❗ *Lat. 'porta, -ae' (f.) = door*	Portalseite
		seldom ['seldəm]	*We very seldom go out in the evening.* *= rarely* *≠ often*	selten
70	2a	**evolution** [ˌi:və'lu:ʃn]	*The internet has a big role in driving the evolution of our lifestyle.* ❗ *Lat. 'evolvere (evolvo, evolvi, evolutum)' = to evolve*	Evolution; Entwicklung
		linguist ['lɪŋgwɪst]	*Linguist David Crystal says that the vast majority of English is exactly the same today as it was 20 years ago.*	Sprachwissenschaftler(in); Linguist(in)
		linguistics [lɪŋ'gwɪstɪks]	*The linguist wrote a book about internet linguistics.*	Linguistik
		transcript ['trænskrɪpt]	*There is an 18th-century transcript of a speech George Washington gave.* ❗ *Lat. 'transcribere (transcribo, transcripsi, transcriptum)'* *= to transcribe*	Abschrift; Niederschrift
		translator [trænz'leɪtə]	*I'm a translator, translating texts from German into English.*	Übersetzer(in)
		abbreviated [ə'bri:vieɪtɪd]	*I use abbreviated phrases like LOL when I write texts.*	abgekürzt
		to shift [ʃɪft]	*Language shifts and grows as a result of outside influences.* *= change* *≠ stay the same*	verändern
		dynamic [daɪ'næmɪk]	*The internet has added a new dynamic to the process of global warming.*	Dynamik
71	4a	**to draft** [drɑ:ft]	*May is drafting a blog post about the results of her mini-survey.*	entwerfen
		margin ['mɑ:dʒɪn]	*Look at her notes in the margin and rewrite the sentences.*	Rand
		unexpected [ˌʌnɪk'spektɪd]	*The storm was unexpected, so we didn't have an umbrella.*	unerwartet
		to surprise [sə'praɪz]	*I must say the number of you who responded surprised me.*	überraschen
	5	**cyberbullying** ['saɪbəbʊliɪŋ]	*Look at the picture about cyberbullying and do the tasks.*	Cyber-Mobbing
		to convey [kən'veɪ]	*I understand the message the author conveys.*	vermitteln
		thought-provoking ['θɔ:t prəvəʊkɪŋ]	*Did you find the film thought-provoking?*	zum Nachdenken anregend
		to trigger ['trɪgə]	*Do these beautiful pictures trigger any emotion from you?*	auslösen
		emotion [ɪ'məʊʃn]	*Describe your emotion in a few words.* ❗ *Fr. 'émotion' (f.)*	Emotion; Gefühl

page	exercise	Workshop 2		
72	1a	**erratic** [ɪ'rætɪk]	*During puberty your behaviour can be erratic and you can feel low.*	erratisch; sprunghaft
		moody ['mu:di]	*My son has been moody since he turned twelve.*	launisch
	1b	**depression** [dɪ'preʃn]	*I knew what depression was at the time, but I wasn't familiar with how best to deal with the situation.*	Depression
		stigma ['stɪgmə]	*Stigma is a problem when treating mental disorders.*	Stigma
		sophomore ['sɒfəmɔ:r]	*A sophomore is a student in the second year of high school or university.*	Student im 2. Studienjahr
		adolescent [ˌædə'lesnt]	*Adolescents are very young adults.* ! *Lat. 'adolescere (adolesco, adolevi, adultum)' = to grow up*	Jugendliche; Jugend...
		wellness ['welnəs]	*= health* *≠ illnes*	Wohlbefinden
		biased ['baɪəst]	*I'm a bit biased, but I enjoy the youth Innovation panel that I'm on.*	parteiisch; voreingenommen
		intriguing [ɪn'tri:gɪŋ]	*The questions the audience asked were intriguing.*	faszinierend
		capacity [kə'pæsəti]	*The company which focuses on mental wellness has the capacity to make a powerful impact in the community.*	Fähigkeit
		desire [dɪ'zaɪə]	*When you have a desire to get involved then pursue your passion right away.*	Wunsch
		passion ['pæʃn]	*Because I've got a passion for nature, I'm involved in environmental activism.*	Leidenschaft
73	2	**advocate (for)** ['ædvəkət]	*How did you end up as an advocate for mental wellness?*	Fürsprecher(in)
	5	**nephew** ['nefju:]	*My uncle has three nephews, two are my cousins.* ! *Fr. 'neveu' (m.)*	Neffe
		bipolar [ˌbaɪ'pəʊlə]	*He has suffered from bipolar disorder and alcohol addiction.*	bipolar
		addiction [ə'dɪkʃn]	*My father suffered from alcohol addiction.*	Sucht; Süchtigkeit
74	S2	**analysis** [ə'næləsɪs]	*Use the notes to help you write a short description and analysis of the information.*	Analyse; Untersuchung
		to state [steɪt]	*A majority of the teens who were interviewed stated that they had been bullied.*	erklären; festlegen
		caution ['kɔ:ʃn]	*The number of young people who received a caution or sentence increased last year.*	Verwarnung; Warnung

page	exercise	Workshop 2		
		to convict [kən'vɪkt]	*She was convicted for theft.*	verurteilen
		conviction [kən'vɪkʃn]	*The most youth convictions were in the 16 – 18-year-old group.*	Verurteilung
		to motivate ['məʊtɪveɪt]	*What motivates teenagers to do physical exercise?*	motivieren; anregen
	S3	**repetition** [ˌrepə'tɪʃn]	*The others should ask for repetition and clarification if necessary.* ❗ *Lat. 'repetere (repeto, repetivi, repetitum)' = to repeat*	Wiederholung
75	S1	**cyberthreat** ['saɪbəθret]	*Many teens have experienced cyberthreats through their cell phones.*	Cyber-Bedrohung
76	1b	**meanwhile** ['mi:nwaɪl]	*Meanwhile, I have met my new brothers.*	inzwischen; mittlerweile
	2a	**unnatural** [ʌn'nætʃrəl]	*Working too late into the night is tiring and feels unnatural.*	unnatürlich
		obliged: to be obliged (to) [bi 'ɒblɪgeɪtɪd]	*In the UK, you are not obliged to include a headshot photo in your CV.*	müssen; verpflichtet sein
77	3	**to accuse** [ə'kju:z]	*She was accused of shoplifting and is in court.*	beschuldigen; anklagen
		client ['klaɪənt]	*My client does accept responsibility for her actions.*	Mandant(in); Kunde/Kundin
		guard [gɑ:d]	*The shop is watched by security guards.* ❗ *Fr. 'gardien' (m.)*	Sicherheitsbeamter(in); Wächter(in)
		to resist [rɪ'zɪst]	*When the police arrested her she didn't resist.*	widerstehen
	4	**substantial** [səb'stænʃl]	*It's good to have a substantial breakfast that includes protein.*	reichlich
		to overrate [ˌəʊvə'reɪt]	*= think too much of*	überbewerten
		dietician [ˌdaɪə'tɪʃn]	*In the studio we've got two experts: Amanda Grace, who is a dietician and Bob Taylor, a fitness instructor.*	Ernährungswissen-schaftler(in)
		porridge ['pɒrɪdʒ]	*A bowl of porridge for breakfast will give you a lot of energy.*	Haferbrei
		muesli ['mju:zli]	*Start by having something like yoghurt and fruit or something more substantial like a bowl of porridge or muesli.*	Müsli
		unnecessary [ʌn'nesəsəri]	*All of the plastic packaging products are wrapped in is unnecessary.*	unnötig; überflüssig
		skinny ['skɪni]	*She wants to look fit but is too skinny.* *= very thin* *≠ fat*	mager; dünn
	5	**to acknowledge** [ək'nɒlɪdʒ]	*People acknowledge that advertisers look for an opportunity for free advertising.*	bestätigen; anerkennen

page	exercise	Workshop 2		
80	1	**unconventional** [ˌʌnkənˈvenʃənl]	*My family may seem unconventional to other people, but to me it's normal.*	unkonventionell
		tolerant [ˈtɒlərənt]	*In my community people are tolerant and try to respect others.* *≠ intolerant* **!** *Lat. 'tolerare (tolero, toleravi, toleratum)' = to tolerate*	tolerant
	2	**constant** [ˈkɒnstənt]	*I don't like websites with constant advertising.*	ständig
		to target [ˈtɑːɡɪt]	*Advertising is constantly targeting teenagers.*	zielen auf
81	4	**to punch** [pʌntʃ]	*She punched her teacher and ran out of the room.*	schlagen
	5	**priority** [praɪˈɒrəti]	*Our priorities are buying food and paying the bills.* **!** *Lat. 'prioritas, -atis' (f.)*	Priorität

page	exercise	Workshop 3		
88		**commerce** [ˈkɒmɜːs]	*International commerce has grown in the last decade.*	Handel; Kommerz
		military [ˈmɪlətri]	*Israel is one of the few countries where women also have to do military service.*	militärisch; Militär...
		signpost [ˈsaɪnpəʊst]	*There is a signpost with different directions.*	Wegweiser; Schild
		apprenticeship [əˈprentɪʃɪp]	*Some school leavers go to university but others start an apprenticeship.* **!** *Fr. 'apprentissage' (f.)*	Lehrstelle; Ausbildung
89		**scheme** [skiːm]	*I heard that there are apprenticeship schemes for 16 year-olds.*	Programm
		vocational [vəʊˈkeɪʃənl]	*You can get vocational qualifications at many colleges.*	beruflich
		apprentice [əˈprentɪs]	*I've managed to secure an interview for a job as an apprentice software developer.*	Auszubildende(r); Lehrling
		to trade [treɪd]	*Use your language skills with businesses that trade internationally.*	handeln
90	1a	**leaver** [ˈliːvə]	*Why do many school leavers choose to take a gap year?*	Schulabgänger(in)
	1b	**start-up** [ˈstɑːtʌp]	*After university, I worked at a technology startup and learned a lot.*	junges Unternehmen
		undergraduate [ˌʌndəˈɡrædʒuət]	*My sister will be an undergraduate at the university next year.*	Student(in) (ohne Abschluss)
		activist [ˈæktɪvɪst]	*In the student activist group that I'm in, we focus on looking at social issues like discrimination.* **!** *Lat. 'activus, -a, -um' = active*	Aktivist(in)

page	exercise	Workshop 3		
		discrimination [dɪˌskrɪmɪˈneɪʃn]	*At school I am in a student activist group that deals with social issues like discrimination.*	Diskriminierung; Ausgrenzung
		determined [dɪˈtɜːmɪnd]	*I really want a job in science, I'm determined to get one.*	entschlossen
		computing [kəmˈpjuːtɪŋ]	*You don't really need a degree to start in computing, you need to be good at programming.* **!** *Lat. 'computare (computo, computavi, computatum)'* *= to compute*	Computing
		to secure [sɪˈkjʊər]	*I've managed to secure a job interview.* *= to get*	sichern; ergattern
		developer [dɪˈveləpə]	*Software developers are always needed.*	Entwickler(in)
		vintage [ˈvɪntɪdʒ]	*I buy vintage clothes, make changes and then sell them at markets.*	alt; klassisch; Vintage
		incubator [ˈɪŋkjubeɪtər]	*We applied to an incubator for training and help with our idea.*	Inkubator; Unterstützer von Start-ups
91	2b	**advisor** [ədˈvaɪzə]	*The careers advisor suggested a gap year while I decide what to do.*	Berater(in)
	3	**patch** [pætʃ]	*I like those jeans with colouful patches.*	Fleck; Flicken
		flea [fliː]	*I discovered a stall at the local flea market.*	Floh
	4a	**publisher** [ˈpʌblɪʃə]	*I worked in the marketing department of a book publisher.*	Verleger(in)
		motivation [ˌməʊtɪˈveɪʃn]	*What's your motivation for taking a gap year?*	Motivation; Begründung
92	2a	**unpaid** [ˌʌnˈpeɪd]	*Unpaid internships are difficult if you don't have anybody to support you financially.*	unbezahlt
	4	**traineeship** [ˌtreɪˈniːʃɪp]	*Traineeships are short education programmes for 16 – 23-year-olds who haven't got a job or an apprenticeship.*	Praktikumsplatz
		flexible [ˈfleksəbl]	*Traineeships are short, flexible education programmes.*	flexibel
		self-employed [ˌself ɪmˈplɔɪd]	*Being self-employed means you run your own business.*	selbständig
		employee [ɪmˈplɔɪiː]	*New employees are shown around the workplace on the first day.* **!** *Fr. 'employé' (m.)*	Angestellte(r)
93	2a	**to tutor** [ˈtjuːtə]	*I earn some money tutoring younger students in math.*	unterrichten; Nachhilfe geben
		to flip [flɪp]	*Are you serving customers or flipping the burgers?*	umdrehen

page	exercise	Workshop 3		
		pushy ['pʊʃi]	*My boss is kind of pushy and loud.* *= aggressive* *≠ friendly*	aggressiv
		schoolwork ['sku:lwɜ:k]	*So the evening shifts don't affect your schoolwork too much?*	Schulaufgaben
	2c	**profile** ['prəʊfaɪl]	*Write a profile for a job.*	Profil
	TIP	**intonation** [ˌɪntə'neɪʃn]	*Does the intonation go up and down or is it flat and monotone?*	Intonation
		monotone ['mɒnətəʊn]	*When you speak in front of people try not to let your voice be monotone.*	monoton
		eyebrow ['aɪbraʊ]	*Do his eyes, mouth or eyebrows move a lot when he speaks?*	Augenbraue
		to slump [slʌmp]	*Does he or she sit up with a straight back or slump in the chair?*	abrutschen; zusammensacken
		gesture ['dʒestər]	*Does she use hand gestures when she speaks?* *! Fr. 'geste' (m.)*	Geste
94	1a	**brief** [bri:f]	*Make your statement clear and brief.*	kurz
		format ['fɔ:mæt]	*Your CV should have a clear format and structure.*	Format
		to discriminate [dɪ'skrɪmɪneɪt]	*Employers shouldn't discriminate any groups of people.*	unterschiedlich behandeln; diskriminieren
		headshot ['hedʃɒt]	*A headshot is a photograph of your head and shoulders.*	Portraitfoto
		ought to ['ɔ:t tə]	*If you have special skills, you ought to highlight them here.*	sollte
		interpersonal [ˌɪntə'pɜ:sənl]	*I have strong communication and interpersonal skills and work well as part of a team.*	interpersonell; zwischenmenschlich
		impression [ɪm'preʃn]	*You need to leave a strong final impression.* *! Lat. 'imprimere (imprimo, impressi, impressum)' = to impress*	Eindruck
	1b	**applicant** ['æplɪkənt]	*A job applicant's CV doesn't always have to include a photo.*	Bewerber(in); Anmelder(in)
95	2a	**obligation** [ˌɒblɪ'geɪʃn]	*We have an obligation to slow climate change.*	Pflicht
	4a	**overly** ['əʊvəli]	*Don't feel obliged to act overly cheerful.*	übermäßig
		interviewer ['ɪntəvju:ə]	*You shouldn't ask your interviewer any personal questions.*	Interviewer(in)
		flowing ['fləʊɪŋ]	*An interview that is flowing and smooth is good for both participants.* *≠ slow*	fließend
		thoughtful ['θɔ:tfl]	*Offer help whenever you can – this shows that you're thoughtful and willing to give time to others.*	aufmerksam; rücksichtsvoll

page	exercise	Workshop 3		
	4b	**salary** ['sæləri]	*If they offer you the position, that's when you ought to ask about the salary.* ❗ *Lat. 'salarium' (n.)*	Gehalt; Lohn
96	1	**typist** ['taɪpɪst]	*Today, a typist should have good computer skills.*	Schreibkraft
		transcriber [træn'skraɪbə]	*My grandmother worked as a part-time typist and transcriber.* ❗ *Fr. 'transcripteur' (m.)*	Transkribierer(in)
		to transcribe [træn'skraɪb]	*I will help transcribe listening materials for learning software.*	abschreiben; transkribieren
		activism ['æktɪvɪzəm]	*Community activism is important to me.*	Aktivismus
	2	**sector** ['sektə]	*As a part-time waiter I learned about the hospitality sector.*	Bereich
		helper ['helpə]	*My neighbour is old and needs a helper.*	Helfer(in)
	4	**rewarding** [rɪ'wɔːdɪŋ]	*You'll work hard as a legal aid lawyer, but it's a very rewarding job.*	lohnend
97	6a	**thankfully** ['θæŋkfəli]	*Thankfully, it didn't rain and we didn't have to cancel our hike.*	zum Glück
98		**poll** [pəʊl]	*In a recent poll 21% of millennials said they had changed jobs in the last year.* *= survey*	Umfrage
		millennial [mɪ'leniəl]	*In a recent poll 21% of millennials said they had changed jobs in the last year.*	Millennium-Generation; Millenial
		insecure [ˌɪnsɪ'kjʊər]	*Freelancers are often in an insecure position, at least in terms of finances.*	unsicher; instabil
		aside [ə'saɪd]	*It is harder to put money aside for those big-ticket items like a car, apartment or house.*	beiseite
		youngster ['jʌŋstə]	*Youngsters and teenagers have greater career choices nowadays.* *= young person*	Jugendliche
		loyalty ['lɔɪəlti]	*One consequence of gig work is that young people feel less loyalty towards their employers.*	Loyalität
		whereas [ˌweər'æz]	*I thought he was impolite, whereas he's just shy.*	während
		to quit [kwɪt]	*I can always quit and look for another job.*	kündigen
		uncertainty [ʌn'sɜːtnti]	*Many young people feel uncertainty about their jobs.*	Unsicherheit
		incentive [ɪn'sentɪv]	*When people aren't paid well they have little incentive to work harder.*	Anreiz; Antrieb

page	exercise	Workshop 3		
		transferable [træns'fɜːrəbl]	*Transferrable skills like problem solving become more important.*	übertragbar
99	4b	**talent** ['tælənt]	*If you have talent and can work hard, you can succeed.*	Talent
		analyst ['ænəlɪst]	*My father works as an analyst who looks at data about climate change.*	Analytiker(in); Analyst(in)
		someday ['sʌmdeɪ]	*Someday I'll be done with school and can move to a different place.*	eines Tages; irgendwann
		entrepreneur [ˌɒntrəprə'nɜː]	*Are you a young entrepreneur with an outstanding and innovative business?* ❗ *Fr. 'entrepreneur' (m.)*	Unternehmer(in)
		motivational [ˌməʊtɪ'veɪʃənl]	*The motivational speaker talked about the importance of self-confidence.*	anregend; Motivations...
	5a	**to value** ['væljuː]	*When someone thanks you for your work, you feel valued.*	wertschätzen
		happiness ['hæpinəs]	*Money and success are good, but happiness is more important.*	Glück; Freude
		ambition [æm'bɪʃn]	*I have a lot of ambition, so I want to go to university.* ❗ *Lat. 'ambitio, -onis' (f.)*	Ehrgeiz; Ambition
100	S1	**to optimize** ['ɒptɪmaɪz]	*We work to optimize communication in our office.*	optimieren
	TIP	**to rephrase** [ˌriː'freɪz]	*Rephrase a statement in your own words to confirm understanding.*	neu formulieren; umformulieren
	S2	**besides** [bɪ'saɪdz]	*Besides, I think graphic design is the perfect job for me.* *= in addition*	außerdem
		arty ['ɑːti]	*I've always been the arty type and like to draw.*	gewollt künstlerisch
		to code [kəʊd]	*I am interested in coding and designed my own website.* *= to program*	kodieren; programmieren
	S3	**gig** [gɪg]	*I am working a few part-time gigs to top up my income.*	Gig; Auftritt; Mini-Job
101	S1	**evaluation** [ɪˌvælju'eɪʃn]	*Use the interview evaluation sheet to assess the candidate.*	Bewertung
	S3	**observer** [əb'zɜːvə]	*In groups of three, take turns role playing as a candidate interviewing for a job, as the interviewer and as an observer.*	Beobachter(in)
		to expand [ɪk'spænd]	*You will get practical training to expand your skills.* ❗ *Lat. 'expandere (expando, expansi, expansum)'*	wachsen; ausbauen

page	exercise
102	

Workshop 3

The world of work

applicant ['æplɪkənt]	Bewerber(in); Anmelder(in)
apprentice [ə'prentɪs]	Auszubildende(r); Lehrling
apprenticeship [ə'prentɪʃɪp]	Lehrstelle; Ausbildung
contractor [kən'træktə]	Auftragnehmer(in)
economy [ɪ'kɒnəmi]	Ökonomie; Wirtschaft
employee [ɪm'plɔɪi:]	Angestellte(r)
employer [ɪm'plɔɪə]	Arbeitgeber(in)
enterprise ['entəpraɪz]	Unternehmen
entrepreneur [ˌɒntrəprə'nɜ:]	Unternehmer(in)
freelance ['fri:lɑ:ns]	freiberuflich
freelancer ['fri:lɑ:nsə]	Freiberufler(in)
gig economy [gɪg ɪ'kɒnəmi]	*In einer Gig-Economy gibt es keine festen Angestellten, die Arbeitskräfte werden für Einzelaufträge (Gigs) bezahlt.*
intern [ɪn'tɜ:n]	Praktikant(in); Volontär(in)
internship ['ɪntɜ:nʃɪp]	Praktikum
job hopping [dʒɒb 'hɒpɪŋ]	wiederholter Stellenwechsel
letter of reference [ˌletə əv 'refrəns]	Referenzschreiben; Empfehlungsschreiben
menial ['mi:niəl]	untergeordnet; nieder
overtime ['əʊvətaɪm]	Überstunden
to quit [kwɪt], **quit, quit**	kündigen
salary ['sæləri]	Gehalt; Lohn
sector ['sektə]	Bereich
self-employed [ˌself ɪm'plɔɪd]	selbstständig
to shadow sb ['ʃædəʊ]	bei jdm hospitieren
sideline ['saɪdlaɪn]	Nebenberuf
start-up ['stɑ:tʌp]	junges Unternehmen
traineeship [ˌtreɪ'ni:ʃɪp]	Praktikumsplatz
unemployed [ˌʌnɪm'plɔɪd]	arbeitslos
unpaid [ˌʌn'peɪd]	unbezahlt
venture ['ventʃə]	Unternehmen
vocational [vəʊ'keɪʃənl]	beruflich
workforce ['wɜ:kfɔ:s]	Arbeitskräfte

exercise	word	example	German
2a	**economy** [ɪ'kɒnəmi]	*The gig economy offers new opportunities for young people.* ! *Fr. 'économie' (f.)*	Ökonomie; Wirtschaft
	norm [nɔ:m]	*Working long hours seems to be the norm these days.*	Regel; Standard
	job hopping [dʒɒb 'hɒpɪŋ]	*Job hopping is when you change jobs frequently.*	wiederholter Stellenwechsel
	contractor [kən'træktə]	*Many companies hire independent contractors for short-term work.*	Auftragnehmer(in)
	demand [dɪ'mɑ:nd]	*The demand for consumer products has increased.*	Nachfrage; Verlangen
	delivery [dɪ'lɪvəri]	*Many gig workers are delivery drivers.*	Zustellung; Zustellung
	sideline ['saɪdlaɪn]	*Some people run their own business as a sideline, while working a regular job.*	Nebenberuf
	freelance ['fri:lɑ:ns]	*I work as a freelance journalist.*	freiberuflich

page	exercise	Workshop 3		
		freelancer ['fri:la:nsə]	*Freelancers can set up a personal profile to find jobs that match their skills.*	Freiberufler(in)
		to bid for [bɪd]**, bid, bid**	*I publish my profile, so I can bid for jobs that match my skills.*	sich bewerben um; ein Angebot machen
		to commute [kə'mju:t]	*Employees used to commute, now they can work anywhere.*	pendeln
103	3	**to handwrite** ['hændraɪt]**, handwrote, handwritten** ['hændrəʊt, 'hændrɪtn]	*My grandmother often still handwrites letters.*	mit der Hand schreiben
		overtime ['əʊvətaɪm]	*In the past, my dad stayed late at work and he got paid overtime.*	Überstunden
		menial ['mi:niəl]	*Women often had to do menial tasks like typing.*	untergeordnet; nieder
	4a	**banking** ['bæŋkɪŋ]	*Most jobs are in service industries these days, like in education, banking and tourism.*	Banking; Bankwesen
		breadwinner ['bredwɪnə]	*My mother was the family breadwinner and my father stayed home with the children.*	Ernährer(in); Brotverdiener(in)
		housewife ['haʊswaɪf]	*When I was growing up, my mum was a housewife.*	Hausfrau
		pay gap ['peɪ gæp]	*The pay gap between men and women is still there.*	Lohngefälle
		workforce ['wɜ:kfɔ:s]	*Women are almost half the workforce, but the gender pay gap is still there.*	Arbeitskräfte
		smart [sma:t]	*Technological devices become smarter.*	schlau
	5	**pit** [pɪt]	*Your great-grandfather was a coal miner who worked down in the pit.*	Grube
		to retire [rɪ'taɪər]	*Then, after he had retired, he began to travel.*	in Rente gehen
		pigeon ['pɪdʒɪn]	*Pigeon are birds that live mainly in cities.*	Taube
	6a	**spiky** ['spaɪki]	*I used to have long hair, but now I have short, spiky hair.*	stachelig; spitz
104	1	**wealth** [welθ]	*Industry and trade generate wealth.* ≠ *poverty*	Reichtum
		claim [kleɪm]	*One claim is that children fear stabbings so much, they don't go out.*	Behauptung
		poverty ['pɒvəti]	*We want to raise awareness about different social issues like food poverty.* **!** *Lat. 'paupertas, -tatis' (f.)*	Armut
	2	**housing** ['haʊzɪŋ]	*Today it is much harder to get on the housing ladder than it used to be.*	Wohn...; Wohnungs...
		food bank ['fu:d bæŋk]	*Foodbanks help people in poverty.*	Essensausgabe; Lebensmittelsammelstelle

page	exercise	Workshop 3		
		buyer ['baɪə]	*The average age of a first-time home buyer is 33.*	Käufer(in)
		unemployed [ˌʌnɪm'plɔɪd]	*He doesn't have job, he's unemployed.*	arbeitslos
	3a	**stability** [stə'bɪləti]	*In the future there will likely be less economic stability but more freedom to choose your lifestyle.*	Stabilität
		aware [ə'weər]	*Would you say that Generation Z-ers are one of the most socially aware groups in society?*	bewusst
	3a	**proportion** [prə'pɔ:ʃn]	*The proportion of young people donating money to charities has fallen in the past few years.* ❗ *Lat. 'proportio, -onis' (f.)*	Anteil
		economic [ˌi:kə'nɒmɪk]	*Economic security and stability is difficult in a gig economy.*	wirtschaftlich
		usable ['ju:zəbl]	*We recycle and find a new purpose for usable packaging.*	nutzbar; verwendbar
		carrier ['kæriə]	*We've been collecting re-usable carrier bags for the local food bank.*	Trage...
		gang [gæŋ]	*The charity tries to prevent young people from getting caught up in gang violence.*	Bande; Gang
		to campaign (for) [kæm'peɪn]	*We are campaigning to raise awareness about social injustice.* ❗ *Fr. 'faire campagne'*	kämpfen (um); sich einsetzen (für)
105	2	**to place** [pleɪs]	*We designed posters, which were placed on noticeboards.*	anbringen; vermitteln
		initially [ɪ'nɪʃəli]	*Initially the response was disappointedly slow.* ❗ *Lat. 'initium, -i' (n.)*	zunächst; anfangs
		to **surpass** [sə'pɑ:s]	*We collected more than 5,000 carrier bags, surpassing our original target of 2,000.*	übertreffen
		to **alleviate** [ə'li:vieɪt]	*Many of us feel there is far more we could do to help alleviate food poverty.*	lindern; erleichtern
		well-being ['wel bi:ɪŋ]	*I am interested in issues that affect children's health and well-being.* *= wellness*	Wohlbefinden
	4a	**toolkit** ['tu:lkɪt]	*We have created a toolkit for schools to use when teaching kids about health.*	Toolkit; Werkzeugkiste
		pandemic [pæn'demɪk]	*The charity was founded in 2020 during the Corona pandemic to help musicians.* ❗ *Fr. 'pandémie' (f.)*	Pandemie
		to subscribe to [səb'skraɪb]	*If you're interested in getting involved, subscribe to our platform.*	abonnieren; anmelden

page	exercise	Workshop 3		
	4b	**to convince** [kən'vɪns]	*Can the writer convince the reader about the importance of the charity?*	überzeugen
106	1	**internship** ['ɪntɜ:nʃɪp]	*Daniela did an internship abroad.* *= placement*	Praktikum
		intern [ɪn'tɜ:n]	*As you are not getting paid while you are working as an intern, you have to cover the cost yourself, and it's expensive.*	Praktikant(in); Volontär(in)
	2a	**review** [rɪ'vju:]	*Read Daniela's review of the movie and say whether it sounds interesting.*	Kritik; Review
		letter of reference [ˌletə əv 'refrəns]	*I filled in an online application and sent my CV and letters of reference.*	Referenzschreiben; Empfehlungsschreiben
		to shadow sb ['ʃædəʊ]	*She shadowed a doctor to get hospital experience.*	bei jdm hospitieren
		clinic ['klɪnɪk]	*She was really great at explaining things to me and letting me watch her both in the clinic and in surgery.*	Klinik
		surgery ['sɜ:dʒəri]	*The doctor's surgery is open on Mondays, Tuesdays and Fridays.*	Sprechstunde; Praxis
		thoroughly ['θʌrəli]	*= really*	völlig; durchaus
		genuinely ['dʒenjuɪnli]	*Looking back, I can genuinely say I had a fantastic experience.* *= really*	echt
107		**simultaneous** [ˌsɪml'teɪniəs]	*= happening at the same time*	gleichzeitig; simultan
	3	**to rate** [reɪt]	*How do they rate their experience with the computer software?*	bewerten; beurteilen
		psychology [saɪ'kɒlədʒi]	*I want to study medicine and afterwards psychology.*	Psychologie
		psychologist [saɪ'kɒlədʒɪst]	*The more cultures I can begin to understand, the better prepared I will be for my future career as a psychologist or non-profit worker.*	Psychologe/Psychologin
		city hall [ˌsɪti 'hɔ:l]	*The city hall is an old building in the centre.*	Rathaus
		paragliding ['pærəglaɪdɪŋ]	*My friend thinks paragliding is dangerous, but I like it.*	Gleitschirmfliegen
		cage [keɪdʒ]	*We shouldn't keep animals in cages.*	Käfig
		roommate ['rumˌmeɪt]	*After work and on weekends, I explored the city with my roommates.* **!** *BE = flatmate*	Mitbewohner(in)
108	2	**supervisor** ['su:pərvaɪzə]	*The supervisor wrote a report about Daniela's stay.* **!** *Lat. 'videre (video, vidi, visum)' = to view*	Leiter(in)
		initial [ɪ'nɪʃl]	*She had initial reservations but now she is happy in the programme.*	ursprünglich; anfänglich
109	3	**to opt** [ɒpt]	*I opted not to travel after finishing school and did an internship instead.*	(sich) entscheiden (für/gegen)

page	exercise	Workshop 3		
	4a	**finalist** ['faɪnəlɪst]	*Her idea was so good that she became one of the finalists.*	Finalist(in)
		enterprise ['entəpraɪz]	*Send in your application with a short description of your business idea or start-up enterprise.*	Unternehmen
		gelato ['dʒelɑ:təʊ]	*I learned how to make Italian ice cream, which is called gelato.*	italienische Eiscreme
		retail ['ri:teɪl]	*The pay in retail is fairly low and far more women then men have jobs in shops.*	Einzelhandel
		gelateria ['dʒelə'tɪəriə]	*She visited many gelaterias around the world and has eaten a lot of gelato.*	italienisches Eiscafé
		venture ['ventʃə]	*She started a new venture renting clothes for special events.*	Unternehmen
		paperwork ['peɪpəwɜ:k]	*This platform allows people to work smart and spend less time on paperwork.*	Schreibarbeit
		electrical [ɪ'lektrɪkl]	*He was employed as an electrical engineer and worked at testing electrical equipment.*	elektrisch; elektronisch
		artificial intelligence [ˌɑ:tɪfɪʃl ɪn'telɪdʒəns]	*The computer programme uses artificial intelligence to help people make decisions.* ! *Fr. 'intelligence artificielle' (f.)*	künstliche Intelligenz
		algorithm ['ælgərɪðəm]	*An algorithm is a process in problem-solving operations normally executed by a computer.*	Algorithmus
		to **empower** [ɪm'paʊə]	*We use technology to help empower young people.*	stärken; ermächtigen
110	2a	**outer space** [ˌaʊtə 'speɪs]	*My generation will continue to explore outer space.*	Weltraum
		spacewalker ['speɪswɔ:kə]	*Almost all of the spacewalkers in the world have been men.*	Spacewalker; jemand, der im Weltraum spazieren geht
	3	**merit** ['merɪt]	*People should be judged on merit, not on whether they are male or female.*	Wert; Leistung
		glass ceiling [ˌglɑ:s 'si:lɪŋ]	*The glass ceiling prevents women from getting better jobs.*	gläserne Decke; unsichtbare Barriere
		critic ['krɪtɪk]	*She is an observer and a critic of the developments.*	Kritiker(in)
		nursing ['nɜ:sɪŋ]	*Nursing became an important job during the pandemic.*	Krankenpflege
		invisible [ɪn'vɪzəbl]	*The invisible barrier for women and minorities is called the glass ceiling.*	unsichtbar
		progression [prə'greʃn]	*Career progression is not important to everyone.*	Fortschreiten; Entwicklung
		counterpart ['kaʊntəpɑ:t]	*Women often earn less than their male counterparts.*	Kollege/Kollegin

Workshop 3

page	exercise			
111	4b	**Chief Executive Officer (CEO)** [ˌtʃi:f ɪgˌzekjətɪv ˈɒfɪsə]	*Of the top 100 companies in the UK only six had a female Chief Executive Officer in 2020.*	Geschäftsführer(in)
		nursery [ˈnɜ:səri]	*Most nursery and primary school teachers in the UK are women.*	Kindergarten; Kindertagesstätte
		occupied: to be occupied [bi ˈɒkjupaɪd]	*In the US, only 26% of jobs in computing or math are occupied by women.*	beschäftigt sein
		airline [ˈeəlaɪn]	*In 2019, only 5% of airline pilots were female.*	Fluggesellschaft
112	S1a	**forklift** [ˌfɔ:klɪft]	*A forklift is a small electric vehicle that can lift heavy boxes and things.*	Gabelstapler
		induction [ɪnˈdʌkʃn]	*The office is new to him, so he's getting an induction.* ! *Lat. 'inducere (induco, induxi, inductum)' = to induce*	Einführung
		horizontal [ˌhɒrɪˈzɒntl]	*≠ vertical*	horizontal
		thermostat [ˈθɜ:məstæt]	*Use the thermostat to change the room temperature.*	Thermostat; Temperaturregler
		spirit level [ˈspɪrɪt levl]	*Check the surface with a spirit level to see whether it is straight.*	Wasserwaage
	TIP	**dispenser** [dɪˈspensə]	*There are water dispensers on every floor of the office building.*	Spender
	S2a	**timer** [ˈtaɪmər]	*You select the function here, then you set the timer like this.*	Timer; Zeituhr
		rota [ˈrəʊtə]	*My roommates and I have organized a cleaning rota for the apartment.* ! *Lat. 'rotare (roto, rotavi, rotatum)' = to rotate*	abwechselnder Dienst
		breakout area [ˈbreɪkaʊt ˈeəriə]	*We have offices, open plan areas and breakout areas for informal meetings.*	Gruppenfläche; Breakout-Bereich
		ID card (identification card) [ˌaɪ ˈdi: kɑ:d]	*I need to issue you your office ID card.*	Ausweis
		to clip to [klɪp tə]	*The best way not to lose your ID card is to clip it to a lanyard.*	klemmen an
		lanyard [ˈlænjɑ:d]	*I have a clip on a lanyard for my ID card.*	Umhängeband; Kordel
		sticky note [ˌstɪki ˈnəʊt]	*People put sticky notes with their names on some things like yoghurt.*	Haftnotiz
113	S1	**e-scooter** [ˈi:sku:tə]	*In big cities you can now rent scooters by the minute using an app on your phone.*	E-Roller
		yoga [ˈjəʊgə]	*Practising yoga keeps you fit.*	Yoga
	S2a	**toner cartridge** [ˈtəʊnə ˈkɑ:trɪdʒ]	*The printer needs a new toner cartridge in order to print properly.*	Tonerkartusche
		legal pad [ˈli:gl pæd]	*Take your notes on a legal pad first.*	Schreibblock mit speziellem Papier

page	exercise	Workshop 3		
		to transfer [træns'fɜ:r]	*All your notes from the legal pad have to be transferred to the client's electronic file and the paper shredded.* ❗ *Fr. 'transférer'*	übertragen
	S1	**fire escape** ['faɪər ɪskeɪp]	*That's one of two fire escapes on the house.*	Fluchtweg
	S2a	**fire extinguisher** ['faɪər ɪkstɪŋgwɪʃə]	*There is a fire extinguisher under the kitchen sink.*	Feuerlöscher
		cabinet ['kæbɪnət]	*The fire extinguishers are in that cabinet over there.*	Schrank; Kabinett
115	3	**typewriter** ['taɪpraɪtə]	*A traditional typewriter is difficult to use.*	Schreibmaschine
		dial phone ['daɪəl fəʊn]	*When my mother was a girl they had dial phones.*	Telefon mit Wählscheibe
118	1	**MBA (Masters of Business Administration)** [ˌem bi: 'eɪ]	*When I finish university I'm planning go to the USA and take an MBA.*	MBA
	3	**mechanical** [mə'kænɪkl]	*I am studying engineering because I 'm interested in mechanical things.*	mechanisch

page	exercise	Workshop 4		
128	1a	**graphic novel** [ˌgræfɪk 'nɒvl]	*Graphic novels contain mainly pictures and short texts.*	Bildroman
		murder ['mɜ:dər]	*This award-winning graphic novel has an exciting murder mystery plot and an amazing art style.*	Mord
		mystery ['mɪstri]	*I read history books and love mystery novels.*	Geheimnis; Rätsel
		ember ['embər]	*An ember fell out of the fire and burned my foot.*	glühende Kohle
		dystopian [dɪs'təʊpiən]	*Dystopian fiction shows a future society that is very bad for the people who live in it. Humans often have to fight for survival and against evel powers.* *≠ utopian*	dystopisch
		darkness ['dɑ:knəs]	*Many children are afraid of darkness.*	Dunkelheit
		underworld ['ʌndəwɜ:ld]	*The story is about two children who grow up in an underworld.*	Unterwelt
		builder ['bɪldə]	*The builder of the house finished on time.*	Baumeister(in); Bauherr(in)
		memoir ['memwɑ:]	*The book is a memoir of a young girl who was not allowed to go to school.*	Memoiren; Erinnerung
		oppression [ə'preʃn]	*There is war and oppression in many areas of the world.* ❗ *Lat. 'oppressio, -onis' (f.)*	Unterdrückung
		afterlife ['ɑ:ftəlaɪf]	*After he is killed, his spirit lives on in the afterlife.*	Leben nach dem Tod

page	exercise	Workshop 4		
	1b	**to associate (with)** [ə'səʊsieɪt]	*What types stories do you associate with graphic novels.*	assoziieren; in Verbindung bringen
	2a	**glimpse** [glɪmps]	*Dystopian novels can give you a glimpse of the future.*	flüchtiger Blick
	2b	**evil** ['i:vl]	*The evil in the movie was really scary.*	Übel; Böse
129	3	**setting** ['setɪŋ]	*The setting is the location and time in which a story takes place.*	Setting; Umgebung
	4b	**intolerant** [ɪn'tɒlərənt]	*My neighbour is very intolerant and doesn't respect people who are different.*	intolerant
		impatient [ɪm'peɪʃnt]	*Kids can be impatient in the days before their birthday.* *= patient*	ungeduldig
		narrow-minded [ˌnærəʊ 'maɪndɪd]	*We want to help narrow-minded people to be more open.*	engstirnig
		uncaring [ʌn'keərɪŋ]	*The man seemed to uncaring when he spoke to the poor people.*	gefühllos
	7	**coyote** [kaɪ'əʊti]	*The coyote helps people to cross the border.*	Kojote; hier: Schlepper(in)
	CC	**enforcement** [ɪn'fɔ:smənt]	*ICE is the USA's Immigration and Customs Enforcement.*	Vollstreckung
		to smuggle ['smʌgl]	*There us a lot of smuggling at the border.*	schmuggeln
130		**to vandalize** ['vændəlaɪzd]	*After the party the park was vandalized.*	mutwillig beschädigen
132		**to scavenge** ['skævɪndʒ]	*My brother scavenged in the garbage for things to sell.*	nach etw. suchen
133		**to pick a fight** [pɪk ə faɪt]	*She went and picked a fight with the boss of the gang.*	einen Streit mit anzetteln
136		**to worship** ['wɜ:ʃɪp]	*Bastian said he worshipped the lady of death, Santa Muerte.*	verehren
		runaway ['rʌnəweɪ]	*She protects poor runaways who have no home or security.*	Ausreißer(in)
137		**raid** [reɪd]	*There was a police raid and people were arrested.*	Razzia
		hell [hel]	*It was so hot, it was like hell.*	Hölle
140	1b	**to sympathize (with)** ['sɪmpəθaɪz]	*I sympathize with people who can't speak in front of groups.* **!** *Fr. 'sympythiser avec'*	mitfühlen (mit jmd)
	2	**cameraman** ['kæmrəmæn]	*The cameraman is well known for working on action films.*	Kameramann
	3b	**violent** ['vaɪələnt]	*Kids who have extremely violent behaviour need help and guidance.* **!** *Lat. 'violare (violo, violavi, violatum)' = to violate*	gewalttätig
		to beg [beg]	*My dog begs for food.*	betteln

page	exercise	Workshop 4		
141	4b	**trainer** ['treɪnər]	*When you buy trainers, you should question how they were made.* ❗ *AE = sneaker*	Turnschuh
		certified ['sɜːtɪfaɪd]	*Are the products certified as fair trade?* ❗ *Fr. 'certifié'*	beglaubigt; anerkannt
		label ['leɪbl]	*Look at the labels on the clothing you buy to see where they're made.*	Etikett
	6	**slum** [slʌm]	*Many big cities have slums where the poor live.*	Slum; Elendsviertel
	8	**genre** ['ʒɒnrə]	*Graphic novels are a genre similar to comic books.*	Genre

Dictionary: English – German

A

abbreviated [ə'bri:vieɪtɪd] abgekürzt **WS 2**, 70

abbreviation [əˌbri:vi'eɪʃn] Abkürzung OT 2

ability [ə'bɪləti] Fähigkeit; Möglichkeit OT 4

to **be able** [bi 'eɪbl] fähig sein; können OT 2

aboard [ə'bɔ:d] an Bord OT 4

about [ə'baʊt] über; wegen; ungefähr OT 1

above [ə'bʌv] oben; oberhalb OT 2

abroad [ə'brɔ:d] im Ausland OT 2

to **abseil** ['æbseɪl] (sich) abseilen OT 2

absolutely ['æbsəlu:tli] absolut; wirklich OT 2

abstract ['æbstrækt] Zusammenfassung; Auszug OT 4

academic [ˌækə'demɪk] akademisch OT 4

accent ['æksənt] Akzent OT 2

to **accept** [ək'sept] annehmen OT 2

acceptance [ək'septəns] Akzeptanz **WS 1**, 33

access ['ækses] Zugang OT 2

to **access** ['ækses] zugreifen auf OT 4

accessible [ək'sesəbl] zugänglich; barrierefrei OT 2

accessory [ək'sesəri] Zubehör OT 3

accident ['æksɪdənt] Unfall OT 1

by accident [baɪ 'æksɪdənt] versehentlich OT 2

to **cause an accident** [ˌkɔ:z ən 'æksɪdənt] einen Unfall verursachen OT 2

Accident and Emergency ['æksɪdənt ənd iˌmɜ:dʒənsi] Notaufnahme OT 1

accidentally [ˌæksɪ'dentəli] zufällig; versehentlich OT 3

accommodation [əˌkɒmə'deɪʃn] Unterkunft OT 4

accompanied [ə'kʌmpəni:d] in Begleitung OT 3

according to [ə'kɔ:dɪŋ tə] nach; gemäß OT 4

accordion [ə'kɔ:diən] Akkordeon OT 2

account [ə'kaʊnt] Konto OT 3

to **account for** [ə'kaʊnt fər] ausmachen **WS 2**, 58

to **hold accountable** [həʊld ə'kaʊntəbl] zur Rechenschaft ziehen **WS 2**, 64

accurate ['ækjərət] genau; präzise OT 4

to **accuse** [ə'kju:z] beschuldigen; anklagen **WS 2**, 77

ache [eɪk] Schmerz OT 3

to **achieve** [ə'tʃi:v] erreichen; schaffen OT 4

achievement [ə'tʃi:vmənt] Errungenschaft OT 4

acidic [ə'sɪdɪk] sauer **WS 1**, 28

to **acknowledge** [ək'nɒlɪdʒ] bestätigen; anerkennen **WS 2**, 77

acoustic [ə'ku:stɪk] akustisch OT 2

acquaintance [ə'kweɪntəns] Bekannte(r); Bekanntschaft OT 3

acre ['eɪkə] Morgen (Fläche) OT 4

across [ə'krɒs] auf der anderen Seite; hinüber OT 1

act [ækt] Gesetz; Verordnung **WS 1**, 43

to **act** [ækt] sich verhalten; handeln; Theater spielen OT 1

to **act out** [ækt aʊt] ausspielen OT 2

action ['ækʃn] Aktion OT 2

in action [ɪn 'ækʃn] im Einsatz OT 2

actively ['æktɪvli] aktiv OT 4

activism ['æktɪvɪzəm] Aktivismus **WS 3**, 96

activist ['æktɪvɪst] Aktivist(in) **WS 3**, 90

activity [æk'tɪvəti] Aktivität OT 1

actor ['æktə] Schauspieler(in) OT 1

actual ['æktʃuəl] richtig; wirklich OT 4

actually ['æktʃuəli] eigentlich; um genau zu sein OT 3

ad [æd] Werbung OT 2

AD (Anno Domini) [ˌeɪ 'di:] n. Chr.; unserer Zeitrechnung OT 2

adaptation [ˌædæp'teɪʃn] Adaptierung OT 4

to **add** [æd] hinzufügen; addieren OT 1

addiction [ə'dɪkʃn] Sucht; Süchtigkeit **WS 2**, 73

addition [ə'dɪʃn] Zusatz; Ergänzung OT 4

additional [ə'dɪʃənl] zusätzlich; ergänzend **WS 2**, 57

address [ə'dres] Adresse OT 1

to **address** [ə'dres] ansprechen **WS 1**, 37

adjective ['ædʒɪktɪv] Adjektiv OT 2

to **admire** [əd'maɪə] bewundern OT 4

admission [əd'mɪʃn] Eintritt OT 2

to **admit** [əd'mɪt] zugeben **WS 1**, 20

adolescent [ˌædə'lesnt] Jugendliche; Jugend... **WS 2**, 72

to **adopt** [ə'dɒpt] annehmen **WS 1**, 32

to **adore** [ə'dɔ:] anbeten; bewundern OT 4

adult ['ædʌlt] Erwachsene(r) OT 1

advance [əd'vɑ:ns] Fortschritt OT 4

advantage [əd'vɑ:ntɪdʒ] Vorteil OT 3

advent ['ædvent] Beginn; Einführung **WS 1**, 25

adventure [əd'ventʃə] Abenteuer OT 1

adventurous [əd'ventʃərəs] abenteuerlustig OT 2

advert ['ædvɜ:t] Werbung OT 2

to **advertise** ['ædvətaɪz] Werbung machen für OT 2

advertisement [əd'vɜ:tɪsmənt] Werbung OT 1

advertising ['ædvətaɪzɪŋ] Werbung OT 2

advice [əd'vaɪs] Rat OT 2

to **advise** [əd'vaɪz] raten OT 4

advisor [əd'vaɪzə] Berater(in) **WS 3**, 91

advocate (for) ['ædvəkət] Fürsprecher(in) **WS 2**, 73

aeroplane ['eərəpleɪn] Flugzeug OT 4

aerospace ['eərəʊspeɪs] Luftfahrt OT 4

affair [ə'feə] Angelegenheit; Affäre OT 4

to **affect** [ə'fekt] sich auswirken auf OT 3

affirmative [ə'fɜ:mətɪv] zustimmend OT 3

to **afford** [ə'fɔ:d] sich leisten OT 2

afraid [ə'freɪd] ängstlich OT 2

African ['æfrɪkən] afrikanisch OT 2

after ['ɑ:ftə] nach; hinter OT 1

afterlife ['ɑ:ftəlaɪf] Leben nach dem Tod **WS 4**, 128

afternoon [ˌɑ:ftə'nu:n] Nachmittag OT 1

afterwards ['ɑ:ftəwədz] danach OT 4

again [ə'gen] wieder OT 1

against [ə'genst] gegen OT 1

age [eɪdʒ] Alter; Zeitalter OT 1

aged ['eɪdʒd] im Alter von OT 3

agency ['eɪdʒənsi] Agentur; Organisation OT 4

agenda [ə'dʒendə] Tagesordnung OT 3

agent ['eɪdʒənt] Mittel **WS 1**, 27

aggravated assault [ˌægrəveɪtɪd ə'sɔ:lt] schwere Körperverletzung **WS 2**, 64

aghast [ə'gɑ:st] entsetzt OT 3

agile ['ædʒaɪl] beweglich OT 3

ago [ə'gəʊ] vor OT 1

agonizingly ['ægənaɪzɪŋli] quälend; sehr OT 3

agrarian [ə'greəriən] landwirtschaftlich **WS 1**, 24
to **agree** [ə'gri:] sich einig sein; zustimmen OT 1
agreement [ə'gri:mənt] Vereinbarung OT 3
agricultural [ˌægrɪ'kʌltʃərəl] landwirtschaftlich OT 4
agriculture ['ægrɪkʌltʃə] Landwirtschaft OT 2
ahead [ə'hed] weiter vorn OT 2
aid [eɪd] Hilfe; Unterstützung **WS 2**, 59
first aid [ˌfɜ:st 'eɪd] Erste Hilfe OT 2
aim [eɪm] Ziel OT 4
to **aim** [eɪm] zielen; beabsichtigen OT 4
air [eə] Luft OT 2
airline ['eəlaɪn] Fluggesellschaft **WS 3**, 111
airplane ['eəpleɪn] Flugzeug OT 2
airport ['eəpɔ:t] Flughafen OT 1
alarm [ə'lɑ:m] Wecker; Alarm OT 2
alarmed [ə'lɑ:md] beunruhigt OT 3
alarming [ə'lɑ:mɪŋ] erschreckend OT 4
Alaskan [ə'læskən] alaskisch OT 2
album ['ælbəm] Album OT 3
alcohol ['ælkəhɒl] Alkohol OT 3
alcoholic [ˌælkə'hɒlɪk] alkoholisch OT 3
to **alert** [ə'lɜ:t] alarmieren OT 2
algorithm ['ælgərɪðəm] Algorithmus **WS 3**, 109
alien ['eɪliən] Außerirdische(r); Alien OT 2
alike [ə'laɪk] ebenso OT 4
alive [ə'laɪv] lebendig OT 2
all [ɔ:l] alles; alle OT 1
to **alleviate** [ə'li:vieɪt] lindern; erleichtern **WS 3**, 105
to **allocate** ['æləkeɪt] zuordnen OT 4
to **allow** [ə'laʊ] erlauben OT 3
allowed [ə'laʊd] erlaubt OT 2
almost ['ɔ:lməʊst] fast OT 2
alone [ə'ləʊn] allein OT 2
to **leave alone** [li:v ə'ləʊn] in Ruhe lassen OT 2
along [ə'lɒŋ] entlang OT 2
aloud [ə'laʊd] laut; mit lauter Stimme OT 2
alpaca [æl'pækə] Alpaka OT 2
alphabet ['ælfəbet] Alphabet OT 1
alphabetical [ˌælfə'betɪkl] alphabetisch OT 2
already [ɔ:l'redi] schon OT 2
alright [ɔ:l'raɪt] in Ordnung **WS 1**, 14
also ['ɔ:lsəʊ] auch OT 1
alternative [ɔ:l'tɜ:nətɪv] alternativ **WS 1**, 27
alternatively [ɔ:l'tɜ:nətɪvli] alternativ OT 4
although [ɔ:l'ðəʊ] obwohl OT 2
always ['ɔ:lweɪz] immer OT 1
amazed [ə'meɪzd] erstaunt; überrascht OT 3
amazing [ə'meɪzɪŋ] fantastisch OT 1
ambition [æm'bɪʃn] Ehrgeiz; Ambition **WS 3**, 99
ambitious [æm'bɪʃəs] ehrgeizig OT 3
ambulance ['æmbjələns] Krankenwagen OT 1
amends [ə'mendz] Wiedergutmachung; Schadenersatz **WS 2**, 64
amendment [ə'mendmənt] Ergänzung OT 4
amenity [ə'mi:nəti] Einrichtung OT 4
American [ə'merɪkən] amerikanisch OT 1
among [ə'mʌŋ] unter; zwischen OT 3
amount [ə'maʊnt] Betrag OT 2
amused [ə'mju:zd] amüsiert OT 3
to **analyse** ['ænəlaɪz] analysieren OT 3
analysis [ə'næləsɪs] Analyse; Untersuchung **WS 2**, 74
analyst ['ænəlɪst] Analytiker(in); Analyst(in) **WS 3**, 99
ancestor ['ænsestə] Vorfahr(in) OT 3
ancestral [æn'sestrəl] zur Familie gehörend; den Vorfahren gehörend OT 4
ancestry ['ænsestri] Abstammung OT 3
to **anchor** ['æŋkə] ankern OT 4
ancient ['eɪnʃənt] antik OT 2
and [ənd] und OT 1
anecdote ['ænɪkdəʊt] Anekdote OT 4
Anglican ['æŋglɪkən] anglikanisch OT 3
Anglo-Saxon [ˌæŋgləʊ'sæksn] angelsächsisch OT 3
angry ['æŋgri] wütend; verärgert OT 1
animal ['ænɪml] Tier OT 1
animated ['ænɪmeɪtɪd] animiert OT 4
ankle ['æŋkl] Knöchel; Fußknöchel OT 1
to **announce** [ə'naʊns] ansagen; bekannt geben OT 2
announcement [ə'naʊnsmənt] Bekanntgabe; Ansage OT 2
announcer [ə'naʊnsə] Ansager(in) OT 2
to **annoy** [ə'nɔɪ] ärgern; aufregen **WS 2**, 68
annoyed [ə'nɔɪd] verärgert OT 3
annoying [ə'nɔɪɪŋ] ärgerlich OT 2
annual ['ænjuəl] jährlich **WS 2**, 56
another [ə'nʌðə] noch ein(e); ein(e) andere(r, -s) OT 1
answer ['ɑ:nsə] Antwort OT 1
to **answer** ['ɑ:nsə] antworten; beantworten OT 1
antelope ['æntɪləʊp] Antilope OT 4
anthem ['ænθəm] Nationalhymne; Hymne **WS 1**, 33
anthropology [ˌænθrə'pɒlədʒi] Anthropologie OT 4
anxiety [æŋ'zaɪəti] Sorge; Ängstlichkeit **WS 1**, 34
anxious ['æŋkʃəs] besorgt; ängstlich **WS 2**, 50
anxiously ['æŋkʃəsli] besorgt OT 3
any ['eni] irgendein(e) OT 1
anybody ['enibɒdi] irgend jemand OT 1
any more [ˌeni 'mɔ:] nicht mehr OT 3
anymore [ˌeni'mɔ:] nicht mehr OT 4
anyone ['eniwʌn] (irgend)jemand OT 2
anything ['eniθɪŋ] irgend etwas OT 1
anytime ['enitaɪm] jederzeit OT 3
anyway ['eniweɪ] trotzdem; sowieso OT 1
anywhere ['eniweə] irgendwo OT 2
apart [ə'pɑ:t] auseinander **WW**, 11
apart from [ə'pɑ:t] abgesehen von OT 3
apartment [ə'pɑ:tmənt] Wohnung OT 1
to **apologize** [ə'pɒlədʒaɪz] sich entschuldigen OT 2
apology [ə'pɒlədʒi] Entschuldigung OT 3
app [æp] App OT 3
apparently [ə'pærəntli] anscheinend OT 3
appeal [ə'pi:l] Aufruf OT 2
to **appear** [ə'pɪə] erscheinen; scheinen; auftauchen OT 3
appearance [ə'pɪərəns] Aussehen OT 2
appetizing ['æpɪtaɪzɪŋ] appetitlich OT 3
to **applaud** [ə'plɔ:d] applaudieren OT 2
applause [ə'plɔ:z] Applaus OT 2
round of applause [ˌraʊnd əv ə'plɔ:z] ein Applaus OT 2
apple ['æpl] Apfel OT 1
appliance [ə'plaɪəns] Gerät OT 3
applicant ['æplɪkənt] Bewerber(in); Anmelder(in) **WS 3**, 94
application [ˌæplɪ'keɪʃn] Anwendung OT 4
to **apply** [ə'plaɪ] sich bewerben OT 3
to **appoint** [ə'pɔɪnt] ernennen OT 4
appointment [ə'pɔɪntmənt] Termin OT 3
to **appreciate** [ə'pri:ʃieɪt] anerkennen; schätzen OT 4
apprentice [ə'prentɪs] Auszubildende(r); Lehrling **WS 3**, 89

apprenticeship [ə'prentɪʃɪp] Lehrstelle; Ausbildung **WS 3**, 88
approach [ə'prəʊtʃ] Vorgehen; Ansatz **WS 2**, 59
to **approach** [ə'prəʊtʃ] näher kommen; sich nähern OT 3
approachable [ə'prəʊtʃəbl] aufgeschlossen OT 4
appropriate [ə'prəʊpriət] angemessen OT 4
to **approve** [ə'pru:v] zustimmen; genehmigen OT 4
approximately [ə'prɒksɪmətli] ungefähr; etwa **WW**, 10
April ['eɪprəl] April OT 1
aquarium [ə'kweəriəm] Aquarium OT 2
aqueduct ['ækwɪdʌkt] Aquädukt OT 3
arch [ɑ:tʃ] Bogen OT 3
archaeological [ˌɑ:kiə'lɒdʒɪkl] archäologisch OT 2
archaeologist [ˌɑ:ki'ɒlədʒɪst] Archäologe(-in) OT 2
archer ['ɑ:tʃə] Bogenschütze(-in) OT 3
architect ['ɑ:kɪtekt] Architekt(in) OT 4
architecture ['ɑ:kɪtektʃə] Architektur OT 4
archive ['ɑ:kaɪv] Archiv **WS 2**, 68
arctic ['ɑ:ktɪk] arktisch; Arktis OT 4
area ['eəriə] Gebiet; Gegend OT 1
arena [ə'ri:nə] Arena OT 1
to **argue** ['ɑ:gju:] sich streiten OT 3
argument ['ɑ:gjumənt] Streit; Auseinandersetzung OT 1
arid ['ærɪd] dürr; trocken **WS 1**, 25
arm [ɑ:m] Arm OT 1
armchair ['ɑ:mtʃeə] Sessel OT 1
armed [ɑ:md] bewaffnet **WS 2**, 55
armed forces [ˌɑ:md 'fɔ:sɪz] Streitkräfte OT 4
army ['ɑ:mi] Armee OT 2
around [ə'raʊnd] um; um...herum OT 1
to **arrange** [ə'reɪndʒ] planen; vereinbaren OT 2
arrangement [ə'reɪndʒmənt] Vereinbarung **WS 2**, 53
to **arrest** [ə'rest] gefangen nehmen; verhaften OT 4
arrival [ə'raɪvl] Ankunft OT 2
to **arrive** [ə'raɪv] ankommen OT 1
arrow ['ærəʊ] Pfeil OT 3
art [ɑ:t] Kunst OT 1
artefact ['ɑ:tɪfækt] Artefakt OT 2
article ['ɑ:tɪkl] Artikel OT 1
  definite article ['defɪnət ˌɑ:tɪkl] bestimmter Artikel OT 1
artificial [ˌɑ:tɪ'fɪʃl] künstlich OT 4
artificial intelligence [ˌɑ:tɪfɪʃl ɪn'telɪdʒəns] künstliche Intelligenz **WS 3**, 109
artist ['ɑ:tɪst] Künstler(in) OT 1
arty ['ɑ:ti] gewollt künstlerisch **WS 3**, 100
as [æz] als; wie OT 1
asexual [ˌeɪ'sekʃuəl] asexuell **WS 2**, 55
ash [æʃ] Asche OT 2
ashamed [ə'ʃeɪmd] beschämt OT 3
aside [ə'saɪd] beiseite **WS 3**, 98
to **ask** [ɑ:sk] fragen OT 1
asleep [ə'sli:p] schlafend OT 2
aspect ['æspekt] Aspekt OT 4
assault [ə'sɔ:lt] Angriff; Überfall **WS 2**, 64
assembly [ə'sembli] Versammlung OT 1
assembly hall [ə'sembli hɔ:l] Aula OT 1
to **assess** [ə'ses] beurteilen OT 4
assignment [ə'saɪnmənt] Aufgabe OT 4
assimilation [əˌsɪmə'leɪʃn] Assimilation; Anpassung OT 4
to **assist** [ə'sɪst] unterstützen OT 4
assistance [ə'sɪstəns] Unterstützung **WS 2**, 57
assistant [ə'sɪstənt] Assistent(in); Verkäufer(in) OT 4
to **associate (with)** [ə'səʊsieɪt] assoziieren; in Verbindung bringen **WS 4**, 128
astonishingly [ə'stɒnɪʃɪŋli] erstaunlicherweise OT 3
astronaut ['æstrənɔ:t] Astronaut(in) OT 3
at [ət] an; in; bei OT 1
athlete ['æθli:t] Sportler(in) OT 2
athletics [æθ'letɪks] Leichtathletik; Sport OT 1
atmosphere ['ætməsfɪə] Atmosphäre OT 3
attack [ə'tæk] Angriff OT 2
to **attack** [ə'tæk] angreifen OT 4
attacking [ə'tækɪŋ] angreifend OT 3
attainment [ə'teɪnmənt] Leistungen **WS 2**, 58
attempt [ə'tempt] Versuch OT 2
to **attend** [ə'tend] besuchen OT 2
attendant [ə'tendənt] Aufseher(in); Diener(in) OT 2
attention deficit hyperactivity disorder (ADHD) [əˌtenʃn 'defɪsɪt haɪpəræk'tɪvəti dɪsɔ:də] Aufmerksamkeitsdefizit-Hyperaktivitätsstörung **WS 2**, 57
attention [ə'tenʃn] Aufmerksamkeit OT 2
  to **pay attention** [ˌpeɪ ə'tenʃn] aufpassen OT 2
attic ['ætɪk] Dachboden OT 2
attitude ['ætɪtju:d] Ansicht; Einstellung OT 4
to **attract** [ə'trækt] anziehen OT 4
attraction [ə'trækʃn] Sehenswürdigkeit OT 2
attractive [ə'træktɪv] reizvoll **WS 1**, 32
audience ['ɔ:diəns] Publikum OT 1
audio ['ɔ:diəʊ] Audio... OT 2
audition [ɔ:'dɪʃn] Vorsprechen OT 3
to **audition** [ɔ:'dɪʃn] vorsingen; vorsprechen OT 3
August [ɔ:'gʌst] August OT 1
aunt [ɑ:nt] Tante OT 1
auntie ['ɑ:nti] Tantchen OT 2
authentic [ɔ:'θentɪk] authentisch; echt OT 4
author ['ɔ:θə] Autor(in) OT 2
authority [ɔ:'θɒrəti] Autorität; Behörde OT 3
autism ['ɔ:tɪzəm] Autismus **WS 2**, 57
automobile ['ɔ:təməbi:l] Automobil OT 4
autonomous [ɔ:'tɒnəməs] unabhängig; autonom OT 4
autumn ['ɔ:təm] Herbst OT 2
availability [əˌveɪlə'bɪləti] Verfügbarkeit OT 4
available [ə'veɪləbl] verfügbar; erhältlich OT 4
avatar ['ævətɑ:] Avatar OT 3
average ['ævərɪdʒ] durchschnittlich OT 3
  on average [ɒn 'ævərɪdʒ] im Durchschnitt **WS 1**, 21
avocado [ˌævə'kɑ:dəʊ] Avocado **WS 1**, 34
to **avoid** [ə'vɔɪd] vermeiden OT 4
awake [ə'weɪk] wach OT 2
award [ə'wɔ:d] Auszeichnung OT 2
to **award** [ə'wɔ:d] vergeben; verleihen OT 4
aware [ə'weər] bewusst **WS 3**, 104
to **be aware** [bi ə'weə] sich bewusst sein; vorsichtig sein OT 4
awareness [ə'weənəs] Bewusstsein OT 4
away [ə'weɪ] weg OT 2
awesome ['ɔ:səm] toll OT 2
awful ['ɔ:fl] fürchterlich; schrecklich OT 1
aye [aɪ] ja OT 2

B

baby ['beɪbi] Säugling; Baby OT 1
to have a baby [ˌhæv ə 'beɪbi] ein Baby bekommen OT 2
back [bæk] zurück OT 1
back [bæk] Rücken; hinterer Teil OT 1
backbone ['bækbəʊn] Rückgrat OT 2
to backfire [ˌbæk'faɪə] fehlschlagen; daneben gehen OT 4
background ['bækgraʊnd] Hintergrund... OT 3
backing ['bækɪŋ] Unterstützung OT 4
backpack ['bækpæk] Rucksack OT 2
to backpack ['bækpæk] mit dem Rucksack reisen OT 3
backstage [ˌbæk'steɪdʒ] hinter der Bühne OT 3
backwards ['bækwədz] nach hinten; rückwärts OT 3
backyard [ˌbæk'jɑ:d] Garten hinter dem Haus; Hinterhof **WS 2**, 65
bacon ['beɪkən] Speck OT 1
bad [bæd] schlecht OT 1
badge [bædʒ] Abzeichen; Plakette **WS 2**, 60
badminton ['bædmɪntən] Badminton OT 1
bag [bæg] Tasche OT 1
bagger [bægə] Packer(in) OT 4
bagless ['bægles] ohne Beutel OT 4
to bake [beɪk] backen OT 1
baked beans [beɪkt 'bi:ns] weiße Bohnen in Tomatensoße OT 1
baker ['beɪkə] Bäcker(in) OT 4
to balance ['bæləns] ausgleichen **WS 1**, 13
balance ['bæləns] Balance OT 3
bald [bɔ:ld] kahl OT 3
ball [bɔ:l] Ball OT 1
ballet ['bæleɪ] Ballett OT 4
ban [bæn] Verbot; Sperre **WS 1**, 27
to ban [bæn] verbieten OT 3
banana [bə'nɑ:nə] Banane OT 1
band [bænd] Band OT 1
bandage ['bændɪdʒ] Verband OT 2
bank [bæŋk] Ufer; Bank OT 3
banking ['bæŋkɪŋ] Banking; Bankwesen **WS 3**, 103
banner ['bænə] Transparent OT 4
bar [bɑ:] Bar; Riegel OT 1
barbecue ['bɑ:bɪkju:] Grillen OT 2
barge [bɑ:dʒ] Frachtkahn OT 3
to bark [bɑ:k] bellen OT 2
barn [bɑ:n] Scheune OT 2
barrier ['bæriə] Barriere OT 3
barrow ['bærəʊ] Karre OT 4
base [beɪs] Fuß; Basis **WS 1**, 27
baseball ['beɪsbɔ:l] Baseball OT 1
based on ['beɪst ɒn] basierend auf; bezogen auf OT 4
basic ['beɪsɪk] Grund-; grundsätzlich; einfach OT 4
basically ['beɪsɪkli] im Grunde OT 3
basics ['beɪsɪks] Grundlagen OT 2
basin ['beɪsn] Becken OT 3
basis ['beɪsɪs] Grundlage; Basis OT 4
basket ['bɑ:skɪt] Korb OT 4
basketball ['bɑ:skɪtbɔ:l] Basketball OT 3
double bass [ˌdʌbl 'beɪs] Kontrabass OT 2
bat [bæt] Fledermaus; Schläger (Sport) OT 1
bath [bɑ:θ] Badewanne; Bad OT 1
bathhouse ['bɑ:θhaʊs] Badehaus OT 2
bathroom ['bɑ:θru:m] Badezimmer OT 1
to batter ['bætə] schlagen; zertrümmern OT 4
battery ['bætri] Batterie OT 2
battle ['bætl] Schlacht OT 4
battleship ['bætlʃɪp] Schlachtschiff OT 3
bay [beɪ] Bucht OT 2
BCE (before the Common Era) [ˌbi: si: 'i:] v. Chr.; vor unserer Zeitrechnung OT 2
to be [bi:] sein OT 1
to be into [bi: 'ɪntʌ:] auf etwas stehen OT 2
to be fed up [fed 'ʌp] satthaben OT 1
beach [bi:tʃ] Strand OT 1
beam [bi:m] Balken OT 3
bean [bi:n] Bohne OT 1
bear [beə] Bär OT 1
to bear [beər] ertragen **WS 1**, 34
beard [bɪəd] Bart OT 1
beast [bi:st] Tier OT 2
beat [bi:t] Schlag; Takt OT 4
to beat [bi:t] schlagen; übertreffen OT 4
beautiful ['bju:tɪfl] schön OT 1
beauty ['bju:ti] Schönheit OT 3
beaver ['bi:və] Biber OT 4
because [bɪ'kɒz] weil OT 1
to become [bɪ'kʌm] werden OT 2
bed [bed] Bett; Beet OT 1
bedroom ['bedru:m] Schlafzimmer OT 1
bedtime ['bedtaɪm] Schlafenszeit OT 2
bee [bi:] Biene OT 1
beef [bi:f] Rindfleisch OT 2
beer [bɪə] Bier OT 1
before [bɪ'fɔ:] vor OT 1
to beg [beg] betteln **WS 4**, 140
to begin [bɪ'gɪn] anfangen OT 2
beginning [bɪ'gɪnɪŋ] Beginn; Anfang OT 1
to behave [bɪ'heɪv] sich benehmen OT 2
behaviour [bɪ'heɪvjə] Benehmen; Verhalten OT 2
to behead [bɪ'hed] köpfen OT 3
behind [bɪ'haɪnd] hinter OT 1
to behold [bɪ'həʊld] anschauen OT 3
being ['bi:ɪŋ] Wesen OT 4
belief [bɪ'li:f] Glaube OT 3
to believe [bɪ'li:v] glauben OT 2
bell [bel] Glocke OT 1
to belong [bɪ'lɒŋ] gehören OT 2
belongings [bɪ'lɒŋɪŋz] persönliche Gegenstände OT 4
below [bɪ'ləʊ] unter OT 2
bench [bentʃ] Bank OT 3
beneath [bɪ'ni:θ] unten; unter OT 3
beneficial [ˌbenɪ'fɪʃl] vorteilhaft OT 2
benefit ['benɪfɪt] Vorteil OT 4
to benefit ['benɪfɪt] profitieren OT 4
berry ['beri] Beere OT 4
beside [bɪ'said] neben OT 2
besides [bɪ'saɪdz] außerdem **WS 3**, 100
best [best] beste(r, -s) OT 1
to bet [bet] wetten OT 1
better ['betə] besser OT 1
between [bɪ'twi:n] zwischen OT 1
to beware [bɪ'weə] vorsichtig sein OT 2
beyond [bɪ'jɒnd] dahinter OT 3
bias ['baɪəs] Voreingenommenheit **WS 2**, 54
biased ['baɪəst] parteiisch; voreingenommen **WS 2**, 72
bicultural [ˌbaɪ'kʌltʃərəl] bikulturell OT 4
bicycle ['baɪsɪkl] Fahrrad OT 3
to bid for [bɪd] sich bewerben um; ein Angebot machen **WS 3**, 102
big [bɪg] groß OT 1
bike [baɪk] Fahrrad OT 1
bilingual [ˌbaɪ'lɪŋgwəl] zweisprachig OT 3
bilingualism [ˌbaɪ'lɪŋgwəlɪzəm] Zweisprachigkeit OT 4
bill [bɪl] Gesetz; Rechnung OT 4
billion ['bɪljən] Milliarde OT 4
bin [bɪn] Tonne OT 4
binoculars [bɪ'nɒkjələz] Fernglas OT 2
biofuel ['baɪəʊfju:əl] Biokraftstoff OT 3
biography [baɪ'ɒgrəfi] Biografie OT 4

biological [ˌbaɪəˈlɒdʒɪkl] biologisch WS 1, 32
biology [baɪˈɒlədʒi] Biologie OT 1
bipolar [ˌbaɪˈpəʊlə] bipolar WS 2, 73
bird [bɜːd] Vogel OT 1
birth [bɜːθ] Geburt OT 2
 date of birth [ˌdeɪt əv ˈbɜːθ] Geburtsdatum OT 2
birthday [ˈbɜːθdeɪ] Geburtstag OT 1
birthplace [ˈbɜːθpleɪs] Geburtsort OT 4
biscuit [ˈbɪskɪt] Keks OT 1
bisexual [ˌbaɪˈsekʃuəl] bisexuell WS 2, 51
bison [ˈbaɪsn] Bison OT 4
bit [bɪt] Stück OT 2
 a bit [bɪt] Stück; ein bisschen OT 1
bite [baɪt] Biss OT 2
bitterly [ˈbɪtəli] bitterlich WS 1, 26
black [blæk] schwarz OT 1
blackberry [ˈblækbəri] Brombeere OT 1
blackbird [ˈblækbɜːd] Amsel OT 1
blackboard [ˈblækbɔːd] Tafel OT 1
bladder [ˈblædə] Blase OT 4
blame [bleɪm] Schuld; Vorwurf OT 4
blank [blæŋk] leer OT 4
blanket [ˈblæŋkɪt] Decke OT 2
blast [blɑːst] Tuten OT 3
to **blast** [blɑːst] bombadieren WS 2, 68
blazer [ˈbleɪzər] Blazer; leichte Sportjacke WS 2, 60
bleak [bliːk] düster OT 4
blended [ˈblendɪd] gemischt WS 2, 52
block [blɒk] Block OT 4
to **block** [blɒk] blockieren WS 2, 69
blocker [blɒkər] Blocker WS 2, 55
blog [blɒg] Blog OT 1
blogger [blɒgə] Blogger(in) OT 3
blogpost [blɒgpəʊst] Blogeintrag OT 4
blonde [blɒnd] blond OT 1
blood [blʌd] Blut OT 2
bloodshed [ˈblʌdʃed] Blutvergießen WS 1, 26
to **blow** [bləʊ] blasen; pfeifen; wehen OT 2
blubber [ˈblʌbə] Walspeck OT 2
BMXing [ˌbiː em ˈeksɪŋ] BMX-Rad fahren WS 2, 55
to **board** [bɔːd] an Bord gehen OT 4
boarding pass [ˈbɔːdɪŋ pɑːs] Bordkarte OT 2
boat [bəʊt] Boot OT 1
boater [ˈbəʊtə] Bootsfahrer(in) OT 3
boating [ˈbəʊtɪŋ] Bootfahren OT 3
body [ˈbɒdi] Körper OT 1
to **boil** [bɔɪl] kochen OT 1
boiling [ˈbɔɪlɪŋ] kochend heiß OT 1
bold [bəʊld] mutig; fettgedruckt OT 1
bone [bəʊn] Knochen OT 1
book [bʊk] Buch; Heft OT 1
to **book** [bʊk] buchen OT 4
bookcase [ˈbʊkkeɪs] Bücherregal OT 1
booking [ˈbʊkɪŋ] Buchung OT 2
booklet [ˈbʊklət] Broschüre OT 2
to **bookmark** [ˈbʊkmɑːk] markieren OT 4
boot [buːt] Stiefel; Kofferraum OT 1
border [ˈbɔːdə] Grenze OT 3
to **border** [ˈbɔːdə] angrenzen; begrenzen OT 4
bored [bɔːd] gelangweilt OT 1
boring [ˈbɔːrɪŋ] langweilig OT 1
to **be born** [bi bɔːn] geboren sein OT 2
to **borrow** [ˈbɒrəʊ] (aus)leihen OT 2
boss [bɒs] Chef(in) OT 2
bossy [ˈbɒsi] herrisch OT 3
botanical [bəˈtænɪkl] botanisch OT 4
both [bəʊθ] beide OT 1
to **bother** [ˈbɒðə] stören OT 4
bottle [ˈbɒtl] Flasche OT 1
bottom [ˈbɒtəm] Boden; unterster Teil OT 1
boundary [ˈbaʊndri] Grenze OT 4
bow [bəʊ] Bogen OT 2
bowl [bəʊl] Schüssel OT 1
box [bɒks] Kiste; Kasten OT 1
boy [bɔɪ] Junge OT 1
boyband [ˈbɔɪbænd] Boygroup OT 2
bracket [ˈbrækɪt] Klammer OT 2
brain [breɪn] Gehirn OT 2
to **brainstorm** [ˈbreɪnstɔːm] brainstormen OT 2
branch [brɑːntʃ] Ast OT 2
brand [brænd] Marke WS 2, 68
brave [breɪv] tapfer OT 1
bravery [ˈbreɪvəri] Mut OT 2
bread [bred] Brot OT 1
bread roll [ˌbredˈrəʊl] Brötchen OT 1
breadwinner [ˈbredwɪnə] Ernährer(in); Brotverdiener(in) WS 3, 103
break [breɪk] Pause OT 1
to **break** [breɪk] brechen OT 1
 to **break down** [breɪk daʊn] in Schritte unterteilen; aufschlüsseln WS 2, 59
breakfast [ˈbrekfəst] Frühstück OT 1
breakout area [ˈbreɪkaʊt ˈeəriə] Gruppenfläche; Breakout-Bereich WS 3, 112
breakthrough [ˈbreɪkθruː] Durchbruch OT 4
breath [breθ] Atem(zug) OT 2
 to **take a deep breath** [ˌteɪk ə ˈdiːp breθ] tief einatmen OT 2
to **breathe** [briːð] atmen OT 2
breathless [ˈbreθləs] atemlos OT 3
breathtaking [ˈbreθteɪkɪŋ] atemberaubend OT 2
breeches [ˈbrɪtʃɪz] Kniehose OT 3
to **breed** [briːd] brüten; züchten WS 2, 51
breeze [briːz] Brise OT 3
bridge [brɪdʒ] Brücke OT 1
brief [briːf] kurz WS 3, 94
briefly [ˈbriːfli] kurz OT 3
bright [braɪt] leuchtend OT 1
brilliant [ˈbrɪliənt] genial OT 1
to **bring** [brɪŋ] bringen OT 1
British [ˈbrɪtɪʃ] britisch OT 1
Briton [ˈbrɪtn] Brite OT 2
broadcast [ˈbrɔːdkɑːst] Sendung OT 3
broccoli [ˈbrɒkəli] Brokkoli OT 1
brochure [ˈbrəʊʃə] Broschüre OT 1
broken [ˈbrəʊkən] gebrochen OT 1
broom [bruːm] Besen OT 4
brother [ˈbrʌðə] Bruder OT 1
brown [braʊn] braun OT 1
brush [brʌʃ] Bürste; Pinsel OT 2
to **brush** [brʌʃ] putzen; bürsten OT 4
bubble [ˈbʌbl] Blase OT 2
bucket [ˈbʌkɪt] Eimer OT 3
buddy [ˈbʌdi] Kumpel OT 2
to **budget** [ˈbʌdʒɪt] einplanen OT 3
budgie [ˈbʌdʒi] Wellensittich OT 1
buffalo [ˈbʌfələʊ] Büffel OT 4
buffet [ˈbʊfeɪ] Buffet OT 4
to **build** [bɪld] bauen OT 1
builder [ˈbɪldə] Baumeister(in); Bauherr(in) WS 4, 128
 fire-builder [ˈfaɪə bɪldə] Feuermacher(in) OT 2
building [ˈbɪldɪŋ] Gebäude OT 1
to **bulk up** [bʌlk ʌp] Masse zusetzen; hier: Muskeln aufbauen WS 2, 66
bullet [ˈbʊlɪt] Kugel OT 2
to **bully** [ˈbʊli] mobben OT 3
to **bump into** [bʌmp ˈɪntə] anstoßen OT 2
bumpy [ˈbʌmpi] holprig; uneben OT 4
bundle [ˈbʌndl] Bündel OT 2
to **buoy** [bɔɪ] Auftrieb geben OT 3
burden [ˈbɜːdn] Last OT 3
burger [ˈbɜːgə] Hamburger OT 1
to **burn** [bɜːn] brennen OT 2
bus [bʌs] Bus OT 1
bush [bʊʃ] Busch; Gebüsch; Buschland WS 1, 13
bushfire [ˈbʊʃfaɪər] Buschfeuer WS 1, 28
bushland [ˈbʊʃlænd] Buschland WS 1, 28
business [ˈbɪznəs] Geschäft(e) OT 3

businessman, -woman ['bɪznəsmæn, -wʊmən] Geschäftsmann, -frau OT 4
busker ['bʌskər] Straßenmusiker(in) **WS 1**, 29
busload ['bʌsləʊd] Busladung **WS 1**, 27
busted ['bʌstɪd] kaputt OT 4
busy ['bɪzi] beschäftigt OT 1
butter ['bʌtə] Butter OT 1
butternut squash ['bʌtənʌt skwɒʃ] Butternut-Kürbis OT 3
button ['bʌtn] Knopf OT 1
to **buy** [baɪ] kaufen OT 1
buyer ['baɪə] Käufer(in) **WS 3**, 104
buzzard ['bʌzəd] Bussard OT 2
by [faɪv] bei; von OT 1
bye [baɪ] Tschüss! OT 1

C

cab [kæb] Taxi OT 1
cabbage ['kæbɪdʒ] Kohl OT 1
cabin ['kæbɪn] Kabine OT 2
cabinet ['kæbɪnət] Schrank; Kabinett **WS 3**, 113
cabinet minister ['kæbɪnət] Kabinettsminister(in) OT 4
cable ['keɪbl] Kabel OT 3
cactus ['kæktəs] Kaktus OT 4
caddie ['kædi] Caddie OT 4
café ['kæfeɪ] Café OT 1
cafeteria [ˌkæfə'tɪəriə] Cafeteria OT 2
caffeine ['kæfi:n] Koffein **WS 2**, 66
cage [keɪdʒ] Käfig **WS 3**, 107
cake [keɪk] Kuchen OT 1
calendar ['kælɪndə] Kalender OT 1
call [kɔ:l] Anruf OT 2
to **take a call** [teɪk ə kɔ:l] einen Anruf entgegennehmen OT 2
to **call** [kɔ:l] anrufen; nennen OT 1
called [kɔ:ld] namens OT 1
caller ['kɔ:lə] Anrufer(in) OT 2
calm [kɑ:m] ruhig OT 2
to **keep calm** [ki:p kɑ:m] Ruhe bewahren OT 2
to **calm down** [kɑ:m daʊn] beruhigen OT 2
calmly ['kɑ:mli] ruhig OT 3
calorie ['kæləri] Kalorie **WS 2**, 66
camel ['kæml] Kamel **WS 1**, 25
camera ['kæmərə] Fotoapparat; Kamera OT 1
cameraman ['kæmrəmæn] Kameramann **WS 4**, 140
camp [kæmp] Camp; Lager OT 1
to **camp** [kæmp] zelten OT 1
to **camp out** [kæmp aʊt] zelten **WS 1**, 25
campaign [kæm'peɪn] Kampagne; Aktion OT 3
to **campaign (for)** [kæm'peɪn] kämpfen (um); sich einsetzen (für) **WS 3**, 104
camper ['kæmpə] Camper(in) OT 2
campfire ['kæmpfaɪə] Lagerfeuer OT 2
to **build a campfire** [ˌbɪld ə 'kæmpfaɪə] ein Lagerfeuer machen OT 2
campground ['kæmpgraʊnd] Zeltplatz OT 2
campsite ['kæmpsaɪt] Zeltplatz; Campingplatz OT 2
campus ['kæmpəs] Campus OT 2
can [kæn] Dose OT 2
can [kæn] können OT 1
canal [kə'næl] Kanal OT 3
canary [kə'neəri] Kanarienvogel OT 2
candidate ['kændɪdət] Kandidat(in) OT 4
candle ['kændl] Kerze OT 2
candlelight ['kændllaɪt] Kerzenlicht OT 4
canned [kænd] Dosen... OT 2
canoe [kə'nu:] Kanu OT 2
canoeing [kə'nu:ɪŋ] Kanufahren OT 2
canteen [kæn'ti:n] Kantine OT 1
canvas ['kænvəs] Leinen OT 3
canyon ['kænjən] Schlucht; Canyon OT 3
cap [kæp] Mütze; Deckel OT 1
capable ['keɪpəbl] fähig OT 4
capacity [kə'pæsəti] Fähigkeit **WS 2**, 72
capital ['kæpɪtl] Hauptstadt OT 1
caption ['kæpʃn] Bildunterschrift OT 2
to **capture** ['kæptʃə] einfangen; festnehmen OT 4
car [kɑ:] Auto OT 1
caravan ['kærəvæn] Wohnwagen OT 1
carbohydrate [ˌkɑ:bəʊ'haɪdreɪt] Kohlenhydrat **WS 2**, 66
carbon ['kɑ:bən] Kohlenstoff OT 4
carbon dioxide [ˌkɑ:bəndaɪ'ɒksaɪd] Kohlendioxid OT 3
carbon emission [ˌkɑ:bəni'mɪʃn] CO2-Ausstoß OT 3
carbon footprint [ˌkɑ:bən'fʊtprɪnt] CO2-Bilanz; ökologischer Fußabdruck OT 3
card [kɑ:d] Karte; Karton OT 1
care [keə] Betreuung; Sorge OT 2
to **care** [keə] besorgt sein OT 2
I don't care! [aɪ dəʊnt keə] Das ist mir egal! OT 2
career [kə'rɪə] Karriere OT 3
careful ['keəfl] vorsichtig; sorgfältig OT 1
careless ['keələs] sorglos OT 2
carer ['keərər] Betreuer(in) **WS 2**, 54
caretaker ['keəteɪkə] Hausmeister(in) OT 1
cargo ['kɑ:gəʊ] Ladung OT 3
caribou ['kærɪbu:] Karibu OT 4
carnival ['kɑ:nɪvl] Karneval OT 4
car park ['kɑ: pɑ:k] Parkplatz OT 2
carpenter ['kɑ:pəntə] Zimmermann; Tischler(in) OT 3
carriage ['kærɪdʒ] Wagen OT 2
carrier ['kæriə] Trage... **WS 3**, 104
carrot ['kærət] Karotte OT 1
to **carry** ['kæri] tragen OT 1
cartoonist [kɑ:'tu:nɪst] Karikaturist(in) OT 4
to **carve** [kɑ:v] schnitzen OT 2
carver [kɑ:və] Schnitzer(in) OT 4
carving ['kɑ:vɪŋ] Schnitzerei OT 4
case [keɪs] Koffer; Tasche; Fall OT 1
cash [kæʃ] Kleingeld; Bargeld OT 1
cashier [kæ'ʃɪə] Kassierer(in) OT 4
cast [kɑ:st] Besetzung OT 3
castle ['kɑ:sl] Burg; Schloss OT 1
casual ['kæʒuəl] locker; lässig **WS 2**, 68
cat [kæt] Katze OT 1
to **catch** [kætʃ] fangen OT 1
category ['kætəgəri] Kategorie OT 3
catering ['keɪtərɪŋ] Versorgung; Catering OT 3
cathedral [kə'θi:drəl] Kathedrale OT 1
Catholic ['kæθəlɪk] katholisch OT 3
Catholic ['kæθlɪk] Katholik(in) OT 3
cattle ['kætl] Rinder OT 4
to **cause** [kɔ:z] verursachen OT 2
caution ['kɔ:ʃn] Verwarnung; Warnung **WS 2**, 74
cavalry ['kævlri] Kavallerie OT 3
cave [keɪv] Höhle OT 3
CE (Common Era) [ˌsi: 'i:] n. Chr.; unserer Zeitrechnung OT 2
ceiling ['si:lɪŋ] Decke OT 2
to **celebrate** ['selɪbreɪt] feiern OT 3
celebration [ˌselɪ'breɪʃn] Feier OT 2
celebrity [sə'lebrəti] Prominente(r) **WS 2**, 66
cello ['tʃeləʊ] Cello OT 1
cell phone ['sel fəʊn] Handy OT 4
Celtic ['keltɪk] Keltisch OT 2
center ['sentə] Mitte; Zentrum OT 2
centimetre ['sentɪmi:tə] Zentimeter OT 2
central ['sentrəl] Zentral- OT 1
central heating [ˌsentrəl 'hi:tɪŋ] Zentralheizung OT 2
centre ['sentə] Mitte OT 1

century ['sentʃəri] Jahrhundert OT 2
cereal ['sɪəriəl] Cerealien; Frühstücksflocken OT 1
cerebral palsy [sə'ri:brəl 'pɔ:lzi] zerebrale Kinderlähmung **WS 2**, 57
ceremonial [ˌserɪ'məʊniəl] zeremoniell; feierlich OT 3
ceremony ['serəməni] Feier OT 2
certain ['sɜ:tn] sicher OT 3
certainly ['sɜ:tnli] sicher; sicherlich OT 2
certainty ['sɜ:tnti] Gewissheit OT 4
certificate [sə'tɪfɪkət] Zeugnis; Zertifikat OT 2
certified ['sɜ:tɪfaɪd] beglaubigt; anerkannt **WS 4**, 141
chain [tʃeɪn] Kette OT 3
chair [tʃeə] Stuhl; Vorsitz OT 1
chairlift ['tʃeəlɪft] Sessellift **WS 1**, 31
challenge ['tʃælɪndʒ] Herausforderung OT 3
to **challenge** ['tʃælɪndʒ] herausfordern OT 4
challenging ['tʃælɪndʒɪŋ] schwierig OT 2
chamber ['tʃeɪmbə] Kammer OT 2
chamber pot ['tʃeɪmbə pɒt] Nachttopf OT 3
champion ['tʃæmpiən] Champion OT 4
chance [tʃɑ:ns] Zufall; Möglichkeit OT 2
chandelier [ˌʃændə'lɪə] Kronleuchter OT 2
change [tʃeɪndʒ] Wechselgeld OT 1
to **change** [tʃeɪndʒ] ändern; sich umziehen; wechseln OT 1
channel [tʃænl] Kanal OT 3
chaos ['keɪɒs] Chaos OT 4
chapter ['tʃæptə] Kapitel OT 1
character ['kærəktə] Charakter OT 2
characteristic [ˌkærəktə'rɪstɪk] charakteristisches Merkmal OT 2
charge: in charge ['ɪn tʃɑ:dʒ] zuständig OT 1
to **charge** [tʃɑ:dʒ] aufladen OT 2
to **charge (with)** [tʃɑ:dʒ] anklagen (wegen) **WS 2**, 64
charity ['tʃærəti] Wohlfahrtsorganisation OT 2
charming ['tʃɑ:mɪŋ] charmant OT 3
chart [tʃɑ:t] Diagramm; Chart OT 4
to **chase** [tʃeɪs] jagen OT 2
to **chat** [tʃæt] plaudern OT 3
to **chatter** ['tʃætə] plaudern OT 2
chatty ['tʃæti] gesprächig **WS 1**, 36
cheap [tʃi:p] billig OT 2
to **cheat** [tʃi:t] schummeln; mogeln OT 4
to **check** [tʃek] überprüfen OT 1
check-out ['tʃekaʊt] Kasse OT 4
checklist ['tʃeklɪst] Checkliste OT 2
cheek [tʃi:k] Backe OT 4
cheeky ['tʃi:ki] frech OT 3
cheerful ['tʃɪəfl] fröhlich OT 2
cheerleader ['tʃɪəli:də] Cheerleader(in) OT 3
to **cheer up** ['tʃɪə ʌp] aufmuntern OT 1
to **cheer up** [tʃɪə ʌp] fröhlich sein OT 3
cheese [tʃi:z] Käse OT 1
cheetah ['tʃi:tə] Gepard OT 3
chef [ʃef] Küchenchef(in); Koch/Köchin OT 1
chemical ['kemɪkl] Chemikalie OT 3
chemistry ['kemɪstri] Chemie **WS 2**, 56
cheque [tʃek] Scheck OT 4
cherry ['tʃeri] Kirsche OT 4
chess [tʃes] Schach OT 1
chest [tʃest] Truhe; Brust OT 1
chest of drawers [ˌtʃest əv 'drɔ:z] Kommode OT 1
chicken ['tʃɪkɪn] Huhn; Hähnchen OT 1
Chief Executive Officer (CEO) [ˌtʃi:f ɪgˌzekjətɪv 'ɒfɪsə] Geschäftsführer(in) **WS 3**, 111
child [tʃaɪld] Kind OT 1
childhood ['tʃaɪldhʊd] Kindheit OT 3
childish ['tʃaɪldɪʃ] kindisch OT 3
chili ['tʃɪli] Chili OT 2
chimney ['tʃɪmni] Schornstein OT 3
Chinese [ˌtʃaɪ'ni:z] chinesisch OT 1
chip [tʃɪp] Chip; Fritte OT 1
choc-chip ['tʃɒk tʃɪp] Schockoladensplitter OT 1
chocoholic [ˌtʃɒkə'hɒlɪk] Schokoladensüchtige(r) OT 3
chocolate ['tʃɒklət] Schokolade OT 1
choice [tʃɔɪs] Wahl OT 1
choir ['kwaɪə] Chor OT 1
cholera ['kɒlərə] Cholera OT 4
to **choose** [tʃu:z] auswählen OT 1
to **chop** [tʃɒp] schneiden OT 3
chopped [tʃɒpt] gehackt OT 2
chore [tʃɔ:] Hausarbeit OT 4
chowder ['tʃaʊdə] dickflüssige Fischsuppe OT 3
chromosome ['krəʊməsəʊm] Chromosom **WS 2**, 61
chronological [ˌkrɒnə'lɒdʒɪkl] chronologisch OT 4
church [tʃɜ:tʃ] Kirche OT 1
cinema [sɪnəmə] Kino OT 1
circle ['sɜ:kl] Kreis OT 2
to **circulate** ['sɜ:kjəleɪt] kursieren; zirkulieren OT 4
circumstance ['sɜ:kəmstəns] Umstand; Lage **WS 2**, 64
to **cite** [saɪt] anführen OT 2
citizen ['sɪtɪzn] Einwohner(in) OT 2
city ['sɪti] Stadt OT 1
city hall [ˌsɪti 'hɔ:l] Rathaus **WS 3**, 107
civilized ['sɪvəlaɪz] zivilisiert; kultiviert **WS 1**, 27
claim [kleɪm] Behauptung **WS 3**, 104
to **claim** [kleɪm] behaupten OT 3
clam [klæm] Venusmuschel OT 3
clan [klæn] Stamm **WS 1**, 26
to **clap** [klæp] klatschen OT 1
clarification [ˌklærəfɪ'keɪʃn] Abklärung OT 4
to **clarify** ['klærəfaɪ] etw. klären OT 4
clarinet [ˌklærə'net] Klarinette OT 2
class [klɑ:s] Stunde; Klasse OT 1
classic ['klæsɪk] klassisch OT 2
classical ['klæsɪkl] klassisch OT 2
to **classify** ['klæsɪfaɪ] etw. einstufen OT 4
classmate ['klɑ:smeɪt] Klassenkamerad(in) OT 3
classroom ['klɑ:sru:m] Klassenzimmer OT 1
to **clean** [kli:n] putzen OT 1
cleaner ['kli:nə] Reinigungsmittel OT 3
clear [klɪə] klar OT 2
clearly ['klɪəli] deutlich OT 3
clever ['klevə] intelligent OT 2
to **click** [klɪk] klicken OT 3
client ['klaɪənt] Mandant(in); Kunde/Kundin **WS 2**, 77
cliff [klɪf] Klippe; Felsen **WS 1**, 24
climate ['klaɪmət] Klima OT 2
to **climb** [klaɪm] klettern; steigen OT 1
climber ['klaɪmə] Kletterer(in) OT 2
climbing ['klaɪmɪŋ] Klettern; Bergsteigen OT 1
clinic ['klɪnɪk] Klinik **WS 3**, 106
clip [klɪp] Ausschnitt OT 2
to **clip to** [klɪp tə] klemmen an **WS 3**, 112
cloak [kləʊk] Umhang OT 2
cloakroom ['kləʊkru:m] Garderobe OT 4
clock [klɒk] Uhr OT 1
to **clog** [klɒg] verstopfen OT 4
to **close** [kləʊz] schließen OT 1
close [kləʊs] nah OT 1
closed [kləʊzd] geschlossen OT 1
closely ['kləʊsli] eng OT 3

cloth [klɒθ] Stoff OT 2
clothes [kləʊðz] Kleidung; Kleider OT 1
clothing ['kləʊðɪŋ] Kleidung OT 4
cloud [klaʊd] Wolke OT 1
cloudy ['klaʊdi] wolkig OT 1
club [klʌb] Klub; Verein OT 1
clue [klu:] Hinweis; Anhaltspunkt OT 1
clumsy ['klʌmzi] ungeschickt OT 2
coach [kəʊtʃ] Reisebus; Trainer(in) OT 1
coal [kəʊl] Kohle OT 2
coast [kəʊst] Küste OT 1
coastal ['kəʊstl] Küsten...; an der Küste OT 4
coastguard ['kəʊstgɑ:d] Küstenwache OT 2
coastline ['kəʊstlaɪn] Küstenlinie; Küste **WS 1**, 36
coat [kəʊt] Mantel OT 2
cocoa ['kəʊkəʊ] Kakao OT 4
code [kəʊd] Code; Vorwahl OT 2
to **code** [kəʊd] kodieren; programmieren **WS 3**, 100
co-ed, co-educational [ˌkəʊ'ed] gemischtgeschlechtlich OT 2
coffee ['kɒfi] Kaffee OT 1
coffin ['kɒfɪn] Sarg OT 4
coin [kɔɪn] Münze OT 1
cold [kəʊld] kalt OT 1
collaboration [kəˌlæbə'reɪʃn] Zusammenarbeit; Kollaboration OT 4
collar ['kɒlə] Halsband OT 2
colleague ['kɒli:g] Kollege, Kollegin; Mitarbeiter(in) OT 4
to **collect** [kə'lekt] sammeln; einsammeln OT 1
collection [kə'lekʃn] Sammlung OT 2
college ['kɒlɪdʒ] Hochschule; Universität OT 2
colonial [kə'ləʊniəl] kolonial OT 3
colonialism [kə'ləʊniəlɪzəm] Kolonialismus **WW**, 10
colonist ['kɒlənɪst] Kolonist(in) OT 4
colonization [ˌkɒlənaɪ'zeɪʃn] Kolonialisierung **WS 1**, 24
to **colonize** ['kɒlənaɪz] kolonisieren OT 3
colony ['kɒləni] Kolonie OT 3
colour ['kʌlə] Farbe OT 1
to **colour** ['kʌlə] ausmalen OT 1
coloured ['kʌləd] farbig; bunt OT 1
colourful ['kʌləfl] farbenfroh OT 3
column ['kɒləm] Säule; Spalte OT 1
comb [kəʊm] Kamm OT 2
combination [ˌkɒmbɪ'neɪʃn] Kombination OT 4
to **combine** [kəm'baɪn] kombinieren; mischen OT 4
combustion: internal combustion [ɪn'tɜ:nl kəm'bʌstʃən] Verbrennungs- OT 4
to **come** [kʌm] kommen OT 1
to **come first / second / third** [kʌm 'fɜ:st / 'sekənd / 'θɜ:d] den ersten / zweiten / dritten Platz belegen OT 2
to **come from** [kʌm frəm] kommen aus **WW**, 11
to **come to know** [kʌm tə nəʊ] erfahren; kennenlernen **WW**, 11
comedy ['kɒmədi] Komödie OT 4
comfortable ['kʌmftəbl] bequem OT 1
comic ['kɒmɪk] Comicheft OT 1
comma ['kɒmə] Komma OT 3
commander [kə'mɑ:ndə] Kommandant(in) OT 2
Commander-in-Chief [kəˌmɑ:ndər ɪn 'tʃi:f] Oberbefehlshaber(in) OT 4
commanding [kə'mɑ:ndɪŋ] befehlshabend OT 2
comment ['kɒment] Bemerkung OT 3
to **comment** ['kɒment] bemerken; kommentieren OT 3
commerce ['kɒmɜ:s] Handel; Kommerz **WS 3**, 88
commercial [kə'mɜ:ʃl] kommerziell OT 4
to **commit** [kə'mɪt] begehen OT 3
committee [kə'mɪti] Kommission; Komitee OT 4
common ['kɒmən] Gemeindeland OT 2
Common Era [ˌkɒmən 'ɪərə] unsere Zeitrechnung OT 2
commonly ['kɒmənli] gewöhnlich; häufig **WW**, 10
to **communicate** [kə'mju:nɪkeɪt] kommunizieren; etw. vermitteln OT 4
communication [kəˌmju:nɪ'keɪʃn] Kommunikation OT 1
community [kə'mju:nəti] Gemeinschaft OT 2
to **commute** [kə'mju:t] pendeln **WS 3**, 102
commuter [kə'mju:tə] Pendler(in) OT 2
commuter rail [kəˌmju:tə 'reɪl] Pendlerbahn OT 2
company ['kʌmpəni] Unternehmen OT 1
comparable to ['kɒmpərəbl tə] vergleichbar mit **WS 2**, 56
comparative [kəm'pærətɪv] Komparativ OT 2
to **compare** [kəm'peə] vergleichen OT 1
comparison [kəm'pærɪsn] Vergleich **WS 1**, 29
compass ['kʌmpəs] Kompass OT 2
compatible [kəm'pætəbl] kompatibel **WS 2**, 56
compensation [ˌkɒmpen'seɪʃn] Entschädigung **WS 2**, 64
to **compete** [kəm'pi:t] konkurrieren OT 2
competent ['kɒmpɪtənt] fähig; kompetent OT 4
competition [ˌkɒmpə'tɪʃn] Konkurrenz; Wettbewerb OT 1
competitive [kəm'petətɪv] konkurrenzorientiert OT 3
competitively [kəm'petətɪvli] konkurrierend; wetteifernd OT 4
competitor [kəm'petɪtə] Konkurrent(in); Wettbewerber(in) OT 4
to **complain** [kəm'pleɪn] sich beklagen; sich beschweren OT 3
complaint [kəm'pleɪnt] Beschwerde OT 2
to **complete** [kəm'pli:t] vervollständigen OT 1
completely [kəm'pli:tli] ganz; komplett OT 4
completion [kəm'pli:ʃn] Vervollständigung; Erfüllung OT 4
complex ['kɒmpleks] Anlage; Komplex OT 4
complicated ['kɒmplɪkeɪtɪd] kompliziert OT 3
to **compliment** ['kɒmplɪmənt] loben OT 3
compliment ['kɒmplɪmənt] Kompliment OT 3
to **compose** [kəm'pəʊz] komponieren OT 3
composer [kəm'pəʊzə] Komponist(in) OT 2
compost ['kɒmpɒst] Kompost OT 3
composting ['kɒmpɒstɪŋ] Kompostierungs- OT 4
composting toilet ['kɒmpɒstɪŋ 'tɔɪlət] kompostierende Toilette OT 3
computer [kəm'pju:tər] Computer **WW**, 11
computer lab [kəm'pju:tə ˌlæb] Computerraum OT 2
computing [kəm'pju:tɪŋ] Computing **WS 3**, 90
to **conceal** [kən'si:l] verbergen **WS 2**, 55
to **concentrate** ['kɒnsntreɪt] konzentrieren OT 3
concept ['kɒnsept] Konzept; Begriff OT 4

concern [kən'sɜːn] Sorge; Bedenken **WS 1**, 37
concerned [kən'sɜːnd] besorgt OT 3
concerning [kən'sɜːn] betreffend; bezüglich **WS 2**, 67
concert ['kɒnsət] Konzert OT 1
to **conclude** [kən'kluːd] schließen (aus etwas); beenden OT 3
conclusion [kən'kluːʒn] Schluss OT 3
concrete ['kɒŋkriːt] Beton OT 2
condition [kən'dɪʃn] Zustand OT 2
condor ['kɒndɔː] Condor OT 3
to **conduct** [kən'dʌkt] durchführen OT 3
conference ['kɒnfərəns] Konferenz OT 3
confidence ['kɒnfɪdəns] Selbstvertrauen **WS 2**, 50
confident ['kɒnfɪdənt] selbstsicher OT 3
to **confirm** [kən'fɜːm] bestätigen OT 4
conflict ['kɒnflɪkt] Konflikt OT 4
to **conform (to)** [kən'fɔːm] (sich) anpassen an; übereinstimmen (mit) **WS 2**, 54
confused [kən'fjuːzd] verwirrt OT 2
confusing [kən'fjuːzɪŋ] verwirrend OT 2
congestion [kən'dʒestʃən] Stau; Stauung OT 4
to **congratulate** [kən'grætʃuleɪt] gratulieren OT 2
congratulations [kən,grætʃu'leɪʃnz] Glückwünsche OT 2
congressman, -woman ['kɒŋgrəsmən, -wʊmən] Abgeordnete(r) OT 4
conjunction [kən'dʒʌŋkʃn] Konjunktion OT 2
to **connect** [kə'nekt] verbinden OT 2
connection [kə'nekʃn] Verbindung OT 2
to **conquer** ['kɒŋkə] erobern OT 2
con [kɒn] Nachteil OT 2
consequence ['kɒnsɪkwəns] Folge; Konsequenz OT 4
conservation [,kɒnsə'veɪʃn] Schutz OT 2
to **consider** [kən'sɪdə] nachdenken über OT 3
to **consist** [kən'sɪst] bestehen OT 3
consistent [kən'sɪstənt] konsequent **WS 2**, 59
console: game console ['geɪm kənsəʊl] Spielekonsole OT 4
consonant ['kɒnsənənt] Konsonant; Mitlaut OT 1
constant ['kɒnstənt] ständig **WS 2**, 80
constantly ['kɒnstəntli] ständig; konstant OT 4
constituency [kən'stɪtʃuənsi] Wahlbezirk; Interessengemeinschaft OT 4
constituent [kən'stɪtʃuənt] Wähler OT 4
constitution [,kɒnstɪ'tjuːʃn] Verfassung OT 4
constitutional [,kɒnstɪ'tjuːʃənl] konstitutionell; Verfassungs... OT 4
to **construct** [kən'strʌkt] bauen; errichten OT 4
construction [kən'strʌkʃn] Bau OT 4
consultant [kən'sʌltənt] Berater(in) **WS 2**, 51
to **consume** [kən'sjuːm] konsumieren; verbrauchen OT 4
consumer [kən'sjuːmər] Verbraucher(in) **WS 2**, 68
to **contact** ['kɒntækt] kontaktieren OT 2
contact ['kɒntækt] Kontakt; Kontaktperson OT 1
to **contain** [kən'teɪn] etw. enthalten OT 4
container [kən'teɪnə] Behälter; Container OT 4
to **contaminate** [kən'tæmɪneɪt] verunreinigen; kontaminieren **WS 1**, 34
contemporary [kən'temprəri] zeitgenössisch OT 4
contents [kən'tents] Inhalt OT 2
contestant [kən'testənt] Wettkämpfer(in) OT 4
context ['kɒntekst] Kontext; Zusammenhang OT 4
continent ['kɒntɪnənt] Kontinent **WS 1**, 12
to **continue** [kən'tɪnjuː] weitermachen OT 2
continuous [kən'tɪnjuəs] laufend; kontinuierlich OT 4
contract ['kɒntrækt] Vertrag OT 4
contractor [kən'træktə] Auftragnehmer(in) **WS 3**, 102
contrast ['kɒntrɑːst] Gegenteil; Kontrast OT 3
to **contribute (to)** [kən'trɪbjuːt] mitarbeiten (an); beitragen (zu) **WS 1**, 29
control [kən'trəʊl] Kontrolle OT 2
to **control** [kən'trəʊl] kontrollieren OT 4
controversial [,kɒntrə'vɜːʃl] umstritten OT 3
controversy ['kɒntrəvɜːsi] Kontroverse OT 4
convenience [kən'viːniəns] Bequemlichkeit; zweckmäßiges Gerät OT 4
convenient [kən'viːniənt] günstig; praktisch OT 4
conversation [,kɒnvə'seɪʃn] Gespräch OT 1
conversational [,kɒnvə'seɪʃənl] Gesprächs... **WS 1**, 29
to **convey** [kən'veɪ] vermitteln **WS 2**, 71
convict ['kɒnvɪkt] Verurteilte(r) **WS 1**, 17
to **convict** [kən'vɪkt] verurteilen **WS 2**, 74
conviction [kən'vɪkʃn] Verurteilung **WS 2**, 74
to **convince** [kən'vɪns] überzeugen **WS 3**, 105
to **cook** [kʊk] kochen OT 1
cooker ['kʊkə] Herd OT 3
cookery ['kʊkəri] Kochen OT 2
cookie ['kʊki] Keks OT 3
cooking ['kʊkɪŋ] Kochen OT 1
cool [kuːl] kühl; cool OT 1
to **cool** [kuːl] abkühlen **WS 1**, 26
cooling system ['kuːlɪŋ 'sɪstəm] Kühlsystem OT 3
cooperation [kəʊ,ɒpə'reɪʃn] Zusammenarbeit **WS 2**, 53
to **cope** [kəʊp] zurechtkommen **WS 2**, 57
copy ['kɒpi] Kopie OT 1
to **copy** ['kɒpi] kopieren; nachahmen OT 1
core [kɔː] Kern; Haupt... OT 4
corn [kɔːn] Mais OT 3
corner ['kɔːnə] Ecke OT 1
coronation [,kɒrə'neɪʃn] Krönung OT 3
correct [kə'rekt] richtig OT 1
to **correct** [kə'rekt] verbessern; korrigieren OT 1
correction [kə'rekʃn] Korrektur OT 4
correspondent [,kɒrə'spɒndənt] Korrespondent(in); Reporter(in) OT 4
corridor ['kɒrɪdɔː] Korridor OT 2
corset ['kɔːsɪt] Korsett OT 3
cosmopolitan city [,kɒzməpɒlɪtən 'sɪti] Weltstadt OT 4
cost [kɒst] Kosten OT 1
to **cost** [kɒst] kosten OT 1
costume ['kɒstjuːm] Kostüm OT 2
cottage ['kɒtɪdʒ] Häuschen OT 3
cotton ['kɒtn] Baumwolle OT 4
cougar ['kuːgə] Puma OT 2
could [kʊd] konnte; könnte(n) OT 1
council ['kaʊnsl] Rat OT 3
counselling ['kaʊnsəlɪŋ] Beratung **WS 2**, 64
counselor ['kaʊnsələ] Jugendbetreuer(in) OT 2

to **count** [kaʊnt] zählen OT 2
countable ['kaʊntəbl] zählbar OT 1
counterpart ['kaʊntəpɑ:t] Kollege/Kollegin **WS 3**, 110
country ['kʌntri] Land OT 1
countryside ['kʌntrisaɪd] Land(schaft) OT 1
couple ['kʌpl] Paar OT 2
coupon ['ku:pɒn] Gutschein OT 2
courier ['kʊriə] Kurier(in) OT 2
course [kɔ:s] Kurs OT 3
coursework ['kɔ:swɜ:k] Facharbeit OT 4
court [kɔ:t] Gericht OT 4
cousin ['kʌzn] Cousin(e) OT 1
to **cover** ['kʌvə] abdecken OT 2
covered ['kʌvəd] bedeckt OT 2
cow [kaʊ] Kuh OT 1
coyote [kaɪ'əʊti] Kojote; hier: Schlepper(in) **WS 4**, 129
cracker ['krækə] Cracker OT 3
cradle ['kreɪdl] Wiege OT 3
craft [krɑ:ft] Handwerk; Kunsthandwerk OT 4
cramp [kræmp] Krampf OT 2
cramped [kræmpt] beengt OT 3
cranberry ['krænbəri] Preiselbeere OT 3
to **crash** [kræʃ] abstürzen OT 3
crash diet ['kræʃ 'daɪət] Crash-Diät **WS 2**, 66
crate [kreɪt] Kiste OT 4
to **crawl** [krɔ:l] krabbeln; kriechen **WS 1**, 38
crazy ['kreɪzi] verrückt OT 2
cream [kri:m] Sahne OT 1
to **create** [kri'eɪt] schaffen; kreieren OT 2
creation [kri'eɪʃn] Schöpfung **WS 1**, 26
creative [kri'eɪtɪv] kreativ OT 2
creativity [ˌkri:eɪ'tɪvəti] Kreativität OT 3
creator [kri'eɪtər] Schöpfer(in); Erschaffer(in) **WS 1**, 26
creature ['kri:tʃər] Geschöpf; Lebewesen **WS 1**, 26
credit ['kredɪt] Credit; Notenpunkt **WS 2**, 56
credit card ['kredɪt kɑ:d] Kreditkarte OT 1
creepy ['kri:pi] gruselig **WS 1**, 13
creepy-crawly [ˌkri:pi'krɔ:li] Krabbeltier OT 2
crew [kru:] Mannschaft; Personal OT 2
cricket ['krɪkɪt] Kricket; Grille OT 1
crime [kraɪm] Verbrechen OT 4
criminal ['krɪmɪnl] Kriminelle(r) OT 3
criminal record [ˌkrɪmɪnl 'rekɔ:d] Vorstrafregister **WS 2**, 64
crisis ['kraɪsɪs] Krise OT 4
crisp [krɪsp] Kartoffelchip OT 1
criterion [kraɪ'tɪəriən] Kriterium **WS 2**, 56
critic ['krɪtɪk] Kritiker(in) **WS 3**, 110
critical ['krɪtɪkl] kritisch OT 4
criticism ['krɪtɪsɪzəm] Kritik OT 3
to **criticize** ['krɪtɪsaɪz] kritisieren OT 3
crop [krɒp] Getreide; Feldfrüchte OT 3
cross [krɒs] verärgert OT 2
to **cross** [krɒs] überqueren; sich kreuzen OT 1
cross country [ˌkrɒs 'kʌntri] Querfeldein- OT 2
cross-country skiing [ˌkrɒs ˌkʌntri 'ski:ɪŋ] Langlaufen; Skilanglauf **WS 1**, 13
crossly ['krɒsli] mürrisch OT 3
crow [krəʊ] Krähe OT 3
crowd [kraʊd] Menge; Menschenmenge OT 1
crowded ['kraʊdɪd] überfüllt OT 2
to **crown** [kraʊn] krönen OT 1
crown [kraʊn] Krone OT 1
cruel ['kru:əl] grausam OT 3
to **cruise** [kru:z] mit dem Boot fahren; eine Kreuzfahrt machen OT 3
cruise ship ['kru:z ʃɪp] Kreuzfahrtschiff OT 2
crush: to have a crush (on) [həv ə 'krʌʃ] in jmdn. verknallt sein OT 4
crutch [krʌtʃ] Krücke OT 2
to **cry** [kraɪ] weinen OT 1
cub [kʌb] Junge(s) OT 2
cucumber ['kju:kʌmbə] Gurke OT 1
cuddly ['kʌdli] knuddelig OT 3
cue [kju:] Hinweis; Stichwort **WS 2**, 61
cuisine [kwɪ'zi:n] Küche OT 3
to **cull** [kʌl] keulen; selektiv schlachten **WS 1**, 25
cull [kʌl] Schlachten; Keulen **WS 1**, 25
cultural ['kʌltʃərəl] kulturell OT 4
culture ['kʌltʃə] Kultur OT 1
Cumbrian ['kʌmbriən] von/aus Cumbria OT 2
cup [kʌp] Tasse; Pokal OT 1; Meisterschaft **WS 1**, 21
cupboard ['kʌbəd] Schrank OT 1
curb [kɜ:b] Bordstein **WS 2**, 64
curfew ['kɜ:fju:] Ausgangssperre OT 3
curious ['kjʊəriəs] neugierig; gespannt OT 4
curlew ['kɜ:lju:] Brachvogel OT 2
curling ['kɜ:lɪŋ] Curling OT 4
curly ['kɜ:li] gelockt OT 3
current ['kʌrənt] aktuell OT 2
currently ['kʌrəntli] derzeit; gerade OT 4
curriculum [kə'rɪkjələm] Curriculum; Lehrplan OT 4
curry ['kʌri] Currygericht OT 1
curtain ['kɜ:tn] Vorhang OT 2
cushion ['kʊʃn] Kissen OT 1
custard ['kʌstəd] Vanillesoße OT 1
custodial sentence [kʌ'stəʊdiəl 'sentəns] Freiheitsstrafe **WS 2**, 65
custody ['kʌstədi] Verwahrung; Schutz; Sorgerecht **WS 2**, 64
customer ['kʌstəmə] Kunde(-in) OT 2
customs ['kʌstəmz] Zoll OT 2
to **cut** [kʌt] schneiden OT 2
cute [kju:t] niedlich OT 3
cutlery ['kʌtləri] Besteck OT 3
CV (curriculum vitae) [ˌsi: 'vi:] Lebenslauf OT 4
cyberbullying ['saɪbəbʊliɪŋ] Cyber-Mobbing **WS 2**, 71
cyberthreat ['saɪbəθret] Cyber-Bedrohung **WS 2**, 75
cycle ['saɪkl] Periode; Zyklus OT 4
to **cycle** ['saɪkl] radfahren OT 1
cyclist ['saɪklɪst] Radfahrer(in) OT 3
cyclone ['saɪkləʊn] Zyklon **WS 1**, 34

D

dad [dæd] Papa OT 1
daily ['deɪli] täglich OT 2
dairy ['deəri] Milchprodukte OT 4
damage ['dæmɪdʒ] Beschädigung OT 3
to **damage** ['dæmɪdʒ] beschädigen OT 3
damaged ['dæmɪdʒd] beschädigt OT 2
dance [dɑ:ns] Tanz **WS 1**, 31
dancing ['dɑ:nsɪŋ] Tanzen OT 1
danger ['deɪndʒə] Gefahr OT 2
dangerous ['deɪndʒərəs] gefährlich OT 1
to **dare** [deə] wagen OT 2
dark [dɑ:k] dunkel OT 1
dark-haired [ˌdɑ:k 'heəd] dunkelhaarig OT 3
darkness ['dɑ:knəs] Dunkelheit **WS 4**, 128
data ['deɪtə] Daten **WS 2**, 54
date [deɪt] Verabredung OT 3
to **date back** [deɪt bæk] stammen aus OT 4
daughter ['dɔ:tə] Tochter OT 1
dawn [dɔ:n] Morgendämmerung OT 3

day [deɪ] Tag OT 1
one day ['wʌn deɪ] eines Tages; später einmal OT 2
day out [deɪ 'aʊt] Tagesausflug OT 2
dead [ded] tot OT 1
deadly ['dedli] tödlich **WS 1**, 13
deaf [def] taub OT 3
deal [di:l] Geschäft; hier: Angelegenheit **WS 1**, 21
to **deal with** [di:l wɪð] umgehen OT 2
death [deθ] Tod OT 2
date of death [ˌdeɪt əv 'deθ] Todesdatum OT 2
debate [dɪ'beɪt] Debatte OT 4
debut ['deɪbju:] Debüt; Auftreten OT 4
decade ['dekeɪd] Dekade; Jahrzehnt OT 4
December [dɪ'sembə] Dezember OT 1
to **decide** [dɪ'saɪd] entscheiden OT 1
decision [dɪ'sɪʒn] Entscheidung OT 1
deck [dek] Deck OT 3
to **declare** [dɪ'kleə] ausrufen; verkünden OT 4
decline [dɪ'klaɪn] Rückgang **WS 1**, 24
to **decline** [dɪ'klaɪn] verfallen **WW**, 11
to **decorate** ['dekəreɪt] dekorieren; schmücken OT 2
decoration [ˌdekə'reɪʃn] Dekoration OT 3
to **decrease** [dɪ'kri:s] fallen; zurückgehen **WS 2**, 62
deed [di:d] Urkunde **WS 1**, 26
deep [di:p] tief OT 1
deer [dɪə] Hirsch OT 1
deerskin ['dɪəskin] Hirschleder OT 3
de facto [ˌdeɪ 'fæktəʊ] de facto **WW**, 10
default [dɪ'fɔ:lt] Standard OT 3
defence [dɪ'fens] Verteidigung **WS 2**, 65
to **defend** [dɪ'fend] verteidigen **WS 1**, 25
to **define** [dɪ'faɪn] definieren; bestimmen OT 4
defining [dɪ'faɪnɪŋ] bestimmend OT 2
definite ['defɪnət] eindeutig OT 1
definitely ['defɪnətli] bestimmt; definitiv OT 2
definition [ˌdefɪ'nɪʃn] Definition OT 1
deforestation [ˌdi:ˌfɒrɪ'steɪʃn] Abholzung **WS 1**, 39
degree [dɪ'gri:] Grad **WS 1**, 28
dehydrated [ˌdi:haɪ'dreɪtɪd] dehydriert OT 2
delay [dɪ'leɪ] Verzögerung; Verspätung OT 4
delegate ['delɪgət] Abgeordnete(r) OT 4
deli ['deli] Feinkostladen **WS 1**, 15
delicious [dɪ'lɪʃəs] lecker OT 1

to **deliver** [dɪ'lɪvə] liefern OT 3
delivery [dɪ'lɪvəri] Zustellung; Zustellung **WS 3**, 102
demand [dɪ'mɑ:nd] Nachfrage; Verlangen **WS 3**, 102
demanding [dɪ'mɑ:ndɪŋ] anspruchsvoll OT 4
democracy [dɪ'mɒkrəsi] Demokratie OT 3
to **demolish** [dɪ'mɒlɪʃ] abreißen **WS 1**, 25
to **demonstrate** ['demənstreɪt] zeigen; vorführen **WS 2**, 58
demonstration [ˌdemən'streɪʃn] Demonstration **WS 1**, 28
demonstrative [dɪ'mɒnstrətɪv] Demonstrativbegleiter OT 1
deny [dɪ'naɪ] leugnen OT 4
department store [dɪ'pɑ:tmənt stɔ:] Kaufhaus OT 4
department [dɪ'pɑ:tmənt] Abteilung OT 4
departure [dɪ'pɑ:tʃə] Abfahrt; Abflug OT 2
to **depend** [dɪ'pend] abhängen OT 2
depression [dɪ'preʃn] Depression **WS 2**, 72
to **descend (from)** [dɪ'send] abstammen (von) **WS 2**, 53
to **be descended** [bi dɪ'sendɪd] abstammen von OT 3
descendant [dɪ'sendənt] Nachkomme OT 3
descent [dɪ'sent] Abstammung **WS 1**, 33
to **describe** [dɪ'skraɪb] beschreiben OT 1
description [dɪ'skrɪpʃn] Beschreibung OT 1
descriptive [dɪ'skrɪptɪv] beschreibend OT 4
desert ['dezət] Wüste OT 3
to **deserve** [dɪ'zɜ:v] verdienen OT 2
design [dɪ'zaɪn] Entwurf; Design OT 1
to **design** [dɪ'zaɪn] planen OT 4
designated ['dezɪgneɪtɪd] bestimmt OT 3
designer [dɪ'zaɪnə] Designer(in) OT 3
desire [dɪ'zaɪə] Wunsch **WS 2**, 72
desk [desk] Schreibtisch OT 1
desperate ['despərət] verzweifelt OT 3
desperately ['despərətli] verzweifelt OT 3
despite [dɪ'spaɪt] obwohl; trotz OT 4
dessert [dɪ'zɜ:t] Nachtisch OT 1
destination [ˌdestɪ'neɪʃn] Reiseziel OT 4

to **destroy** [dɪ'strɔɪ] zerstören OT 2
destruction [dɪ'strʌkʃn] Zerstörung OT 4
detail ['di:teɪl] Detail OT 2
detailed ['di:teɪld] detailliert; ausführlich OT 4
determination [dɪˌtɜ:mɪ'neɪʃn] Entschlossenheit OT 4
to **determine** [dɪ'tɜ:mɪn] ausmachen; bestimmen OT 4
determined [dɪ'tɜ:mɪnd] entschlossen **WS 3**, 90
determiner [dɪ'tɜ:mɪnə] Bestimmungswort OT 1
devastating ['devəsteɪtɪŋ] verheerend **WS 1**, 34
to **develop** [dɪ'veləp] entwickeln OT 2
developer [dɪ'veləpə] Entwickler(in) **WS 3**, 90
development [dɪ'veləpmənt] Entwicklung OT 4
device [dɪ'vaɪs] Gerät OT 3
devoted [dɪ'vəʊtɪd] verbunden OT 4
diagram ['daɪəgræm] Schaubild; Diagramm OT 1
to **dial** ['daɪəl] wählen OT 2
dial phone ['daɪəl fəʊn] Telefon mit Wählscheibe **WS 3**, 115
dialect ['daɪəlekt] Dialekt OT 4
dialogue ['daɪəlɒg] Dialog OT 1
diaper ['daɪəpə] Windel OT 3
diary ['daɪəri] Terminkalender; Tagebuch OT 1
to **dictate** [dɪk'teɪt] bestimmen **WS 2**, 54
dictionary ['dɪkʃənri] Wörterbuch OT 2
didgeridoo [ˌdɪdʒəri'du:] Didgeridoo **WS 1**, 23
to **die** [daɪ] sterben OT 1
diesel ['di:zl] Diesel OT 3
diet ['daɪət] Diät OT 3
dietary ['daɪətəri] diätetisch **WS 2**, 67
dietician [ˌdaɪə'tɪʃn] Ernährungswissenschaftler(in) **WS 2**, 77
dieting ['daɪətɪŋ] Schlankheitskuren; Diäten **WS 2**, 66
difference ['dɪfrəns] Unterschied OT 1
different ['dɪfrənt] unterschiedlich OT 1
difficult ['dɪfɪkəlt] schwer; schwierig OT 1
difficulty ['dɪfɪkəlti] Schwierigkeit OT 2
to **dig** [dɪg] graben **WS 1**, 28
digit ['dɪdʒɪt] Ziffer OT 2
digital ['dɪdʒɪtl] digital OT 1
dilemma [dɪ'lemə] Dilemma **WS 1**, 14

dimension [daɪˈmenʃn] Abmessung OT 2
dingo [ˈdɪŋgəʊ] Dingo **WS 1**, 25
dining room [ˈdaɪnɪŋ ruːm] Esszimmer OT 1
dinner [ˈdɪnə] Abendessen OT 1
dinosaur [ˈdaɪnəsɔː] Dinosaurier OT 1
to **dip** [dɪp] tauchen OT 4
diploma [dɪˈpləʊmə] Diplom; Urkunde OT 4
to **direct** [dəˈrekt] Regie führen OT 3
direction [dəˈrekʃn] Anweisung OT 2
directions [dəˈrekʃnz] Wegbeschreibungen OT 2
directly [dəˈrektli] direkt OT 3
director [dəˈrektə] Leiter(in) OT 2
dirt [dɜːt] Dreck; Schmutz OT 4
dirty [ˈdɜːti] schmutzig OT 1
disability [ˌdɪsəˈbɪləti] Behinderung OT 2
disabled [dɪsˈeɪbld] Behinderte(r) OT 4
disadvantage [ˌdɪsədˈvɑːntɪdʒ] Nachteil OT 4
disadvantaged [ˌdɪsədˈvɑːntɪdʒd] benachteiligt **WS 2**, 56
to **disagree** [ˌdɪsəˈgriː] anderer Meinung sein OT 1
disagreement [ˌdɪsəˈgriːmənt] Uneinigkeit OT 3
to **disappear** [ˌdɪsəˈpɪə] verschwinden OT 3
disappointed [ˌdɪsəˈpɔɪntɪd] enttäuscht OT 2
disappointing [ˌdɪsəˈpɔɪntɪŋ] enttäuschend OT 4
disaster [dɪˈzɑːstə] Katastrophe OT 2
discount [ˈdɪskaʊnt] Rabatt; Nachlass OT 4
to **discover** [dɪˈskʌvə] entdecken OT 2
discovery [dɪˈskʌvəri] Entdeckung OT 4
to **discriminate** [dɪˈskrɪmɪneɪt] unterschiedlich behandeln; diskriminieren **WS 3**, 94
discrimination [dɪˌskrɪmɪˈneɪʃn] Diskriminierung; Ausgrenzung **WS 3**, 90
to **discuss** [dɪˈskʌs] besprechen; diskutieren OT 1
discussion [dɪˈskʌʃn] Besprechung; Diskussion OT 1
disease [dɪˈziːz] Krankheit OT 2
disgusted [dɪsˈgʌstɪd] empört; angewidert **WS 2**, 55
disgusting [dɪsˈgʌstɪŋ] ekelhaft OT 2
dish [dɪʃ] Gericht; Schale OT 2
dishes [ˈdɪʃɪz] Geschirr OT 2
to **do the dishes** [ˌduː ðə ˈdɪʃɪz] den Abwasch machen OT 2
disinfectant [ˌdɪsɪnˈfektənt] Desinfektionsmittel OT 3
to **dislike** [dɪsˈlaɪk] nicht mögen OT 2
to **disobey** [ˌdɪsəˈbeɪ] nicht gehorchen OT 3
disorder [dɪsˈɔːdə] Störung **WS 2**, 61
disorganized [dɪsˈɔːgənaɪzd] chaotisch OT 2
dispenser [dɪˈspensə] Spender **WS 3**, 112
display [dɪˈspleɪ] Ausstellung OT 2
disrespectful [ˌdɪsrɪˈspektfl] respektlos OT 3
disruption [dɪsˈrʌpʃn] Störung; Unterbrechung OT 4
dissatisfaction [ˌdɪsˌsætɪsˈfækʃn] Unzufriedenheit **WS 2**, 67
distance [ˈdɪstəns] Entfernung OT 2
to **distance oneself** [ˈdɪstəns] (sich) distanzieren OT 4
distant [ˈdɪstənt] weit entfernt OT 4
distinct [dɪˈstɪŋkt] eindeutig; eigenständig **WS 1**, 24
distinctive [dɪˈstɪŋktɪv] unverwechselbar; ausgeprägt **WS 1**, 32
to **distribute** [dɪˈstrɪbjuːt] verteilen OT 4
district [ˈdɪstrɪkt] Bezirk **WS 2**, 56
to **disturb** [dɪˈstɜːb] stören OT 3
to **dive** [daɪv] tauchen; hineinspringen OT 3
diver [ˈdaɪvər] Taucher(in) OT 3
diverse [daɪˈvɜːs] vielfältig; verschieden OT 4
diversity [daɪˈvɜːsəti] Vielfältigkeit OT 4
to **divide** [dɪˈvaɪd] (sich) teilen OT 2
diving [ˈdaɪvɪŋ] Tauchen OT 1
divorce [dɪˈvɔːs] Scheidung OT 3
divorced: get divorced [get dɪˈvɔːst] sich scheiden lassen OT 3
dizzy [ˈdɪzi] schwindlig OT 3
to **do** [duː] tun; machen OT 1
doctor [ˈdɒktə] Arzt/Ärztin; Doktor(in) OT 1
document [ˈdɒkjumənt] Dokument OT 4
documentary [ˌdɒkjuˈmentri] Dokumentation OT 2
dog [dɒg] Hund OT 1
doll [dɒl] Puppe OT 2
dollar [ˈdɒlə] Dollar OT 1
dolphin [ˈdɒlfɪn] Delfin OT 1
dome [dəʊm] Kuppel OT 4
dominant [ˈdɒmɪnənt] wichtig; überwiegend OT 4
to **donate** [dəʊˈneɪt] spenden OT 2
donation [dəʊˈneɪʃn] Spende OT 2
donkey [ˈdɒŋki] Esel OT 4
door [dɔː] Tür OT 1
doorbell [ˈdɔːbel] Klingel OT 2
doorstep [ˈdɔːstep] Türschwelle **WS 1**, 19
double [ˈdʌbl] doppelt; Doppel... OT 1
to **double** [ˈdʌbl] sich verdoppeln **WS 1**, 17
doublet [ˈdʌblət] Wams OT 3
doubt [daʊt] Zweifel **WW**, 11
doughnut [ˈdəʊnʌt] Krapfen OT 2
down [daʊn] (nach) unten OT 1
downhill [ˌdaʊnˈhɪl] bergab **WS 1**, 13
to **download** [ˈdaʊnləʊd] herunterladen OT 3
downside [ˈdaʊnsaɪd] Nachteil OT 3
to **downsize** [ˈdaʊnsaɪz] reduzieren; sich einschränken OT 3
downstairs [ˈdaʊnsteəz] im unteren Stockwerk OT 1
Down syndrome [ˈdaʊn sɪndrəʊm] Downsyndrom **WS 2**, 61
downtown [ˌdaʊnˈtaʊn] Innenstadt OT 4
to **doze** [dəʊz] ein Nickerchen machen OT 2
dozen [ˈdʌzn] Dutzend OT 4
to **draft** [drɑːft] entwerfen **WS 2**, 71
draft [drɑːft] Entwurf OT 2
to **drain** [dreɪn] abgießen OT 2
drained [dreɪnd] abgetropft OT 2
drama [ˈdrɑːmə] Drama OT 1
dramatic [drəˈmætɪk] dramatisch OT 4
drastic [ˈdræstɪk] drastisch; extrem **WS 1**, 24
to **draw** [drɔː] ziehen; zeichnen OT 1
drawer [drɔː] Schublade OT 1
drawing [ˈdrɔːɪŋ] Zeichnung OT 4
dreadful [ˈdredfl] schrecklich OT 2
dream [driːm] Traum OT 2
dreamtime [ˈdriːmtaɪm] Traumzeit **WS 1**, 26
dress [dres] Kleid **WS 2**, 55
to **dress** [dres] anziehen; sich anziehen OT 3
dried [draɪd] getrocknet OT 3
drink [drɪŋk] Getränk OT 1
to **drink** [drɪŋk] trinken OT 1
to **drip** [drɪp] tropfen OT 3
drive [draɪv] Fahrt **WS 1**, 19
to **drive** [draɪv] fahren OT 1; treiben **WS 1**, 24
driver [ˈdraɪvə] Fahrer(in) OT 2

driveway [ˈdraɪvweɪ] Zufahrt; Auffahrt OT 4
drone [drəʊn] Drone OT 4
to **drop** [drɒp] fallen (lassen) OT 1
drop kick [ˈdrɒp kɪk] Dropkick **WS 1**, 30
drought [draʊt] Dürre **WS 1**, 25
to **drown** [draʊn] ertrinken OT 3
drug [drʌg] Droge OT 3
drummer [ˈdrʌmə] Schlagzeuger(in) OT 2
drums [drʌmz] Schlagzeug OT 1
dry [draɪ] trocken OT 2
dual [ˈdjuːəl] zweifach; dual OT 4
duality [djuːˈæləti] Dualität OT 4
duck [dʌk] Ente OT 2
due to [djuː tə] wegen **WS 1**, 28
dumb [dʌm] blöd; dumm **WS 2**, 65
to **dump** [dʌmp] abkippen OT 2
dumpster [ˈdʌmpstə] Müllcontainer OT 4
dunk [dʌŋk] Treffer OT 3
during [ˈdjʊərɪŋ] während OT 2
dust [dʌst] Staub OT 2
dusty [ˈdʌsti] verstaubt OT 4
duty free [ˌdjuːti ˈfriː] zollfrei OT 2
duvet [ˈduːveɪ] Bettdecke OT 2
dwelling [ˈdwelɪŋ] Behausung OT 4
to **dye** [daɪ] färben OT 3
dynamic [daɪˈnæmɪk] Dynamik **WS 2**, 70
dyscalculia [ˌdɪskælˈkjuːliə] Dyskalkulie **WS 2**, 57
dyslexia [dɪsˈleksiə] Legasthenie **WS 2**, 57
dyslexic [dɪsˈleksɪk] legasthenisch **WS 2**, 58
dyspraxia [dɪsˈpræksiə] Dyspraxie **WS 2**, 61
dystopian [dɪsˈtəʊpiən] dystopisch **WS 4**, 128

E

each [iːtʃ] jede(r, -s) OT 1
each other [ˌiːtʃ ˈʌðə] (sich) gegenseitig OT 3
eager [ˈiːgə] eifrig OT 2
eagle [ˈiːgl] Adler OT 2
ear [ɪə] Ohr OT 1
early [ˈɜːli] früh OT 1
to **earn** [ɜːn] verdienen OT 3
earring [ˈɪərɪŋ] Ohrring OT 3
Earth [ɜːθ] Erde OT 1
earthquake [ˈɜːθkweɪk] Erdbeben OT 2
east [iːst] Ost- OT 2
eastern [ˈiːstən] östlich OT 2
easy [ˈiːzi] einfach OT 1
to **eat** [iːt] essen OT 1
to **echo** [ˈekəʊ] nachhallen; nachklingen **WS 1**, 14
eco-friendly [ˌiːkəʊ ˈfrendli] umweltfreundlich OT 3
ecological [ˌiːkəˈlɒdʒɪkl] ökologisch **WS 1**, 25
economic [ˌiːkəˈnɒmɪk] wirtschaftlich **WS 3**, 104
economy [ɪˈkɒnəmi] Ökonomie; Wirtschaft **WS 3**, 102
ecotourism [ˈikəʊtʊərɪzəm] Ökotourismus OT 3
edge [edʒ] Rand OT 3
edit [ˈedɪt] Überarbeitung; Schnitt OT 4
to **edit** [ˈedɪt] bearbeiten OT 4
editor [ˈedɪtə] Redakteur(in); Herausgeber(in) OT 2
education [ˌedjʊˈkeɪʃən] Ausbildung OT 3
educational [ˌedʒuˈkeɪʃənl] Bildungs- OT 4
effect [ɪˈfekt] Wirkung OT 3
special effects [ˌspeʃlɪˈfekts] Spezialeffekte OT 2
effective [ɪˈfektɪv] wirksam OT 3
efficient [ɪˈfɪʃnt] effizient; wirksam **WS 2**, 59
efficiently [ɪˈfɪʃntli] effizient OT 3
effort [ˈefət] Anstrengung; Mühe OT 3
egg [eg] Ei OT 1
eight [eɪt] acht OT 1
eighteen [ˌeɪˈtiːn] achtzehn OT 1
eighty [ˈeɪti] achtzig OT 1
either [ˈaɪðə] auch nicht OT 2
elbow [ˈelbəʊ] Ellbogen OT 1
elder [ˈeldə] Älteste(r) OT 4
elderly [ˈeldəli] älter OT 4
to **elect** [ɪˈlekt] wählen; auswählen OT 4
election [ɪˈlekʃn] Wahl OT 3
elective [ɪˈlektɪv] Auswahlfach OT 4
elector [ɪˈlektə] Wahlmann OT 4
electoral [ɪˈlektərəl] Wahl- OT 4
electric [ɪˈlektrɪk] elektrisch OT 1
electrical [ɪˈlektrɪkl] elektrisch; elektronisch **WS 3**, 109
electrician [ɪˌlekˈtrɪʃn] Elektriker(in) **WS 1**, 20
electricity [ɪˌlekˈtrɪsəti] Strom OT 2
electronic [ɪˌlekˈtrɒnɪk] elektronisch OT 2
element [ˈelɪmənt] Element OT 4
elementary school [ˌelɪˈmentri skuːl] Grundschule OT 2
elephant [ˈelɪfənt] Elefant OT 1
eleven [ɪˈlevn] elf OT 1
to **eliminate** [ɪˈlɪmɪneɪt] beseitigen OT 3
else [els] sonst noch OT 1
emaciated [ɪˈmeɪsieɪtɪd] ausgemergelt OT 3
email [ˈiːmeɪl] Email OT 3
to **email** [ˈiːmeɪl] emailen OT 3
embarrassing [ɪmˈbærəsɪŋ] peinlich OT 2
ember [ˈembər] glühende Kohle **WS 4**, 128
to **emerge** [iˈmɜːdʒ] ans Licht kommen OT 3
emergency [iˈmɜːdʒənsi] Notfall OT 1
to **emigrate** [ˈemɪgreɪt] auswandern OT 4
emission [ɪˈmɪʃn] Ausstoss; Emission OT 4
emoji [ɪˈməʊdʒi] Emoji OT 2
emotion [ɪˈməʊʃn] Emotion; Gefühl **WS 2**, 71
emotional [ɪˈməʊʃənl] emotional OT 4
emperor [ˈempərə] Kaiser OT 2
emphasis (on) [ˈemfəsɪs] Betonung (auf) **WS 2**, 60
to **emphasize** [ˈemfəsaɪz] betonen OT 4
emphatic [ɪmˈfætɪk] emphatisch **WS 2**, 66
empire [ˈempaɪə] Reich OT 2
to **employ** [ɪmˈplɔɪ] beschäftigen OT 4
employee [ɪmˈplɔiː] Angestellte(r) **WS 3**, 92
employer [ɪmˈplɔɪə] Arbeitgeber(in) OT 3
employment [ɪmˈplɔɪmənt] Beschäftigung; Arbeit OT 4
to **empower** [ɪmˈpaʊə] stärken; ermächtigen **WS 3**, 109
to **empty out** [ˌemptiˈaʊt] ausleeren; herausfließen OT 3
empty [ˈempti] leer OT 1
to **enable** [ɪˈneɪbl] ermöglichen OT 4
to **encounter** [ɪnˈkaʊntə] begegnen OT 3
to **encourage** [ɪnˈkʌrɪdʒ] ermutigen OT 4
encyclopedia [ɪnˌsaɪkləˈpiːdiə] Enzyklopädie; Lexikon OT 4
end [end] Ende OT 1
to **end** [end] enden; beenden OT 1
to **endanger** [ɪnˈdeɪndʒər] gefährden **WS 1**, 28
endangered [ɪnˈdeɪndʒəd] gefährdet OT 2
ending [ˈendɪŋ] Ende; Schluss OT 1
endless [ˈendləs] endlos; unendlich OT 4

end zone ['end zəʊn] Endzone OT 3
enemy ['enəmi] Feind(in) OT 3
energetic [ˌenəˈdʒetɪk] aktiv OT 2
energy ['enədʒi] Energie OT 2
to **enforce** [ɪnˈfɔːs] durchsetzen OT 4
enforcement [ɪnˈfɔːsmənt] Vollstreckung **WS 4**, 129
to **engage** [ɪnˈgeɪdʒ] fesseln; engagieren **WS 1**, 36
to **engage with** [ɪnˈgeɪdʒ wɪð] sich befassen mit OT 4
engagement [ɪnˈgeɪdʒmənt] Engagement; Einsatz OT 4
engine ['endʒɪn] Motor; Lokomotive OT 2
engineer [ˌendʒɪˈnɪə] Ingenieur(in); Lokführer(in) OT 2
engineering [ˌendʒɪˈnɪərɪŋ] Ingenieurwesen OT 2
English ['ɪŋglɪʃ] englisch OT 1
to **engrave** [ɪnˈgreɪv] gravieren; eingravieren OT 4
to **enhance** [ɪnˈhɑːns] verbessern OT 4
to **enjoy** [ɪnˈdʒɔɪ] genießen OT 1
enjoyable [ɪnˈdʒɔɪəbl] angenehm OT 2
enormous [ɪˈnɔːməs] riesig OT 1
enough [ɪˈnʌf] genug OT 1
to **enrich** [ɪnˈrɪtʃ] verbessern; bereichern OT 4
to **ensure** [ɪnˈʃʊə] sicherstellen OT 4
to **entail** [ɪnˈteɪl] beinhalten OT 4
to **enter** ['entə] eintreten; eintragen OT 2
enterprise ['entəpraɪz] Unternehmen **WS 3**, 109
to **entertain** [ˌentəˈteɪn] unterhalten OT 4
entertainment [ˌentəˈteɪnmənt] Unterhaltung OT 2
enthusiastic [ɪnˌθjuːziˈæstɪk] begeistert OT 3
entire [ɪnˈtaɪə] ganze(r,-s) OT 3
entrance ['entrəns] Eingang OT 1
entrance hall ['entrəns ˌhɔːl] Eingangsbereich; Eingangshalle OT 1
entrepreneur [ˌɒntrəprəˈnɜː] Unternehmer(in) **WS 3**, 99
entrepreneurship [ˌɒntrəprəˈnɜːʃɪp] Unternehmertum OT 4
entry ['entri] Eintrag; Einsendung OT 2
envelope ['envələʊp] Briefumschlag OT 2
environment [ɪnˈvaɪrənmənt] Umfeld; Umwelt OT 2
environmental [ɪnˌvaɪrənˈmentl] Umwelt-; ökologisch OT 4
environmentally [ɪnˌvaɪrənˈmentəli] umwelt... OT 3
environmentalist [ɪnˌvaɪrənˈmentəlɪst] Umweltschützer(in) OT 3
to **envy** ['envi] beneiden **WS 2**, 53
epidemic [ˌepɪˈdemɪk] epidemisch **WS 1**, 24
equal ['iːkwəl] gleich; gleichberechtigt OT 4
equality [iˈkwɒləti] Gleichberechtigung **WS 1**, 43
equator [ɪˈkweɪtər] Äquator **WS 1**, 13
equipment [ɪˈkwɪpmənt] Ausrüstung OT 2
equivalent (to) [ɪˈkwɪvələnt] entsprechend **WS 2**, 56
to **erect** [ɪˈrekt] errichten OT 4
errand ['erənd] Besorgung OT 4
erratic [ɪˈrætɪk] erratisch; sprunghaft **WS 2**, 72
to **erupt** [ɪˈrʌpt] ausbrechen OT 2
escalator ['eskəleɪtə] Rolltreppe OT 1
to **escape** [ɪˈskeɪp] entkommen OT 2
e-scooter ['iːskuːtə] E-Roller **WS 3**, 113
to **escort** ['eskɔːt] begleiten OT 4
especially [ɪˈspeʃəli] besonders OT 2
essay ['eseɪ] Aufsatz OT 3
essence: in essence [ɪn ˈesns] im Wesentlichen OT 4
essential [ɪˈsenʃl] wichtig; wesentlich OT 4
to **establish** [ɪˈstæblɪʃ] gründen **WS 1**, 17
to **estimate** ['estɪmeɪt] schätzen OT 4
ETA (estimated time of arrival) [ˌiː tiː ˈeɪ] geschätzte Ankunftszeit OT 2
etc. [ˌet ˈsetərə] usw.; und so weiter OT 3
ethical ['eθɪkl] ethisch; moralisch vertretbar OT 3
ethnic ['eθnɪk] ethnisch **WS 1**, 33
eureka moment [juˈriːkə ˈməʊmənt] Heureka-Erlebnis OT 4
European [ˌjʊərəˈpiːən] Europäer(in) OT 3
to **evacuate** [ɪˈvækjueɪt] verlassen; evakuieren OT 4
evacuation [ɪˌvækjuˈeɪʃn] Evakuierung OT 4
to **evaluate** [ɪˈvæljueɪt] bewerten OT 4
evaluation [ɪˌvæljuˈeɪʃn] Bewertung **WS 3**, 101
even ['iːvn] sogar OT 1
evening ['iːvnɪŋ] Abend OT 1
event [ɪˈvent] Ereignis; Veranstaltung OT 1
eventually [ɪˈventʃuəli] schließlich OT 3
ever ['evə] je OT 1
every ['evri] jede(r,-s) OT 1
everybody ['evribɒdi] jeder; alle OT 1
everyday ['evrideɪ] alltäglich OT 3
everyone ['evriwʌn] jeder OT 1
everything ['evriθɪŋ] alles OT 1
everywhere ['evriweə] überall OT 1
evidence ['evɪdəns] Nachweis; Beweis OT 4
evil ['iːvl] Übel; Böse **WS 4**, 128
evolution [ˌiːvəˈluːʃn] Evolution; Entwicklung **WS 2**, 70
to **evolve** [ɪˈvɒlv] sich entwickeln OT 4
ewe [juː] Mutterschaf OT 2
exact [ɪgˈzækt] genau OT 2
exaggerated [ɪgˈzædʒəreɪtɪd] übertrieben **WS 1**, 21
exaggeration [ɪgˌzædʒəˈreɪʃn] Übertreibung OT 4
exam [ɪgˈzæm] Prüfung OT 1
to **examine** [ɪgˈzæmɪn] untersuchen OT 4
example [ɪgˈzɑːmpl] Beispiel OT 1
to **excavate** ['ekskəveɪt] ausgraben OT 2
excavation [ˌekskəˈveɪʃn] Ausgrabung OT 2
to **excel** [ɪkˈsel] sich selbst übertreffen; sich hervortun OT 4
excellent ['eksələnt] ausgezeichnet OT 2
except [ɪkˈsept] außer OT 2
exception [ɪkˈsepʃn] Ausnahme **WS 2**, 56
excerpt [ekˈsɜːpt] Ausschnitt; Auszug OT 4
to **exchange** [ɪksˈtʃeɪndʒ] austauschen; wechseln **WS 1**, 14
exchange [ɪksˈtʃeɪndʒ] Austausch OT 1
excited [ɪkˈsaɪtɪd] begeistert; aufgeregt OT 1
exciting [ɪkˈsaɪtɪŋ] aufregend OT 1
to **exclaim** [ɪkˈskleɪm] rufen OT 3
excuse [ɪkˈskjuːs] Entschuldigung **WS 2**, 64
to **excuse** [ɪkˈskjuːz] entschuldigen OT 1
to **execute** ['eksɪkjuːt] hinrichten OT 3
executive [ɪgˈzekjətɪv] Exekutive; ausführend OT 4
exercise ['eksəsaɪz] körperliche Bewegung; Übung OT 1
exercise book ['eksəsaɪz bʊk] Übungsheft OT 1
exhausted [ɪgˈzɔːstɪd] erschöpft OT 2

to exhibit [ɪɡ'zɪbɪt] ausstellen OT 2
exhibition [ˌeksɪ'bɪʃn] Ausstellung OT 1
to exist [ɪɡ'zɪst] existieren OT 3
existence [ɪɡ'zɪstəns] Existenz OT 4
exit ['eksɪt] Ausgang; Abfahrt OT 2
to expand [ɪk'spænd] wachsen; ausbauen **WS 3**, 101
to expect [ɪk'spekt] erwarten OT 2
expectation [ˌekspek'teɪʃn] Erwartung OT 4
expedition [ˌekspə'dɪʃn] Expedition OT 2
expense [ɪk'spens] Kosten; Ausgabe OT 4
expensive [ɪk'spensɪv] teuer OT 1
experience [ɪk'spɪəriəns] Erfahrung OT 2
to experience [ɪk'spɪəriəns] erfahren; erleben **WS 2**, 53
experienced [ɪk'spɪəriənst] erfahren OT 3
experiential [ɪkˌspɪəri'enʃl] erfahrungsmäßig; auf Erfahrung beruhend OT 4
experiment [ɪk'sperɪmənt] Experiment OT 2
to experiment [ɪk'sperɪmənt] experimentieren OT 4
expert ['ekspɜ:t] Experte / Expertin OT 3
to explain [ɪk'spleɪn] erklären OT 1
explanation [ˌeksplə'neɪʃn] Erklärung OT 1
to explode [ɪk'spləʊd] explodieren **WS 1**, 25
to exploit [ɪk'splɔɪt] ausbeuten OT 3
exploration [ˌeksplə'reɪʃn] Exploration; Erforschung **WS 1**, 39
to explore [ɪk'splɔ:] erforschen; erkunden OT 1
explorer [ɪk'splɔ:rə] Forscher(in) OT 3
exporter [ek'spɔ:tər] Exporteur(in) **WS 1**, 28
exposure [ɪk'spəʊʒə] Sichtbarkeit OT 4
to express [ɪk'spres] äußern; etw. ausdrücken OT 4
expression [ɪk'spreʃn] Ausdruck OT 1
extended [ɪk'stendɪd] erweitert **WS 2**, 53
extent [ɪk'stent] Ausmaß OT 3
extinct [ɪk'stɪŋkt] ausgestorben OT 2
extinction [ɪk'stɪŋkʃn] Aussterben OT 4
extra ['ekstrə] Extra... OT 1
extract [ɪk'strækt] Auszug OT 3
extreme [ɪk'stri:m] Extrem OT 4
extreme [ɪk'stri:m] extrem OT 4
  extremely [ɪk'stri:mli] extrem OT 3
eye [aɪ] Auge OT 1
eyebrow ['aɪbraʊ] Augenbraue **WS 3**, 93
eyelid ['aɪlɪd] Augenlid OT 2
eyepiece ['aɪpi:s] Okular OT 2

F

fabulous ['fæbjələs] fabelhaft OT 2
face [feɪs] Gesicht OT 1
  to make a face [ˌmeɪk ə 'feɪs] eine Grimasse schneiden OT 2
to face [feɪs] begegnen OT 4
facial ['feɪʃl] Gesichts- OT 4
facility [fə'sɪləti] Anlage OT 3
fact [fækt] Tatsache; Fakt OT 1
factor ['fæktə] Faktor OT 3
factory ['fæktri] Fabrik OT 2
factual ['fæktʃuəl] sachlich OT 4
to fail [feɪl] scheitern OT 4
failure ['feɪljə] Misserfolg OT 4
faint [feɪnt] schwindlig OT 2
to faint [feɪnt] ohnmächtig werden OT 2
fair [feə] Jahrmarkt OT 2
fair [feə] gerecht OT 1
fairground ['feəgraʊnd] Jahrmarkt OT 2
fairy tale ['feəri teɪl] Märchen OT 1
faith [feɪθ] Vertrauen; Glaube OT 3
fall [fɔ:l] Herbst; Wasserfall OT 1
to fall [fɔ:l] fallen; stürzen OT 1
  to fall in love [fɔ:l ɪn lʌv] sich verlieben **WS 2**, 50
  to fall over [fɔ:l 'əʊvə] hinfallen; umfallen OT 2
false [fɔ:ls] falsch OT 1
familiar [fə'mɪliə] vertraut; bekannt OT 2
familiarity [fəˌmɪli'ærəti] Vertrautheit OT 4
family ['fæməli] Familie OT 1
famine ['fæmɪn] Hungersnot OT 2
famous ['feɪməs] berühmt OT 1
fan [fæn] Fan OT 1
fanatic [fə'nætɪk] Fanatiker(in) **WS 1**, 15
fantastic [fæn'tæstɪk] fantastisch OT 1
fantasy ['fæntəsi] Fantasy; Fantasie OT 2
FAQ [ˌefeɪ'kju:] FAQ; häufig gestellte Fragen OT 3
far [fɑ:] weit OT 1
  far-off ['fɑ: ɒf] fern OT 2
faraway ['fɑ:rəweɪ] fern **WS 1**, 28
farewell [ˌfeə'wel] Lebe wohl! OT 2
farm [fɑ:m] Bauernhof OT 1
farmer ['fɑ:mə] Bauer / Bäuerin OT 2
farmhouse ['fɑ:mhaʊs] Bauernhaus OT 2
farming ['fɑ:mɪŋ] Landwirtschaft OT 2
farmland ['fɑ:mlænd] Ackerland OT 4
farmyard ['fɑ:mjɑ:d] Hof OT 2
to fascinate ['fæsɪneɪt] faszinieren OT 4
fascinating ['fæsɪneɪtɪŋ] faszinierend OT 2
fascination [ˌfæsɪ'neɪʃn] Faszination OT 3
fashion ['fæʃn] Trend; Mode OT 1
fashionable ['fæʃnəbl] modisch OT 2
fast [fɑ:st] schnell; fest OT 1
fat [fæt] Fett OT 2
father ['fɑ:ðə] Vater OT 1
fault [fɔ:lt] Schuld OT 2
to fault [fɔ:lt] bemängeln OT 2
in favour [ɪn 'feɪvə] für; zugunsten OT 4
favoured ['feɪvəd] favorisiert; bevorzugt OT 4
favourite ['feɪvərɪt] Lieblings... OT 1
fear [fɪə] Angst; Furcht OT 3
to fear [fɪər] befürchten **WS 1**, 38
feast [fi:st] Fest OT 3
feat [fi:t] Meisterleistung OT 2
feather ['feðə] Feder OT 2
to feature ['fi:tʃə] haben; präsentieren OT 2
February ['februəri] Februar OT 1
federal ['fedərəl] Bundes... OT 4
fee [fi:] Gebühr OT 3
to feed [fi:d] füttern OT 2
feedback ['fi:dbæk] Feedback OT 2
feeding ['fi:dɪŋ] Füttern OT 2
to feel [fi:l] (sich) fühlen; fühlen; anfassen OT 1
feeling ['fi:lɪŋ] Gefühl OT 2
fell [fel] (in Nordengland) Berg OT 2
female ['fi:meɪl] weiblich OT 2
fence [fens] Zaun OT 1
feral ['ferəl] wild **WS 1**, 25
fertilizer ['fɜ:təlaɪzə] Dünger OT 3
festival ['festɪvl] Festival; Fest OT 1
festival-goer ['festɪvl 'gəʊə] Festivalbesucher(in) OT 4
few [fju:] wenige OT 1
fictional ['fɪkʃənl] erfunden OT 2
field [fi:ld] Feld OT 1
field trip ['fi:ld trɪp] Schulausflug OT 2
fifteen [ˌfɪf'ti:n] fünfzehn OT 1
fifty ['fɪfti] fünfzig OT 1
fight [faɪt] Kampf OT 1
to fight [faɪt] kämpfen OT 1
fighter ['faɪtə] Kämpfer(in) OT 2
figure ['fɪgə] Zahl; Figur OT 3
file [faɪl] Datei OT 2
file card ['faɪl ˌkɑ:d] Karteikarte OT 2
to fill [fɪl] füllen OT 1

film [fɪlm] Film OT 1
to film [fɪlm] drehen; filmen **WS 1**, 31
filmmaker ['fɪlm meɪkə] Filmemacher(in) OT 4
filter ['fɪltə] Filter OT 4
final ['faɪnl] endgültig; letzte(r, -s) OT 2
finalist ['faɪnəlɪst] Finalist(in) **WS 3**, 109
to finalize ['faɪnəlaɪz] fertigstellen; abschließen OT 4
finally ['faɪnəli] schließlich OT 1
to finance ['faɪnæns] finanzieren OT 4
financial [faɪ'nænʃl] finanziell OT 4
to find [faɪnd] finden OT 1
to find out [faɪnd aʊt] herausfinden OT 2
finding ['faɪndɪŋ] Ergebnis; Erkenntnis OT 4
fine [faɪn] gut; prima OT 1
finger ['fɪŋgə] Finger OT 1
fingernail ['fɪŋgəneɪl] Fingernagel OT 2
to finish ['fɪnɪʃ] abschließen; aufhören OT 1
fire ['faɪə] Feuer OT 2
to fire ['faɪə] schießen; feuern OT 4
fire escape ['faɪər ɪskeɪp] Fluchtweg **WS 3**, 113
fire extinguisher ['faɪər ɪkstɪŋgwɪʃə] Feuerlöscher **WS 3**, 113
firefighter ['faɪəfaɪtə] Feuerwehrmann; Feuerwehrfrau OT 2
firefighting [faɪəfaɪtɪŋ] Brandbekämpfung OT 2
fireplace ['faɪəpleɪs] Kamin OT 1
firewood ['faɪəwʊd] Brennholz OT 4
fireworks ['faɪəwɜ:ks] Feuerwerk OT 3
firmly ['fɜ:mli] fest OT 4
first [fɜ:st] erste(r,-s) OT 1
at first [ət 'fɜ:st] zuerst; anfangs OT 2
for the first time [fɔ: ðə 'fɜ:st taɪm] zum ersten Mal OT 2
firstly ['fɜ:stli] zuerst OT 3
fish [fɪʃ] Fisch OT 1
fish finger ['fɪʃ ˌfɪŋgə] Fischstäbchen OT 1
fisherman ['fɪʃəmən] Fischer OT 2
fishing ['fɪʃɪŋ] Fischerei OT 3
fit [fɪt] in Form; geeignet OT 2
to keep fit [ki:p 'fɪt] sich fit halten OT 2
fitness ['fɪtnəs] Fitness **WS 2**, 66
five [faɪv] fünf OT 1
to fix [fɪks] korrigieren OT 2
fizzy ['fɪzi] kohlensäurehaltig OT 2
flag [flæg] Fahne **WW**, 10
flagship ['flægʃɪp] Flaggschiff OT 3
flamingo [flə'mɪŋgəʊ] Flamingo OT 2
flash [flæʃ] Blitz OT 4
flashlight ['flæʃlaɪt] Taschenlampe OT 2
flat [flæt] Wohnung OT 1
flea [fli:] Floh **WS 3**, 91
fleet [fli:t] Flotte OT 3
flexible ['fleksəbl] flexibel **WS 3**, 92
flight [flaɪt] Flug; Flucht OT 1
to flip [flɪp] umdrehen **WS 3**, 93
to float [fləʊt] treiben; schweben OT 3
flood [flʌd] Hochwasser; Flut OT 2
flooding ['flʌdɪŋ] Fluten; Flut **WS 1**, 34
floor [flɔ:] Boden; Stock(werk) OT 1
flora ['flɔ:rə] Flora OT 4
flour ['flaʊə] Mehl OT 2
flower ['flaʊə] Blume OT 1
flowing ['fləʊɪŋ] fließend **WS 3**, 95
fluent ['flu:ənt] fließend OT 3
fluently ['flu:əntli] fließend OT 3
fluffy ['flʌfi] flauschig OT 2
flute [flu:t] Querflöte OT 1
to fly [flaɪ] fliegen OT 1
flyer ['flaɪə] Flyer OT 4
to focus ['fəʊkəs] fokusieren OT 2
to focus on ['fəʊkəs ɒn] sich konzentrieren **WS 2**, 56
foggy ['fɒgi] nebelig OT 3
foil [fɔɪl] Folie OT 2
folk [fəʊk] Volks... OT 2
folklore ['fəʊklɔ:r] Folklore **WS 1**, 26
folks [fəʊks] Leute OT 2
to follow ['fɒləʊ] folgen OT 2
follower ['fɒləʊə] Anhänger(in) OT 3
food [fu:d] Nahrungsmittel; Essen OT 1
food bank ['fu:d bæŋk] Essensausgabe; Lebensmittelsammelstelle **WS 3**, 104
food poisoning ['fu:d pɔɪzənɪŋ] Lebensmittelvergiftung OT 2
food supplement ['fu:d ˌsʌplɪmənt] Nahrungsergänzungsmittel **WS 2**, 66
foolishly ['fu:lɪʃli] unvernünftig **WS 2**, 65
foot [fʊt] Fuß OT 1
footage ['fʊtɪdʒ] Filmmaterial; Filmaufnahmen OT 4
football ['fʊtbɔ:l] Fußball; Football OT 1
footprint ['fʊtprɪnt] Fußabdruck OT 2
footstep ['fʊtstep] Fußstapfen **WS 2**, 59
for ['fə] für OT 1
to force [fɔ:s] zwingen **WS 2**, 55
force [fɔ:s] Wasserfall; Kraft OT 2
forecast ['fɔ:kɑ:st] Prognose OT 2
forefather ['fɔ:fɑ:ðə] Ahne; Urvater OT 4
foreground ['fɔ:graʊnd] Vordergrund OT 4
foreign ['fɒrən] ausländisch; fremd OT 1
forest ['fɒrɪst] Wald OT 1
forested ['fɒrɪstɪd] bewaldet OT 4
forever [fər'evə] für immer OT 2
to forget [fə'get] vergessen OT 1
to forgive [fə'gɪv] vergeben OT 2
forklift [ˌfɔ:klɪft] Gabelstapler **WS 3**, 112
form [fɔ:m] Form; Formular OT 1
to form [fɔ:m] gründen; bilden OT 4
formal ['fɔ:ml] förmlich; formell OT 3
format ['fɔ:mæt] Format **WS 3**, 94
formation [fɔ:'meɪʃn] Formation **WS 1**, 26
former ['fɔ:mə] frühere(r) **WS 2**, 69
formula ['fɔ:mjələ] Formel OT 2
fort [fɔ:t] Festung OT 2
fortunate ['fɔ:tʃənət] glücklich OT 3
fortune ['fɔ:tʃu:n] Glück; Reichtum OT 3
forty ['fɔ:ti] vierzig OT 1
forum ['fɔ:rəm] Forum OT 2
forwards ['fɔ:wədz] vorwärts OT 2
fossil ['fɒsl] fossil OT 3
foul [faʊl] Foul OT 3
to foul [faʊl] foulen OT 3; verschmutzen; verseuchen **WS 1**, 25
to found [faʊnd] gründen OT 4
foundation [faʊn'deɪʃn] Grundlage; Fundament OT 4
to founder ['faʊndə] sinken OT 3
fountain ['faʊntən] Springbrunnen OT 1
four [fɔ:] vier OT 1
fourteen [ˌfɔ:'ti:n] vierzehn OT 1
fox [fɒks] Fuchs OT 1
to frack [fræk] fracken **WS 1**, 28
frame [freɪm] Rahmen OT 3
framework ['freɪmwɜ:k] Rahmen OT 4
frankly ['fræŋkli] offen gesagt; ehrlich gesagt OT 4
frantic ['fræntɪk] hektisch; aufgeregt OT 3
freckles ['frekelz] Sommersprossen OT 3
free [fri:] frei; kostenlos OT 1
freedom ['fri:dəm] Freiheit OT 3
freelance ['fri:lɑ:ns] freiberuflich **WS 3**, 102
freelancer ['fri:lɑ:nsə] Freiberufler(in) **WS 3**, 102
freezer ['fri:zə] Gefrierschrank OT 3
freezing ['fri:zɪŋ] kalt OT 2
freight [freɪt] Fracht OT 2

French [frentʃ] französisch OT 1
French fries [ˌfrentʃˈfraɪz] Pommes frites OT 2
frequency [ˈfriːkwənsi] Häufigkeit OT 3
frequent [ˈfriːkwənt] häufig **WS 1**, 28
frequently [ˈfriːkwəntli] häufig OT 3
fresh [freʃ] frisch OT 3
freshman [ˈfreʃmən] Student im ersten Jahr; Studienanfänger(in) OT 4
Friday [ˈfraɪdeɪ] Freitag OT 1
fridge [frɪdʒ] Kühlschrank OT 1
fried [fraɪd] frittiert OT 2
friend [frend] Freund(in) OT 1
friendliness [ˈfrendlinəs] Freundlichkeit OT 4
friendly [ˈfrendli] freundlich OT 1
frightened [ˈfraɪtnd] verängstigt OT 1
frightening [ˈfraɪtnɪŋ] erschreckend OT 1
frizzy [ˈfrɪzi] kraus OT 3
from [frəm] von; aus OT 1
front [frʌnt] Vorderseite OT 1
to **frown** [fraʊn] die Stirn runzeln OT 3
frozen [ˈfrəʊzn] gefroren OT 4
fruit [fruːt] Obst OT 1
frustrated [frʌˈstreɪtɪd] frustriert OT 4
fuel [ˈfjuːəl] Brennstoff OT 2
full [fʊl] voll OT 1
full-time [ˌfʊl ˈtaɪm] ganztags **WS 2**, 53
fun [fʌn] Spaß OT 1
function [ˈfʌŋkʃn] Funktion OT 4
fund [fʌnd] Geldmittel OT 4
fundraiser [ˈfʌndreɪzə] Wohltätigkeitsveranstaltung OT 2
fundraising [ˈfʌndreɪzɪŋ] Spendensammlung OT 2
funeral [ˈfjuːnərəl] Beerdigung OT 4
funny [ˈfʌni] lustig; merkwürdig OT 1
fur [ˈfɜː] Fell OT 4
fur-lined [ˈfɜː laɪnd] mit Fell gefüttert OT 4
furniture [ˈfɜːnɪtʃə] Möbel OT 1
further [ˈfɜːðə] weiter OT 4
furthest [ˈfɜːðɪst] am weitesten entfernt OT 2
future [ˈfjuːtʃə] Zukunft OT 2
fuzz [fʌz] Fussel OT 4

G

gadget [ˈgædʒɪt] Gerät; technische Spielerei OT 4
to **gain** [geɪn] bekommen; erreichen OT 4
gallery [ˈgæləri] Galerie OT 1
galley [ˈgæli] Kombüse OT 3
gallon [ˈgælən] Gallone OT 3
game [geɪm] Spiel OT 1
gamer [ˈgeɪmə] Gamer(in); Spieler(in) OT 4
gang [gæŋ] Bande; Gang **WS 3**, 104
gap [gæp] Lücke OT 1
garage [ˈgærɑːʒ] Garage; Werkstatt OT 4
garbage [ˈgɑːbɪdʒ] Abfall OT 2
garden [ˈgɑːdn] Garten OT 1
gardener [ˈgɑːdnə] Gärtner(in) OT 4
gardening [ˈgɑːdnɪŋ] Gartenarbeit OT 1
gas [gæs] Gas OT 4
gas cooker [ˈgas kʊkə] Gaskocher OT 3
gate [geɪt] Tor OT 1
gateway [ˈgeɪtweɪ] Zugang; Gateway **WS 1**, 39
to **gather** [ˈgæðə] sammeln OT 4
gay [geɪ] schwul; früher: fröhlich **WS 2**, 50
to **gaze** [geɪz] blicken **WS 1**, 29
GCSE (General Certificate of Secondary Education) [ˌdʒiː siː es ˈiː] mittlerer Schulabschluss OT 4
geared: to be geared towards [bi gɪər təˈwɔːdz] auf etw. ausgerichtet sein **WS 2**, 56
geek [giːk] Geek; Spezialist(in) **WS 2**, 68
gel [dʒel] Gel OT 2
gelateria [ˈdʒeləˈtɪəriə] italienisches Eiscafé **WS 3**, 109
gelato [ˈdʒelɑːtəʊ] italienische Eiscreme **WS 3**, 109
gender [ˈdʒendə] Geschlecht; Gender OT 4
gendered [ˈdʒendəd] geschlechtsspezifisch **WS 2**, 54
genderless [ˈdʒendələs] geschlechtslos **WS 2**, 54
gender-neutral [ˌdʒendə ˈnjuːtrəl] geschlechtsneutral **WS 2**, 54
general [ˈdʒenrəl] allgemein; generell OT 4
generalization [ˌdʒenrəlaɪˈzeɪʃn] Generalisierung **WS 2**, 56
generally [ˈdʒenrəli] im Allgemeinen; hauptsächlich OT 4
general manager [ˈdʒenrəl ˈmænɪdʒər] Geschäftsführer(in) OT 3
to **generate** [ˈdʒenəreɪt] erzeugen OT 4
generation [ˌdʒenəˈreɪʃn] Generation OT 3
genetic [dʒəˈnetɪk] genetisch **WS 2**, 61
genre [ˈʒɒnrə] Genre **WS 4**, 141
gently [ˈdʒentli] sachte OT 3
genuinely [ˈdʒenjuɪnli] echt **WS 3**, 106
geocache [ˈdʒiːəʊkæʃ] Geocache OT 2
geocaching [ˈdʒiːəʊkæʃɪŋ] Geocaching OT 2
geographical [ˌdʒiːəˈgræfɪkl] geografisch OT 4
geography [dʒiˈɒgrəfi] Erdkunde; Geografie OT 1
geology [dʒiˈɒlədʒi] Geologie OT 2
German [ˈdʒɜːmən] deutsch OT 1
gesture [ˈdʒestər] Geste **WS 3**, 93
to **get** [get] bekommen OT 1
to **get** [get] werden OT 2
to **get in** [get ɪn] einsteigen OT 1
to **get off** [get ɒf] aussteigen OT 2
to **get on** [get ɒn] zusteigen OT 2
to **get out** [ˈget aʊt] aussteigen OT 1
Get out! [get aʊt] Raus hier! OT 2
to **get ready** [ˈget redi] vorbereiten OT 1
to **get rid of** [get rɪd əv] los werden OT 3
to **get there** [get ðeə] ankommen OT 2
to **get to (a place)** [get tʌː] ankommen OT 2
to **get up** [ˈget ʌp] aufstehen OT 1
ghost [gəʊst] Geist OT 2
ghyll [gɪl] (in Nordengland) enges Tal OT 2
giant [ˈdʒaɪənt] riesig OT 2
gift [gɪft] Geschenk OT 1
gifted [ˈgɪftɪd] begabt **WS 2**, 51
gig [gɪg] Gig; Auftritt; Mini-Job **WS 3**, 100
ginger [ˈdʒɪndʒə] Ingwer; rötlich braun OT 1
giraffe [dʒəˈrɑːf] Giraffe OT 1
girl [gɜːl] Mädchen OT 1
Girl Scout [ˌgɜːlˈskaʊt] Pfadfinderin OT 3
to **give** [gɪv] geben OT 1
to **give up** [gɪv ʌp] aufgeben OT 2
glad [glæd] froh OT 2
gladiator [ˈglædieɪtə] Gladiator(in) OT 2
glam [glæm] schick OT 4
glamorous [ˈglæmərəs] glamourös OT 4
glamping [ˈglæmpɪŋ] glamouröses Zelten OT 4
glass [glɑːs] Glas OT 1
glass ceiling [ˌglɑːs ˈsiːlɪŋ] gläserne Decke; unsichtbare Barriere **WS 3**, 110
glimpse [glɪmps] flüchtiger Blick **WS 4**, 128
global [ˈgləʊbl] global; weltweit OT 4
globe [gləʊb] Globus; Erdkugel **WS 1**, 13

glove [glʌv] Handschuh OT 1
glue [glu:] Klebstoff OT 1
to **go** [gəʊ] gehen; fahren OT 1
to **go ahead** [ˌgəʊ ə'hed] weitermachen OT 2
goal [gəʊl] Tor; Ziel OT 1
goalkeeper ['gəʊlki:pə] Torwart OT 4
goat [gəʊt] Ziege OT 3
God [gɒd] Gott OT 3
godmother ['gɒdmʌðər] Patentante **WS 1**, 15
gold [gəʊld] Gold OT 2
golden ['gəʊldən] golden OT 2
gold rush ['gəʊld rʌʃ] Goldrausch **WS 1**, 17
golf [gɒlf] Golf OT 4
golfer ['gɒlfə] Golfer(in) OT 4
to **gongoozle** [gɒŋ'gu:zl] gaffen OT 3
gongoozler [gɒŋ'gu:zlə] Gaffer OT 3
good [gʊd] gut OT 1
goody ['gʊdi] tolle Kleinigkeit OT 2
goods [gʊdz] Güter OT 3
to **govern** ['gʌvn] regieren OT 3
government ['gʌvənmənt] Regierung OT 2
governmental [ˌgʌvn'mentl] Regierungs- OT 4
governor ['gʌvənə] Gouverneur(in) OT 3
GPS (global positioning system) [ˌdʒi: pi: 'es] Navigationssystem; Globales Positionsbestimmungssystem OT 2
to **grab** [græb] greifen OT 3
grade [greɪd] Klassenstufe OT 2
sixth grader ['sɪksθ ˌgreɪdə] Sechstklässler(in) OT 2
grading ['greɪdɪŋ] Noten... **WS 2**, 59
to **graduate** ['grædʒuət] den Schulabschluss machen OT 4
grain [greɪn] Getreide **WS 2**, 66
gram [græm] Gramm OT 2
grammar ['græmə] Grammatik OT 1
grandchild ['græntʃaɪld] Enkel(in); Enkelkind OT 1
grandfather ['grænfa:ðə] Großvater OT 1
grandma ['grænma:] Oma OT 1
grandmother ['grænmʌðə] Großmutter OT 1
grandpa ['grænpa:] Opa OT 1
grandparents ['grænpeərənts] Großeltern OT 1
grandson ['grænsʌn] Enkel OT 1
grant [gra:nt] Förderung; Zuschuss OT 4
graph [gra:f] Diagramm **WS 2**, 59
graphic ['græfɪk] Grafik OT 3
graphic novel [ˌgræfɪk 'nɒvl] Bildroman **WS 4**, 128
to **grasp** [gra:sp] greifen; festhalten **WS 2**, 61
grass [gra:s] Gras OT 1
grassland ['gra:slænd] Grasland; Grünland OT 4
grateful ['greɪtfl] dankbar OT 3
gravy ['greɪvi] Bratensoße OT 1
great [greɪt] groß; toll; toll OT 1
Greek [gri:k] Grieche(-in) OT 2
green [gri:n] grün OT 1
to **greet** [gri:t] grüßen OT 2
greeting ['gri:tɪŋ] Gruß OT 2
grey [greɪ] grau OT 1
to **grin** [grɪn] grinsen OT 2
grizzly ['grɪzli] Grizzlybär OT 2
grocery ['grəʊsəri] Lebensmittel OT 4
gross [grəʊs] ätzend OT 3
grouchy ['graʊtʃi] griesgrämig OT 2
ground [graʊnd] Boden; Erde; Platz OT 2
group [gru:p] Gruppe OT 1
to **group** [gru:p] gruppieren OT 4
to **grow** [grəʊ] wachsen; anbauen OT 1
grown up ['grəʊn ʌp] erwachsen OT 2
growth [grəʊθ] Wachstum **WS 2**, 66
to **guarantee** [ˌgærən'ti:] garantieren OT 4
guard [ga:d] Sicherheitsbeamter(in); Wächter(in) **WS 2**, 77
guardian ['ga:diən] Betreuer(in) OT 2
guess [ges] Schätzung OT 1
to **guess** [ges] schätzen; raten OT 1
guest [gest] Gast OT 2
guestbook ['gestbʊk] Gästebuch OT 2
guidance ['gaɪdns] Anleitung OT 4
guidance counsellor ['gaɪdns'kaʊnsələ] Beratungslehrer(in) OT 3
guide [gaɪd] Führer(in) OT 1
to **guide** [gaɪd] führen; leiten OT 1
guidebook ['gaɪdbʊk] Reiseführer OT 3
guide dog ['gaɪd dɒg] Blindenführhund OT 2
guideline ['gaɪdlaɪn] Richtlinie; Regel OT 3
guilty ['gɪlti] schuldig OT 4
guitar [gɪ'ta:] Gitarre OT 1
guitarist [gɪ'ta:rɪst] Gitarrist(in) OT 4
gun [gʌn] Schusswaffe OT 3
gunfire ['gʌnfaɪə] Schießerei; Schüsse OT 3
gunman ['gʌnmən] Schütze OT 4
gurning ['gɜ:nɪŋ] Grimassieren OT 2
guy [gaɪ] Kerl; Typ **WS 1**, 30
guys [gaɪz] Leute OT 2
gym [dʒɪm] Turnen; Turnhalle OT 1
gymnasium [dʒɪm'neɪziəm] Sporthalle; Turnhalle OT 4
gymnastics [dʒɪm'næstɪks] Gymnastik OT 1

H

habit ['hæbɪt] Angewohnheit OT 4
habitable ['hæbɪtəbl] bewohnbar OT 4
habitat ['hæbɪtæt] Habitat **WS 1**, 34
to **hail** [heɪl] grüßen OT 2
hair [heə] Haare OT 1
haircut ['heəkʌt] Haarschnitt OT 2
half [ha:f] halbe(r, -s); halb OT 1
half past ['ha:f pa:st] eine halbe Stunde nach OT 1
halfway [ˌha:f'weɪ] halbwegs; halb OT 4
hall [hɔ:l] Halle; Flur OT 1
Halloween [ˌhæləʊ'i:n] Halloween OT 2
halt [hɔ:lt] Haltestelle OT 2
ham [hæm] Schinken OT 1
hamster ['hæmstə] Hamster OT 1
hand [hænd] Hand OT 1
to **hand in** [hænd ɪn] einreichen OT 2
handbag ['hændbæg] Handtasche OT 3
handbook ['hændbʊk] Handbuch OT 3
handful ['hændfʊl] Handvoll OT 4
handicraft ['hændikra:ft] Handwerk; Handarbeit OT 4
handle ['hændl] Griff OT 2
to **handle** ['hændl] handhaben OT 4
handout ['hændaʊt] Handout; Flugblatt OT 4
handset ['hændset] Handapparat OT 2
handsome ['hænsəm] gut aussehend OT 1
to **handwrite** ['hændraɪt] mit der Hand schreiben **WS 3**, 103
handwriting ['hændraɪtɪŋ] Handschrift OT 2
to **hang on** [ˌhæŋ'ɒn] warten OT 2
to **hang out** [hæŋ aʊt] herumhängen OT 3
to **happen** ['hæpən] geschehen; passieren OT 1
to **happen upon** ['hæpən ə'pɒn] zufällig entdecken OT 4
happiness ['hæpinəs] Glück; Freude **WS 3**, 99
happy ['hæpi] glücklich OT 1
harbour ['ha:bə] Hafen OT 4
hard [ha:d] hart OT 2
hardly ['ha:dli] kaum OT 4
harm [ha:m] Schaden OT 3

harmful ['hɑ:mfl] schädlich **WS 2**, 65
harpoon [hɑ:'pu:n] Harpune OT 4
harsh [hɑ:ʃ] rau OT 3
harvest ['hɑ:vɪst] Ernte OT 3
to **harvest** ['hɑ:vɪst] ernten OT 4
hat [hæt] Hut OT 1
to **hate** [heɪt] hassen OT 1
to **have got** ['hæv gɒt] haben OT 1
hazardous ['hæzədəs] gefährlich OT 4
head [hed] Kopf OT 1
headache ['hedeɪk] Kopfschmerzen OT 1
header ['hedə] Kopfball OT 3
heading ['hedɪŋ] Überschrift OT 3
headline ['hedlaɪn] Schlagzeile OT 2
to **headline** ['hedlaɪn] hier: der wichtigste Künstler sein OT 3
headset ['hedset] Headset; Kopfhörer **WS 2**, 58
headphones ['hedfəʊnz] Kopfhörer OT 2
headshot ['hedʃɒt] Portraitfoto **WS 3**, 94
head teacher [ˌhed 'ti:tʃə] Schulleiter(in) OT 1
headword ['hedwɜ:d] Stichwort OT 2
health [helθ] Gesundheit OT 3
healthcare ['helθkeə] Gesundheitsfürsorge OT 4
healthy ['helθi] gesund OT 2
heap [hi:p] Haufen **WS 1**, 16
to **hear** [hɪə] hören OT 1
heart [hɑ:t] Herz OT 2
to **heat** [hi:t] heizen OT 2
heater ['hi:tə] Ofen OT 2
heatwave ['hi:tweɪv] Hitzewelle **WS 1**, 28
heavy ['hevi] schwer OT 1
hectic ['hektɪk] hektisch OT 4
hedgehog ['hedʒhɒg] Igel OT 1
height [haɪt] Höhe OT 1
hell [hel] Hölle **WS 4**, 137
hello [hə'ləʊ] Hallo! OT 1
helmet ['helmɪt] Helm OT 1
to **help** [help] helfen OT 1
helper ['helpə] Helfer(in) **WS 3**, 96
helpful ['helpfl] hilfreich OT 1
helpline ['helplaɪn] Hotline OT 2
hemisphere ['hemɪsfɪər] Hemisphäre **WS 1**, 13
hen [hen] Henne; Huhn OT 4
heptathlon [hep'tæθlən] Siebenkampf OT 2
her [hə] sie; ihr OT 1
herb [hɜ:b] Kraut; Heilkraut OT 3
herd [hɜ:d] Herde **WS 1**, 25
to **herd** [hɜ:d] treiben OT 2
herder ['hɜ:də] Hirte / Hirtin OT 3
here [hɪə] hier OT 1
heritage ['herɪtɪdʒ] Erbe; Tradition OT 4
hero ['hɪərəʊ] Held(in) OT 4
hers [hɜ:z] ihre(r,-s) OT 3
hesitantly ['hezɪtəntli] zögerlich OT 4
to **hesitate** ['hezɪteɪt] zögern OT 3
hesitation [ˌhezɪ'teɪʃn] Zögern OT 3
heterosexual [ˌhetərə'sekʃuəl] heterosexuell **WS 2**, 55
hi-fi ['haɪ faɪ] Hi-Fi-Anlage OT 3
to **hide** [haɪd] sich verstecken OT 3
high [haɪ] Höchststand OT 1
high-heeled [ˌhaɪ 'hi:ld] hochhackig OT 3
to **highlight** ['haɪlaɪt] betonen **WS 1**, 32
highly ['haɪli] höchst; äußerst OT 4
highway ['haɪweɪ] Highway; Landstraße OT 3
to **hike** [haɪk] wandern OT 1
hill [hɪl] Hügel OT 1
him [hɪm] ihn; ihm OT 1
Hindu ['hɪndu:] hinduistisch OT 1
to **hint** [hɪnt] andeuten OT 4
hip [hɪp] Hüfte OT 1
to **hire** ['haɪə] mieten OT 3
his [hɪz] seine(r,-s) OT 1
Hispanic [hɪ'spænɪk] hispanisch OT 3
historian [hɪ'stɔ:riən] Historiker(in) OT 2
historic [hɪ'stɒrɪk] historisch OT 2
historical [hɪ'stɒrɪkl] geschichtlich OT 2
history ['hɪstri] Geschichte OT 1
to **hit** [hɪt] schlagen OT 1
hob [hɒb] Kochfeld OT 3
hobby ['hɒbi] Hobby OT 1
hockey ['hɒki] Hockey OT 1
to **hold** [həʊld] halten OT 1
hole [həʊl] Loch OT 1
holiday ['hɒlədeɪ] Urlaub OT 1
hologram ['hɒləgræm] Hologramm OT 2
home [həʊm] Zuhause OT 1
homecoming ['həʊmkʌmɪŋ] traditionelles Event in Highschools **WS 2**, 60
homeland ['həʊmlænd] Heimat **WS 1**, 28
homeless ['həʊmləs] obdachlos; Obdachlose(r) OT 4
homemade ['həʊmmeɪd] selbst gemacht OT 1
home-schooled [ˌhəʊm'sku:ld] zu Hause unterrichtet OT 4
homesick ['həʊmsɪk] voll Heimweh OT 2
homesickness ['həʊmsɪknəs] Heimweh **WS 1**, 30
homework ['həʊmwɜ:k] Hausaufgaben OT 1
honest ['ɒnɪst] ehrlich OT 2
honey ['hʌni] Honig; Schatz (als Kosename) OT 2
to **honour** ['ɒnə] ehren OT 4
hoodie ['hʊdi] Kapuzenpullover OT 1
to **hope** [həʊp] hoffen OT 1
hopeful ['həʊpfl] hoffnungsvoll OT 4
hopefully ['həʊpfəli] hoffentlich OT 3
hopeless ['həʊpləs] hoffnungslos OT 4
horizon [hə'raɪzn] Horizont **WS 1**, 38
horizontal [ˌhɒrɪ'zɒntl] horizontal **WS 3**, 112
hormone ['hɔ:məʊn] Hormon **WS 2**, 55
horn [hɔ:n] Horn; Hupe OT 3
horrible ['hɒrəbl] furchtbar OT 2
horrified ['hɒrɪfaɪd] entsetzt **WW**, 11
horror ['hɒrə] Schrecken; Horror OT 4
horse [hɔ:s] Pferd OT 1
on **horseback** ['hɔ:sbæk] zu Pferde OT 3
horse riding ['raɪdɪŋ] Reiten OT 1
hospital ['hɒspɪtl] Krankenhaus OT 1
hospitality [ˌhɒspɪ'tæləti] Gastfreundlichkeit OT 2
host [həʊst] Gastgeber(in) OT 3
to **host** [həʊst] ausrichten OT 3
hot [hɒt] heiß; scharf OT 1
hotel [həʊ'tel] Hotel OT 1
hound [haʊnd] Spürhund OT 2
hour ['aʊə] Stunde OT 1
house [haʊs] Haus OT 1
household ['haʊshəʊld] häuslich; Haushalts- OT 4
housekeeper ['haʊski:pə] Haushälter(in) OT 3
housewife ['haʊswaɪf] Hausfrau **WS 3**, 103
housework ['haʊswɜ:k] Hausarbeit OT 1
housing ['haʊzɪŋ] Wohn...; Wohnungs... **WS 3**, 104
how [haʊ] wie OT 1
however [haʊ'evə] jedoch OT 2
howl [haʊl] Geheul **WS 1**, 25
hug [hʌg] Umarmung OT 1
huge [hju:dʒ] riesig OT 2
hull [hʌl] Rumpf OT 3
to **hum** [hʌm] summen OT 4
human ['hju:mən] menschlich OT 2
human being [ˌhju:mən'bi:ɪŋ] Mensch OT 2

humanities [hjuːˈmænətis] Geisteswissenschaften OT 4
human right [ˌhjuːmən ˈraɪt] Menschenrecht **WW**, 11
humid [ˈhjuːmɪd] humid; feucht OT 4
humour [ˈhjuːmə] Humor OT 4
hundred [ˈhʌndrəd] hundert OT 1
Hungarian [hʌŋˈgeəriən] ungarisch OT 2
hunger [ˈhʌŋgə] Hunger OT 3
hungry [ˈhʌŋgri] hungrig OT 1
to **hunt** [hʌnt] jagen OT 2
hunter [ˈhʌntə] Jäger(in) OT 3
hunter-gatherer [ˌhʌntə ˈgæðərər] Jäger und Sammler **WS 1**, 24
hunting [ˈhʌntɪŋ] Jagen OT 2
hurricane [ˈhʌrɪkən] Hurrikan; Orkan OT 4
to **hurry** [ˈhʌri] sich beeilen OT 1
to **hurry up** [ˈhʌri ʌp] sich beeilen OT 2
hurt [hɜːt] verletzt OT 1
to **hurt** [hɜːt] schmerzen; wehtun OT 1
husband [ˈhʌzbənd] Ehemann; Mann OT 2
hydro-electric [ˌhaɪdrəʊɪˈlektrɪk] Wasserkraft OT 4
hyper [ˈhaɪpə] über- OT 4
hyperactive [ˌhaɪpərˈæktɪv] hyperaktiv **WS 2**, 57
hypothermia [ˌhaɪpəˈθɜːmiə] Unterkühlung OT 2

I
ice [aɪs] Eis OT 1
ice cream [ˌaɪsˈkriːm] Eis; Eiscreme OT 1
iconic [aɪˈkɒnɪk] ikonisch; Kult... OT 3
ICT (information and communications technology) [ˌaɪ siːˈtiː] Informations- und Kommunikationstechnologie; Informatikunterricht OT 1
icy [ˈaɪsi] eisig **WS 2**, 64
ID card (identification card) [ˌaɪ ˈdiː kɑːd] Ausweis **WS 3**, 112
idea [aɪˈdɪə] Idee OT 1
ideal [aɪˈdiːəl] ideal OT 4
to **identify** [aɪˈdentɪfaɪ] identifizieren OT 4
identity [aɪˈdentəti] Identität OT 3
idol [ˈaɪdl] Idol **WS 2**, 66
if [ɪf] falls OT 1
igloo [ˈɪgluː] Iglu OT 4
to **ignore** [ɪgˈnɔː] ignorieren OT 4
ill [ɪl] krank OT 2
illegal [ɪˈliːgl] illegal OT 3
illiterate [ɪˈlɪtərət] analphabetisch OT 4
illness [ˈɪlnəs] Krankheit OT 2
to **illustrate** [ˈɪləstreɪt] verdeutlichen; illustrieren OT 4
illustration [ˌɪləˈstreɪʃn] Illustration OT 2
image [ˈɪmɪdʒ] Bild OT 3
imaginary [ɪˈmædʒɪnəri] erfunden; fiktiv OT 4
to **imagine** [ɪˈmædʒɪn] sich etwas vorstellen OT 1
immediate [ɪˈmiːdiət] unmittelbar; umgehend **WS 1**, 24
immediately [ɪˈmiːdiətli] sofort OT 4
immigrant [ˈɪmɪgrənt] Einwanderer(in) OT 4
to **immigrate** [ˈɪmɪgreɪt] einwandern **WS 2**, 53
immigration [ˌɪmɪˈgreɪʃn] Einwanderung OT 2
impact [ˈɪmpækt] Auswirkung OT 3
impaired [ɪmˈpeəd] beeinträchtigt **WS 2**, 61
to **impart** [ɪmˈpɑːt] vermitteln OT 4
impatient [ɪmˈpeɪʃnt] ungeduldig **WS 4**, 129
imperative [ɪmˈperətɪv] Imperativ; Befehlsform OT 1
to **implement** [ˈɪmplɪment] umsetzen; durchführen OT 4
importance [ɪmˈpɔːtns] Wichtigkeit; Bedeutung OT 3
important [ɪmˈpɔːtnt] wichtig OT 1
impossible [ɪmˈpɒsəbl] unmöglich OT 2
to **impress** [ɪmˈpres] beeindrucken OT 4
impression [ɪmˈpreʃn] Eindruck **WS 3**, 94
impressive [ɪmˈpresɪv] beeindruckend OT 2
to **improve** [ɪmˈpruːv] sich verbessern OT 3
improvement [ɪmˈpruːvmənt] Verbesserung OT 3
in [ɪn] in OT 1
inaccessible [ˌɪnækˈsesəbl] unzugänglich OT 3
inaccurate [ɪnˈækjərət] ungenau OT 4
incentive [ɪnˈsentɪv] Anreiz; Antrieb **WS 3**, 98
inch [ɪntʃ] Zoll (2,54 cm) OT 2
incident [ˈɪnsɪdənt] Vorfall; Ereignis **WS 2**, 65
to **include** [ɪnˈkluːd] einschließen OT 2
including [ɪnˈkluːdɪŋ] einschließlich OT 1
inclusive [ɪnˈkluːsɪv] integrativ OT 4
income [ˈɪnkʌm] Einkommen **WS 1**, 27
incomplete [ˌɪnkəmˈpliːt] unvollständig **WS 2**, 53
incorrectly [ˌɪnkəˈrektli] falsch; fehlerhaft **WS 2**, 66
increase [ˈɪnkriːs] Zunahme OT 3
to **increase** [ɪnˈkriːs] erhöhen **WS 1**, 34
increased [ɪnˈkriːst] erhöht **WS 1**, 34
increasingly [ɪnˈkriːsɪŋli] zunehmend **WS 2**, 52
incredible [ɪnˈkredəbl] unglaublich OT 2
incubator [ˈɪŋkjubeɪtər] Inkubator; Unterstützer von Start-ups **WS 3**, 90
independence [ˌɪndɪˈpendəns] Unabhängigkeit OT 2
independent [ˌɪndɪˈpendənt] unabhängig OT 4
to **indicate** [ˈɪndɪkeɪt] angeben; zeigen OT 4
indigenous [ɪnˈdɪdʒənəs] einheimisch OT 4
individual [ˌɪndɪˈvɪdʒuəl] individuell OT 3
individually [ˌɪndɪˈvɪdʒuəli] einzeln **WS 1**, 31
indoor [ˈɪndɔː] Innen... OT 2
indoors [ˌɪnˈdɔːz] drinnen OT 3
induction [ɪnˈdʌkʃn] Einführung **WS 3**, 112
industrial [ɪnˈdʌstriəl] Industrie... OT 2
industry [ˈɪndəstri] Industrie OT 2
infamous [ˈɪnfəməs] berüchtigt OT 4
infection [ɪnˈfekʃn] Entzündung OT 2
infinitive [ɪnˈfɪnətɪv] Infinitiv OT 1
influence [ˈɪnfluəns] Einfluss **WW**, 11
to **influence** [ˈɪnfluəns] beeinflussen OT 3
influencer [ˈɪnfluənsə] Influencer(in) **WS 2**, 69
influenza [ˌɪnfluˈenzə] Grippe; Influenza **WS 1**, 24
infographic [ˌɪnfəʊˈgræfɪk] Infografik OT 3
infomercial [ˌɪnfəʊˈmɜːʃl] Infomercial OT 4
to **inform** [ɪnˈfɔːm] informieren OT 4
informal [ɪnˈfɔːml] informell **WS 1**, 16
information [ˌɪnfəˈmeɪʃn] Information OT 1
informative [ɪnˈfɔːmətɪv] informativ OT 4

infrastructure [ˈɪnfrəstrʌktʃə] Infrastruktur OT 4
ingredient [ɪnˈgriːdiənt] Zutat OT 2
to **inhabit** [ɪnˈhæbɪt] bewohnen OT 4
to **inherit** [ɪnˈherɪt] erben OT 4
initial [ɪˈnɪʃl] ursprünglich; anfänglich **WS 3**, 108
initially [ɪˈnɪʃəli] zunächst; anfangs **WS 3**, 105
initiative [ɪˈnɪʃətɪv] Initiative; Kampagne OT 4
to **injure** [ˈɪndʒə] verletzen OT 2
injury [ˈɪndʒəri] Verletzung OT 2
inn [ɪn] Gasthaus OT 2
to **innovate** [ˈɪnəveɪt] innovieren; verbessern OT 4
innovation [ˌɪnəˈveɪʃn] Innovation; Neuheit OT 4
innovative [ˈɪnəveɪtɪv] innovativ OT 4
innovator [ˈɪnəveɪtə] Innovator(in) OT 4
insect [ˈɪnsekt] Insekt OT 2
insecure [ˌɪnsɪˈkjʊər] unsicher; instabil **WS 3**, 98
inside [ˌɪnˈsaɪd] in; innerhalb OT 1
inspiration [ˌɪnspəˈreɪʃn] Inspiration; Eingebung OT 4
to **inspire** [ɪnˈspaɪə] inspirieren; anregen OT 4
to **install** [ɪnˈstɔːl] installieren OT 3
installation [ˌɪnstəˈleɪʃn] Installation OT 4
instance: for instance [fə ˈɪnstəns] zum Beispiel OT 4
instead [ɪnˈsted] stattdessen OT 2
institution [ˌɪnstɪˈtjuːʃn] Einrichtung OT 4
instruction [ɪnˈstrʌkʃn] Anweisung OT 1
instructive [ɪnˈstrʌktɪv] instruktiv; lehrreich **WS 1**, 29
instructor [ɪnˈstrʌktə] Lehrer(in) OT 2
instrument [ˈɪnstrəmənt] Instrument OT 1
to **insult** [ˈɪnsʌlt] beleidigen; verletzen **WS 1**, 26
to **integrate** [ˈɪntɪgreɪt] integrieren OT 4
integration [ˌɪntɪˈgreɪʃn] Integration **WS 2**, 57
intelligence [ɪnˈtelɪdʒəns] Intelligenz OT 4
intelligent [ɪnˈtelɪdʒənt] intelligent OT 2
to **intend** [ɪnˈtend] beabsichtigen OT 4
intense [ɪnˈtens] stark; ernsthaft **WS 1**, 32
intention [ɪnˈtenʃn] Absicht **WS 2**, 66
to **interact** [ˌɪntərˈækt] interagieren OT 4
interaction [ˌɪntərˈækʃn] Interaktion OT 4
interactive [ˌɪntərˈæktɪv] interaktiv OT 4
interest [ˈɪntrəst] Interesse OT 1
interested [ˈɪntrəstɪd] interessiert OT 1
interesting [ˈɪntrəstɪŋ] interessant OT 1
interior [ɪnˈtɪəriər] Binnenland; das Innere **WS 1**, 13
intern [ɪnˈtɜːn] Praktikant(in); Volontär(in) **WS 3**, 106
international [ˌɪntəˈnæʃnəl] international OT 1
internet [ˈɪntənet] Internet OT 3
internship [ˈɪntɜːnʃɪp] Praktikum OT 4
interpersonal [ˌɪntəˈpɜːsənl] interpersonell; zwischenmenschlich **WS 3**, 94
to **interpret** [ɪnˈtɜːprət] interpretieren OT 4
interpreter [ɪnˈtɜːprɪtə] Dolmetscher(in) OT 3
to **interrupt** [ˌɪntəˈrʌpt] unterbrechen OT 2
intersex [ˈɪntəseks] Intersex **WS 2**, 55
to **intervene** [ˌɪntəˈviːn] eingreifen **WS 2**, 64
intervention [ˌɪntəˈvenʃn] Eingriff; Eingreifen **WS 2**, 65
interview [ˈɪntəvjuː] Vorstellungsgespräch; Interview OT 1
to **interview** [ˈɪntəvjuː] ein Vorstellungsgespräch führen mit; interviewen OT 1
interviewee [ˌɪntəvjuˈiː] Interviewte(r) OT 3
interviewer [ˈɪntəvjuːə] Interviewer(in) **WS 3**, 95
into [ˈɪntuː] in OT 1
intolerant [ɪnˈtɒlərənt] intolerant **WS 4**, 129
intonation [ˌɪntəˈneɪʃn] Intonation **WS 3**, 93
intriguing [ɪnˈtriːgɪŋ] faszinierend **WS 2**, 72
to **introduce** [ˌɪntrəˈdjuːs] vorstellen OT 2
introduction [ˌɪntrəˈdʌkʃn] Vorstellung; Einführung OT 2
introductory [ˌɪntrəˈdʌktəri] Anfangs...; Einführungs... **WS 1**, 15
to **invade** [ɪnˈveɪd] einmarschieren OT 3
invader [ɪnˈveɪdə] Angreifer(in) OT 3
invasive [ɪnˈveɪsɪv] invasiv **WS 1**, 25
to **invent** [ɪnˈvent] erfinden OT 2
invention [ɪnˈvenʃn] Erfindung OT 2
inventor [ɪnˈventə] Erfinder(in) OT 2
to **invert** [ɪnˈvɜːt] umkehren; umstellen **WS 1**, 31
inverted commas [ɪnˌvɜːtɪd ˈkɒməz] Anführungszeichen OT 3
to **invest** [ɪnˈvest] investieren OT 4
to **investigate** [ɪnˈvestɪgeɪt] untersuchen OT 3
investment [ɪnˈvestmənt] Investition OT 4
investor [ɪnˈvestə] Investor(in); Geldgeber(in) OT 4
invisible [ɪnˈvɪzəbl] unsichtbar **WS 3**, 110
invitation [ˌɪnvɪˈteɪʃn] Einladung OT 1
to **invite** [ɪnˈvaɪt] einladen OT 2
to **involve** [ɪnˈvɒlv] einbeziehen; umfassen OT 4
involved [ˈvnɒlvd] beteiligt OT 3
Irish [ˈaɪrɪʃ] irisch OT 1
iron [ˈaɪən] Eisen OT 3
ironing [ˈaɪənɪŋ] Bügeln **WS 2**, 54
irregular [ɪˈregjələ] unregelmäßig OT 1
irritated [ˈɪrɪteɪtɪd] verärgert OT 2
island [ˈaɪlənd] Insel OT 1
islander [ˈaɪləndə] Insulaner(in) OT 4
issue [ˈɪsjuː] Thema; Ausgabe OT 2
to **issue** [ˈɪsjuː] erteilen OT 4
it [ɪt] es; ihm OT 1
Italian [ɪˈtæliən] italienisch OT 2
to **itch** [ɪtʃ] jucken OT 2
itchy [ˈɪtʃi] juckend OT 2
item [ˈaɪtəm] Gegenstand; Punkt OT 3
its [ɪts] sein; ihr OT 1
itself [ɪtˈself] sich (selbst) OT 3
ivory [ˈaɪvəri] Elfenbein OT 4

J

jacket [ˈdʒækɪt] Jacke OT 1
jam [dʒæm] Marmelade; Stau OT 1
January [ˈdʒænjuəri] Januar OT 1
Japanese [ˌdʒæpəˈniːz] japanisch OT 1
jar [dʒɑː] Einweckglas OT 2
jazz [dʒæz] Jazz OT 2
jealous [ˈdʒeləs] eifersüchtig OT 2
jerk chicken [ˌdʒɜːk ˈtʃɪkɪn] gegrilltes Huhn OT 4
jewel [ˈdʒuːəl] Edelstein; Schmuckstück OT 3
jewelry [ˈdʒuːəlri] Schmuck OT 2
job [dʒɒb] Stelle; Job OT 1
job hopping [dʒɒb ˈhɒpɪŋ] wiederholter Stellenwechsel **WS 3**, 102
to **join** [dʒɔɪn] Mitglied werden in; eintreten in OT 1
to **join up** [dʒɔɪn ʌp] verbinden OT 2

joke [dʒəʊk] Witz OT 2
to take a joke [teɪk ə dʒəʊk] Spaß verstehen OT 2
to joke [dʒəʊk] Witze machen OT 2
journal ['dʒɜ:nl] Journal; Fachzeitschrift OT 3
journalism ['dʒɜ:nəlɪzəm] Journalismus OT 4
journalist ['dʒɜ:nəlɪst] Journalist(in) OT 2
journey ['dʒɜ:ni] Reise; Fahrt OT 1
joust [dʒaʊst] Turnier OT 2
joyride ['dʒɔɪraɪd] Spritztour (mit einem gestohlenen Auto) **WS 2**, 64
judge [dʒʌdʒ] Richter(in) OT 2
to judge [dʒʌdʒ] einschätzen OT 2
judging ['dʒʌdʒɪŋ] Beurteilen OT 2
judicial [dʒu'dɪʃl] Justiz- OT 4
judo ['dʒu:dəʊ] Judo OT 1
juice [dʒu:s] Saft OT 1
July [dʒu'laɪ] Juli OT 1
to jump [dʒʌmp] springen OT 2
jumper ['dʒʌmpə] Pullover OT 1
June [dʒu:n] Juni OT 1
junior ['dʒu:niə] Junior(in) OT 2
junk food ['dʒʌŋk fu:d] ungesundes Essen OT 4
just [dʒʌst] genau; nur OT 1
justice ['dʒʌstɪs] Justiz **WS 2**, 64
to justify ['dʒʌstɪfaɪ] rechtfertigen OT 4

K

kangaroo [ˌkæŋgə'ru:] Känguru OT 3
kayak ['kaɪæk] Kajak OT 4
kayaking ['kaɪækɪŋ] Kajakfahren OT 2
keen [ki:n] leidenschaftlich OT 2
to keep [ki:p] bleiben; behalten OT 2
keeper ['ki:pə] Hüter(in) OT 4
ketchup ['ketʃəp] Ketchup OT 3
kettle ['ketl] Kessel OT 2
key [ki:] Schlüssel; Taste OT 1
to key [ki:] tippen OT 2
keyboard ['ki:bɔ:d] Tastatur; Keyboard OT 1
keyword ['ki:wɜ:d] Stichwort OT 2
to kick [kɪk] treten OT 1
kid [kɪd] Kind OT 1
to kidnap ['kɪdnæp] entführen OT 3
kidnapper ['kɪdnæpə] Entführer(in) OT 2
kidney bean ['kɪdni bi:n] Kidneybohne OT 2
to kill [kɪl] töten OT 1
kiln [kɪln] Brennofen OT 3
kilo ['ki:ləʊ] Kilo OT 2
kilometre ['kɪləmi:tə] Kilometer OT 1
kilt [kɪlt] Schottenrock; Kilt OT 2
kind [kaɪnd] Art OT 1
kind [kaɪnd] freundlich; nett OT 1
kindling ['kɪndlɪŋ] Kleinholz OT 2
king [kɪŋ] König OT 1
kinsman ['kɪnzmən] Verwandter OT 4
kiss [kɪs] Kuss OT 2
to kiss [kɪs] küssen OT 2
kit [kɪt] Ausrüstung OT 2
kitchen ['kɪtʃɪn] Küche OT 1
kiwi ['ki:wi:] Kiwi OT 1
knee [ni:] Knie OT 1
knife [naɪf] Messer OT 2
to knock [nɒk] klopfen; stoßen OT 2
to knock over [nɒk əʊvə] umstoßen OT 2
to know [nəʊ] wissen; kennen OT 1
knowledge ['nɒlɪdʒ] Wissen OT 4
knowledgeable ['nɒlɪdʒəbl] kenntnisreich OT 3
koala [kəʊ'ɑ:lə] Koala **WS 1**, 13
kookaburra ['kʊkəbʌrə] Kookaburra; Lachender Hans **WS 1**, 13
Korean [kə'ri:ən] koreanisch OT 1

L

lab [læb] Labor OT 4
label ['leɪbl] Etikett **WS 4**, 141
to label ['leɪbl] beschriften OT 1
labour ['leɪbər] Arbeits... **WS 2**, 63
lack [læk] Mangel OT 3
lacrosse [lə'krɒs] Lacrosse OT 4
lad [læd] Bursche; Kerl **WS 2**, 65
ladder ['lædə] Leiter OT 3
lady ['leɪdi] Dame OT 2
lake [leɪk] See OT 1
lamb [læm] Lamm OT 2
lamp [læmp] Lampe OT 1
land [lænd] Land OT 2
to land [lænd] landen OT 2
landfill ['lændfɪl] Mülldeponie OT 3
landline ['lændlaɪn] Festnetz OT 4
landmark ['lændmɑ:k] Wahrzeichen OT 3
landscape ['lændskeɪp] Landschaft OT 2
lane [leɪn] Fahrbahn; Gasse OT 4
laneway [leɪnweɪ] Sträßchen **WS 1**, 29
language ['læŋgwɪdʒ] Sprache OT 1
lantern ['læntən] Laterne OT 2
lanyard ['lænjɑ:d] Umhängeband; Kordel **WS 3**, 112
laptop ['læptɒp] Laptop OT 3
large [lɑ:dʒ] groß OT 1
last [lɑ:st] letzte(r, -s) OT 1
at last [ət 'lɑ:st] endlich OT 2
to last [lɑ:st] dauern; anhalten OT 2
late [leɪt] spät OT 1
Latin ['lætɪn] Latein OT 2
Latino [læ'ti:nəʊ] lateinamerikanisch OT 2
to laugh [lɑ:f] lachen OT 1
to laugh at [lɑ:f ət] auslachen OT 2
to launch [lɔ:ntʃ] starten; auf den Markt bringen OT 4
laundry ['lɔ:ndri] Wäsche; Wäscherei OT 3
lava ['lɑ:və] Lava **WS 1**, 26
law [lɔ:] Gesetz OT 3
lawn [lɔ:n] Rasen **WS 2**, 54
lawyer ['lɔɪə] Rechtsanwalt, Rechtsanwältin OT 4
lazy ['leɪzi] faul OT 2
to lead [li:d] führen OT 3
leading ['li:dɪŋ] führend OT 2
leader ['li:də] Leiter(in) OT 2
leadership ['li:dəʃɪp] Führung OT 2
leaflet ['li:flət] Reklamezettel OT 2
league [li:g] Liga OT 2
lean [li:n] mager **WS 2**, 66
to lean [li:n] lehnen OT 3
to learn [lɜ:n] lernen OT 1
learner ['lɜ:nə] Lernende(r); Fahranfänger(in) OT 3
least: at least [ət 'li:st] mindestens OT 1
leather ['leðə] Leder OT 3
leatherback turtle ['leðəbæk ˌtɜ:tl] Lederrückenschildkröte OT 2
to leave [li:v] verlassen OT 1
to leave behind [ˌli:v bɪ'haɪnd] hinterlassen OT 2
leaver ['li:və] Schulabgänger(in) **WS 3**, 90
leaving ['li:vɪŋ] Abschieds... OT 2
lecture ['lektʃə] Vorlesung OT 4
leftover ['leftəʊvə] übriggeblieben OT 4
leg [leg] Bein OT 1
legacy ['legəsi] Vermächtnis; Erbe OT 4
legal ['li:gl] rechtlich; legal OT 3
to legalize ['li:gəlaɪz] legalisieren **WS 2**, 52
legal pad ['li:gl pæd] Schreibblock mit speziellem Papier **WS 3**, 113
legend ['ledʒənd] Legende; Sage OT 4
legion ['li:dʒən] Legion OT 2
legislative ['ledʒɪslətɪv] Legislative; gesetzgebend OT 4
leisure ['leʒə] Freizeit OT 3
lemonade [ˌlemə'neɪd] Zitronenlimonade OT 1

to lend [lend] leihen OT 2
length [leŋθ] Länge OT 3
lens [lenz] Objektiv; Linse OT 2
lesbian ['lezbiən] Lesbe **WS 2**, 51
less [les] weniger OT 2
lesson ['lesn] Unterricht; Lektion OT 1
to let [let] lassen; vermieten OT 1
letter ['letə] Brief; Buchstabe OT 1
letter of reference [,letə əv 'refrəns] Referenzschreiben; Empfehlungsschreiben **WS 3**, 106
letterbox ['letəbɒks] Briefkasten OT 1
lettuce ['letɪs] Kopfsalat OT 2
levee ['levi] Deich OT 4
level ['levl] Niveau; Stufe OT 1
to level off ['levl ɒf] sich ebnen; abflachen **WS 2**, 62
lexicon ['leksɪkən] Wortschatz **WW**, 11
LGBT (lesbian, gay, bisexual, transgender) [el dʒi: bi: 'ti:] LGBT **WS 2**, 51
liberty ['lɪbəti] Freiheit OT 2
library ['laɪbrəri] Bücherei; Bibliothek OT 1
licence ['laɪsns] Erlaubnis OT 3
lid [lɪd] Deckel OT 2
to lie [laɪ] liegen OT 1
life [laɪf] Leben OT 1
lifebuoy ['laɪfbɔɪ] Rettungsring OT 3
lifeguard ['laɪfgɑ:d] Rettungsschwimmer(in) OT 4
life jacket ['laɪf dʒækɪt] Schwimmweste OT 3
lifeline ['laɪflaɪn] Rettungsleine OT 3
lifestyle ['laɪfstaɪl] Lebensstil; Lifestyle OT 4
life-threatening ['laɪf θretnɪŋ] lebensbedrohlich OT 2
lifetime ['laɪftaɪm] Lebenszeit; Lebensdauer OT 3
lift [lɪft] Anheben; Lift; Mitfahrgelegenheit OT 3
to lift [lɪft] heben OT 3
to light [laɪt] anzünden OT 2
light [laɪt] Licht OT 1
light bulb ['laitbʌlb] Glühbirne OT 4
lightheartedly [,laɪt 'hɑ:tɪdli] unbeschwert OT 4
like [laɪk] wie OT 1
like [laɪk] halt **WW**, 11
to like [laɪk] gernhaben; mögen OT 1
likely ['laɪkli] wahrscheinlich OT 2
to limit ['lɪmɪt] begrenzen OT 4
limit ['lɪmɪt] Grenze OT 4
limited ['lɪmɪtɪd] begrenzt OT 4
line [laɪn] Linie; Reihe; Zeile OT 1
linen ['lɪnɪn] Leinen OT 3
linguist ['lɪŋgwɪst] Sprachwissenschaftler(in); Linguist(in) **WS 2**, 70
linguistic [lɪŋ'gwɪstɪk] sprachlich OT 4
linguistics [lɪŋ'gwɪstɪks] Linguistik **WS 2**, 70
link [lɪŋk] Verbindung OT 2
linked [lɪŋkt] verbunden OT 2
lion ['laɪən] Löwe(-in) OT 1
lip [lɪp] Lippe OT 2
liquid ['lɪkwɪd] flüssig OT 2
list [lɪst] Liste OT 1
to list [lɪst] auflisten; listen **WW**, 11
to listen ['lɪsn] hören; zuhören OT 1
listener ['lɪsnə] Hörer(in) OT 3
litre ['li:tə] Liter OT 4
litter bin ['lɪtə bɪn] Abfalleimer OT 2
little ['lɪtl] klein OT 1
little-known ['lɪtlnəʊn] wenig bekannt OT 2
to live [lɪv] leben; wohnen OT 1
lively ['laɪvli] lebhaft OT 2
liver ['lɪvər] Leber **WS 2**, 66
livestock ['laɪvstɒk] Vieh; Viehbestand **WS 1**, 28
living room ['lɪvɪŋ ru:m] Wohnzimmer OT 1
to load [ləʊd] (be)laden OT 3
loads of [ləʊds əv] jede Menge OT 3
loaf [ləʊf] Brotlaib OT 1
loan [ləʊn] Darlehen; Leihgabe OT 4
to loath [ləʊð] hassen; verabscheuen **WS 1**, 25
local ['ləʊkl] Einheimische(r) OT 2
local ['ləʊkl] einheimisch OT 2
locally ['ləʊkəli] örtlich; am Ort OT 4
located [ləʊ'keɪtid] gelegen OT 4
location [ləʊ'keɪʃn] Standort OT 2
lock [lɒk] Schleuse OT 3
locker ['lɒkə] Spind; Schließfach OT 2
lock keeper ['lɒk ki:pə] Schleusenwärter(in) OT 3
lodge [lɒdʒ] Pension OT 2
log [lɒg] Holzscheit OT 3
to log on [lɒg ɒn] sich einloggen OT 3
logical ['lɒdʒɪkl] logisch; folgerichtig **WS 1**, 36
logically ['lɒdʒɪkli] logisch OT 4
logline [lɒglaɪn] Logline OT 4
logo ['ləʊgəʊ] Logo OT 1
lonely ['ləʊnli] einsam OT 3
long [lɒŋ] lang OT 1
long-eared bat ['lɒŋɪəd ,bæt] (Fledermaus) Braunes Langohr OT 2
loo [lu:] Klo OT 2
look [lʊk] Aussehen; Blick OT 2
to take a look [,teɪk ə 'lʊk] einen Blick werfen OT 2
to look [lʊk] sehen; aussehen OT 1
to look after [lʊk 'ɑ:ftə] auf jdn. aufpassen OT 1
to look forward to ['fɔ:wəd] sich auf etwas freuen OT 1
lord [lɔ:d] Herr OT 2
to lose [lu:z] verlieren OT 1
loss [lɒs] Verlust OT 4
lot: a lot [lɒt] eine Menge; viel OT 1
lots, a lot [lɒts] viel OT 1
loud [laʊd] laut OT 1
loudspeaker [,laʊd'spi:kə] Lautsprecher OT 2
lounge [laʊndʒ] Aufenthaltsraum OT 4
to love [lʌv] lieben OT 1
lovely ['lʌvli] hübsch; schön OT 1
low [ləʊ] tief OT 2
loyal ['lɔɪəl] treu OT 4
loyalty ['lɔɪəlti] Loyalität **WS 3**, 98
luck [lʌk] Glück OT 1
luckily ['lʌkɪli] glücklicherweise OT 3
lucky ['lʌki] glücklich OT 4
to be lucky [bi 'lʌki] Glück haben OT 3
luggage ['lʌgɪdʒ] Gepäck OT 4
lunch [lʌntʃ] Mittagessen OT 1
lunch break ['lʌntʃ breɪk] Mittagspause OT 1
lunchtime ['lʌntʃtaɪm] Mittagszeit OT 1
lung [lʌŋ] Lunge OT 3
luxurious [lʌg'ʒʊəriəs] luxuriös OT 2
lynx [lɪŋks] Luchs OT 2

M

ma'am [mæm] gnädige Frau OT 2
machine [mə'ʃi:n] Maschine OT 2
machinery [mə'ʃi:nəri] Maschinen OT 2
mad [mæd] böse (AmE); verrückt (BrE) OT 2
madam ['mædəm] gnädige Frau OT 1
magazine [,mægə'zi:n] Zeitschrift OT 1
magic ['mædʒɪk] Zauber OT 1
magical ['mædʒɪkl] magisch OT 2
magician [mə'dʒɪʃn] Zauberer/Zauberin OT 1
magnet ['mægnət] Magnet OT 4
magnetic [mæg'netɪk] magnetisch OT 2
magnificent [mæg'nɪfɪsnt] großartig; herrlich **WS 1**, 29
magnifying glass ['mægnɪfaɪɪŋ glɑ:s] Lupe OT 2
magpie ['mægpaɪ] Elster OT 1

mail [meɪl] Post OT 4
mailbox ['meɪlbɒks] Briefkasten; Mailbox OT 4
mail carrier ['meɪl kæriə] Postbote; Postbotin OT 4
snail mail ['sneɪl meɪl] Schneckenpost OT 4
main [meɪn] Haupt... OT 1
main course ['meɪn kɔ:s] Hauptgang OT 1
mainland ['meɪnlænd] Festland OT 3
mainstream school ['meɪnstri:m'sku:l] Regelschule **WS 2**, 57
to **maintain** [meɪn'teɪn] pflegen; aufrechterhalten OT 4
maintenance ['meɪntənəns] Wartung OT 3
majestic [mə'dʒestɪk] majestätisch OT 4
major ['meɪdʒə] wichtig OT 3
majority [mə'dʒɒrəti] Mehrheit OT 4
to **make** [meɪk] kochen; machen OT 1
makeup ['meɪk ʌp] Schminke **WS 2**, 68
malaria [mə'leəriə] Malaria **WS 1**, 34
male [meɪl] männlich OT 2
mall [mɔ:l] Einkaufszentrum OT 3
mammal ['mæml] Säugetier OT 2
man [mæn] Mann; Mensch OT 1
to **manage** ['mænɪdʒ] leiten; managen; zurechtkommen OT 1
management ['mænɪdʒmənt] Management; Geschäftsführung OT 4
manager ['mænɪdʒə] Geschäftsführer(in); Manager(in); Leiter(in) OT 1
mandatory ['mændətəri] verpflichtend OT 4
manifesto [,mænɪ'festəʊ] Manifest OT 4
manner ['mænə] Art und Weise OT 3
manual ['mænjuəl] Handbuch OT 3
to **manufacture** [,mænju'fæktʃə] herstellen OT 4
manure [mə'njʊə] Dung OT 3
many ['meni] viele OT 1
map [mæp] Karte OT 1
marathon ['mærəθən] Marathon OT 2
March [mɑ:tʃ] März OT 1
march [mɑ:tʃ] Marsch **WS 1**, 42
to **march** [mɑ:tʃ] marschieren OT 4
margin ['mɑ:dʒɪn] Rand **WS 2**, 71
marine [mə'ri:n] marin; Meeres... **WS 1**, 26
to **mark** [mɑ:k] korrigieren OT 2
marker ['mɑ:kə] Markierung; Textmarker OT 1
market ['mɑ:kɪt] Markt OT 1
marketing ['mɑ:kɪtɪŋ] Marketing **WS 2**, 68
marquee [mɑ:'ki:] Festzelt OT 2
marriage ['mærɪdʒ] Ehe OT 3
to **marry** ['mæri] heiraten OT 1
marshmallow [,mɑ:ʃ'mæləʊ] Marshmallow OT 2
mascot ['mæskət] Maskottchen OT 2
mashed potato [,mæʃt pə'teɪtəʊ] Kartoffelbrei OT 1
mask [mɑ:sk] Maske OT 3
mass [mæs] Masse **WW**, 11
massacre ['mæsəkər] Massaker **WS 1**, 24
massage ['mæsɑ:ʒ] Massage OT 2
massive ['mæsɪv] riesig OT 3
to **master** ['mɑ:stə] beherrschen OT 4
masterpiece ['mɑ:stəpi:s] Meisterstück OT 4
match [mætʃ] Spiel; Wettkampf OT 1; Streichholz OT 2
mate [meɪt] Kumpel OT 4
material [mə'tɪəriəl] Material OT 4
maths [mæθs] Mathematik OT 1
to **matter** ['mætə] von Bedeutung sein OT 2
matter ['mætə] Angelegenheit; Problem OT 2
no matter [nəʊ 'mætər] was auch immer; egal wie **WW**, 11
What's the matter? [wɒts ðə 'mætə] Was ist los? OT 2
mattress ['mætrəs] Matratze OT 4
maximum ['mæksɪməm] Maximum OT 2
May [meɪ] Mai OT 1
maybe ['meɪbi] vielleicht OT 1
mayonnaise [,meɪə'neɪz] Mayonnaise OT 1
mayor [meə] Bürgermeister(in) OT 3
maze [meɪz] Irrgarten OT 3
MBA (Masters of Business Administration) [,em bi: 'eɪ] MBA **WS 3**, 118
me [mi:] mich; mir; ich OT 1
meadow ['medəʊ] Wiese OT 2
meal [mi:l] Mahlzeit OT 1
to **mean** [mi:n] bedeuten OT 1
meaning ['mi:nɪŋ] Sinn; Bedeutung OT 1
meaningful ['mi:nɪŋfl] sinnvoll OT 4
meanwhile ['mi:nwaɪl] inzwischen; mittlerweile **WS 2**, 76
measles ['mi:zlz] Masern **WS 1**, 24
measure ['meʒə] Maßnahme **WS 1**, 25
to **measure** ['meʒə] messen OT 1
measurement ['meʒəmənt] Maß; Maßeinheit OT 2
meat [mi:t] Fleisch OT 1
meat loaf ['mi:t ləʊf] Hackbraten OT 3
meatball ['mi:tbɔ:l] Fleischklößchen; Hackfleischbällchen OT 1
mechanical [mə'kænɪkl] mechanisch **WS 3**, 118
medal ['medl] Medaille OT 2
median ['mi:diən] Median; Durchschnitt **WS 2**, 62
medical ['medɪkl] ärztliche Untersuchung; medizinisch OT 2
medicine ['medsn] Medizin **WS 2**, 55
medieval [,medi'i:vl] mittelalterlich OT 2
medium ['mi:diəm] Mittel; Medium OT 2
medium-sized ['mi:diəm saɪzd] mittelgroß OT 2
to **meet** [mi:t] treffen OT 1
meeting ['mi:tɪŋ] Besprechung; Treffen OT 1
to **melt** [melt] schmelzen OT 4
member ['membə] Mitglied OT 1
memoir ['memwɑ:] Memoiren; Erinnerung **WS 4**, 128
memorable ['memərəbl] unvergesslich OT 3
memorial [mə'mɔ:riəl] Denkmal OT 4
memory ['meməri] Gedächtnis OT 2
to **mend** [mend] reparieren OT 3
menial ['mi:niəl] untergeordnet; nieder **WS 3**, 103
mental ['mentl] mental; geistig OT 4
to **mention** ['menʃn] erwähnen OT 2
menu ['menju:] Speisekarte OT 1
merchant ['mɜ:tʃənt] Händler(in) OT 3
merit ['merɪt] Wert; Leistung **WS 3**, 110
mess [mes] Unordnung OT 2
to **mess up** [,mes'ʌp] in Unordnung bringen; vergeigen OT 2
message ['mesɪdʒ] Nachricht; Botschaft OT 1
metal ['metl] Metall OT 1
method ['meθəd] Methode OT 1
metre ['mi:tə] Meter OT 1
metro ['metrəʊ] U-Bahn OT 1
microphone ['maɪkrəfəʊn] Mikrofon **WS 2**, 58
microwave ['maɪkrəweɪv] Microwelle OT 4
middle ['mɪdl] Mitte OT 1
midnight ['mɪdnaɪt] Mitternacht OT 1
might [maɪt] könnte(n) OT 2
mighty ['maɪti] sehr OT 3
migrant ['maɪgrənt] Migrant(in) OT 4
to **migrate** [maɪ'greɪt] migrieren OT 3

migration [maɪˈgreɪʃn] Migration OT 3
mile [maɪl] Meile (etwa 1,6 km) OT 1
milestone [ˈmaɪlstəʊn] Meilenstein OT 3
military [ˈmɪlətri] militärisch; Militär… **WS 3**, 88
milk [mɪlk] Milch OT 1
millennial [mɪˈleniəl] Millennium-Generation; Millenial **WS 3**, 98
million [ˈmɪljən] Million OT 1
minced [mɪnst] fein gehackt OT 2
mind [maɪnd] Verstand OT 1
  to **change one's mind** [tʃeɪndʒ wʌnz maɪnd] seine Meinung ändern OT 2
  mind map [ˈmaɪnd mæp] Gedankenkarte; Mindmap OT 1
mine [maɪn] meine(r, -s) OT 1; Bergwerk OT 2
miner [ˈmaɪnə] Bergarbeiter OT 3
mini [ˈmɪni] klein; winzig **WS 1**, 12
miniature [ˈmɪnətʃə] Miniatur OT 2
minibus [ˈmɪnibʌs] Kleinbus OT 2
minimum [ˈmɪnɪməm] Mindest… OT 1
mining [ˈmaɪnɪŋ] Bergbau… OT 3
minister [ˈmɪnɪstə] Minister(in) OT 4
minor [ˈmaɪnə] Minderjährige(r) OT 2
minority [maɪˈnɒrəti] Minderheit OT 4
mint [mɪnt] Minze; Pfefferminzbonbon OT 1
minute [ˈmɪnɪt] Minute OT 1
mirror [ˈmɪrə] Spiegel OT 1
miserable [ˈmɪzrəbl] unglücklich OT 2
to **miss** [mɪs] vermissen OT 2
Miss [mɪs] Frau; Fräulein OT 2
missing [ˈmɪsɪŋ] verschwunden; vermisst OT 1
mistake [mɪˈsteɪk] Fehler OT 1
  by mistake [baɪ mɪˈsteɪk] versehentlich OT 2
  to **make a mistake** [ˌmeɪk ə mɪˈsteɪk] einen Fehler machen OT 2
to **misunderstand** [ˌmɪsʌndəˈstænd] missverstehen **WS 2**, 61
misunderstanding [ˌmɪsʌndəˈstændɪŋ] Missverständnis OT 3
mitten [ˈmɪtn] Fausthandschuh OT 4
mix [mɪks] Mischung OT 2
mixed up [ˌmɪkst ˈʌp] durcheinander OT 2
mixture [ˈmɪkstʃə] Mischung OT 2
mob [mɒb] Meute **WS 1**, 28
mobile phone [ˈməʊbaɪl] Handy OT 1
modal [ˈməʊdl] Modalverb OT 2
model [ˈmɒdl] Modell OT 1
modern [ˈmɒdn] modern OT 1
modest [ˈmɒdɪst] bescheiden OT 2
module [ˈmɒdjuːl] Modul OT 4
moment [ˈməʊmənt] Moment OT 1
monarch [ˈmɒnək] Monarch(in); Herrscher(in) OT 4
monarchy [ˈmɒnəki] Monarchie OT 4
Monday [ˈmʌndeɪ] Montag OT 1
money [ˈmʌni] Geld OT 1
monk [mʌŋk] Mönch OT 3
monolingual [ˌmɒnəˈlɪŋgwəl] einsprachig **WS 1**, 24
monopoly [məˈnɒpəli] Monopol OT 4
monotone [ˈmɒnətəʊn] monoton **WS 3**, 93
monster [ˈmɒnstə] Monster OT 1
month [mʌnθ] Monat OT 1
monument [ˈmɒnjumənt] Monument; Denkmal OT 4
mood [muːd] Stimmung OT 3
moody [ˈmuːdi] launisch **WS 2**, 72
moon [muːn] Mond OT 1
moor [mɔː] Heidelandschaft OT 3
to **moor** [mɔː] vertäuen; anlegen OT 3
mooring [ˈmɔːrɪŋ] Anlegeplatz OT 3
moose [muːs] Elch OT 4
moped [ˈməʊped] Moped OT 4
moral [ˈmɒrəl] Moral OT 2
more [mɔː] mehr OT 1
moreover [mɔːrˈəʊvə] außerdem OT 4
morning [ˈmɔːnɪŋ] Morgen; Vormittag OT 1
mortgage [ˈmɔːgɪdʒ] Hypothek OT 4
mosaic [məʊˈzeɪɪk] Mosaik OT 2
mosquito [məˈskiːtəʊ] Stechmücke OT 2
most [məʊst] der / die / das meiste; die meisten OT 1
motel [məʊˈtel] Motel OT 3
mother [ˈmʌðə] Mutter OT 1
to **motivate** [ˈməʊtɪveɪt] motivieren; anregen **WS 2**, 74
motivated [ˈməʊtɪveɪtɪd] motiviert OT 4
motivation [ˌməʊtɪˈveɪʃn] Motivation; Begründung **WS 3**, 91
motivational [ˌməʊtɪˈveɪʃənl] anregend; Motivations… **WS 3**, 99
to **motor** [ˈməʊtə] fahren OT 3
motorized [ˈməʊtəraɪzd] motorisiert OT 4
motto [ˈmɒtəʊ] Motto OT 4
mountain [ˈmaʊntən] Berg OT 1
mountain biking [ˈmaʊntən baɪkɪŋ] Mountainbiken OT 2
mountain range [ˈmaʊntən reɪndʒ] Gebirge OT 4
mouse [maʊs] Maus OT 1
mouth [maʊθ] Mund OT 1
mouthguard [maʊθgɑːd] Mundschutz OT 2
to **move** [muːv] bewegen; umziehen OT 1
movement [ˈmuːvmənt] Bewegung OT 4
movie [ˈmuːvi] Film OT 2
to **mow** [məʊ] mähen **WS 2**, 54
MP (member of parliament) [ˌem ˈpiː] Abgeordnete(r) OT 4
Mr [ˈmɪstə] Herr OT 1
Mrs [ˈmɪsɪz] Frau OT 1
Ms [mɪz] Frau OT 2
much [mʌtʃ] viel; sehr OT 1
to **muck around** [mʌk əˈraʊnd] Spaß haben; vertrödeln **WS 2**, 55
mud [mʌd] Schlamm OT 3
muddy [ˈmʌdi] schlammig; matschig OT 4
mudslide [ˈmʌdslaɪd] Schlammlawine **WS 1**, 34
muesli [ˈmjuːzli] müsli **WS 2**, 77
muffin [ˈmʌfɪn] Muffin OT 1
mule [mjuːl] Maultier OT 3
multicultural [ˌmʌltiˈkʌltʃərəl] multikulturell OT 4
multiculturalism [ˌmʌltiˈkʌltʃərəlɪzəm] Multikulturalismus OT 4
multi-functional [ˌmʌltiˈfʌŋkʃənl] multi-funktional OT 4
multinational [ˌmʌltiˈnæʃnəl] multinational OT 4
multiple [ˈmʌltɪpl] vielfach OT 2
mum [mʌm] Mama OT 1
mural [ˈmjʊərəl] Wandgemälde OT 2
murder [ˈmɜːdər] Mord **WS 4**, 128
to **murder** [ˈmɜːdə] ermorden OT 2
murky [ˈmɜːki] trübe OT 4
muscle [ˈmʌsl] Muskel OT 2
museum [mjuːˈziːəm] Museum OT 1
mushroom [ˈmʌʃrʊm] Pilz OT 2
music [ˈmjuːzɪk] Musik OT 1
musical [ˈmjuːzɪkl] Musik…; musikalisch OT 2
musician [mjuˈzɪʃn] Musiker(in) OT 2
must [mʌst] müssen OT 1
mustard [ˈmʌstəd] Senf OT 1
my [maɪ] mein OT 1
myself [maɪˈself] (ich) selbst OT 3
mystery [ˈmɪstri] Geheimnis; Rätsel **WS 4**, 128
myth [mɪθ] Mythos; Legende OT 4
mythology [mɪˈθɒlədʒi] Mythologie OT 2

N

name [neɪm] Name OT 1
to **nap** [næp] ein Nickerchen machen OT 2

nappy ['næpi] Windel OT 3
narrator [nə'reɪtə] Erzähler(in) OT 2
narrow ['nærəʊ] eng OT 2
narrowboat ['nærəʊbəʊt] schmales Kanalboot; Hausboot OT 3
narrow-minded [ˌnærəʊ 'maɪndɪd] engstirnig **WS 4**, 129
nasty ['nɑ:sti] unangenehm OT 2
nation ['neɪʃn] Nation OT 2
national ['næʃnəl] national OT 1
nationality [ˌnæʃə'næləti] Staatsangehörigkeit OT 2
native ['neɪtɪv] Einheimische(r); einheimisch OT 3
natural ['nætʃrəl] natürlich OT 1
naturalist ['nætʃrəlɪst] Naturforscher(in) OT 2
nature ['neɪtʃə] Natur OT 2
naughty ['nɔ:ti] ungezogen OT 2
navy ['neɪvi] Marine OT 3
near [nɪə] nahe; in der Nähe von OT 1
nearby [ˌnɪə'baɪ] in der Nähe OT 3
nearly ['nɪəli] fast OT 2
neat [ni:t] ordentlich OT 4
necessarily [ˌnesə'serəli] unbedingt; notwendig OT 4
necessary ['nesəsəri] notwendig OT 3
necessity [nə'sesəti] Notwendigkeit OT 4
neck [nek] Hals; Nacken OT 1
necklace ['nekləs] Halskette OT 3
to **need** [ni:d] brauchen OT 1
negative ['negətɪv] Verneinung; Negativ OT 1
negativity [ˌnegə'tɪvəti] Negativität; negative Einstellung OT 4
neighbourhood ['neɪbəhʊd] Nachbarschaft OT 4
neighbour ['neɪbə] Nachbar OT 2
neither ['naɪðə] auch nicht OT 3
neither ... nor ['naɪðə 'nɔ:] weder ... noch OT 4
nephew ['nefju:] Neffe **WS 2**, 73
nerve [nɜ:v] Nerv OT 3
nervous ['nɜ:vəs] nervös OT 2
nest [nest] Nest OT 3
net [net] Netz OT 4
netball ['netbɔ:l] Netzball **WS 1**, 15
network ['netwɜ:k] Netzwerk OT 4
neurological [ˌnjʊərə'lɒdʒɪkl] neurologisch **WS 2**, 61
neutral ['nju:trəl] neutral OT 3
never ['nevə] nie OT 1
new [nju:] neu OT 1
brand new [ˌbrænd 'nju:] brandneu OT 2
news [nju:z] Neuigkeit(en); Nachrichten OT 1
newsletter ['nju:zletə] Mitteilungsblatt; Newsletter OT 3
newspaper ['nju:zpeɪpə] Zeitung OT 1
next [nekst] als Nächstes; nächste(r) OT 3
next to ['nekst tu:] neben OT 1
nice [naɪs] schön; nett OT 1
nickname ['nɪkneɪm] Spitzname OT 4
niece [ni:s] Nichte OT 4
night [naɪt] Nacht OT 1
nine [naɪn] neun OT 1
ninety ['naɪnti] neunzig OT 1
nobleman ['nəʊblmən] Adliger OT 3
nobody ['nəʊbədi] niemand OT 1
to **nod** [nɒd] nicken OT 3
noise [nɔɪz] Geräusch; Lärm OT 1
noisy ['nɔɪzi] laut OT 1
nomadic [nəʊ'mædɪk] nomadisch OT 3
none [nʌn] keine(r, -s) OT 3
nonsense ['nɒnsns] Unsinn OT 1
noodle ['nu:dl] Nudel OT 2
noon [nu:n] Mittag OT 4
norm [nɔ:m] Regel; Standard **WS 3**, 102
normal ['nɔ:ml] normal OT 1
Norman ['nɔ:mən] normannisch OT 3
north [nɔ:θ] Nord- OT 1
north-east ['nɔ:θ i:st] Nordosten OT 1
northern [nɔ:ðən] nördlich OT 2
nose [nəʊz] Nase OT 2
nostalgia [nɒ'stældʒə] Nostalgie OT 4
notable ['nəʊtəbl] bemerkenswert OT 4
note [nəʊt] Notiz; Zettel OT 1
notebook ['nəʊtbʊk] Notizbuch OT 2
nothing ['nʌθɪŋ] nichts OT 1
notice ['nəʊtɪs] Schild; Aushang OT 1
to **notice** ['nəʊtɪs] bemerken OT 4
noticeboard ['nəʊtɪsbɔ:d] Anschlagbrett OT 1
noun [naʊn] Substantiv; Nomen; Hauptwort OT 1
novel ['nɒvl] Roman OT 2
novelist ['nɒvəlɪst] Schriftsteller(in) OT 4
November [nəʊ'vembə] November OT 1
now [naʊ] jetzt OT 1
nowadays ['naʊədeɪz] heutzutage OT 3
nowhere ['nəʊweə] nirgendwo OT 2
nuclear ['nju:kliə] Atom...; Nuklear... OT 3
number ['nʌmbə] Zahl; Nummer OT 1
numerical [nju:'merɪkl] numerisch **WS 2**, 59
nun [nʌn] Nonne OT 3
nurse [nɜ:s] Krankenschwester / -pfleger OT 1
nursery ['nɜ:səri] Kindergarten; Kindertagesstätte **WS 3**, 111
nursing ['nɜ:sɪŋ] Krankenpflege **WS 3**, 110
nut [nʌt] Nuss; hier: Verrückte(r) **WS 1**, 14
nutritious [nju'trɪʃəs] nahrhaft OT 4

O

o'clock [ə'klɒk] Uhr OT 1
object ['ɒbdʒɪkt] Gegenstand; Objekt OT 1
objection [əb'dʒekʃn] Einwand OT 3
obligation [ˌɒblɪ'geɪʃn] Pflicht **WS 3**, 95
obliged: to be obliged (to) [bi 'ɒblɪgeɪtɪd] müssen; verpflichtet sein **WS 2**, 76
observation [ˌɒbzə'veɪʃn] Beobachtung OT 3
to **observe** [əb'zɜ:v] beobachten OT 4
observer [əb'zɜ:və] Beobachter(in) **WS 3**, 101
obsession [əb'seʃn] Obsession; Besessenheit **WS 2**, 50
obstacle ['ɒbstəkl] Hindernis OT 4
obvious ['ɒbviəs] offensichtlich OT 3
obviously ['ɒbviəsli] offensichtlich OT 3
occasion [ə'keɪʒn] Gelegenheit OT 3
occasionally [ə'keɪʒnəli] hin und wieder; gelegentlich OT 4
occupation [ˌɒkju'peɪʃn] Tätigkeit; Beschäftigung OT 4
occupied: to be occupied [bi 'ɒkjupaɪd] beschäftigt sein **WS 3**, 111
ocean ['əʊʃn] Ozean OT 2
October [ɒk'təʊbə] Oktober OT 1
odd [ɒd] eigenartig OT 2
of [əv] von OT 1
of course [əv 'kɔ:s] natürlich OT 1
off [ɒf] von; aus; weg OT 1
to **be off beat** [ˌɒf'bi:t] aus dem Takt kommen OT 4
off-road ['ɒf rəʊd] geländetauglich OT 2
offence [ə'fens] Straftat **WS 2**, 64
to **offend** [ə'fend] beleidigen OT 3
offender [ə'fendə] Täter(in) **WS 2**, 64
offer ['ɒfə] Angebot OT 2
to **offer** ['ɒfə] anbieten OT 2
offering ['ɒfərɪŋ] Angebot OT 4
office ['ɒfɪs] Büro OT 2
officer ['ɒfɪsə] Offizier(in) OT 2

official [əˈfɪʃl] Beamter; Beamtin; offiziell OT 2
officially [əˈfɪʃəli] offiziell OT 4
offstage [ˌɒfˈsteɪdʒ] aus dem Off OT 2
often [ˈɒfn] oft OT 1
oil [ɔɪl] Öl OT 3
OK [əʊˈkeɪ] in Ordnung OT 1
old [əʊld] alt OT 1
old-fashioned [ˌəʊldˈfæʃnd] altmodisch OT 2
Olympic [əˈlɪmpɪk] olympisch OT 2
on [ɒn] auf; an; in OT 1
once [wʌns] einmal OT 2
one [wʌn] eins OT 1
onion [ˈʌnjən] Zwiebel OT 2
online [ˌɒnˈlaɪn] online OT 3
only [ˈəʊnli] nur OT 1
onscreen [ˌɒn ˈskriːn] auf dem Bildschirm; auf der Leinwand OT 2
onto [ˈɒntuː] auf OT 1
open [ˈəʊpən] offen OT 1
to **open** [ˈəʊpən] aufmachen; öffnen OT 1
opening times [ˈəʊpnɪŋ taɪmz] Öffnungszeiten OT 1
to **operate** [ˈɒpəreɪt] bedienen; operieren OT 3
operation [ˌɒpəˈreɪʃn] Verfahren; Vorgang OT 4
operator [ˈɒpəreɪtə] Leitstellendisponent(in) OT 2
opinion [əˈpɪnjən] Meinung OT 3
opponent [əˈpəʊnənt] Gegner(in) OT 2
opportunity [ˌɒpəˈtjuːnəti] Gelegenheit OT 2
opposite [ˈɒpəzɪt] Gegenteil OT 1
oppression [əˈpreʃn] Unterdrückung **WS 4**, 128
to **opt** [ɒpt] (sich) entscheiden (für / gegen) **WS 3**, 109
optimistic [ˌɒptɪˈmɪstɪk] optimistisch OT 4
to **optimize** [ˈɒptɪmaɪz] optimieren **WS 3**, 100
option [ˈɒpʃn] Wahl OT 2
optional [ˈɒpʃənl] optional; freiwillig OT 4
or [ɔː] oder OT 1
oral [ˈɔːrəl] mündlich OT 1
orange [ˈɒrɪndʒ] Apfelsine; Orange OT 1
orange [ˈɒrɪndʒ] orange OT 1
orbit [ˈɔːbɪt] Orbit; Umlaufbahn OT 4
orchard [ˈɔːtʃəd] Obstgarten OT 4
orchestra [ˈɔːkɪstrə] Orchester OT 1
order [ˈɔːdə] Reihenfolge; Bestellung; Befehl OT 1
to **order** [ˈɔːdə] befehlen; in eine Reihenfolge bringen; bestellen OT 1
ordinary [ˈɔːdnri] normal OT 2
organ [ˈɔːgən] Organ **WS 2**, 55
organic [ɔːˈgænɪk] biologisch OT 4
organization [ˌɔːgənaɪˈzeɪʃn] Organisation; Gesellschaft OT 3
organizational [ˌɔːgənaɪˈzeɪʃənl] organisatorisch OT 4
to **organize** [ˈɔːgənaɪz] organisieren OT 1
organizer [ˈɔːgənaɪzə] Organisator(in) OT 4
orientated [ˈɔːrienteɪt] orientiert **WS 2**, 56
origin [ˈɒrɪdʒɪn] Ursprung OT 3
original [əˈrɪdʒənl] ursprünglich; Original... OT 3
originally [əˈrɪdʒənəli] ursprünglich OT 2
other [ˈʌðə] andere(r, -s) OT 1
otherwise [ˈʌðəwaɪz] sonst; ansonsten OT 4
otter [ˈɒtə] Otter OT 4
ought to [ˈɔːt tə] sollte **WS 3**, 94
our [ˈaʊə] unser OT 1
ours [ɑːz,ˈaʊəz] unsere(r, -s) OT 3
ourselves [ɑːˈselvz,ˌaʊəˈselvz] uns OT 3
out [aʊt] heraus; aus; draußen OT 1
outback [ˈaʊtbæk] Busch; Hinterland **WS 1**, 13
outdoor [ˈaʊtdɔː] im Freien OT 2
outer space [ˌaʊtə ˈspeɪs] Weltraum **WS 3**, 110
outgoing [ˌaʊtˈgəʊɪŋ] kontaktfreudig OT 4
to **outline** [ˈaʊtlaɪn] umreißen; zusammenfassen OT 4
outside [ˌaʊtˈsaɪd] draußen OT 1
outstanding [aʊtˈstændɪŋ] herausragend OT 3
oven [ˈʌvn] Ofen OT 2
over [ˈəʊvə] drüben OT 2
over there [ˈəʊvə ˌðeə] dort drüben OT 2
overall [ˌəʊvərˈɔːl] allgemein **WS 2**, 62
overboard [ˈəʊvəbɔːd] über Bord OT 3
to **overcome** [ˌəʊvəˈkʌm] überwinden; bewältigen OT 4
to **overdo** [ˌəʊvəˈduː] übertreiben **WS 2**, 66
to **overflow** [ˌəʊvəˈfləʊ] überlaufen OT 4
overly [ˈəʊvəli] übermäßig **WS 3**, 95
overnight [ˌəʊvəˈnaɪt] über Nacht OT 2
to **overrate** [ˌəʊvəˈreɪt] überbewerten **WS 2**, 77
overseas [ˌəʊvəˈsiːz] ausländisch OT 2
to **oversee** [ˌəʊvəˈsiː] überwachen; beaufsichtigen OT 4
to **oversleep** [ˌəʊvəˈsliːp] verschlafen OT 4
overtime [ˈəʊvətaɪm] Überstunden **WS 3**, 103
overview [ˈəʊvəvjuː] Überblick; Übersicht OT 4
own [əʊn] eigene(r, -s) OT 1
on one's own [ɒn wʌnz əʊn] allein OT 2
to **own** [əʊn] besitzen OT 2
owner [ˈəʊnə] Besitzer(in) OT 2
oxygen [ˈɒksɪdʒən] Sauerstoff **WS 1**, 39

P

PA (public address) system [ˌpiː ˈeɪ sɪstɪm] Beschallungsanlage OT 2
pack [pæk] Rudel OT 4
to **pack** [pæk] packen OT 2
package [ˈpækɪdʒ] Paket OT 3
packaging [ˈpækɪdʒɪŋ] Verpackung OT 3
packed lunch [ˈpækt lʌntʃ] Lunchpaket OT 1
packet [ˈpækɪt] Paket OT 2
to **paddle** [ˈpædl] paddeln OT 3
pad [pæd] Polster OT 2
page [peɪdʒ] Seite OT 1
pain [peɪn] Schmerz; Nervensäge OT 2
painkiller [ˈpeɪnkɪlə] Schmerzmittel OT 2
to **paint** [peɪnt] malen OT 1
painting [ˈpeɪntɪŋ] Malen; Gemälde OT 1
pair [peə] Paar OT 2
palace [ˈpæləs] Palast; Schloss OT 1
pale [peɪl] blass OT 3
pan [pæn] Pfanne OT 2
pandemic [pænˈdemɪk] Pandemie **WS 3**, 105
panel [ˈpænl] Gremium; Forum OT 4
to **panic** [ˈpænɪk] in Panik geraten OT 2
panther [ˈpænθə] Panther OT 2
pants [pænts] Hose **WW**, 11
paper [ˈpeɪpə] Papier OT 1
paperwork [ˈpeɪpəwɜːk] Schreibarbeit **WS 3**, 109
to **parachute** [ˈpærəʃuːt] Fallschirm springen OT 4
parade [pəˈreɪd] Umzug; Parade OT 2
paradise [ˈpærədaɪs] Paradies **WS 1**, 21
paragliding [ˈpærəglaɪdɪŋ] Gleitschirmfliegen **WS 3**, 107
paragraph [ˈpærəgrɑːf] Absatz OT 1

paramedic [ˌpærəˈmedɪk] Rettungssanitäter(in) OT 1
to **paraphrase** [ˈpærəfreɪz] umschreiben OT 3
parcel [ˈpɑːsl] Paket OT 2
parent [ˈpeərənt] Elternteil OT 1
park [pɑːk] Park OT 1
park ranger [ˈpɑːk ˌreɪndʒə] Forstbeamter; Forstbeamtin OT 2
to **park** [pɑːk] parken OT 2
parking [ˈpɑːkɪŋ] Parken OT 2
parliament [ˈpɑːləmənt] Parlament; Abgeordnetenhaus OT 4
part [pɑːt] Teil OT 1
part of speech [ˌpɑːt əv ˈspiːtʃ] Wortart OT 2
participant [pɑːˈtɪsɪpənt] Teilnehmer(in) OT 4
to **participate** [pɑːˈtɪsɪpeɪt] teilnehmen OT 4
participation [pɑːˌtɪsɪˈpeɪʃn] Beteiligung **WS 2**, 58
participle [pɑːˈtɪsɪpl] Partizip OT 2
particular [pəˈtɪkjələ] bestimmt; besondere OT 4
particularly [pəˈtɪkjələli] besonders OT 4
partly [ˈpɑːtli] teilweise OT 4
partner [ˈpɑːtnə] Partner(in) OT 1
partnership [ˈpɑːtnəʃɪp] Partnerschaft; Kooperation OT 4
part-time [ˌpɑːt ˈtaɪm] nebenberuflich; teilzeitlich **WS 1**, 14
party [ˈpɑːti] Party; Partei; Gruppe OT 1
to **pass** [pɑːs] zuspielen; an etw. vorbeifahren OT 2
passenger [ˈpæsɪndʒə] Passagier(in) OT 2
passion [ˈpæʃn] Leidenschaft **WS 2**, 72
passionate [ˈpæʃənət] leidenschaftlich OT 4
passport [ˈpɑːspɔːt] Pass OT 2
past [pɑːst] nach; vorbei OT 1
pasta [ˈpæstə] Nudeln OT 1
to **paste** [peɪst] kleben OT 2
pat [pæt] Klaps OT 3
patch [pætʃ] Fleck; Flicken **WS 3**, 91
patchy [ˈpætʃi] lückenhaft; ungleichmäßig OT 4
to **patent** [ˈpætnt] patentieren OT 4
path [pɑːθ] Weg OT 1
patient [ˈpeɪʃnt] Patient(in) OT 1
patriot [ˈpeɪtriət] Patriot OT 2
pattern [ˈpætn] Muster OT 4
to **pause** [pɔːz] eine Pause machen OT 3

to **pay** [ˈpeɪ] bezahlen OT 1
pay gap [ˈpeɪ gæp] Lohngefälle **WS 3**, 103
PE (physical education) [ˌpiːˈiː] Sport; Sportunterricht OT 1
pea [piː] Erbse OT 1
peace [piːs] Frieden OT 3
peaceful [ˈpiːsfl] friedlich OT 3
peak [piːk] Gipfel; Spitzen... OT 4
pear [peə] Birne OT 1
pedigree [ˈpedɪgriː] Rasse... OT 3
peer [pɪə] Peer OT 4
pen [pen] Stift OT 1
penal [ˈpiːnl] strafrechtlich **WS 1**, 22
penalty [ˈpenəlti] Strafe; Strafstoß OT 3
pencil [ˈpensl] Bleistift OT 1
pencil case [ˈpensl ˌkeɪs] Federtasche OT 1
penguin [ˈpeŋgwɪn] Pinguin OT 2
peninsula [pəˈnɪnsjələ] Halbinsel **WS 1**, 32
penny [ˈpeni] Penny OT 1
people [ˈpiːpl] Leute OT 1
pepper [ˈpepə] Pfeffer; Paprika OT 2
per [pə] per; je OT 4
percent [pəˈsent] Prozent OT 3
percentage [pəˈsentɪdʒ] Prozentsatz; Anteil OT 4
perfect [ˈpɜːfɪkt] perfekt OT 2
to **perform** [pəˈfɔːm] auftreten OT 2
performance [pəˈfɔːməns] Aufführung OT 2
perhaps [pəˈhæps] vielleicht OT 3
period [ˈpɪəriəd] Zeit; Epoche OT 3
permanent [ˈpɜːmənənt] permanent; dauerhaft OT 4
permanently [ˈpɜːmənəntli] permanent; immer OT 3
permission [pəˈmɪʃn] Erlaubnis OT 2
permit [pəˈmɪt] Erlaubnis OT 3
to **permit** [pəˈmɪt] erlauben OT 4
perseverance [ˌpɜːsəˈvɪərəns] Ausdauer; Durchhaltevermögen OT 4
person [ˈpɜːsn] Person OT 1
personal [ˈpɜːsənl] persönlich OT 1
personality [ˌpɜːsəˈnæləti] Persönlichkeit; Prominente OT 4
to **personalize** [ˈpɜːsənəlaɪz] personalisieren **WS 2**, 68
perspective [pəˈspektɪv] Sichtweise; Perspektive **WS 1**, 35
to **persuade** [pəˈsweɪd] überreden; überzeugen OT 3
persuasive [pəˈsweɪsɪv] überzeugend **WS 1**, 37

pest [pest] Plage; Schädling **WS 1**, 25
pet [pet] Haustier OT 1
to **pet** [pet] streicheln OT 4
petition [pəˈtɪʃn] Antrag OT 3
petrochemical [ˌpetrəʊˈkemɪkl] Petrochemikalie OT 4
petrol [ˈpetrəl] Benzin OT 1
pharmacist [ˈfɑːməsɪst] Apotheker(in) OT 2
pharmacy [ˈfɑːməsi] Apotheke OT 2
phenomenon [fəˈnɒmɪnən] Phänomen **WS 1**, 32
philosophy [fəˈlɒsəfi] Philosophie OT 4
phone [fəʊn] Telefon; telefonieren OT 1
photo [ˈfəʊtə] Foto OT 1
to **take a photo** [ˌteɪk ə ˈfəʊtəʊ] ein Foto machen OT 1
photograph [ˈfəʊtəgrɑːf] Foto OT 1
photographer [fəˈtɒgrəfə] Fotograf(in) OT 2
phrase [freɪz] Wendung OT 1
physical [ˈfɪzɪkl] körperlich OT 2
physics [ˈfɪzɪks] Physik **WS 2**, 56
pianist [ˈpɪənɪst] Pianist(in) OT 2
piano [piˈænəʊ] Klavier OT 1
to **pick** [pɪk] pflücken; aussuchen OT 2
to **pick a fight** [pɪk ə faɪt] einen Streit mit anzetteln **WS 4**, 133
to **pick up** [pɪk ʌp] aufheben; abholen OT 2
picker [ˈpɪkə] Pflücker(in) OT 4
picnic [ˈpɪknɪk] Picknick OT 1
picture [ˈpɪktʃə] Bild OT 1
picturesque [ˌpɪktʃəˈresk] malerisch OT 4
pie [paɪ] gedeckter Obstkuchen OT 1
pie chart [ˈpaɪ tʃɑːt] Tortendiagramm OT 4
piece [piːs] Stück; Teil OT 1
in one piece [ɪn ˈwʌn ˌpiːs] heil OT 2
pier [pɪər] Kai **WS 1**, 29
pierced [pɪəsed] durchstochen OT 3
pig [pɪg] Schwein OT 1
pigeon [ˈpɪdʒɪn] Taube **WS 3**, 103
to **pile** [paɪl] auftürmen OT 3
pill [pɪl] Tablette **WS 2**, 66
pillow [ˈpɪləʊ] Kopfkissen OT 2
pillowcase [ˈpɪləʊkeɪs] Kopfkissenbezug OT 3
to **pin** [pɪn] heften OT 1
pin [pɪn] Stecknadel OT 1
pineapple [ˈpaɪnæpl] Ananas OT 2
ping-pong [ˈpɪŋ pɒŋ] Tischtennis OT 4
pink [pɪŋk] rosa OT 1
pioneer [ˌpaɪəˈnɪə] Pionier(in) OT 4
pipe [paɪp] Leitung OT 4

pipeline [ˈpaɪplaɪn] Pipeline OT 4
pit [pɪt] Grube **WS 3**, 103
pitch [pɪtʃ] Spielfeld OT 3
pity: it's a pity [ɪts ə ˈpɪti] das ist schade OT 2
place [pleɪs] Ort OT 1
to **place** [pleɪs] anbringen; vermitteln **WS 3**, 105
placement [ˈpleɪsmənt] Platzierung **WS 2**, 68
plagiarism [ˈpleɪdʒərɪzəm] Plagiat OT 2
to **plagiarize** [ˈpleɪdʒəraɪz] plagiieren OT 2
plague [pleɪɡ] Pest OT 3
plain [pleɪn] Ebene; Flachland OT 4
to **plan** [plæn] planen OT 1
plane [pleɪn] Flugzeug; Ebene OT 1
planet [ˈplænɪt] Planet OT 2
planner [ˈplænə] Planer(in) OT 4
plant [plɑːnt] Pflanze OT 2
plantain [ˈplæntɪn] Kochbanane OT 4
plaster [ˈplɑːstə] Gips; Pflaster OT 1
plastic [ˈplæstɪk] Plastik; aus Plastik; Plastik… OT 3
plate [pleɪt] Teller OT 1
platform [ˈplætfɔːm] Bahnsteig; Plattform OT 1
platypus [ˈplætɪpəs] Schnabeltier **WS 1**, 13
to **play** [pleɪ] spielen OT 1
play [pleɪ] Theaterstück OT 1
player [ˈpleɪə] Spieler(in) OT 1
playground [ˈpleɪɡraʊnd] Spielplatz; Schulhof OT 1
playwright [ˈpleɪraɪt] Dramatiker(in) OT 4
to **plead guilty** [pliːd ˈɡɪlti] sich schuldig bekennen **WS 2**, 65
pleasant [ˈpleznt] angenehm OT 3
please [pliːz] bitte OT 1
pleased [pliːzd] zufrieden OT 1
pleasure [ˈpleʒə] Freude OT 1
plenty [ˈplenti] reichlich; viel OT 2
plot [plɒt] Handlung OT 3
to **plug in** [plʌɡ] einstecken OT 1
plum [plʌm] Pflaume OT 1
plural [ˈplʊərəl] Plural; Mehrzahl OT 1
pocket [ˈpɒkɪt] Tasche OT 2
pocketknife [ˈpɒkɪtnaɪf] Taschenmesser OT 2
podcast [ˈpɒdkɑːst] Podcast OT 3
poem [ˈpəʊɪm] Gedicht OT 1
poet [ˈpəʊɪt] Dichter(in) OT 1
poetry [ˈpəʊətri] Dichtung OT 4
point [pɔɪnt] Punkt OT 1
to **point (to)** [pɔɪnt] zeigen (auf) OT 1
poison [ˌpɔɪzn] Gift OT 1
poison ivy [ˌpɔɪzn ˈaɪvi] giftiger Efeu OT 2
poisonous [ˈpɔɪzənəs] giftig **WS 1**, 35
polar bear [ˈpəʊlə beə] Eisbär OT 4
pole [pəʊl] Stange; Pol OT 4
police [pəˈliːs] Polizei OT 1
policy [ˈpɒləsi] Politik; politische Linie **WS 2**, 57
Polish [ˈpəʊlɪʃ] polnisch OT 2
polite [pəˈlaɪt] höflich OT 1
political [pəˈlɪtɪkl] politisch OT 3
politician [ˌpɒləˈtɪʃn] Politiker(in) OT 3
politics [ˈpɒlətɪks] Politik OT 4
poll [pəʊl] Umfrage **WS 3**, 98
to **pollute** [pəˈluːt] verschmutzen; verseuchen **WS 1**, 25
pollution [pəˈluːʃn] Verschmutzung OT 3
polo shirt [ˈpəʊləʊ ʃɜːt] Polohemd **WS 2**, 60
polyp [ˈpɒlɪp] Polyp **WS 1**, 28
pond [pɒnd] Teich OT 1
ponderously [ˈpɒndərəsli] gemächlich OT 3
pony [ˈpəʊni] Pony OT 3
pool [puːl] Pfütze; Schwimmbecken; Schwimmbecken OT 1
poor [pʊə] arm OT 1
pop [pɒp] Pop- OT 2
popcorn [ˈpɒpkɔːn] Popcorn OT 2
Pope [pəʊp] Papst OT 3
popular [ˈpɒpjələ] beliebt OT 1
popularity [ˌpɒpjuˈlærəti] Popularität OT 4
populated [ˈpɒpjuleɪtɪd] bevölkert; besiedelt **WS 1**, 28
population [ˌpɒpjəˈleɪʃən] Bevölkerung OT 3
pork [pɔːk] Schweinefleisch OT 2
porridge [ˈpɒrɪdʒ] Haferbrei **WS 2**, 77
port [pɔːt] Hafen OT 2
portable [ˈpɔːtəbl] tragbar OT 4
portal [ˈpɔːtl] Portalseite **WS 2**, 69
position [pəˈzɪʃn] Position OT 3
positive [ˈpɒzətɪv] Positiv OT 1
to **possess** [pəˈzes] besitzen OT 4
possession [pəˈzeʃn] Besitz OT 4
possessive [pəˈzesɪv] besitzergreifend; besitzanzeigend OT 1
possibility [ˌpɒsəˈbɪləti] Möglichkeit OT 4
possible [ˈpɒsəbl] möglich OT 2
post [pəʊst] Post OT 2; Beitrag OT 3
to **post** [pəʊst] posten; verschicken OT 4
postcard [ˈpəʊstkɑːd] Postkarte OT 1
poster [ˈpəʊstə] Plakat; Poster OT 1
postman [ˈpəʊstmən] Briefträger(in) OT 2
posture [ˈpɒstʃə] Körperhaltung OT 4
postwoman [ˈpəʊstwʊmən] Briefträgerin OT 2
pot [pɒt] Topf OT 2
potato [pəˈteɪtəʊ] Kartoffel OT 1
potential [pəˈtenʃl] möglich OT 4
pottery [ˈpɒtəri] Töpfern; Töpferwaren OT 3
poultry [ˈpəʊltri] Geflügel OT 2
pound [paʊnd] Pfund OT 1
to **pour** [pɔː] gießen OT 1
poverty [ˈpɒvəti] Armut **WS 3**, 104
power [ˈpaʊə] Kraft; Macht OT 4
to **power** [ˈpaʊə] antreiben OT 4
powerful [ˈpaʊəfl] mächtig OT 2
practical [ˈpræktɪkl] praktisch OT 2
practice [ˈpræktɪs] Praxis; Übung OT 1
to **practise** [ˈpræktɪs] üben OT 1
to **praise** [preɪz] loben OT 4
prawn [prɔːn] Garnele OT 3
to **pray** [preɪ] beten OT 3
prayer [preə] Gebet OT 4
predator [ˈpredətər] Raubtier; Räuber **WS 1**, 25
to **predict** [prɪˈdɪkt] vorhersagen OT 2
predictable [prɪˈdɪktəbl] vorhersehbar **WS 1**, 24
predicting [prɪˈdɪktɪŋ] Vorhersagen OT 2
prediction [prɪˈdɪkʃn] Vorhersage OT 2
to **prefer** [prɪˈfɜː] vorziehen OT 1
preference [ˈprefrəns] Vorliebe; Präferenz OT 4
pregnant [ˈpreɡnənt] schwanger OT 3
premier [ˈpremiə] erste OT 2
preparation [ˌprepəˈreɪʃn] Vorbereitung OT 2
to **prepare** [prɪˈpeə] vorbereiten; zubereiten OT 1
preposition [ˌprepəˈzɪʃn] Präposition; Verhältniswort OT 1
preschool [ˈpriːskuːl] vorschulisch **WS 2**, 63
to **prescribe** [prɪˈskraɪb] vorschreiben; festsetzen **WS 2**, 56
to **present** [prɪˈzent] überreichen; vorstellen OT 1
present [ˈpreznt] Geschenk; Gegenwart OT 1
presentation [ˌpreznˈteɪʃn] Präsentation OT 1
presenter [prɪˈzentə] Moderator(in) OT 4

to preserve [prɪ'zɜ:v] erhalten OT 3
president ['prezɪdənt] Präsident(in) OT 3
presidential [ˌprezɪ'denʃl] präsidentiell OT 4
to press [pres] drücken OT 1
pressure ['preʃə] Druck OT 3
to pretend [prɪ'tend] vorgeben; so tun, als ob OT 1
pretty ['prɪti] hübsch OT 1
to prevent [prɪ'vent] verhindern; abhalten OT 4
prevention [prɪ'venʃn] Verhütung OT 2
previous ['pri:viəs] früher **WS 1**, 33
previously ['pri:viəsli] vorher; früher OT 4
price [praɪs] Preis OT 1
pride [praɪd] Stolz **WS 1**, 32
to pride oneself [praɪd wʌn'self] Stolz auf etwas sein **WS 2**, 57
primary ['praɪməri] Haupt...; primär OT 1
primary school ['praɪməri ˌsku:l] Primärschule; Grundschule OT 1
prince [prɪns] Prinz OT 1
principal ['prɪnsəpl] Rektor(in) OT 2
principle ['prɪnsəpl] Prinzip OT 4
printed [prɪnt] gedruckt **WS 1**, 24
priority [praɪ'ɒrəti] Priorität **WS 2**, 81
prison ['prɪzn] Gefängnis OT 4
privacy ['prɪvəsi] Privatsphäre OT 3
privacy settings ['prɪvəsi 'setɪŋz] Datenschutzeinstellungen OT 3
private ['praɪvət] privat OT 3
privilege ['prɪvəlɪdʒ] Privileg; Recht OT 4
prize [praɪz] (Gewinn)Preis OT 1
proactive [ˌprəʊ'æktɪv] proaktiv OT 4
probably ['prɒbəbli] wahrscheinlich OT 2
probation [prə'beɪʃn] Bewährung **WS 2**, 64
problem ['prɒbləm] Problem OT 1
problem-solver ['prɒbləm sɒlvə] Problemlöser(in) OT 4
procedure [prə'si:dʒə] Prozedur; Verfahren OT 4
process ['prəʊses] Prozess OT 4
procession [prə'seʃn] Umzug OT 2
to produce [prə'dju:s] erzeugen OT 3
product ['prɒdʌkt] Produkt OT 2
production [prə'dʌkʃn] Produktion; Inszenierung **WS 2**, 60
professional [prə'feʃənl] professionell OT 3
proficiency [prə'fɪʃnsi] Kompetenz OT 4
profile ['prəʊfaɪl] Profil **WS 3**, 93
profit ['prɒfɪt] Profit; Gewinn OT 4
program ['prəʊgræm] Programm; Kurs OT 3
to programme ['prəʊgræm] programmieren OT 2
programme ['prəʊgræm] Programm; Sendung OT 1
programming ['prəʊgræmɪŋ] Programmierung OT 2
to progress ['prəʊgres] fortschreiten **WS 2**, 50
progress ['prəʊgres] Fortschritt OT 4
progression [prə'greʃn] Fortschreiten; Entwicklung **WS 3**, 110
progressive [prə'gresɪv] fortschrittlich; progressiv OT 1
project ['prɒdʒekt] Projekt OT 1
projector [prə'dʒektə] Projektor; Beamer OT 1
prolonged [prə'lɒŋd] anhaltend; verlängert **WS 1**, 25
prom [prɒm] Schulball OT 3
promenade [ˌprɒmə'nɑ:d] Promenade **WS 1**, 29
prominent ['prɒmɪnənt] bedeutend OT 4
to promise ['prɒmɪs] versprechen OT 2
promise ['prɒmɪs] Versprechen OT 2
to promote [prə'məʊt] fördern OT 4
prompt [prɒmpt] Hinweis OT 3
pronoun ['prəʊnaʊn] Pronomen; Fürwort OT 1
to pronounce [prə'naʊns] aussprechen OT 3
pronounced [prə'naʊnst] ausgesprochen OT 2
pronunciation [prəˌnʌnsi'eɪʃn] Aussprache OT 2
proof [pru:f] ...sicher; undurchdringlich **WS 1**, 12
prop [prɒp] Stütze; Requisite OT 1
proper ['prɒpə] richtig; anständig OT 1
property ['prɒpəti] Eigentum; Immobilie OT 4
proportion [prə'pɔ:ʃn] Anteil **WS 3**, 104
pro [prəʊ] Vorteil OT 2
prosecution [ˌprɒsɪ'kju:ʃn] Staatsanwaltschaft **WS 2**, 65
prosecutor ['prɒsɪkju:tə] Staatsanwalt / -anwältin **WS 2**, 64
prospectus [prə'spektəs] Prospekt OT 4
to prosper ['prɒspə] florieren OT 2
to protect [prə'tekt] schützen OT 2
protein ['prəʊti:n] Protein **WS 2**, 66
to protest ['prəʊtest] protestieren OT 4
protest ['prəʊtest] Protest OT 4
Protestant ['prɒtɪstənt] Protestantisch OT 3
protester [prə'testə] Demonstrant(in); Protestierer(in) OT 4
prototype ['prəʊtətaɪp] Prototyp OT 4
proud [praʊd] stolz OT 2
to prove [pru:v] beweisen OT 4
to provide [prə'vaɪd] zur Verfügung stellen; versorgen (mit) OT 4
province ['prɒvɪns] Provinz OT 4
provision [prə'vɪʒn] Maßnahme **WS 2**, 57
psychologist [saɪ'kɒlədʒɪst] Psychologe / Psychologin **WS 3**, 107
psychology [saɪ'kɒlədʒi] Psychologie **WS 3**, 107
pub [pʌb] Kneipe OT 2
puberty ['pju:bəti] Pubertät **WS 2**, 55
public ['pʌblɪk] Öffentlichkeit OT 3
publication [ˌpʌblɪ'keɪʃn] Veröffentlichung OT 4
to publish ['pʌblɪʃ] veröffentlichen OT 4
publisher ['pʌblɪʃə] Verleger(in) **WS 3**, 91
puck [pʌk] Puck OT 4
pueblo ['pwebləʊ] Pueblo OT 3
to pull [pʊl] ziehen OT 1
pulse [pʌls] Hülsenfrucht OT 4
pump [pʌmp] Pumpe OT 2
pumpkin ['pʌmpkɪn] Kürbis OT 2
pun [pʌn] Witz; Wortspiel OT 4
to punch [pʌntʃ] schlagen **WS 2**, 81
punctual ['pʌŋktʃuəl] pünktlich OT 4
to punctuate ['pʌŋktʃueɪt] mit Satzzeichen versehen OT 3
punctuation [ˌpʌŋktʃu'eɪʃn] Zeichensetzung OT 3
to punish ['pʌnɪʃ] bestrafen OT 3
puppy ['pʌpi] Welpe OT 2
purpose ['pɜ:pəs] Zweck **WS 1**, 36
on purpose [ɒn 'pɜ:pəs] absichtlich OT 2
to pursue [pə'sju:] verfolgen OT 4
pursuit [pə'sju:t] Beschäftigung; Verfolgung OT 4
to push [pʊʃ] stoßen OT 2
pushy ['pʊʃi] aggressiv **WS 3**, 93
to put [pʊt] setzen; stellen; legen OT 1
to put on [pʌt 'ɒn] sich anziehen; veranstalten OT 1
to put up [pʊt 'ʌp] errichten OT 1
puzzled ['pʌzld] verblüfft; verwirrt **WS 1**, 14

pyjamas [pəˈdʒɑːməz] Schlafanzug OT 3

Q

quack! [kwæk] Quak! (Ente) OT 2
qualification [ˌkwɒlɪfɪˈkeɪʃn] Qualifikation; Eignung OT 4
qualified [ˈkwɒlɪfaɪd] qualifiziert OT 4
quality [ˈkwɒləti] Eigenschaft; Qualität OT 3
quarter [ˈkwɔːtə] Viertel OT 1
quarter to [ˈkwɔːtə tə] viertel vor OT 1
quarterback [ˈkwɔːtəbæk] Quarterback OT 2
queen [kwiːn] Königin OT 1
queer [kwɪər] schwul; queer **WS 2**, 55
question [ˈkwestʃən] Frage OT 1
to **question** [ˈkwestʃən] fragen OT 4
questionnaire [ˌkwestʃəˈneə] Fragebogen OT 1
queue [kjuː] Schlange; Warteschlange OT 1
quick [kwɪk] schnell OT 3
quiet [ˈkwaɪət] still; ruhig OT 1
to **quit** [kwɪt] kündigen **WS 3**, 98
quite [kwaɪt] ziemlich OT 3
quiz [kwɪz] Quiz OT 2
quotation [kwəʊˈteɪʃn] Zitat OT 2
quotation mark [kwəʊˈteɪʃn mɑːk] Anführungszeichen OT 2
to **quote** [kwəʊt] zitieren OT 2

R

rabbit [ˈræbɪt] Kaninchen OT 1
race [reɪs] Rennen OT 2
to **race** [reɪs] rasen **WS 1**, 31
racing [ˈreɪsɪŋ] Rennsport OT 2
racoon [rəˈkuːn] Waschbär OT 4
radical [ˈrædɪkl] radikal; grundlegend OT 4
radio [ˈreɪdiəʊ] Radio OT 1
raid [reɪd] Razzia **WS 4**, 137
rail [reɪl] Bahn; Geländer OT 3
railway [ˈreɪlweɪ] Bahn; Eisenbahn OT 2
to **rain** [reɪn] regnen OT 1
rainbow [ˈreɪnbəʊ] Regenbogen **WS 1**, 13
rainfall [ˈreɪnfɔːl] Regen; Niederschlag OT 4
rainforest [ˈreɪnfɒrɪst] Regenwald OT 2
rainstorm [ˈreɪnstɔːm] Regenschauer; Gewitter **WS 1**, 38
rainwater [ˈreɪnwɔːtə] Regenwasser OT 4
rainy [ˈreɪni] regnerisch OT 4
to **raise** [reɪz] einwerben; erheben; erhöhen OT 2
ramp [ræmp] Rampe OT 2
random [ˈrændəm] zufällig; willkürlich **WS 1**, 24
range [reɪndʒ] Angebot; Palette OT 4
ranger [ˈreɪndʒə] Aufseher(in); Förster(in) OT 3
to **rank** [ræŋk] in eine Reihenfolge bringen OT 4
rank [ræŋk] Position; Rang OT 4
ranking [ˈræŋkɪŋ] Reihenfolge OT 4
rap [ræp] Rap OT 4
rapid [ˈræpɪd] schnell OT 3
rare [reə] selten OT 2
raspberry [ˈrɑːzbəri] Himbeere OT 1
rat [ræt] Ratte OT 3
rate [reɪt] Rate; Geschwindigkeit OT 4
to **rate** [reɪt] bewerten; beurteilen **WS 3**, 107
rather [ˈrɑːðə] ziemlich OT 3
ratter [ˈrætə] Rattenfänger (Hund) OT 3
raven [ˈreɪvn] Rabe OT 2
to **reach** [riːtʃ] erreichen OT 3
to **react** [riˈækt] reagieren OT 3
reaction [riˈækʃn] Reaktion OT 3
to **read** [riːd] lesen OT 1
reader [ˈriːdə] Leser(in) OT 2
reading [ˈriːdɪŋ] Lesen OT 1
ready [ˈredi] bereit OT 1
real [rɪəl] echt OT 1
realistic [ˌriːəˈlɪstɪk] realistisch OT 4
reality [riˈæləti] Realität **WS 1**, 28
to **realize** [ˈriːəlaɪz] erkennen OT 2
really [ˈriːəli] wirklich; sehr OT 1
to **rearrange** [ˌriːəˈreɪndʒ] umstellen OT 2
reason [ˈriːzn] Grund OT 1
to **rebel** [ˈrebl] rebellieren; sich auflehnen OT 4
rebel [ˈrebl] Rebell(in) OT 4
rebellion [rɪˈbeljən] Aufstand OT 3
to **rebuild** [ˌriːˈbɪld] wieder aufbauen OT 2
to **receive** [rɪˈsiːv] erhalten OT 2
receiver [rɪˈsiːvə] Empfänger(in) OT 4
recent [ˈriːsnt] neueste(r) OT 3
recently [ˈriːsntli] neulich OT 3
reception [rɪˈsepʃn] Rezeption; Empfang OT 1
receptionist [rɪˈsepʃənɪst] Rezeptionist(in) OT 1
recess [ˈriːses] Pause OT 4
recipe [ˈresəpi] Rezept OT 2
recognizable [ˈrekəgnaɪzəbl] erkennbar OT 4
to **recognize** [ˈrekəgnaɪz] erkennen OT 3
to **recommend** [ˌrekəˈmend] empfehlen OT 3
recommendation [ˌrekəmenˈdeɪʃn] Empfehlung OT 4
to **reconstruct** [ˌriːkənˈstrʌkt] wiederaufbauen OT 3
to **record** [rɪˈkɔːd] aufnehmen OT 1
recording studio [ˈrɪkɔːdɪŋ ˌstjuːdiəʊ] Aufnahmestudio OT 3
to **recover** [rɪˈkʌvə] (sich) erholen OT 4
recovery [rɪˈkʌvəri] Rettung; Wiederherstellung OT 3
recreation [ˌriːkriˈeɪʃn] Modell OT 4
recreational [ˌrekriˈeɪʃənl] Freizeit... OT 3
rectangular [rekˈtæŋgjələ] rechteckig OT 2
to **recycle** [ˌriːˈsaɪkl] wiederverwerten OT 2
recycler [ˌriːˈsaɪklə] Wiederverwerter(in) OT 3
red [red] rot; Rotwein OT 1
to **reduce** [rɪˈdjuːs] reduzieren; verringern OT 4
reef [riːf] Riff **WS 1**, 26
reenactment [ˌriː ɪˈnæktmənt] Nachstellung OT 4
to **refer** [rɪˈfɜː] sich beziehen OT 3
referee [ˌrefəˈri] Schiedsrichter(in) OT 3
to **refine** [rɪˈfaɪn] verfeinern OT 4
to **reflect** [rɪˈflekt] spiegeln OT 2
reformation [ˌrefəˈmeɪʃn] Reformation OT 3
refreshment [rɪˈfreʃmənt] Erfrischung OT 4
to **refuse** [rɪˈfjuːz] sich weigern OT 4
to **regard** [rɪˈgɑːd] betrachten; ansehen OT 4
regardless [rɪˈgɑːdləs] unabhängig von OT 4
reggae [ˈregeɪ] Reggae OT 2
region [ˈriːdʒən] Region OT 3
regional [ˈriːdʒənl] regional **WS 1**, 32
register [ˈredʒɪstə] Kasse OT 2
registration plate [ˌredʒɪˈstreɪʃnpleɪt] Nummernschild OT 4
to **regret** [rɪˈgret] bereuen OT 2
regular [ˈregjələ] regelmäßig OT 1
rehearsal [rɪˈhɜːsl] Probe OT 2
to **rehearse** [rɪˈhɜːs] proben OT 3
reindeer [ˈreɪndɪə] Rentier OT 3
to **reinforce** [ˌriːɪnˈfɔːs] verstärken; bekräftigen **WS 2**, 54

to **rejoin** [ˌriːˈdʒɔɪn] wieder beitreten OT 4
to **relate to** [rɪˈleɪt tə] mit etw. in Zusammenhang stehen; sich auf etw. beziehen **WS 1**, 34
related [rɪˈleɪtɪd] verwandt OT 3
relation [rɪˈleɪʃn] Beziehung; Verhältnis **WS 1**, 30
relationship [rɪˈleɪʃnʃɪp] Beziehung OT 3
relative [ˈrelətɪv] Verwandte(r) OT 3
relatively [ˈrelətɪvli] relativ; ziemlich OT 4
to **relax** [rɪˈlæks] sich entspannen OT 3
relaxing [rɪˈlæksɪŋ] erholsam OT 2
to **release** [rɪˈliːs] veröffentlichen; auf den Markt bringen OT 4
relevant [ˈreləvənt] wichtig OT 4
reliable [rɪˈlaɪəbl] verlässlich OT 4
relief [rɪˈliːf] Erleichterung; Hilfe OT 2
relieved [rɪˈliːvd] erleichtert OT 3
religion [rɪˈlɪdʒən] Religion OT 3
religious [rɪˈlɪdʒəs] religiös; fromm OT 3
religious studies [rɪˈlɪdʒəs stʌdiz] Religionsunterricht OT 1
to **relocate** [ˌriːləʊˈkeɪt] umziehen OT 4
reluctance [rɪˈlʌktəns] Abneigung OT 4
to **rely on** [rɪˈlaɪ ɒn] sich verlassen auf OT 4
to **remain** [rɪˈmeɪn] bleiben OT 4
remarriage [ˌriːˈmærɪdʒ] Wiederverheiratung **WS 2**, 62
to **remember** [rɪˈmembə] sich erinnern an OT 1
to **remind** [rɪˈmaɪnd] erinnern OT 2
remorse [rɪˈmɔːs] Reue **WS 2**, 64
remote [rɪˈməʊt] Fernbedienung OT 3; entfernt; abgelegen OT 4
remotely [rɪˈməʊtli] aus der Ferne OT 4
removal van [rɪˈmuːvl væn] Umzugswagen OT 4
to **remove** [rɪˈmuːv] entfernen OT 2
renewable [rɪˈnjuːəbl] erneuerbar OT 4
to **rent** [rent] mieten OT 3
repair [rɪˈpeə] Reparatur OT 2
to **repair** [rɪˈpeər] beheben; reparieren **WS 2**, 64
to **repeat** [rɪˈpiːt] wiederholen OT 1
repetition [ˌrepəˈtɪʃn] Wiederholung **WS 2**, 74
repetitive [rɪˈpetətɪv] repetitiv; sich wiederholend **WS 2**, 57
to **rephrase** [ˌriːˈfreɪz] neu formulieren; umformulieren **WS 3**, 100
to **replace** [rɪˈpleɪs] ersetzen OT 3
replica [ˈreplɪkə] Kopie OT 4
reply [rɪˈplaɪ] Antwort OT 1
to **reply** [rɪˈplaɪ] antworten OT 1
to **report** [rɪˈpɔːt] berichten; melden; sich melden OT 1
reporter [rɪˈpɔːtə] Reporter(in) OT 1
to **represent** [ˌreprɪˈzent] vertreten OT 3
representative [ˌreprɪˈzentətɪv] Vertreter(in); Abgeordnete(r) OT 4
reptile [ˈreptaɪl] Reptil OT 2
republic [rɪˈpʌblɪk] Republik OT 4
request [rɪˈkwest] Bitte OT 1
to **require** [rɪˈkwaɪə] benötigen OT 4
required [rɪˈkwaɪəd] erforderlich OT 3
requirement [rɪˈkwaɪəmənt] Voraussetzung **WS 1**, 37
rescue [ˈreskjuː] Rettung OT 2
research [rɪˈsɜːtʃ] Forschung OT 2
to **research** [rɪˈsɜːtʃ] erforschen OT 4
researcher [rɪˈsɜːtʃə] Forscher(in) OT 2
reservation [ˌrezəˈveɪʃn] Reservierung; Vorbehalt; Reservat OT 1
reserved [rɪˈzɜːvd] reserviert OT 2
reservoir [ˈrezəvwɑːr] Reservoir; Behälter **WS 1**, 34
resident [ˈrezɪdənt] Bewohner(in) OT 4
residential [ˌrezɪˈdenʃl] Wohn- OT 4
to **resign** [rɪˈzaɪn] zurücktreten OT 4
to **resist** [rɪˈzɪst] widerstehen **WS 2**, 77
resistance [rɪˈzɪstəns] Widerstand; hier: Resistenz **WS 1**, 24
resort [rɪˈzɔːt] Urlaubsort OT 3
resource [rɪˈsɔːs] Ressource; Mittel OT 4
to **respect** [rɪˈspekt] achten OT 3
respect [rɪˈspekt] Respekt **WS 1**, 30
respectful [rɪˈspektfl] respektvoll OT 3
to **respond** [rɪˈspɒnd] antworten OT 1
respondent [rɪˈspɒndənt] Befragte(r) **WS 2**, 52
response [rɪˈspɒns] Reaktion; Antwort OT 4
responsibility [rɪˌspɒnsəˈbɪləti] Verantwortung OT 3
responsible [rɪˈspɒnsəbl] verantwortlich OT 3
rest [rest] Ruhe; Pause; Rest OT 1
restaurant [ˈrestrɒnt] Restaurant OT 1
to **restore** [rɪˈstɔː] wiederherstellen OT 3
to **restrict** [rɪˈstrɪkt] einschränken OT 4
restriction [rɪˈstrɪkʃn] Einschränkung OT 4
result [rɪˈzʌlt] Ergebnis OT 2
to **resume** [rɪˈzjuːm] übernehmen; wieder annehmen **WS 1**, 26
retail [ˈriːteɪl] Einzelhandel **WS 3**, 109
to **retire** [rɪˈtaɪər] in Rente gehen **WS 3**, 103
to **return** [rɪˈtɜːn] zurückkehren OT 2
reusable [ˌriːˈjuːzəbl] wiederverwendbar OT 3
to **reuse** [ˌriːˈjuːz] wiederverwenden OT 4
to **reveal** [rɪˈviːl] zeigen OT 4
review [rɪˈvjuː] Kritik; Review **WS 3**, 106
to **review** [rɪˈvjuː] überprüfen; beurteilen OT 3
to **revise** [rɪˈvaɪz] revidieren OT 2
revival [rɪˈvaɪvl] Wiederbelebung **WS 2**, 58
revolting [rɪˈvəʊltɪŋ] abstoßend OT 2
revolution [ˌrevəˈluːʃn] Revolution OT 2
to **revolutionize** [ˌrevəˈluːʃənaɪz] revolutionieren OT 4
to **reward** [rɪˈwɔːd] belohnen **WS 2**, 59
rewarding [rɪˈwɔːdɪŋ] lohnend **WS 3**, 96
to **rewrite** [ˌriːˈraɪt] neu schreiben OT 2
rhyme [ˈraɪm] Reim OT 2
rib [rɪb] Rippe OT 3
rice [raɪs] Reis OT 1
rich [rɪtʃ] reich OT 1
ride [raɪd] Ritt; Fahrt OT 1
to **ride** [raɪd] fahren **WS 1**, 29
right [raɪt] rechte(r, -s); richtig OT 1
rights [raɪts] Rechte OT 3
rigid [ˈrɪdʒɪd] starr; rigide **WS 2**, 61
rim [rɪm] Rand OT 3
to **ring** [rɪŋ] klingeln OT 1
rink [rɪŋk] Bahn; Eisbahn OT 4
to **rise** [raɪz] aufsteigen OT 3
risk [rɪsk] Risiko; Gefahr OT 4
ritual [ˈrɪtʃuəl] Ritual OT 4
rivalry [ˈraɪvlri] Konkurrenz **WS 1**, 30
river [ˈrɪvə] Fluss OT 1
road [rəʊd] Straße OT 1
the open road [ðə ˈəʊpən ˌrəʊd] die freie Straße OT 2
to **roam** [rəʊm] herumschweifen; durchschweifen **WS 1**, 25
roast [rəʊst] gebraten OT 1
rock [rɒk] Stein OT 2
rocket [ˈrɒkɪt] Rakete OT 4
role [rəʊl] Rolle OT 1
to **role-play** [ˈrəʊlpleɪ] ein Rollenspiel machen OT 2
roleplay [ˈrəʊlpleɪ] Rollenspiel OT 2
roll [rəʊl] Rolle; Filmrolle OT 2
roller skate [ˈrəʊlə skeɪt] Rollschuh **WS 1**, 29

roman ['rəʊmən] römisch OT 2
roof ['ru:f] Dach OT 1
room ['ru:m] Raum OT 1
roommate ['rum,meɪt] Mitbewohner(in) **WS 3**, 107
root [ru:t] Wurzel OT 3
rope [rəʊp] Seil OT 3
to rot ['rəʊtə] verfaulen **WS 1**, 25
rota ['rəʊtə] abwechselnder Dienst **WS 3**, 112
rough [rʌf] rau OT 3
roughly ['rʌfli] ungefähr OT 3
round [raʊnd] rund OT 1
route [ru:t] Strecke OT 2
routine [ru:'ti:n] Routine **WS 2**, 61
row [rəʊ] Reihe OT 2
rowing boat ['rəʊɪŋ bəʊt] Ruderboot OT 1
royal ['rɔɪəl] königlich OT 1
to rub [rʌb] reiben OT 3
rubber ['rʌbə] Gummi; Radiergummi OT 1
rubbish ['rʌbɪʃ] Müll OT 4
rucksack ['rʌksæk] Rucksack OT 1
rude [ru:d] unhöflich OT 2
rugby ['rʌgbi] Rugby OT 1
ruin ['ru:ɪn] Ruine OT 2
ruined ['ru:ɪnd] verfallen OT 3
to rule [ru:l] herrschen OT 2
rule [ru:l] Regel; Herrschaft OT 1
rulebook ['ru:l bʊk] Regelwerk OT 2
ruler ['ru:lə] Lineal; Herrscher(in) OT 1
to run [rʌn] laufen; rennen; leiten OT 1
  to run out [rʌn aʊt] zu Ende gehen OT 2
runaway ['rʌnəweɪ] Ausreißer(in) **WS 4**, 136
runner ['rʌnə] Läufer(in) OT 2
running ['rʌnɪŋ] Führung OT 1
to rush [rʌʃ] eilen OT 2
  rush hour ['rʌʃ aʊə] Hauptverkehrszeit OT 1
  to rush off [rʌʃ ɒf] loshasten OT 2

S

sack [sæk] Sack OT 2
  sack race ['sæk reɪs] Sackhüpfen OT 2
sacred ['seɪkrɪd] heilig OT 4
sad [sæd] traurig OT 1
saddened ['sædnd] betrübt **WS 1**, 26
safari [sə'fɑ:ri] Safari OT 2
safe [seɪf] sicher OT 1
safety ['seɪfti] Sicherheit OT 2
to sail [seɪl] (mit dem Schiff) fahren OT 2
sail [seɪl] Segel **WS 1**, 43
sailing ['seɪlɪŋ] Segeln OT 1
sailor ['seɪlə] Seemann OT 3
saint [seɪnt] Heilige(r) OT 3
salad ['sæləd] Salat OT 1
salary ['sæləri] Gehalt; Lohn **WS 3**, 95
sale [seɪl] Verkauf OT 3
sales [seɪlz] Verkäufe OT 2
sales assistant [,seɪlzə'sɪstənt] Verkäufer(in) OT 2
salmon ['sæmən] Lachs OT 1
salt [sɔ:lt] Salz OT 2
salty ['sɔ:lti] salzig OT 3
salute [sə'lu:t] militärischer Gruß OT 3
to salvage ['sælvɪdʒ] Bergungs… OT 3
salvaged ['sælvɪdʒ] geborgen OT 3
same [seɪm] gleich OT 1
to sample ['sɑ:mpl] probieren OT 4
sanctuary ['sæŋktʃuəri] Schutzgebiet **WS 1**, 29
sand [sænd] Sand OT 1
sandstone ['sændstəʊn] Sandstein OT 4
sandwich ['sænwɪtʃ] Sandwich OT 1
sandy ['sændi] sandig **WS 1**, 29
sash [sæʃ] Schärpe OT 4
sachet ['sæʃeɪ] kleine Tüte OT 3
satellite ['sætəlaɪt] Satellit OT 4
Saturday ['sætədeɪ] Samstag OT 1
sauce [sɔ:s] Soße OT 1
sauna ['sɔ:nə] Sauna OT 2
sausage ['sɒsɪdʒ] Wurst; Würstchen OT 1
to save [seɪv] retten; sparen OT 2
savoury ['seɪvəri] pikant OT 3
savvy ['sævi] klug; schlau **WS 2**, 68
saxophone ['sæksəfəʊn] Saxofon OT 2
to say [seɪ] sagen OT 1
scale [skeɪl] Maßstab OT 2
  large scale ['lɑ:dʒ skeɪl] großskalig OT 2
  small scale ['smɔ:l skeɪl] kleinskalig OT 2
to scan [skæn] überfliegen; scannen OT 2
to scare [skeə] Angst machen OT 2
scared [skeəd] verängstigt OT 1
scarf [skɑ:f] Schal OT 1
scary ['skeəri] unheimlich; beängstigend OT 2
to scavenge ['skævɪndʒ] nach etw. suchen **WS 4**, 132
scene [si:n] Szene OT 2
  behind the scenes [bɪ,haɪnd ðə 'si:nz] hinter den Kulissen OT 2
scenery ['si:nəri] Landschaft; Kulisse OT 2
schedule ['ʃedju:l] Stundenplan OT 2
scheme [ski:m] Programm **WS 3**, 89
scholarship ['skɒləʃɪp] Stipendium **WS 2**, 56
school [sku:l] Schule OT 1
school bag ['sku:l bæg] Schultasche OT 1
school day [sku:l deɪ] Schultag OT 1
schoolmate ['sku:lmeɪt] Schulkamerad(in) OT 4
schoolwork ['sku:lwɜ:k] Schulaufgaben **WS 3**, 93
science ['saɪəns] Wissenschaft; Naturwissenschaft OT 1
scientific [,saɪən'tɪfɪk] wissenschaftlich OT 3
scientist ['saɪəntɪst] Naturwissenschaftler(in) OT 1
scissors ['sɪzəz] Schere OT 1
scone [skəʊn] brötchenartiges, süßes Gebäck OT 1
scorching ['skɔ:tʃɪŋ] glühend **WS 1**, 21
score [skɔ:r] Note **WS 2**, 59
to score [skɔ:] punkten OT 1
Scottish ['skɒtɪʃ] schottisch OT 2
scout [skaʊt] Scout; Kundschafter(in) OT 3
to scrape [skreɪp] kratzen; schrubben OT 2
scrapple [skræpl] Scrapple OT 3
to scratch [skrætʃ] kratzen OT 2
to scream [skri:m] schreien OT 3
screen [skri:n] Bildschirm; Leinwand OT 1
script [skrɪpt] Drehbuch OT 2
scroll [skrəʊl] Schriftrolle OT 2
sculpture ['skʌlptʃə] Skulptur OT 2
sea [si:] Meer OT 1
seabed ['si:bed] Meeresboden OT 3
seabird ['si:bɜ:d] Seevogel **WS 1**, 26
seafaring ['si:feərɪŋ] seefahrend OT 3
seafood ['si:fu:d] Meeresfrüchte OT 4
seal [si:l] Robbe OT 1
seaman ['si:mən] Seemann OT 3
search [sɜ:tʃ] Suche OT 2
to search [sɜ:tʃ] (durch)suchen OT 4
seashell ['si:ʃel] Muschel OT 3
seashore ['si:ʃɔ:] Strand OT 4
seasick ['si:sɪk] seekrank OT 3
seaside ['si:saɪd] Meeresküste OT 3
season ['si:zn] Jahreszeit OT 2
seasoning ['si:zənɪŋ] Gewürz OT 2
to seat [si:t] setzen **WS 2**, 59
seat [si:t] Sitzplatz OT 2
seating ['si:tɪŋ] Sitzplätze OT 2
second ['sekənd] Sekunde; Zweite(r, -s) OT 1

secondary ['sekəndri] weiterführend; sekundär OT 1
secondary school ['sekəndri ˌsku:l] Sekundarschule; weiterführende Schule OT 1
secondly ['sekəndli] zweitens OT 2
secret ['si:krət] Geheimnis OT 2
secretary ['sekrətri] Sekretär(in) OT 1
section ['sekʃn] Teil OT 2
sector ['sektə] Bereich **WS 3**, 96
secure [sɪ'kjʊə] sicher OT 3
to **secure** [sɪ'kjʊər] sichern; ergattern **WS 3**, 90
security [sɪ'kjʊərəti] Sicherheit **WS 1**, 28
to **see** [si:] sehen OT 1
seed [si:d] Samen OT 2
to **seek** [si:k] suchen **WS 1**, 16
to **seem** [si:m] scheinen OT 2
segment ['segmənt] Segment; Abschnitt **WS 1**, 32
seldom ['seldəm] selten **WS 2**, 69
to **select** [sɪ'lekt] wählen; auswählen OT 4
selection [sɪ'lekʃn] Auswahl OT 4
selective [sɪ'lektɪv] getrennt OT 4
self-belief [ˌselfbɪ'li:f] Selbstwertgefühl; Selbstbewusstsein **WS 2**, 50
self-employed [ˌself ɪm'plɔɪd] selbständig **WS 3**, 92
selfie ['selfi] Selfie OT 4
selfish ['selfɪʃ] egoistisch OT 3
self-service [ˌself 's3:vɪs] Selbstbedienung OT 4
self-sufficient [ˌself sə'fɪʃnt] selbstständig; unabhängig OT 4
to **sell** [sel] verkaufen OT 1
semester [sɪ'mestə] Semester OT 4
semi- ['semi] halb- OT 3
semi-detached house [ˌsemidɪtætʃt 'haʊs] Doppelhaushälfte OT 4
senator ['senətə] Senator(in) OT 4
to **send** [send] schicken OT 1
senior ['si:niə] Oberstufenschüler(in); Senior(in) OT 4
senior citizen [ˌsi:niə'sɪtɪzn] Senior(in) OT 2
sense [sens] Sinn OT 2
sensible ['sensəbl] vernünftig OT 2
sensitive ['sensətɪv] einfühlsam OT 4
sensory ['sensəri] sensorisch **WS 2**, 61
sentence ['sentəns] Satz; Strafe OT 1; Verurteilung; Strafe **WS 2**, 64
to **sentence** ['sentəns] verurteilen **WS 2**, 64
separate ['seprət] getrennt OT 2
September [sep'tembə] September OT 1
sequel ['si:kwəl] Folge; Fortsetzung OT 4
to **sequence** ['si:kwəns] in eine Reihenfolge bringen OT 3
sequence ['si:kwəns] Aufeinanderfolge OT 3
sequencing ['si:kwənsɪŋ] Sequenzierung; Reihenfolge OT 3
sequentially [sɪ'kwenʃəli] der Reihe nach OT 4
series ['sɪəri:z] Serie OT 4
serious ['sɪəriəs] ernst OT 2
seriousness ['sɪəriəsnəs] Ernsthaftigkeit **WS 2**, 64
serpent ['s3:pənt] Schlange **WS 1**, 13
servant ['s3:vənt] Diener(in) OT 3
to **serve** [s3:v] servieren; bedienen OT 1
server ['s3:və] Kellner(in) OT 3
service ['s3:vɪs] Dienst OT 2
session ['seʃn] Session ; Sitzung OT 4
to **set** [set] stellen OT 2
to **set off** [ˌset'ɒf] aufbrechen OT 2
to **set the table** [set ðə teɪbl] den Tisch decken OT 2
setting ['setɪŋ] Setting; Umgebung **WS 4**, 129
to **settle** ['setl] sich niederlassen; besiedeln OT 4
to **settle down** ['setl daʊn] sich beruhigen OT 2
to **settle in** ['setl ɪn] sich eingewöhnen **WS 1**, 21
settlement ['setlmənt] Siedlung OT 4
settler ['setlə] Siedler(in) OT 3
seven ['sevn] sieben OT 1
seventeen [ˌsevn'ti:n] siebzehn OT 1
seventy ['sevnti] siebzig OT 1
several ['sevrəl] mehrere; einige OT 1
severe [sɪ'vɪə] schwer; stark OT 4
to **sew** [səʊ] nähen OT 3
sex [seks] Geschlecht; Sex **WS 2**, 52
shade [ʃeɪd] Schatten **WS 1**, 16
shadow ['ʃædəʊ] Schatten OT 3
to **shadow sb.** ['ʃædəʊ] bei jdm. hospitieren **WS 3**, 106
to **shake** [ʃeɪk] schütteln OT 2
shall [ʃæl] werden OT 2
shame [ʃeɪm] Schamgefühl **WS 2**, 58
it's a shame [ɪts ə 'ʃeɪm] das ist schade OT 2
shampoo [ʃæm'pu:] Shampoo OT 3
shape [ʃeɪp] Form OT 1
to **shape** [ʃeɪp] formen OT 4
to **share** [ʃeə] teilen OT 2
shark [ʃɑ:k] Hai OT 2
sharp [ʃɑ:p] scharf OT 4
she [ʃi] sie OT 1
shed [ʃed] Schuppen OT 1
sheep [ʃi:p] Schaf OT 1
sheepdog ['ʃi:pdɒg] Hütehund OT 2
to **sheer** [ʃɪə] sich losmachen OT 3
sheet [ʃi:t] Betttuch; Blatt OT 1
shelf [ʃelf] Regal OT 2
shellfish ['ʃelfɪʃ] Meeresfrüchte OT 3
shelter ['ʃeltə] Unterschlupf OT 2
shepherd ['ʃepəd] Schäfer OT 2
shift [ʃɪft] Veränderung **WS 2**, 58
to **shift** [ʃɪft] verändern **WS 2**, 70
to **shine** [ʃaɪn] leuchten OT 1
ship [ʃɪp] Schiff OT 1
shirt [ʃ3:t] Hemd OT 1
to **shiver** ['ʃɪvə] zittern OT 3
shock [ʃɒk] Überraschung OT 3
to **shock** [ʃɒk] überraschen; schockieren OT 4
shoe [ʃu:] Schuh OT 1
to **shoot** [ʃu:t] schießen OT 3
to **shop** [ʃɒp] kaufen; einkaufen OT 1
shop [ʃɒp] Laden OT 1
shoplifting ['ʃɒplɪftɪŋ] Ladendiebstahl **WS 2**, 50
shopper ['ʃɒpə] Käufer(in) OT 4
shopping ['ʃɒpɪŋ] Einkaufen OT 1
shopping centre ['ʃɒpɪŋ sentə] Einkaufszentrum OT 1

shore [ʃɔ:] Küste OT 2
shoreline ['ʃɔ:laɪn] Küste OT 4
short [ʃɔ:t] kurz OT 1
shortage ['ʃɔ:tɪdʒ] Mangel **WS 1**, 34
to **shorten** ['ʃɔ:tn] kürzen; abkürzen OT 4
shortlist ['ʃɔ:tlɪst] Auswahlliste OT 2
shorts [ʃɔ:ts] kurze Hosen OT 3
shot [ʃɒt] Schuss; Schnappschuss OT 2
should [ʃəd] sollte OT 2
shoulder ['ʃəʊldə] Schulter OT 1
to **shout** [ʃaʊt] laut rufen OT 1
to **show** [ʃəʊ] zeigen OT 1
show-and-tell [ˌʃəʊ ən 'tel] Kurzvortrag über einen mitgebrachten Gegenstand OT 2
shower ['ʃaʊə] Dusche; Schauer OT 1
showground ['ʃəʊgraʊnd] Ausstellungsgelände OT 2
to **shred** [ʃred] zerfetzen OT 2
shredded ['ʃredɪd] zerkleinert OT 2
to **shut** [ʃʌt] zumachen; schließen OT 2
to **shut up** [ʃʌt ʌp] den Mund halten OT 2
shy [ʃaɪ] schüchtern OT 2

sibling ['sɪblɪŋ] Geschwister(kind); Bruder; Schwester **WS 1**, 27
sick [sɪk] krank; übel OT 1
side [saɪd] Seite OT 1
sideline ['saɪdlaɪn] Nebenberuf **WS 3**, 102
to **sigh** [saɪ] seufzen **WS 1**, 15
sight [saɪt] Sehenswürdigkeit; Sehvermögen; Anblick OT 1
sightseeing ['saɪtsiːɪŋ] Besichtigungen OT 1
sign [saɪn] Schild; Zeichen OT 1
to **sign** [saɪn] unterschreiben OT 2
to **sign up** [saɪn ʌp] sich anmelden OT 2
signal ['sɪgnəl] Signal OT 2
significance [sɪg'nɪfɪkəns] Bedeutung; Wichtigkeit **WS 1**, 32
to **signify** ['sɪgnɪfaɪ] bedeuten OT 4
signpost ['saɪnpəʊst] Wegweiser; Schild **WS 3**, 88
silence ['saɪləns] Schweigen; Ruhe **WS 1**, 14
silly ['sɪli] dumm; albern OT 1
silver ['sɪlvə] Silber...; silbern OT 1
similar ['sɪmələ] ähnlich OT 1
similarity [ˌsɪmə'lærəti] Ähnlichkeit OT 3
to **simmer** ['sɪmə] köcheln OT 2
simple ['sɪmpl] einfach OT 1
simultaneous [ˌsɪml'teɪniəs] gleichzeitig; simultan **WS 3**, 107
since [sɪns] seit OT 2
sincerely [sɪn'sɪəli] aufrichtig; mit freundlichen Grüßen OT 3
to **sing** [sɪŋ] singen OT 1
singer ['sɪŋə] Sänger(in) OT 1
single ['sɪŋgl] Einzel... OT 3
to **sink** [sɪŋk] sinken OT 3
sink [sɪŋk] Spülbecken OT 3
sir [sɜː] (mein) Herr OT 1
siren ['saɪrən] Sirene OT 3
sister ['sɪstə] Schwester OT 1
to **sit** [sɪt] sitzen OT 1
site [saɪt] Platz OT 2
situated ['sɪtʃueɪtɪd] gelegen OT 4
situation [ˌsɪtʃu'eɪʃn] Lage; Situation OT 1
six [sɪks] sechs OT 1
sixteen [ˌsɪks'tiːn] sechzehn OT 1
sixty ['sɪksti] sechzig OT 1
size [saɪz] Größe OT 2
to **skate** [skeɪt] Schlittschuh laufen OT 2
skateboard ['skeɪtbɔːd] Skateboard OT 1
skeletal ['skelətl] Skelett... OT 3
skeleton ['skelɪtn] Skelett OT 2
sketch [sketʃ] Skizze; Sketch OT 2
to **ski** [skiː] Ski laufen OT 3
skiing ['skiːɪŋ] Skifahren OT 3
skill [skɪl] Fertigkeit; Fähigkeit OT 1
skilled [skɪld] geschickt; ausgebildet OT 4
to **skim** [skɪm] querlesen; überfliegen OT 2
skin [skɪn] Haut OT 2
skinny ['skɪni] mager; dünn **WS 2**, 77
to **skip** [skɪp] auslassen OT 3
skirt [skɜːt] Rock OT 1
skit [skɪt] Sketch OT 2
skull [skʌl] Schädel OT 2
sky [skaɪ] Himmel OT 1
skydiver ['skaɪdaɪvər] Fallschirmspringer(in) **WS 1**, 29
skyline ['skaɪlaɪn] Skyline OT 4
skyscraper ['skaɪskreɪpə] Wolkenkratzer OT 3
slang [slæŋ] Slang OT 4
to **slap on** [slæp ɒn] draufklatschen **WS 1**, 16
slave [sleɪv] Sklave / Sklavin OT 3
sled [sled] Schlitten OT 4
to **sleep** [sliːp] schlafen OT 1
to **go to sleep** [ˌgəʊ tə 'sliːp] einschlafen OT 1
sleep [sliːp] Schlaf **WS 1**, 20
sleepover ['sliːpoʊvə] Pyjama-Party OT 1
sleeved [sliːvd] mit Ärmeln OT 3
slice [slaɪs] Scheibe OT 1
slide ['slaɪd] Folie OT 1
to **slide on** [slaɪd ɒn] aufschieben **WS 1**, 16
slideshow ['slaɪdʃəʊ] Diaschau **WW**, 11
slightly ['slaɪtli] etwas; ein bisschen OT 3
to **slip on** ['slɪp ɒn] rasch anziehen **WS 1**, 16
slipper ['slɪpə] Pantoffel OT 4
slippery ['slɪpəri] glatt OT 3
slogan ['sləʊgən] Slogan OT 2
to **slop on** ['slɒp ɒn] schwappen **WS 1**, 16
slow [sləʊ] langsam OT 2
to **slow down** [sləʊ'daʊn] verlangsamen OT 4
slum [slʌm] Slum; Elendsviertel **WS 4**, 141
to **slump** [slʌmp] abrutschen; zusammensacken **WS 3**, 93
small [smɔːl] klein OT 1
smallpox ['smɔːlpɒks] Pocken **WS 1**, 17
smart [smɑːt] schlau **WS 3**, 103
smartly ['smɑːtli] schick; klug OT 4
smartphone ['smɑːtfəʊn] Smartphone OT 3
to **smell** [smel] riechen OT 1
smelly ['smeli] übel riechend OT 3
to **smile** [smaɪl] lächeln OT 1
smoke [sməʊk] Rauch OT 2
smooth [smuːð] glatt OT 4
smoothly ['smuːðli] glatt OT 3
to **smuggle** ['smʌgl] schmuggeln **WS 4**, 129
snack [snæk] Snack OT 1
snake [sneɪk] Schlange OT 1
to **snap** [snæp] zerbrechen OT 3
sneaker ['sniːkə] Turnschuh **WS 2**, 68
snow [snəʊ] Schnee OT 1
to **snow** [snəʊ] schneien OT 1
snowboarding ['snəʊbɔːdɪŋ] Snowboardfahren OT 3
snow-capped ['snəʊ kæpt] schneebedeckt OT 4
snowmobile ['snəʊməbiːl] Schneemobil OT 4
snowy ['snəʊi] verschneit OT 4
so [səʊ] also; so OT 1
soaked [səʊkd] durchnässt OT 3
to **soak up** [səʊk ʌp] aufnehmen; hier: (Sonne) tanken **WS 1**, 29
soap [səʊp] Seife OT 2
to **soar** [sɔː] schweben OT 3
soccer ['sɒkə] Fußball OT 2
social ['səʊʃl] gesellschaftlich OT 3
social media [ˌsəʊʃl 'miːdiə] soziale Medien OT 2
to **socialize** ['səʊʃəlaɪz] Kontakte pflegen OT 4
society [sə'saɪəti] Gesellschaft OT 3
sock [sɒk] Socke OT 1
soda ['səʊdə] Limo; Sprudel **WS 2**, 66
sofa ['səʊfə] Sofa OT 1
soft [sɒft] weich OT 1
soil [sɔɪl] Erde; Erdreich OT 4
solar ['səʊlə] Sonnen... OT 3
soldier ['səʊldʒə] Soldat(in) OT 1
solid ['sɒlɪd] fest; massiv OT 4
solo ['səʊləʊ] solo OT 2
solution [sə'luːʃn] Lösung OT 3
to **solve** [sɒlv] lösen OT 4
some [sʌm] etwas; einige OT 1
somebody ['sʌmbədi] jemand OT 1
someday ['sʌmdeɪ] eines Tages; irgendwann **WS 3**, 99
somehow ['sʌmhaʊ] irgendwie OT 4
someone ['sʌmwʌn] jemand OT 1

something ['sʌmθɪŋ] etwas OT 1
sometime ['sʌmtaɪm] irgendwann OT 3
sometimes ['sʌmtaɪmz] manchmal OT 1
somewhere ['sʌmweə] irgendwo OT 1
son [sʌn] Sohn OT 1
to have a son [hæv ə 'sʌn] einen Sohn bekommen OT 1
song [sɒŋ] Lied OT 1
songwriter ['sɒŋraɪtər] Texter(in); Liederkomponist(in) **WS 2**, 50
soon [su:n] bald OT 1
sophomore ['sɒfəmɔ:r] Student im 2. Studienjahr **WS 2**, 72
sorry ['sɒri] Entschuldigung OT 1
sort [sɔ:t] Art OT 2
to sort [sɔ:t] sortieren OT 4
to sort out [sɔ:t 'aʊt] klären; aussortieren OT 4
soul [səʊl] Seele OT 2
sound [saʊnd] Geräusch; Ton; Klang OT 1
to sound [saʊnd] klingen OT 4
soup [su:p] Suppe OT 1
source [sɔ:s] Quelle OT 2
south [saʊθ] Süd- OT 2
southern ['sʌðən] südlich OT 4
southwest [ˌsaʊθ'west] südwestlich OT 3
souvenir [ˌsu:və'nɪə] Andenken OT 3
spa [spɑ:] Heilbad OT 2
space [speɪs] Platz; Weltraum OT 1
spacecraft ['speɪskra:ft] Raumfahrzeug OT 4
spacewalker ['speɪswɔ:kə] Spacewalker; jemand, der im Weltraum spazieren geht **WS 3**, 110
spaghetti [spə'geti] Spaghetti OT 1
spaniel ['spænjəl] Spaniel OT 2
Spanish ['spænɪʃ] spanisch OT 1
spare [speə] übrig; zusätzlich OT 3
spark [spɑ:k] Funke OT 4
to speak [spi:k] sprechen; reden OT 1
speaker ['spi:kə] Redner(in) OT 2
spear [spɪə] Speer OT 4
to spear [spɪər] aufspießen **WS 1**, 26
special ['speʃl] besondere(r, -s) OT 1
specialist ['speʃəlɪst] Spezialist(in); Expert(in) **WS 2**, 61
to specialize ['speʃəlaɪz] sich spezialisieren OT 3
species ['spi:ʃi:z] Spezies; Art **WS 1**, 21
specific [spə'sɪfɪk] bestimmt; konkret; spezifisch OT 2
spectacular [spek'tækjələ] spektakulär OT 2
spectator [spek'teɪtə] Zuschauer(in) OT 2
to speculate ['spekjuleɪt] spekulieren; nachdenken OT 4
speech [spi:tʃ] Rede OT 2
speed [spi:d] Geschwindigkeit OT 2
to spell [spel] buchstabieren OT 1
spelling ['spelɪŋ] Rechtschreibung; Schreibweise OT 1
to spend [spend] ausgeben; verbringen OT 1
to spice [spaɪs] würzen OT 4
spice [spaɪs] Gewürz OT 2
spicy ['spaɪsi] scharf; würzig OT 4
spider ['spaɪdə] Spinne OT 1
spiky ['spaɪki] stachelig; spitz **WS 3**, 103
to spill [spɪl] verschütten OT 2
spirit ['spɪrɪt] Geist OT 2
spirit level ['spɪrɪt levl] Wasserwaage **WS 3**, 112
spite: in spite of [ɪn spaɪt əv] trotz **WS 1**, 25
to splash [splæʃ] platschen OT 2
to split [splɪt] trennen OT 3
to split up [ˌsplɪt'ʌp] sich trennen OT 2
to spoil [spɔɪl] verderben OT 2
spoilage ['spɔɪlɪdʒ] Verderben OT 4
sponsor ['spɒnsə] Sponsor(in) OT 2
to sponsor ['spɒnsə] finanziell unterstützen OT 2
sponsorship ['spɒnsəʃɪp] finanzielle Unterstützung OT 2
spoon [spu:n] Löffel OT 2
sport [spɔ:t] Sport OT 1
good sport [gʊd spɔ:t] kein(e) Spielverderber(in) OT 2
sporting ['spɔ:tɪŋ] sportlich; Sport... **WS 1**, 15
sportswoman ['spɔ:tswʊmən] Sportler(in) OT 2
sporty ['spɔ:ti] sportlich OT 3
to spot [spɒt] erspähen OT 1
sprain [spreɪn] Verstauchung OT 2
to sprain [spreɪn] verstauchen OT 2
to spray [spreɪ] sprühen OT 3
to spread [spred] verbreiten OT 4
spring [sprɪŋ] Frühling; Quelle OT 2
hot spring ['hɒt sprɪŋ] Thermalquelle OT 2
to sprinkle ['sprɪŋkl] streuen OT 2
square [skweə] Quadrat; Feld; Platz OT 1
squirrel ['skwɪrəl] Eichhörnchen OT 1
stability [stə'bɪləti] Stabilität **WS 3**, 104
stable ['steɪbl] Stall OT 4
to stack [stæk] stapeln OT 4
stadium ['steɪdiəm] Stadion OT 1
staff [stɑ:f] Personal OT 1
stage [steɪdʒ] Phase; Bühne OT 2
staggering ['stægərɪŋ] erschreckend; atemberaubend OT 4
stairs ['steəz] Treppe, Treppenstufen OT 1
stall [stɔ:l] Stand OT 4
stamp [stæmp] Briefmarke OT 1
to stand [stænd] stehen OT 1
standard ['stændəd] standardmäßig; normal **WS 1**, 16
star [stɑ:] Stern; Star OT 1
to stare [steə] starren OT 2
to start [stɑ:t] anfangen; beginnen OT 1
start [stɑ:t] Anfang OT 1
starter ['stɑ:tə] Vorspeise; Teilnehmer(in) OT 1
start-up ['stɑ:tʌp] junges Unternehmen **WS 3**, 90
to starve [stɑ:v] hungern(lassen); verhungern OT 1
to state [steɪt] erklären; festlegen **WS 2**, 74
state [steɪt] Staat; Bundesstaat OT 1
statement ['steɪtmənt] Aussage OT 1
station ['steɪʃn] Station; Bahnhof OT 1
statistic [stə'tɪstɪk] Statistik OT 3
statue ['stætʃu:] Statue OT 1
status ['steɪtəs] Status **WW**, 11
to stay [steɪ] bleiben; wohnen OT 1
steady ['stedi] ruhig; stabil OT 3
steak [steɪk] Steak OT 1
to steal [sti:l] klauen OT 2
steam [sti:m] Dampf OT 2
steel [sti:l] Stahl OT 2
steep [sti:p] steil OT 2
to steer [stɪə] steuern OT 3
step [step] Schritt; Stufe OT 1
to step [step] treten OT 4
to step in [step 'ɪn] eintreten OT 4
to step up [step ʌp] vortreten **WS 2**, 53
stereotype ['steriətaɪp] Stereotype; Klischee **WS 2**, 54
stereotypical [ˌsteriə'tɪpɪkl] stereotypisch **WS 2**, 54
steroid ['sterɔɪd] Steroid **WS 2**, 50
stew [stju:] Eintopf OT 3
stick [stɪk] Zweig OT 2
to stick [stɪk] stecken; kleben OT 1
to stick to [stɪk tə] dabei bleiben **WS 2**, 59
sticky note [ˌstɪki 'nəʊt] Haftnotiz **WS 3**, 112

stiff [stɪf] steif; starr **WS 2**, 61
stigma ['stɪgmə] Stigma **WS 2**, 72
still [stɪl] immer noch; still OT 1
to **sting** [stɪŋ] stechen OT 2
stingray ['stɪŋreɪ] Stachelrochen **WS 1**, 21
to **stir** [stɜ:] rühren OT 2
to **stock up** [stɒk 'ʌp] sich bevorraten; auffüllen OT 4
stomach ['stʌmək] Magen OT 1
stone [stəʊn] Stein OT 1
stop [stɒp] Halt OT 1
to **stop** [stɒp] anhalten; aufhören OT 1
storage ['stɔ:rɪdʒ] Lagerung OT 3
to **store** [stɔ:] aufbewahren OT 2
storm [stɔ:m] Sturm OT 2
story ['stɔ:ri] Geschichte OT 1
storyboard ['stɔ:ribɔ:d] Storyboard; Szenenbuch OT 4
storybook ['stɔ:ribʊk] Geschichtenbuch OT 2
storyteller ['stɔ:ritelə] Geschichtenerzähler(in) OT 2
storytelling ['stɔ:ritelɪŋ] Geschichtenerzählen OT 4
stove [stəʊv] Ofen OT 3
straight [streɪt] gerade; direkt OT 3; heterosexuell **WS 2**, 55
straight away ['streɪt ə,weɪ] sofort OT 2
strange [streɪndʒ] seltsam OT 1
stranger ['streɪndʒə] Fremde(r) OT 3
strategy ['strætədʒi] Strategie **WS 1**, 15
straw [strɔ:] Trinkhalm; Strohhalm; Stroh OT 4
strawberry ['strɔ:bəri] Erdbeere OT 1
stream [stri:m] Bach OT 2
streaming ['stri:mɪŋ] Streaming **WS 2**, 58
street [stri:t] Straße OT 1
strength [streŋkθ] Stärke OT 4
to **strengthen** ['streŋkθn] stärker werden; stärker machen OT 4
stress [stres] Stress; Betonung OT 1
stressed [strest] gestresst; angestrengt OT 2
stressful ['stresfl] stressig OT 4
to **stretch** [stretʃ] sich erstrecken OT 3
strict [strɪkt] streng OT 2
strike [straɪk] Streik OT 4
to **strike** [straɪk] streiken OT 4
striking ['straɪkɪŋ] auffallend OT 4
string [strɪŋ] Schnur; Saite OT 2
strip [strɪp] Streifen OT 2
to **stroke** [strəʊk] streicheln OT 3
strong [strɒŋ] stark OT 2
structure ['strʌktʃə] Struktur OT 1
to **structure** ['strʌktʃə] strukturieren; aufbauen **WS 1**, 29
to **struggle** ['strʌgl] sich anstrengen; sich bemühen **WS 2**, 53
student ['stju:dnt] Student(in); Schüler(in) OT 1
studies [stʌdiz] Studium; Wissenschaft OT 1
studio ['stju:diəʊ] Studio **WS 1**, 32
study ['stʌdi] Studie; Untersuchung OT 1
to **study** ['stʌdi] studieren; lernen OT 1
stuff [stʌf] Zeug OT 2
stuffing ['stʌfɪŋ] Füllung OT 3
stunning ['stʌnɪŋ] toll; atemberaubend **WS 1**, 28
stupid ['stju:pɪd] dumm OT 2
style [staɪl] Stil OT 2
stylish ['staɪlɪʃ] schick OT 4
sub-heading [,sʌb 'hedɪŋ] Unterüberschrift OT 2
subject ['sʌbdʒɪkt] Thema; Fach OT 1
to **change the subject** [,tʃeɪndʒ ðə 'sʌbdʒekt] das Thema wechseln OT 2
to **subscribe to** [səb'skraɪb] abonnieren; anmelden **WS 3**, 105
substance ['sʌbstəns] Substanz OT 3
substantial [səb'stænʃl] reichlich **WS 2**, 77
substitute ['sʌbstɪtju:t] Ersatz OT 3
substitution [,sʌbstɪ'tju:ʃn] Ersatz; Ersetzen OT 3
subway ['sʌbweɪ] U-Bahn; Unterführung OT 1
to **succeed** [sək'si:d] Erfolg haben OT 2
success [sək'ses] Erfolg OT 3
successful [sək'sesfl] erfolgreich OT 2
such [sʌtʃ] so OT 2
to **suck** [sʌk] saugen OT 4
sudden ['sʌdn] plötzlich OT 3
suddenly ['sʌdənli] plötzlich OT 2
to **suffer** ['sʌfə] leiden OT 4
sugar ['ʃʊgə] Zucker OT 1
to **suggest** [sə'dʒest] vorschlagen OT 1
suggestion [sə'dʒestʃən] Vorschlag OT 1
suit [su:t] Anzug; Kostüm OT 1
to **suit** [su:t] passen; sich eignen (für) **WS 1**, 36
suitable ['su:təbl] geeignet OT 4
sum [sʌm] Rechenaufgabe OT 2
to **summarize** ['sʌməraɪz] zusammenfassen OT 2
summary ['sʌməri] Zusammenfassung OT 1
summer ['sʌmə] Sommer OT 1
sun [sʌn] Sonne OT 1
sunburn ['sʌnbɜ:n] Sonnenbrand OT 2
Sunday ['sʌndeɪ] Sonntag OT 1
sundial ['sʌndaɪəl] Sonnenuhr OT 3
sunny ['sʌni] sonnig OT 1
sunscreen ['sʌnskri:n] Sonnenschutzmittel OT 2
sunset ['sʌnset] Sonnenuntergang OT 3
sunshine ['sʌnʃaɪn] Sonnenschein OT 3
sunstroke ['sʌnstrəʊk] Sonnenstich OT 2
super ['su:pər] super; besonders **WS 2**, 66
superhero ['su:pəhɪərəʊ] Superheld **WS 2**, 66
superlative [su'pɜ:lətɪv] unübertrefflich OT 2
supermarket ['su:pəmɑ:kɪt] Supermarkt OT 1
to **supervise** ['su:pəvaɪz] beaufsichtigen OT 3
supervision [,su:pə'vɪʒn] Überwachung; Aufsicht **WS 2**, 65
supervisor ['su:pərvaɪzə] Leiter(in) **WS 3**, 108
supply [sə'plaɪ] Vorrat; Lieferung OT 3
to **support** [sə'pɔ:t] unterstützen OT 1
supporter [sə'pɔ:tə] Anhänger(in) OT 3
supportive [sə'pɔ:tɪv] unterstützend **WS 1**, 14
to **suppose** [sə'pəʊz] vermuten; annehmen OT 1
sure [ʃʊə] sicher OT 1
surely ['ʃʊəli] sicherlich OT 4
surface ['sɜ:fɪs] Oberfläche OT 3
surfing ['sɜ:fɪŋ] Surfen OT 1
surgeon ['sɜ:dʒən] Chirurg(in) OT 3
surgery ['sɜ:dʒəri] Sprechstunde; Praxis **WS 3**, 106
to **surpass** [sə'pɑ:s] übertreffen **WS 3**, 105
surprise [sə'praɪz] Überraschung OT 1
to **surprise** [sə'praɪz] überraschen **WS 2**, 71
surprised [sə'praɪzd] überrascht OT 2
surprising [sə'praɪzɪŋ] überraschend OT 2
to **surrender** [sə'rendə] aufgeben; übergeben OT 4
to **surround** [sə'raʊnd] umgeben OT 4
survey ['sɜ:veɪ] Umfrage; Studie OT 1
to **survey** ['sɜ:veɪ] befragen **WS 2**, 62
survival [sə'vaɪvl] Überleben OT 2
to **survive** [sə'vaɪv] überleben OT 3
survivor [sə'vaɪvə] Überlebende(r) OT 3

suspense [sə'spens] Anspannung OT 3
suspicious [sə'spɪʃəs] misstrauisch; verdächtig OT 3
to **sustain** [sə'steɪn] erhalten OT 4
sustainability [səˌsteɪnə'bɪləti] Nachhaltigkeit OT 3
sustainable [sə'steɪnəbl] nachhaltig OT 3
sustainably [sə'steɪnəbli] nachhaltig OT 3
to **swap** [swɒp] tauschen OT 3
to **sweat** ['swet] schwitzen OT 2
sweatshirt ['swetʃɜːt] Sweatshirt OT 1
to **sweep** [swiːp] fegen OT 4
sweet [swiːt] süß OT 1; Bonbon; Nachtisch OT 1
sweetheart ['swiːthɑːt] Liebste(r); Liebes **WS 1**, 30
swelling ['swelɪŋ] Schwellung OT 2
to **swim** [swɪm] schwimmen OT 1
swimmer ['swɪmə] Schwimmer(in) OT 3
swimming ['swɪmɪŋ] Schwimmen OT 1
swimwear ['swɪmweər] Badebekleidung **WW**, 11
switch [swɪtʃ] Umstellung; Umstieg **WS 1**, 19
to **switch on** [swɪtʃ on] anmachen OT 3
swollen ['swəʊln] geschwollen OT 2
sword [sɔːd] Schwert OT 1
syllable ['sɪləbl] Silbe OT 3
symbol ['sɪmbl] Symbol OT 1
sympathetic [ˌsɪmpə'θetɪk] mitfühlend OT 2
to **sympathize (with)** ['sɪmpəθaɪz] mitfühlen (mit jmd.) **WS 4**, 140
synaesthesia [ˌsɪnəs'θiːziə] Synästhesie OT 2
synonym ['sɪnənɪm] Synonym OT 2
syrup ['sɪrəp] Sirup OT 3
system ['sɪstəm] System OT 2
systematically [ˌsɪstə'mætɪkli] systematisch **WS 1**, 24

T

tab [tæb] Tab; Tabulator OT 4
table ['teɪbl] Tisch; Tabelle OT 1
tablecloth ['teɪblklɒθ] Tischdecke OT 2
tablespoon ['teɪblspuːn] Esslöffel OT 2
tablet ['tæblət] Tafel; Tablet OT 2
to **tackle** ['tækl] tackeln; angreifen OT 2
taco ['tækəʊ] Taco OT 3
tag [tæg] Etikett; kurze Schnur, die gelochte Blätter zusammenhält OT 2
tail [teɪl] Schwanz OT 2
to **tailor** ['teɪlə] schneidern OT 4
to **take** [teɪk] nehmen OT 1
to **take apart** [teɪk ə'pɑːt] zerlegen; auseinandernehmen OT 4
to **take a day off** [teɪk ə deɪ ɒf] einen Tag freimachen OT 2
to **take for granted** [teɪk fə 'grɑːntɪd] als selbstverständlich ansehen OT 4
to **take part** [teɪk 'pɑːt] teilnehmen OT 2
to **take turns** ['teɪk tɜːnz] sich abwechseln OT 1
tale [teɪl] Geschichte OT 2
talent ['tælənt] Talent **WS 3**, 99
talented ['tæləntɪd] begabt; talentiert **WS 1**, 32
to **talk** [tɔːk] reden OT 1
tall [tɔːl] groß; hoch OT 1
tally ['tæli] Gesamtliste OT 4
tank [tæŋk] Tank OT 3
tap [tæp] Wasserhahn OT 3
to **tap** [tæp] tippen **WS 2**, 68
target ['tɑːgɪt] Ziel OT 4
to **target** ['tɑːgɪt] zielen auf **WS 2**, 80
task [tɑːsk] Aufgabe OT 1
taste [teɪst] Geschmack **WS 2**, 67
to **taste** [teɪst] schmecken; probieren OT 1
tasty ['teɪsti] schmackhaft OT 2
tattoo [tə'tuː] Tätowierung OT 3
tax [tæks] Steuer OT 4
tea [tiː] Tee OT 1
to **teach** [tiːtʃ] unterrichten; lehren OT 1
teacher ['tiːtʃə] Lehrer(in) OT 1
team [tiːm] Mannschaft; Team OT 1
teammate ['tiːmmeɪt] Manschaftskollege / -kollegin OT 2
tear [tɪə] Träne OT 2
to **tease** [tiːz] ärgern OT 2
tech [tek] technisch OT 2
technical ['teknɪkl] technisch OT 2
technique [tek'niːk] Technik OT 4
technological [ˌteknə'lɒdʒɪkl] technisch; technologisch OT 4
technology [tek'nɒlədʒi] Technologie OT 1
teen [tiːn] Teenager OT 2
teenage ['tiːneɪdʒ] Teenager... OT 3
teenager ['tiːneɪdʒə] Teenager OT 2
tooth [tuːθ] Zahn OT 2
television ['telɪvɪʒn] Fernseher OT 2
to **tell** [tel] erzählen OT 1
to **tell off** [tel ɒf] ausschimpfen OT 2
temperature ['temprətʃə] Temperatur OT 2
template ['templeɪt] Vorlage OT 4
temple ['templ] Tempel OT 1
temporary ['temprəri] befristet; temporär OT 4
tempt [tempt] locken OT 4
ten [ten] zehn OT 1
to **tend to** [tend tə] zu etw. neigen **WS 2**, 54
tennis ['tenɪs] Tennis OT 1
tense [tens] Zeitform; Tempus OT 1
tension ['tenʃn] Anspannung OT 3
tent [tent] Zelt OT 1
term [tɜːm] Semester OT 2
terrible ['terəbl] schrecklich OT 1
terrier ['teriə] Terrier OT 2
terrified ['terɪfaɪd] verängstigt OT 3
territory ['terətri] Gebiet OT 4
test [test] Test OT 1
to **text** [tekst] simsen OT 2
text [tekst] SMS; Text OT 2
textbook ['tekstbʊk] Lehrbuch OT 3
than [ðən] als OT 1
thankfully ['θæŋkfəli] zum Glück **WS 3**, 97
thanks [θæŋks] Danke! OT 1
Thanksgiving [ˌθæŋks'gɪvɪŋ] amerikanisches Erntedankfest OT 2
that [ðæt] dieser / diese / dieses OT 1
theatre ['θɪətə] Theater OT 1
theft [θeft] Diebstahl **WS 2**, 65
their [ðeə] ihr OT 1
theirs [ðeəz] ihre(r, -s) OT 3
theme [θiːm] Thema OT 2
themed [θiːmd] thematisch OT 4
themselves [ðəm'selvz] sich (selbst) OT 3
then [ðen] dann OT 1
theoretical [ˌθɪə'retɪkl] theoretisch OT 4
therapy ['θerəpi] Therapie **WS 2**, 61
there [ðeə] da; dort OT 1
therefore ['ðeəfɔːr] daher; deshalb; darum **WS 1**, 13
thermostat ['θɜːməstæt] Thermostat; Temperaturregler **WS 3**, 112
these [ðiːz] diese OT 1
thick [θɪk] dick OT 1
thigh [θaɪ] Oberschenkel OT 1
thin [θɪn] dünn OT 1
thing [θɪŋ] Ding OT 1
to **think** [θɪŋk] denken; glauben OT 1
to **think about** ['θɪŋk əbaʊt] denken an; nachdenken über OT 1
to **think of** ['θɪŋk əv] denken an; halten von OT 1
third [θɜːd] Dritte(r, -s) OT 1

thirsty ['θɜ:sti] durstig OT 1
thirteen [ˌθɜ:'ti:n] dreizehn OT 1
thirty ['θɜ:ti] dreißig OT 1
this [ðɪs] diese(r, -s) OT 1
thoroughly ['θʌrəli] völlig; durchaus **WS 3**, 106
those [ðəʊz] diese da; jene dort OT 1
though [ðəʊ] obwohl; jedoch OT 2
thought [θɔ:t] Gedanke OT 4
thought-provoking ['θɔ:t prəvəʊkɪŋ] zum Nachdenken anregend **WS 2**, 71
thoughtful ['θɔ:tfl] aufmerksam; rücksichtsvoll **WS 3**, 95
threat [θret] Gefahr OT 4
to **threaten** ['θretn] gefährden OT 4
three [θri:] drei OT 1
throat [θrəʊt] Kehle; Hals OT 4
throne [θrəʊn] Thron OT 4
throng [θrɒŋ] Menschenmenge OT 2
through [θru:] durch OT 1
throughout [θru:'aʊt] während OT 3
to **throw** [θrəʊ] werfen OT 1
to **throw up** [θrəʊ ʌp] sich übergeben OT 2
thumbs up [θʌmz 'ʌp] Daumen hoch OT 4
to **thunder** ['θʌndə] donnern OT 4
thunderstorm ['θʌndəstɔ:m] Gewitter OT 2
Thursday ['θɜ:zdeɪ] Donnerstag OT 1
tick [tɪk] Haken; Häkchen OT 1
ticket ['tɪkɪt] Eintrittskarte; Fahrschein OT 1
to **tidy** ['taɪdi] aufräumen OT 1
tie [taɪ] Krawatte OT 1; Verbindung **WW**, 11
to **tie** [taɪ] binden; zubinden **WS 2**, 61
tiger ['taɪgə] Tiger OT 1
tight-knit [ˌtaɪt 'nɪt] eng verbunden OT 4
tightly ['taɪtli] fest OT 3
tights [taɪts] Strumpfhose OT 2
tile [taɪl] Fliese OT 2
till [tɪl] bis OT 2
tiller ['tɪlər] Ruderpinne OT 3
to **tilt** [tɪlt] sich neigen OT 3
time [taɪm] Zeit OT 1
full time [ˌfʊl 'taɪm] vollzeit OT 2
in (two) months' time [ɪn 'tu: mʌnθs taɪm] in (zwei) Monaten OT 2
some of the time [səm əv ðə taɪm] manchmal OT 2
timeline ['taɪmlaɪn] Zeitachse OT 2
timely ['taɪmli] rechtzeitig; passend OT 3
timer ['taɪmər] Timer; Zeituhr **WS 3**, 112
times [taɪmz] mal **WS 1**, 12
timetable ['taɪmteɪbl] Fahrplan; Stundenplan OT 1
timing ['taɪmɪŋ] Zeitpunkt OT 3
tin [tɪn] Zinn; Dose OT 2
tinder ['tɪndə] Zunder OT 2
tiny ['taɪni] winzig OT 1
tip [tɪp] Spitze; Tipp OT 1
to **tip over** [tɪp 'əʊvə] umkippen **WS 1**, 31
tipping point ['tɪpɪŋ pɔɪnt] Kipppunkt; Trendwende **WS 1**, 28
tiring ['taɪərɪŋ] ermüdend OT 4
tired ['taɪəd] müde OT 1
title ['taɪtl] Titel OT 1
to [tu:] zu OT 1
toast [təʊst] Toast; Trinkspruch OT 2
tobacco [tə'bækəʊ] Tabak OT 4
today [tə'deɪ] heute OT 1
toe [təʊ] Zehe OT 1
together [tə'geðə] zusammen OT 1
toilet ['tɔɪlət] Toilette OT 2
tolerance ['tɒlərəns] Toleranz **WS 2**, 50
tolerant ['tɒlərənt] tolerant **WS 2**, 80
tomato [tə'mɑ:təʊ] Tomate OT 1
tomboy ['tɒmbɔɪ] burschikoses Mädchen; Wildfang **WS 2**, 55
tomorrow [tə'mɒrəʊ] morgen OT 1
ton [tʌn] Tonne OT 4
tone [təʊn] Ton OT 4
toner cartridge ['təʊnə 'kɑ:trɪdʒ] Tonerkartusche **WS 3**, 113
tongue [tʌŋ] Zunge OT 3
tonight [tə'naɪt] heute Abend OT 1
too [tu:] zu; auch OT 1
tool [tu:l] Werkzeug OT 2
toolkit ['tu:lkɪt] Toolkit; Werkzeugkiste **WS 3**, 105
toothbrush ['tu:θbrʌʃ] Zahnbürste OT 4
top [tɒp] obere(r, -s) OT 1
topic ['tɒpɪk] Thema OT 1
torch [tɔ:tʃ] Taschenlampe; Fackel OT 1
tornado [tɔ:'neɪdəʊ] Tornado OT 4
tortoise ['tɔ:təs] Schildkröte OT 1
to **toss** [tɒs] werfen; schwenken OT 1
total ['təʊtl] Gesamtmenge; gesamt OT 3
totally ['təʊtəli] völlig OT 3
to **touch** [tʌtʃ] berühren; anfassen OT 1
touch [tʌtʃ] Kontakt; Berührung OT 2
in touch [ɪn tʌtʃ] in Verbindung; in Kontakt OT 2
touchdown ['tʌtʃdaʊn] Touchdown OT 2
tough [tʌf] hart OT 3
to **tour** [tʊə] besuchen; besichten **WS 1**, 31
tour [tʊə] Reise; Tour OT 1
tourism ['tʊərɪzm,'tɔ:rɪzm] Tourismus OT 3
tourist ['tʊərɪst] Tourist(in) OT 1
tournament ['tɔ:nəmənt] Turnier OT 3
toward(s) [tə'wɔ:dz] in Richtung OT 2
towel ['taʊəl] Handtuch OT 2
tower ['taʊə] Turm OT 1
town [taʊn] Stadt OT 1
townspeople ['taʊnzpi:pl] Stadtbewohner(innen) OT 4
towpath ['təʊpɑ:θ] Treidelpfad OT 3
to **trace** [treɪs] folgen; zurückverfolgen OT 3
track [træk] Weg OT 2
tractor ['træktə] Traktor OT 2
to **trade** [treɪd] handeln **WS 3**, 89
trade [treɪd] Handwerk OT 4; Handel **WW**, 11
tradition [trə'dɪʃn] Tradition OT 2
traditional [trə'dɪʃənl] traditionell OT 2
traffic ['træfɪk] Verkehr OT 1
tragic ['trædʒɪk] tragisch OT 3
trail [treɪl] Pfad; Spur OT 2
trailer ['treɪlər] Trailer **WS 1**, 27
to **train** [treɪn] ausbilden; trainieren OT 2
train [treɪn] Zug OT 1
traineeship [ˌtreɪ'ni:ʃɪp] Praktikumsplatz **WS 3**, 92
trainer ['treɪnər] Turnschuh **WS 4**, 141
training ['treɪnɪŋ] Ausbildung OT 2
tram ['træm] Straßenbahn OT 2
trans [trænz] trans... **WS 2**, 51
transatlantic [ˌtrænzət'læntɪk] transatlantisch OT 3
to **transcribe** [træn'skraɪb] abschreiben; transkribieren **WS 3**, 96
transcriber [træn'skraɪbə] Transkribierer(in) **WS 3**, 96
transcript ['trænskrɪpt] Abschrift; Niederschrift **WS 2**, 70
to **transfer** [træns'fɜ:r] übertragen **WS 3**, 113
transferable [træns'fɜ:rəbl] übertragbar **WS 3**, 98
to **transform** [træns'fɔ:m] verändern OT 4
transgender [trænz'dʒendər] transsexuell **WS 2**, 55
transition [træn'zɪʃn] Wechsel; Übergang **WS 2**, 55
translation [træns'leɪʃn] Übersetzung OT 2
translator [trænz'leɪtə] Übersetzer(in) **WS 2**, 70

to transport [træn'spɔ:t] transportieren OT 3
trap [træp] Falle OT 4
to trap [træp] fangen **WS 2**, 55
trash [træʃ] Abfall OT 2
to travel ['trævl] reisen OT 1
travel agent ['trævl eɪdʒənt] Reisekauffrau / -mann OT 3
traveller ['trævələ] Reisende(r) OT 3
tray [treɪ] Tablett OT 2
treasure ['treʒə] Schatz OT 3
treasurer ['treʒərə] Schatzmeister(in) OT 3
to treat [tri:t] behandeln OT 2
treat [tri:t] Genuss; Vergnügen **WS 1**, 29
treatment ['tri:tmənt] Behandlung OT 4
treaty ['tri:ti] Vertrag OT 4
tree [tri:] Baum OT 1
tremor ['tremə] Zittern OT 3
trend [trend] Trend OT 4
trendy ['trendi] modern OT 2
trial ['traɪəl] Prozess OT 2
tribal ['traɪbl] Stammes... OT 3
tribe [traɪb] Stamm OT 2
tribunal [traɪ'bju:nl] Tribunal; Gericht **WS 2**, 65
trick [trɪk] Trick **WS 2**, 68
to trickle ['trɪkl] rinnen OT 3
tricky ['trɪki] kompliziert OT 4
to trigger ['trɪgə] auslösen **WS 2**, 71
trilogy ['trɪlədʒi] Trilogie **WS 1**, 31
trip [trɪp] Reise; Ausflug OT 1
to trip [trɪp] stolpern OT 2
triumphant [traɪ'ʌmfənt] triumphierend OT 3
trolley ['trɒli] Wagen; Straßenbahn (AmE) OT 2
shopping trolley ['ʃɒpɪŋ trɒli] Einkaufswagen OT 1
troop [tru:p] Truppe OT 3
trophy ['trəʊfi] Pokal OT 2
tropical ['trɒpɪkl] Tropen- OT 4
trouble ['trʌbl] Schwierigkeit; Ärger OT 2
to be in trouble [ˌbi ɪn 'trʌbl] Ärger bekommen OT 2
trough [trɒf] Trog OT 3
trousers ['traʊzəz] Hose OT 2
trout [traʊt] Forelle OT 4
truck [trʌk] LKW OT 1
true [tru:] wahr; richtig OT 1
truly ['tru:li] wirklich OT 4
trumpet ['trʌmpɪt] Trompete OT 4
trunk [trʌŋk] Kofferraum OT 2
to trust [trʌst] vertrauen OT 2
truth [tru:θ] Wahrheit OT 3
to try [traɪ] versuchen OT 1
T-shirt ['ti:ʃɜ:t] Hemd; T-Shirt OT 1
tube [tju:b] Schlauch; Londoner U-Bahn OT 1
to tuck in [tʌk 'ɪn] einstecken OT 4
tuck shop [tʌk ʃɒp] Laden; Kiosk **WS 2**, 60
Tuesday ['tju:zdeɪ] Dienstag OT 1
tuition [tju'ɪʃn] Studiengebühr(en) **WS 2**, 56
tune [tju:n] Melodie OT 4
tunic ['tju:nɪk] Tunika OT 2
tunnel ['tʌnl] Tunnel OT 3
tup [tʌp] Widder OT 2
turkey ['tɜ:ki] Truthahn OT 3
to turn [tɜ:n] drehen OT 2
turn [tɜ:n] Wende; Drehung OT 1
It's your turn! [ɪts 'jɔ: tɜ:n] Du bist dran! OT 1
turntable ['tɜ:nteɪbl] Drehscheibe OT 2
turtle ['tɜ:tl] Wasserschildkröte OT 2
tutor ['tju:tə] Tutor(in) OT 2
to tutor ['tju:tə] unterrichten; Nachhilfe geben **WS 3**, 93
tutorial [tju:'tɔ:riəl] Lernprogramm OT 4
TV [ˌti:'vi:] Fernsehen OT 1
twelve [twelv] zwölf OT 1
twenty ['twenti] zwanzig OT 1
twice [twaɪs] zweimal OT 2
twig [twɪg] Zweig OT 2
twin [twɪn] Zwilling OT 1
to twist [twɪst] Drehung OT 3
two [tu:] zwei OT 1
to type [taɪp] tippen **WS 2**, 59
type [taɪp] Art OT 2
typewriter ['taɪpraɪtə] Schreibmaschine **WS 3**, 115
typical ['tɪpɪkl] typisch OT 2
typist ['taɪpɪst] Schreibkraft **WS 3**, 96

U

ugly ['ʌgli] hässlich OT 1
umbrella [ʌm'brelə] Regenschirm OT 1
unable [ʌn'eɪbl] unfähig; nicht imstande OT 4
unacceptable [ˌʌnək'septəbl] inakzeptabel **WS 1**, 27
unaccompanied [ˌʌnə'kʌmpənid] unbegleitet OT 2
unattended [ˌʌnə'tendɪd] unbeaufsichtigt OT 4
unbelievable [ˌʌnbɪ'li:vəbl] unglaublich OT 4
uncaring [ʌn'keərɪŋ] gefühllos **WS 4**, 129
uncertainty [ʌn'sɜ:tnti] Unsicherheit **WS 3**, 98
uncle ['ʌŋkl] Onkel OT 1
uncomfortable [ʌn'kʌmftəbl] unbequem OT 2
uncommon [ʌn'kɒmən] ungewöhnlich; selten **WS 1**, 17
unconventional [ˌʌnkən'venʃənl] unkonventionell **WS 2**, 80
undecided [ˌʌndɪ'saɪdɪd] unentschieden; unentschlossen **WS 1**, 19
under ['ʌndə] unter OT 1
to undergo [ˌʌndə'gəʊ] durchmachen **WS 2**, 58
undergraduate [ˌʌndə'grædʒuət] Student(in) (ohne Abschluss) **WS 3**, 90
underground ['ʌndəgraʊnd] U-Bahn OT 1
underneath [ˌʌndə'ni:θ] unterhalb; darunter **WS 1**, 13
to understand [ˌʌndə'stænd] verstehen OT 1
underworld ['ʌndəwɜ:ld] Unterwelt **WS 4**, 128
undocumented [ˌʌn'dɒkjumentɪd] nicht erfasst OT 4
undrained [ˌʌn'dreɪnd] nicht abgetropft OT 2
undrinkable [ʌn'drɪŋkəbl] untrinkbar **WS 1**, 25
unelected [ˌʌnɪ'lektɪd] nicht gewählt OT 4
unemployed [ˌʌnɪm'plɔɪd] arbeitslos **WS 3**, 104
unemployment [ˌʌnɪm'plɔɪmənt] Arbeitslosigkeit OT 3
unexpected [ˌʌnɪk'spektɪd] unerwartet **WS 2**, 71
unexpectedly [ˌʌnɪk'spektɪdli] unerwarteterweise OT 3
unfair [ˌʌn'feə] nicht fair OT 2
unfamiliar [ˌʌnfə'mɪliə] unbekannt OT 2
unfit [ʌn'fɪt] ungeeignet; nicht in Form OT 2
unforgettable [ˌʌnfə'getəbl] unvergesslich **WS 1**, 29
unfortunately [ʌn'fɔ:tʃənətli] leider OT 2
unhappy [ʌn'hæpi] unglücklich OT 1
unhealthy [ʌn'helθi] nicht gesund OT 3
uni ['ju:ni] Uni OT 3
uniform ['ju:nɪfɔ:m] Uniform OT 1
uninhabitable [ˌʌnɪn'hæbɪtəbl] unbewohnbar OT 4

uninterested [ʌnˈɪntrəstɪd] desinteressiert **WS 1**, 14
union [ˈjuːniən] Union; Bund OT 4
unique [juˈniːk] einzigartig OT 2
unisex [ˈjuːnɪseks] Unisex...; nicht geschlechtsspezifisch **WS 2**, 54
unit [ˈjuːnɪt] Einheit OT 4
to **unite** [juˈnaɪt] sich vereinigen **WS 1**, 13
unity [ˈjuːnəti] Einheit OT 4
universe [ˈjuːnɪvɜːs] Universum OT 4
university [ˌjuːnɪˈvɜːsəti] Universität; Hochschule OT 1
unkind [ˌʌnˈkaɪnd] unfreundlich OT 3
unknown [ˌʌnˈnəʊn] unbekannt OT 3
unless [ənˈles] außer wenn OT 4
unmarried [ˌʌnˈmærid] unverheiratet **WS 2**, 52
unnatural [ʌnˈnætʃrəl] unnatürlich **WS 2**, 76
unnecessary [ʌnˈnesəsəri] unnötig; überflüssig **WS 2**, 77
unofficial [ˌʌnəˈfɪʃl] inoffiziell **WS 1**, 33
unpaid [ˌʌnˈpeɪd] unbezahlt **WS 3**, 92
unpleasant [ʌnˈpleznt] unangenehm **WS 1**, 35
unspoilt [ˌʌnˈspɔɪlt] unberührt OT 3
unsurprisingly [ˌʌnsəˈpraɪzɪŋlɪ] erwartungsgemäß OT 3
until [ʌnˈtɪl] bis OT 3
unusual [ʌnˈjuːʒuəl] ungewöhnlich OT 2
unwilling [ʌnˈwɪlɪŋ] widerwillig OT 4
to **unwrap** [ʌnˈræp] auspacken **WS 2**, 51
up [ʌp] hinauf; nach oben OT 1
upcycling [ˈʌpsaɪklɪŋ] Abfallveredlung; Wiederverwertung OT 4
to **update** [ˈʌpdeɪt] aktualisieren OT 3
to **upload** [ˈʌpləʊd] hochladen OT 3
upper [ˈʌpə] obere OT 4
upset [ˈʌpset] verärgert; traurig OT 2
upstairs [ˌʌpˈsteəz] oben; im oberen Stockwerk OT 1
upstream [ˌʌpˈstriːm] flussaufwärts OT 3
uptight [ˌʌpˈtaɪt] verklemmt **WS 2**, 52
upwards [ˈʊpwədz] aufwärts; nach oben OT 3
urban [ˈɜːbən] städtisch; urban OT 4
urgently [ˈɜːdʒəntli] dringend OT 4
us [ʌs] uns; wir OT 1
usable [ˈjuːzəbl] nutzbar; verwendbar **WS 3**, 104
to **use** [juːz] gebrauchen OT 1
useful [ˈjuːsfl] nützlich OT 1
user [ˈjuːzə] Benutzer(in) OT 2
usual [ˈjuːʒuəl] üblich OT 2
usually [ˈjuːʒuəli] normalerweise OT 1

V

vacation [veɪˈkeɪʃn] Urlaub OT 2
to **vacuum** [ˈvækjuːm] staubsaugen **WS 2**, 54
vacuum cleaner [ˈvækjuːm kliːnə] Staubsauger OT 4
vague [veɪg] unbestimmt; vage **WS 1**, 27
valley [ˈvæli] Tal OT 1
valuable [ˈvæljuəbl] wertvoll OT 2
value [ˈvæljuː] Wert OT 4
to **value** [ˈvæljuː] wertschätzen **WS 3**, 99
vampire [ˈvæmpaɪə] Vampir(in) OT 2
van [væn] Lieferwagen OT 2
to **vandalize** [ˈvændəlaɪz] mutwillig beschädigen **WS 4**, 130
vanilla [vəˈnɪlə] Vanille OT 1
to **vanish** [ˈvænɪʃ] verschwinden OT 4
variation [ˌveəriˈeɪʃn] Variante; Variation **WS 1**, 33
varied [ˈveərid] unterschiedlich OT 4
variety [vəˈraɪəti] Vielfalt; Auswahl OT 4
various [ˈveəriəs] verschiedene OT 4
to **vary** [ˈveəri] variieren **WS 2**, 56
vast [vɑːst] enorm; groß OT 4
vaulting horse [ˈvɔːltɪŋ hɔːs] Pferd (Geräteturnen) OT 3
vegan [ˈviːgən] vegan; Veganer(in) OT 4
vegetable [ˈvedʒtəbl] Gemüse OT 1
vegetarian [ˌvedʒəˈteəriən] vegetarisch OT 2
veggie [ˈvedʒi] vegetarisch OT 2; Gemüse **WS 1**, 30
vehicle [ˈviːəkl] Fahrzeug OT 2
velvety [ˈvelvəti] samtartig OT 2
vending machine [ˈvendɪŋ məʃiːn] Automat OT 1
venture [ˈventʃə] Unternehmen **WS 3**, 109
verb [vɜːb] Verb; Zeitwort OT 1
verbal [ˈvɜːbl] verbal; mündlich **WS 2**, 57
verse [vɜːs] Vers OT 3
version [ˈvɜːʒn] Version OT 2
very [ˈveri] sehr OT 1
vessel [ˈvesl] Schiff OT 3
via [ˈviːə] über OT 2
vibrant [ˈvaɪbrənt] dynamisch; lebhaft **WS 1**, 19
vice-president [ˌvaɪs ˈprezɪdənt] Vizepräsident(in) OT 4
victim [ˈvɪktɪm] Opfer **WS 2**, 64
victory [ˈvɪktəri] Sieg OT 4
video [ˈvɪdiəʊ] Videokassette; Video OT 1
video game [ˈvɪdiəʊ geɪm] Videospiel OT 2
to **view** [vjuː] betrachten; besichtigen OT 1
view [vjuː] Sicht; Blick; Aussicht OT 1
viewer [ˈvjuːə] Zuschauer(in) OT 3
viewpoint [ˈvjuːpɔɪnt] Aussichtspunkt; Standpunkt OT 3
village [ˈvɪlɪdʒ] Dorf OT 1
vine [vaɪn] Weinrebe OT 4
vintage [ˈvɪntɪdʒ] alt; klassisch; Vintage **WS 3**, 90
violence [ˈvaɪələns] Gewalt OT 4
violent [ˈvaɪələnt] gewalttätig **WS 4**, 140
violet [ˈvaɪələt] violett OT 2
violin [ˌvaɪəˈlɪn] Geige OT 1
viral [ˈvaɪrəl] viral OT 4
virtual [ˈvɜːtʃuəl] virtuell **WS 1**, 29
visible [ˈvɪzəbl] sichtbar OT 4
to **visit** [ˈvɪzɪt] besuchen OT 1
visit [ˈvɪzɪt] Besuch OT 1
visitor [ˈvɪzɪtə] Besucher(in) OT 1
visual [ˈvɪʒuəl] visuell OT 2
visualization [ˌvɪʒuəlaɪˈzeɪʃn] Visualisierung OT 3
to **visualize** [ˈvɪʒuəlaɪz] veranschaulichen OT 4
vital [ˈvaɪtl] lebenswichtig OT 3
to **vlog** [vlɒg] vloggen; einen Vlog erstellen OT 3
vlog [ˈvlɒg] Vlog; Video-Blog OT 3
vlogger [ˈvlɒgə] Vlogger(in) OT 3
vocalist [ˈvəʊkəlɪst] Sänger(in) OT 2
vocals [ˈvəʊklz] Gesang OT 2
vocational [vəʊˈkeɪʃənl] beruflich **WS 3**, 89
voice [vɔɪs] Stimme OT 2
volcano [vɒlˈkeɪnəʊ] Vulkan OT 2
volleyball [ˈvɒlibɔːl] Volleyball **WS 1**, 21
volume [ˈvɒljuːm] Lautstärke OT 3
voluntary [ˈvɒləntri] freiwillig OT 4
to **volunteer** [ˌvɒlənˈtɪə] sich freiwillig melden; ein Ehrenamt haben OT 2
to **vote** [vəʊt] wählen OT 1
vote [vəʊt] Wahlstimme; Stimme; Wahlrecht **WS 1**, 36
voter [ˈvəʊtə] Wähler(in) OT 4
vowel [ˈvaʊəl] Vokal; Selbstlaut OT 1
voyage [ˈvɔɪɪdʒ] Reise OT 3

W

waffle [ˈwɒfl] Waffel OT 3

wage [weɪdʒ] Gehalt OT 3
wagon ['wægən] Wagen OT 4
to **wait** [weɪt] warten OT 1
waiter ['weɪtə] Kellner(in) OT 1
to **wake up** ['weɪk ʌp] aufwachen OT 1
to **walk** [wɔ:k] laufen; gehen (zu Fuß) OT 1
wall [wɔ:l] Wand OT 1
wallet ['wɒlɪt] Brieftasche OT 1
walrus ['wɔ:lrəs] Walross OT 4
to **want** [wɒnt] wollen OT 1
war [wɔ:] Krieg OT 2
wardrobe ['wɔ:drəʊb] Kleiderschrank OT 1
warm [wɔ:m] warm OT 1
warmth [wɔ:mθ] Wärme OT 4
to **warn** [wɔ:n] warnen OT 2
warning ['wɔ:nɪŋ] Warnung OT 2
warrior ['wɒriə] Krieger(in) OT 2
warship ['wɔ:ʃɪp] Kriegsschiff OT 3
wartime ['wɔ:taɪm] Kriegszeit; im Krieg OT 3
to **wash** [wɒʃ] waschen OT 2
washing up [ˌwɒʃɪŋ 'ʌp] Geschirrspülen OT 2
washer ['wɒʃə] Wäscher(in) OT 4
wasp [wɒsp] Wespe OT 3
waste [weɪst] Abfall OT 3
to **waste** [weɪst] verschwenden OT 3
to **watch** [wɒtʃ] beobachten; zuschauen OT 1
water ['wɔ:tə] Wasser OT 1
waterfall ['wɔ:təfɔ:l] Wasserfall OT 1
water fountain ['wɔ:tə faʊntən] Trinkwasserbrunnen OT 2
waterhole ['wɔ:təhəʊl] Wasserloch **WS 1**, 38
watering hole ['wɔ:tərɪŋ həʊl] Wasserstelle **WS 1**, 25
waterproof ['wɔ:təpru:f] wasserdicht OT 2
wave [weɪv] Welle OT 1
way [weɪ] Weg OT 1
  all the way ['ɔ:l ðə weɪ] der ganze Weg OT 2
  Way to go! ['weɪ to gəʊ] Gut gemacht! OT 2
waypoint ['weɪpɔɪnt] Zwischenstation OT 2
we [wi] wir OT 1
weak [wi:k] schwach OT 4
to **weaken** ['wi:kən] schwächer werden; schwächen OT 4
weakness ['wi:knəs] Schwäche OT 4
wealth [welθ] Reichtum **WS 3**, 104
wealthy ['welθi] reich OT 4
weapon ['wepən] Waffe OT 3
to **wear** [weə] tragen OT 1
weather ['weðə] Wetter OT 1
to **wed** [wed] heiraten OT 3
Wednesday ['wenzdeɪ] Mittwoch OT 1
weed [wi:d] Unkraut **WS 1**, 30
week [wi:k] Woche OT 1
weekend ['wikˌend] Wochenende OT 1
weekly ['wi:kli] wöchentlich OT 4
to **weigh** [weɪ] wiegen OT 3
weight [weɪt] Gewicht OT 2
weird [wɪəd] seltsam OT 1
welcome ['welkəm] Willkommen! OT 1
to **welcome** ['welkəm] begrüßen OT 1
well [wel] also; nun OT 1
  well done [wel 'dʌn] gut gemacht OT 1
well-being ['wel bi:ɪŋ] Wohlbefinden **WS 3**, 105
wellness ['welnəs] Wohlbefinden **WS 2**, 72
Welsh [welʃ] walisisch OT 1
west [west] West... OT 1
mid-western [ˌmɪd'westən] des mittleren Westens OT 4
wet [wet] nass OT 1
wetsuit ['wetsu:t] Taucheranzug; Neoprenanzug OT 1
whale [weɪl] Wal OT 2
whaling ['weɪlɪŋ] Walfang OT 2
what [wɒt] was OT 1
whatever [wɒ'tevə] Was auch immer. OT 2
wheat [wi:t] Weizen **WS 1**, 28
wheel [wi:l] Rad OT 1
wheelbarrow ['wi:lbærəʊ] Schubkarre OT 4
wheelchair ['wi:ltʃeə] Rollstuhl OT 2
  wheelchair user ['wi:ltʃeə ˌju:zə] Rollstuhlfahrer(in) OT 2
when [wen] wann; wenn OT 1
whenever [wen'evə] jedes Mal, wenn OT 3
where [weə] wo OT 1
whereas [ˌweər'æz] während **WS 3**, 98
wherever [weər'evə] wo (auch) immer OT 3
whether ['weðə] ob OT 2
which [wɪtʃ] welche(r, -s) OT 1
while [waɪl] während OT 2
whipped cream [ˌwɪpt'kri:m] Schlagsahne OT 3
whistle [wɪsl] Pfeife OT 2
white [waɪt] weiß OT 1
whiteboard ['waɪtbɔ:d] Weißwandtafel; Whiteboard OT 1
to **whizz** [wɪz] zischen OT 2
who [hu:] wer; wen; wem OT 1
whoever [hu:'evə] egal wer OT 4
whole [həʊl] ganz OT 1
whose [hu:z] wessen OT 1
why [waɪ] warum OT 1
wicked ['wɪkɪd] böse; krass OT 2
wide [waɪd] weit OT 2
wife [waɪf] Frau; Ehefrau OT 1
wild [waɪld] wild OT 2
wilderness ['wɪldənəs] Wildnis OT 2
wildfire ['waɪldfaɪə] Großfeuer OT 2
wildlife ['waɪldlaɪf] Tierwelt OT 2
willing: to be willing [bi 'wɪlɪŋ] bereit sein OT 4
to **win** [wɪn] gewinnen OT 1
winch [wɪntʃ] Winde OT 3
wind [wɪnd] Wind OT 2
winding ['waɪndɪŋ] gewunden OT 3
windlass ['wɪndləs] Winsch OT 3
window ['wɪndəʊ] Fenster OT 1
to **windsurf** ['wɪndsɜ:f] windsurfen OT 1
windsurfing ['wɪndsɜ:fɪŋ] Windsurfen OT 1
windturbine ['wɪnd tɜ:baɪn] Windrad OT 4
wind-up radio ['waɪnd ʌp 'reɪdiəʊ] Radio mit Kurbel OT 4
windy ['wɪndi] windig OT 2
wing [wɪŋ] Flügel OT 2
winner ['wɪnə] Gewinner(in); Sieger(in) OT 1
winning ['wɪnɪŋ] gewinnend OT 2
winter ['wɪntə] Winter OT 1
to **wipe** [waɪp] wischen **WS 1**, 39
  to **wipe out** ['waɪp aʊt] vernichten **WS 1**, 39
wish [wɪʃ] Wunsch OT 2
to **wish** [wɪʃ] wünschen OT 2
witch [wɪtʃ] Hexe OT 2
with [wɪð] mit OT 1
within [wɪ'ðɪn] innerhalb OT 4
without [wɪ'ðaʊt] ohne OT 1
to **witness** ['wɪtnəs] Zeuge sein von OT 3
wolf [wʊlf] Wolf OT 4
woman ['wʊmən] Frau OT 1
wombat ['wɒmbæt] Wombat **WS 1**, 28
to **wonder** ['wʌndə] sich fragen; sich wundern OT 4
wonder ['wʌndə] Wunder OT 4
wonderful ['wʌndəfl] wunderbar OT 1
wood [wʊd] Holz OT 2
wooded ['wʊdɪd] bewaldet OT 4
wooden ['wʊdn] hölzern OT 2

woodland ['wʊdlənd] Wald; Waldfläche OT 4
woods [wʊdz] Wald OT 2
wool [wʊl] Wolle OT 3
woolly ['wʊli] wollig OT 2
word [wɜːd] Wort OT 1
wordlist ['wɜːdlɪst] Wortliste OT 2
to **work** [wɜːk] arbeiten OT 1
work [wɜːk] Arbeit OT 2
at work [ət wɜːk] bei der Arbeit OT 2
worker ['wɜːkə] Arbeiter(in) OT 2
workforce ['wɜːkfɔːs] Arbeitskräfte **WS 3**, 103
workout ['wɜːkaʊt] Fitnesstraining OT 3
workplace ['wɜːkpleɪs] Arbeitsplatz **WS 1**, 20
worksheet ['wɜːkʃiːt] Arbeitsblatt OT 2
workshop ['wɜːkʃɒp] Werkstatt OT 1
world [wɜːld] Welt OT 1
from around the world [frəm ə'raʊnd ði ˌwɜːld] aus aller Welt OT 1
worldwide [ˌwɜːld'waɪd] weltweit OT 3
worm [wɜːm] Wurm OT 1
worried ['wʌrid] besorgt OT 1
worry ['wʌri] Sorge **WW**, 10
to **worry** ['wʌri] sich Sorgen machen OT 1
to **worship** ['wɜːʃɪp] verehren **WS 4**, 136
worth [wɜːθ] wert OT 4
worthwhile [ˌwɜːθ'waɪl] lohnend OT 2
to **wrap** [ræp] einwickeln OT 2
wreath [riːθ] Kranz OT 3
wreck [rek] Wrack OT 3
to **wrestle** ['resl] ringen OT 2
wrestling ['reslɪŋ] Ringen OT 2
wrist [rɪst] Handgelenk OT 1
to **write** [raɪt] schreiben OT 1
writer ['raɪtə] Schriftsteller(in); Verfasser(in) OT 1
writing ['raɪtɪŋ] Schreiben OT 1
wrong [rɒŋ] falsch OT 1
What's wrong? [wɒts rɒŋ] Was ist los? OT 2

X
X-ray ['eks reɪ] Röntgen OT 1

Y
yacht [jɒt] Jacht; Yacht **WS 1**, 43
yard [jɑːd] Yard (= 91,44 cm) OT 2
yawn [jɔːn] Gähnen OT 2
year [jɪə] Jahr OT 1
yearbook ['jɪəbʊk] Jahrbuch OT 4
yellow ['jeləʊ] gelb OT 1
yesterday ['jestədeɪ] gestern OT 1
yet [jet] noch; schon OT 2
yoga ['jəʊgə] Yoga **WS 3**, 113
yoghurt ['jɒgət] Joghurt OT 1
you [ju] du / Sie; man OT 1
young [jʌŋ] jung OT 1
youngster ['jʌŋstə] Jugendliche **WS 3**, 98
your [jɔː] dein / Ihr; euer / Ihr OT 1
yours [jɔːz] deine(r, -s) / Ihre(r, -s) OT 3
yourself [jɔː'self] dich / sich; dich / sich (selbst) OT 2
yourselves [jɔː'selvz,jə'selvz] euch (selbst) OT 3
youth [juːθ] Jugend OT 2
youth hostel ['juːθ hɒstl] Jugendherberge OT 2
yuck [jʌk] Igitt! OT 3
yummy ['jʌmi] lecker **WS 1**, 29

Z
zebra ['zebrə] Zebra OT 1
zip line ['zɪp laɪn] Seilrutsche OT 1
zone [zəʊn] Zone OT 2
end zone ['end zəʊn] Endzone OT 2
zoo [zuː] Zoo OT 1
to **zoom** [zuːm] einzoomen OT 2
zucchini [zu'kiːni] Zucchini OT 3

Dictionary: German – English

A
abdecken to cover OT 2
Abend evening OT 1
Abendessen dinner OT 1; supper OT 2
Abenteuer adventure OT 1
abenteuerlustig adventurous OT 2
Abfahrt exit; departure OT 2
Abfall garbage, trash OT 2; waste OT 3
Abfalleimer litter bin OT 2
Abfallveredlung upcycling OT 4
abflachen to level off **WS 2**, 62
Abflug departure OT 2
abgekürzt abbreviated **WS 2**, 70
abgelegen remote OT 4
Abgeordnetenhaus parliament OT 4
Abgeordnete(r) delegate; representative; MP (member of parliament) OT 4
abgesehen von apart from OT 3
abgetropft drained OT 2
abgießen to drain OT 2
abhalten to prevent OT 4
abhängen to depend OT 2
abholen to pick up OT 2
Abholzung deforestation **WS 1**, 39
abkippen to dump OT 2
Abklärung clarification OT 4
abkühlen to cool **WS 1**, 26
abkürzen to shorten OT 4
Abkürzung abbreviation OT 2
Abmessung dimension OT 2
Abneigung reluctance OT 4
abonnieren to subscribe to **WS 3**, 105
abreißen to demolish **WS 1**, 25
abrutschen to slump **WS 3**, 93
Absatz paragraph OT 1
Abschieds... leaving OT 2
abschließen to finalize OT 4
Abschnitt segment **WS 1**, 32
abschreiben to transcribe **WS 3**, 96
Abschrift transcript **WS 2**, 70
(sich) abseilen to abseil OT 2
Absicht intention **WS 2**, 66
Absicht aim **WS 1**, 25
absichtlich on purpose OT 2
absolut absolutely OT 2
abstammen (von) to be descended (from) OT 3; to descend (from) **WS 2**, 53
Abstammung ancestry OT 3; descent **WS 1**, 33
abstoßend revolting OT 2
abstürzen to crash OT 3
Abteilung department OT 4
(ab)warten to hang on OT 4
(sich) abwechseln to take turns OT 1
Abzeichen badge **WS 2**, 60
acht eight OT 1
achten to respect OT 3
achtzehn eighteen OT 1
achtzig eighty OT 1
Ackerland farmland OT 4
Adaptierung adaptation OT 4
Adjektiv adjective OT 2

Adler eagle OT 2
Adliger nobleman OT 3
Adresse address OT 1
Affäre affair OT 4
afrikanisch African OT 2
Agentur agency OT 4
aggressiv pushy **WS 3**, 93
Ahne forefather OT 4
ähnlich similar OT 1
Ähnlichkeit similarity OT 3
akademisch academic OT 4
Akkordeon accordion OT 2
Aktion action OT 2; campaign OT 3
aktiv energetic OT 2; actively OT 4
Aktivismus activism **WS 3**, 96
Aktivist(in) activist **WS 3**, 90
Aktivität activity OT 1
aktualisieren to update OT 3
aktuell current OT 2
akustisch acoustic OT 2
Akzent accent OT 2
Akzeptanz acceptance **WS 1**, 33
Alarm alarm OT 2
alarmieren to alert OT 2
alaskisch Alaskan OT 2
albern silly OT 1
Album album OT 3
Algorithmus algorithm **WS 3**, 109
Alien alien OT 2
Alkohol alcohol OT 3
alkoholisch alcoholic OT 3
alle everybody; all OT 1
allein alone; on one's own OT 2
alles everything; all OT 1
allgemein general OT 4; overall **WS 2**, 62
  im Allgemeinen generally OT 4
alltäglich everyday OT 3
Alpaka alpaca OT 2
Alphabet alphabet OT 1
alphabetisch alphabetical OT 2
als as; than OT 1
also well; so OT 1
alt old OT 1; vintage **WS 3**, 90
Alter age OT 1
älter elderly OT 4
alternativ alternatively OT 4; alternative **WS 1**, 27
Älteste(r) elder OT 4
altmodisch old-fashioned OT 2
Ambition ambition **WS 3**, 99
amerikanisch American OT 1
  amerikanisches Erntedankfest Thanksgiving OT 2
Amsel blackbird OT 1
amüsiert amused OT 3
an at OT 1
analphabetisch illiterate OT 4
Analyse analysis **WS 2**, 74
analysieren to analyse OT 3
Analyst(in) analyst **WS 3**, 99
Analytiker(in) analyst **WS 3**, 99
Ananas pineapple OT 2
anbauen to grow OT 1
anbeten to adore OT 4
anbieten to offer OT 2
anbringen to place **WS 3**, 105
Andenken souvenir OT 3
andere(r, -s) other OT 1
  ein(e) andere(r, -s) another OT 1
ändern to change OT 1
andeuten to hint OT 4
Anekdote anecdote OT 4
anerkannt certified **WS 4**, 141
anerkennen to appreciate OT 4, to acknowledge **WS 2**, 77
Anfang start; beginning OT 1
anfangen to start OT 1; to begin OT 2
anfänglich initial **WS 3**, 108
anfangs at first OT 2; initially **WS 3**, 105
Anfangs... introductory **WS 1**, 15
anfassen to touch; to feel OT 1
anführen to cite OT 2
Anführungszeichen quotation mark OT 2; inverted commas OT 3
angeben to indicate OT 4
Angebot offer OT 2; range OT 4; offering OT 4
  ein Angebot machen to bid for **WS 3**, 102
Angelegenheit matter OT 2; affair OT 4
angelsächsisch Anglo-Saxon OT 3
angemessen appropriate OT 4
angenehm enjoyable OT 2; pleasant OT 3
Angestellte(r) employee **WS 3**, 92
angestrengt stressed OT 2
angewidert disgusted **WS 2**, 55
Angewohnheit habit OT 4
anglikanisch Anglican OT 3
angreifen to tackle OT 2; to attack OT 4
Angreifer(in) invader OT 3
angrenzen to border OT 4
Angriff attack OT 2; assault **WS 2**, 64
Angst fear OT 3
  Angst machen to scare OT 2
ängstlich afraid OT 2; anxious **WS 2**, 50
Ängstlichkeit anxiety **WS 1**, 34
anhalten to stop OT 1; to last OT 2
anhaltend prolonged **WS 1**, 25
Anhänger(in) supporter; follower OT 3
animiert animated OT 4
ankern to anchor OT 4
anklagen (wegen) to charge (with) **WS 2**, 64, to accuse **WS 2**, 77
ankommen to arrive OT 1; to get to OT 2
Ankunft arrival OT 2
  geschätzte Ankunftszeit ETA (estimated time of arrival) OT 2
Anlage facility OT 3; complex OT 4
anlegen to moor OT 3
Anlegeplatz mooring OT 3
Anleitung guidance OT 4
anmachen to switch on OT 3
(sich) anmelden to sign up OT 2; to subscribe to **WS 3** 105
Anmelder(in) applicant **WS 3**, 94
annehmen to suppose OT 1; to accept OT 2; to adopt **WS 1**, 32
Anpassung assimilation OT 4
anregen to inspire OT 4; to motivate **WS 2**, 74
anregend motivational **WS 3**, 99
Anreiz incentive **WS 3**, 98
anrufen to call OT 1
Anrufer(in) caller OT 2
Ansage announcement OT 2
ansagen to announce OT 2
Ansager(in) announcer OT 2
Ansatz approach **WS 2**, 59
anschauen to behold OT 3
anscheinend apparently OT 3
Anschlagbrett noticeboard OT 1
ansehen to look OT 1; to regard OT 4
Ansicht attitude OT 4
ansonsten otherwise OT 4
Anspannung suspense; tension OT 3
ansprechen to address **WS 1**, 37
anspruchsvoll demanding OT 4
anständig proper OT 1
anstoßen to bump into OT 4
sich anstrengen to struggle **WS 2**, 53
Anstrengung effort OT 3
Anteil percentage OT 4; proportion **WS 3**, 104
antik ancient OT 2
Antilope antelope OT 4
Antrag petition OT 3
antreiben to power OT 4
Antrieb incentive **WS 3**, 98
Antropologie anthropology OT 4
Antwort answer; reply OT 1; response OT 4
antworten to answer; to respond; to reply OT 1
Anweisung instruction OT 1; direction OT 2
Anwendung application OT 4

(sich) anziehen to put on OT 1; to dress OT 3; to attract OT 4
Anzug suit OT 1
anzünden to light OT 2
Apfel apple OT 1
Apfelsine orange OT 1
Apotheke pharmacy OT 2
Apotheker(in) pharmacist OT 2
App app OT 3
appetitlich appetizing OT 3
applaudieren to applaud OT 2
Applaus applause OT 2
Aquädukt aqueduct OT 3
Aquarium aquarium OT 2
Äquator equator **WS 1**, 13
Arbeit employment OT 4
arbeiten to work OT 1
Arbeiter(in) worker OT 2
Arbeitgeber(in) employer OT 3
Arbeits... labour **WS 2**, 63
Arbeitsblatt worksheet OT 2
Arbeitskräfte workforce **WS 3**, 103
arbeitslos unemployed **WS 3**, 104
Arbeitslosigkeit unemployment OT 3
Arbeitsplatz workplace **WS 1**, 20
Archäologe / Archäologin archaeologist OT 2
archäologisch archaeological OT 2
Architekt(in) architect OT 4
Architektur architecture OT 4
Archiv archive **WS 2**, 68
Arena arena OT 1
Ärger trouble OT 2
ärgerlich annoying OT 2
ärgern to tease OT 2; to annoy **WS 2**, 68
Arktis arctic OT 4
arktisch arctic OT 4
Arm arm OT 1
arm poor OT 1
Armee army OT 4
Armut poverty **WS 3**, 104
Art kind OT 1; type; sort OT 2, species **WS 1**, 21
  Art und Weise manner OT 3
Artefakt artefact OT 2
Artikel article OT 1
Arzt, Ärztin doctor OT 1
ärztliche Untersuchung medical OT 2
Asche ash OT 2
asexuell asexual **WS 2**, 55
Aspekt aspect OT 4
Assimilation assimilation OT 4
Assistent(in) assistant OT 4
assoziieren to associate (with) **WS 4**, 128
Ast branch OT 2
Astronaut(in) astronaut OT 3
atemberaubend breathtaking OT 2; staggering OT 4; stunning **WS 1**, 28
atemlos breathless OT 3
Atem(zug) breath OT 2
atmen to breathe OT 2
Atmosphäre atmosphere OT 3
Atom... nuclear OT 3
ätzend gross OT 3
auch also; too OT 1
  auch nicht either OT 2; neither OT 3
Audio... audio OT 2
auf on; onto OT 1
aufbauen to structure **WS 1**, 29
  wieder aufbauen to rebuild OT 2
aufbewahren to store OT 2
aufbrechen to set off OT 2
Aufdeckung exposure OT 4
Aufeinanderfolge sequence OT 3
Aufenthaltsraum lounge OT 4
Auffahrt driveway OT 4
auffallend striking OT 4
Aufführung performance OT 2
auffüllen to stock up OT 4
Aufgabe job; task OT 1; assignment OT 4
aufgeben to give up OT 2; to surrender OT 4
aufgeregt excited OT 1; frantic OT 3
aufgeschlossen approachable OT 4
aufheben to pick up OT 2
aufhören to finish; to stop OT 1
aufladen to charge OT 2
sich auflehnen to rebel OT 4
auflisten to list **WW**, 11
aufmachen to open OT 1
aufmerksam thoughtful **WS 3**, 95
Aufmerksamkeit attention OT 2
Aufmerksamkeitsdefizit-Hyperaktivitätsstörung attention deficit hyperactivity disorder (ADHD) **WS 2**, 57
aufmuntern to cheer up OT 1
Aufnahmestudio recording studio OT 3
aufnehmen to record OT 1; to soak up **WS 1**, 29
aufpassen to pay attention OT 2
  auf jdn. aufpassen to look after OT 1
aufräumen to tidy OT 1
aufrechterhalten to maintain OT 4
aufregen to annoy **WS 2**, 68
aufregend exciting OT 1
aufrichtig sincerely OT 3
Aufruf appeal OT 2
Aufsatz essay OT 3
aufschlüsseln to break down **WS 2**, 59
Aufseher(in) attendant OT 2; ranger OT 3
Aufsicht supervision **WS 2**, 65
aufspießen to spear **WS 1**, 26
Aufstand rebellion OT 3
aufstehen to get up OT 1
aufsteigen to rise OT 3
auftauchen to appear OT 3
Auftragnehmer(in) contractor **WS 3**, 102
auftreten to perform OT 2
Auftreten debut OT 4
Auftrieb geben to buoy OT 3
Auftritt gig **WS 3**, 100
auftürmen to pile OT 3
aufwachen to wake up OT 1
aufwärts upwards OT 3
Auge eye OT 1
Augenbraue eyebrow **WS 3**, 93
Augenlid eyelid OT 2
August August OT 1
Aula assembly hall OT 1
aus from OT 1
ausbauen to expand **WS 3**, 101
ausbeuten to exploit OT 3
ausbilden to train OT 2
Ausbildung training OT 2; education OT 3; apprenticeship **WS 3**, 88
ausbrechen to erupt OT 2
Ausdauer perseverance OT 4
Ausdruck expression OT 1
ausdrücken to express OT 4
auseinander apart **WW**, 11
auseinandernehmen to take apart OT 4
Auseinandersetzung argument OT 1
Ausflug trip OT 1
ausführend executive OT 4
ausführlich detailed OT 4
Ausgabe issue OT 2; expense OT 4
Ausgang exit OT 2
Ausgangssperre curfew OT 3
ausgebildet skilled OT 4
ausgemergelt emaciated OT 3
ausgeprägt distinctive **WS 1**, 32
ausgerichtet sein to be geared towards **WS 2**, 56
ausgesprochen pronounced OT 2
ausgestorben extinct OT 2
ausgezeichnet excellent OT 2
ausgleichen to balance **WS 1**, 13
ausgraben to excavate OT 2
Ausgrabung excavation OT 2
Ausgrenzung discrimination **WS 3**, 90
Aushang notice OT 1
auslachen to laugh at OT 2
Ausland: im Ausland abroad OT 2

ausländisch foreign OT 1; overseas OT 2
auslassen to skip OT 3
ausleeren to empty out OT 3
ausleihen to borrow OT 2
auslösen to trigger **WS 2**, 71
ausmachen to determine OT 4; to account for **WS 2**, 58
Ausmaß extent OT 3
Ausnahme exception **WS 2**, 56
auspacken to unwrap **WS 2**, 51
Ausreißer(in) runaway **WS 4**, 136
ausrichten to host OT 3
ausrufen to declare OT 4
Ausrüstung equipment; kit OT 2
Aussage statement OT 1
ausschimpfen to tell off OT 2
Ausschnitt clip OT 2; excerpt OT 4
Aussehen appearance OT 2
außer except OT 2
außer wenn unless OT 4
außerdem moreover OT 4; besides **WS 3**, 100
Außerirdische(r) alien OT 2
äußern to express OT 4
äußerst highly OT 4
Aussicht view OT 1
Aussichtspunkt viewpoint OT 3
aussortieren to sort out OT 4
ausspielen to act out OT 2
Aussprache pronunciation OT 2
aussprechen to pronounce OT 3
aussteigen to get out OT 1; to get off OT 2
ausstellen to exhibit OT 2
Ausstellung exhibition OT 1; display OT 2
Ausstellungsgelände showground OT 2
Aussterben extinction OT 4
Ausstoss emission OT 4
Austausch exchange OT 1
austauschen to exchange **WS 1**, 14
Auswahl selection; variety OT 4
auswählen to choose OT 1; to elect; to select OT 4
Auswahlfach elective OT 4
Auswahlliste shortlist OT 2
auswandern to emigrate OT 4
Ausweis ID card (identification card) **WS 3**, 112
sich auswirken auf to affect OT 3
Auswirkung impact OT 3
Auszeichnung award OT 2
Auszubildende(r) apprentice **WS 3**, 89
Auszug extract OT 3; abstract; excerpt OT 4
authentisch authentic OT 4
Autismus autism **WS 2**, 57
Auto car OT 1
Automat vending machine OT 1
Automobil automobile OT 4
autonom autonomous OT 4
Autor(in) author OT 2
Autorität authority OT 3
Avatar avatar OT 3
Avocado avocado **WS 1**, 34

B
Baby baby OT 1
Bach stream OT 2
Backe cheek OT 4
backen to bake OT 1
Bäcker(in) baker OT 4
Bad bath OT 1
Badebekleidung swimwear **WW**, 11
Badehaus bathhouse OT 2
Badewanne bath OT 1
Badezimmer bathroom OT 1
Badminton badminton OT 1
Bahn railway OT 2; rail OT 3; rink OT 4
Bahnhof station OT 1
Bahnsteig platform OT 1
Balance balance OT 3
bald soon OT 1
Balken beam OT 3
Ball ball OT 1
Ballett ballet OT 4
Banane banana OT 1
Band band OT 1
Bande gang **WS 3**, 104
Bank bench; bank OT 3
Banking banking **WS 3**, 103
Bankwesen banking **WS 3**, 103
Bar bar OT 1
Bär bear OT 1
Bargeld cash OT 1
Barriere barrier OT 3
barrierefrei accessible OT 2
Bart beard OT 1
Baseball baseball OT 1
basierend auf based on OT 4
Basis basis OT 4; base **WS 1**, 27
Basketball basketball OT 3
Batterie battery OT 2
Bau construction OT 4
bauen to build OT 1; to construct OT 4
Bauer, Bäuerin farmer OT 2
Bauernhaus farmhouse OT 2
Bauernhof farm OT 1
Bauherr(in) builder **WS 4**, 128
Baum tree OT 1
Baumeister(in) builder **WS 4**, 128
Baumwolle cotton OT 4
beabsichtigen to intend; to aim OT 4
Beamer projector OT 1
Beamter, Beamtin official OT 2
beängstigend scary OT 2
beantworten to answer OT 1
bearbeiten to edit OT 4
beaufsichtigen to supervise OT 3; to oversee OT 4
Becken basin OT 3
bedeckt covered OT 2
Bedenken concern **WS 2**, 37
bedeuten to mean OT 1; to signify OT 4
bedeutend prominent OT 4
Bedeutung meaning OT 1; importance OT 3; significance **WS 1**, 32
von Bedeutung sein to matter OT 2
bedienen to serve OT 1; to operate OT 3
sich beeilen to hurry OT 1; to hurry up OT 2
beeindrucken to impress OT 4
beeindruckend impressive OT 2
beeinflussen to influence OT 3
beeinträchtigt impaired **WS 2**, 61
beenden to finish OT 1; to conclude OT 3
beengt cramped OT 3
Beerdigung funeral OT 4
Beere berry OT 4
Beet bed OT 1
sich befassen mit to engage with OT 4
Befehlsform imperative OT 1
befehlshabend commanding OT 2
befragen to survey **WS 2**, 62
Befragte(r) respondent **WS 2**, 52
befristet temporary OT 4
befürchten to fear **WS 1**, 38
begabt talented **WS 1**, 32; giftet **WS 2**, 51
begegnen to encounter OT 3; to face OT 4
begehen to commit OT 3
begeistert excited OT 1; enthusiastic OT 3
Beginn beginning OT 1; advent **WS 1**, 25
beginnen to start OT 1
beglaubigt certified **WS 4**, 141
begleiten to escort OT 4
Begleitung: in Begleitung accompanied OT 3
begrenzen to limit; to border OT 4
begrenzt limited OT 4
Begriff concept OT 4
Begründung motivation **WS 3**, 91
begrüßen to welcome OT 1
behalten to keep OT 2
Behälter container OT 4; reservoir **WS 1**, 34
behandeln to treat OT 2

Behandlung treatment OT 4
behaupten to claim OT 3
Behauptung claim **WS 3**, 104
Behausung dwelling OT 4
beheben to repair **WS 2**, 64
beherrschen to master OT 4
Behinderte(r) disabled OT 4
Behinderung disability OT 2
Behörde authority OT 3
bei at; by OT 1
beide both OT 1
Bein leg OT 1
beinhalten to entail OT 4
beiseite aside **WS 3**, 98
Beispiel example OT 1
  zum Beispiel for instance OT 4
Beitrag post OT 3
beitragen (zu) to contribute (to) **WS 1**, 29
bekannt familiar OT 2
  bekannt geben to announce OT 2
Bekannte(r) acquaintance OT 3
Bekanntgabe announcement OT 2
Bekanntschaft acquaintance OT 3
sich beklagen to complain OT 3
bekommen to get OT 1; to gain OT 4
bekräftigen to reinforce **WS 2**, 54
beladen to load OT 3
beleidigen to offend OT 3; to insult **WS 1**, 26
beliebt popular OT 1
bellen to bark OT 2
belohnen to reward **WS 2**, 59
bemängeln to fault OT 2
bemerken to comment OT 3; to notice OT 4
bemerkenswert notable OT 4
Bemerkung comment OT 3
sich bemühen to struggle **WS 2**, 53
benachteiligt disadvantaged **WS 2**, 56
sich benehmen to behave OT 2
Benehmen behaviour OT 2
beneiden to envy **WS 2**, 53
benötigen to require OT 4
benutzen to use OT 1
Benutzer(in) user OT 2
Benzin petrol OT 1
beobachten to watch OT 1; to observe OT 4
Beobachter(in) observer **WS 3**, 101
Beobachtung observation OT 3
bequem comfortable OT 1
Bequemlichkeit convenience OT 4
Berater(in) consultant **WS 2**, 51; advisor **WS 3**, 91
Beratung counselling **WS 2**, 64
Beratungslehrer(in) guidance counsellor OT 3
Bereich sector **WS 3**, 96
bereichern to enrich OT 4
bereit ready OT 1
bereuen to regret OT 2
Berg mountain OT 1
bergab downhill **WS 1**, 13
Bergarbeiter miner OT 3
Bergbau... mining OT 3
Bergsteigen climbing OT 1
Bergungs... salvage OT 3
Bergwerk mine OT 2
berichten to report OT 1
berüchtigt infamous OT 4
beruflich vocational **WS 3**, 89
(sich) beruhigen to settle down; to calm down OT 2
berühmt famous OT 1
berühren to touch OT 1
beschädigen to damage OT 3
Beschädigung damage OT 3
beschäftigen to employ OT 4
beschäftigt busy OT 1; occupied **WS 3**, 111
Beschäftigung pursuit; employment; occupation OT 4
Beschallungsanlage PA (public address) system OT 2
beschämt ashamed OT 3
bescheiden modest OT 2
beschreiben to describe OT 1
beschreibend descriptive OT 4
Beschreibung description OT 1
beschriften to label OT 1
beschuldigen to accuse **WS 2**, 77
Beschwerde complaint OT 2
sich beschweren to complain OT 3
beseitigen to eliminate OT 3
Besen broom OT 4
Besessenheit obsession **WS 2**, 50
Besetzung cast OT 3
besichtigen to tour **WS 1**, 31
Besichtigungen sightseeing OT 1
besiedelt populated **WS 1**, 28
Besitz possession OT 4
besitzen to own OT 2; to possess OT 4
besitzergreifend possessive OT 1
Besitzer(in) owner OT 2
besondere(r, -s) special OT 1; particular OT 4
besonders especially OT 2; particularly OT 4; super **WS 2**, 66
besorgt worried OT 1; anxiously; concerned OT 3; anxious **WS 2**, 50
  besorgt sein to care OT 2
Besorgung errand OT 4
besprechen to discuss OT 1
Besprechung discussion; meeting OT 1
besser better OT 1
bestätigen to confirm OT 4; to acknowledge **WS 2**, 77
Besteck cutlery OT 3
bestehen to consist OT 3
bestellen to order OT 1
Bestellung order OT 1
beste(r,-s) best OT 1
bestimmen to define; to determine OT 4; to dictate **WS 2**, 54
bestimmt definitely; specific OT 2; particular OT 4
  bestimmter Artikel definite article OT 1
Bestimmungswort determiner OT 1
bestrafen to punish OT 3
besuchen to visit OT 1; to attend OT 2; to tour **WS 1**, 31
Besucher(in) visitor OT 1
beteiligt sein to be involved OT 3
Beteiligung participation **WS 2**, 58
beten to pray OT 3
Beton concrete OT 2
betonen to emphasize OT 4
Betonung stress OT 1; emphasis (on) **WS 2**, 60
betrachten to regard OT 4
Betrag amount OT 2
betreffend concerning **WS 1**, 67
Betreuer(in) guardian OT 2; carer **WS 2**, 64
Betreuung care OT 2
betrübt saddened **WS 1**, 26
Bett bed OT 1
Bettdecke duvet OT 2
betteln to beg **WS 4**, 140
Betttuch sheet OT 1
beunruhigt alarmed OT 3
Beurteilen judging OT 2
beurteilen to review OT 3; to assess OT 4; to rate **WS 3**, 107
bevölkert populated **WS 1**, 28
Bevölkerung population OT 3
sich bevorraten to stock up OT 4
bevorzugt favoured OT 4
bewaffnet armed **WS 2**, 55
Bewährung probation **WS 2**, 64
bewaldet forested; wooded OT 4
bewältigen to overcome OT 4
bewegen to move OT 1
beweglich agile OT 3
Bewegung movement OT 4
Beweis evidence OT 4

beweisen to prove OT 4
sich bewerben (um) to apply (for) OT 3; to bid (for) **WS 3**, 102
Bewerber(in) applicant **WS 3**, 94
bewerten to evaluate OT 4; to rate **WS 3**, 107
Bewertung evaluation **WS 3**, 101
bewohnbar habitable OT 4
bewohnen to inhabit OT 4
Bewohner(in) resident OT 4
bewundern to admire; to adore OT 4
bewusst aware **WS 3**, 104
sich bewusst sein to be aware OT 4
Bewusstsein awareness OT 4
bezahlen to pay OT 1
sich beziehen to refer to OT 3; to relate to **WS 1**, 34
Beziehung relationship OT 3; relation **WS 1**, 30
Bezirk district **WS 2**, 56
bezogen auf based on OT 4
bezüglich concerning **WS 1**, 67
Biber beaver OT 4
Bibliothek library OT 1
Biene bee OT 1
Bier beer OT 1
bikulturell bicultural OT 4
Bild picture OT 1; image OT 3
Bildroman graphic novel **WS 4**, 128
Bildschirm screen OT 1
Bildungs- educational OT 4
Bildunterschrift caption OT 2
billig cheap OT 2
binden to tie **WS 2**, 61
Binnenland interior **WS 1**, 13
Biografie biography OT 4
Biokraftstoff biofuel OT 3
Biologie biology OT 1
biologisch organic OT 4; biological **WS 1**, 32
bipolar bipolar **WS 2**, 73
Birne pear OT 1
bis till OT 2; until OT 3
bisexuell bisexual **WS 2**, 51
Bison bison OT 4
Biss bite OT 2
ein bisschen a bit OT 1
bitte please OT 1
Bitte request OT 1
bitterlich bitterly **WS 1**, 26
Blase bubble OT 2; bladder OT 4
blasen to blow OT 2
blass pale OT 3
Blatt sheet OT 1
Blazer blazer **WS 2**, 60
bleiben to stay OT 1; to keep OT 2; to remain OT 4
Bleistift pencil OT 1
Blick: flüchtiger Blick glimpse **WS 4**, 128
blicken to gaze **WS 1**, 29
Blindenführhund guide dog OT 2
Blitz flash OT 4
Block block OT 4
Blocker blocker **WS 2**, 55
blockieren to block **WS 2**, 69
blöd dumb **WS 2**, 65
Blog blog OT 1
Blogeintrag blogpost OT 4
Blogger(in) blogger OT 3
blond blonde OT 1
Blume flower OT 1
Blut blood OT 2
Blutvergießen bloodshed **WS 1**, 26
BMX-Rad fahren BMXing **WS 2**, 55
Boden bottom OT 1; ground OT 2
Bogen bow OT 2; arch OT 3
Bogenschütze / Bogenschützin archer OT 3
Bohne bean OT 1
bombadieren to blast **WS 2**, 68
Bonbon sweet OT 1
Boot boat OT 1
mit dem Boot fahren to cruise OT 3
Bootfahren boating OT 3
Bootsfahrer(in) boater OT 3
Bord to board OT 4
an Bord aboard OT 4
über Bord overboard OT 3
Bordkarte boarding pass OT 2
Bordstein curb **WS 2**, 64
Böse evil **WS 4**, 128
böse angry OT 1; wicked; mad (AE) OT 2
botanisch botanical OT 4
Boygroup boyband OT 2
Brachvogel curlew OT 2
brainstormen to brainstorm OT 2
Brandbekämpfung firefighting OT 2
brandneu brand new OT 2
Bratensoße gravy OT 1
brauchen to need OT 1
braun brown OT 1
brechen to break OT 1
brennen to burn OT 2
Brennholz firewood OT 4
Brennofen kiln OT 3
Brennstoff fuel OT 2
Brief letter OT 1
Briefkasten letterbox OT 1; mailbox OT 4
Briefmarke stamp OT 1
Brieftasche wallet OT 1
Briefträger(in) postman OT 2
Briefumschlag envelope OT 2
bringen to bring OT 1
Brise breeze OT 3
Brite Briton OT 2
britisch British OT 1
Brokkoli broccoli OT 1
Brombeere blackberry OT 1
Broschüre brochure OT 1; booklet OT 2
Brot bread OT 1
Brötchen bread roll OT 1
Brotlaib loaf OT 1
Brotverdiener(in) breadwinner **WS 3**, 103
Brücke bridge OT 1
Bruder brother OT 1
Brust chest OT 1
brüten to breed **WS 2**, 51
Buch book OT 1
buchen to book OT 4
Bücherei library OT 1
Bücherregal bookcase OT 1
Buchstabe letter OT 1
buchstabieren to spell OT 1
Bucht bay OT 4
Buchung booking OT 2
Büffel buffalo OT 4
Buffet buffet OT 4
Bügeln ironing **WS 2**, 54
Bühne stage OT 2
hinter der Bühne backstage OT 3
Bund union OT 4
Bündel bundle OT 2
Bundes... federal OT 4
Bundesstaat state OT 1
bunt coloured OT 1
Burg castle OT 1
Bürgermeister(in) mayor OT 3
Büro office OT 2
Bursche lad **WS 2**, 65
Bürste brush OT 2
bürsten to brush OT 4
Bus bus OT 1
Busch bush **WS 1**, 13
Busch outback **WS 1**, 13
Buschfeuer bushfire **WS 1**, 28
Buschland bush **WS 1**, 13; bushland **WS 1**, 28
Busladung busload **WS 1**, 27
Bussard buzzard OT 2
Butter butter OT 1

C

Caddie caddie OT 4
Café café OT 1
Cafeteria cafeteria OT 2
Camp camp OT 1

Camper(in) camper OT 2
Campingplatz campsite OT 2
Campus campus OT 4
Canyon canyon OT 3
Cartoonist cartoonist OT 4
Catering catering OT 3
Cello cello OT 1
Cerealien cereal OT 1
Champion champion OT 4
Chaos chaos OT 4
chaotisch disorganized OT 2
Charakter character OT 2
charmant charming OT 3
Chart chart OT 4
Checkliste checklist OT 2
Cheerleader(in) cheerleader OT 3
Chef(in) boss OT 2
Chemie chemistry **WS 2**, 56
Chemikalie chemical OT 3
Chili chili OT 2
chinesisch Chinese OT 1
Chirurg(in) surgeon OT 3
Cholera cholera OT 4
Chor choir OT 1
Chromosom chromosome **WS 2**, 61
chronologisch chronological OT 4
CO2-Ausstoß carbon emission OT 3
CO2-Bilanz carbon footprint OT 3
Comicheft comic OT 1
Computer computer **WW**, 11
Computerraum computer lab OT 2
Condor condor OT 3
Container container OT 4
cool cool OT 1
Cousin(e) cousin OT 1
Cracker cracker OT 3
Curling curling OT 4
Curriculum curriculum OT 4
Currygericht curry OT 1
Cyber-Mobbing cyberbullying **WS 2**, 71; cyberthreat **WS 2**, 75

D

da there OT 1
dabei bleiben to stick to **WS 2**, 59
Dach roof OT 1
Dachboden attic OT 2
daher therefore **WS 1**, 13
dahinter beyond OT 3
Dame lady OT 2
Dampf steam OT 2
danach afterwards OT 4
daneben gehen to backfire OT 4
dankbar grateful OT 3
Danke! thanks OT 1
dann then OT 1
Darlehen loan OT 4
darum therefore **WS 1**, 13
darunter underneath **WS 1**, 13
Datei file OT 2
Daten data **WS 2**, 54
Datenschutzeinstellungen privacy settings OT 3
dauerhaft permanent OT 4
dauern to last OT 2
Daumen hoch thumbs up OT 4
Debatte debate OT 4
Debüt debut OT 4
Deck deck OT 3
Decke ceiling; blanket OT 2
Deckel lid OT 2
definieren to define OT 4
Definition definition OT 1
definitiv definitely OT 2
dehydriert dehydrated OT 2
Deich levee OT 4
dein / Ihr your OT 1
deine(r, -s) / Ihre(r, -s) yours OT 3
Dekade decade OT 4
Dekoration decoration OT 3
dekorieren to decorate OT 2
Delfin dolphin OT 1
Demokratie democracy OT 3
Demonstrant(in) protester OT 4
Demonstration demonstration **WS 1**, 28
Demonstrativbegleiter demonstrative OT 1
denken to think OT 1
  denken an to think about; to think of OT 1
Denkmal memorial; monument OT 4
Depression depression **WS 2**, 72
derzeit currently OT 4
deshalb therefore **WS 1**, 13
Design design OT 1
Designer(in) designer OT 3
Desinfektionsmittel disinfectant OT 3
desinteressiert uninterested **WS 1**, 14
Detail detail OT 2
detailliert detailed OT 4
deutlich clearly OT 3
deutsch German OT 1
Diagramm diagram OT 1; chart OT 4; graph **WS 2**, 5
Dialekt dialect OT 4
Dialog dialogue OT 1
Diaschau slideshow **WW**, 11
Diät diet OT 3
Diäten dieting **WS 2**, 66
diätetisch dietary **WS 2**, 67
dich / sich (selbst) yourself OT 2
Dichter(in) poet OT 1
Dichtung poetry OT 4
dick thick OT 1
Didgeridoo didgeridoo **WS 1**, 23
Diebstahl theft **WS 2**, 65
Diener(in) attendant OT 2; servant OT 3
Dienst service OT 2
Dienstag Tuesday OT 1
Diesel diesel OT 3
digital digital OT 1
Dilemma dilemma **WS 1**, 14
Ding thing OT 1
Dingo dingo **WS 1**, 25
Dinosaurier dinosaur OT 1
Diplom diploma OT 4
direkt straight; directly OT 3
diskriminieren to discriminate **WS 3**, 94
Diskriminierung discrimination **WS 3**, 90
Diskussion discussion OT 1
sich distanzieren to distance oneself OT 4
Dokument document OT 4
Dokumentation documentary OT 2
Dollar dollar OT 1
Dolmetscher(in) interpreter OT 3
donnern to thunder OT 4
Donnerstag Thursday OT 1
Doppel... double OT 1
Doppelhaushälfte semi-detached house OT 4
doppelt double OT 1
Dorf village OT 1
dort there OT 1
  dort drüben over there OT 2
Dose can OT 2, tin (AE) OT 2
Dosen... canned OT 2
Downsyndrom Down syndrome **WS 2**, 61
Drama drama OT 1
Dramatiker(in) playwright OT 4
dramatisch dramatic OT 4
drastisch drastic **WS 1**, 24
draufklatschen to slap on **WS 1**, 16
draußen outside OT 1
Dreck dirt OT 4
Drehbuch script OT 2
drehen to turn OT 2; to film **WS 1**, 31
Drehscheibe turntable OT 2
Drehung to twist OT 3
drei three OT 1
dreißig thirty OT 1
dreizehn thirteen OT 1
dringend urgently OT 4
drinnen indoors OT 3
Dritte(r, -s) third OT 1
Droge drug OT 3
Drone drone OT 4

drüben over OT 2
Druck pressure OT 3
drücken to press OT 1
du / Sie you OT 1
dual dual OT 4
Dualität duality OT 4
dumm silly OT 1; stupid OT 2; dumb **WS 2**, 65
Dung manure OT 3
Dünger fertilizer OT 3
dunkel dark OT 1
dunkelhaarig dark-haired OT 3
Dunkelheit darkness **WS 4**, 128
dünn thin OT 1; skinny **WS 2**, 77
durch through OT 1
durchaus thoroughly **WS 3**, 106
Durchbruch breakthrough OT 4
durcheinander mixed up OT 2
durchführen to conduct OT 3; to implement OT 4
Durchhaltevermögen perseverance OT 4
durchmachen to undergo **WS 2**, 58
durchnässt soaked OT 3
Durchschnitt average OT 1; median **WS 2**, 62
  im Durchschnitt on average **WS 1**, 21
durchschnittlich on average OT 3
durchschweifen to roam **WS 1**, 25
durchsetzen to enforce OT 4
durchstochen pierced OT 3
dürr arid **WS 1**, 25
Dürre drought **WS 1**, 25
durstig thirsty OT 1
Dusche shower OT 1
düster bleak OT 4
Dutzend dozen OT 4
Dynamik dynamic **WS 2**, 70
dynamisch vibrant **WS 1**, 19
Dyskalkulie dyscalculia **WS 2**, 57
Dyspraxie dyspraxia **WS 2**, 61
dystopisch dystopian **WS 4**, 128

E

Ebene plain OT 4
ebenso alike OT 4
(sich) ebnen to level off **WS 2**, 62
echt real OT 1; authentic OT 4; genuine **WS 3**, 106
Ecke corner OT 1
Edelstein jewel OT 3
Efeu poison ivy OT 2
effizient efficient OT 3
egal: es ist egal it doesn't matter OT 1
  egal wer whoever OT 4
  egal wie no matter **WW**, 11
egoistisch selfish OT 3
Ehe marriage OT 3
Ehefrau wife OT 1
Ehemann husband OT 2
ehren to honour OT 4
ein Ehrenamt haben to volunteer OT 2
Ehrgeiz ambition **WS 3**, 99
ehrgeizig ambitious OT 3
ehrlich honest OT 2
Ei egg OT 1
Eichhörnchen squirrel OT 1
eifersüchtig jealous OT 2
eifrig eager OT 2
eigenartig odd OT 2
eigene(r, -s) own OT 1
Eigenschaft quality OT 3
eigenständig distinct **WS 1**, 24
eigentlich actually OT 3
Eigentum property OT 4
sich eignen (für) to suit **WS 1**, 36
Eignung qualification OT 4
eilen to rush OT 2
Eimer bucket OT 3
einbeziehen to involve OT 4
eindeutig definite OT 1; distinct **WS 1**, 24
Eindruck impression **WS 3**, 94
einfach simple; easy OT 1, basic OT 4
einfangen to capture OT 4
Einfluss influence **WW**, 11
einfühlsam sensitive OT 4
Einführung induction **WS 3**, 112
Einführung introduction OT 2; advent **WS 1**, 25; induction **WS 3**, 112
Einführungs... introductory **WS 1**, 15
Eingang entrance OT 1
Eingangsbereich entrance hall OT 1
Eingangshalle entrance hall OT 1
Eingebung inspiration OT 4
sich eingewöhnen to settle in **WS 1**, 21
eingravieren to engrave OT 4
eingreifen to intervene **WS 2**, 64
Eingriff intervention **WS 2**, 65
einheimisch local OT 2
Einheimische(r) local OT 2; native OT 3
Einheit unity; unit OT 4
sich einig sein to agree OT 1
einige some; several OT 1
Einkaufen shopping OT 1
einkaufen to shop OT 1
Einkaufswagen shopping trolley OT 1
Einkaufszentrum shopping centre OT 1; mall OT 3
Einkommen income **WS 1**, 27
einladen to invite OT 2
Einladung invitation OT 1
sich einloggen to log on OT 3
einmal once OT 2
einmarschieren to invade OT 3
einplanen to budget OT 3
einreichen to hand in OT 2
Einrichtung institution OT 4
Einrichtung amenity OT 4
eins one OT 1
einsam lonely OT 3
einsammeln to collect **WS 1**, 32
Einsatz engagement OT 4
einschätzen to judge OT 2
einschlafen to go to sleep OT 1
einschließen to include OT 2
einschließlich including OT 1
einschränken to restrict OT 4
  sich einschränken to downsize OT 3
Einschränkung restriction OT 4
Einsendung entry OT 2
sich einsetzen (für) to campaign (for) **WS 3**, 104
einsprachig monolingual **WS 1**, 24
einstecken to plug in OT 1
einsteigen to get in OT 1
Einstellung attitude OT 4
einstufen to classify OT 4
Eintopf stew OT 3
Eintrag entry OT 2
eintragen to enter OT 2
eintreten to enter OT 2; to step in OT 4
  eintreten in to join OT 1
Eintritt admission OT 2
Eintrittskarte ticket OT 1
einverstanden sein to be willing OT 4
Einwand objection OT 3
Einwanderer / Einwanderin immigrant OT 4
einwandern to immigrate **WS 2**, 53
Einwanderung immigration OT 2
Einweckglas jar OT 2
einwerben to raise OT 2
einwickeln to wrap OT 2
Einwohner(in) citizen OT 2
Einzel... single OT 3
Einzelhandel retail **WS 3**, 109
einzeln individually **WS 1**, 31
einzigartig unique OT 2
Eis ice; ice cream OT 1
Eisbahn rink OT 4
Eisbär polar bear OT 4
Eiscreme ice cream OT 1
Eisenbahn railway OT 2
eisig icy **WS 2**, 64
ekelhaft disgusting OT 2
Elch moose OT 4
Elefant elephant OT 1
Elektriker(in) electrician **WS 1**, 20

elektrisch electric OT 1; electrical **WS 3**, 109
elektronisch electronic OT 2
Element element OT 4
Elendsviertel slum **WS 4**, 141
elf eleven OT 1
Elfenbein ivory OT 4
Ellbogen elbow OT 1
Elster magpie OT 1
Elternteil parent OT 1
emailen to email OT 3
Emission emission OT 4
Emoji emoji OT 2
Emotion emotion **WS 2**, 71
emotional emotional OT 4
Empfang reception OT 1
Empfänger(in) receiver OT 4
Empfangschef(in) receptionist OT 1
empfehlen to recommend OT 3
Empfehlung recommendation OT 4
Empfehlungsschreiben letter of reference **WS 3**, 106
emphatisch emphatic **WS 2**, 66
empört disgusted **WS 2**, 55
Ende ending; end OT 1
  zu Ende gehen to run out OT 2
enden to end OT 1
endgültig final OT 2
endlich at last OT 2
endlos endless OT 4
Endung ending OT 1
Endzone end zone OT 2
Energie energy OT 2
eng narrow OT 2; closely OT 3
  eng verbunden tight-knit OT 4
Engagement engagement OT 4
engagieren to engage **WS 1**, 36
englisch English OT 1
engstirnig narrow-minded **WS 4**, 129
Enkel grandson OT 1
Enkel(in) grandchild OT 1
enorm vast OT 4
entdecken to discover OT 2
Entdeckung discovery OT 4
Ente duck OT 2
entfernen to remove OT 2
entfernt remote OT 4
Entfernung distance OT 2
entführen to kidnap OT 3
Entführer(in) kidnapper OT 2
enthalten to contain OT 4
entkommen to escape OT 2
entlang along OT 2
Entschädigung compensation **WS 2**, 64
entscheiden to decide OT 1; to opt **WS 3**, 109
Entscheidung decision OT 1
entschlossen determined **WS 3**, 90
Entschlossenheit determination OT 4
entschuldigen to excuse OT 1
  sich entschuldigen to apologize OT 2
Entschuldigung sorry OT 1; apology OT 3; excuse **WS 2**, 64
entsetzt aghast OT 3; horrified **WW**, 11
sich entspannen to relax OT 3
entsprechend equivalent (to) **WS 2**, 56
enttäuschend disappointingly OT 3; disappointing OT 4
enttäuscht disappointed OT 2
entwerfen to draft **WS 2**, 71
entwickeln to develop OT 2
  sich entwickeln to evolve OT 4
Entwickler(in) developer **WS 3**, 90
Entwicklung development OT 4; evolution **WS 2**, 70; progression **WS 3**, 110
Entwurf draft OT 2
Entzündung infection OT 2
Enzyklopädie encyclopedia OT 4
epidemisch epidemic **WS 1**, 24
Epoche period OT 3
Erbe heritage; legacy OT 4
erben to inherit OT 4
Erbse pea OT 1
Erdbeben earthquake OT 2
Erdbeere strawberry OT 1
Erde Earth OT 1; ground OT 2; soil OT 4
Erdkugel globe **WS 1**, 13
Erdkunde geography OT 1
Erdreich soil OT 4
Ereignis event OT 1; incident **WS 2**, 65
erfahren to come to know **WW**, 11; to experience **WS 2**, 53
erfahren experienced OT 3
Erfahrung experience OT 2
erfahrungsmäßig experiential OT 4
erfinden to invent OT 2
Erfinder(in) inventor OT 2
Erfindung invention OT 2
Erfolg success OT 3
  Erfolg haben to succeed OT 2
erfolgreich successful OT 2
erforderlich required OT 3
erforschen to explore OT 1
Erforschung exploration **WS 1**, 39
Erfrischung refreshment OT 4
Erfüllung completion OT 4
erfunden fictional OT 2; imaginary OT 4
ergänzend additional **WS 2**, 57
Ergänzung amendment; addition OT 4
ergattern to secure **WS 3**, 90
Ergebnis result OT 2; finding OT 4
erhalten to receive OT 2; to preserve OT 3; to sustain OT 4
erhältlich available OT 4
erheben to raise OT 2
erhöhen to raise OT 2; to increase **WS 1**, 34
erhöht increased **WS 1**, 34
sich erholen to recover OT 4
erholsam relaxing OT 2
erinnern to remind OT 2
  (sich) erinnern an to think of; to remember OT 1
Erinnerung memoir **WS 4**, 128
erkennbar recognizable OT 4
erkennen to realize OT 2; to recognize OT 3
Erkenntnis finding OT 4
erklären to explain OT 1; to state **WS 2**, 74
Erklärung explanation OT 1
erkunden to explore OT 1
erlauben to allow OT 3; to permit OT 4
Erlaubnis permission OT 2; permit; licence OT 3
erlaubt allowed OT 2
erleben to experience **WS 2**, 53
erleichtern to alleviate **WS 3**, 105
erleichtert relieved OT 3
Erleichterung relief OT 2
ermächtigen to empower **WS 3**, 109
ermöglichen to enable OT 4
ermorden to murder OT 2
ermüdend tiring OT 4
ermutigen to encourage OT 4
Ernährer(in) breadwinner **WS 3**, 103
Ernährungswissenschaftler(in) dietician **WS 2**, 77
ernennen to appoint OT 4
erneuerbar renewable OT 4
ernst serious OT 2
ernsthaft intense **WS 1**, 32
Ernsthaftigkeit seriousness **WS 2**, 64
Ernte harvest OT 3
Ernte to harvest OT 4
erobern to conquer OT 2
E-Roller e-scooter **WS 3**, 113
erratisch erratic **WS 2**, 72
erreichen to reach OT 3; to gain; to achieve OT 4
errichten to put up OT 1; to construct; to errect OT 4
Errungenschaft achievement OT 4
Ersatz substitute OT 3
Erschaffer(in) creator **WS 1**, 26
erscheinen to appear OT 3
erschöpft exhausted OT 2

erschreckend frightening OT 1; alarming; staggering OT 4
ersetzen to replace OT 3
Ersetzen substitution OT 3
erspähen to spot OT 1
erstaunlich amazing OT 1
erstaunlicherweise astonishingly OT 3
erstaunt amazed OT 3
erste(r, -s) first OT 1; premier OT 2
Erste Hilfe first aid OT 2
sich erstrecken to stretch OT 3
erteilen to issue OT 4
ertragen to bear **WS 1**, 34
ertrinken to drown OT 3
erwachsen grown up OT 2
Erwachsene(r) adult OT 1
erwähnen to mention OT 2
erwarten to expect OT 2
Erwartung expectation OT 4
erwartungsgemäß unsurprisingly OT 3
erweitert extended **WS 2**, 53
erzählen to tell OT 1
Erzähler(in) narrator OT 2
erzeugen to produce OT 3; to generate OT 4
es it OT 1
Esel donkey OT 4
essen to eat OT 1
Essen food OT 1
Essensausgabe food bank **WS 3**, 104
Esslöffel tablespoon OT 2
Esszimmer dining room OT 1
ethisch ethical OT 3
ethnisch ethnic **WS 1**, 33
Etikett tag OT 2, label **WS 4**, 141
etwa approximately **WW**, 10
etwas some OT 1; something; slightly OT 3
euch (selbst) yourselves OT 3
euer / Ihr your OT 1
Europäer(in) European OT 3
evakuieren to evacuate OT 4
Evakuierung evacuation OT 4
Evolution evolution **WS 2**, 70
Exekutive executive OT 4
Existenz existence OT 4
existieren to exist OT 3
Expedition expedition OT 2
Experiment experiment OT 2
experimentieren to experiment OT 4
Experte(in) expert OT 3; specialist **WS 2**, 61
explodieren to explode **WS 1**, 25
Exploration exploration **WS 1**, 39
Exporteur(in) exporter **WS 1**, 28
Extra... extra OT 1
extrem extremely OT 3; extreme OT 4; drastic **WS 1**, 24
Extrem extreme OT 4

F

fabelhaft fabulous OT 2
Fabrik factory OT 2
Fach subject OT 1
Facharbeit coursework OT 4
Fachzeitschrift journal OT 3
fähig capable OT 4
fähig sein to be able OT 2
Fähigkeit ability OT 4; capacity **WS 2**, 72
Fahne flag **WW**, 10
Fahranfänger(in) learner OT 3
Fahrbahn lane OT 4
fahren to go; to drive OT 1; to motor OT 3; to ride **WS 2**, 29
Fahrer(in) driver OT 2
Fahrplan timetable OT 1
Fahrrad bike OT 1; bicycle OT 3
mit dem Fahrrad fahren to cycle OT 1
Fahrt drive **WS 1**, 19
Fahrt journey; ride OT 1
Fahrzeug vehicle OT 2
Fakt fact OT 1
Faktor factor OT 3
Fall case OT 1
Falle trap OT 4
fallen to fall OT 1; drop OT 4; to decrease **WS 2**, 62
fallen lassen to drop OT 1
falls if OT 1
Fallschirm springen to parachute OT 4
Fallschirmspringer(in) skydiver **WS 1**, 29
falsch incorrectly **WS 2**, 66
Familie family OT 1
Fan fan OT 1
Fanatiker(in) fanatic **WS 1**, 15
fangen to catch OT 1; to trap **WS 2**, 55
Fantasie fantasy OT 2
fantastisch fantastic OT 1
Fantasy fantasy OT 2
FAQ FAQ OT 3
Farbe colour OT 1
färben to dye OT 3
farbenfroh colourful OT 3
farbig coloured OT 1
fast almost; nearly OT 2
Faszination fascination OT 3
faszinieren to fascinate OT 4
faszinierend fascinating OT 2; intriguing **WS 2**, 72
faul lazy OT 2
Fausthandschuh mitten OT 4
favorisiert favoured OT 4
Feder feather OT 2
Federtasche pencil case OT 1
Feedback feedback OT 2
fegen to sweep OT 4
fehlend missing OT 1
Fehler mistake OT 1
fehlerhaft incorrectly **WS 2**, 66
fehlschlagen to backfire OT 4
Feier party OT 1; celebration; ceremony OT 2
feierlich ceremonial OT 3
feiern to celebrate OT 3
Feind(in) enemy OT 3
Feinkostladen deli **WS 1**, 15
Feld field; square; space OT 1
Feldfrüchte crop OT 3
Fell fur OT 4
Felsen cliff **WS 1**, 24
Fenster window OT 1
Ferienlager camp OT 1
fern far-off OT 2; faraway **WS 1**, 28
Fernbedienung remote OT 3
Ferne: aus der Ferne remotely OT 4
Fernglas binoculars OT 2
Fernsehen TV OT 1
Fernseher television OT 2
fertigstellen to finalize OT 4
fesseln to engage **WS 1**, 36
fest tightly OT 3; firmly; solid OT 4
Fest festival OT 1; feast OT 3
festhalten to grasp **WS 2**, 61
Festival festival OT 1
Festivalbesucher(in) festival-goer OT 4
Festland mainland OT 3
festlegen to state **WS 2**, 74
festnehmen to capture OT 4
Festnetz landline OT 4
festsetzen to prescribe **WS 2**, 56
Festung fort OT 2
Festzelt marquee OT 2
Fett fat OT 2
fettgedruckt bold OT 1
feucht humid OT 4
Feuer fire OT 2
Feuerlöscher fire extinguisher **WS 3**, 113
Feuermacher(in) fire-builder OT 2
Feuerwehrfrau firefighter OT 2
Feuerwehrmann firefighter OT 2
Feuerwerk fireworks OT 3
Figur figure OT 3
fiktiv imaginary OT 4
Film film OT 1; movie OT 2
Filmaufnahmen footage OT 4
Filmemacher(in) filmmaker OT 4
filmen to film **WS 1**, 31
Filmmaterial footage OT 4

Filmrolle roll OT 2
Filter filter OT 4
Filzstift marker OT 1
Finalist(in) finalist **WS 3**, 109
finanziell financial OT 4
finanziell unterstützen to sponsor OT 2
finanzieren to finance OT 4
finden to find OT 1
Finger finger OT 1
Fingernagel fingernail OT 2
Fisch fish OT 1
Fischer fisherman OT 2
Fischerei fishing OT 3
Fischstäbchen fish finger OT 1
sich fit halten to keep fit OT 2
Fitness fitness **WS 2**, 66
Fitnesstraining workout OT 3
Flachland plain OT 4
Flaggschiff flagship OT 3
Flamingo flamingo OT 2
Flasche bottle OT 1
flauschig fluffy OT 2
Fleck patch **WS 3**, 91
Fledermaus bat OT 1
Fleisch meat OT 1
Fleischklößchen meatball OT 1
flexibel flexible **WS 3**, 92
Flicken patch **WS 3**, 91
fliegen to fly OT 1
Fliese tile OT 2
fließen to flow OT 1
fließend fluent OT 3; flowing **WS 3**, 95
Floh flea **WS 3**, 91
Flora flora OT 4
florieren to prosper OT 2
Flotte fleet OT 3
Fluchtweg fire escape **WS 3**, 113
Flug flight OT 1
Flugblatt handout OT 4
Flügel wing OT 2
Fluggesellschaft airline **WS 3**, 111
Flughafen airport OT 1
Flugzeug plane OT 1; airplane OT 2; aeroplane OT 4
Fluss river OT 1
flussaufwärts upstream OT 3
flüssig liquid OT 2
Flut flood OT 2; flooding **WS 1**, 34
Flyer flyer OT 4
fokusieren to focus OT 2
Folge consequence; sequel OT 4
Fortsetzung sequel OT 4
folgen to follow OT 2; to trace OT 3
folgerichtig logical **WS 1**, 36
Folie slide OT 1; foil OT 2
Folklore folklore **WS 1**, 26
fördern to promote OT 4
Förderung grant OT 4
Forelle trout OT 4
Form form; shape OT 1
Format format **WS 3**, 94
Formation formation **WS 1**, 26
Formel formula OT 2
formell formal OT 3
formen to shape OT 4
förmlich formal OT 3
Formular form OT 4
forschen to research OT 4
Forscher(in) researcher OT 2; explorer OT 3
Forschung research OT 2
Forstbeamter, -beamtin park ranger OT 2
Förster(in) ranger OT 3
Fortschreiten progression **WS 3**, 110
fortschreiten to progress **WS 2**, 50
Fortschritt advance; progress OT 4
fortschrittlich progressive OT 1
Forum forum OT 2; panel OT 4
fossil fossil OT 3
Foto photograph OT 1
Fotoapparat camera OT 1
Fotograf(in) photographer OT 2
Foul foul OT 3
foulen to foul OT 3
Fracht freight OT 2
Frachtkahn barge OT 3
fracken to frack **WS 1**, 28
Frage question OT 1
Fragebogen questionnaire OT 1
fragen to ask OT 1; to question OT 4
sich fragen to wonder OT 4
französisch French OT 1
Frau Mrs, Ms; woman; wife OT 1
Fräulein Miss OT 2
frech cheeky OT 3
frei free OT 1
im Freien outdoor OT 2
Freiberufler(in) freelancer **WS 3**, 102
freiberuflich freelance **WS 3**, 102
Freiheit liberty OT 2; freedom OT 3
Freiheitsstrafe custodial sentence **WS 2**, 65
Freitag Friday OT 1
freiwillig optional; voluntary OT 4
sich freiwillig melden to volunteer OT 2
Freizeit leisure OT 3
Freizeit... recreational OT 3
fremd foreign OT 1
Fremde(r) stranger OT 3
Freude pleasure OT 1; happiness **WS 3**, 99
freuen: sich auf etwas freuen to look forward to OT 1
Freund(in) friend OT 1
freundlich friendly; kind OT 1
Freundlichkeit friendliness OT 4
Frieden peace OT 3
friedlich peaceful OT 3
frisch fresh OT 3
Fritte chip OT 1
frittiert fried OT 2
froh glad OT 2
fröhlich cheerful OT 2
fromm religious OT 3
früh early OT 1
früher previous OT 4
frühere(r) former **WS 2**, 69
Frühling spring OT 2
Frühstück breakfast OT 1
Frühstücksflocken cereal OT 1
frustriert frustrated OT 4
Fuchs fox OT 1
(sich) fühlen to feel OT 1
führen to guide OT 1; to lead OT 3
führend leading OT 2
Führer(in) guide OT 1
Führung leadership OT 2
füllen to fill OT 1
Füllung stuffing OT 3
Fundament foundation OT 4
fünf five OT 1
fünfzehn fifteen OT 1
fünfzig fifty OT 1
Funke spark OT 4
Funktion function OT 4
für for OT 1; in favour OT 4
Furcht fear OT 3
furchtbar horrible OT 2
Fürsprecher(in) advocate (for) **WS 2**, 73
Fürwort pronoun OT 1
Fuß foot OT 1; base **WS 1**, 27
Fußabdruck footprint OT 2
Fußball football OT 1; soccer OT 2
Fußboden floor OT 1
Fussel fuzz OT 4
Fußknöchel ankle OT 1
Fußstapfen footstep **WS 2**, 59
füttern to feed OT 2
Füttern feeding OT 2

G

Gabelstapler forklift **WS 3**, 112
Gähnen yawn OT 2
Galerie gallery OT 1
Gallone gallon OT 3
Gamer(in) gamer OT 4

ganz whole OT 1; completely OT 4
ganze(r, -s) entire OT 3
ganztags full-time **WS 2**, 53
Garage garage OT 4
garantieren to guarantee OT 4
Garderobe cloakroom OT 4
Garnele prawn OT 3
Garten garden OT 1
Gartenarbeit gardening OT 1
Gärtner(in) gardener OT 4
Gas gas OT 4
Gaskocher gas cooker OT 3
Gasse lane OT 4
Gast guest OT 2
Gästebuch guestbook OT 2
Gastfreundlichkeit hospitality OT 2
Gastgeber(in) host OT 3
Gasthaus inn OT 2
Gebäude building OT 1
geben to give OT 1
Gebet prayer OT 4
Gebiet area OT 1; territory OT 4
Gebirge mountain range OT 4
geboren sein to be born OT 2
gebraten roast OT 1
Gebühr fee OT 3
Geburt birth OT 2
Geburtsdatum date of birth OT 2
Geburtsort birthplace OT 4
Geburtstag birthday OT 1
Gebüsch bush **WS 1**, 13
Gedächtnis memory OT 2
Gedanke thought OT 4
Gedicht poem OT 1
gedruckt printed **WS 1**, 24
geeignet fit OT 2; suitable OT 4
Gefahr danger OT 2; threat; risk OT 4
gefährden to threaten OT 4; to endanger **WS 1**, 28
gefährdet endangered OT 2
gefährlich dangerous OT 1; hazardous OT 4
gefangen nehmen to arrest OT 4
Gefängnis prison OT 4
Geflügel poultry OT 2
Gefrierschrank freezer OT 3
gefroren frozen OT 4
Gefühl feeling OT 2; emotion **WS 2**, 71
gefühllos uncaring **WS 4**, 129
gegen against OT 1
Gegend area OT 1
gegenseitig each other OT 3
Gegenstand object OT 1; item OT 3
Gegenteil opposite OT 1; contrast OT 3
Gegner(in) opponent OT 2
gehackt chopped OT 2
Gehalt wage OT 3; salary **WS 3**, 95
Geheimnis secret OT 2, mystery **WS 4**, 128
gehen to go; to walk OT 1
Geheul howl **WS 1**, 25
Gehirn brain OT 2
gehorchen obey OT 3
  nicht gehorchen to disobey OT 3
gehören to belong OT 2
Geige violin OT 1
Geist spirit; ghost OT 2
Geisteswissenschaften humanities OT 4
geistig mental OT 4
Gel gel OT 2
Geländer rail OT 3
geländetauglich off-road OT 2
gelangweilt bored OT 1
gelb yellow OT 1
Geld money OT 1
Geldgeber(in) investor OT 4
Geldmittel fund OT 4
gelegen located; situated OT 4
Gelegenheit opportunity OT 2; occasion OT 3
gelegentlich occasionally OT 4
gemächlich ponderously OT 3
Gemälde painting OT 1
gemäß according to OT 4
Gemeindeland common OT 2
Gemeinschaft community OT 2
gemischt blended **WS 2**, 52
gemischtgeschlechtlich co-ed, co-educational OT 2
Gemüse vegetable OT 1; veggie **WS 1**, 30
genau just OT 1; exact OT 2; accurate OT 4
genehmigen to approve OT 4
Generalisierung generalization **WS 2**, 56
Generation generation OT 3
generell general OT 4
genetisch genetic **WS 2**, 61
genial brilliant OT 1
genießen to enjoy OT 1
Genre genre **WS 4**, 141
genug enough OT 1
Genuss treat **WS 1**, 29
Geocache geocache OT 2
Geocaching geocaching OT 2
Geografie geography OT 1
geografisch geographical OT 4
Geologie geology OT 2
Gepäck luggage OT 4
Gepard cheetah OT 3
gerade straight OT 3; currently OT 4
Gerät appliance; device OT 3; gadget OT 4
Geräusch sound; noise OT 1
gerecht fair OT 1
Gericht dish OT 2; court OT 4; tribunal **WS 2**, 65
gernhaben to like OT 1
Gesamtliste tally OT 4
Gesamtmenge total OT 3
Gesang vocals OT 2
Geschäft(e) business OT 3; deal **WS 1**, 21
Geschäftsführer(in) manager OT 1; Chief Executive Officer (CEO) **WS 3**, 111
Geschäftsführung management OT 4
Geschäftsmann, -frau businessman, -woman OT 4
geschehen to happen OT 1
Geschenk gift OT 1
Geschichte history OT 1
Geschichtenbuch storybook OT 2
Geschichtenerzählen storytelling OT 4
Geschichtenerzähler(in) storyteller OT 2
geschichtlich historical OT 2
Geschick skill OT 1
geschickt skilled OT 4
Geschirr dishes OT 2
Geschirrspülen washing up OT 2
Geschlecht gender OT 4; sex **WS 2**, 52
geschlechtslos genderless **WS 2**, 54
geschlechtsneutral gender-neutral **WS 2**, 54
geschlechtsspezifisch gendered **WS 2**, 54
Geschlechtswort article OT 1
geschlossen closed OT 1
Geschmack taste **WS 2**, 67
Geschöpf creature **WS 1**, 26
Geschwindigkeit speed OT 2; rate OT 4
Geschwister(kind) sibling **WS 1**, 27
geschwollen swollen OT 2
Gesellschaft society; organization OT 3
gesellschaftlich social OT 3
Gesetz law OT 3; bill OT 4; act **WS 1**, 43
gesetzgebend legislative OT 4
Gesicht face OT 1
Gesichts- facial OT 4
gespannt curious OT 4
Gespräch conversation OT 1
gesprächig chatty **WS 1**, 36
Gesprächs... conversational **WS 1**, 29
Geste gesture **WS 3**, 93
gestern yesterday OT 1
gestresst stressed OT 2
gesund healthy OT 2
Gesundheit health OT 3
Gesundheitsfürsorge healthcare OT 4
Getränk drink OT 1

Getreide crop OT 3, grain **WS 2**, 66
getrennt separate OT 2; selective OT 4
getrocknet dried OT 3
Gewalt violence OT 4
gewalttätig violent **WS 4**, 140
Gewicht weight OT 2
Gewinn prize OT 1; profit OT 4
gewinnen to win OT 1
gewinnend winning OT 2
Gewinner(in) winner OT 1
Gewissheit certainty OT 4
Gewitter thunderstorm OT 2; rainstorm **WS 1**, 38
gewöhnlich commonly **WW**, 10
gewunden winding OT 3
Gewürz spice; seasoning OT 2
gewürzt spicy OT 4
gießen to pour OT 1
giftig poisonous **WS 1**, 35
Gig gig **WS 3**, 100
Gipfel peak OT 4
Gips plaster OT 1
Giraffe giraffe OT 1
Gitarre guitar OT 1
Gitarrist(in) guitarist OT 4
Gladiator(in) gladiator OT 2
glamourös glamorous OT 4
  glamouröses Zelten glamping OT 4
Glas glass OT 1
glatt slippery OT 3; smooth OT 4
Glaube faith; belief OT 3
glauben to believe OT 2
gleich same OT 1; equal OT 4
gleichberechtigt equal OT 4
Gleichberechtigung equality **WS 1**, 43
gleichzeitig simultaneous **WS 3**, 107
Gleitschirmfliegen paragliding **WS 3**, 107
global global OT 4
Globus globe **WS 1**, 13
Glocke bell OT 1
Glück luck OT 1; fortune OT 3; happiness **WS 3**, 99
  Glück haben to be lucky OT 3
  zum Glück thankfully **WS 3**, 97
glücklich happy OT 1; fortunate OT 3; lucky OT 4
glücklicherweise luckily OT 3
Glückwünsche congratulations OT 2
Glühbirne light bulb OT 4
glühend scorching **WS 1**, 21
Gold gold OT 2
golden golden OT 2
Goldrausch gold rush **WS 1**, 17
Golf golf OT 4
Golfer(in) golfer OT 4
Gott God OT 3
Gouverneur(in) governor OT 3
graben to dig **WS 1**, 28
Grad degree **WS 1**, 28
Grafiken graphics OT 3
Gramm gram OT 2
Grammatik grammar OT 1
Gras grass OT 1
Grasland grassland OT 4
gratulieren to congratulate OT 2
grau grey OT 1
grausam cruel OT 3
gravieren to engrave OT 4
greifen to grab OT 3; to grasp **WS 2**, 61
Gremium panel OT 4
Grenze border OT 3; limit; boundary OT 4
Grieche / Griechin Greek OT 2
griesgrämig grouchy OT 2
Griff handle OT 2
Grillen barbecue OT 2
grinsen to grin OT 2
Grippe influenza **WS 1**, 24
Grizzlybär grizzly OT 2
groß big, tall, large; great OT 1; vast OT 4
großartig magnificent **WS 1**, 29
Größe size OT 2
Großeltern grandparents OT 1
Großmutter grandmother OT 1
Großvater grandfather OT 1
Grube pit **WS 3**, 103
grün green OT 1
Grund reason OT 1
Grund... basic OT 4
gründen to found; to form OT 4; to establish **WS 1**, 17
Grundlage basis; foundation OT 4
grundlegend radical OT 4
grundsätzlich basic OT 4
Grundschule primary school OT 1; elementary school OT 2
Grünland grassland OT 4
Gruppe group OT 1
Gruppenfläche breakout area **WS 3**, 112
gruppieren to group OT 4
gruselig creepy **WS 1**, 13
Gruß greeting OT 2
  militärischer Gruß salute OT 3
  mit freundlichen Grüßen sincerely OT 3
grüßen to greet; to hail OT 2
Gummi rubber OT 1
günstig convenient OT 4
Gurke cucumber OT 1
gut good OT 1
  gut aussehend handsome OT 1
  gut gemacht well done OT 1
Güter goods OT 3
Gutschein coupon OT 2
Gymnastik gymnastics OT 1

H

Haare hair OT 1
Haarschnitt haircut OT 2
haben to have got OT 1; to feature OT 2
Habitat habitat **WS 1**, 34
Hackbraten meat loaf OT 3
Hackfleischbällchen meatball OT 1
Hafen port OT 2; harbour OT 4
Haferbrei porridge **WS 2**, 77
Haftnotiz sticky note **WS 3**, 112
Hähnchen chicken OT 1
Hai shark OT 2
Häkchen tick OT 1
Haken tick OT 1
halb half OT 1; halfway OT 4
halb... semi- OT 3
Halbinsel peninsula **WS 1**, 32
halbwegs halfway OT 4
Halle hall OT 1
Hallo! hello OT 1
Halloween Halloween OT 2
Hals neck OT 1; throat OT 4
Halsband collar OT 2
Halskette necklace OT 3
Halt stop OT 1
halten to hold OT 1
Haltestelle halt OT 2
Hamburger burger OT 1
Hamster hamster OT 1
Hand hand OT 1
  mit der Hand schreiben to handwrite **WS 3**, 103
Handapparat handset OT 2
Handarbeit handicraft OT 4
Handbuch handbook; manual OT 3
Handel trade **WW**, 11; commerce **WS 3**, 88
handeln to trade **WS 3**, 89
Handgelenk wrist OT 1
handhaben to handle OT 4
Händler(in) merchant OT 3
Handlung plot OT 3
Handout handout OT 4
Handschrift handwriting OT 2
Handschuh glove OT 1
Handtasche handbag OT 3
Handtuch towel OT 2
Handvoll handful OT 4
Handwerk handicraft; trade; craft OT 4

Handy mobile phone OT 1; cell phone OT 4
Harpune harpoon OT 4
hart hard; tough OT 2
hassen to hate OT 1; to loath **WS 1**, 25
hässlich ugly OT 1
Haufen heap **WS 1**, 16
häufig frequent OT 3; common **WW,** 10
Häufigkeit frequency OT 3
Haupt primary; main OT 1; core OT 4
Hauptgang main course OT 1
hauptsächlich generally OT 4
Hauptstadt capital OT 1
Hauptverkehrszeit rush hour OT 1
Hauptwort noun OT 1
Haus house OT 1
Hausarbeit housework OT 1; chore OT 4
Hausaufgaben homework OT 1
Hausboot narrowboat OT 3
Häuschen cottage OT 3
Hausfrau housewife **WS 3**, 103
Haushälter(in) housekeeper OT 3
Haushalts... household OT 4
häuslich household OT 4
Hausmeister(in) caretaker OT 1
Haustier pet OT 1
Haut skin OT 2
heben to lift OT 3
heften to pin OT 1
Heidelandschaft moor OT 3
heil in one piece OT 2
Heilbad spa OT 2
heilig sacred OT 4
Heilige(r) saint OT 3
Heilkraut herb OT 3
Heimat homeland **WS 1**, 28
Heimweh homesickness **WS 1**, 30
  voll Heimweh homesick OT 2
heiraten to marry OT 1; to wed OT 3
heiß hot OT 1
heizen to heat OT 2
hektisch frantic OT 3; hectic OT 4
Held(in) hero OT 4
helfen to help OT 1
Helfer(in) helper **WS 3**, 96
Helm helmet OT 1
Hemd shirt OT 1
Hemisphäre hemisphere **WS 1**, 13
Henne hen OT 4
heraus out OT 1
herausfinden to find out OT 2
herausfließen to empty out OT 3
herausfordern to challenge OT 4
Herausforderung challenge OT 3
Herausgeber(in) editor OT 2
herausragend outstanding OT 3
Herbst autumn OT 2
Herd cooker OT 3
Herde herd **WS 1**, 25
Herr Mr OT 1; lord OT 2
herrisch bossy OT 3
herrlich magnificent **WS 1**, 29
herrschen to rule OT 2
Herrscher(in) monarch OT 4
herstellen to manufacture OT 4
herumhängen to hang out OT 3
herumschweifen to roam **WS 1**, 25
herunterladen to download OT 3
sich hervortun to excel OT 4
Herz heart OT 2
heterosexuell heterosexual **WS 2**, 55; straight **WS 2**, 55
Heureka-Erlebnis eureka moment OT 4
heute today OT 1
  heute Abend tonight OT 1
heutzutage nowadays OT 3
Hexe witch OT 2
Hi-Fi-Anlage hi-fi OT 3
hier here OT 1
Highway highway OT 3
Hilfe aid **WS 2**, 59
Hilfe relief OT 2
hilfreich helpful OT 1
Himbeere raspberry OT 1
Himmel sky OT 1
hinauf up OT 1
Hindernis obstacle OT 4
hinduistisch Hindu OT 1
hineinspringen to dive OT 3
hinfallen to fall over OT 2
hinrichten to execute OT 3
hinten at the back OT 3
  nach hinten backwards OT 3
hinter behind OT 1
Hintergrund... background OT 3
Hinterhof backyard **WS 2**, 65
Hinterland outback **WS 1**, 13
hinterlassen to leave behind OT 2
hinüber across OT 1
hin und wieder occasionally OT 4
hinunter down OT 1
Hinweis clue OT 1; prompt OT 3; cue **WS 2**, 61
hinzufügen to add OT 1
Hirsch deer OT 1
Hirschleder deerskin OT 3
Hirte / Hirtin herder OT 3
hispanisch Hispanic OT 3
Historiker(in) historian OT 2
historisch historic OT 2
Hitzewelle heatwave **WS 1**, 28
Hobby hobby OT 1
hoch high; tall OT 1
hochhackig high-heeled OT 3
hochladen to upload OT 3
Hochschule college OT 2
höchst highly OT 4
höchste(r, -s) highest OT 1
Hochwasser flood OT 2
Hockey hockey OT 1
Hof farmyard OT 2
hoffen to hope OT 1
hoffentlich hopefully OT 3
hoffnungslos hopeless OT 4
hoffnungsvoll hopeful OT 4
höflich polite OT 1
Höhe height OT 1
Höhepunkt high OT 1
Höhle cave OT 3
Hölle hell **WS 4**, 137
Hologramm hologram OT 2
holprig bumpy OT 4
Holz wood OT 2
hölzern wooden OT 2
Holzhacken wood cutting OT 2
Holzscheit log OT 3
Honig honey OT 2
hören to listen; to hear OT 1
Hörer(in) listener OT 3
Horizont horizon **WS 1**, 38
horizontal horizontal **WS 3**, 112
Hormon hormone **WS 2**, 55
Horn horn OT 3
Horror horror OT 4
Hose trousers OT 1; pants **WW,** 11
  kurze Hosen shorts OT 3
bei jdm. hospitieren to shadow sb. **WS 3**, 106
Hotel hotel OT 1
Hotline helpline OT 2
hübsch pretty; lovely OT 1
Hüfte hip OT 1
Hügel hill OT 1
Huhn chicken OT 1, hen OT 4
Hülsenfrucht pulse OT 4
humid humid OT 4
Humor humour OT 4
Hund dog OT 1
hundert hundred OT 1
Hunger hunger OT 3
hungern (lassen) to starve OT 1
Hungersnot famine OT 2
hungrig hungry OT 1
Hupe horn OT 3
Hurrikan hurricane OT 4
Hut hat OT 1
Hütehund sheepdog OT 2

Hüter(in) keeper OT 4
Hymne anthem **WS 1**, 33
hyperaktiv hyperactive **WS 2**, 57
Hypothek mortgage OT 4

I

ich me OT 1
ideal ideal OT 4
Idee idea OT 1
identifizieren to identify OT 4
Identität identity OT 3
Idol idol **WS 2**, 66
Igel hedgehog OT 1
Igitt! yuck OT 3
Iglu igloo OT 4
ignorieren to ignore OT 4
ihm, ihn him OT 1
ihre(r, -s) hers; theirs OT 3
ikonisch iconic OT 3
illegal illegal OT 3
Illustration illustration OT 2
illustrieren to illustrate OT 4
immer always OT 1; permanently OT 3
  für immer forever OT 2
  immer noch still OT 1
Immobilie property OT 4
Imperativ imperative OT 1
in in; on; at OT 1
inakzeptabel unacceptable **WS 1**, 27
individuell individual OT 3
Industrie industry OT 2
Industrie... industrial OT 2
Infinitiv infinitive OT 1
Influencer(in) influencer **WS 2**, 69
Influenza influenza **WS 1**, 24
Infografik infographic OT 3
Informatikunterricht ICT (information and communications technology) OT 1
Informationen information OT 1
Informations- und Kommunikations-technologie ICT (information and communications technology) OT 1
informativ informative OT 4
informell informal **WS 1**, 16
informieren to inform OT 4
Infrastruktur infrastructure OT 4
Ingenieur(in) engineer OT 2
Ingenieurwesen engineering OT 2
Ingwer ginger OT 1
Inhalt contents OT 2
Initiative initiative OT 4
Inkubator incubator **WS 3**, 90
Innen... indoor OT 2
Innenstadt downtown OT 4
Innere: das Innere interior **WS 1**, 13
innerhalb inside OT 1; within OT 4
Innovation innovation OT 4
innovativ innovative OT 4
Innovator(in) innovator OT 4
innovieren to innovate OT 4
inoffiziell unofficial **WS 1**, 33
Insekt insect OT 2
Insel island OT 1
Inspiration inspiration OT 4
inspirieren to inspire OT 4
instabil insecure **WS 3**, 98
Installation installation OT 4
installieren to install OT 3
instruktiv instructive **WS 1**, 29
Instrument instrument OT 1
Insulaner(in) islander OT 4
Inszenierung production **WS 2**, 60
Integration integration **WS 2**, 57
integrativ inclusive OT 4
integrieren to integrate OT 4
intelligent clever OT 2; intelligent OT 3
Intelligenz intelligence OT 4
interagieren to interact OT 4
Interaktion interaction OT 4
interaktiv interactive OT 4
interessant interesting OT 1
Interesse interest OT 1
Interessengemeinschaft constituency OT 4
interessiert interested OT 1
international international OT 1
Internet internet OT 3
interpersonell interpersonal **WS 3**, 94
interpretieren to interpret OT 4
Interview interview OT 1
interviewen to interview OT 1
Interviewer(in) interviewer **WS 3**, 95
Interviewte(r) interviewee OT 3
intolerant intolerant **WS 4**, 129
Intonation intonation **WS 3**, 93
invasiv invasive **WS 1**, 25
investieren to invest OT 4
Investition investment OT 4
Investor(in) investor OT 4
inzwischen meanwhile **WS 2**, 76
irgendein(e) any OT 1
irgend etwas anything OT 1
irgend jemand anybody; anyone OT 1
irgendwann sometime OT 3; someday **WS 3**, 99
irgendwie somehow OT 4
irgendwo somewhere; anywhere OT 1
irisch Irish OT 1
Irrgarten maze OT 3
italienisch Italian OT 2

J

ja aye OT 2
Jacht yacht **WS 1**, 43
Jacke jacket OT 1
jagen to hunt; to chase OT 2
Jäger(in) hunter OT 3
  Jäger und Sammler hunter-gatherer **WS 1**, 24
Jahr year OT 1
Jahrbuch yearbook OT 4
Jahreszeit season OT 2
Jahrhundert century OT 2
jährlich annual **WS 2**, 56
Jahrmarkt fairground; fair OT 2
Jahrzehnt decade OT 4
japanisch Japanese OT 1
Jazz jazz OT 2
je ever OT 1; per OT 4
jede(r, -s) every; each; everyone, everybody OT 1
jederzeit anytime OT 3
jedoch however OT 1; though OT 2
jemand someone; somebody OT 1
jetzt now OT 1
Job job OT 1
Joghurt yoghurt OT 1
Journal journal OT 3
Journalismus journalism OT 4
Journalist(in) journalist OT 2
jubeln to cheer up OT 1
jucken to itch OT 2
juckend itchy OT 2
Judo judo OT 1
Jugend youth OT 2
Jugend... adolescent **WS 2**, 72
Jugendbetreuer(in) counselor OT 2
Jugendherberge youth hostel OT 2
Jugendliche adolescent **WS 2**, 72
Jugendliche youngster **WS 3**, 98
Juli July OT 1
jung young OT 1
Junge boy OT 1
Junge(s) cub OT 2
Junior(in) junior OT 2
Justiz justice **WS 2**, 64
Justiz... judicial OT 4

K

Kabel cable OT 3
Kabine cabin OT 2
Kabinett cabinet **WS 3**, 113
Kabinettsminister(in) cabinet minister OT 4
Kaffee coffee OT 1
Käfig cage **WS 3**, 107
kahl bald OT 3

Kai pier **WS 1**, 29
Kaiser emperor OT 2
Kajak kayak OT 4
Kakao cocoa OT 4
Kaktus cactus OT 4
Kalender calendar OT 1
Kalorie calorie **WS 2**, 66
kalt cold OT 1; freezing OT 2
Kamel camel **WS 1**, 25
Kamera camera OT 1
Kameramann cameraman **WS 4**, 140
Kamin fireplace OT 1
Kamm comb OT 2
Kammer chamber OT 2
Kampagne campaign OT 3; initiative OT 4
Kampf fight OT 1
kämpfen (um) to fight OT 1; to campaign (for) **WS 3**, 104
Kämpfer(in) fighter OT 2
Kanal canal; channel OT 3
Kanarienvogel canary OT 2
Kandidat(in) candidate OT 4
Känguru kangaroo OT 3
Kaninchen rabbit OT 1
Kantine canteen OT 1
Kanu canoe OT 2
Kapitel chapter OT 1
kaputt busted OT 4
Kapuzenpullover hoodie OT 1
Karibu caribou OT 4
Karneval carnival OT 4
Karotte carrot OT 1
Karre barrow OT 4
Karriere career OT 3
Karte card OT 1
Karteikarte file card OT 2
Kartoffel potato OT 1
Kartoffelbrei mashed potato OT 1
Kartoffelchip crisp OT 1
Käse cheese OT 1
Kasse register OT 2; check-out OT 4
Kassierer(in) cashier OT 4
Katastrophe disaster OT 2
Kategorie category OT 3
Kathedrale cathedral OT 1
Katholik(in) Catholic OT 3
katholisch Catholic OT 3
Katze cat OT 1
kaufen to shop; to buy OT 1
Käufer(in) shopper OT 4; buyer **WS 3**, 104
Kaufhaus department store OT 4
kaum hardly OT 4
Kavallerie cavalry OT 3
Kehle throat OT 4
keine(r, -s) none OT 3
Keks biscuit OT 1; cookie (AE) OT 3
Kellner(in) waiter OT 1; server (AE) OT 3
Keltisch Celtic OT 2
kennen to know OT 1
kennenlernen to come to know **WW**, 11
kenntnisreich knowledgeable OT 3
Kerl guy **WS 1**, 30; lad **WS 2**, 65
Kern core OT 4
Kerze candle OT 2
Kerzenlicht candlelight OT 4
Kessel kettle OT 2
Ketchup ketchup OT 3
Kette chain OT 3
keulen to cull **WS 1**, 25
Keulen cull **WS 1**, 25
Keyboard keyboard OT 1
Kidneybohne kidney bean OT 2
Kilo kilo OT 2
Kilometer kilometre OT 1
Kilt kilt OT 2
Kind child; kid OT 1
Kindergarten nursery **WS 3**, 111
Kindertagesstätte nursery **WS 3**, 111
Kindheit childhood OT 3
kindisch childish OT 3
Kino cinema OT 1
Kiosk tuck shop **WS 2**, 60
Kirche church OT 1
Kirsche cherry OT 4
Kissen cushion OT 1
Kiste box OT 1; crate OT 4
Kiwi kiwi OT 1
Klammer bracket OT 2
Klaps pat OT 3
klar clear OT 2
klären to clarify; to sort out OT 4
Klarinette clarinet OT 2
Klasse class OT 1
Klassenkamerad(in) classmate OT 3
Klassenstufe grade OT 2
Klassenzimmer classroom OT 1
klassisch classic; classical OT 2; vintage **WS 3**, 90
klatschen to clap OT 1
klauen to steal OT 2
Klavier piano OT 1
kleben to stick OT 1; to paste OT 2
Klebstoff glue OT 1
Kleid dress OT 1
Kleider clothes OT 1
Kleiderschrank wardrobe OT 1
Kleidung clothes OT 1; clothing OT 4
klein small; little OT 1; mini **WS 1**, 12
Kleinbus minibus OT 2
Kleingeld cash OT 1
Kleinholz kindling OT 2
klemmen an to clip to **WS 3**, 112
Kletterer(in) climber OT 2
klettern to climb OT 1
klicken to click OT 3
Klima climate OT 2
Klingel doorbell OT 2
klingeln to ring OT 1; to sound OT 4
Klinik clinic **WS 3**, 106
Klippe cliff **WS 1**, 24
Klischee stereotype **WS 2**, 54
Klo loo OT 2
klopfen to knock OT 2
klug smart OT 4, savvy **WS 2**, 68
Kneipe pub OT 2
Knie knee OT 1
Kniehose breeches OT 3
Knöchel ankle OT 1
Knochen bone OT 1
Knopf button OT 1
knuddelig cuddly OT 3
Koala koala **WS 1**, 13
Koch, Köchin chef OT 1
köcheln to simmer OT 2
kochen to cook; to boil; to make OT 1
Kochen cooking OT 1; cookery OT 2
Kochfeld hob OT 3
kodieren to code **WS 3**, 100
Koffein caffeine **WS 2**, 66
Kofferraum trunk OT 2
Kohl cabbage OT 1
Kohle coal OT 2
Kohlendioxid carbon dioxide OT 3
Kohlenhydrat carbohydrate **WS 2**, 66
kohlensäurehaltig fizzy OT 2
Kohlenstoff carbon OT 4
Kojote coyote **WS 4**, 129
Kollaboration collaboration OT 4
Kollege, Kollegin colleague OT 4; counterpart **WS 3**, 110
kolonial colonial OT 3
Kolonialisierung colonization **WS 1**, 24
Kolonialismus colonialism **WW**, 10
Kolonie colony OT 3
kolonisieren to colonize OT 3
Kolonist(in) colonist OT 4
Kombination combination OT 4
kombinieren to combine OT 4
Kombüse galley OT 3
Komitee committee OT 4
Komma comma OT 3
Kommandant(in) commander OT 2
kommen to come OT 1
kommentieren to comment OT 3
Kommerz commerce **WS 3**, 88
kommerziell commercial OT 4

Kommission committee OT 4
Kommode chest of drawers OT 1
Kommunikation communication OT 1
kommunizieren to communicate OT 4
Komödie comedy OT 4
Komparativ comparative OT 2
Kompass compass OT 2
kompatibel compatible **WS 2**, 56
kompetent competent OT 4
Kompetenz proficiency OT 4
komplett completely OT 4
Komplex complex OT 4
Kompliment compliment OT 3
kompliziert complicated OT 3; tricky OT 4
komponieren to compose OT 3
Komponist(in) composer OT 2
Kompost compost OT 3
Kompostierungs- composting OT 4
Konferenz conference OT 3
Konflikt conflict OT 4
König king OT 1
Königin queen OT 1
königlich royal OT 1
Konjunktion conjunction OT 2
konkret specific OT 2
Konkurrent(in) competitor OT 4
Konkurrenz competition OT 1; rivalry **WS 1**, 30
konkurrenzorientiert competitive OT 3
konkurrieren to compete OT 2
konkurrierend competitively OT 4
können can OT 1; to be able OT 2
konnte could OT 1
könnte(n) could OT 1; might OT 2
konsequent consistent **WS 2**, 59
Konsequenz consequence OT 4
Konsonant consonant OT 1
konstant constantly OT 4
konstitutionell constitutional OT 4
konsumieren to consume OT 4
Kontakt contact OT 1
  in Kontakt in touch OT 2
  Kontakte pflegen to socialize OT 4
kontaktfreudig outgoing OT 4
kontaktieren to contact OT 2
kontaminieren to contaminate **WS 1**, 34
Kontext context OT 4
Kontinent continent **WS 1**, 12
kontinuierlich continuous OT 4
Konto account OT 3
Kontrabass double bass OT 2
Kontrast contrast OT 3
kontrastieren to contrast OT 4
Kontrolle control OT 2
kontrollieren to control OT 4
Kontroverse controversy OT 4
(sich) konzentrieren to concentrate OT 3; to focus on **WS 2**, 56
Konzept concept OT 4
Konzert concert OT 1
Kooperation partnership OT 4
Kopf head OT 1
Kopfball header OT 3
köpfen to behead OT 3
Kopfhörer headphones OT 2; headset **WS 2**, 58
Kopfkissen pillow OT 2
Kopfkissenbezug pillowcase OT 3
Kopfsalat lettuce OT 2
Kopfschmerzen headache OT 1
Kopie replica OT 4
kopieren to copy OT 1
Korb basket OT 4
Kordel lanyard **WS 3**, 112
koreanisch Korean OT 1
Körper body OT 1
Körperhaltung posture OT 4
körperlich physical OT 2
  körperliche Bewegung exercise OT 1
(schwere) Körperverletzung aggravated assault **WS 2**, 64
Korrektur correction OT 4
Korrespondent(in) correspondent OT 4
Korridor corridor OT 2
korrigieren to correct OT 1
Korsett corset OT 3
Kosten cost OT 1; expense OT 4
kosten to cost OT 1
kostenlos free OT 1
Kostüm costume OT 2
krabbeln to crawl **WS 1**, 38
Krabbeltier creepy-crawly OT 2
Kraft force OT 2; power OT 4
Krähe crow OT 3
Krampf cramp OT 2
krank sick OT 1; ill OT 2
Krankenhaus hospital OT 1
Krankenpflege nursing **WS 3**, 110
Krankenpfleger nurse OT 1
Krankenschwester nurse OT 1
Krankenwagen ambulance OT 1
Krankheit disease; illness OT 2
Kranz wreath OT 3
Krapfen doughnut OT 2
krass wicked OT 2
kratzen to scrape; to scratch OT 2
kraus frizzy OT 3
Kraut herb OT 3
Krawatte tie OT 1
kreativ creative OT 2
Kreativität creativity OT 3
Kreditkarte credit card OT 1
kreieren to create OT 2
Kreis circle OT 2
Kreuzfahrtschiff cruise ship OT 2
Kricket cricket OT 1
kriechen to crawl **WS 1**, 38
Krieg war OT 2
Krieger(in) warrior OT 2
Kriegsschiff warship OT 3
Kriegszeit wartime OT 3
Kriminelle(r) criminal OT 3
Krise crisis OT 4
Kriterium criterion **WS 2**, 56
Kritik criticism OT 3; review **WS 3**, 106
Kritiker(in) critic **WS 3**, 110
kritisch critical OT 4
kritisieren to criticize OT 3
Krone crown OT 1
krönen to crown OT 1
Kronleuchter chandelier OT 2
Krönung coronation OT 3
Krücke crutch OT 2
Küche kitchen OT 1; cuisine OT 3
Kuchen cake OT 1
Küchenchef(in) chef OT 1
Kugel bullet OT 2
Kuh cow OT 1
kühl cool OT 1
Kühlschrank fridge OT 1
Kühlsystem cooling system OT 3
Kult... iconic OT 3
kultiviert civilized **WS 1**, 27
Kultur culture OT 1
kulturell cultural OT 4
Kumpel buddy OT 2; mate OT 4
Kunde, Kundin customer OT 2; client **WS 2**, 77
kündigen to quit **WS 3**, 98
Kundschafter(in) scout OT 3
Kunst art OT 1
Kunsthandwerk craft OT 4
Künstler(in) artist OT 1
künstlich artificial OT 4
  künstliche Intelligenz artificial intelligence **WS 3**, 109
Kuppel dome OT 4
Kürbis pumpkin OT 2
Kurier(in) courier OT 2
Kurs program; course OT 3
kursieren to circulate OT 4
kurz short OT 1; brief OT 3
kürzen to shorten OT 4
Kuss kiss OT 2
Küste coast OT 1; shore OT 2; shoreline OT 4; coastline **WS 1**, 36
Küsten... coastal OT 4

Küstenlinie coastline **WS 1**, 36
Küstenwache coastguard OT 2

L
Labor lab OT 4
Lache pool OT 1
lächeln to smile OT 1
lachen to laugh OT 1
Lachs salmon OT 1
Lacrosse lacrosse OT 4
Laden tuck shop **WS 2**, 60
Laden shop OT 1
Ladendiebstahl shoplifting **WS 2**, 50
Ladung cargo OT 3
Lage circumstance **WS 2**, 64
Lage situation OT 1
Lagerfeuer campfire OT 2
Lagerung storage OT 3
Lamm lamb OT 2
Lampe lamp OT 1
Land country; countryside OT 1; land OT 2
landen to land OT 2
Landkarte map OT 1
Landschaft landscape; scenery OT 2
Landstraße highway OT 3
Landwirtschaft farming; agriculture OT 2
landwirtschaftlich agrarian **WS 1**, 24
lang long OT 1
Länge length OT 3
Langlaufen cross-country skiing **WS 1**, 13
langsam slow OT 2
langweilig boring OT 1
Laptop laptop OT 3
Lärm noise OT 1
lassen to let OT 1
lässig casual **WS 2**, 68
Last burden OT 3
Latein Latin OT 2
lateinamerikanisch Latino OT 2
Laterne lantern OT 2
Laufen running OT 1
laufen to walk; to run OT 1
laufend continuous OT 4
Läufer(in) runner OT 2
launisch moody **WS 2**, 72
laut loud; noisy OT 1; aloud OT 2
  laut rufen to shout OT 1
Lautsprecher loudspeaker OT 2
Lautstärke volume OT 3
Lava lava **WS 1**, 26
Leben life OT 1
  Leben nach dem Tod afterlife **WS 4**, 128
leben to live OT 1
lebendig alive OT 2
lebensbedrohlich life-threatening OT 2
Lebensdauer lifetime OT 3
Lebenslauf CV (curriculum vitae) OT 4
Lebensmittel grocery OT 4
Lebensmittelsammelstelle food bank **WS 3**, 104
Lebensmittelvergiftung food poisoning OT 2
Lebensstil lifestyle OT 4
lebenswichtig vital OT 3
Lebenszeit lifetime OT 3
Leber liver **WS 2**, 66
Lebewesen creature **WS 1**, 26
lebhaft lively OT 2; vibrant **WS 1**, 19
lecker delicious OT 1; yummy **WS 1**, 29
Leder leather OT 3
leer empty OT 1, blank OT 4
legal legal OT 3
legalisieren to legalize **WS 2**, 52
Legasthenie dyslexia **WS 2**, 57
legasthenisch dyslexic **WS 2**, 58
Legende legend; myth OT 4
Legion legion OT 2
Legislative legislative OT 4
lehnen to lean OT 3
Lehrbuch textbook OT 3
Lehrer(in) teacher OT 1; instructor OT 2
Lehrling apprentice **WS 3**, 89
Lehrplan curriculum OT 4
lehrreich instructive **WS 1**, 29
Lehrstelle apprenticeship **WS 3**, 88
leicht easy OT 1
Leichtathletik athletics OT 1
leiden to suffer OT 4
Leidenschaft passion **WS 2**, 72
leidenschaftlich keen OT 2; passionate OT 4
leider unfortunately OT 2
leihen to lend OT 2
Leihgabe loan OT 4
Leinen canvas OT 3
Leinen linen OT 3
Leinwand screen OT 1
sich leisten to afford OT 2
Leistung merit **WS 3**, 110
Leistungen attainment **WS 2**, 58
leiten to run; to manage; to guide OT 1
Leiter ladder OT 3
Leiter(in) manager OT 1; leader; director OT 2; supervisor **WS 3**, 108
Leitung pipe OT 4
lernen to learn OT 1
Lernende(r) learner OT 3
Lernprogramm tutorial OT 4
Lesbe lesbian **WS 2**, 51
lesen to read OT 1
Leser, Leserin reader OT 2
letzte(r, -s) last OT 1; last OT 2
leuchtend bright OT 1
leugnen deny OT 4
Leute people OT 1; folks; guys OT 2
Lexikon encyclopedia OT 4
Licht light OT 1
  ans Licht kommen to emerge OT 3
lieben to love OT 1
Liebes sweetheart **WS 1**, 30
Lieblings... favourite OT 1
Liebste(r) sweetheart **WS 1**, 30
Lied song OT 1
liefern to deliver OT 3
Lieferung supply OT 3
Lieferwagen van OT 2
liegen to lie OT 1
Lifestyle lifestyle OT 4
Lift lift OT 3
Liga league OT 2
Limo soda **WS 2**, 66
lindern to alleviate **WS 3**, 105
Lineal ruler OT 1
Linguist(in) linguist **WS 2**, 70
Linguistik linguistics **WS 2**, 70
Linie line OT 1
Linse lens OT 2
Lippe lip OT 2
Liste list OT 1
listen to list **WW**, 11
Liter litre OT 4
LKW truck OT 1
loben to compliment OT 3; to praise OT 4
Loch hole OT 1
locken tempt OT 4
locker casual **WS 2**, 68
Löffel spoon OT 2
logisch logical OT 4
Logline logline OT 4
Logo logo OT 1
Lohn salary **WS 3**, 95
lohnend worthwhile OT 2; rewarding **WS 3**, 96
Lohngefälle pay gap **WS 3**, 103
Lokführer(in) engineer OT 2
Lokomotive engine OT 2
lösen to solve OT 4
loshasten to rush off OT 2
(sich) losmachen to sheer OT 3
Lösung solution OT 3
los werden to get rid of OT 3
Löwe lion OT 1
Loyalität loyalty **WS 3**, 98
Luchs lynx OT 2

Lücke gap OT 1
lückenhaft patchy OT 4
Luft air OT 2
Luftfahrt aerospace OT 4
Lunchpaket packed lunch OT 1
Lunge lung OT 3
Lupe magnifying glass OT 2
lustig funny OT 1
luxuriös luxurious OT 2

M
machen to do OT 1, to make OT 1
  selbst gemacht homemade OT 1
Macht power OT 4
mächtig powerful OT 2
Mädchen girl OT 1
Magen stomach OT 1
mager lean **WS 2**, 66; skinny **WS 2**, 77
magisch magical OT 2
Magnet magnet OT 4
magnetisch magnetic OT 2
mähen to mow **WS 2**, 54
Mahlzeit meal OT 1
Mailbox mailbox OT 4
Mais corn OT 3
majestätisch majestic OT 4
mal times **WS 1**, 12
Malaria malaria **WS 1**, 34
malen to paint OT 1
malerisch picturesque OT 4
man you OT 1
Management management OT 4
managen to manage OT 1
Manager(in) manager OT 1
manchmal sometimes OT 1
Mandant(in) client **WS 2**, 77
Mangel lack OT 3; shortage **WS 1**, 34
Manifest manifesto OT 4
Mann man OT 1; husband OT 2
männlich male OT 2
Mannschaft team OT 1; crew OT 2
Manschaftskollege, -kollegin teammate OT 2
Mantel coat OT 2
Marathon marathon OT 2
Märchen fairy tale OT 1
marin marine **WS 1**, 26
Marine navy OT 3
Marke brand **WS 2**, 68
Marketing marketing **WS 2**, 68
markieren to bookmark OT 4
Markierung marker OT 1
Markt market OT 1
  auf den Markt bringen to release; to launch OT 4
Marmelade jam OT 1
Marsch march **WS 1**, 42
marschieren to march OT 4
Maschine machine OT 2
  Maschinen machinery OT 2
Masern measles **WS 1**, 24
Maske mask OT 3
Maskottchen mascot OT 2
Maß measurement OT 2
Massage massage OT 2
Massaker massacre **WS 1**, 24
Masse mass **WW**, 11
Maßeinheit measurement OT 2
Massen... mass OT 4
massiv solid OT 4
Maßnahme measure **WS 1**, 25; provision **WS 2** 57
Maßstab scale OT 2
Material material OT 4
Mathematik maths OT 1
Matratze mattress OT 4
matschig muddy OT 4
Maultier mule OT 3
Maus mouse OT 1
Maximum maximum OT 2
Mayonnaise mayonnaise OT 1
MBA MBA (Masters of Business Administration) **WS 3**, 118
mechanisch mechanical **WS 3**, 118
Medaille medal OT 2
Median median **WS 2**, 62
Medium medium OT 2
  soziale Medien social media OT 2
Medizin medicine **WS 2**, 55
medizinisch medical OT 2
Meer sea OT 1
Meeres... marine **WS 1**, 26
Meeresboden seabed OT 3
Meeresfrüchte shellfish OT 3; seafood OT 4
Meeresküste seaside OT 3
Mehl flour OT 2
mehr more OT 1
  nicht mehr anymore OT 4
Mehrheit majority OT 4
Mehrzahl plural OT 1
Meile (etwa 1,6 km) mile OT 1
Meilenstein milestone OT 3
mein my, mine OT 1
Meinung opinion OT 3
  anderer Meinung sein to disagree OT 1
Meisterleistung feat OT 2
Meisterschaft cup **WS 1**, 21
Meisterstück masterpiece OT 4
sich melden to report OT 1
Melodie tune OT 4
Memoiren memoir **WS 4**, 128
Menge crowd OT 1
  eine Menge a lot OT 1
  jede Menge loads of OT 3
Mensch person OT 1; human being OT 2
Menschenmenge crowd OT 1; throng OT 2
Menschenrecht human right **WW**, 11
menschlich human OT 2
mental mental OT 4
merkwürdig funny OT 1
messen to measure OT 1
Messer knife OT 2
Metall metal OT 1
Meter metre OT 1
Methode method OT 1
Meute mob **WS 1**, 28
mich me OT 1
mieten to hire; to rent OT 3
Migrant(in) migrant OT 4
Migration migration OT 3
migrieren to migrate OT 3
Mikrofon microphone **WS 2**, 58
Mikrowelle microwave OT 4
Milch milk OT 1
Milchprodukte dairy OT 4
Militär... military **WS 3**, 88
militärisch military **WS 3**, 88
Millenial millennial **WS 3**, 98
Millennium-Generation millennial **WS 3**, 98
Milliarde billion OT 4
Million million OT 1
Minderheit minority OT 4
Minderjährige(r) minor OT 2
Mindest... minimum OT 1
mindestens at least OT 1
Mindmap mind map OT 1
Mini-Job gig **WS 3**, 100
Miniatur miniature OT 2
Minister(in) minister OT 4
Minute minute OT 1
Minze mint OT 1
mir me OT 1
mischen to combine OT 4
Mischung mixture; mix OT 2
Misserfolg failure OT 4
misstrauisch suspicious OT 3
Missverständnis misunderstanding OT 3
missverstehen to misunderstand **WS 2**, 61
mit with OT 1
mitarbeiten (an) to contribute (to) **WS 1**, 29
Mitarbeiter(in) colleague OT 4

Mitbewohner(in) roommate **WS 3**, 107
Mitfahrgelegenheit lift OT 3
mitfühlen (mit jmd.) to sympathize (with) **WS 4**, 140
mitfühlend sympathetic OT 2
Mitglied member OT 1
Mitglied werden in to join OT 1
Mitlaut consonant OT 1
Mittag noon OT 4
Mittagessen lunch OT 1
Mittagspause lunch break OT 1
Mittagszeit lunchtime OT 1
Mitte centre; middle OT 1
Mitteilungsblatt newsletter OT 3
Mittel medium OT 2; resource OT 4; agent **WS 1**, 27
mittelalterlich medieval OT 2
mittelgroß medium-sized OT 2
Mitternacht midnight OT 1
mittlerweile meanwhile **WS 2**, 76
Mittwoch Wednesday OT 1
mobben to bully OT 3
Möbel furniture OT 1
möchte(n) would like OT 1
Mode fashion OT 1
Modell model OT 1; recreation OT 4
Moderator(in) presenter OT 4
modern modern OT 1; trendy OT 2
modisch fashionable OT 2
Modul module OT 4
mogeln to cheat OT 4
mögen to like OT 1
nicht mögen to dislike OT 2
möglich possible OT 2; potential OT 4
Möglichkeit chance OT 2; possibility OT 4
Moment moment OT 1
Monarchie monarchy OT 4
Monarch(in) monarch OT 4
Monat month OT 1
Mönch monk OT 3
Mond moon OT 1
Monopol monopoly OT 4
monoton monotone **WS 3**, 93
Monster monster OT 1
Montag Monday OT 1
Monument monument OT 4
Moped moped OT 4
Moral moral OT 2
Mord murder **WS 4**, 128
Morgen morning OT 1; acre (Fläche) OT 4
morgen tomorrow OT 1
Morgendämmerung dawn OT 3
Mosaik mosaic OT 2
Motel motel OT 3
Motivation motivation **WS 3**, 91
Motivations... motivational **WS 3**, 99
motivieren to motivate **WS 2**, 74
motiviert motivated OT 4
Motor engine OT 2
motorisiert motorized OT 4
Motto motto OT 4
Mountainbiken mountain biking OT 2
müde tired OT 1
Muffin muffin OT 1
Mühe effort OT 3
Müll rubbish OT 4
Müllcontainer dumpster OT 4
Mülldeponie landfill OT 3
multi-funktional multi-functional OT 4
Multikulturalismus multiculturalism OT 4
multikulturell multicultural OT 4
multinational multinational OT 4
Mund mouth OT 1
mündlich oral OT 1; verbal **WS 2**, 57
Mundschutz mouthguard OT 2
Münze coin OT 1
mürrisch crossly OT 3
Muschel seashell OT 3
Museum museum OT 1
Musik music OT 1
Musik... musical OT 2
musikalisch musical OT 2
Musiker(in) musician OT 2
Muskel muscle OT 2
Müsli muesli **WS 2**, 77
müssen to be obliged (to) **WS 2**, 76
müssen must OT 1
Muster pattern OT 4
Mut bravery OT 2
mutig bold OT 1
Mutter mother OT 1
Mutterschaf ewe OT 2
Mutti mum OT 1
mutwillig beschädigen to vandalize **WS 4**, 130
Mütze cap OT 1
Mythologie mythology OT 2
Mythos myth OT 4

N

nach after; past OT 1; according to OT 4
Nachbar neighbour OT 2
Nachbarschaft neighbourhood OT 4
nachdenken to speculate OT 4
nachdenken über to think about OT 1; consider OT 3
Nachfrage demand **WS 3**, 102
nachhallen to echo **WS 1**, 14
nachhaltig sustainable OT 3
Nachhaltigkeit sustainability OT 3
Nachhilfe geben to tutor **WS 3**, 93
nachklingen to echo **WS 1**, 14
Nachkomme descendant OT 3
Nachlass discount OT 4
Nachmittag afternoon OT 1
Nachricht message OT 1
Nachstellung reenactment OT 4
nächste(r) next OT 3
als Nächstes next OT 3
Nacht night OT 1
über Nacht overnight OT 2
Nachteil con OT 2; downside OT 3; disadvantage OT 4
Nachtisch dessert OT 1
Nachttopf chamber pot OT 3
Nachweis evidence OT 4
nah near; close OT 1; nearby OT 3
näher kommen to approach OT 3
nähen to sew OT 3
(sich) nähern to approach OT 3
nahrhaft nutritious OT 4
Nahrungsergänzungsmittel food supplement **WS 2**, 66
Name name OT 1
namens called OT 1
Nase nose OT 2
nass wet OT 1
Nation nation OT 2
national national OT 1
Nationalhymne anthem **WS 1**, 33
Natur nature OT 2
Naturforscher(in) naturalist OT 2
natürlich of course; natural OT 1
Naturwissenschaften science OT 1
Naturwissenschaftler(in) scientist OT 1
Navigationssystem GPS (global positioning system) OT 2
nebelig foggy OT 3
neben next to; by OT 1; beside OT 2
Nebenberuf sideline **WS 3**, 102
nebenberuflich part-time **WS 1**, 14
Neffe nephew **WS 2**, 73
Negativ negative OT 1
Negativität negativity OT 4
nehmen to take OT 1
(sich) neigen to tilt OT 3
zu etw. neigen to tend to **WS 2**, 54
nennen to call OT 1
Neoprenanzug wetsuit OT 1
Nerv nerve OT 3
Nervensäge pain OT 2
nervös nervous OT 2
Nest nest OT 3
nett kind; nice OT 1
Netz net OT 4
Netzball netball **WS 1**, 15

Netzwerk network OT 4
neu new OT 1
neueste(r) recent OT 3
neugierig curious OT 4
Neuheit innovation OT 4
Neuigkeit(en) news OT 1
neulich recently OT 3
neun nine OT 1
neunzig ninety OT 1
neurologisch neurological **WS 2**, 61
neutral neutral OT 3
Newsletter newsletter OT 3
Nichte niece OT 4
nichts nothing OT 1
nicken to nod OT 3
nie never OT 1
nieder menial **WS 3**, 103
Niederschlag rainfall OT 4
Niederschrift transcript **WS 2**, 70
niedlich cute OT 3
niemand nobody; no one OT 1
nirgendwo nowhere OT 2
Niveau level OT 1
noch yet OT 2
  noch ein(e, -r) another OT 1
nomadisch nomadic OT 3
Nomen noun OT 1
Nonne nun OT 3
Nord- north OT 1
nördlich northern OT 2
Nordosten north-east OT 1
normal normal OT 1; ordinary OT 2; standard **WS 1**, 16
normalerweise usually OT 1
normannisch Norman OT 3
Nostalgie nostalgia OT 4
Notaufnahme Accident and Emergency OT 1
Note score **WS 2**, 59
Noten... grading **WS 2**, 59
Notenpunkt credit **WS 2**, 56
Notfall emergency OT 1
Notiz note OT 1
Notizbuch notebook OT 2
notwendig necessary OT 3; necessarily OT 4
Notwendigkeit necessity OT 4
Nudel noodle OT 2
  Nudeln pasta OT 1
Nuklear... nuclear OT 3
numerisch numerical **WS 2**, 59
Nummer number OT 1
Nummernschild registration plate OT 4
nun well OT 1
nur just; only OT 1
Nuss nut **WS 1**, 14
nutzbar usable **WS 3**, 104
nützlich useful OT 1

O
ob whether OT 2
obdachlos homeless OT 4
Obdachlose(r) homeless OT 4
oben upstairs OT 1; above OT 2
  nach oben up OT 1; upwards OT 3
Oberbefehlshaber Commander-in-Chief OT 4
obere(r, -s) top; upper OT 1
Oberfläche surface OT 3
oberhalb above OT 2
Oberschenkel thigh OT 1
Oberstufenschüler(in) senior OT 4
Objekt object OT 1
Objektiv lens OT 2
Obsession obsession **WS 2**, 50
Obst fruit OT 1
Obstgarten orchard OT 4
obwohl though; although OT 2; despite OT 4
oder or OT 1
Ofen oven; heater OT 2; stove OT 3
offen open OT 1
  offen gesagt frankly OT 4
offensichtlich obvious OT 3
Öffentlichkeit public OT 3
offiziell official OT 2
Offizier(in) officer OT 2
öffnen to open OT 1
Öffnungszeiten opening times OT 1
oft often OT 1
ohne without OT 1
ohnmächtig werden to faint OT 2
Ohr ear OT 1
Ohrring earring OT 3
ökologisch ecological **WS 1**, 25
  ökologischer Fußabdruck carbon footprint OT 3
Ökonomie economy **WS 3**, 102
Ökotourismus ecotourism OT 3
Okular eyepiece OT 2
Öl oil OT 3
olympisch Olympic OT 2
Oma grandma OT 1
Onkel uncle OT 1
online online OT 3
Opa grandpa OT 1
operieren to operate OT 3
Opfer victim **WS 2**, 64
optimieren to optimize **WS 3**, 100
optimistisch optimistic OT 4
optional optional OT 4
Orange orange OT 1
orange orange OT 1
Orbit orbit OT 4
Orchester orchestra OT 1
ordentlich neat OT 4
Ordnung order OT 1
  in Ordnung OK; alright OT 1
Organ organ **WS 2**, 55
Organisation organization OT 3; agency OT 4
Organisator(in) organizer OT 4
organisatorisch organizational OT 4
organisieren to organize OT 1
orientiert orientated **WS 2**, 56
Original... original OT 3
Orkan hurricane OT 4
Ort place OT 1
örtlich locally OT 4
Ost- east OT 2
östlich eastern OT 2
Otter otter OT 4
Ozean ocean OT 2

P
Paar couple; pair OT 2
packen to pack OT 2
Packer(in) bagger OT 4
paddeln to paddle OT 3
Paket packet OT 2
Palast palace OT 1
Palette range OT 4
Pandemie pandemic **WS 3**, 105
Panik: in Panik geraten to panic OT 2
Panther panther OT 2
Pantoffel slipper OT 4
Papa dad OT 1
Papier paper OT 1
Paprika pepper OT 2
Papst pope OT 2
Parade parade OT 2
Paradies paradise **WS 1**, 21
Park park OT 1
parken to park OT 2
Parkplatz car park OT 2
Parlament parliament OT 4
parteiisch biased **WS 2**, 72
Partizip participle OT 2
Partner(in) partner OT 1
Partnerschaft partnership OT 4
Party party OT 1
Pass passport OT 2
Passagier(in) passenger OT 2
passen to suit **WS 1**, 36
passend timely OT 3
passieren to happen OT 1
Patentante godmother **WS 1**, 15
patentieren to patent OT 4

Patient(in) patient OT 1
Patriot(in) patriot OT 2
Pause break; rest OT 1; recess OT 4
  eine Pause machen to pause OT 3
peinlich embarrassing OT 2
pendeln to commute **WS 3**, 102
Pendler(in) commuter OT 2
Pendlerbahn commuter rail OT 2
Penny penny OT 1
Pension lodge OT 2
per per OT 4
perfekt perfect OT 2
Periode cycle OT 4
permanent permanent OT 4
Personal staff OT 1; crew OT 2
personalisieren to personalize **WS 2**, 68
persönlich personal OT 1
Persönlichkeit personality OT 4
Perspektive perspective **WS 1**, 35
Pest plague OT 3
Petrochemikalie petrochemical OT 4
Pfad trail OT 2
Pfadfinder(in) Scout OT 3
Pfanne pan OT 2
Pfeffer pepper OT 2
Pfeife whistle OT 2
pfeifen to blow OT 2
Pfeil arrow OT 3
Pferd horse OT 1
  zu Pferde on horseback OT 3
Pflanze plant OT 2
Pflaster plaster OT 1
Pflaume plum OT 1
pflegen to maintain OT 4
Pflicht obligation **WS 3**, 95
Pflücker(in) picker OT 4
Pfund pound OT 1
Phänomen phenomenon **WS 1**, 32
Phase stage OT 2
Philosophie philosophy OT 4
Physik physics **WS 2**, 56
Pianist(in) pianist OT 2
Picknick picnic OT 1
pikant savoury OT 3
Pilz mushroom OT 2
Pinguin penguin OT 2
Pinsel brush OT 2
Pionier(in) pioneer OT 4
Pipeline pipeline OT 4
Plage pest **WS 1**, 25
Plagiat plagiarism OT 2
plagiieren to plagiarize OT 2
Plakat poster OT 1
Plakette badge **WS 2**, 60
planen to plan OT 1; to arrange OT 2; to design OT 4
Planer(in) planner OT 4
Planet planet OT 2
Plastik plastic OT 3
Plastik... plastic OT 3
platschen to splash OT 2
Platz square; space OT 1; site; ground OT 2
Platzierung placement **WS 2**, 68
plaudern to chatter OT 2; to chat OT 3
plötzlich suddenly OT 2; sudden OT 3
Plural plural OT 1
Pocken smallpox **WS 1**, 17
Podcast podcast OT 3
Pokal trophy OT 2
Pol pole OT 4
Politik politics OT 4; policy **WS 2**, 57
Politiker(in) politician OT 3
politisch political OT 3
Polizei police OT 1
polnisch Polish OT 2
Polohemd polo shirt **WS 2**, 60
Polster pad OT 2
Polyp polyp **WS 1**, 28
Pommes frites French fries OT 2
Pony pony OT 3
Popcorn popcorn OT 2
Popularität popularity OT 4
Portalseite portal **WS 2**, 69
Portraitfoto headshot **WS 3**, 94
Position position OT 3; rank OT 4
Positiv positive OT 1
Post post OT 2; mail OT 4
Postbote, -botin mail carrier OT 4
posten to post OT 4
Postkarte postcard OT 1
Präferenz preference OT 4
Praktikant(in) intern **WS 3**, 106
Praktikum internship OT 4
Praktikumsplatz traineeship **WS 3**, 92
praktisch practical OT 2; convenient OT 4
Präposition preposition OT 1
Präsentation presentation OT 1
präsentieren to feature OT 2
präsidentiell presidential OT 4
Präsident(in) president OT 3
Praxis practice OT 1; surgery **WS 3**, 106
präzise accurate OT 4
Preis price; prize OT 1
Preiselbeere cranberry OT 3
prima fine OT 1
primär primary OT 1
Prinz prince OT 1
Prinzip principle OT 4
Priorität priority **WS 2**, 81
privat private OT 3
Privatsphäre privacy OT 3
Privileg privilege OT 4
proaktiv proactive OT 4
Probe rehearsal OT 2
proben to rehearse OT 3
probieren to sample OT 4
Problem problem OT 1; matter OT 2
Problemlöser(in) problem-solver OT 4
Produkt product OT 2
Produktion production **WS 2**, 60
professionell professional OT 3
Profil profile **WS 3**, 93
Profit profit OT 4
profitieren to benefit OT 4
Prognose forecast OT 2
Programm programme OT 1; program OT 3; scheme **WS 3**, 89
programmieren to programme OT 2; to code **WS 3**, 100
progressiv progressive OT 1
Projekt project OT 1
Projektor projector OT 1
Promenade promenade **WS 1**, 29
Prominente(r) personality OT 4; celebrity **WS 2**, 66
Pronomen pronoun OT 1
Prospekt prospectus OT 4
Protein protein **WS 2**, 66
Protest protest OT 4
Protestantisch Protestant OT 3
protestieren to protest OT 4
Protestierer(in) protester OT 4
Prototyp prototype OT 4
Provinz province OT 4
Prozedur procedure OT 4
Prozent percent OT 3
Prozentsatz percentage OT 4
Prozess trial OT 2; process OT 4
Prüfung exam OT 1
Psychologe, Psychologin psychologist **WS 3**, 107
Psychologie psychology **WS 3**, 107
Pubertät puberty **WS 2**, 55
Publikum audience OT 1
Pueblo pueblo OT 3
Pullover jumper OT 1
Puma cougar OT 2
Pumpe pump OT 2
Punkt point OT 1; item OT 3
punkten to score OT 1
pünktlich punctual OT 4
Puppe doll OT 2
putzen to clean OT 1; to brush OT 4
Pyjama-Party sleepover OT 1

Q
Quadrat square OT 1
quälend agonizingly OT 3
Qualifikation qualification OT 4
qualifiziert qualified OT 4
Qualität quality OT 3
Quarterback quarterback OT 2
Quelle spring; source OT 2
Querfeldein... cross country OT 2
Querflöte flute OT 1
querlesen to skim OT 2
Quiz quiz OT 2

R
Rabatt discount OT 4
Rabe raven OT 2
Rad bike; wheel OT 1
Radfahrer(in) cyclist OT 3
Radiergummi rubber OT 1
radikal radical OT 4
Radio radio OT 1
Rahmen frame OT 3; framework OT 4
Rakete rocket OT 4
Rampe ramp OT 2
Rand rim; edge OT 3; margin **WS 2**, 71
Rang rank OT 4
rasen to race **WS 1**, 31
Rasen lawn **WS 2**, 54
Rasse... pedigree OT 3
Rat advice OT 2; council OT 3
Rate rate OT 4
raten to advise OT 4
Rathaus city hall **WS 3**, 107
Rätsel mystery **WS 4**, 128
Ratte rat OT 3
Rattenfänger ratter OT 3
rau rough; harsh OT 3
Räuber predator **WS 1**, 25
Raubtier predator **WS 1**, 25
Rauch smoke OT 2
Raum room OT 1
Raumfahrzeug spacecraft OT 4
Razzia raid **WS 4**, 137
reagieren to react OT 3
Reaktion reaction OT 3; response OT 4
realistisch realistic OT 4
Realität reality **WS 1**, 28
rebellieren to rebel OT 4
Rebell(in) rebel OT 4
Rechenaufgabe sum OT 2
Rechenschaft: zur Rechenschaft ziehen to hold accountable **WS 2**, 64
Rechnung bill OT 4
Recht privilege OT 4
rechteckig rectangular OT 2
rechte(r, -s) right OT 1
rechtfertigen to justify OT 4
rechtlich legal OT 3
rechts right OT 4
Rechtsanwalt, -anwältin lawyer OT 4
Rechtschreibung spelling OT 1
rechtzeitig timely OT 3
Redakteur(in) editor OT 2
Rede speech OT 2
reden to talk OT 1
Redner(in) speaker OT 2
reduzieren to downsize OT 3; to reduce OT 4
Referenzschreiben letter of reference **WS 3**, 106
Reformation Reformation OT 3
Regal shelf OT 2
Regel rule OT 1; guideline OT 3; norm **WS 3**, 102
regelmäßig regular OT 1
Regelschule mainstream school **WS 2**, 57
Regelwerk rulebook OT 2
Regen rainfall OT 4
Regenbogen rainbow **WS 1**, 13
Regenschauer rainstorm **WS 1**, 38
Regenschirm umbrella OT 1
Regenwald rainforest OT 2
Regenwasser rainwater OT 4
Reggae reggae OT 2
Regie: Regie führen to direct OT 3
regieren to govern OT 3
Regierung government OT 2
Regierungs... governmental OT 4
Region region OT 3
regional regional **WS 1**, 32
regnen to rain OT 1
regnerisch rainy OT 4
reiben to rub OT 3
Reich empire OT 2
reich rich OT 1; wealthy OT 4
reichlich plenty OT 2; substantial **WS 2**, 77
Reichtum fortune OT 3; wealth **WS 3**, 104
Reihe row OT 2
  der Reihe nach sequentially OT 4
Reihenfolge order OT 1; sequencing OT 3; ranking OT 4
  in eine Reihenfolge bringen to sequence OT 3; to rank OT 4
Reim rhyme OT 2
Reinigungsmittel cleaner OT 3
Reis rice OT 1
Reise journey; trip, tour OT 1; voyage OT 3
Reisebus coach OT 1
Reiseführer guidebook OT 3
Reisekaufmann, -kauffrau travel agent OT 3
reisen to travel OT 1
Reisende(r) traveller OT 3
Reiseziel destination OT 4
Reiten horse riding OT 1
reizvoll attractive **WS 1**, 32
Reklamezettel leaflet OT 2
Rektor(in) principal OT 2
relativ relatively OT 4
Relativsatz relative clause OT 2
Religion religion OT 3
Religionsunterricht religious studies OT 1
religiös religious OT 3
Rennen race OT 2
rennen to run OT 1
Rennsport racing OT 2
Rente: in Rente gehen to retire **WS 3**, 103
Rentier reindeer OT 3
Reparatur repair OT 2
reparieren to mend OT 3; to repair **WS 2**, 64
repetitiv repetitive **WS 2**, 57
Reporter(in) reporter OT 1; correspondent OT 4
Reptil reptile OT 2
Republik republic OT 4
Requisite prop OT 1
reserviert reserved OT 2
Reservierung reservation OT 1
Reservoir reservoir **WS 1**, 34
Respekt respect **WS 1**, 30
respektlos disrespectful OT 3
respektvoll respectful OT 3
Ressource resource OT 4
Restaurant restaurant OT 1
retten to save OT 2
Rettung rescue OT 2; recovery OT 3
Rettungsleine lifeline OT 3
Rettungsring lifebuoy OT 3
Rettungssanitäter(in) paramedic OT 1
Rettungsschwimmer(in) lifeguard OT 4
Reue remorse **WS 2**, 64
revidieren to revise OT 2
Review review **WS 3**, 106
Revolution revolution OT 2
revolutionieren to revolutionize OT 4
Rezept recipe OT 2
Rezeption reception OT 1
Rezeptionist(in) receptionist OT 1
Richter(in) judge OT 2
richtig right; correct; true; proper OT 1; actual OT 4
Richtlinie guideline OT 3

Richtung: in Richtung toward(s) OT 2
riechen to smell OT 1
übel riechend smelly OT 3
Riegel bar OT 1
riesig enormous OT 1; huge; giant OT 2; massive OT 3
Riff reef **WS 1**, 26
rigide rigid **WS 2**, 61
Rinder cattle OT 4
Rindfleisch beef OT 2
ringen to wrestle OT 2
Ringen wrestling OT 2
rinnen to trickle OT 3
Rippe rib OT 3
Risiko risk OT 4
Ritt ride OT 1
Ritual ritual OT 4
Robbe seal OT 1
Rock skirt OT 1
Rolle role OT 1; roll OT 2
Rollenspiel roleplay OT 2
Rollschuh roller skate **WS 1**, 29
Rollstuhl wheelchair OT 2
Rollstuhlfahrer(in) wheelchair user OT 2
Rolltreppe escalator OT 1
Roman novel OT 2
römisch Roman OT 2
Röntgen X-ray OT 1
rosa pink OT 1
rot red OT 1
Rotwein red OT 1
Routine routine **WS 2**, 61
Rücken back OT 1
Rückgang decline **WS 1**, 24
Rückgrat backbone OT 2
Rucksack rucksack OT 1; backpack OT 2
mit dem Rucksack reisen to backpack OT 3
rücksichtsvoll thoughtful **WS 3**, 95
rückwärts backwards OT 3
Rudel pack OT 4
Ruderboot rowing boat OT 1
Ruderpinne tiller OT 3
rufen to exclaim OT 3
Rugby rugby OT 1
Ruhe rest OT 1; silence **WS 1**, 14
in Ruhe lassen to leave alone OT 2
Ruhe bewahren to keep calm OT 2
ruhig quiet OT 1; calm OT 2; steady OT 3
rühren to stir OT 2
Ruine ruin OT 2
Rumpf hull OT 3
rund round OT 1
Rundgang tour OT 1

S

sachlich factual OT 4
sachte gently OT 3
Sack sack OT 2
Sackhüpfen sack race OT 2
Safari safari OT 2
Saft juice OT 1
Sage legend OT 4
sagen to say OT 1
Sahne cream OT 1
Saite string OT 2
Salat salad OT 1
Salz salt OT 2
salzig salty OT 3
Samen seed OT 2
sammeln to collect OT 1; to gather OT 4
Sammlung collection OT 2
Samstag Saturday OT 1
samtartig velvety OT 2
Sand sand OT 1
sandig sandy **WS 1**, 29
Sandstein sandstone OT 4
Sandwich sandwich OT 1
Sänger(in) singer OT 1; vocalist OT 2
Sarg coffin OT 4
Satellit satellite OT 4
satthaben to be fed up OT 1
Satz sentence OT 1
sauer acidic **WS 1**, 28
Sauerstoff oxygen **WS 1**, 39
saugen to suck OT 4
Säugetier mammal OT 2
Säugling baby OT 1
Säule column OT 1
Sauna sauna OT 2
Saxofon saxophone OT 2
scannen to scan OT 2
Schach chess OT 1
Schädel skull OT 2
Schaden harm OT 3
Schadenersatz amends **WS 2**, 64
schädlich harmful **WS 2**, 65
Schädling pest **WS 1**, 25
Schaf sheep OT 1
Schäfer(in) shepherd OT 2
schaffen to create OT 2; to achieve OT 4
Schal scarf OT 1
Schale dish OT 2
Schamgefühl shame **WS 2**, 58
scharf hot OT 1; spicy; sharp OT 4
Schärpe sash OT 4
Schatten shade **WS 1**, 16
Schatten shadow OT 3
Schatz treasure OT 3
schätzen to guess OT 1; to estimate; to appreciate OT 4
Schatzmeister(in) treasurer OT 3
Schätzung guess OT 1
Schaubild diagram OT 1
Schauspieler(in) actor OT 1
Scheck cheque OT 4
Scheibe slice OT 1
(sich) scheiden lassen to get divorced OT 3
Scheidung divorce OT 3
Schein note OT 1
scheinen to shine OT 1; to seem OT 2; to appear OT 3
scheitern to fail OT 4
Schere scissors OT 1
Scheune barn OT 2
schick smartly; stylish; glam OT 4
schicken to send OT 1
Schiedsrichter(in) referee OT 3
schießen to shoot OT 3; to fire OT 4
Schießerei gunfire OT 3
Schiff ship OT 1; vessel OT 3
mit dem Schiff fahren to sail OT 2
Schild sign; notice OT 1; signpost **WS 3**, 88
Schildkröte tortoise OT 1
Schinken ham OT 1
Schlacht battle OT 4
schlachten to cull **WS 1**, 25
Schlachtschiff battleship OT 3
Schlaf sleep **WS 1**, 20
Schlafanzug pyjamas OT 3
schlafen to sleep OT 1
schlafend asleep OT 2
Schlafenszeit bedtime OT 2
Schlafzimmer bedroom OT 1
Schlag beat OT 4
schlagen to hit OT 1; to beat; to batter OT 4; to punch **WS 2**, 81
Schlagsahne whipped cream OT 3
Schlagzeile headline OT 2
Schlagzeug drums OT 1
Schlagzeuger(in) drummer OT 2
Schlamm mud OT 3
schlammig muddy OT 4
Schlammlawine mudslide **WS 1**, 34
Schlange snake; queue OT 1; serpent **WS 1**, 13
Schlankheitskuren dieting **WS 2**, 66
schlau savvy **WS 2**, 68; smart **WS 3**, 103
Schlauch tube OT 1
schlecht bad OT 1
Schlepper(in) coyote **WS 4**, 129
Schleuse lock OT 3
Schleusenwärter(in) lock keeper OT 3
schließen to close OT 1; to shut OT 2; to conclude OT 3

Schließfach locker OT 2
schließlich finally OT 1; eventually OT 3
Schlitten sled OT 4
Schlittschuh laufen to skate OT 2
Schlucht canyon OT 3
Schluss conclusion OT 3
Schlüssel key OT 1
schmackhaft tasty OT 2
schmecken to taste OT 1
schmelzen to melt OT 4
Schmerz pain OT 2; ache OT 3
schmerzen to hurt OT 1
Schmerzmittel painkiller OT 2
Schminke makeup **WS 2**, 68
Schmuck jewelry OT 2
schmücken to decorate OT 2
Schmuckstück jewel OT 3
schmuggeln to smuggle **WS 4**, 129
Schmutz dirt OT 4
schmutzig dirty OT 1
Schnabeltier platypus **WS 1**, 13
Schnappschuss shot OT 2
Schneckenpost snail mail OT 4
Schnee snow OT 1
schneebedeckt snow-capped OT 4
Schneemobil snowmobile OT 4
schneiden to cut OT 2; to chop OT 3
schneidern to tailor OT 4
schnell fast OT 1; quick; rapid OT 3
Schnitt edit OT 4
schnitzen to carve OT 2
Schnitzer(in) carver OT 4
Schnitzerei carving OT 4
Schnur string OT 2
schockieren to shock OT 4
Schokolade chocolate OT 1
Schokoladensplitter choc-chip OT 1
Schokoladensüchtige(r) chocoholic OT 3
schon already; yet OT 2
schön lovely; beautiful; nice OT 1
Schönheit beauty OT 3
Schöpfer(in) creator **WS 1**, 26
Schöpfung creation **WS 1**, 26
Schornstein chimney OT 3
Schottenrock kilt OT 2
schottisch Scottish OT 2
Schrank cupboard OT 1; cabinet **WS 3**, 113
Schrecken horror OT 4
schrecklich awful; terrible OT 1; dreadful OT 2
Schreibarbeit paperwork **WS 3**, 109
Schreibblock (mit speziellem Papier) legal pad **WS 3**, 113
schreiben to write OT 1
  neu schreiben to rewrite OT 2
Schreibkraft typist **WS 3**, 96
Schreibmaschine typewriter **WS 3**, 115
Schreibtisch desk OT 1
Schreibweise spelling OT 1
schreien to scream OT 3
Schriftrolle scroll OT 2
Schriftsteller(in) writer OT 1; novelist OT 4
Schritt step OT 1
schrubben to scrape OT 2
Schubkarre wheelbarrow OT 4
Schublade drawer OT 1
schüchtern shy OT 2
Schuh shoe OT 1
Schulabgänger(in) leaver **WS 3**, 90
Schulaufgaben schoolwork **WS 3**, 93
Schulausflug field trip OT 2
Schulball prom OT 3
Schuld fault OT 2; blame OT 4
schuldig guilty OT 4
  sich schuldig bekennen to plead guilty **WS 2**, 65
Schule school OT 1
Schüler(in) student OT 1
Schulhof playground OT 1
Schulkamerad(in) schoolmate OT 4
Schulleiter(in) head teacher OT 1
Schultag school day OT 1
Schultasche school bag OT 1
Schulter shoulder OT 1
schummeln to cheat OT 4
Schuppen shed OT 1
Schuss shot OT 2
Schüsse gunfire OT 3
Schüssel bowl OT 1
Schusswaffe gun OT 3
schütteln to shake OT 2
Schutz conservation OT 2; custody **WS 2**, 64
Schütze gunman OT 4
schützen to protect OT 2
Schutzgebiet sanctuary **WS 1**, 29
schwach weak OT 4
Schwäche weakness OT 4
schwächen to weaken OT 4
schwanger pregnant OT 3
Schwanz tail OT 2
schwappen to slop **WS 1**, 16
schwarz black OT 1
schweben to float; to soar OT 3
Schweigen silence **WS 1**, 14
Schwein pig OT 1
Schweinefleisch pork OT 2
Schwellung swelling OT 2
schwer difficult; heavy OT 1; severe OT 4
Schwert sword OT 1
Schwester sister OT 1
schwierig difficult; challenging OT 1
Schwierigkeit difficulty; trouble OT 2
Schwimmbecken pool OT 1
schwimmen to swim OT 1
Schwimmer(in) swimmer OT 3
Schwimmweste life jacket OT 3
schwindlig faint OT 2; dizzy OT 3
schwitzen to sweat OT 2
schwul gay **WS 2**, 50; queer **WS 2**, 55
Scout scout OT 3
sechs six OT 1
Sechstklässler(in) sixth grader OT 2
sechzehn sixteen OT 1
sechzig sixty OT 1
See lake OT 1
seefahrend seafaring OT 3
seekrank seasick OT 3
Seele soul OT 2
Seemann sailor; seaman OT 3
Seevogel seabird **WS 1**, 26
Segel sail **WS 1**, 43
Segeln sailing OT 1
Segment segment **WS 1**, 32
sehen to look; to see OT 1
Sehenswürdigkeit sight OT 1; attraction OT 2
sehr very; really OT 1; agonizingly OT 3
Sehvermögen sight OT 1
Seife soap OT 2
Seil rope OT 3
Seilrutsche zip line OT 1
sein to be OT 1
seine(r, -s) his OT 1
seit since OT 2
Seite side OT 1; page OT 1
  auf der anderen Seite across OT 1
Sekretär(in) secretary OT 1
sekundär secondary OT 1
Sekundarschule secondary school OT 1
Sekunde second OT 1
selbständig self-employed **WS 3**, 92
Selbstbedienung self-service OT 4
Selbstbewusstsein self-belief **WS 2**, 50
Selbstlaut vowel OT 1
selbstsicher confident OT 3
selbstständig self-sufficient OT 4
Selbstvertrauen confidence **WS 2**, 50
Selbstwertgefühl self-belief **WS 2**, 50
Selfie selfie OT 4
selten rare OT 2; uncommon **WS 1** , 17; seldom **WS 2**, 69
seltsam strange; weird OT 1
Semester term OT 2; semester OT 4
Senator(in) senator OT 4

Sendung programme OT 1; broadcast OT 3
Senf mustard OT 1
Senior(in) senior citizen OT 2
sensorisch sensory **WS 2**, 61
Serie series OT 4
servieren to serve OT 1
Sessel armchair OT 1
Sessellift chairlift **WS 1**, 31
Session session OT 4
Setting setting **WS 4**, 129
setzen to seat **WS 2**, 59
seufzen to sigh **WS 1**, 15
Sex sex **WS 2**, 52
Shampoo shampoo OT 3
sicher sure; safe OT 1; secure; certain OT 3
... sicher proof **WS 1**, 12
Sicherheit safety OT 2; security **WS 1**, 28
Sicherheitsbeamter(in) guard **WS 2**, 77
sicherlich certainly OT 2; surely OT 4
sichern to secure **WS 3**, 90
sicherstellen to ensure OT 4
Sicht view OT 1
sichtbar visible OT 4
Sichtweise perspective **WS 1**, 35
sie she; her OT 1
sieben seven OT 1
Siebenkampf heptathlon OT 2
siebzehn seventeen OT 1
siebzig seventy OT 1
Siedler(in) settler OT 3
Siedlung settlement OT 4
Sieg victory OT 4
Sieger(in) winner OT 1
Signal signal OT 2
Silbe syllable OT 3
Silber silver OT 1
silbern silver OT 1
simultan simultaneous **WS 3**, 107
singen to sing OT 1
sinken to sink OT 3
Sinn sense OT 2
sinnvoll meaningful OT 4
Sirene siren OT 3
Sirup syrup OT 3
Situation situation OT 1
sitzen to sit OT 1
Sitzplatz seat OT 2
Sitzung session OT 4
Skateboard skateboard OT 1
Skelett skeleton OT 2
Skelett... skeletal OT 3
Sketch sketch; skit OT 2
Skifahren skiing OT 3
Skilanglauf cross-country skiing **WS 1**, 13
Ski laufen to ski OT 3
Skizze sketch OT 2
Sklave, Sklavin slave OT 3
Skulptur sculpture OT 2
Skyline skyline OT 4
Slang slang OT 4
Slogan slogan OT 2
Slum slum **WS 4**, 141
Smartphone smartphone OT 3
SMS text OT 2
Snack snack OT 1
Snowboardfahren snowboarding OT 3
so such OT 2
Socke sock OT 1
Sofa sofa OT 1
sofort straight away OT 2; immediately OT 3
sogar even OT 1
Sohn son OT 1
Soldat(in) soldier OT 1
sollte ought to **WS 3**, 94
solo solo OT 2
Sommer summer OT 1
Sommersprossen freckles OT 3
Sonne sun OT 1
Sonnen... solar OT 3
Sonnenbrand sunburn OT 2
Sonnenschein sunshine OT 3
Sonnenschutzmittel sunscreen OT 2
Sonnenstich sunstroke OT 2
Sonnenuhr sundial OT 3
Sonnenuntergang sunset OT 3
sonnig sunny OT 1
Sonntag Sunday OT 1
sonst otherwise OT 4
  sonst noch else OT 1
Sorge care OT 2; worry **WW**, 10; anxiety **WS 1**, 34; concern **WS 2**, 37
  sich Sorgen machen to worry OT 1
Sorgerecht custody **WS 2**, 64
sorgfältig careful OT 1
sorglos careless OT 2
Soße sauce OT 1
sozial social OT 2
soziale Signal social cue **WS 2**, 61
Spacewalker spacewalker **WS 3**, 110
Spaghetti spaghetti OT 1
Spalte column OT 1
Spaniel spaniel OT 2
spanisch Spanish OT 1
sparen to save OT 2
Spaß fun OT 1
  Spaß verstehen to take a joke OT 2
spät late OT 1
  später einmal one day OT 2
Speck bacon OT 1
Speer spear OT 4
Speisekarte menu OT 1
spektakulär spectacular OT 2
spekulieren to speculate OT 4
Spende donation OT 2
spenden to donate OT 2
Spendensammlung fundraising OT 2
Spender dispenser **WS 3**, 112
Sperre ban **WS 1**, 27
Spezialeffekte special effects OT 2
(sich) spezialisieren to specialize OT 3
Spezialist(in) specialist **WS 2**, 61; geek **WS 2**, 68
Spezies species **WS 1**, 21
spezifisch specific OT 2
Spiegel mirror OT 1
spiegeln to reflect OT 2
Spiel match; game OT 1
Spielekonsole game console OT 4
spielen to play OT 1
Spieler(in) player OT 1; gamer OT 4
Spielfeld pitch OT 3
Spielplatz playground OT 1
Spind locker OT 2
Spinne spider OT 1
spitz spiky **WS 3**, 103
Spitze tip; top OT 1
Spitzen... peak OT 4
Spitzname nickname OT 4
Sponsor(in) sponsor OT 2
Sport sport; athletics; PE OT 1
Sport... sporting **WS 1**, 15
Sporthalle gymnasium OT 4
Sportler(in) athlete OT 2
sportlich sporty OT 3; sporting **WS 1**, 15
Sportunterricht PE (physical education) OT 1
Sprache language OT 1
sprachlich linguistic OT 4
Sprachwissenschaftler(in) linguist **WS 2**, 70
sprechen to speak OT 1
Sprechstunde surgery **WS 3**, 106
Springbrunnen fountain OT 1
springen to jump OT 2
Spritztour joyride **WS 2**, 64
Sprudel soda **WS 2**, 66
sprühen to spray OT 3
sprunghaft erratic **WS 2**, 72
Spülbecken sink OT 3
Spur trail OT 2
Spürhund hound OT 2
Staatsangehörigkeit nationality OT 2
Staatsanwalt, -anwältin prosecutor **WS 2**, 64

Staatsanwaltschaft prosecution **WS 2**, 65
stabil steady OT 3
Stabilität stability **WS 3**, 104
stachelig spiky **WS 3**, 103
Stachelrochen stingray **WS 1**, 21
Stadion stadium OT 1
Stadt town; city OT 1
Stadtbewohner(innen) townspeople OT 4
städtisch urban OT 4
Stahl steel OT 2
Stall stable OT 4
Stamm tribe OT 2; clan **WS 1**, 26
stammen aus to date back; to originate OT 4
Stammes… tribal OT 3
Stand stall OT 4
Standard default OT 3; standard **WS 2**, 66; norm **WS 3**, 102
standardmäßig standard **WS 1**, 16
ständig constant OT 4
Standort location OT 2
Standpunkt viewpoint OT 3
Stange pole OT 4
stapeln to stack OT 4
Star star OT 1
stark strong OT 2; severe OT 4; intense **WS 1**, 32
  stärker machen to strengthen OT 4
Stärke strength OT 4
stärken to empower **WS 3**, 109
starr stiff **WS 2**, 61; rigid **WS 2**, 61
starren to stare OT 2
starten to launch OT 4
Station station OT 1
Statistik statistic OT 3
stattdessen instead OT 2
Statue statue OT 1
Status status **WW**, 11
Stau congestion OT 4
Staub dust OT 2
staubsaugen to vacuum **WS 2**, 54
Staubsauger vacuum cleaner OT 4
Steak steak OT 1
stechen to sting OT 2
Stechmücke mosquito OT 2
stecken to stick OT 1
Stecknadel pin OT 1
stehen to stand OT 1
  auf etwas stehen to be into OT 2
steif stiff **WS 2**, 61
steigen to climb OT 1
steil steep OT 2
Stein stone OT 1; rock OT 2
stellen to put OT 1; to set OT 2
sterben to die OT 1
Stereotype stereotype **WS 2**, 54
stereotypisch stereotypical **WS 2**, 54
Stern star OT 1
Steroid steroid **WS 2**, 50
Steuer tax OT 4
steuern to steer OT 3
Stichwort headword; keyword OT 2
Stiefel boot OT 1
Stift pen OT 1
Stigma stigma **WS 2**, 72
Stil style OT 2
still quiet; still OT 1
Stimme voice OT 2; vote **WS 1**, 36
Stimmung mood OT 3
Stipendium scholarship **WS 2**, 56
Stirn forehead OT 3
  die Stirn runzeln to frown OT 3
Stockwerk floor OT 1
  im oberen Stockwerk upstairs OT 1
  im unteren Stockwerk downstairs OT 1
Stoff cloth OT 2
stolpern to trip OT 2
Stolz pride **WS 1**, 32
  Stolz auf etwas sein to pride oneself **WS 2**, 57
stolz proud OT 2
stören to disturb OT 3; to bother OT 4
Störung disruption OT 4; disorder **WS 2**, 61
Storyboard storyboard OT 4
stoßen to knock; to push OT 2
Strafe sentence **WS 2**, 64
Strafe penalty OT 3
strafrechtlich penal **WS 1**, 22
Strafstoß penalty OT 3
Straftat offence **WS 2**, 64
Strand beach OT 1; seashore OT 4
Sträßchen laneway **WS 1**, 29
Straße road; street OT 1
Straßenbahn tram; trolley (AE) OT 2
Straßenmusiker(in) busker **WS 1**, 29
Strategie strategy **WS 1**, 15
Streaming streaming **WS 2**, 58
Strecke route OT 2
streicheln to stroke OT 3; to pet OT 4
Streichholz match OT 2
Streifen strip OT 2
Streik strike OT 4
streiken to strike OT 4
Streit argument OT 1
(sich) streiten to quarrel OT 2; to argue OT 3
Streitkräfte armed forces OT 4
streng strict OT 2
Stress stress OT 1
stressig stressful OT 4
streuen to sprinkle OT 2
Stroh straw OT 4
Strohhalm straw OT 4
Strom electricity OT 2
Struktur structure OT 1
strukturieren to structure **WS 1**, 29
Strumpfhose tights OT 2
Stück piece OT 1; bit OT 2
Student(in) student OT 1
Studie study OT 1
Studienanfänger freshman OT 4
Studiengebühr(en) tuition **WS 2**, 56
studieren to study OT 1
Studio studio **WS 1**, 32
Studium studies OT 1
Stufe step; level OT 1
Stuhl chair OT 1
Stunde hour; class OT 1
Stundenplan timetable OT 1; schedule (AE) OT 2
Sturm storm OT 2
stürzen to fall OT 1
Stütze prop OT 1
Substantiv noun OT 1
Substanz substance OT 3
Suche search OT 2
suchen to search OT 4, to seek **WS 1**, 16
  nach etw. suchen to scavenge **WS 4**, 132
Sucht addiction **WS 2**, 73
Süchtigkeit addiction **WS 2**, 73
Süden south OT 2
südlich southern OT 4
südwestlich southwest OT 3
summen to hum OT 4
super super **WS 2**, 66
Superheld superhero **WS 2**, 66
Supermarkt supermarket OT 1
Suppe soup OT 1
Surfen surfing OT 1
Sweatshirt sweatshirt OT 1
Symbol symbol OT 1
Synästhesie synaesthesia OT 2
Synonym synonym OT 2
System system OT 2
systematisch systematically **WS 1**, 24
Szene scene OT 2
Szenenbuch storyboard OT 4

T

Tabak tobacco OT 4
Tablet tablet OT 2
Tablett tray OT 2
Tablette pill **WS 2**, 66

Tabulator tab OT 4
Tafel blackboard OT 1; tablet; board OT 2
Tag day OT 1
Tagesausflug day out OT 2
Tagesordnung agenda OT 3
täglich daily OT 2
Takt beat OT 4
  aus dem Takt kommen to be off beat OT 4
Tal valley OT 1
Talent talent **WS 3**, 99
talentiert talented **WS 1**, 32
Tank tank OT 3
Tante aunt OT 1
Tanz dance **WS 1**, 31
Tanzen dancing OT 1
tapfer brave OT 1
Tasche case OT 1; pocket OT 2
Taschenlampe torch OT 1; flashlight OT 2
Taschenmesser pocketknife OT 2
Tasse cup OT 1
Tastatur keyboard OT 1
Täter(in) offender **WS 2**, 64
Tätigkeit occupation OT 4
Tätowierung tattoo OT 3
Tatsache fact OT 1
taub deaf OT 3
Taube pigeon **WS 3**, 103
tauchen to dive OT 3; to dip OT 4
Taucheranzug wetsuit OT 1
Taucher(in) diver OT 3
tauschen to swap OT 3
Taxi cab OT 1
Technik technique OT 4
technisch technical; tech OT 2; technological OT 4
Technologie technology OT 1
technologisch technological OT 4
Tee tea OT 1
Teenager teen; teenager OT 2
Teich pond OT 1
Teil part; piece OT 1; section OT 2
Teil... semi... **WS 1**, 24
teilen to share OT 2
  (sich) teilen to divide OT 2
teilnehmen to take part OT 2; to participate OT 4
Teilnehmer(in) participant OT 4
teilweise partly OT 4
teilzeitlich part-time **WS 1**, 14
Telefon phone OT 1
Teller plate OT 1
Tempel temple OT 1
Temperatur temperature OT 2
Temperaturregler thermostat **WS 3**, 112
temporär temporary OT 4
Tempus tense OT 1
Tennis tennis OT 1
Termin appointment OT 3
Terminkalender diary OT 1
Terrier terrier OT 2
Test test OT 1
teuer expensive OT 1
Text text OT 2
Texter(in) songwriter **WS 2**, 50
Theater theatre OT 1
  Theater spielen to act OT 1
Theaterstück play OT 1
Thema topic; subject OT 1; issue OT 2
thematisch themed OT 4
theoretisch theoretical OT 4
Therapie therapy **WS 2**, 61
Thermalquelle hot spring OT 2
Thermostat thermostat **WS 3**, 112
Thron throne OT 4
tief deep OT 1; low OT 2
Tier animal OT 1; beast OT 2
Tierwelt wildlife OT 2
Tiger tiger OT 1
Timer timer **WS 3**, 112
tippen to key OT 2; to type **WS 2**, 59; to tap **WS 1**, 68
Tisch table OT 1
Tischdecke tablecloth OT 2
Tischler(in) carpenter OT 3
Tischtennis ping-pong OT 4
Titel title OT 1
Toast toast OT 2
Tochter daughter OT 1
Tod death OT 2
Todesdatum date of death OT 2
tödlich deadly **WS 1**, 13
Toilette toilet OT 2
tolerant tolerant **WS 2**, 80
Toleranz tolerance **WS 2**, 50
toll great OT 1; awesome OT 2; stunning **WS 1**, 28
Tomate tomato OT 1
Ton tone OT 4
Tonerkartusche toner cartridge **WS 3**, 113
Tonne bin; ton OT 4
Toolkit toolkit **WS 3**, 105
Topf pot OT 2
Töpfern pottery OT 3
Tor goal; gate OT 1
Tornado tornado OT 4
Tortendiagramm pie chart OT 4
Torwart goalkeeper OT 4
tot dead OT 1
töten to kill OT 1
Touchdown touchdown OT 2
Tourismus tourism OT 3
Tourist(in) tourist OT 1
Tradition tradition OT 2; heritage OT 4
traditionell traditional OT 2
tragbar portable OT 4
Trage... carrier **WS 3**, 104
tragen to wear; to carry OT 1
tragisch tragic OT 3
Trailer trailer **WS 1**, 27
Trainer(in) coach OT 1
trainieren to train OT 2
Traktor tractor OT 2
Träne tear OT 2
trans... trans **WS 2**, 51
transatlantisch transatlantic OT 3
transkribieren to transcribe **WS 3**, 96
Transkribierer(in) transcriber **WS 3**, 96
Transparent banner OT 4
transportieren to transport OT 3
transsexuell transgender **WS 2**, 55
Traum dream OT 2
Traumzeit dreamtime **WS 1**, 26
traurig sad OT 1; upset OT 2
treffen to meet OT 1
Treffen meeting OT 1
Treffer dunk OT 3
treiben to herd OT 2; to float OT 3; to drive **WS 1**, 24
Treidelpfad towpath OT 3
Trend fashion OT 1; trend OT 4
Trend trend OT 4
Trendwende tipping point **WS 1**, 28
Treppe stairs OT 1
treten to kick OT 1
treu loyal OT 4
Tribunal tribunal **WS 2**, 65
Trick trick **WS 2**, 68
Trilogie trilogy **WS 1**, 31
trinken to drink OT 1
Trinkhalm straw OT 4
Trinkspruch toast OT 2
Trinkwasserbrunnen water fountain OT 2
triumphierend triumphant OT 3
trocken dry OT 2; arid **WS 1**, 25
Trog trough OT 3
Trompete trumpet OT 4
Tropen... tropical OT 4
tropfen to drip OT 3
trotz in spite of **WS 1**, 25
trotzdem anyway OT 1
trübe murky OT 4
Truhe chest OT 1
Truppe troop OT 3
Truthahn turkey OT 3

Tschüss! bye OT 1
T-Shirt T-shirt OT 1
tun to do; to put OT 1
 so tun, als ob to pretend OT 1
Tunika tunic OT 2
Tunnel tunnel OT 3
Tür door OT 1
Turm tower OT 1
Turnen gym OT 1
Turnhalle gym OT 1; gymnasium OT 4
Turnier joust OT 2; tournament OT 3
Turnschuh sneaker **WS 2**, 68; trainer **WS 4**, 141
Türschwelle doorstep **WS 1**, 19
Tüte bag OT 1
Tuten blast OT 3
Tutor(in) tutor OT 2
Typ guy **WS 1**, 30
typisch typical OT 2

U

U-Bahn metro; subway; underground OT 1
Übel evil **WS 4**, 128
üben to practise OT 1
über about OT 1; via OT 2
über... hyper OT 4
überall everywhere OT 1
Überarbeitung edit OT 4
überbewerten to overrate **WS 2**, 77
Überblick overview OT 4
übereinstimmen (mit) to conform (to) **WS 2**, 54
Überfall assault **WS 2**, 64
überfliegen to scan OT 2; to skim **WS 1**, 32
überflüssig unnecessary **WS 2**, 77
überfüllt crowded OT 2
Übergang transition **WS 2**, 55
übergeben to surrender OT 4
(sich) übergeben to throw up OT 2
überlaufen to overflow OT 4
Überleben survival OT 2
überleben to survive OT 3
Überlebende(r) survivor OT 3
übermäßig overly **WS 3**, 95
übernehmen to resume **WS 1**, 26
überprüfen to check OT 1; to review OT 3
überqueren to cross OT 1
überraschen to shock OT 4; to surprise **WS 2**, 71
überraschend surprising OT 2
überrascht surprised OT 2; amazed OT 3
Überraschung surprise OT 1; shock OT 3
überreden to persuade OT 3
überreichen to present OT 1
Überschrift heading OT 3
Übersetzer(in) translator **WS 2**, 70
Übersetzung translation OT 2
Übersicht overview OT 4
Überstunden overtime **WS 3**, 103
übertragbar transferable **WS 3**, 98
übertragen to transfer **WS 3**, 113
übertreffen to beat OT 4; to surpass **WS 3**, 105
 (sich) selbst übertreffen to excel OT 4
übertreiben to overdo **WS 2**, 66
Übertreibung exaggeration OT 4
übertrieben exaggerated **WS 1**, 21
überwachen to oversee OT 4
Überwachung supervision **WS 2**, 65
überwiegend dominant OT 4
überwinden to overcome OT 4
überzeugen to persuade OT 3; to convince **WS 3**, 105
überzeugend persuasive **WS 1**, 37
üblich usual OT 2
übrig spare OT 3
übriggeblieben leftover OT 4
Übung practice; exercise OT 1
Übungsheft exercise book OT 1
Ufer bank OT 3
Uhr clock; o'clock OT 1
um around OT 1
 um ... herum about OT 1
Umarmung hug OT 1
umdrehen to flip **WS 3**, 93
umfallen to fall over OT 2
umfassen to involve OT 4
Umfeld environment OT 2
umformulieren to rephrase **WS 3**, 100
Umfrage survey OT 1; poll **WS 3**, 98
umgeben to surround OT 4
Umgebung setting **WS 4**, 129
umgehen to deal with OT 2
umgehend immediate **WS 1**, 24
Umhang cloak OT 2
Umhängeband lanyard **WS 3**, 112
umkehren to invert **WS 1**, 31
umkippen to tip over **WS 1**, 31
Umlaufbahn orbit OT 4
umreißen to outline OT 4
umschreiben to paraphrase OT 3
umsetzen to implement OT 4
Umstand circumstance **WS 2**, 64
umstellen to rearrange OT 2; to invert **WS 1**, 31
Umstellung switch **WS 1**, 19
Umstieg switch **WS 1**, 19
umstoßen to knock over OT 2
umstritten controversial OT 3
Umwelt environment OT 2
Umwelt... environmental OT 4
umweltfreundlich eco-friendly OT 3
Umweltschützer(in) environmentalist OT 3
umziehen to move OT 1; to relocate OT 4
Umzug parade; procession OT 2
Umzugswagen removal van OT 4
unabhängig independent; autonomous; self-sufficient OT 4
 unabhängig von regardless OT 4
Unabhängigkeit independence OT 2
unangenehm nasty OT 2; unpleasant **WS 1**, 35
unbeaufsichtigt unattended OT 4
unbedingt necessarily OT 4
unbegleitet unaccompanied OT 2
unbekannt unfamiliar OT 2; unknown OT 3
unbequem uncomfortable OT 2
unberührt unspoilt OT 3
unbeschwert lightheartedly OT 4
unbestimmt vague **WS 1**, 27
unbewohnbar uninhabitable OT 4
unbezahlt unpaid **WS 3**, 92
und and OT 1
uneben bumpy OT 4
Uneinigkeit disagreement OT 3
unendlich endless OT 4
unentschieden undecided **WS 1**, 19
unentschlossen undecided **WS 1**, 19
unerwartet unexpected **WS 2**, 71
unerwarteterweise unexpectedly OT 3
unfähig unable OT 4
Unfall accident OT 1
unfreundlich unkind OT 3
ungarisch Hungarian OT 2
ungeduldig impatient **WS 4**, 129
ungeeignet unfit OT 2
ungefähr about OT 1; roughly OT 3; approximately **WW**, 10
ungenau inaccurate OT 4
ungeschickt clumsy OT 2
ungewöhnlich unusual OT 2; uncommon **WS 1**, 17
ungezogen naughty OT 2
unglaublich incredible OT 2; unbelievable OT 4
ungleichmäßig patchy OT 4
unglücklich unhappy; miserable OT 1
unheimlich scary OT 2
unhöflich rude OT 2
Uni uni OT 3
Uniform uniform OT 1
Union union OT 4

Unisex... unisex **WS 2**, 54
Universität university OT 1; college **WS 1**, 32
Universum universe OT 4
unkonventionell unconventional **WS 2**, 80
Unkraut weed **WS 1**, 30
unmittelbar immediate **WS 1**, 24
unmöglich impossible OT 2
unnatürlich unnatural **WS 2**, 76
unnötig unnecessary **WS 2**, 77
Unordnung mess OT 2
  in Unordnung bringen to mess up OT 2
unregelmäßig irregular OT 1
uns us OT 1; ourselves OT 3
unsere(r, -s) our; ours OT 1
unsicher insecure **WS 3**, 98
Unsicherheit uncertainty **WS 3**, 98
unsichtbar invisible **WS 3**, 110
Unsinn nonsense OT 1
unten beneath OT 3
unter under OT 1; below OT 2; among OT 3
unterbrechen to interrupt OT 2
Unterbrechung disruption OT 4
Unterdrückung oppression **WS 4**, 128
untergeordnet menial **WS 3**, 103
unterhalb underneath **WS 1**, 13
unterhalten to entertain OT 4
Unterhaltung entertainment OT 2
Unterkühlung hypothermia OT 2
Unterkunft accommodation OT 4
Unternehmen company OT 1; venture **WS 3**, 109; enterprise **WS 3**, 109
Unternehmer(in) entrepreneur **WS 3**, 99
Unternehmertum entrepreneurship OT 4
Unterricht lesson OT 1
unterrichten to teach OT 1; to tutor **WS 3**, 93
Unterschied difference OT 1
unterschiedlich different OT 1; varied OT 4
  unterschiedlich behandeln to discriminate **WS 3**, 94
Unterschlupf shelter OT 2
unterschreiben to sign OT 2
unterstützen to support OT 1; to assist OT 4
unterstützend supportive **WS 1**, 14
Unterstützung backing OT 4; assistance **WS 2**, 57; aid **WS 2**, 59
untersuchen to investigate OT 3; to examine OT 4
Untersuchung study OT 1; analysis **WS 2**, 74
Unterwelt underworld **WS 4**, 128
untrinkbar undrinkable **WS 1**, 25
unvergesslich memorable OT 3; unforgettable **WS 1**, 29
unverheiratet unmarried **WS 2**, 52
unvernünftig foolishly **WS 2**, 65
unverwechselbar distinctive **WS 1**, 32
unvollständig incomplete **WS 2**, 53
Unzufriedenheit dissatisfaction **WS 2**, 67
unzugänglich inaccessible OT 3
urban urban OT 4
Urkunde diploma OT 4; deed **WS 1**, 26
Urlaub holiday OT 1; vacation OT 2
Urlaubsort resort OT 3
Ursprung origin OT 3
ursprünglich original OT 3; inital **WS 3**, 108
Urvater forefather OT 4
usw. etc. OT 3

V

vage vague **WS 1**, 27
Vampir vampire OT 2
Vanille vanilla OT 1
Vanillesoße custard OT 1
Variante variation **WS 1**, 33
Variation variation **WS 1**, 33
variieren to vary **WS 2**, 56
Vater father OT 1
vegan vegan OT 4
Veganer(in) vegan OT 4
vegetarisch veggie; vegetarian OT 2
Venusmuschel clam OT 3
Verabredung date OT 3
verabscheuen to loath **WS 1**, 25
verändern to transform OT 4; to shift **WS 2**, 70
Veränderung shift **WS 2**, 58
verängstigt scared; frightened OT 1; terrified OT 3
veranschaulichen to visualize OT 4
veranstalten to put on OT 1
verantwortlich responsible OT 3
Verantwortung responsibility OT 3
verärgert upset; cross OT 2; annoyed OT 3
Verb verb OT 1
verbal verbal **WS 2**, 57
Verband bandage OT 2
verbergen to conceal **WS 2**, 55
verbessern to correct OT 1; to enhance; to enrich OT 4
  (sich) verbessern to improve OT 3
Verbesserung improvement OT 3
verbieten to ban OT 3
verbinden to join up; to connect OT 2
Verbindung connection; link OT 2; tie **WW**, 11
  in Verbindung in touch OT 2
  in Verbindung bringen (mit) to associate (with) **WS 4**, 128
verblüfft puzzled **WS 1**, 14
Verbot ban **WS 1**, 27
verbrauchen to consume OT 4
Verbraucher(in) consumer **WS 2**, 68
Verbrechen crime OT 4
verbreiten to spread OT 4
Verbrennungs... internal combustion OT 4
verbringen to spend OT 1
verbunden linked OT 2; devoted OT 4
verdächtig suspicious OT 3
verderben to spoil OT 2
Verderben spoilage OT 4
verdeutlichen to illustrate OT 4
verdienen to deserve OT 2; to earn OT 3
(sich) verdoppeln to double **WS 1**, 17
verehren to worship **WS 4**, 136
Verein club OT 1
vereinbaren to arrange OT 2
Vereinbarung agreement OT 3; arrangement **WS 2**, 53
vereinigen to unite **WS 1**, 13
Verfahren operation; procedure OT 4
verfallen to decline **WW**, 11
verfallen ruined OT 3
Verfassung constitution OT 4
Verfassungs... constitutional OT 4
verfaulen to rot **WS 1**, 25
verfeinern to refine OT 4
verfolgen to pursue OT 4
Verfolgung pursuit OT 4
verfügbar available OT 4
Verfügbarkeit availability OT 4
vergeben to forgive OT 2; to award OT 4
vergeigen to mess up OT 2
vergessen to forget OT 1
Vergleich comparison **WS 1**, 29
vergleichbar (mit) comparable (to) **WS 2**, 56
vergleichen to compare OT 1
Vergnügen treat **WS 1**, 29
verhaften to arrest OT 4
(sich) verhalten to act OT 1
Verhalten behavior OT 3
Verhältnis relation **WS 1**, 30
Verhältniswort preposition OT 1
verheerend devastating **WS 1**, 34
verhindern to prevent OT 4
verhungern to starve OT 1

Verhütung prevention OT 2
Verkauf sale OT 3
Verkäufe sales OT 2
verkaufen to sell OT 1
Verkäufer(in) sales assistant OT 2
Verkehr traffic OT 1
verklemmt uptight **WS 2**, 52
verknallt: (in jmdn.) verknallt sein to have a crush on OT 4
verkünden to declare OT 4
Verlangen demand **WS 3**, 102
verlängert prolonged **WS 1**, 25
verlangsamen to slow down OT 4
verlassen to leave OT 1; to evacuate OT 4
(sich) verlassen auf to rely on OT 4
verlässlich reliable OT 4
Verleger(in) publisher **WS 3**, 91
verleihen to award OT 4
verletzen to injure OT 2; to insult **WS 1**, 26
verletzt hurt OT 1
Verletzung injury OT 2
verlieben: sich verlieben to fall in love **WS 2**, 50
verlieren to lose OT 1
Verlust loss OT 4
Vermächtnis legacy OT 4
vermeiden to avoid OT 4
vermissen to miss OT 2
vermitteln to impart; to communicate OT 4; to convey **WS 2**, 71
vermuten to suppose OT 1
Verneinung negative OT 1
vernichten to wipe out **WS 1**, 39
vernünftig sensible OT 2
veröffentlichen to release; to publish OT 4
Veröffentlichung publication OT 4
Verordnung act **WS 1**, 43
Verpackung packaging OT 3
verpflichtend mandatory OT 4
verpflichtet sein to be obliged (to) **WS 2**, 76
Verputz plaster OT 1
verringern to reduce OT 4
verrückt crazy; mad OT 2
Verrückte(r) nut **WS 1**, 14
Vers verse OT 3
Versammlung assembly OT 1
verschieden various; diverse OT 4
verschlafen to oversleep OT 4
verschlüsselt in code OT 2
verschmutzen to foul **WS 1**, 25; to pollute **WS 1**, 25
Verschmutzung pollution OT 3
verschneit snowy OT 4
verschütten to spill OT 2
verschwenden to waste OT 3
verschwinden to disappear OT 3; to vanish OT 4
versehentlich by accident; by mistake OT 2; accidentally OT 3
verseuchen to foul **WS 1**, 25; to pollute **WS 1**, 25
Version version OT 2
versorgen mit to provide OT 4
Versorgung catering OT 3
Verspätung delay OT 4
versprechen to promise OT 2
Versprechen promise OT 2
Verstand mind OT 1
verstärken to reinforce **WS 2**, 54
verstaubt dusty OT 4
verstauchen to sprain OT 2
Verstauchung sprain OT 2
(sich) verstecken to hide OT 3
verstehen to understand OT 1
verstopfen to plug in OT 1; to clog OT 4
Versuch attempt OT 2
versuchen to try OT 1
vertäuen to moor OT 3
verteidigen to defend **WS 1**, 25
Verteidigung defence **WS 2**, 65
verteilen to distribute OT 4
Vertrag treaty; contract OT 4
Vertrauen faith OT 3
vertrauen to trust OT 2
vertraut familiar OT 2
Vertrautheit familiarity OT 4
vertreten to represent OT 3
Vertreter(in) representative OT 4
vertrödeln to muck around **WS 2**, 55
verunreinigen to contaminate **WS 1**, 34
verursachen to cause OT 2
verurteilen to sentence **WS 2**, 64; to convict **WS 2**, 74
Verurteilte(r) convict **WS 1**, 17
Verurteilung sentence **WS 2**, 64; conviction **WS 2**, 74
vervollständigen to complete OT 1
Vervollständigung completion OT 4
Verwahrung custody **WS 2**, 64
verwandt related OT 3
Verwandte(r) relative OT 3; kinsman OT 4
Verwarnung caution **WS 2**, 74
verwendbar usable **WS 3**, 104
verwirrend confusing OT 2
verwirrt confused OT 2; puzzled **WS 1**, 14
Verzögerung delay OT 4
verzweifelt desperate OT 3
Video video OT 1
Video-Blog vlog OT 3
Videokassette video OT 1
Videospiel video game OT 2
Vieh livestock **WS 1**, 28
Viehbestand livestock **WS 1**, 28
viel lots; a lot OT 1
viele many OT 1
vielfach multiple OT 2
Vielfalt variety OT 4
vielfältig diverse OT 4
Vielfältigkeit diversity OT 4
vielleicht maybe OT 1; perhaps OT 3
vier four OT 1
Viertel quarter OT 1
viertel vor quarter to OT 1
vierzehn fourteen OT 1
vierzig forty OT 1
Vintage vintage **WS 3**, 90
violett violet OT 2
viral viral OT 4
virtuell virtual **WS 1**, 29
Visualisierung visualization OT 3
visuell visual OT 2
Vizepräsident(in) vice-president OT 4
Vlog vlog OT 3
vloggen to vlog OT 3
Vlogger(in) vlogger OT 3
Vogel bird OT 1
Vokal vowel OT 1
Volks... folk OT 2
voll full OT 1
Volleyball volleyball **WS 1**, 21
völlig totally OT 3; thoroughly **WS 3**, 106
Vollstreckung enforcement **WS 4**, 129
vollzeit full time OT 2
Volontär(in) intern **WS 3**, 106
von by; of from; off OT 1
vor before; ago OT 1
Voraussetzung requirement **WS 1**, 37
vorbereiten to prepare; to get ready OT 1
Vorbereitung preparation OT 2
Vordergrund foreground OT 4
Vorderseite front OT 1
voreingenommen biased **WS 2**, 72
Voreingenommenheit bias **WS 2**, 54
Vorfahr(in) ancestor OT 3
Vorfall incident **WS 2**, 65
vorführen to demonstrate **WS 2**, 58
Vorgang operation OT 4
vorgeben to pretend OT 1
Vorgehen approach **WS 2**, 59
Vorhang curtain OT 2
vorher previously OT 4
Vorhersage prediction OT 2
vorhersagen to predict OT 2

vorhersehbar predictable **WS 1**, 24
Vorlage template OT 4
Vorlesung lecture OT 4
Vorliebe preference OT 4
Vorrat supply OT 3
Vorschlag suggestion OT 1
vorschlagen to suggest OT 1
vorschreiben to prescribe **WS 2**, 56
vorschulisch preschool **WS 2**, 63
vorsichtig careful OT 1
  vorsichtig sein to be aware OT 4
vorsingen to audition OT 3
Vorspeise starter OT 1
Vorsprechen audition OT 3
vorsprechen to audition OT 3
vorstellen to present OT 1; to introduce OT 2
  (sich) etwas vorstellen to imagine OT 1
Vorstellung introduction OT 2
Vorstrafregister criminal record **WS 2**, 64
Vorteil pro OT 2; advantage OT 3; benefit OT 4
vorteilhaft beneficial OT 2
vortreten to step up **WS 2**, 53
vorwärts forwards OT 2
Vorwurf blame OT 4
vorziehen to prefer OT 1
Vulkan volcano OT 2

W
wach awake OT 2
wachsen to grow OT 1; to expand **WS 3**, 101
Wachstum growth **WS 2**, 66
Wächter(in) guard **WS 2**, 77
Waffe weapon OT 3
Waffel waffle OT 3
wagen to dare OT 2
Wagen trolley; carriage OT 2; wagon OT 4
Wahl choice OT 1; option OT 2; election OT 3
Wahl... electoral OT 4
Wahlbezirk constituency OT 4
wählen to elect; to select OT 4
Wähler(in) voter; constituent OT 4
Wahlmann elector OT 4
Wahlrecht vote **WS 1**, 36
Wahlstimme vote **WS 1**, 36
wahr true OT 1
während while OT 2; whereas **WS 3**, 98
Wahrheit truth OT 3
wahrscheinlich probably; likely OT 2
Wahrzeichen landmark OT 3
Wal whale OT 2
Wald forest OT 1; woods OT 2; woodland OT 4
Walfang whaling OT 2
walisisch Welsh OT 1
Walross walrus OT 4
Walspeck blubber OT 2
Wams doublet OT 3
Wand wall OT 1
wandern to hike OT 1
Wandgemälde mural OT 2
wann when OT 1
warm warm OT 1
Wärme warmth OT 4
warnen to warn OT 2
Warnung warning OT 2; caution **WS 2**, 74
warten to wait OT 1; to hang on OT 2
Warteschlange queue OT 1
Wartung maintenance OT 3
warum why OT 1
was what OT 1
Waschbär racoon OT 4
Wäsche laundry OT 3
waschen to wash OT 2
Wäscherei laundry OT 3
Wäscher(in) washer OT 4
Wasser water OT 1
wasserdicht waterproof OT 2
Wasserfall fall; waterfall OT 1
Wasserhahn tap OT 3
Wasserkraft hydro-electric OT 4
Wasserloch waterhole **WS 1**, 38
Wasserschildkröte turtle OT 2
Wasserstelle watering hole **WS 1**, 25
Wasserwaage spirit level **WS 3**, 112
Wechsel transition **WS 2**, 55
Wechselgeld change OT 1
wechseln to change OT 1; to exchange **WS 1**, 14
Wecker alarm OT 2
weder ... noch neither ... nor OT 4
Weg way; path OT 1; track OT 2
weg off OT 1; away OT 2
Wegbeschreibungen directions OT 2
wegen due to **WS 1**, 28
Wegweiser signpost **WS 3**, 88
wehen to blow OT 2
wehtun to hurt OT 1
weiblich female OT 2
weich soft OT 1
(sich) weigern to refuse OT 4
weil because OT 1
weinen to cry OT 1
Weinrebe vine OT 4
weiß white OT 1
weit far OT 1; wide OT 2
  weit entfernt distant OT 4
weiter further OT 4
  weiter vorn ahead OT 2
weiterführend secondary OT 1
  weiterführende Schule secondary school OT 1
weitermachen to continue; to go ahead OT 2
Weizen wheat **WS 1**, 28
welche(r, -s) which OT 1
Welle wave OT 1
Wellensittich budgie OT 1
Welpe puppy OT 2
Welt world OT 1
Weltraum space OT 1; outer space **WS 3**, 110
Weltstadt cosmopolitan city OT 4
weltweit worldwide OT 3; global OT 4
Wendung phrase OT 1
wenige few OT 1
  weniger less OT 2
wer, wen, wem who OT 1
Werbung advertisement OT 1; ad, advert; avdvertising OT 2
  Werbung machen für to advertise OT 2
werden to become; to get OT 2
werden to get OT 2
werfen to throw; to toss OT 1
Werkstatt workshop OT 1; garage OT 4
Werkzeug tool OT 2
Werkzeugkiste toolkit **WS 3**, 105
Wert value OT 4; merit **WS 3**, 110
wert worth OT 4
wertschätzen to value **WS 3**, 99
wertvoll valuable OT 2
Wesen being OT 4
wesentlich essential OT 4
  im Wesentlichen in essence OT 4
Wespe wasp OT 3
wessen whose OT 1
Westen west OT 1
Wettbewerb competition OT 1
Wettbewerber(in) competitor OT 4
wetteifernd competitively OT 4
wetten to bet OT 1
Wetter weather OT 1
Wettkampf match OT 1
Wettkämpfer(in) contestant OT 4
wichtig important OT 1; major OT 3; relevant; essential; dominant OT 4
Wichtigkeit importance OT 3; significance **WS 1**, 32
Widder tup OT 2
Widerstand resistance **WS 1**, 24
widerstehen to resist **WS 2**, 77
widerwillig unwilling OT 4

wie how; as OT 1
wieder again OT 1
wieder annehmen to resume **WS 1**, 26
Wiederbelebung revival **WS 2**, 58
Wiedergutmachung amends **WS 2**, 64
wiederherstellen to restore OT 3
Wiederherstellung recovery OT 3
wiederholen to repeat OT 1
  sich wiederholend repetitive **WS 2**, 57
Wiederholung repetition **WS 2**, 74
Wiederverheiratung remarriage **WS 2**, 62
wiederverwendbar reusable OT 3
wiederverwenden to reuse OT 4
wiederverwerten to recycle OT 2
Wiederverwerter(in) recycler OT 3
Wiederverwertung upcycling OT 4
Wiege cradle OT 3
wiegen to weigh OT 3
Wiese meadow OT 2
wild wild OT 2; feral **WS 1**, 25
Wildfang tomboy **WS 2**, 55
Wildnis wilderness OT 2
Willkommen! welcome OT 1
willkürlich random **WS 1**, 24
Wind wind OT 2
Winde winch OT 3
Windel nappy; diaper (AE) OT 3
windig windy OT 2
Windrad wind turbine OT 4
windsurfen to windsurf OT 1
Winsch windlass OT 3
Winter winter OT 1
winzig tiny OT 1; mini **WS 1**, 12
wir us; we OT 1
wirklich really OT 1; truly; actual OT 4
wirksam effective OT 3; efficient **WS 2**, 59
Wirkung effect OT 3
Wirtschaft economy **WS 3**, 102
wirtschaftlich economic **WS 3**, 104
wissen to know OT 1
Wissen knowledge OT 4
Wissenschaft studies OT 1
wissenschaftlich scientific OT 3
Witz joke OT 2; pun OT 4
  Witze machen to joke OT 2
wo where OT 1
  wo (auch) immer wherever OT 3
Woche week OT 1
Wochenende weekend OT 1
wöchentlich weekly OT 4
Wohlbefinden wellness **WS 2**, 72; well-being **WS 3**, 105
Wohlfahrtsorganisation charity OT 2
Wohltätigkeitsveranstaltung fundraiser OT 2
Wohn... residential OT 4; housing **WS 3**, 104
wohnen to live OT 1
Wohnung flat; apartment OT 1
Wohnungs... housing **WS 3**, 104
Wohnwagen caravan OT 1
Wohnzimmer living room OT 1
Wolf wolf OT 4
Wolke cloud OT 1
Wolkenkratzer skyscraper OT 3
wolkig cloudy OT 1
Wolle wool OT 3
wollen to want OT 1
wollig woolly OT 2
Wombat wombat **WS 1**, 28
Wort word OT 1
Wortart part of speech OT 2
Wörterbuch dictionary OT 2
Wortliste wordlist OT 2
Wortschatz lexicon **WW**, 11
Wortspiel pun OT 4
Wrack wreck OT 3
Wunder wonder OT 4
wunderbar wonderful OT 1
(sich) wundern to wonder OT 4
Wunsch desire **WS 2**, 72
wünschen to wish OT 2
Wurm worm OT 1
Wurst sausage OT 1
Wurzel root OT 3
würzen to spice OT 4
Wüste desert OT 3

Y

Yacht yacht **WS 1**, 43
Yoga yoga **WS 3**, 113

Z

Zahl number OT 1; figure OT 3
zählbar countable OT 1
zählen to count OT 2
Zahn tooth OT 2
Zahnbürste toothbrush OT 4
Zauber magic OT 1
Zauberer, Zauberin magician OT 1
Zaun fence OT 1
Zebra zebra OT 1
Zehe toe OT 1
zehn ten OT 1
Zeichensetzung punctuation OT 3
zeichnen to draw OT 1
Zeichnung drawing OT 4
zeigen to show; to point OT 1; to indicate; to reveal OT 4
Zeit time OT 1; period OT 3
Zeitachse timeline OT 2
Zeitform tense OT 1
zeitgenössisch contemporary OT 4
Zeitpunkt timing OT 3
Zeitschrift magazine OT 1
Zeituhr timer **WS 3**, 112
Zeitung newspaper OT 1
Zeitwort verb OT 1
Zelt tent OT 1
zelten to camp OT 1
Zeltplatz campsite; campground OT 2
Zentimeter centimetre OT 2
Zentral- central OT 1
Zentralheizung central heating OT 2
Zentrum center OT 2
zerbrechen to snap OT 3
zerebrale Kinderlähmung cerebral palsy **WS 2**, 57
zeremoniell ceremonial OT 3
zerfetzen to shred OT 2
zerkleinert shredded OT 2
zerlegen to take apart OT 4
zerstören to destroy OT 2
Zerstörung destruction OT 4
Zertifikat certificate OT 2
zertrümmern to batter OT 4
Zeug stuff OT 2
Zeuge, Zeugin witness OT 3
  Zeuge sein von to witness OT 3
Zeugnis certificate OT 2
Ziege goat OT 3
ziehen to draw; to pull OT 1
Ziel aim; target OT 4
zielen to aim OT 4
  zielen auf to target **WS 2**, 80
ziemlich rather; quite OT 3; relatively OT 4
Ziffer digit OT 2
Zimmermann carpenter OT 3
Zinn tin OT 2
zirkulieren to circulate OT 4
zischen to whizz OT 2
Zitat quotation OT 2
zitieren to quote OT 2
Zitronenlimonade lemonade OT 1
Zittern tremor OT 3
zittern to shiver OT 3
zivilisiert civilized **WS 1**, 27
zögerlich hesitantly OT 4
Zögern hesitation OT 3
zögern to hesitate OT 3
Zoll customs OT 2
Zoll (2,54 cm) inch OT 2
zollfrei duty free OT 2
Zone zone OT 2
Zoo zoo OT 1
zu to; too OT 1

Zubehör accessory OT 3
zubinden to tie **WS 2**, 61
Zucchini zucchini OT 3
züchten to breed **WS 2**, 51
Zucker sugar OT 1
zuerst at first OT 2; firstly OT 3
Zufahrt driveway OT 4
Zufall chance OT 2
zufällig accidental OT 3; random **WS 1**, 24
zufällig entdecken to happen upon OT 4
zufrieden pleased OT 1
Zug train OT 1
Zugang access OT 2; gateway **WS 1**, 39
zugänglich accessible OT 2
zugeben to admit **WS 1**, 20
zugreifen to access OT 4
zugunsten in favour OT 4
Zuhause home OT 1
zuhören to listen OT 1
Zukunft future OT 2
zumachen to shut OT 2
zunächst initially **WS 3**, 105
Zunahme increase OT 3
Zunder tinder OT 2
zunehmend increasingly **WS 2**, 52
Zunge tongue OT 3
zuordnen to allocate OT 4
zurechtkommen to cope **WS 2**, 57
zurück back OT 1
zurückgehen to decrease **WS 2**, 62
zurückkehren to return OT 2
zurücktreten to resign OT 4
zurückverfolgen to trace OT 3
zusammen together OT 1
Zusammenarbeit collaboration OT 4; cooperation **WS 2**, 53
zusammenfassen to summarize OT 2; to outline OT 4
Zusammenfassung summary OT 1; abstract OT 4
Zusammenhang context OT 4
mit etw. in Zusammenhang stehen to relate to **WS 1**, 34
zusammensacken to slump **WS 3**, 93
Zusatz addition OT 4
zusätzlich spare OT 3; additional **WS 2**, 57
Zuschauer(in) spectator OT 2; viewer OT 3
Zuschuss grant OT 4
zuspielen to pass OT 2
Zustand condition OT 2
zuständig in charge OT 1; competent OT 4
zusteigen to get on OT 2
Zustellung delivery **WS 3**, 102
zustimmen to agree OT 1; to approve OT 4
zustimmend affirmative OT 3
Zutat ingredient OT 2
zwanzig twenty OT 1
Zweck purpose **WS 1**, 36
zwei two OT 1
zweifach dual OT 4
Zweifel doubt **WW**, 11
Zweig stick; twig OT 2
zweimal twice OT 2
zweisprachig bilingual OT 3
Zweisprachigkeit bilingualism OT 4
zweitens secondly OT 2
Zweite(r, -s) second OT 1
Zwiebel onion OT 2
Zwilling twin OT 1
zwingen to force **WS 2**, 55
zwischen between OT 1; among OT 3
zwischenmenschlich interpersonal **WS 3**, 94
Zwischenstation waypoint OT 2
zwölf twelve OT 1
Zyklon cyclone **WS 1**, 34
Zyklus cycle OT 4

Dictionary: Names

A

Abingdon House [ˌæbɪŋtən ˈhaʊs] SEN school in England **WS 2**, 61
Aesha [aɪˈiːʃə] girl's name **WW**, 11
Alain [əˈleɪn] boy's name **WW**, 11
Amir [eˈmɪə] boy's name **WS 3**, 90
Auckland [ˈɔːklənd] city in the North Island of New Zealand **WS 1**, 13
Ayers Rock [eɪərs ˈrɒk] former colonial name of Uluru **WS 1**, 26

B

Barkindji [baˈkindʒiː] an Australian Aboriginal tribal group in New South Wales, Australia **WS 1**, 15
Ben Ockrent [ben ˈɔkrent] contemporary British writer and theatre director **WS 3**, 122
Brad [bræd] boy's name **WW**, 11

C

Canberra [ˈkænbərə] capital of Australia **WS 1**, 13
Cardiff [ˈkɑːdɪf] capital of Wales **WS 3**, 90
Christchurch [ˈkraɪstʃɜːtʃ] largest city in the South Island of New Zealand **WS 1**, 13
Conny [ˈkɒni] girl's name **WS 2**, 58

D

David Ignatow [ˈdeɪvɪd ˈignatov] American poet (1914 – 1997) **Extra pages**, 142

E

Eleni [əˈleɪni] girl's name **WS 1**, 14

F

Fred [fred] boy's name **WS 1**, 18

G

Graham [ˈgreɪəm] boy's name **WS 2**, 58
Great Barrier Reef [greɪt ˈbæriə ˌriːf] the world's largest coral reef system, off the coast of Queensland, Australia **WS 1**, 26
Greton [ˈgretən] SEN school in England **WS 2**, 61
Guatemala [ˌgwɑːtəˈmɑːlə] country in Central America **WS 4**, 132

H

Hosier Lane [ˌhəʊzɪə ˈleɪn] popular street and tourist attraction in Melbourne **WS 1**, 29

I

Iain Murray Rose [ˈiːən mʌri ˈrəʊz] Australian swimmer and six-time Olympic medalist (1939 – 2012) **WS 1**, 22

J

Jacinda Ardern [dʒəˈsɪndə] Prime Minister of New Zealand, born 26th July 1980 **WS 1**, 33
James Cook [dʒeɪmz ˈkʊk] British explorer (1728 – 1799) **WS 1**, 17
Jason [ˈdʒeɪsn] boy's name **WS 1**, 14

Acknowledgements

Audio credits

Dialogues and words and phrases produced by Anne Rosenfeld for RBA Productions (rbaproductions.co.uk). Recording engineer Mark Smith.
Track 18: "First Nation". Text (OT): Hirst, Rovert George / Tasman, Keith. © SFM Publishing Pty Ltd/Sony/ATV Music Publishing (Germany) GmbH, Berlin
Track 19: "Brown Girl". Text (OT): Silverman, Jeffrey Scott / d´Annunzio, Vincent John jr / Patel, Aaradhna Jayantilal. © Jeffrey Scott Productions LLC/Vincent John Music/Kobalt Music Publishing/Printrechte Hal Leonard Europe GmbH

Video credits

Videos 1, 2, 4: produced by Anne Rosenfeld for RBA Productions, Brighton (rbaproductions.co.uk). Editor: David Rafique
Video 1 (picture credits): Anatoly Vartanov / Rozhnovskaya, Tanya; Forster, Stuart; The Print Collector; Long, Suzanne; Delimont, Danita; FLHC Y1; Corbishley, Guy; PA Images; public domain sourced / access rights from PJF Military Collection; McAllister, Neil; Henry Westheim Photography; Horree, Peter; Aflo Co. Ltd.; Mayo, Marcelo; edhar yuralaits
Video 2 (picture credits): structuresxx / iStockphoto.com; Classic Image / Alamy Stock Photo; Rainbird, John / Alamy Stock Photo; Lake Erie Maps and Prints / Alamy Stock Photo; geogphotos / Alamy Stock Photo; Hellier, Chris / Alamy Stock Photo; Swanepoel, Johan / Alamy Stock Photo; simonbradfield / iStockphoto.com; zetter / iStockphoto.com; slowmotiongli / iStockphoto.com; Aristine / iStockphoto.com; Griffiths, Ken / Alamy Stock Photo; Fare, Andrew / Alamy Stock Photo; Totajla / iStockphoto.com; DoraDalton / iStockphoto.com; FiledIMAGE / iStockphoto.com; Crux, John / Alamy Stock Photo; DPK-Photo / Alamy Stock Photo
Video 4 (picture credits): South, David / Alamy Stock Photo; Lesniewski, Rainer / Alamy Stock Photo; World History Archive / Alamy Stock Photo; Granger Historical Picture Archive / Alamy Stock Photo; McLaren, Kirsty / Alamy Stock Photo; Classic Image / Alamy Stock Photo; public domain sourced / access rights from Lakeview Images / Alamy Stock Photo; public domain sourced / access rights from Historic Collection / Alamy Stock Photo; Miceking / Shutterstock.com; Robert Wallace / Wallace Media Network / Alamy Stock Photo
Video 6: provided courtesy of My Genderation. www.mygenderation.com
Videos 7-12: produced by James Vyner and Luke Vyner for Creative Listening, London (www.creativelistening.co.uk).

Picture credits

|123RF.com, Hong Kong: stefaninahill 22.3. |Alamy Stock Photo, Abingdon/Oxfordshire: Action Plus Sports Images 33.2; agefotostock 22.4, 31.5; Allstar Picture Library Ltd 15.1; Arcaid Images/Gollings, John 143.1; Arnold, Rob 29.2; Bachman, Bill 23.2, 38.1; Barraud, Martin 60.4; Ben-Ari, Rafael 12.2; Berg, Georg 23.6; Bialasiewicz, Katarzyna 61.2; Bildagentur-online/Schoening 45.1; Black, Ruth 36.1; Blake, Gary 42.4; Blue Jean Images 111.5; Blulz60 21.3; Bujdoso, Andor 91.1; Cavoretto, Stefano 111.3; Classic Image 17.3; clivestock 152.2; Crossick, Matt 122.1; Daemmrich, Bob 141.2; david a eastley 23.5; Davydov, Aleksandr 93.2; Demidova, Ekaterina 111.2; Dorney, Chris 43.1; DPK-Photo 32.2; du Feu, Geoff 90.2; E.D. Torial 61.1; Ekstrand, Jim 94.1; eldar nurkovic 67.1; Fuchslocher, Mike 19.3; Gekko Studios 12.4; Genevieve Vallee 23.3; Gerbino, Silvia 58.5; Gilbert, Jeff 104.1; Gingell, Ben 66.2; Gino's Premium Images 66.3; Hasenkopf, Juergen 25.1; Imagebroker 25.3; imageBROKER 35.3, 36.2; Ison, Chris 25.2; Janine Wiedel Photolibrary 50.3; Jeffrey Isaac Greenberg 17+ 5.2, 60.2; Jeffrey Isaac Greenberg 8+ 23.4; jeremy sutton-hibbert 17.4; Johnson, Mark A. 21.2; Jon Arnold Images Ltd 13.4, 26.1; Jon D 81.1; Jordan, Peter 105.1; KGPA Ltd 22.2; Klepo, Emir 111.4; L.S. Sandiford 151.1; Marinic, Borislav 60.5; Maskot 111.1; Maurice Savage 104.3; MBI 11.1, 60.3, 118.1; Michael, Andrew 241.2; Milnes, Richard 22.5; Naoumova, Irina 35.2; Neelon(misc), Michael 152.1; New Illustrations by Alfonsodetomas / Alamy Vektorgrafik 68.1; Nine Elms Regeneration 104.2; Oeland, Ingo 12.1; Outback Australia 28.2; PA Images 144.1, 145.1; parkerphotography 90.4, 109.1; paul kennedy 35.6; Pearsall, Chris 102.1; Pictorial Press Ltd 22.1; Popov, Andriy 93.1; Prisma by Dukas Presseagentur GmbH 13.1; public domain sourced / access rights from History and Art Collection 41.1; public domain sourced / access rights from Lakeview Images 17.1; Quayle, Paul 88.2, 88.4; rakus 97.1; robertharding 31.4; Science Photo Library 91.2; Selinger, Andy 42.2; Shakirov, Albert 109.2; Spiers, Nigel 35.5; Sykes, Homer 99.1; Tallec, Tony 98.1; Tetra Images 90.5; Thalhofer, Karoline 20.2; tommaso altamura 50.1; Travel Pictures 23.1; travellinglight 32.1; Travelscape Images 42.1, 42.5; uknip 64.2; Uliasz, Marek 99.3; UPI 147.4; Urban Napflin 36.3; Wall, David 31.1; Wavebreak Media ltd 108.3; WENN Rights Ltd 73.1, 73.2; Wheal, Kevin 35.4; Williams, Jane 109.3; Windsor, Joshua 51.2; Wiskerke, Wim 241.1; Wisniewska, Monika 51.4; World History Archive 17.2; ZUMA Press, Inc. 33.1, 120.1, 146.1. |Alamy Stock Photo (RMB), Abingdon/Oxfordshire: Travelscape Images 142.1; Willett, A. T. 35.1. |Bayerisches

Staatsministerium für Unterricht und Kultus, München: 116.1. |Buccellato, Steve, Los Angeles: 128.1, 128.2, 129.1, 131.1, 133.1, 134.1, 137.1, 139.1, 140.1, 141.1. |CartoonStock.com, Bath: Stahler, Jeff 54.1; www.CartoonStock.com/Hardin, Patrick 24.2. |Creative Listening, Newick: 90.1, 93.4, 96.1, 101.1, 101.2, 107.1. |Domke, Franz-Josef, Hannover: 3.1, 10.1, 258.1, 259.1. |Donnelly, Karen, Brighton: 14.1, 14.2, 16.1, 18.1, 20.1, 30.1, 30.2, 30.3, 31.2, 31.3, 31.6, 56.1, 58.1, 58.2, 58.3, 58.4, 71.1, 89.1, 89.2, 89.3, 89.4, 89.5, 110.1, 110.2, 112.1, 112.2, 150.1. |fotolia.com, New York: cevahir87 10.3; totajla 5.1, 44.1. |Hoth, Katharina, Erfurt: 63.1, 75.1. |iStockphoto.com, Calgary: AJ_Watt 11.2; AurielAki 76.1; AzmanJaka 102.4; bennymarty 19.1; Brainsil 11.5; Carillet, Joel 111.6; chokkicx 72.2; Damocean 28.3; davidf 11.4; duncan1890 24.1; engabito 81.2; FatCamera 76.2; fcscafeine 154.1; ferrantraite 50.2; Irina_Strelnikova 148.1; JackF 117.2; jenifoto 77.1; Kapliuk, Maksym 106.2; kokkai 13.2; LazingBee 147.1, 147.2, 147.3; ljubaphoto 102.5; mgkaya 123.1; mollypix 21.1; monkeybusinessimages 93.3; Moore Media 52.3; MStudioImages 52.2; Patil, Nikhil 11.3; pawel.gaul 106.1; pixelfit 117.5; Plahutar, Ziga 117.3; Prostock-Studio 72.1; Ridofranz 66.1; RoBeDeRo 90.3; ROMAOSLO 114.1; Sladic 61.4; Totajla 19.2; travellinglight 39.1; undefined undefined 117.1; VectorStory 70.1; ViewApart 64.1; Vignjevic, Dobrila 103.2; VioletaStoimenova 103.1; xavierarnau 37.2. |My Genderation: 55.1. |Oxford Designers and Illustrators, Oxford: 149.2, 153.1. |Picture-Alliance GmbH, Frankfurt a.M.: Fiedler, Doreen 78.1; SAKUMA, PAUL 99.2. |Shutterstock.com, New York: Alizada Studios 142.3; Andrey_Popov 108.1; Balasko, Rudy 33.4; Bogdan, Serban 13.3; de Marmore, Cabeca 115.4; delcarmat 122.2; Everett Collection 115.5; Filimonov, Iakov 108.2; Franzi 51.3; Frog, Jack 115.6; Galexia 29.1; Guillem, Antonio 117.4; Huebner, Daniel 33.3; James, Alexander S 28.1; LightField Studios 115.2; marekuliasz 88.1; Markin, Aleksandr 51.1; Miceking 10.2; Monkey Business Images 61.3; Nerud, Roman 115.3; Parker, Isabella 106.3; Pete Niesen 142.2; Ragelis, Girts 102.3; sirtravelalot 60.1; stockpexel 42.3; Trueffelpix 119.1; Wildfoto 12.3; xavier gallego morell 115.1; YAKOBCHUK VIACHESLAV 68.2. |Shutterstock.com (RM), New York: Moviestore 27.1. |stock.adobe.com, Dublin: Brivio, Marco 26.2; klyaksun 71.2; LIGHTFIELD STUDIOS 52.1; moodboard 102.2; Palmer, Matt 37.1; Race, Dan 7.1, 95.1; suwatwongkham 88.3; ©AntonioDiaz 149.1. |United Nations Office for Outer Space Affairs, Wien: 110.3. |Williamson, Pete, Kent, Southorough, Tunbridge Wells: 46.1, 47.1, 47.2, 48.1, 48.2, 49.1, 49.2, 84.1, 85.1, 86.1, 86.2, 87.1, 87.2, 87.3, 124.1, 125.1, 125.2, 127.1.

Abbreviations:

BIH	Bosnia and Herzegovina	UK	United Kingdom
MNE	Montenegro	USA	United States of America
RKS	Kosovo		

0 500 1,000 1,500 2,000 2,500 km

Russia
Moscow
Belarus
Ukraine
Crimea
Georgia
Armenia
Azer-
baijan
Turkey
Syria
Lebanon
Israel
Jordan
Iraq
Iran
Kuwait
Bahrain
Qatar
United
Arab
Emirates
Oman
Saudi
Arabia
Yemen
Egypt
Sudan
Eritrea
Djibouti
Ethiopia
South
Sudan
Somalia
Uganda
Kenya
Rwanda
Burundi
Tanzania
Seychelles
Comoros
Malawi
Zambia
Zimbabwe
Mozam-
bique
Madagascar
Mauritius
Pretoria
Swaziland
Lesotho
Kazakhstan
Uzbekistan
Turkmenistan
Kyrgyzstan
Tajikistan
Afghanistan
Pakistan
New Delhi
India
Nepal
Bhutan
Bangla-
desh
Sri Lanka
Maldives
Mongolia
China
Beijing
North Korea
South
Korea
Japan
Tokyo
Taiwan
Myanmar
Laos
Thailand
Vietnam
Cambodia
Philippines
Brunei
Malaysia
Singapore
Indonesia
Timor-Leste
Papua
New Guinea
Australia
Canberra
New Zealand
Wellington
Pacific
Ocean
Indian
Ocean
Iceland
Reykjavik
Norway
Oslo
Sweden
Stockholm
Finland
Helsinki
Tallinn
Estonia
Riga
Latvia
Lithuania
Vilnius
Minsk
Belarus
Russia
Moscow
North
Sea
Baltic Sea
Ireland
Dublin
Irish
Sea
United
Kingdom
London
Denmark
Copenhagen
Nether-
lands
Amsterdam
Berlin
Warsaw
Poland
Germany
Brussels
Belgium
English Channel
Paris
Luxembourg
Luxem-
bourg
Prague
Czechia
Slovakia
Kiev
Ukraine
France
Liechten-
stein
Vienna
Bratislava
Budapest
Bern
Vaduz
Austria
Hungary
Moldova
Chişinău
Switzerland
Slovenia
Ljubljana
Zagreb
Belgrade
Romania
Bucharest
Croatia
BIH
Serbia
Monaco
San
Marino
Black Sea
Bulgaria
Sofia
MNE
RKS
Portugal
Lisbon
Madrid
Andorra
Spain
Rome
Italy
Tirana
Albania
North
Macedonia
Ankara
Turkey
Greece
Athens
Gibraltar
(UK)
Mediterranean Sea
Valletta
Malta
Cyprus
0 250 500 750 km

The British Isles